FAMILY PLANNING
AND
CHILD SURVIVAL
100 DEVELOPING COUNTRIES

John A. Ross, Marjorie Rich
Janet P. Molzan, Michael Pensak

Center for Population and Family Health
Columbia University
1988

Center for Population and Family Health
Columbia University
60 Haven Avenue
New York, N.Y. 10032

Cover: Original painting and photograph
by Dr. David Bichell, inspired by a visit to
a Mozambique maternity ward

Printing: The William Byrd Press

ISBN 0–9620952–0–6

Library of Congress Catalog Number 88–72069

Contents

Demographic and Social Setting

Family Planning Programs

Government Policies

Family Planning Budgets and Expenditures

Imports, Contraceptive Supplies, and Costs

Personnel and Facilities

Program Effort and Coverage

Acceptor Numbers and Characteristics

Prevalence of Contraceptive Use

Adolescents

Child Survival Programs

Health Personnel and Hospital Beds

Infant, Child, and Maternal Mortality

Program Outcomes

Preface

Rates of population growth have been very high in many developing countries during the past two or three decades because of rapid decreases in mortality. Many governments have responded by developing policies and programs designed to lower fertility. The primary policy instruments advocated have been programs organized to promote the use of contraception, and similar programs have been widely established on grounds of health and human rights. International organizations and many donor countries have responded by providing money, supplies, and technical assistance in support of family planning programs. It is estimated that donor countries and organizations spend $500 million per year in support of these programs. It is more difficult to estimate the costs to developing countries, primarily because of the varying ways in which programs are budgeted, but estimates vary from approximately $500 million to $1 billion per year.

Much information is generated and published about population programs by individual countries and by several donors, notably the World Bank, the United Nations Fund for Population Activities, and the United States Agency for International Development. However, no agency compiles and publishes information covering all developing countries. Starting in 1969, the Population Council published Fact Books on population programs annually until 1976, biennially until 1982, and a final edition in 1985. Those Fact Books provided comparative information about family planning programs in almost all developing countries that had established population policies and programs.

It is somewhat surprising that the population field does not have a reliable, regularly updated source of information on the large number of population programs, with systematic coverage of essential features —their policies and action objectives, their principal characteristics, their budgets, the means they use (institutional channels, method mixes, types of personnel and service sites, communication techniques), their performance trends, and the probable reasons for marked shifts in performance.

Numerous publications provide partial information: these include the World Bank's *World Development Reports,* the *Population Reports* series of the Population Information Program of Johns Hopkins University, the Demographic and Health Surveys, the UN Population Division's biennial *Monitoring Reports*, and others. The time between collection of data and publication lessens the value of many of these reports. Further, no agency serves as a central source that collects, regularly updates, interprets, and publishes data on all aspects of population action programs for developing countries.

Moreover, relevant data from the child survival side have not been put alongside the family planning data, even though the same agencies implement both kinds of programs in many countries. Fertility and early mortality are interconnected, with mutually causative relationships; yet programmatic information across large numbers of countries has not been brought together as it should have been.

The Center for Population and Family Health, Columbia University, seeks to fill both gaps: the one that was created by the Population Council's decision to cease regular publication of a Fact Book on population programs, and the one that exists between family planning and child survival information. I take particular pleasure in the publication of this volume inasmuch as it is, in a sense, a continuation of the Fact Books of the Population Council, which I initiated (see the first two editions) and which were so ably carried out by Dorothy Nortman. This volume provides a historical series of family planning information, child survival data, and background statistics. It is planned that these materials will be updated approximately every two years.

W. Parker Mauldin
Senior Associate,
The Population Council, and
Consultant,
The Rockefeller Foundation

Acknowledgments

We owe a heavy debt to many persons and agencies for their contributions to this volume. First mention must go to Dorothy Nortman, who over some 15 years compiled and published 12 editions of the world's best comparative statistics on family planning programs. To this information she added perceptive commentary, and she used the information in a number of technical analyses.

Respondents to our questionnaire, though anonymous here, know who they are and know the labor they invested in assembling information and statistics. We can only thank them, and ask their forbearance for any maladroit handling of their responses in the long chain from questionnaire entries to published tables.

We received unpublished data and other assistance from the United Nations Population Division and Statistical Office, the United Nations Children's Fund, the World Health Organization, the World Bank, the Population Council, the Rockefeller Foundation, the U.S. Census Bureau's Center for International Research, and the World Resources Institute. Staff at these agencies willingly gave their time and expertise, and we wish to thank especially Mary Beth Weinberger, Birgitta Bucht, Alice Clague, Leo Goldstone, Carol Chan, Angélica Marin-Lira, Randy Bulatao, Althea Hill, John Bongaarts, Robert Sendek, W. Parker Mauldin, Sylvia Quick, Peter Johnson, and Alan Brewster. Materials for certain tables were prepared by Tessa Wardlaw and Dana Schwartz.

Jay Kantor provided early computer assistance that formed the structures for the tables. Subsequently, Sharon Guillory performed a complex series of data transformations, including many computations. Other colleagues at the Center for Population and Family Health assisted the project, and we particularly thank Norman Weatherby for valuable advice on data management, and Susan Pasquariella and Carole Oshinski of the Library for extensive help with the literature of the field. Aundres Brenyah and Nina Gray provided secretarial assistance not only with speed and accuracy, but with much cheerful goodwill.

Primary funding for the project was provided by the Rockefeller Foundation, the Ford Foundation, and the Andrew W. Mellon Foundation, and we are grateful to them for their traditions of respecting the complete scientific independence of their grantees.

In the last few months of the project we received valuable assistance from several individuals:

Angela Iacca LaValle graciously produced the figures on a tight schedule and through our series of changes.

Walter Watson examined every table and the entire text, and made many suggestions that materially improved the volume.

Dore Hollander served as copy editor for the book and, as in our earlier collaborations, performed magic on every draft. Her contributions were many and are much appreciated.

We are deeply indebted to Luther Sperberg, whose professional expertise in desktop publishing saw the manuscript through from rough tables to camera-ready copy.

John A. Ross
Marjorie Rich
Janet P. Molzan
Michael Pensak

August 8, 1988

Introduction

This volume provides statistics on family planning and child survival programs, with stress on time trends and broad geographic coverage. The 100 developing countries with populations over 1 million are covered (the developed world is omitted), and some provincial data are included for China, India, and Indonesia, the three most populous of the 100 countries. These three account for 54 percent of the total population of the developing world, and the 100 account for over 98 percent of it.

The special features of the volume are as follows:
- It presents a historical series of family planning information, drawn mainly from three sources: the 12 editions of the Nortman Fact Book,* a questionnaire inquiry to the 100 countries in 1987, and the general literature.
- It includes a set of child survival tables based on the 1987 questionnaire and on compilations held by international agencies, chiefly the World Health Organization, the United Nations Children's Fund, and the United Nations Population Division.
- It provides time trends not previously available on the number of married women of reproductive age, by country, as well as the latest UN estimates for infant and child mortality and total fertility rates. Partial information is also given for adolescent fertility, mortality, and contraceptive use.

The detailed information on both family planning and child survival programs, assembled together here for the first time, permits linkage between the two. Little analysis has been done that cross-classifies programmatic information, over time, between family planning and child survival, and this compendium may advance that. The information published here is held in a computerized data bank, and portions are available on request.

No data set on substantial numbers of countries and features can aspire to high and uniform accuracy throughout. The user of such a compendium must proceed cautiously and critically. All data here are sub-

ject to error, some more than others, and although we have attempted to remove mistakes and improve quality, many shortcomings doubtless remain. Certain concepts changed from year to year, and in many cases respondents who compiled the data for each country were different in different years. Some qualifications are included in the footnotes, and the Technical Notes section supplies a number of points about each table. Readers with special interests will benefit by going to the original sources of secondary data for additional details.

Notwithstanding such problems, we have considered it important to preserve and extend the world's statistical information in a common format, across countries and across time periods, for these large-scale programs. Indeed, if basic information on these programs were unavailable, there would surely be an urgent call to obtain it, in a field receiving as large investments as this one.

In compiling the tables we proceeded as follows:

For much of the family planning data, we constructed the historical series by consolidating information from the 12 editions of the Nortman Fact Books, published from 1969 to 1985 (data through 1983). Because this body of information had never been computerized, we entered the data into computer files after a laborious process of merging the information from all editions. Duplicated entries were removed and contradictory ones reconciled, usually by accepting the most recent entries submitted by country respondents.

Information concerning sterilization came largely from another Fact Book,** a compilation based upon numerous sources, including tables in the Nortman series.

A new questionnaire was sent to the 100 developing countries having populations above 1 million, to update the former series and to gather certain additional information on child survival programs. As of early 1988, replies were received from two-thirds of the countries; most of the remainder have no national fami-

* D. Nortman, *Population and Family Planning Programs: A Fact Book,* The Population Council, New York, 1969–1976, 1978, 1980, 1982, 1985.

** J. A. Ross, S. Hong, and D. H. Huber, *Voluntary Sterilization: An International Fact Book,* Association for Voluntary Sterilization, New York, 1985.

ly planning program and are quite small, totaling only 9.9 percent of the population of the developing world. Moreover, these countries appear in the historical data in certain tables and in some of the tables that were provided by the United Nations and other agencies.

Child survival tables, including information for such topics as immunization, oral rehydration supplies, and breast-feeding, as well as mortality and fertility estimates, were provided by courtesy of staff at the World Health Organization, the United Nations Children's Fund, the United Nations Population Division, the United Nations Statistical Office, and the World Bank. The World Resources Institute and the U.S. Census Bureau's Center for International Research also provided secondary data. Responses to the 1987 questionnaire supplemented parts of tables obtained from other agencies.

To repeat, this volume is an effort to capture the world's comparative information on family planning and child survival programs. It is, we believe, valuable as it stands, but beyond that it can serve to guide improvements in the systems that gather such data.

Illustrative Results

Although this volume is meant primarily as a data compendium, we draw attention in this section to some results that illustrate the kind of information contained in the tables.

Family Planning

It is now abundantly clear that large numbers of couples in developing countries wish to intervene in the child-bearing process—to delay the next pregnancy or to cease giving birth entirely. Many women are sufficiently desperate to risk illicit abortions; many have more children than they want or can raise humanely. Public programs have appeared to meet these needs, and to reduce fertility rates in the interest of society at large. Since the mid-1960s, many governments have promulgated sympathetic policies toward public family planning programs, and many have implemented these programs vigorously. By no means, however, are the

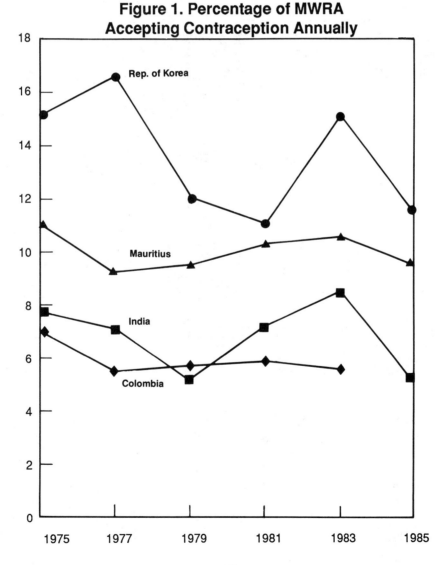

Figure 1. Percentage of MWRA Accepting Contraception Annually

Figure 2. Contraceptive Prevalence: Percentage of MWRA Currently Using a Method

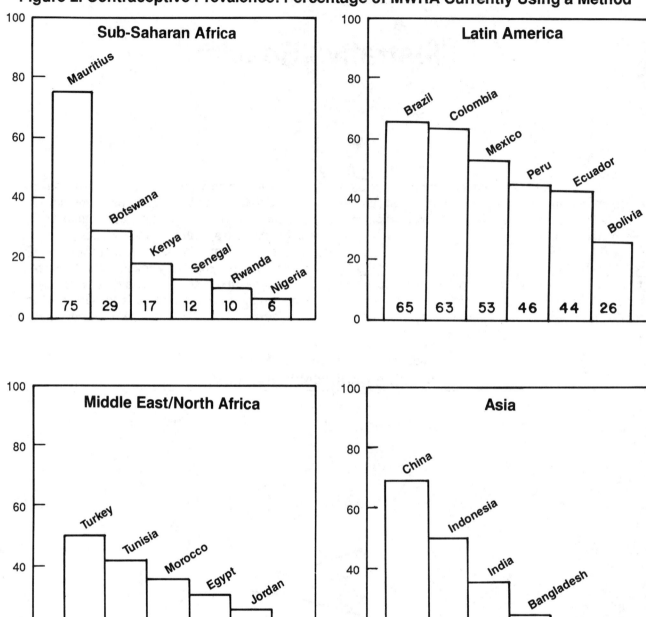

programs of uniform effectiveness, and the figures presented here illustrate the considerable variation among them.

Contraceptive Acceptance

Family planning statistics often start with the direct response to programs, in terms of the numbers adopting contraceptive methods. These numbers can be converted to rates, as in Figure 1, which shows a pattern over time for a variety of countries. Levels of 10–15 percent of married women of reproductive age (MWRA) accepting a contraceptive method each year are typical for the strongest programs, and levels down to 1 or 2 percent are registered by weak programs. Rates in most countries, of course, fall between these extremes.

Figure 3. Percentage of Contraceptive Users Relying on Public Programs[a]

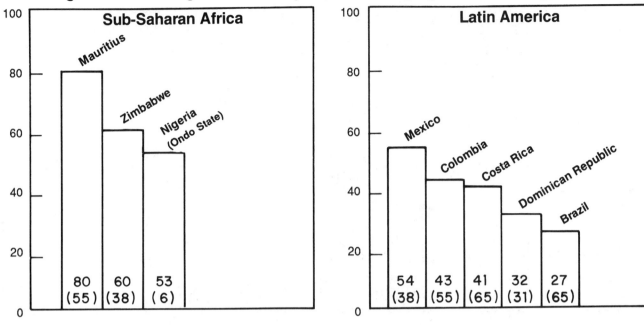

Sub-Saharan Africa

Mauritius
Zimbabwe
Nigeria (Ondo State)

| 80 (55) | 60 (38) | 53 (6) |

Latin America

Mexico
Colombia
Costa Rica
Dominican Republic
Brazil

| 54 (38) | 43 (55) | 41 (65) | 32 (31) | 27 (65) |

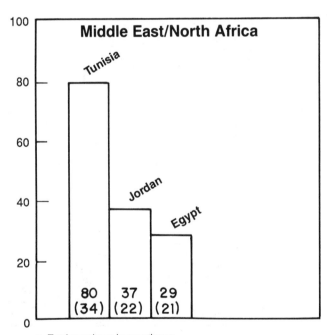

Middle East/North Africa

Tunisia
Jordan
Egypt

| 80 (34) | 37 (22) | 29 (21) |

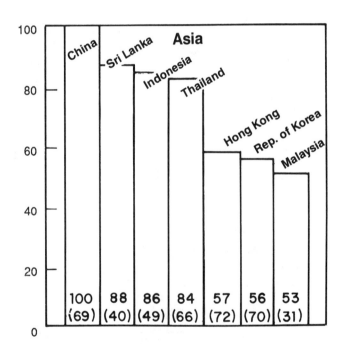

Asia

China
Sri Lanka
Indonesia
Thailand
Hong Kong
Rep. of Korea
Malaysia

| 100 (69) | 88 (40) | 86 (49) | 84 (66) | 57 (72) | 56 (70) | 53 (31) |

a. Total prevalence in parentheses.

Contraceptive Prevalence

Straight numbers of acceptors (Table 23) mean little without a high continuation rate, and these two factors produce the prevalence of contraceptive use at any point in time. Over the last 20 years a true revolution has occurred in birth control, with contraceptive use in some of the world's largest developing countries changing from almost negligible levels to very high levels, similar to ones in the West. Figure 2 illustrates some of these, as well as some that remain lower (see also Table 26).

Sterilization, because of its popularity and long continuation, has built up sufficient users worldwide to give protection against pregnancy to more couples than any other method. Oral contraception is a very close second. Many more women try it than seek steriliza-

Figure 4. Number of MWRA (000s) per Public-Sector Service Point

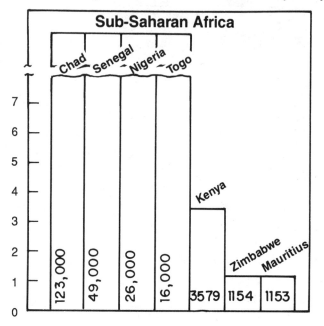

Sub-Saharan Africa

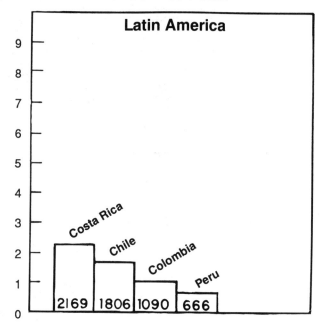

Latin America

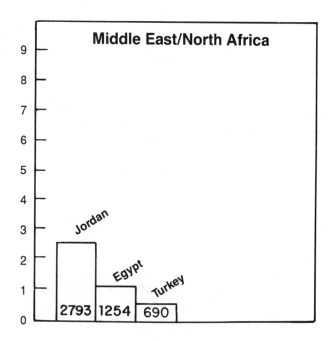

Middle East/North Africa

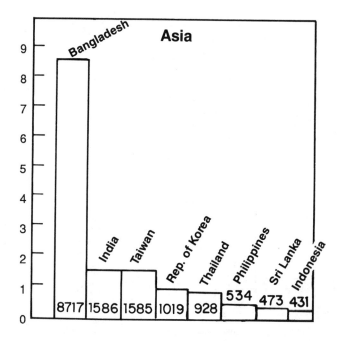

Asia

tion, but women tend to use the pill for much shorter periods because they are simply spacing pregnancies or because of side effects and various nuisance factors.

Role of Programs
Large-scale family planning programs tend to dominate contraceptive supply and service, including sterilization (Figure 3). This is true, for example, in China and Indonesia in Asia, Mexico in Latin America, and Tunisia in North Africa. Brazil, however, the most populous country in Latin America, is an exception; most contraceptive use there is obtained through the private sector (although many sterilizations are provided by physicians working in the Social Security system; see Table 27).

Figure 5. Trends in Total Fertility Rates

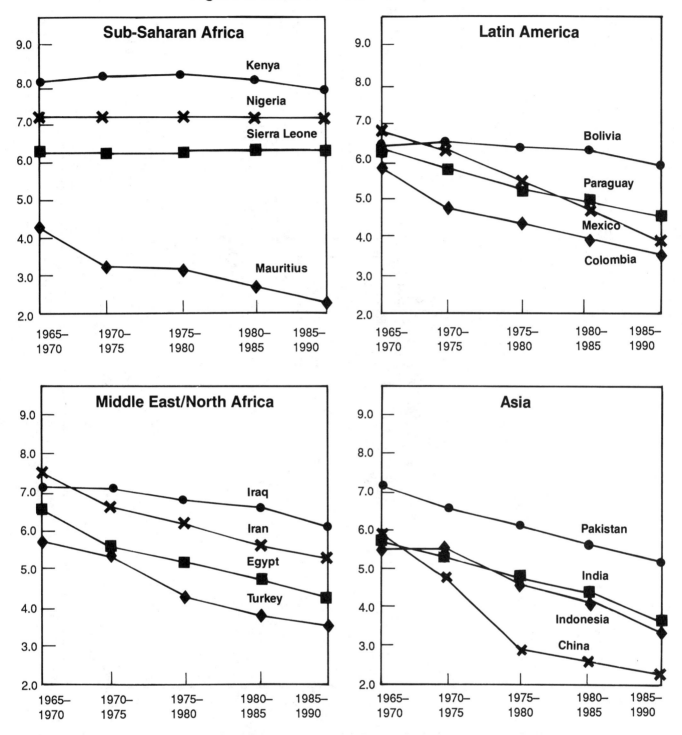

Service Points

The creation of a public family planning program may mean little unless the program can establish a large number of service points, well dispersed. The better programs have shown impressive improvement in the number of MWRA per service point, with some down to the 500–1000 range (Figure 4). Indonesia is one of the most advanced in this respect; it began with rela- tively small numbers of established clinics and branched out gradually until it had established small vil- lage depots, mothers' clubs, and acceptor groups of various types in most of its villages. These distribute pills and condoms and act as referral points for clinical methods. China has done much the same, and offers every birth control method, including sterilization and abortion. (See Table 17 for data on service points.)

7

Figure 6. Infant and Child Mortality: Three Largest Developing Countries, 1987

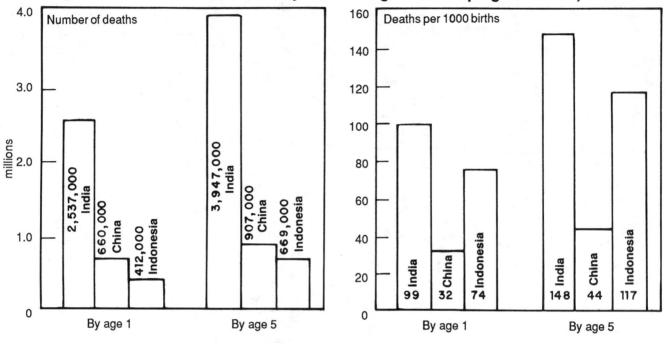

Figure 7. Regional Infant Mortality Rates

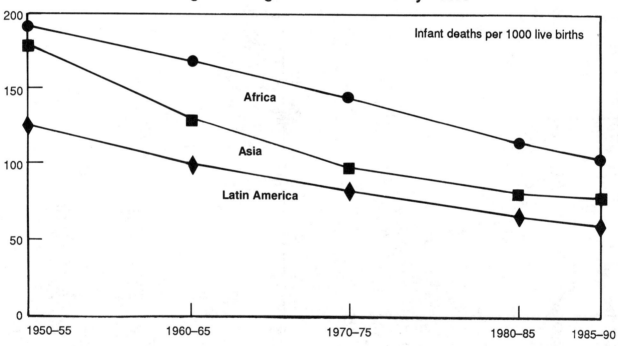

Child Survival

An immense task repeats itself every year: that of providing basic medical care to a new group of infants. A fresh cohort arrives annually, needing attendance at birth, immunizations, treatment for diarrhea, and adequate nutrition. The magnitude of this task has been halved in China, as its birthrate has fallen from the 40s to the 20s. China now has only two-thirds as many births as India, even though it has 25 percent more people. (See Table 35.)

Fertility Rates

A convenient measure of differences in childbearing is the total fertility rate: the numbers of births a young woman would have if she experienced through life the fertility rates that now prevail at each age (neglecting

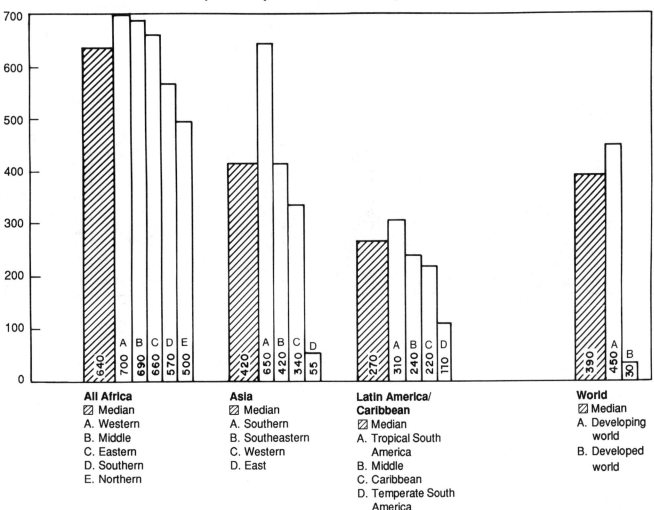

**Figure 8. Estimates for Maternal Mortality
(Deaths per 100,000 births), 1983**

All Africa	**Asia**	**Latin America/ Caribbean**	**World**
▨ Median	▨ Median	**Caribbean**	▨ Median
A. Western	A. Southern	▨ Median	A. Developing world
B. Middle	B. Southeastern	A. Tropical South America	B. Developed world
C. Eastern	C. Western	B. Middle	
D. Southern	D. East	C. Caribbean	
E. Northern		D. Temperate South America	

female mortality). Illustrative trends for several countries appear in Figure 5. Fertility estimates show declines in many countries, but there are important exceptions; in many countries in Africa and elsewhere, declines are absent or small. (See Table 3.)

Infant and Child Mortality
In parts of the developing world, one-third of pregnant women will lose the pregnancy or see the child die before age one. The potential for improvement is again illustrated by comparing China and India: there are far more infant and child deaths in India despite its smaller population. These result from its larger number of births, as well as its higher mortality rates. China has lowered both its fertility rate and its mortality rate; consequently, the numbers of early deaths is much reduced (see Figure 6 and Table 30).

The two countries are relatively closer on rates than on numbers of deaths. China's infant mortality rate

is one-third that of India; its number of deaths is one-fourth India's. This is because China's infant mortality rate is applied to its smaller number of births, giving a small number of infant deaths.

Overall trends in infant mortality rates appear in Figure 7; these data are from United Nations estimates. Declines have occurred for whole regions over the last three decades, but there are, of course, large variations among countries (see Table 31).

Maternal Mortality
Maternal deaths arise from complications of pregnancy and childbearing, including the high risks that accompany the illegal abortions associated with unwanted pregnancies. The risk of maternal death in some areas approaches 1 percent at each birth. The highest regional average, for all of Africa, is estimated at 640 deaths per 100,000 births, or 0.64 percent (Figure 8); again, levels in some countries are well

Figure 9. Percentage of Infants Immunized against Measles, 1984–87

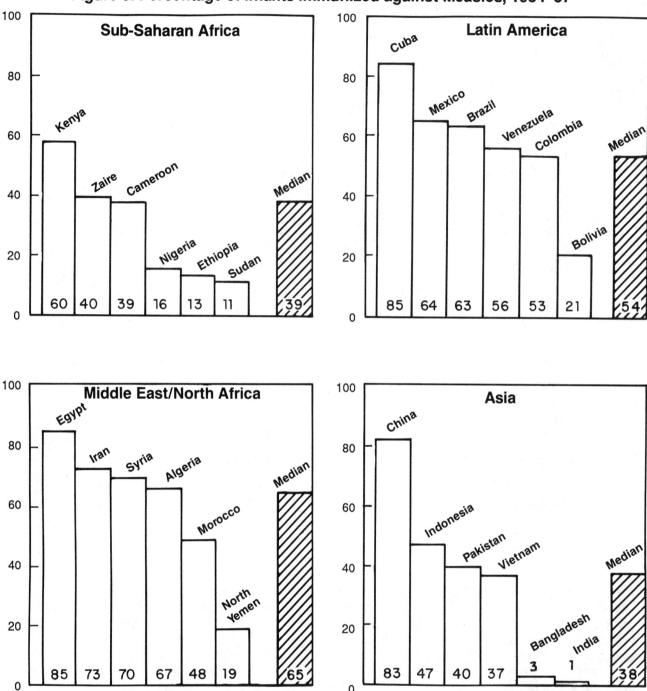

above this. This risk, when taken repeatedly birth after birth, accumulates to a chance of 1 in 21 of death over the childbearing career (see Table 34).

Immunizations
At one time, health authorities could do little to protect infants against certain major causes of death. It is now technically possible with the immunizations and oral rehydration supplies (ORS) that have emerged in recent years to revolutionize the rates of child survival. The constraints on this are financial and administrative, as well as shortfalls in trained personnel. Many countries and donors, particularly UNICEF and WHO, have undertaken vigorous programs to alleviate these difficulties. This work is in midstream, and much remains to be done. The percentage of children receiving im-

Figure 10. Percentage of Diarrhea Cases Treated with ORS, 1987

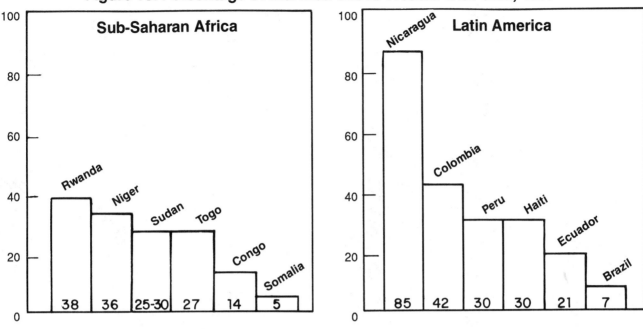

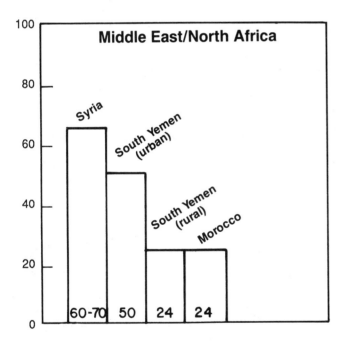

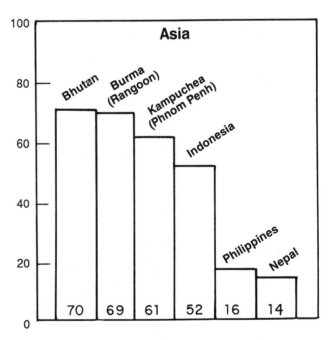

munizations, illustrated in Figure 9 for measles, is still unsatisfactory in every region. Figure 9 shows medians for 32 countries in Sub-Saharan Africa, 23 in Latin America and the Caribbean, 16 in the Middle East and North Africa, and 20 in Asia. (See Table 35.)

ORS

Oral rehydration salts can save thousands of infants from death if treatment is administered properly during diarrhea episodes. This is now possible through the discovery of the correct ingredients, their ratios to each other, and the right dilution in water. WHO, UNICEF, and other organizations, as mentioned above, are investing great efforts in conjunction with governments to establish the use of ORS among populations in developing countries.

Figure 11. Percentage of Births Attended by Trained Personnel, 1984

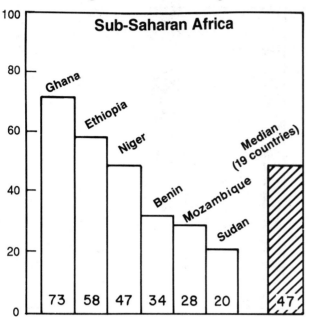

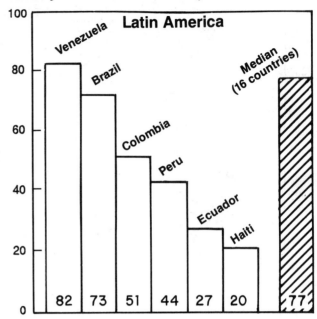

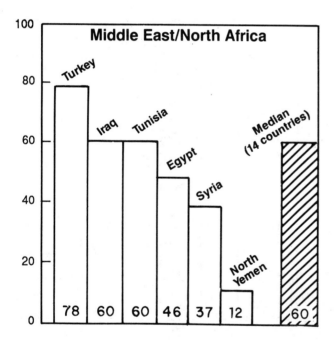

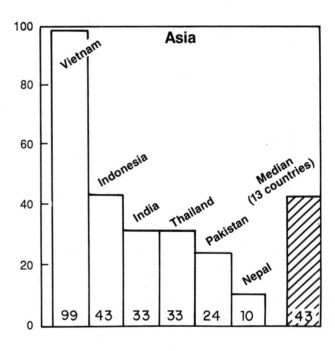

Figure 10 shows the percentage of diarrhea cases treated with oral rehydration solution (see also Table 36). The supplies themselves are more available than these percentages suggest (see Table 20); much remains to be done to translate availability into use. Nevertheless, treatment with ORS was entirely unknown not many years ago, and it now has a strong foothold in numerous countries.

Maternal Coverage

Both maternal mortality and infant mortality can be reduced by raising the percentage of births that are attended by trained personnel (Figure 11). In some ways, however, this is more difficult to do than is increasing the percentage of infants immunized, since nurse-midwives and more facilities can be provided to village populations only over a long period. Improvements in

Figure 12. Percentage of Rural Population with Access to Safe Drinking Water

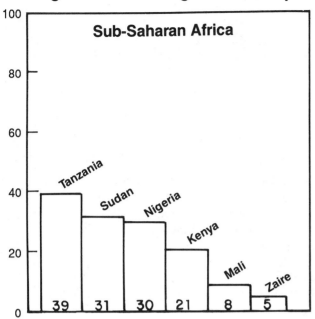

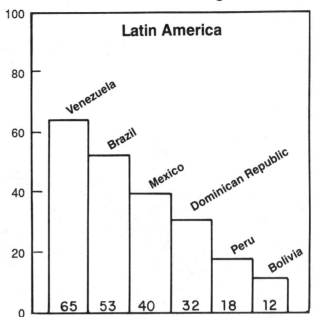

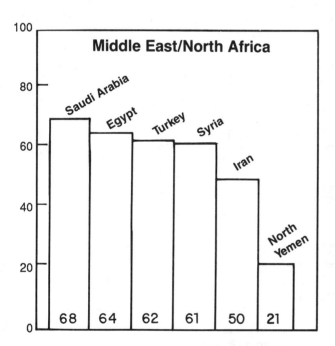

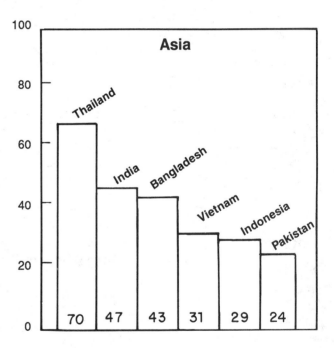

maternal coverage are at an intermediate stage; considerable progress has been made in many countries, but substantial proportions of births still occur without formal medical attention (see Table 37).

Water

Much childhood disease, including much diarrhea, is traceable to impure water and poor environmental sanitation. These are, of course, not the only determinants; sheer quantities of water for washing are also important, and household habits regarding preparation of food, use of soap, excretion, and management of animals are also important determinants. Access to safe water, however, remains important as one index to monitor, and Figure 12 gives illustrative information for selected countries (see Table 39).

Acronyms and Abbreviations

ABEPF	Associação Brasileira de Entidades de Planejamento Familiar
ADC	Asociacion Demografica Costarricense
APPBF	Asociacion Puertorriqueña Pro Bienestar de la Familia
APROFAM	Asociacion Pro-Bienestar de la Familia de Guatemala
ASCOFAME	Asociacion Colombiana de Facultades de Medicina
BEMFAM	Sociedade Civil de Bem Estar Familiar no Brasil
CBD	Community-based distribution
CEPEP	Centro Paraguayo de Estudios en Poblacion
CPS	Contraceptive prevalence survey
CSM	Contraceptive social marketing
CYP	Couple-years of protection
DHS	Demographic and Health Surveys
FEPAC	Fundación para Estudios de la Población, Mexico A.C.
FGAE	Family Guidance Association of Ethiopia
FP	Family planning
FPA	Family Planning Association
FPAL	Family Planning Association of Liberia
FY	Fiscal year
IMSS	Instituto Mexicano del Seguro Social
INPPARES	Instituto Peruano de Paternidad Responsable
IPPF	International Planned Parenthood Federation
KIFP	Korea Institute for Family Planning
KIPH	Korea Institute for Population and Health
MCH	Maternal and child health
MEXFAM	La Fundación Mexicana Para la Planeación Familiar, A.C.
MOH	Ministry of Health
MWRA	Married women of reproductive age
NGO	Nongovernmental organization
OC	Oral contraceptive
ORS	Oral rehydration solution
PAHO	Pan American Health Organization
PHC	Primary health care; primary health center
PROFAM	Asociación Boliviana de Protección de la Familia
PROFAMILIA	Asociación Pro-Bienestar de la Familia Colombiana
SIDA	Swedish International Development Authority
UNDIESA	United Nations Department of International Economic and Social Affairs
UNESCO	United Nations Educational, Scientific, and Cultural Organization
UNFPA	United Nations Fund for Population Activities
UNICEF	United Nations Children's Fund
USAID	United States Agency for International Development
WFS	World Fertility Survey
WHO	World Health Organization

Technical Notes

Table 1. Selected Demographic, Social, and Economic Characteristics

Sources: World Bank unpublished data, and *World Development Report 1987,* Oxford University Press, New York, 1987; United Nations, Population Division, Department of International Economic and Social Affairs, *World Demographic Estimates and Projections, 1950–2025,* New York, 1988; ———, *World Population Prospects: Estimates and Projections as Assessed in 1982,* New York, 1985; ———, *Demographic Indicators of Countries: Estimates and Projections as Assessed in 1980,* New York, 1982; and UNESCO's *Statistical Yearbooks,* Paris.

Table 1 gives standard demographic, social, and economic indices for 100 developing countries. The first six columns show the total population in 1988 and as projected to 2000; the population density; the proportion of the population that is urban, beginning in 1984 and as projected to 2000; and the dependency ratio, that is, the ratio of the population in the dependent ages (0–14 and 65+) to the population in the economically productive ages (15–64). High values of the dependency ratio, as in Botswana and Kenya, indicate that a relatively small work force must support a relatively large burden of children and elderly people.

The next three columns show vital rates: the crude birthrate, crude death rate, and life expectancy. The crude birthrate and crude death rate are the numbers of births and deaths per 1,000 population; they give only a rough idea of the levels of fertility and mortality in the country, since both are affected by the age distribution. (See Table 3 for total fertility rates.)

Life expectancy is a refined measure of mortality, independent of any peculiarities in the age composition of the population. It summarizes a nation's health and mortality situation by indicating the mean number of years that a newborn infant would live if subjected throughout life to the current mortality rate at each age. For related information on infant and child mortality, see Tables 31–33.

The next six columns give literacy and primary and secondary school enrollment rates by sex. The literacy rate indicates the proportion of the population 15 years old and over who can read and write. For the school enrollment rates, primary and secondary school enrollment figures are divided by the total number of children of primary and secondary school age in the population. Because the figures come from different sources, and because enrollment patterns are not always well standardized by age and are not uniform across countries, it is possible for primary enrollment rates artifically to exceed 100 percent.

The per capita gross national product is a measure of the economic level of the country. It divides the total population into the gross national product (the total dollar value of all the goods and services produced in the country), with adjustments for the value of goods and services produced by nationals abroad and by foreigners residing within the country.

The per capita food production index relates food production in 1983–85 to that of 1979–81. The value of the latter within each country is taken as 100. Thus, a value of 121 (Benin) indicates that 1983–85 food production per capita exceeded that of 1979–81 by 21 percent. A value of 96 (Botswana) indicates that per capita food production in the latter years was only 96 percent as great as that in 1979–81.

The final column shows per capita daily calorie supply. It divides the total population into the calorie equivalent of the food supply, which is domestic production plus imports less exports; animal feed, seeds for agriculture, and food lost in processing and distribution are excluded.

Table 2. Number of Married Women of Reproductive Age (000s), 1975–2000

Source: This table was provided courtesy of the Center for International Research, U.S. Census Bureau. To our knowledge, no time trend for the number of married women of reproductive age has been previously published, and we are grateful to the Center for International Research for producing these estimates.

This table covers married women aged 15–44 for each country over a range of years, starting as early as 1975. For each country, the time trend was created in two steps. First, from a baseline census (or, in a few cases, from a sample survey) the population of all women in each age-group was projected through the usual component method, giving the time trend for all women by age. As a second step, these figures were reduced to the numbers married or cohabiting, by using the same percentage married or cohabiting by age as was reported in the base census. The age-groups were then summed to obtain the total number of married women aged 15–44.

The figures were also subjected to various corrections and adjustments—for example, to make all figures apply to midyear, to adjust where a census did not use standard five-year age-groups, and to smooth the age distribution to correct for age misstatement and heaping.

These adjustments produce what we believe to be the best international time series available. Projections from a recent census are reasonably secure for 15 years into the future, since the female population aged 0–14 has already been born at the time of the count. Thus, errors in fertility assumptions can affect only the later years, and then only for the younger age-groups. Projections vary little when alternative mortality assumptions are applied, and in most countries migration is not significant at the national level.

The baseline information is not as recent as we would like; 1970 information is often used, since detailed tabulations by sex, age, and marital status from the 1980 censuses were unavailable in many cases. In some instances, changes in the proportions married by age may have been rapid enough and substantial enough to produce consequential differences from the figures given here, especially in the younger age-groups. These, however, are only one component in the 15–44 total.

This table is the source for the estimates of married women of reproductive age used to calculate the last column of Tables 16 and 17.

Table 3. Total Fertility Rates, 1955–2000

Source: United Nations Population Division.

Programs that address high fertility rates and the health needs of infants must take into account likely time trends in childbearing. A useful indicator is the trend in the total fertility rate, the number of lifetime births a woman would have, given the current fertility rates at each age (neglecting female mortality). For each country, Table 3 gives the total fertility rate as estimated from 1955 onward. Each figure is the number of lifetime births expected in a new cohort of 1,000 women. Thus, for example, for Angola in 1955–60, the total fertility rate was 6,386 births per 1,000 women, or an average of 6.4 births per woman.

Table 4. Government Positions on Population Growth, and Interventions, 1986

Source: United Nations, Population Division, Department of International Economic and Social Affairs,

World Population Trends and Policies: 1987 Monitoring Report, New York, Table 3.5.

This table is derived from the Population Division's biennial questionnaire sent to all countries. The table categorizes countries as to the government's appraisal of the rate of population growth as too high, too low, or satisfactory and as to whether direct interventions are being undertaken to modify or maintain the growth rate. We have condensed the breakdown on these questions into the five categories shown in the table.

Table 5. Legal Status of Female Sterilization, 1987

Sources: The 1987 questionnaire; and J. A. Ross, S. Hong, and D. H. Huber, *Voluntary Sterilization: An International Fact Book,* Association for Voluntary Sterilization, New York, 1985, Table 3.1.

A very few countries make female sterilization entirely illegal. Most permit it, either on very restrictive grounds, such as to save the life of the mother, or for broader health reasons, eugenic considerations, or socioeconomic reasons. Some permit it simply on request. In countries that have no relevant law, the climate varies from permissive to restrictive. This table shows these policy variations.

Table 5 is closely related to Table 6, which summarizes procedural conditions for sterilization.

For additional information on female sterilization and on vasectomy, consult the publication listed above, Table 3.2.

Table 6. Conditions for Performing Sterilization, 1987

Sources: The 1987 questionnaire; and J. A. Ross, S. Hong, and D. H. Huber, *Voluntary Sterilization: An International Fact Book,* Association for Voluntary Sterilization, New York, 1985, Table 3.1.

Countries that permit sterilization often set conditions under which it may be performed. Frequently these vary between male and female sterilization. Conditions may include approval by a committee (usually medical), by the spouse, or by other parties, such as the parents for underage applicants. Most countries require that the procedure be done only by doctors, while others permit it by paramedics. Some specify a minimum age; some, a minimum number of children.

Table 8 provides similar information for abortion, plus price information. For sterilization prices, see Tables 13 and 14. For estimates of the proportion of the population for whom male and female sterilization is reasonably accessible, see Table 20.

Table 7. Legal Status of Abortion, 1987

Sources: The 1987 questionnaire; and C. Tietze and S. K. Henshaw, *Induced Abortion: A World Review, 1986,* Alan Guttmacher Institute, New York, 1986, Table 1. A revised edition is forthcoming.

This table parallels Table 5 for female sterilization.

It shows those countries that make abortion illegal without exception and those that permit it on grounds relating to the mother's survival or health, eugenic grounds, juridical grounds (rape or incest), socio-economic grounds, or simply on the woman's request.

Table 8. Conditions for Performing Legal Abortion, and Average Price of Abortion, 1987

Source: The 1987 questionnaire.

In some countries, abortion is illegal with no exceptions but it is often available in the private sector. Countries that make abortion legal may specify any of several conditions, including approval by a committee (usually medical), or with the husband's consent. Many require that it be performed by a physician, and some set a maximum gestational age.

The 1987 questionnaire asked for the average cost of abortion in the private sector, and in the public sector if it was available there. These prices appear in the final two columns.

See Table 20 for estimates of the proportion of the population for whom abortion services are reasonably accessible.

Table 9. Annual Family Planning, Health, and Total Government Budgets

Sources: Nortman Fact Books and the 1987 questionnaire.

This table gives, to the extent available, a time trend for the budgets of each country. Budgets are given in terms of expenditures (the preferred measure) or allocations. In some instances, when neither of these is available, planned budgets are shown. The table shows the figures for the family planning program, the health ministry, and the entire national budget; then the family planning budget as a percentage of the health ministry budget and of the national budget; and the health budget as a percentage of the national budget. (The percentages are derived from the budgets shown.) Thus, this table provides some sense of the priority given to family planning within (or relative to) the health sector and, similarly, the importance given to health within the entire national budget.

Caution must be observed with regard to the family planning figures and to family planning as a percentage of the other budgets. Many countries have no special family planning budget and instead report their maternal and child health budget, with an indication that family planning is contained within that. Such figures overstimate expenditures on family planning alone.

A further caution is that Table 9 gives all budgets in terms of local currency, and the rapid inflation experienced in many countries has undermined the value of the amounts shown for more recent years. However, the proportions in the final three columns are not affected by this difficulty.

Table 10. Annual Total and Per Capita Funding for Family Planning Programs, by Major Source

Sources: Nortman Fact Books and the 1987 questionnaire.

Funds for family planning are given in Table 10 as a time series for each country, by source. The qualifications noted for Table 9 apply here as well. In Table 10, each domestic budget is converted to U.S. dollars, on the basis of the exchange rate shown for each year. Exchange rates sometimes fluctuate widely, because of market changes in the value of the dollar, the value of the local currency, or both. In any year when a government devalued its own currency, sometimes by a large fraction, the converted dollar amount in Table 10 may be considerably below that for the previous year, but this does not necessarily imply a drop in real inputs to the program.

This table attempts to capture the overall monetary inputs into the family planning program: from the government (these figures are sometimes inflated by the inclusion of maternal and child health monies); such international agencies as the World Bank and the United Nations Fund for Population Activities; foreign government sources of bilateral aid, such as the U.S. Agency for International Development and the Swedish International Development Authority; and private organizations, such as the International Planned Parenthood Federation, the Ford Foundation, and the Population Council.

The final two columns use the population base in each year to provide the per capita expenditure for the government and for all sources, including the government. The time trend in any country for the per capita budgets is, of course, subject to the qualifications given above. Donor amounts were sometimes under-reported, since the country respondent did not always have access to full information. These figures are therefore often minimum estimates.

Table 11. Percentage Distribution of Family Planning Program Expenditures, by Type of Expenditure

Sources: Nortman Fact Books and the 1987 questionnaire.

This table divides the program's total budget (see Table 10) in percentage terms along traditional budgetary lines. It shows the salaries paid to different categories of personnel, and salaries paid for special efforts to recruit contraceptive clients through information and education campaigns and other promotional work. It also gives the percentage for contraceptive supplies, for maintenance and operations (including rent, electricity, telephone, postage, stationery, office equipment, vehicles, and computers), and for capital construction and improvement (longer-range outlays for buildings, either for central headquarters or for outlying facilities).

Table 12. Percentage Distribution of Family Planning Program Expenditures, by Program Function

Sources: Nortman Fact Books and the 1987 questionnaire.

Like Table 11, this table gives the percentage distribution of the total country budget, but does so by functional categories, to show the amount going for the purpose specified in each column heading: actual contraceptive services, public information and education, research and evaluation, personnel training, administration, and other activities. Tables 11 and 12 both give the available time series.

Table 13. Import Regulations, Contraceptive Supplies Available, and Price Range in Private Sector

Sources: Nortman Fact Books and the 1987 questionnaire.

As this table shows, many governments require commercial firms, such as pharmaceutical concerns, to obtain a license to import contraceptives. Also, duty may be charged, as a percentage of either the import value or the CIF (cost insurance freight) price. In some countries, even the Ministry of Health must pay duty to another ministry on contraceptives it imports.

Table 13 also shows the quantity of contraceptive supplies available in each country, both the total and as broken down between imports and those manufactured domestically. In general, orals are counted by cycles and condoms by dozens, unless otherwise stated. The final two columns give the typical retail price range of each contraceptive in the private sector.

Table 14. Charges and Payments to Acceptors of Family Planning Services and Supplies

Sources: Nortman Fact Books and the 1987 questionnaire.

Many countries provide contraceptive services free, some charge for some or all services, and a few pay the acceptor (usually only for sterilization or the IUD). Table 14 presents information for both charges and payments, by country and method, for each year for which data are available.

This table is closely related to Table 15, which covers payments made to program personnel.

As with all financial information, these figures are subject to the cautions explained for Tables 9 and 10.

Table 15. Payments to Personnel for Specified Family Planning Services, by Type of Service and Category of Worker

Sources: Nortman Fact Books and the 1987 questionnaire.

Payments to personnel for family planning services are made on different bases. Doctors or nurses may be paid, for example, per clinic session, or a monthly salary, or for each IUD insertion or sterilization.

In a few countries, the individual who recruits each client is paid a finder's fee on a per case basis. Table 15 shows payments to physicians, nurses or midwives, and other workers, and indicates for each country the basis on which payment is made. Payments are shown in both local currency and U.S. dollars.

For some early years the exchange rates shown here differ from those in Table 10, usually only by a small amount. These differences have been retained from the original sources.

Table 16. Personnel Specifically Allocated for Family Planning Services

Sources: Nortman Fact Books (modified information) and the 1987 questionnaire.

For the Nortman Fact Books, country respondents were asked to list personnel specifically allocated for family planning services, by type. In the new questionnaire, respondents were instructed that if family planning activities were merged with maternal and child health services, they should indicate that and enter personnel figures for the combined program.

The personnel mentioned over the years were of many types, with great variety in titles. We have combined them into five categories, as shown in Table 16. Respondents were asked to give both the total number of personnel involved (that is, counts of individuals) and the full-time equivalent of any part-time personnel. For example, four half-time physicians represent two full-time equivalents. Table 16 shows only the full-time equivalents.

The first column gives the total for the others, even when a "u" (for unknown) is entered in one or more columns; the total number is therefore a minimum. This total is used as the denominator for the final column; the numerator is the number of married women of reproductive age (MWRA), taken from Table 2. MWRA estimates were not available for certain years for some countries; where estimates existed for two years somewhat apart, interpolation was used to calculate intermediate MWRA values. In many instances baseline figures prior to the beginning date of 1975 in Table 2 were used; these come from the same U.S. Census Bureau source noted in Table 2. In a few cases extrapolation was used to obtain values for nearby years; however, where this seemed unwise, "u" was entered in the final column.

Caution must be exercised to distinguish between sharp breaks in time trends that may be due to reporting problems and those that represent genuine programmatic change. For example, in Thailand there is a sharp break in the number of personnel between 1972 and 1973, corresponding to a national decision to authorize a large rural corps of auxiliary nurse-midwives to prescribe and resupply oral contraceptives, a real programmatic change.

Table 17. Facilities Specifically Allocated for Family Planning Services

Sources: Nortman Fact Books and the 1987 questionnaire.

Data on facilities specifically allocated for family planning services are given in Table 17. Where family planning is merged with maternal and child health services, the respondent was asked to indicate that and to give the number of facilities offering integrated services. The table shows the total, then the allocation to the various facility types.

The total is the sum of the entries in the cells, and, as in Table 16, it is a minimum wherever the row contains one or more "u" entries. In some cases (for example, Burkina Faso), only the total is known and not the distribution.

The final column shows estimates of the number of married women of reproductive age per service point. The numerator, MWRA, is drawn from Table 2, and the denominator is the entry in the total column.

Table 18. Family Planning Program Effort Scores, by Effort Level and Program Component, 1982; and Contraceptive Prevalence, Selected Years

Sources: R. J. Lapham and W. P. Mauldin, "Contraceptive Prevalence: The Influence of Organized Family Planning Programs," *Studies in Family Planning* 16(3): 117–137, 1985. See also R. J. Lapham and W. P. Mauldin, "Family Planning Program Effort and Birthrate Decline in Developing Countries," *International Family Planning Perspectives* 10(4): 109–118, 1984.

Earlier publications based upon similar scores include R. Freedman and B. Berelson, "The Record of Family Planning Programs," *Studies in Family Planning* 7(1):1–40, 1976; and W. P. Mauldin and B. Berelson, "Conditions of Fertility Decline in Developing Countries, 1965–1975," *Studies in Family Planning* 9(5): 84–148, 1978.

Lapham and Mauldin undertook a major survey to establish effort measures for large family planning programs, with 1982 as the reference point. Thirty indices emerged from this work,* which were classified under the four general headings shown in Table 18. The score on each index ranged from 0 to 4. Thus, with eight indices under "policy and stage setting," a maximum score of 32 was possible for this category; the 13 indices under "service and service-related" gave a

maximum of 52; the three under "record keeping and evaluation" gave a maximum of 12; and the six under "availability and accessibility" gave a maximum of 24 (all shown in the first row of the table). Countries are ranked in the table by the total score attained, starting with China at 101.1, and are grouped according to level of effort: strong (total score of 80–120), moderate (55–79), weak (25–54), and very weak or none (0–24). Lapham and Mauldin also provided the contraceptive prevalence level prevailing in each country for 1982 or for the closest year available (final two columns).

Table 19. Family Planning Activities Performed by Paramedics, 1987

Source: The 1987 questionnaire.

In many family planning programs paramedics are allowed to screen potential users of oral contraceptives. In most of these cases they are required, at least formally, to follow a checklist of medical contraindications such as varicose veins, a history of other cardiovascular problems, or headaches. The diligence with which such checklists are actually employed in practice naturally varies. Appropriately trained paramedics are also permitted to insert IUDs in some family planning programs. This table summarizes these policies for the countries for which the information is available.

Table 20. Percentage of Population with Access to Family Planning and Health Services, 1987

Source: The 1987 questionnaire.

Respondents to the 1987 questionnaire were asked to provide expert judgments on the proportion of the population in the urban and rural sectors having ready physical access to each of several family planning and child survival services. It was explained that ready access meant that "travel time and distance are not serious barriers to getting the service." The proportions reported for the family planning items appear on the lefthand page, and those for the child survival items appear on the righthand page.

The origin of the use of expert judgments of accessibility is found in the work of Lapham and Mauldin (see notes to Table 18). The articles cited there were concerned largely with overall program effort, as measured by the 30 scores described. Accessibility was one part of that work, and the measure used in our 1987 ques-

---

* These headings, and indices, were as follows: **Policy- and stage-setting activities**—policy regarding fertility reduction and family planning, statements by leaders, level of program leadership, policy regarding age at marriage, import laws and legal regulations, advertising of contraceptives allowed, other ministries/public agencies involved, in-country budget for program; **service and service-related activities**—involvement of private-sector agencies and groups, civil bureaucracy used, community-based distribution, social marketing,

postpartum program, home-visiting workers, administrative structure, training program, carry out assigned tasks, logistics and transport, supervision system, mass media for IEC, incentives/disincentives; **record keeping and evaluation**—record keeping, evaluation, management use of evaluation findings; **availability and accessibility of fertility control supplies and services**—male sterilization, female sterilization, pills (and injectables), condoms (and other conventionals), IUDs, abortion.

tionnaire was closely similar to that of Lapham and Mauldin.

The columns of Table 20 are largely self-explanatory. Related information for oral rehydration supplies (ORS) is found in Table 36. For countries that appear in both tables, the information on ORS in Table 36 is identical to that presented here, although the rural-urban breakdown is not shown there.

Differences between the estimated percentage with access to delivery by trained midwives shown in this table and the percentage of births attended by trained health personnel shown in Table 37, as supplied by UNICEF, reflect different years, different definitions of the question, and different respondents. Such disparities are illustrative of data problems in this field. Similar discrepancies occur between the information regarding infant and maternal immunizations given here and in Table 35.

Table 21. Community-Based Distribution Programs, 1987

Source: The 1987 questionnaire.

Community-based distribution programs deliver simple family planning and health services at the local level, sometimes to the doorstep and sometimes through neighborhood depots. Our questionnaire elicited the information shown, which, while not extensive, is up to date. The various columns indicate the number of agents or providers, the number of villages and the population covered, the types of services, and whether or not the program charges for services and supplies. For a comprehensive though older review, see A. Kols and M. Wawer, "Community-Based Health and Family Planning," *Population Reports* series L, no. 3, Nov.–Dec. 1982.

Table 22. Social Marketing Programs

Sources: The 1987 questionnaire and supplementary information. Some figures come from *Social Marketing Forum,* which regularly issues price data. Other information comes from J. Cherris, B. Ravenholt, and R. Blackburn, "Contraceptive Social Marketing: Lessons from Experience," *Population Reports* series J, no. 30, July–Aug. 1985. This comprehensive treatment includes extensive descriptive information on numerous social marketing programs. We are grateful to Ward Rinehart for unpublished figures on time trends in sales shown only graphically in this source.

Social marketing programs offer contraceptives through commercial outlets, but at a subsidized price. Typically, a donor provides contraceptive supplies either free or at a reduced price to one or more wholesale commercial firms, which then sell the contraceptives through their regular channels. Such programs now operate in numerous countries. This table provides coverage estimates, sales figures, and typical prices for each of the contraceptive methods.

Table 23. Number of Acceptors of Family Planning Services (000s), by Method and Year

Sources: Nortman Fact Books and the 1987 questionnaire. Acceptor data for IUDs and sterilizations for Chinese provinces in 1984 were kindly provided by Xizhe Peng, drawn from the *Handbook of China's Family Planning Statistics,* compiled by China's Population Information Centre.

Most large-scale programs maintain records to show the number of acceptors of each contraceptive method, and this table compiles that information for all years available.

A caution is that "acceptor" is defined variously in these record systems. A few countries attempt to restrict "acceptor" to a first-time adopter of any method, and if the individual later switches to any other method, he or she is not counted again as an acceptor. But most countries are unable to maintain such precision. They generally count each woman taking a first IUD as an acceptor, even if she previously used another method, and most countries include reinsertions in the IUD count. Individuals accepting sterilization are nearly always included in the sterilization count, even if they previously used another method, and this is an advantage from the standpoint of knowing the number and characteristics of persons choosing a permanent method.

More troublesome are acceptor counts for the resupply methods: pill, injectable, condom, and spermicide. While some countries identify first-time adopters of each such method and avoid counting them again when they return for fresh supplies, this is difficult to do in practice, and many systems simply track the total quantity of supplies given out. Some of them convert these figures to couple-years of protection to provide some indication of the number of "couple-equivalents" who are covered. Thirteen cycles of the pill, for example, are counted as one couple-year of protection. Assuming an average coital frequency, for example, of 100 per year, 100 condoms or 100 applications of spermicide are counted as one couple-year of protection (sometimes with a discount for wastage and nonuse). Exact formulas vary from country to country. For injectables, which usually protect for three months, four doses are counted as one couple-year of protection. Country definitions, conventions, and formulas may have changed in some programs over the years; hence, long time series are not always completely standardized.

Another difficulty concerns provider agencies. In a number of the large Asian countries, the private family planning associations perform various specialized functions; and some do rather little in service delivery. In Latin America, however, and in some African countries, family planning associations are major providers, along with government health ministries and other agencies, and frequently began activities prior to the development of government-sponsored programs. Practice differs as to whether the various provider agencies and respondents consolidate their figures into national totals, report separately, or underreport. In a number of instances, we have reported data for the major provider agencies separately, and we have attempted to clarify their various contributions in current and past statistics. However, readers should proceed cautiously.

Tables 24–25. Acceptors Distributed by Age and Number of Living Children

Table 24. Acceptors Distributed by Method and Age of Wife, and Median Age of Wife

Table 25. Acceptors Distributed by Method and Number of Living Children, and Median Number of Living Children

Sources: Nortman Fact Books and the 1987 questionnaire.

Acceptors vary by age (Table 24) and by number of living children (Table 25). The distributions given in these two tables are sometimes based upon a sample rather than upon the total shown in Table 23. Table 24 gives the year in question, the sample size (which can be quite large where all acceptors were analyzed), the percentage distribution by age of wife, and wife's median age. For every method but vasectomy and condoms, "age of wife" refers to the acceptor herself; for those two methods, wife's age is used to permit uniform comparisons among methods. (No medians were calculated when age was unknown for 15 percent or more of acceptors.)

Table 25 is exactly parallel to Table 24, but distributes acceptors of each method by number of living children.

Time trends in age and number of living children by method can be calculated from the data given. In many countries there has been a trend toward acceptance by younger women and those with fewer children as family planning has spread through the population.

Table 26. Contraceptive Prevalence: Percentage of Married Women of Reproductive Age (or Spouses) Currently Using Each Method

Sources: We relied particularly upon these compilations of prevalence information:

(1) United Nations, Population Division, Department of International Economic and Social Affairs, "Recent Levels and Trends of Contraceptive Use as Assessed in 1983," New York, 1984, and *World Population Trends and Policies: 1987 Monitoring Report,* New York, 1988.

(2) W. P. Mauldin and S. J. Segal, *Prevalence of Contraceptive Use in Developing Countries: A Chart Book,* Rockefeller Foundation, New York, 1986.

The authors of the above were most generous in supplying supplementary unpublished information.

We are grateful to Chi-shien Tuan for prepublication data on contraceptive prevalence in China. See his *Contraceptive Revolution in China,* New World Press, forthcoming.

The 1987 questionnaire yielded data for some countries, as did the Demographic and Health Surveys series. A further source was K. London et al., "Fertility and Family Planning Surveys: An Update," *Population Reports* series M, no. 8, Sept.–Oct. 1985, pp. 289–348. Finally, survey reports and publications from various other sources and country surveys were helpful.

Prevalence of contraceptive use pertains to the proportion of all couples of childbearing age who are *currently using* a particular method. Current use is quite different from the number *accepting* given in Table 23, since many acceptors terminate use for one reason or another, and many past acceptors have passed out of the childbearing ages. Others have been counted as an "acceptor" more than once because they tried more than one method; now they use only one, or none. In epidemiological terms, an annual acceptance figure is comparable to incidence, whereas the proportion of couples currently using a method is comparable to prevalence.

The column on all methods gives the total percentage using contraception (including sterilization). The next column provides a subtotal for the use of "modern" methods, which we have restricted to sterilization, IUD, orals, and injectables, the methods with best acceptability, continuation, and reliability in actual practice.

The symbol "u" is entered in a cell when an exact figure is unavailable. Nevertheless, we have calculated totals for the figures shown. Frequently a method for which "u" is entered is covered for that country in the "other" column, so the total is essentially correct. For example, a survey may obtain information on use of rhythm, withdrawal, and abstinence, but the survey report combines these under "other." In such a case we enter "u" in the columns for rhythm, withdrawal, and abstinence.

Most entries in Table 26 come from surveys. In some cases, generally only where the program is the primary source of supply, the estimates given are from program service statistics. China, India, and Indonesia are three such cases, and the table gives both survey and service statistics information for each. The different sources are identified in the footnotes.

Surveys are able to detect use of methods obtained in the private sector, and methods not provided in either sector, such as withdrawal, abstinence, and folk methods. Abortion is also included in many surveys, but underreporting is common. Surveys, in fact, produce prevalence percentages that are subject to undercounts of all methods in the numerator and to sampling and other errors in the denominator of married (or cohabiting) women.

Service statistics in some countries give a better picture of program-supplied contraception than surveys do, and this is important for assessing the public program's contribution (see Table 27). In the case of China, virtually all contraception is provided in the public sector, so the service statistics cover essentially all prevalence of use. However, in all countries it is difficult to know how many past IUD acceptors still retain the device, and there are other tendencies for program officials (and some couples) to overstate the level of contraceptive use. The Chinese survey of 1982 is thought to contain less overreporting than the service statistics; still, prevalence almost certainly rose after 1982, with a changing method mix toward more sterilization.

In the case of India, the 1980 survey shows 34 percent prevalence, whereas service statistics for adjoining years show only about 23 percent supplied through the program. This reflects a good deal of private-sector use, including reliance on methods difficult to obtain through the program.

Indonesia has always issued monthly reports showing program-supplied prevalence. It also has survey estimates, and an estimate from the 1980 census. Some of the considerations mentioned above apply, including omission of certain methods in the program and undercounts of use in the census. Until 1980, at least, there was excellent agreement between the surveys and the service statistics on a method-specific and province-specific basis. See J. Ross and S. Poedjastoeti, "Contraceptive Use and Program Development: New Information from Indonesia," *International Family Planning Perspectives* 9(3): 68–77, 1983; and J. Sinquefield and B. Sungkono, "Fertility and Family Planning Trends in Java and Bali," *International Family Planning Perspectives* 5(2):43–58, 1979.

Table 27. Contraceptive Prevalence by Sector: Percentage of Married Women of Reproductive Age (or Spouses) Obtaining Contraception through the Public and Private Sectors

Sources: Nortman Fact Books, the 1987 questionnaire, and country survey reports (see sources for Table 26).

Table 27 provides estimates of the proportion of couples using contraception, but separately for those relying on public programs and those relying on the private sector of pharmacies, shops, physicians, and paramedic practitioners for supplies and services. Private use also includes nonsupply methods, such as withdrawal, which is important in Turkey and certain other countries. This division permits an approximate picture of the role of each sector in providing contraceptive supplies and services, including sterilizations.

The sum of the two figures shown in each row equals the total prevalence of contraceptive use. However, the figures shown here may not entirely reconcile with those in Table 26. In some cases, the division by sector was available only from a survey earlier than the latest one represented in Table 26. In other cases, figures come from different sources or derive from different techniques of analysis.

Table 28. Adolescents: Vital Statistics for Women 15–19

Sources: This table was made possible by courtesy of the United Nations Statistical Office, which provided prepublication information from the 1987 *Demographic Yearbook.* The age-specific fertility rates are from the United Nations Population Division. Contraceptive prevalence figures are from K. London et al., "Fertility and Family Planning Surveys: An Update," *Population Reports* series M, no. 8, Sept.–Oct. 1985, pp. 289–348.

We have included this table to provide basic indicators for teenage women, since these are generally unavailable on a cross-country or time-trend basis. As the table shows, time trends are extremely limited, making it difficult to trace progress in large-scale programs directed to younger women. The percentage using contraception can be traced in somewhat more detail than shown by further reference to contraceptive prevalence surveys.

Table 29. Health Manpower Coverage

Sources: The numbers of personnel and beds shown here were compiled by the World Health Organization as of 1982, and the population figures are from the United Nations Population Division. See also the United Nations 1983/84 *Statistical Yearbook,* Table 53; and the Nortman Fact Book, 12th ed.

The World Health Organization discontinued its annual efforts to compile these figures as of 1982; however, it has recently renewed the activity and plans a publication in late 1988 or early 1989 giving new estimates (see comments under Table 37).

See also Table 17, which gives the number of facilities devoted to family planning or, for some countries, to maternal and child health.

Both manpower and facilities tend to be concentrated in the urban sector. If separate figures for rural areas were available, they would show a very much lower level of coverage for many countries.

Tables 30–33. Infant and Child Mortality

Table 30. Numbers of Infant and Child Deaths, 1987
Table 31. Infant Mortality: Proportion of Infants Dying before Age One
Table 32. Child Mortality between Ages One and Five: Proportion of One-Year-Olds Dying before Age Five
Table 33. Child Mortality through Age Five: Proportion of Infants Dying before Age Five

Sources: Data for these four tables were provided by courtesy of the United Nations Population Division and UNICEF. The figures were produced from technical work by Population Division staff from original country materials, subjected to indirect demographic estimation techniques. See United Nations, Population Division, Department of International Economic and Social Affairs, *Mortality of Children under Age 5: World Estimates and Projections, 1950–2025, Population Studies,* no. 105, New York, 1988. See also United Nations, Population Division, Department of International Economic and Social Affairs, *World Demographic Estimates and Projections, 1950–2025,* New York, 1988; and UNICEF, *The State of the World's Children 1988,* New York, Oxford University Press, Table 1 (see also Table 1 in the 1987 edition).

Table 30 gives numbers of infant and child deaths in each country for 1987. These come from a two-step calculation: first, the number of annual births was calculated as the product of the population size and the crude birthrate; second, the number of deaths was calculated as the product of births and mortality probabilities taken from Tables 31–33. The table shows numbers of deaths before the first birthday, from exact age one to five, and from birth to exact age five.

Data in Table 30 are given in absolute numbers, since these indicate the magnitude of services needed. Attention tends typically to be on rates rather than on numbers, but that focus can obscure striking differences. India, for example, has five times as many child deaths as China.

Tables 31–33 give time trends for the probability of dying at young ages. Technically, these are mortality probabilities rather than mortality rates. The distinction is simply that a mortality probability is based on the number of infants alive at the start of the time interval in question, whereas a mortality rate uses the average number alive during the interval, which is a smaller denominator.

Table 31 gives the classic infant mortality rate—the probability of dying between birth and age one—expressed as the number of deaths in the first year per 1,000 births. Table 32 gives the probability of dying between exact ages one and five—that is, of 1,000 infants who are still alive at age one, the number who die before the fifth birthday. Table 33 gives the number of deaths between birth and age five among 1,000 births.

Table 34. Estimates of Maternal Mortality, by Region, ca. 1983

Sources: World Health Organization, Division of Family Health, *Maternal Mortality Rates: A Tabulation of Available Information,* 2nd ed., Geneva, 1986. See also B. Herz and A. Measham, *The Safe Motherhood Initiative: Proposals for Action,* World Bank, Washington, D.C., 1987.

A maternal mortality rate refers to pregnancy- and delivery-related deaths per 100,000 live births. It includes abortion-related deaths, which in some locations account for a significant proportion of maternal deaths. Measurement of maternal mortality rates is difficult; much information is unreliable because the absolute number of deaths is relatively small and is subject to severe underreporting. Nevertheless, the risk to the typical mother in many developing countries is far from trivial. Some rates approach 1,000 maternal deaths per 100,000 live births. This 1 percent chance, taken 10 or 12 times during a lifetime, may cumulate to be approximately equivalent to a 10 percent probability of dying during the childbearing career.

Averages across whole regions are below this level, but they conceal wide variations by country. Because of the large uncertainty that accompanies many country estimates, we present here only regional figures. The WHO source cited above covers an exhaustive collection of studies, with references, on maternal mortality for a large number of developing countries. The regions shown in Table 34 and Figure 8 follow the UN categories, which place North African countries under Africa (Northern), and Middle East countries under Asia (Western).

Although the measurement of maternal mortality has been difficult, innovative methods are under trial. For example, see W. Graham, W. Brass, and R. Snow, "Estimating Maternal Mortality," *Lancet* Feb. 20, 1988, pp. 416–417.

Table 35. Immunization Coverage as of 1984–87

Source: World Health Organization, Expanded Programme on Immunization.

Extraordinary efforts have been devoted to immunization programs in many developing countries, largely under the aegis of the Expanded Programme on Immunization of the World Health Organization. The Programme office has also recommended a standard method for estimating the proportions of children who are immunized against each of several leading childhood diseases, using a cluster sampling approach that interviews families in selected villages. While this method appears reliable insofar as sampling considerations are concerned, it is subject to difficult problems of memory and record keeping, as all household surveys are. The figures in Table 35 are based only partly upon that method; they come also from other surveys and, in some cases, from the judgments of country experts.

Table 35 includes 1986 estimates for numbers of births, the infant mortality rate, and surviving infants (the product of births and the infant survival rate, which is one minus the infant mortality rate). The 1986 infant mortality rate is not always consistent with the rate used for Table 31, but we have retained the figures without change from their original source. The purpose here is to give a sense of the service requirements for health programs. For child survival objectives such as immunizations, it is important to know the number of births and the number of surviving infants each year, since most injections must occur within the first year, and the objective is complete coverage of the country.

Table 36. Availability and Use of Oral Rehydration Solution

Sources: World Health Organization and the 1987 questionnaire.

Table 36 gives the typical market price of oral rehydration solution (ORS) packets, and shows which countries are known to provide them free. It also presents estimates of the percentage of all diarrhea cases that are treated with ORS; the number of packets used per 100 diarrhea episodes; and the percentage of the population with ready access to ORS, as estimated by country respondents to the 1987 questionnaire (see Table 20). The last column indicates which governments promote home mixes of ORS, as distinct from prepackaged supplies to which water is added.

The columns in Table 36 represent some of the main points of interest concerning the use of oral rehydration supplies to replace fluids lost as a result of diarrhea. However, the information available on each point is skimpy, and one function of this table, with its numerous empty cells, is to illustrate this unfortunate lack of information. Clearly, the various agencies working to extend the use of ORS need to devote greater efforts to the accurate assessment of progress.

Table 37. Percentage of Births Attended by Trained Health Personnel, 1984

Source: UNICEF, *The State of the World's Children 1988,* New York, Oxford University Press, 1988, Table 3.

"Trained health personnel" means physicians, nurses, and midwives with formal training, as distinct from traditional village midwives. Table 37 provides the percentage of births attended by trained health personnel as of approximately 1984. This percentage is one indicator for "maternal coverage," which refers to the extent of health care before, during, and soon after pregnancy.

Other sources of information on maternal coverage provide information in detailed categories by the type of medical personnel in attendance, and also indicate whether the birth occurred in an institution; however, that information is generally older. Most comparative data on maternal coverage originate with inquiries by WHO and are referred to by these other sources (see, for example, the World Bank's annual *World Development Reports,* and the Nortman Fact

Books). WHO discontinued its annual efforts in 1982, but it has reestablished an activity to obtain data from country respondents, and the results may be published within the next year. Closely related to maternal coverage is the proportion of mothers receiving tetanus shots (see Table 35). See also comments under Table 20 regarding accessibility indicators.

Table 38. Prevalence and Duration of Breast-Feeding

Sources: World Health Organization, the 1987 questionnaire, and selected national surveys. Most table entries are selected from an extensive compilation developed by WHO; only national estimates were kept, although where none were available local surveys were sometimes included. These data were supplemented by results from recent Demographic and Health Surveys, conducted under Westinghouse auspices, and from other literature.

Table 38 shows the size and type of the sample; the proportion of women giving birth who ever breast-fed; the proportions who were still breast-feeding at three months, six months, and 12 months; and the median or mean duration of breast-feeding.

For a careful examination of breast-feeding trends from repeated surveys in selected countries, see S. Millman, "Breastfeeding Trends in Eighteen Developing Countries," Final Report to Family Health International, Research Triangle Park, N.C., June 1987.

An earlier version of the WHO data bank on breast-feeding was published as World Health Organization, Division of Family Health, "The Prevalence and Duration of Breastfeeding: A Critical Review of Available Information," *World Health Statistics Quarterly* 35(2): 92–118, 1982.

Table 39. Percentage of Population with Access to Safe Drinking Water and Sanitation, Early 1980s

Sources: World Resources Institute, *World Resources 1987,* New York, Basic Books, 1987, Table 17.2. This publication, in turn, credits the following sources: World Health Organization, *The International Drinking Water Supply and Sanitation Decade: Review of National Baseline Data: December, 1980,* Geneva, 1984; and unpublished WHO data, Geneva, September 1986; and, for urban and rural proportions of total population, United Nations, Population Division, *World Population Prospects: Estimates and Projections as Assessed in 1982,* New York, 1985.

Contributing factors to widespread prevalence of diarrhea in the developing world are polluted water and poor sanitation. Local studies point to household factors as equally or more important, but we give national, urban, and rural estimates here for safe water and adequate sanitation as separate determinants having their own importance. The estimates must, of course, be treated with caution, but they are the best available.

Tables 1–39

Table 1.   Selected Demographic, Social, and Economic Characteristics

Country	Total population (000s) 1988	Total population (000s) 2000	Density (population per sq. km) 1988	Urban population (%) 1984	Urban population (%) 2000	Dependency ratio 1980	Crude birthrate 1985	Crude death rate 1985	Life expectancy 1985
SUB-SAHARAN AFRICA									
Angola	9503	13234[a]	7.6	25[b]	36	89	47.0	20.6[c]	44.0[c]
Benin	4459	6474	39.6	15	53	95	49.2	17.2	49.3
Botswana	1242	1712	2.1	19[b]	33	107	45.7	12.4	57.0
Burkina Faso	7531	12101	27.5	11	12	88	48.6	20.5	45.3
Burundi	5154	7370	185.4	3	21	87	46.9	18.4	47.8
Cameroon	10765	16680	22.6	41	60	85	47.3	13.9	54.9
Central African Republic	2775	3962	4.5	45	55	83	42.1	16.2	45.0[c]
Chad	5408	7281	4.2	21	44	84	43.5	20.5	44.5
Congo	1893	3176	5.5	56	50	87	45.2	11.9	57.5
Côte d'Ivoire	10919	16026	33.9	46	55	91	44.5	13.8	52.7
Ethiopia	47475	65073	38.9	15	17	93	45.7	19.4	45.0
Gabon	1224	1500	4.6	40	54	67	38.4	16.3	51.0
Ghana	15078	19718	63.2	39	38	96	46.2	13.9	53.2
Guinea	6556	8288	26.7	27	33	84	49.9	24.0	40.3
Kenya	23488	36452	40.3	20[b]	32	115	53.6	13.2	54.3
Lesotho	1647	2302	54.2	17[b]	28	84	41.0	14.0	54.4
Liberia	2423	6533	21.7	39	52	95	48.7	16.4	50.2
Madagascar	10950	15969	18.7	21	32	88	46.8	14.9	52.3
Malawi	7696	11351	64.9	12[b]	21	100	53.6	21.9	45.0
Mali	8850	11198	7.1	18[b]	23	95	47.8	19.6	46.2
Mauritania	2077	2555	2.0	26	54	94	45.2	18.7	46.5
Mauritius	1104	1212	581.2	42[b]	46	59	20.0	7.1	66.0
Mozambique	15167	21480	18.9	19[b]	36	91	45.2	18.1	46.8
Namibia	1696	1749	2.1	51[b]	66	89	45.2	15.9	50.6
Niger	6712	10161	5.3	14	24	99	51.4	21.3	43.6
Nigeria	106085	163484	114.8	23[b]	33	102	49.6	16.2	49.8
Rwanda	6735	10240	256.1	5	12	103	52.0	18.6	47.5
Senegal	7004	10270	35.7	35	44	90	46.2	18.5	46.5
Sierra Leone	3821	5339	53.3	24	40	78	48.4	25.1	39.5
Somalia	4963	8462	7.8	34[b]	46	88	49.3	19.5	46.0
South Africa	35009	45008	28.7	57	64	83	37.2	13.1	54.8
Sudan	23557	33694	9.4	21	26	91	45.2	17.0	48.4
Tanzania	25198	37046	26.7	14	41	103	50.1	15.3	51.9
Togo	3254	4872	57.3	23	33	90	49.1	16.4	50.5
Uganda	17246	23374	73.1	7	14	102	50.4	17.0	49.0
Zaire	32886	47392	14.0	39	46	91	45.1	15.1	51.3
Zambia	7413	11126	9.9	48	65	98	48.7	14.8	51.9
Zimbabwe	9818	13238	25.1	27	35	100	46.7	11.7	57.1
LATIN AMERICA/CARIBBEAN									
Argentina	31953	36541	11.5	85[b]	89	62	23.4	8.9	70.3
Bolivia	6936	9172	6.3	48[b]	58	88	42.1	14.5	52.8
Brazil	144446	178369	17.0	73[b]	83	72	29.3	7.9	64.5
Chile	12607	14550	16.7	83	89	61	21.6	6.7	70.4
Colombia	30577	36831	26.8	67[b]	75	75	27.4	7.2	64.9
Costa Rica	2802	3481	55.3	45	61	72	28.5	4.1	73.5
Cuba	10339	11718[a]	90.6	72[b]	80	63	18.0	6.7[c]	74.0[c]
Dominican Republic	6680	8655	137.2	55	68	88	32.4	7.2	64.4
Ecuador	10220	13569	36.0	47	65	92	35.1	6.9	66.0
El Salvador	6112	6368	291.0	43	44	95	38.2	10.0	63.6
Guatemala	8704	11533	79.9	41	47	88	40.4	9.5	60.2
Guyana	1005	1196[a]	4.7	32	42	76	24.8[c]	7.4	65.4
Haiti	7139	7864	256.8	27	37	89	35.0	12.7	54.4
Honduras	4812	6825	42.9	39	52	102	42.0	9.0	62.0
Jamaica	2447	2777	222.5	53	64	87	25.0	5.7	73.4
Mexico	85005	109861	43.1	69	77	93	32.9	6.5	66.6
Nicaragua	3631	4985	27.9	56	66	99	42.5	10.3	59.2
Panama	2323	2791	30.1	50	60	81	26.4	5.2	71.6
Paraguay	4011	5348	9.9	41	54	86	35.0	6.7	66.1
Peru	21278	25182	16.6	68	75	83	33.0	10.7	58.6

Table 1.

Literacy rate 1985 (%)		Primary school enrollment 1984 (%)[k]		Secondary school enrollment 1984 (%)[k]		GNP per capita (U.S.$) 1985	Food production index[l] 1983–85	Per capita daily calories 1985	Country
Males	Females	Males	Females	Males	Females				
									SUB-SAHARAN AFRICA
49	u	u	u	u	u	470.00[h]	102	u	Angola
37	16	86	42	28	11	250.40	121	2173	Benin
73	69	91	103	23	27	660.50	96	2219	Botswana
21	6	37	22	6	3	135.70	114	1924	Burkina Faso
43[d]	26[d]	58	40	5	3	222.60	106	2116	Burundi
68	55	116	97	29	18	745.00	107	2089	Cameroon
53	29	98	51	u	u	255.30	105	2050	Central African Republic
40	11	55	21	11	2	129.20	106	1504	Chad
71	55	u	u	u	u	1087.40	104	2549	Congo
53	31	91	63	28	12	639.50	115	2505	Côte d'Ivoire
u	u	u	u	14	8	111.20	97	1681	Ethiopia
70	53	u	u	u	u	3431.50	u	u	Gabon
64	43	75	59	45	27	379.40	118	1747	Ghana
40	17	44	20	20	7	298.70	102	1728	Guinea
70	49	101	94	22	16	274.00	99	2151	Kenya
62	84	97	126	17	26	370.00	93	2358	Lesotho
47	23	95	57	u	u	467.80	114	2311	Liberia
74	62	125	118	43	30	217.40	112	2469	Madagascar
52	31	71	53	6	2	145.30	105	2448	Malawi
23	11	u	u	u	u	144.70	114	u	Mali
u	u	45	29	u	u	386.70	94	2078	Mauritania
89	77	105	106	54	48	995.50	105	2740	Mauritius
55	22	94	71	8	4	237.60	98	1678	Mozambique
u	u	u	u	u	u		u	u	Namibia
19	9	34	19	u	u	240.60	96	2250	Niger
54	31	103	81	u	u	757.80	109	2038	Nigeria
61	33	64	60	3	1	282.50	106	1919	Rwanda
37	19	66	44	17	8	368.10	105	2342	Senegal
38	21	u	u	u	u	327.00	108	1817	Sierra Leone
18	6	32	18	23	12	452.90	102	2072	Somalia
u	u	u	u	u	u	1600.10	88	2979	South Africa
33[e, j]	14[e, j]	57	41	23	16	328.80	103	1737	Sudan
93[e, j]	88[e, j]	u	u	u	u	276.30	108	2335	Tanzania
53	28	118	75	32	10	214.20	103	2236	Togo
70	45	65	49	u	u	230.00	125	2083	Uganda
79	45	112	84	81	33	141.10	113	2154	Zaire
84	67	105	95	22	12	317.90	107	2137	Zambia
81	67	135	127	46	31	580.70	100	2054	Zimbabwe
									LATIN AMERICA/CARIBBEAN
96	95	107	107	62	69	1985.50	106	3221	Argentina
84	65	96	85	40	34	419.90	101	2146	Bolivia
79	76	108	99	u	u	1535.90	115	2633	Brazil
97[f, j]	96[f, j]	108	106	63	69	1167.60	103	2602	Chile
89	87	119	119	48	49	1158.20	103	2574	Colombia
94	93	102	100	40	45	1341.10	100	2803	Costa Rica
96[i]	96[i]	110	102	71	79	u	110	u	Cuba
78	77	107	117	u	u	670.00	113	2461	Dominican Republic
85	80	117	117	51	53	1246.10	104	2054	Ecuador
75	69	69	70	23	26	772.60	100	2148	El Salvador
63	47	80	69	17	16	1361.80	108	2294	Guatemala
97	97	u	u	u	u	480.20	u	u	Guyana
40	35	81	72	16	16	324.20	104	1855	Haiti
61	58	102	101	31	36	722.70	104	2211	Honduras
90[h]	93[h]	106	107	56	60	760.90	109	2585	Jamaica
92	88	118	115	56	53	2140.50	110	3177	Mexico
u	u	100	106	39	48	812.20	90	2425	Nicaragua
89	88	107	102	56	63	2080.80	109	2419	Panama
91	85	107	99	u	u	793.40	111	2796	Paraguay
91	78	120	112	u	u	851.10	111	2171	Peru

Table 1. Selected Demographic, Social, and Economic Characteristics *(continued)*

Country	Total population (000s) 1988	Total population (000s) 2000	Density (population per sq. km) 1988	Urban population (%) 1984	Urban population (%) 2000	Dependency ratio 1980	Crude birthrate 1985	Crude death rate 1985	Life expectancy 1985
LATIN AMERICA/CARIBBEAN *(continued)*									
Puerto Rico	3605	4185[a]	405.0	71[b]	79	65	21.0	6.6[c]	74.7[c]
Trinidad and Tobago	1244	1476	243.8	22	75	64	24.0[c]	6.9	69.4
Uruguay	3082	3339	17.5	85	87	60	18.5	9.9	72.2
Venezuela	18768	24000	20.6	85	91	82	31.1	5.2	69.7
MIDDLE EAST/NORTH AFRICA									
Algeria	23984	33585	10.1	47	51	102	41.0	10.0	60.9
Egypt	50285	67278	50.2	45	56	79	35.6	10.1	60.7
Iran	48608	69331	29.5	54	61	91	40.7	11.0	59.8
Iraq	17615	27096	40.5	70	79	97	44.4	8.0	61.4
Jordan	3981	5514	40.7	64[b]	74	111	39.0	7.4	64.5
Kuwait	2062	3007[a]	116.2	94[b]	98	79	37.0	3.1[c]	72.7[c]
Lebanon	2847	2947	273.8	80[b]	88	84	28.1	8.4	65.9
Libya	4040	6082[a]	2.2	65[b]	76	96	45.0	9.4[c]	60.8[c]
Morocco	23546	31267	52.7	43	56	96	32.5[c]	10.7	59.3
Oman	1371	1975	6.6	27	15	87	44.3[c]	13.0	53.6
Saudi Arabia	13009	19824[a]	5.6	72[b]	83	86	41.0	7.4[c]	63.7[c]
Syria	11782	16517	63.6	49	57	103	44.1	8.0	63.6
Tunisia	7568	9847	46.3	54	68	86	31.9	9.0	62.5
Turkey	52504	66808	67.3	46	54	76	30.1	8.4	64.1
United Arab Emirates	1478	1939[a]	17.2	78[b]	70	48	24.9[c]	4.2[c]	69.2[c]
Yemen, North	7495	12335	38.4	19	33	96	48.3	20.8	45.0
Yemen, South	2345	2934	7.0	37	51	95	45.8	18.6	46.1
ASIA									
Afghanistan	19227	26035[a]	30.3	19[b]	29	88	48.0	23.9[c]	39.0[c]
Bangladesh	109605	141092	761.1	18	18	98	40.3	15.2	50.6
Bhutan	1508	1744	32.1	4	8	77	42.7	20.5	43.7
Burma	39367	48770	58.2	29	28	82	29.9	10.5	58.8
China	1098100	1274000	114.9	22	25	71	19.0	6.5	68.9
Hong Kong	5840	6314	5839.5	93	94	47	14.0	5.0	75.8
India	799862	995793	243.3	25	34	74	32.6	12.0	56.0
Indonesia	175499	212407	91.4	25	36	80	32.3	12.2	54.9
Kampuchea	7861	9732	43.4	15	15	55	44.4	19.6	44.5
Korea, Dem. People's Rep.	21917	28166[a]	181.7	64[b]	73	78	30.0	5.4[c]	69.4[c]
Korea, Republic of	43400	49368	440.6	64	80	60	21.0	6.2	68.5
Laos	4435	5373	18.7	15	25	86	41.6	18.9	45.0
Malaysia	16602	20691	50.3	31	50	75	29.8	6.3	67.6
Mongolia	2076	2837[a]	1.1	51[b]	55	86	34.7[c]	7.4[c]	64.5[c]
Nepal	17675	24485	125.5	7	14	87	43.1	18.0	46.8
Pakistan	107488	146000	133.7	29	38	92	44.0	14.6	50.9
Papua New Guinea	3778	4888	8.2	14	20	84	37.2	13.0	52.4
Philippines	58383	75327	194.6	39	49	77	32.7	7.7	62.9
Singapore	2644	2926	4407.3	100	100	47	17.2	5.0	72.6
Sri Lanka	16953	20095	258.4	21	24	70	25.0	6.0	69.8
Taiwan	19800	23233	550.0	73	u	52	16.0	4.9	73.7
Thailand	53992	65647	105.0	20[b]	29	76	25.8	7.5	64.0
Vietnam	63577	87877	191.6	7	27	83	29.6[c]	7.6	65.0

u = unknown.

a. The source for this figure is UNDIESA, *World Demographic Estimates and Projections, 1950–2025,* New York, 1988.

b. Ibid. 1985 data.

c. Ibid.

d. 1982 data.

e. 1986 data.

f. 1984 data.

Table 1. *(continued)*

Literacy rate 1985 (%)		Primary school enrollment 1984 (%)[k]		Secondary school enrollment 1984 (%)[k]		GNP per capita (U.S.$) 1985	Food production index[l] 1983–85	Per capita daily calories 1985	Country
Males	Females	Males	Females	Males	Females				
u	u	u	u	u	u	u	u	u	**LATIN AMERICA/CARIBBEAN** Puerto Rico
97	97	94	98	75	78	6064.00	95	3006	Trinidad and Tobago
93[g]	94[g]	110	107	u	u	1650.00	107	2695	Uruguay
88	85	109	108	40	49	2728.00	101	2583	Venezuela
									MIDDLE EAST/NORTH AFRICA
63	37	106	83	54	39	2594.10	108	2677	Algeria
59	30	94	72	70	46	591.30	115	3263	Egypt
62	39	117	95	51	35	u	109	3122	Iran
90	87	111	98	67	37	1080.00	114	2926	Iraq
87	64	98	99	80	78	1083.10	121	2947	Jordan
76	63	105	102	85	79	14480.00	u	3138	Kuwait
86	69	u	u	u	u	u	112	u	Lebanon
81	50	u	u	u	u	7170.00	u	3612	Libya
45	22	97	62	37	25	507.50	113	2678	Morocco
47[d, j]	12[d, j]	93	72	40	19	7127.50	u	u	Oman
35[d]	12[d]	77	58	47	29	8850.00	u	3128	Saudi Arabia
76	43	115	98	70	47	1517.60	108	3168	Syria
68	41	127	105	37	26	1108.20	114	2836	Tunisia
86[f]	62[f]	116	109	47	28	1022.10	108	3167	Turkey
58[g]	38[g]	97	97	52	65	19270.00	u	3625	United Arab Emirates
27	3	112	22	17	3	515.10	112	2250	Yemen, North
59	25	96	35	26	11	514.80	100	2337	Yemen, South
									ASIA
39	8	u	u	u	u	u	104	u	Afghanistan
43	22	67	55	26	11	159.40	110	1899	Bangladesh
u	u	32	17	6	1	150.50	110	2571	Bhutan
u	u	u	u	u	u	189.50	129	2547	Burma
82	56	129	107	43	31	255.70	125	2602	China
95	81	106	104	66	72	6284.70	108	2698	Hong Kong
57	29	105	73	44	23	258.50	120	2189	India
83	65	121	116	45	34	512.70	117	2533	Indonesia
85[j]	65[j]	u	u	u	u	u	153	u	Kampuchea
u	u	u	u	u	u	u	116	u	Korea, Dem. People's Rep.
96[d]	88[d]	99	99	94	88	2024.60	109	2841	Korea, Republic of
92	76	103	77	22	15	381.60	129	2228	Laos
81	66	98	97	53	53	1859.50	116	2684	Malaysia (Peninsular)
93[d]	86[d]	104	106	84	92	u	111	u	Mongolia
39	12	104	47	35	11	142.10	116	2034	Nepal
40	19	54	29	u	u	350.80	114	2159	Pakistan
55	35	68	55	u	u	618.00	109	2181	Papua New Guinea
86	85	106	107	65	71	581.00	103	2341	Philippines
93	79	118	113	70	73	6931.70	98	2771	Singapore
91	83	105	101	58	64	373.60	98	2385	Sri Lanka
u	u	u	u	u	u	u	u	u	Taiwan
94	88	u	u	u	u	713.20	119	2462	Thailand
88[j]	80[j]	120	105	u	u	u	122	2240	Vietnam

g. 1975 data.

h. 1980 data.

i. 1981 data; include those aged 10 and older.

j. UNICEF field office source.

k. The data in this column refer to a variety of years, generally not more than three years distant from 1984, and are mostly from UNESCO.

l. Average annual quantity of food produced per capita in 1983–85, with 1979–81 production as an index of 100.

Table 2. Number of Married Women of Reproductive Age (000s), 1975–2000

Country	1975	1976	1977	1978	1979	1980	1981	1982	1983
SUB-SAHARAN AFRICA									
Angola	908	911	939	953	976	1017	1038	1061	1082
Benin	—	—	—	—	586	602	618	635	653
Botswana	—	—	—	—	—	—	76	79	82
Burundi	—	—	—	—	544	562	574	593	620
Cameroon	—	1181	1208	1237	1265	1303	1337	1363	1397
Chad	756	767	779	791	790	778	787	821	848
Côte d'Ivoire	1083	1118	1152	1188	1224	1263	1304	1347	1393
Ghana	1399	1423	1447	1467	1482	1493	1511	1544	1703
Guinea	—	—	—	—	—	—	—	—	1194
Kenya	—	—	—	—	2174	2259	2348	2444	2544
Lesotho	—	166	171	176	182	188	194	200	207
Liberia	244	252	259	267	275	283	292	301	311
Madagascar	1001	1028	1055	1084	1116	1149	1185	1223	1263
Malawi	—	—	897	915	933	951	971	994	1019
Mali	—	1100	1124	1149	1175	1201	1228	1257	1287
Mauritius	—	—	—	—	—	—	—	—	135
Mozambique	—	—	—	—	—	1747	1792	1837	1884
Nigeria	—	—	—	—	—	—	—	—	—
Rwanda	—	—	—	632	654	676	701	729	758
Senegal	—	844	—	—	—	—	—	—	—
South Africa	—	—	—	—	—	2582	—	—	—
Sudan	—	—	—	—	—	—	—	—	3128
Tanzania	—	—	—	2654	2728	2804	2883	2966	3055
Togo	—	—	—	—	—	—	370	380	392
Uganda	—	—	—	—	—	1923	1960	2001	2048
Zaire	—	—	—	—	—	—	—	—	—
Zambia	—	—	—	—	—	841	871	907	946
Zimbabwe	—	—	—	—	—	—	—	1044	1086
LATIN AMERICA/CARIBBEAN									
Argentina	—	—	—	—	—	3571	3623	3676	3730
Bolivia	—	630	647	663	681	699	717	736	755
Brazil	—	—	—	—	—	15231	—	—	—
Chile	—	—	—	—	—	—	—	1472	1512
Colombia	2697	2784	2872	2962	3064	3180	3302	3430	3563
Costa Rica	234	245	256	270	283	292	304	317	330
Cuba	—	—	—	—	1317	—	—	—	—
Dominican Republic	619	645	672	701	730	761	794	828	862
Ecuador	—	—	—	—	—	—	—	1080	1119
El Salvador	470	484	499	514	530	541	536	539	559
Guatemala	—	—	—	—	—	—	826	—	1052
Guyana	—	—	—	—	—	79	81	82	84
Honduras	379	393	408	425	441	460	482	501	519
Jamaica	—	—	—	—	—	—	—	—	—
Mexico	—	—	—	—	—	8942	9272	9619	9976
Nicaragua	285	295	306	313	323	340	354	365	375
Panama	—	—	—	—	—	239	247	255	264
Paraguay	319	333	349	365	382	399	416	434	452
Peru	—	—	—	—	—	—	2127	2197	2270
Uruguay	348	347	345	345	345	346	347	349	351
Venezuela	—	—	—	—	—	—	1823	1895	1969
MIDDLE EAST/NORTH AFRICA									
Algeria	—	—	2196	2268	2344	2425	2511	2603	2702
Egypt	—	—	5359	5500	5643	5811	6007	6192	6368
Iran	—	5071	5236	5409	5612	5849	6104	6373	6649
Iraq	—	—	1454	1555	1613	1672	1735	1802	1873
Jordan	—	—	—	—	246	256	267	279	291
Kuwait	140	—	—	—	—	178	—	—	—
Lebanon	384	392	390	388	387	387	386	386	386

30

Table 2.

1984	1985	1986	1987	1988	1989	1990	1995	2000	Country
									SUB-SAHARAN AFRICA
1105	1129	1153	1187	1231	1276	1317	1509	1746	Angola
674	696	720	746	774	804	835	1016	1235	Benin
85	89	92	96	100	104	108	131	156	Botswana
640	661	683	705	727	750	773	887	998	Burundi
1435	1476	1518	1562	1608	1656	1706	1984	2310	Cameroon
847	846	860	879	902	925	949	1044	1154	Chad
1442	1495	1550	1609	1671	1735	1800	2155	2574	Côte d'Ivoire
1841	1911	2018	2089	2164	2241	2323	2762	3187	Ghana
1248	1315	1353	1383	1413	1445	1477	1654	1868	Guinea
2651	2764	2883	3009	3141	3279	3423	4252	5303	Kenya
214	222	229	237	244	252	260	300	347	Lesotho
321	331	342	353	364	376	389	458	542	Liberia
1305	1348	1392	1438	1485	1533	1583	1851	2177	Madagascar
1046	1076	1109	1145	1184	1225	1269	1510	1789	Malawi
1319	1353	1388	1425	1462	1501	1542	1768	2043	Mali
141	147	153	159	165	170	175	196	207	Mauritius
1932	1982	2033	2086	2144	2204	2268	2627	3028	Mozambique
—	18489	18913	19456	20006	20598	21211	—	—	Nigeria
786	816	847	878	910	945	982	1180	1416	Rwanda
—	1041	1073	1107	1143	1181	1220	1437	1693	Senegal
3387	3493	3601	3710	3821	3935	4051	4656	5265	South Africa
3239	3382	3473	3516	3569	3625	3688	4301	5103	Sudan
3148	3245	3347	3456	3571	3691	3818	4537	5404	Tanzania
406	421	435	450	464	479	494	579	693	Togo
2105	2183	2274	2356	2432	2513	2599	3098	3683	Uganda
4886	5003	5124	5249	5380	5517	5666	6563	7725	Zaire
984	1020	1060	1101	1142	1184	1228	1462	1740	Zambia
1131	1176	1222	1271	1323	1377	1434	1753	2127	Zimbabwe
									LATIN AMERICA/CARIBBEAN
3784	3837	3891	3945	3998	4051	4105	4384	4702	Argentina
775	795	816	838	860	882	904	1023	1151	Bolivia
—	18352	18928	19514	20104	20691	21258	24079	26858	Brazil
1551	1590	1628	1663	1697	1729	1759	1894	2005	Chile
3698	3836	3975	4115	4254	4394	4533	5156	5631	Colombia
344	357	370	384	397	409	421	475	525	Costa Rica
—	1577	1617	1658	1697	1734	1768	1890	1932	Cuba
895	929	964	999	1033	1068	1101	1270	1425	Dominican Republic
1160	1202	1245	1290	1335	1382	1429	1670	1921	Ecuador
580	601	622	646	671	696	723	871	1026	El Salvador
1079	1108	1137	1167	1199	1232	1266	1467	1711	Guatemala
85	87	88	90	91	93	94	102	111	Guyana
540	562	586	609	634	658	684	822	977	Honduras
281	290	298	307	315	323	331	372	413	Jamaica
10346	10731	11130	11544	11971	12408	12853	15117	17210	Mexico
386	396	407	420	434	450	468	564	672	Nicaragua
272	281	290	299	308	318	327	375	419	Panama
470	489	507	525	543	562	580	674	771	Paraguay
2346	2425	2506	2591	2678	2767	2858	3330	3812	Peru
354	358	361	365	370	374	379	406	429	Uruguay
2045	2122	2198	2274	2350	2426	2500	2846	3190	Venezuela
									MIDDLE EAST/NORTH AFRICA
2807	2920	3040	3168	3303	3446	3595	4356	5167	Algeria
6550	6735	6923	7113	7310	7516	7726	8906	10384	Egypt
6930	7212	7494	7776	8058	8341	8606	9909	11500	Iran
1949	2030	2115	2206	2301	2400	2503	3072	3731	Iraq
305	320	335	352	369	387	406	512	634	Jordan
—	247	261	275	288	300	313	365	402	Kuwait
386	387	388	392	398	406	415	493	593	Lebanon

Table 2. Number of Married Women of Reproductive Age (000s), 1975–2000 *(continued)*

Country	1975	1976	1977	1978	1979	1980	1981	1982	1983
MIDDLE EAST/NORTH AFRICA *(continued)*									
Libya	312	323	328	336	357	380	400	422	444
Morocco	—	—	—	—	—	—	—	2729	2820
Syria	—	—	—	—	—	—	—	1195	1240
Tunisia	666	—	—	—	—	—	—	—	—
Turkey	5794	—	—	—	—	6688	6884	7089	7304
United Arab Emirates	—	—	—	—	—	—	—	—	—
Yemen, North	803	809	817	826	838	854	872	894	918
ASIA									
Afghanistan	—	—	—	—	2611	2508	2349	2269	2279
Bangladesh	12637	13068	13528	14000	14484	14977	15479	15990	16514
Burma	4017	4114	4218	4329	4446	4569	4698	4832	4969
China	—	—	—	—	—	—	—	146032	152758
Hong Kong	474	483	505	528	550	572	595	635	675
India	101838	104584	107430	110387	113462	116657	119974	123407	126950
Indonesia	—	19060	—	—	—	24219	24862	25528	26215
Korea, Republic of	4531	—	—	—	—	5141	—	—	—
Malaysia	—	—	—	—	—	1996	2067	2138	2210
Nepal	2367	2411	2456	2502	2550	2600	2653	2709	2769
Pakistan	—	—	—	—	—	—	12809	13255	13640
Philippines	5701	5893	6090	6294	6502	6715	6932	7153	7381
Singapore	—	—	—	—	—	319	331	342	354
Sri Lanka	—	—	—	—	—	—	1982	2040	2094
Taiwan	—	—	—	—	—	2449	2541	2633	2725
Thailand	5521	5702	5893	6090	6294	6502	6714	6930	7152

Note: A dash signifies the absence of baseline data to calculate values.

Table 2. *(continued)*

1984	1985	1986	1987	1988	1989	1990	1995	2000	Country
									MIDDLE EAST/NORTH AFRICA
464	472	479	499	518	539	560	684	830	Libya
2916	3016	3122	3235	3354	3478	3609	4309	4987	Morocco
1289	1342	1398	1459	1524	1594	1667	2081	2564	Syria
825	855	887	919	953	989	1027	1229	1434	Tunisia
7529	7766	8014	8273	8541	8815	9094	10514	11870	Turkey
—	—	230	252	273	292	312	402	476	United Arab Emirates
945	975	1008	1041	1075	1108	1138	1349	1627	Yemen, North
									ASIA
2299	2311	2329	2365	2419	2483	2620	3506	4232	Afghanistan
17049	17596	18150	18705	19245	19737	20253	23675	27548	Bangladesh
5109	5251	5397	5546	5698	5851	6005	6804	7585	Burma
158003	163022	167403	172013	179572	187088	193743	220771	229858	China
716	756	796	827	857	886	911	962	941	Hong Kong
130603	134312	137944	141752	145636	149560	153457	172286	190943	India
26926	27658	28396	29185	29999	30843	31711	36413	40333	Indonesia
—	5982	6154	6326	6499	6671	6841	7615	8083	Korea, Republic of
2284	2361	2441	2523	2606	2687	2766	3108	3394	Malaysia
2830	2892	2952	3024	3101	3184	3271	3783	4397	Nepal
14040	14471	14921	15377	15842	16322	16778	19247	22242	Pakistan
7617	7859	8108	8363	8622	8886	9152	10517	11889	Philippines
366	378	390	403	414	425	433	445	431	Singapore
2147	2199	2252	2307	2362	2416	2469	2716	2906	Sri Lanka
2819	2915	3013	3110	3206	3298	3383	3696	3753	Taiwan
7384	7626	7888	8156	8426	8695	8956	10177	11057	Thailand

Table 3. Total Fertility Rates, 1955–2000

Country	1955–1960	1960–1965	1965–1970	1970–1975	1975–1980	1980–1985	1985–1990	1990–1995	1995–2000
SUB-SAHARAN AFRICA									
Angola	6386[a]	6380	6384	6395	6395	6395	6395	6313	6131
Benin	6762	6811	6857	6849	7004	7004	7004	6902	6699
Botswana	6267	6425	6482	6496	6496	6496	6496	6395	6232
Burkina Faso	6531	6504	6510	6512	6496	6496	6496	6395	6232
Burundi	5339	5684	5826	5928	6435	6435	6313	6110	5704
Cameroon	5731	5702	5680	5702	5786	5786	5786	5704	5542
Central African Republic	5595	5656	5690	5719	5887	5887	5887	5806	5643
Chad	5905	5999	6045	5986	5887	5887	5887	5806	5643
Congo	5781	5869	5930	6035	5989	5989	5989	5907	5725
Côte d'Ivoire	6626	6606	6626	6691	6699	6699	6598	6415	6110
Ethiopia	6699	6699	6699	6699	6699	6699	6699	6598	6415
Gabon	4070	4064	4068	4060	4060	4507	5116	5684	5420
Ghana	6421	6478	6565	6496	6496	6496	6496	6374	6232
Guinea	6461	6392	6407	6192	6192	6185	6185	6084	5922
Kenya	8179	8148	8104	8193	8217	8120	7998	7755	7308
Lesotho	5865	5806	5708	5743	5743	5786	5786	5704	5542
Liberia	6226	6267	6267	6368	6902	6902	6902	6801	6618
Madagascar	5749	5790	5834	5905	6090	6090	6090	6009	5826
Malawi	6841	6861	6922	6922	7004	7004	7004	6902	6699
Mali	6390	6455	6575	6598	6699	6699	6699	6598	6415
Mauritania	6837	6861	6865	6908	6902	6902	6902	6699	6395
Mauritius	5980	5726	4247	3252	3068	2761	2454	2250	2086
Mozambique	5562	5704	5867	6090	6090	6090	6090	6009	5826
Namibia	5950	6027	6086	6055	6090	6090	6090	6009	5826
Niger	7036	7058	7103	7095	7105	7105	7105	7004	6801
Nigeria	6825	6872	7105	7105	7105	7105	7105	7004	6801
Rwanda	6618	6821	7004	7308	7308	7511	7308	7186	6943
Senegal	6660	6656	6656	6736	6496	6496	6496	6395	6232
Sierra Leone	6137	6112	6116	6122	6131	6131	6131	6009	5826
Somalia	6598	6598	6598	6598	6598	6598	6598	6496	6313
South Africa	5589	5623	5611	5335	5075	5075	4939	4728	4442
Sudan	6683	6683	6683	6683	6683	6585	6384	6047	5560
Tanzania	6825	6857	6874	7001	7105	7105	7105	7004	6801
Togo	6114	6153	6171	6090	6090	6090	6090	6009	5826
Uganda	6941	6906	6912	6902	6902	6902	6902	6801	6618
Zaire	5966	5942	5976	6090	6090	6090	6090	6009	5826
Zambia	6598	6616	6654	6742	6760	6760	6760	6658	6476
Zimbabwe	6608	6608	6608	6598	6598	6598	6598	6496	6313
LATIN AMERICA/CARIBBEAN									
Argentina	3121	3080	3040	3142	3366	3379	3260	3000	2741
Bolivia	6683	6622	6560	6499	6396	6250	6060	5810	5500
Brazil	6150	6150	5310	4695	4203	3810	3460	3160	2910
Chile	5248	5105	4121	3485	2686	2589	2498	2429	2369
Colombia	6724	6724	5945	4777	4305	3930	3581	3260	3000
Costa Rica	7114	6950	5802	4264	3731	3500	3260	3050	2850
Cuba	3764	4669	4299	3476	2180	1975	1975	2016	2102
Dominican Republic	7503	7319	7011	6314	4797	4182	3629	3157	2809
Ecuador	6909	6909	6704	6048	5392	5000	4650	4321	4000
El Salvador	6806	6847	6622	6335	6007	5556	5105	4736	4449
Guatemala	6929	6847	6601	6458	6396	6120	5770	5360	4900
Haiti	6150	6150	6150	6068	5925	5744	5557	5356	5146
Honduras	7175	7360	7421	7380	7134	6500	5588	5140	5000
Jamaica	5043	5453	5433	5433	3957	3366	2856	2448	2244
Mexico	6745	6745	6704	6396	5392	4610	3981	3430	3000
Nicaragua	7339	7339	7093	6704	6314	5940	5500	5010	4500
Panama	5884	5925	5617	4941	4059	3461	3140	2871	2650

Table 3. Total Fertility Rates, 1955–2000 *(continued)*

Country	1955–1960	1960–1965	1965–1970	1970–1975	1975–1980	1980–1985	1985–1990	1990–1995	1995–2000
LATIN AMERICA/CARIBBEAN *(continued)*									
Paraguay	6622	6622	6396	5699	5207	4852	4480	4106	3748
Peru	6868	6868	6560	6007	5371	5001	4490	3970	3500
Puerto Rico	4818	4367	3403	2993	2747	2539	2438	2336	2235
Trinidad and Tobago	5330	5023	3895	3485	3075	2885	2679	2473	2267
Uruguay	2829	2891	2809	2993	2932	2760	2610	2480	2380
Venezuela	6458	6458	5904	4961	4449	4100	3770	3470	3201
NORTH AFRICA/MIDDLE EAST									
Algeria	7278	7380	7483	7380	7175	6663	6150	5330	4305
Egypt	6970	7073	6560	5535	5269	4818	4305	3793	3383
Iran	8350	8128	7554	6816	6048	5638	5207	4613	3998
Iraq	7175	7175	7175	7114	6970	6663	6048	5433	4818
Jordan	7175	7175	7175	7380	7278	7380	7278	7073	6765
Kuwait	7278	7380	7483	6970	6458	6150	5740	5228	4408
Lebanon	6150	6355	6048	4920	4305	3793	3383	3075	2829
Libya	6970	7175	7483	7585	7380	7175	6868	6458	5843
Morocco	7175	7155	7093	6888	5904	5126	4305	3485	2870
Saudi Arabia	7175	7257	7257	7298	7278	7073	6868	6499	5945
Syria	7093	7462	7790	7483	7442	7175	6827	6253	5433
Tunisia	6970	7175	6827	6150	5638	4818	4100	3383	2870
Turkey	6150	6007	5802	5453	4305	3964	3651	3233	2921
Yemen, North	6970	6970	6970	6970	6970	6970	6765	6560	6314
Yemen, South	6970	6970	6970	6970	6970	6765	6560	6314	5843
ASIA									
Afghanistan	6860	7006	7132	7138	6901	6901	6654	6277	5747
Bangladesh	6622	6681	6906	7017	6656	6150	5535	4920	4305
Bhutan	5988	5918	5892	5945	5740	5535	5330	4920	4510
Burma	6048	5945	5740	5433	4613	4100	3690	3280	2911
China	5371	5904	5966	4736	2891	2365	2109	1910	1910
Hong Kong	4676	5269	3983	2870	2296	1907	1856	1856	1856
India	5918	5810	5689	5426	4826	4305	3690	3280	2870
Indonesia	5672	5420	5568	5527	4809	4100	3485	3075	2665
Kampuchea	6294	6291	6216	5535	4100	5125	4715	4100	3485
Korea, Dem. People's Rep.	5775	5574	5640	5211	4531	4017	3605	3234	2966
Korea, Republic of	6043	5373	4494	4086	3137	2602	2503	2266	2163
Laos	5594	5679	6130	6150	6150	5843	5412	4879	4264
Malaysia (Peninsular)	6911	6691	5912	5125	4141	3914	3296	2884	2472
Mongolia	5740	5715	5886	5558	5355	5125	4818	4510	4100
Nepal	5699	5863	6171	6519	6540	6253	5843	5433	4920
Pakistan	6978	7155	7214	6521	6031	5843	5330	4715	4100
Papua New Guinea	6234	6255	6177	5925	6253	5665	5253	4841	4429
Philippines	7058	6574	6011	5269	4941	4408	3914	3502	3090
Singapore	5927	4871	3417	2595	1845	1695	1649	1699	1751
Sri Lanka	5403	5118	4646	3968	3765	3383	2870	2460	2255
Thailand	6421	6421	6138	5010	4274	3522	2731	2620	2538
Vietnam	6300	7013	6697	5847	5588	4305	3690	3280	2870

a. For example, in Angola there would be 6386 births per 1000 women under the prevailing age-specific fertility rates (ignoring mortality), or 6.4 births per woman.

Table 4. Government Positions on Population Growth, and Interventions, 1986

Country	Growth rate too low — No direct intervention reported	Growth rate too low — Intervention to raise rate	Growth rate satisfactory[a]	Growth rate too high — Intervention to lower rate	Growth rate too high — No direct intervention reported
SUB-SAHARAN AFRICA					
Angola	—	—	X	—	—
Benin	—	—	X	—	—
Botswana	—	—	—	X	—
Burkina Faso	—	—	X	—	—
Burundi	—	—	—	X	—
Cameroon	—	—	—	—	X
Central African Republic	—	—	—	—	X
Chad	—	—	X	—	—
Congo	X	—	—	—	—
Côte d'Ivoire[a]	—	—	X	—	—
Ethiopia	—	—	—	—	X
Gabon	—	X	—	—	—
Gambia	—	—	—	X	—
Ghana	—	—	—	X	—
Guinea	—	—	X	—	—
Kenya	—	—	—	X	—
Lesotho	—	—	—	X	—
Liberia	—	—	—	—	X
Madagascar	—	—	X	—	—
Malawi	—	—	—	—	X
Mali[a]	—	—	X	—	—
Mauritania[a]	—	—	X	—	—
Mauritius	—	—	—	X	—
Mozambique	—	—	X	—	—
Niger	—	—	X	—	—
Nigeria	—	—	—	X	—
Rwanda	—	—	—	X	—
Senegal	—	—	—	X	—
Sierra Leone	—	—	—	—	X
Somalia	—	—	X	—	—
South Africa	—	—	—	X	—
Sudan	—	—	X	—	—
Tanzania	—	—	—	—	X
Togo[a]	—	—	X	—	—
Uganda	—	—	—	X	—
Zaire	—	—	X	—	—
Zambia	—	—	—	—	X
Zimbabwe	—	—	—	X	—
LATIN AMERICA/CARIBBEAN					
Argentina	—	—	X	—	—
Bolivia	X	—	—	—	—
Brazil	—	—	X	—	—
Chile	X	—	—	—	—
Colombia	—	—	X	—	—
Costa Rica	—	—	X	—	—
Cuba	—	—	X	—	—
Dominican Republic	—	—	—	X	—
Ecuador	—	—	X	—	—
El Salvador	—	—	—	X	—
Guatemala	—	—	—	—	X
Guyana	—	—	X	—	—
Haiti	—	—	—	X	—
Honduras	—	—	—	X	—
Jamaica	—	—	—	X	—
Mexico	—	—	—	X	—

Table 4. Government Positions on Population Growth, and Interventions, 1986 *(continued)*

Country	Growth rate too low — No direct intervention reported	Growth rate too low — Intervention to raise rate	Growth rate satisfactory[a]	Growth rate too high — Intervention to lower rate	Growth rate too high — No direct intervention reported
LATIN AMERICA/CARIBBEAN *(continued)*					
Nicaragua	—	—	X	—	—
Panama	—	—	X	—	—
Paraguay	—	—	X	—	—
Peru	—	—	—	X	—
Trinidad and Tobago	—	—	—	X	—
Uruguay	X	—	—	—	—
Venezuela	—	—	X	—	—
MIDDLE EAST/NORTH AFRICA					
Algeria	—	—	—	X	—
Egypt	—	—	—	X	—
Iran	—	—	X	—	—
Iraq	—	X	—	—	—
Jordan	—	—	X	—	—
Kuwait	—	X	—	—	—
Lebanon	—	—	X	—	—
Libya	—	—	X	—	—
Morocco	—	—	—	X	—
Oman	—	X	—	—	—
Saudi Arabia	—	X	—	—	—
Syria	—	—	X	—	—
Tunisia	—	—	—	X	—
Turkey	—	—	—	X	—
United Arab Emirates[a]	—	—	X	—	—
Yemen, North	—	—	X	—	—
Yemen, South	—	—	X	—	—
ASIA					
Afghanistan	—	—	—	—	X
Bangladesh	—	—	—	X	—
Bhutan	X	—	—	—	—
Burma	—	—	X	—	—
China	—	—	—	X	—
India	—	—	—	X	—
Indonesia	—	—	—	X	—
Kampuchea	—	X	—	—	—
Korea, Dem. People's Rep.	—	X	—	—	—
Korea, Republic of	—	—	—	X	—
Laos	—	X	—	—	—
Malaysia[a]	—	—	X	—	—
Mongolia	—	X	—	—	—
Nepal	—	—	—	X	—
Pakistan	—	—	—	X	—
Papua New Guinea	—	—	—	X	—
Philippines	—	—	—	X	—
Singapore	—	X	—	—	—
Sri Lanka	—	—	—	X	—
Thailand[a]	—	—	X	—	—
Vietnam	—	—	—	X	—

a. Of the 37 developing countries in the third column, 30 reported no direct intervention to change the current growth rate. The seven others reported action of different types: Thailand reported efforts to lower the rate; Côte d'Ivoire, Mauritania, and United Arab Emirates, efforts to raise the rate; and Mali, Togo, and Malaysia, efforts to maintain the rate.

Table 5. Legal Status of Female Sterilization, 1987

Country	No relevant law	Illegal, no exceptions	Legal for medical reasons			Legal on request[a]
			Life	Health	Eugenic	
SUB-SAHARAN AFRICA						
Botswana	X	—	—	—	—	X
Burkina Faso	X	—	—	—	—	—
Burundi	X	—	—	—	—	—
Chad	—	X	—	—	—	—
Côte d'Ivoire	—	X	—	—	—	—
Ghana	—	—	—	—	—	X
Kenya	—	—	—	—	—	X
Lesotho	—	—	X	—	—	X
Liberia	—	—	—	—	—	X
Mauritania	—	X	—	—	—	—
Mauritius	—	—	X	—	—	—
Niger	—	—	X	—	—	—
Nigeria	X	—	—	—	—	X
Senegal	—	X	—	—	—	—
Somalia	X	—	—	—	—	—
Sudan	X	—	—	—	—	X
Togo	—	—	X	—	—	—
Zimbabwe	—	—	—	—	—	X
LATIN AMERICA/CARIBBEAN						
Bolivia	—	—	X	—	—	X
Brazil	—	—	X	—	—	—
Chile	—	—	—	X	—	—
Colombia	—	—	—	—	—	X
Costa Rica	—	—	X	X	X	—
Haiti	—	—	—	—	—	X
Honduras	—	—	X	X	—	X
Jamaica	—	—	—	—	—	X
Mexico	X	—	X	X	X	X
Panama	—	—	X	—	—	X
Paraguay	X	—	—	—	—	—
Peru	—	—	X	—	—	—
Puerto Rico	X	—	—	—	—	X
Trinidad and Tobago	X	—	—	—	—	X
MIDDLE EAST/NORTH AFRICA						
Egypt	—	—	X	X	—	—
Iran	—	X	—	—	—	—
Iraq	—	—	X	X	X	—
Jordan	—	—	X	—	—	—
Morocco	—	—	X	X	—	—
Tunisia	—	—	—	—	—	X
Turkey	—	—	—	—	—	X
ASIA						
Bangladesh	—	—	—	—	—	X
China	—	—	—	—	—	X
Hong Kong	X	—	—	—	—	X
India	—	—	—	—	—	X
Korea, Republic of	—	—	—	—	X	X[b]
Laos	—	—	X	—	—	—
Malaysia (Peninsular)	X	—	—	—	—	X
Mongolia	—	—	X	X	—	—
Pakistan	X	—	—	—	—	X
Philippines	—	—	—	—	—	X
Singapore	—	—	—	—	—	X
Sri Lanka	—	—	—	—	—	X
Taiwan	—	—	—	—	—	X
Vietnam	—	—	—	—	—	X

a. If sterilization is allowed for contraceptive purposes, it was coded as legal on request of applicant.

b. Sterilization is available for socioeconomic reasons as well.

38

Table 6. Conditions for Performing Sterilization, 1987

Country	None	Requires approval: Of committee	Requires approval: Of spouse	Requires approval: Other	Must be performed by physician	Minimum age	Minimum number of living children
SUB-SAHARAN AFRICA							
Burkina Faso							
Female	—	—	X	—	—	a	a
Burundi							
Female	X	—	—	—	—	—	—
Male	X	—	—	—	—	—	—
Ghana							
Female	—	—	X	—	X	u	u
Male	—	—	—	—	X	u	u
Kenya							
Female	—	—	X	—	X	u	u
Lesotho							
Female	—	—	X	—	X	u	3[b]
Male	—	—	—	—	X	u	u
Liberia							
Female	—	—	X	—	X	u	u
Male	—	—	X	—	X	u	u
Mauritius							
Female	—	X	X	—	X	30	2
Morocco							
Female	—	—	X	—	X	u	4[j]
Niger							
Female	—	X	X	X[c]	X	u	u
Nigeria							
Female	X	—	—	—	—	—	—
Male	X	—	—	—	—	—	—
Sudan							
Female	—	—	X	—	X	u	3
Male	—	—	—	—	X	u	3
Togo							
Female	—	—	X	—	X	u	d
Zimbabwe							
Female	—	—	X	X[e]	X	u	2
Male	—	—	X	X[e]	X	u	2
LATIN AMERICA/CARIBBEAN							
Bolivia							
Female	—	—	X	X[f]	X	35	4
Male	—	—	X	—	X	u	u
Brazil							
Female	—	X	X	—	X	u	u
Male	—	X	X	—	X	u	u
Chile							
Female	—	X	X	—	X	a	a
Colombia							
Female	—	—	—	X[e]	X	u	u
Male	—	—	—	X[e]	X	u	u
Costa Rica							
Female	—	X	X	X	X	—	—
Male	—	X	X	—	X	—	—

39

Table 6. Conditions for Performing Sterilization, 1987 *(continued)*

Country	None	Requires approval: Of committee	Requires approval: Of spouse	Requires approval: Other	Must be performed by physician	Minimum age	Minimum number of living children
Haiti							
Female	—	—	—	—	—	u	3
Honduras							
Female	—	X	X	X	X	24	1
Male	—	—	—	—	—	a	1
Jamaica							
Female	—	—	X	—	X	u	2
Male	—	—	—	—	X	u	u
Mexico (MEXFAM)							
Female	—	—	—	X[c]	—	u	2[g]
Mexico (IMSS)							
Female	—	—	—	X[h]	X	u	u
Male	—	—	—	X[h]	X	u	u
Panama							
Female	—	—	X	—	X	29	3
Male	—	—	—	—	X	u	u
Paraguay (CEPEP)							
Female	—	—	—	—	X	u	i
Peru							
Female	—	X	X	—	X	35	4
Puerto Rico							
Female	—	—	—	—	X	u	u
Male	—	—	—	—	X	u	u
Trinidad and Tobago							
Female	—	—	—	—	X	u	u
Male	—	—	—	—	X	u	u
MIDDLE EAST/NORTH AFRICA							
Egypt							
Female	—	—	X	—	X	u	u
Male	—	—	X	—	X	u	u
Iraq							
Female	—	X	X	—	X	35	7
Jordan							
Female	—	—	X	—	X	35	6
Tunisia							
Female	—	—	—	—	X	u	u
Male	—	—	—	—	X	u	u
Turkey							
Female	—	—	X	—	—	u	u
Male	—	—	X	—	—	u	u
ASIA							
Bangladesh							
Female	—	—	X	—	X	u	2
Male	—	—	X	—	X	u	2
Hong Kong							
Female	—	—	X	—	X	u	u
Male	—	—	X	—	X	u	u
India							
Female	—	—	—	—	—	20[k]	u
Male	—	—	—	—	—	25	u

Table 6. Conditions for Performing Sterilization, 1987 *(continued)*

Country	None	Requires approval: Of committee	Of spouse	Other	Must be performed by physician	Minimum age	Minimum number of living children
Korea, Republic of							
Female	—	—	X	—	X	15[l]	u
Male	—	—	X	—	X	15[l]	u
Laos							
Female	—	X	—	—	X	u	u
Malaysia							
Female	—	—	X	X[m]	X	30	2
Male	—	—	X	X[m]	X	30[n]	2
Mongolia							
Female	—	X	—	—	X	u	u
Pakistan							
Female	—	—	X	—	X	25	2
Male	—	—	X	—	X	u	2
Philippines							
Female	—	X	X	—	X	30	3
Male	—	X	X	—	X	u	u
Sri Lanka							
Female	—	—	X	—	X	u	2
Male	—	—	X	—	X	u	2
Taiwan							
Female	—	—	X	X[e]	X[o]	u	0
Male	—	—	X	X[e]	X[o]	u	u
Thailand							
Female	—	—	X	—	p	u	1
Male	—	—	—	—	p	u	1
Vietnam							
Female	X	—	—	—	—	—	—
Male	X	—	—	—	—	—	—

u = unknown

a. A specific requirement exists but is unknown.

b. Only two living children are required if the woman has had two cesarean sections. Otherwise, the woman must have at least 12 children.

c. A woman must have the approval of her parents and her husband's parents.

d. A woman must have children from each husband.

e. Mentally incompetent persons need the approval of a parent or guardian.

f. A woman may also need the approval of a close relative.

g. A woman must have had two cesarean sections.

h. Parental approval is needed.

i. A sterilization applicant must receive counseling.

j. At least one of the four children must be male.

k. The maximum age is 45.

l. The maximum age is 44.

m. A physician can refuse to perform a sterilization.

n. The wife's age must be at least 30.

o. The physician performing the sterilization must have a "eugenic protection license."

p. Sterilization may be performed by a paramedic under supervision.

Table 7. Legal Status of Abortion, 1987

Country	Illegal, no exceptions	Legal for medical reasons			Legal for other reasons		
		Life	Health[b]	Eugenic	Juridical	Socioeconomic	On request[c]
SUB-SAHARAN AFRICA							
Benin	—	X	—	—	—	—	—
Botswana	—	X	—	—	—	—	X
Burkina Faso	X	—	—	—	—	—	—
Burundi	—	X	—	—	—	—	—
Cameroon	—	X	—	—	X	—	—
Central African Republic	—	X	—	—	—	—	—
Chad	—	X	—	—	—	—	—
Congo	—	—	X	—	—	—	—
Côte d'Ivoire	X	—	—	—	—	—	—
Ethiopia	—	X	X	X	—	—	—
Gabon	—	X	—	—	—	—	—
Ghana	—	X	—	—	—	—	—
Guinea	—	—	X	—	—	—	—
Kenya	—	—	X	—	—	—	—
Lesotho	—	—	X	—	—	—	—
Liberia	—	X	X	X	X	—	—
Madagascar	—	X	—	—	—	—	—
Malawi	—	X	—	—	—	—	—
Mali	—	X	—	—	—	—	—
Mauritania	X	—	—	—	—	—	—
Mauritius	X	—	—	—	—	—	—
Mozambique	—	X	—	—	—	—	—
Namibia	—	—	X	X	X	—	—
Niger	X	—	—	—	—	—	—
Nigeria	—	X	—	—	—	—	—
Rwanda	—	—	X	—	—	—	—
Senegal	—	X	—	—	—	—	—
Sierra Leone	—	—	X	—	—	—	—
Somalia	—	X	—	—	—	—	—
Sudan	—	X	X[d]	X[e]	—	—	—
Tanzania	—	—	X	—	—	—	—
Togo	—	X	—	—	—	—	—
Uganda	—	—	X	—	—	—	—
Zaire	—	X	—	—	—	—	—
Zambia	—	—	X	X	—	X[f]	—
Zimbabwe	—	X	—	X	X	—	—
LATIN AMERICA/CARIBBEAN							
Argentina	—	X	X	—	X	—	—
Bolivia	—	X	X	—	X	—	—
Brazil	—	X	—	—	X	—	—
Chile	X	—	—	—	—	—	—
Colombia	X	—	—	—	—	—	—
Costa Rica	—	X	X	—	—	—	—
Cuba	—	—	—	—	—	—	X[g]
Dominican Republic	—	X	—	—	—	—	—
Ecuador	—	X	—	—	X	—	—
El Salvador	—	X	—	X	X	—	—
Guatemala	—	X	—	—	—	—	—
Guyana	—	—	X	—	—	—	—
Haiti	X	—	—	—	—	—	—
Honduras	—	X	X	—	—	—	—
Jamaica	X	X	X	—	—	—	—
Mexico	—	X	X	X	X	—	—
Nicaragua	—	X	—	—	—	—	—
Panama	—	X	—	—	—	—	—
Paraguay	X	—	—	—	—	—	—
Peru	X	—	—	—	—	—	—
Puerto Rico	k	—	—	—	—	—	X[f]
Trinidad and Tobago	X	—	—	—	—	—	—
Uruguay	—	X	—	—	X	X[h]	—
Venezuela	—	X	—	—	—	—	—

Table 7. Legal Status of Abortion, 1987 *(continued)*

Country	Illegal, no exceptions	Legal for medical reasons			Legal for other reasons		
		Life	Health[b]	Eugenic	Juridical	Socioeconomic	On request[c]
MIDDLE EAST/NORTH AFRICA							
Algeria	—	—	X	—	—	—	—
Egypt	—	X	X	—	—	—	—
Iran	—	X	—	—	—	—	—
Iraq	—	X	X	X	—	—	—
Jordan	—	X	—	—	—	—	—
Kuwait	—	—	X	X	—	—	—
Lebanon	—	X	—	—	—	—	—
Libya	—	X	—	—	—	—	—
Morocco	—	X	X	—	—	—	—
Saudi Arabia	—	X	—	—	—	—	—
Syria	—	X	—	—	—	—	—
Tunisia	—	—	—	—	—	—	X[i]
Turkey	—	—	—	—	—	—	X[g]
Yemen, North	—	X	—	—	—	—	—
Yemen, South	—	X	—	—	—	—	—
ASIA							
Afghanistan	—	X	—	—	—	—	—
Bangladesh	—	X	—	—	X	—	—
Burma	—	X	—	—	—	—	—
China	—	—	—	—	—	—	X[a]
Hong Kong	—	X	X	—	X	—	—
India	—	X	X	X	X	X[j]	—
Indonesia	—	X	—	—	—	—	—
Korea, Dem. People's Rep.[l]	—	—	X	X	X	X	—
Korea, Republic of	—	X	X	X	X	—	—
Laos	—	X	—	—	—	—	—
Malaysia	—	X	—	—	—	—	—
Mongolia	—	X	X	—	—	—	—
Nepal	—	—	X	—	—	—	—
Pakistan	—	X	X	—	—	—	—
Papua New Guinea	—	—	X	—	—	—	—
Philippines	X	—	—	—	—	—	—
Singapore	—	—	—	—	—	—	X
Sri Lanka	—	X	—	—	—	—	—
Taiwan	—	X	X	X	X	X[f]	—
Thailand	—	—	X	—	X	—	—
Vietnam	—	—	—	—	—	—	X

a. No legal limit, but most abortions are performed during the first trimester.

b. In countries where abortion is permitted if it is necessary to protect a woman's health, the law may not specifically state that condition.

c. In countries where abortion is permitted on request, it is also permitted where necessary to protect a woman's life or health, and on eugenic, juridical, and socioeconomic grounds.

d. This applies only to serious psychiatric cases.

e. Abortion on eugenic grounds is rare because fetal tests are virtually unavailable.

f. Prior to viability of fetus.

g. During the first 10 weeks.

h. Penalty may be waived when abortion is performed during the first three months of pregnancy because of serious economic difficulty.

i. During the first three months or 12 weeks.

j. During the first 20 weeks.

k. Puerto Rican law prohibits abortion; however, since United States law overrules Puerto Rican legislation regarding constitutional rights, the *Roe v. Wade* Supreme Court decision applies and abortion is performed openly.

l. For "important reasons."

Table 8. Conditions for Performing Legal Abortion, and Average Price of Abortion, 1987

Country	None	Requires approval Of committee	Requires approval Of husband	Must be performed by physician	Maximum gestation (weeks)	Average price (U.S.$) Public	Average price (U.S.$) Private[i]
SUB-SAHARAN AFRICA							
Botswana[c]	—	—	X	—	u	u	u
Burundi	—	X	X	X	12	u	173–259
Cameroon	—	—	—	X	18	u	u
Chad	—	—	X	X	u	u	u
Ethiopia	—	—	—	X	u	u	u
Ghana	—	—	X	X	10	0	u
Liberia	—	X	—	—	u	u	u
Morocco	—	—	X[d]	X	u	u	u
Senegal	—	X	—	X	u	u	u
Sudan	—	X	X[e]	X	u	0	u
Tanzania[f]	—	—	X	—	12	u	u
Togo	—	—	X	X	u	0	33
Zimbabwe	—	X	X	X	u	u	u
LATIN AMERICA/CARIBBEAN							
Bolivia	—	X	X	X	12	u	98–246
Brazil	—	X	—	—	u	u	u
Cuba[f]	—	—	—	—	10	u	u
El Salvador[f]	—	—	—	—	16	u	120
Honduras	—	X	X	X	8	na	200
Mexico (IMSS)	—	—	X	X	8	na	35–141
Mexico (MEXFAM)	—	X	—	X	12	u	u
Panama	—	—	—	X	u	u	u
Puerto Rico[a]	—	—	—	X	h	na	250–350
MIDDLE EAST/NORTH AFRICA							
Egypt	—	—	X	X	u	0	u
Iraq	—	X	—	b	12	u	966
Jordan	—	X	X	X	u	43	213
Tunisia	—	—	—	X	12	0	u
Turkey	—	—	X	X	11	1	10
ASIA							
Bangladesh	—	—	—	X	u	u	16
China	X	—	—	—	u	0	na
Hong Kong	—	—	—	X	10	77	513
Korea, Republic of	—	—	X	X	28	0	58
Mongolia[g]	—	X	—	X	12	0	u
Pakistan	—	—	X	X	u	u	u
Singapore	X	—	—	—	u	2	142
Sri Lanka	—	X	—	X	u	u	u
Taiwan	—	—	X	X	24	0	100
Thailand	—	—	—	X	u	u	u
Vietnam	—	—	—	X	u	u	u

u = unknown.

na = not applicable.

a. Puerto Rican law prohibits abortion; however, since U.S. law overrules Puerto Rican legislation regarding constitutional rights, the *Roe v. Wade* Supreme Court decision applies and abortion is performed openly.

b. Abortion may be performed by a paramedic under supervision.

c. 1978 data.

d. If the husband is not available, the approval of the medical director of the facility where the procedure will be performed is required.

e. Husband's consent is preferred, but not required.

f. 1980 data.

g. Mongolia also requires that the woman have at least four children and be at least 40 years old.

h. Prior to viability of fetus.

i. Private-sector prices as of 1987 were reported in the following countries where abortion is illegal: Côte d'Ivoire, U.S.$167; Colombia, $10–$100; Haiti, $15–$200; Jamaica, $92; Peru, $167–$278; and Laos, $50.

Table 9. Annual Family Planning, Health, and Total Government Budgets

Country and year	Budget status[b]	Budget in local currency (in millions)			Family planning		Health as % of total budget
		Family planning program	Health ministry	Total government budget	As % of health budget	As % of total budget	
SUB-SAHARAN AFRICA							
Botswana							
1970	exp.	c	1.050	15.840	u	u	6.60
1971	exp.	c	1.270	19.410	u	u	6.50
1972	exp.	c	1.500	28.600	u	u	5.20
1973	exp.	c	1.800	40.900	u	u	4.40
1974	exp.	c	3.100	62.600	u	u	4.90
1975	alloc.	c	4.000	73.300	u	u	5.40
1976	alloc.	c	4.400	68.000	u	u	6.50
1979	exp.	u	8.900	170.300	u	u	5.20
1980	exp.	u	10.300	223.400	u	u	4.60
1981	exp.	u	15.200	279.300	u	u	5.40
1982	exp.	u	18.700	309.300	u	u	6.00
1982/83	exp.	u	17.580	378.040	u	u	4.65
1983/84	exp.	u	20.510	518.060	u	u	3.96
1984/85	exp.	u	23.550	728.770	u	u	3.23
1985/86	exp.	0.082	27.860	893.070	0.29	0.010	3.12
Ghana[a]							
1972	alloc.	0.700	40.000	603.000	1.75	0.120	6.60
1973	alloc.	0.750	44.900	763.000	1.70	0.100	5.90
1974	alloc.	1.040	81.800	1015.000	1.20	0.100	8.00
1975	alloc.	1.160	79.700	1322.000	1.50	0.090	6.00
Kenya							
1968	u	0.015	3.840	61.300	0.40	0.020	6.30
1969	u	0.010	4.250	67.000	0.20	0.010	6.30
1970	u	0.015	6.070	87.150	0.25	0.010	6.90
1979	prop.	u	45.200	762.700	u	u	5.90
1980	prop.	u	50.500	802.900	u	u	6.30
1981	prop.	u	54.500	909.600	u	u	6.00
1982	prop.	u	58.300	900.900	u	u	6.50
1983	u	63.183[c]	u	u	u	u	u
1984	u	66.827[c]	u	u	u	u	u
1985	u	70.039[c]	u	u	u	u	u
1986	u	73.447[c]	u	u	u	u	u
1987	prop.	76.922[c]	u	u	u	u	u
Mauritius							
1965	exp.	0.100	21.000	262.000	0.48	0.040	8.00
1966	exp.	0.200	22.000	266.000	0.91	0.080	8.30
1967	exp.	0.500	31.000	275.000	1.61	0.180	11.30
1968	exp.	0.500	36.000	295.000	1.39	0.170	12.20
1969	exp.	0.500	26.000	285.000	1.92	0.170	9.10
1970	alloc.	0.500	30.000	364.000	1.70	0.140	8.20
1971	exp.	0.450	31.000	283.000	1.50	0.200	11.00
1972	exp.	0.500	34.000	326.000	1.50	0.200	10.40
1973	exp.	1.200	45.000	535.000	2.70	0.200	8.40
1974	exp.	2.000	66.600	736.000	3.00	0.300	9.00
1975	exp.	3.400	103.500	1071.000	3.30	0.300	9.70
1976	exp.	4.700	116.900	1260.000	4.00	0.400	9.30
1977	exp.	4.600	110.600	1242.000	4.20	0.400	8.90
1978	exp.	9.800[p]	168.500	1770.000	5.80	0.600	9.50
1979	exp.	10.500[p]	185.000	2027.000	5.70	0.600	9.10
1980	exp.	10.500[p]	219.500	2555.000	4.80	0.400	8.60
1981	exp.	11.500[p]	233.000	3075.000	4.90	0.400	7.60
1982	exp.	13.500[p]	241.000	3716.000	5.60	0.400	6.50
Nigeria							
1986	alloc.	u	36.000	u	u	u	u
1987	alloc.	u	166.896	u	u	u	u
Tanzania							
1973	exp.	1.600	202.200	3182.000	0.79	0.050	6.40
1974	exp.	2.000	293.200	4427.000	0.68	0.050	6.60

Country and year	Budget status[b]	Budget in local currency (in millions)			Family planning		Health as % of total budget
		Family planning program	Health ministry	Total government budget	As % of health budget	As % of total budget	
Tanzania *(continued)*							
1975	exp.	2.700	425.600	6183.000	0.63	0.040	6.90
1976	exp.	3.100	384.000	5969.000	0.81	0.050	6.40
1977	alloc.	3.800	493.500	7684.000	0.77	0.050	6.40
Zimbabwe							
1982	exp.	2.400	10.600	212.900	2.30	1.100	5.00
1983	exp.	2.800	12.400	228.300	2.30	1.200	5.40
LATIN AMERICA/CARIBBEAN							
Bolivia							
1971	alloc.	u	84.700	5606.000[s]	u	u	1.50
1972	alloc.	u	85.300	6483.000[s]	u	u	1.32
1973	alloc.	u	125.900	12520.000[s]	u	u	1.00
1974	alloc.	0.569	227.200	17556.000[s]	0.25	0.003	1.29
1975	alloc.	0.452	270.100	26742.000[s]	0.17	0.002	1.01
1976	alloc.	0.452	382.900	37813.000[s]	0.12	0.001	1.01
1977	alloc.	0.180	405.400	u	0.04	u	u
Colombia							
1971	alloc.	3.800	1522.000	17700.000	0.20	0.020	8.60
1972	alloc.	6.200[d]	1528.000	21422.000	0.40	0.030	7.10
1973	alloc.	6.200[d]	2051.000	26212.000	0.30	0.020	7.80
1974	alloc.	8.000[d]	2681.000	30303.000	0.30	0.030	8.80
1975	alloc.	10.100	2819.000	34854.000	0.40	0.030	8.10
Colombia (PROFAMILIA)							
1980	exp.	256.000	u	u	u	u	u
1981	exp.	352.000	u	u	u	u	u
1982	exp.	442.000	u	u	u	u	u
1983	exp.	539.000	u	u	u	u	u
1984	alloc.	685.000	u	u	u	u	u
1986	alloc.	621.635	u	u	u	u	u
Costa Rica							
1970	exp.	1.700[e]	25.400	809.700	6.70	0.200	3.10
1971	exp.	2.600[e]	32.600	1103.900	8.00	0.300	3.20
1972	exp.	3.100[e]	34.600	1114.700	9.00	0.300	3.10
1973	exp.	3.600[e]	37.400	1314.200	9.60	0.300	2.80
1974	exp.	10.000[e]	90.700	1619.900	11.00	0.600	5.60
1975	exp.	14.500[e]	162.900	2906.200	8.90	0.500	5.60
1982	u	u	456.000	16708.000	u	u	2.70
1983	prop.	u	524.000	17714.000	u	u	3.00
1987	alloc.	u	1440.000	52300.000	u	u	2.75
Dominican Republic							
1969	exp.	0.154	16.210	235.330	1.00	0.070	6.90
1970	exp.	0.295	15.130	253.480	1.90	0.120	6.00
1971	exp.	0.270	18.600	304.990	1.50	0.090	6.10
1972	exp.	0.179	21.250	300.900	0.80	0.060	7.10
1973	exp.	0.159	21.470	325.300	0.70	0.050	6.60
1974	exp.	0.454[f]	18.270	440.300	2.50	0.100	4.10
1975	exp.	0.823[f]	65.990	486.300	1.20	0.170	13.60
1976	exp.	1.009[f]	33.800	580.600	3.00	0.170	5.80
1977	alloc.	0.910[f]	79.100	547.700	1.20	0.170	14.40
El Salvador							
1975	exp.	4.200	86.000	710.000	4.90	0.600	12.10
1976	alloc.	6.500	104.000	845.000	6.20	0.800	12.30
1977	alloc.	7.500	120.000	1069.000	6.20	0.700	11.20
1978	alloc.	u	148.000	1251.000	u	u	11.90
1979	alloc.	u	148.000	1452.000	u	u	10.20
1980	alloc.	u	171.000	1676.000	u	u	10.20

Table 9. Annual Family Planning, Health, and Total Government Budgets (continued)

Country and year	Budget status[b]	Budget in local currency (in millions)			Family planning		Health as % of total budget
		Family planning program	Health ministry	Total government budget	As % of health budget	As % of total budget	
Guatemala							
1971	exp.	0.150	20.000	211.000	0.75	0.070	9.50
1972	alloc.	0.034	23.000	292.000	0.15	0.010	7.90
1974	alloc.	0.160	22.500	355.000	0.71	0.050	6.30
Haiti							
1982	alloc.	4.320	u	u	u	u	u
1983	alloc.	7.425	u	u	u	u	u
1984	alloc.	9.060	u	u	u	u	u
1985	alloc.	11.590	u	u	u	u	u
1988	prop.	25.150	u	u	u	u	u
Honduras							
1968	u	0.030	15.260	197.720	0.20	0.020	7.70
1969	u	0.150	19.230	218.260	0.80	0.070	8.80
1970	u	0.100	20.130	225.600	0.50	0.040	8.90
1971	u	0.150	20.260	251.260	0.70	0.060	8.10
1972	u	0.150	21.250	267.280	0.70	0.060	8.00
Jamaica							
1969	exp.	0.531	18.920	212.030	2.80	0.300	8.90
1970	exp.	0.721	22.840	250.480	3.30	0.290	8.80
1971	exp.	1.000	25.000	310.000	4.00	0.300	8.10
1972	exp.	1.100	33.000	372.000	3.30	0.300	8.90
1973	exp.	1.300	50.000	471.000	2.60	0.300	10.60
1974	exp.	1.400	55.000	728.000	2.50	0.200	7.60
1975	alloc.	1.800	70.000	945.000	2.60	0.200	7.40
Mexico							
1983	alloc.	1608.500	311492.000	2778799.000	0.52	0.060	11.20
1984	alloc.	2228.800	424521.000	3611230.000	0.52	0.060	11.70
Mexico (IMSS)							
1985	alloc.	1856.240	u	u	u	u	u
1986	alloc.	2794.295	u	u	u	u	u
1987	alloc.	5744.253	u	u	u	u	u
Panama							
1983	exp.	0.117	u	u	u	u	u
1984	exp.	0.200	u	u	u	u	u
Paraguay							
1986	u	0.000	8459.000	143400.000	0.00	0.000	6.00
Peru							
1986	u	u	2411.815	37463.536	u	u	6.44
Puerto Rico							
1971	exp.	1.100	100.400	u	1.10	u	u
1972	exp.	1.600	109.500	u	1.40	u	u
1973	exp.	1.700	128.900	u	1.30	u	u
1974	exp.	2.600	148.100	u	1.70	u	u
1975	alloc.	3.600	159.900	u	2.30	u	u
1976	alloc.	5.100	160.000	u	3.20	u	u
MIDDLE EAST/NORTH AFRICA							
Egypt							
1978	exp.	2.000	117.000	2084.000	1.70	0.100	5.60
1979	exp.	1.900	131.000	4863.000	1.40	0.040	2.70
1980/81	exp.	1.800	179.000	7366.000	1.00	0.020	2.40
1981/82	exp.	1.900	u	u	u	u	u
1982/83	exp.	2.000	u	u	u	u	u
1983/84	exp.	2.300	u	u	u	u	u
1984/85	exp.	2.800	u	u	u	u	u
1985/86	alloc.	2.700	u	u	u	u	u

47

Table 9. Annual Family Planning, Health, and Total Government Budgets *(continued)*

Country and year	Budget status[b]	Budget in local currency (in millions)			Family planning		Health as % of total budget
		Family planning program	Health ministry	Total government budget	As % of health budget	As % of total budget	
Egypt *(continued)*							
1986/87	alloc.	2.700	u	u	u	u	u
Iran							
1968	u	40.000[k]	10400.000	247600.000	0.38[k]	0.020[k]	4.20
1969	u	70.000[k]	11000.000	330400.000	0.58[k]	0.020[k]	3.30
1970	exp.	250.000[k]	7292.000	336400.000	3.40[k]	0.070[k]	2.20
1971	exp.	405.000[k]	7813.000	548536.000	5.20[k]	0.070[k]	1.40
1972	exp.	650.000[k]	9309.000	578000.000	7.01[k]	0.110[k]	1.60
1973	exp.	871.000[k]	10753.000	785200.000	8.10[k]	0.110[k]	1.40
1974	exp.	1273.000[k]	19971.000	2082636.000	6.40[k]	0.060[k]	1.00
1975	exp.	1945.000[k]	22870.000	2447174.000	8.50[k]	0.080[k]	0.90
1976	exp.	2074.000[k]	23038.000	3105248.000	9.00[k]	0.070[k]	0.70
1977	alloc.	2197.000[k]	45420.000	3530000.000	4.80[k]	0.060[k]	1.30
1983	alloc.	1465.000	202931.000	3531044.000	0.72	0.041	5.75
1984	alloc.	1494.000	268078.000	4087831.000	0.49	0.037	6.56
1985	alloc.	1460.000	297745.000	4134885.000	0.49	0.035	7.47
1986	alloc.	1378.000	308878.000	4157828.000	0.45	0.033	7.43
1987	alloc.	r	259529.000	3970793.000	u	u	6.54
Iraq							
1986	u	0.062	u	u	u	u	u
Jordan							
1982	exp.	0.098	19.664	654.491	0.50	0.015	3.00
1983	exp.	0.113	20.521	717.656	0.55	0.016	2.86
1984	exp.	0.120	19.862	729.435	0.60	0.016	2.72
1985	exp.	0.125	23.956	812.848	0.52	0.015	2.95
1986	exp.	0.130	28.600	1002.633	0.45	0.013	2.85
Morocco							
1968	alloc.	0.800[k]	213.200	3523.000	0.40[k]	0.020[k]	6.00
1969	alloc.	1.200[k]	227.300	3602.000	0.50[k]	0.030[k]	6.30
1970	alloc.	1.300[k]	237.400	3656.000	0.50[k]	0.040[k]	6.50
1971	alloc.	1.200[k]	231.300	3694.000	0.50[k]	0.030[k]	6.30
1972	alloc.	1.600[k]	252.900	3979.000	0.60[k]	0.040[k]	6.40
1973	alloc.	4.000[k]	319.300	3478.000	1.30[k]	0.110[k]	9.20
Tunisia							
1970	exp.	0.067	15.300	214.700	0.40	0.030	7.10
1971	exp.	0.104	15.900	225.300	0.70	0.050	7.10
1972	exp.	0.143	18.300	276.600	0.80	0.050	6.60
1973	exp.	0.500	34.000	449.100	1.50	0.100	7.60
1974	exp.	2.200	38.600	553.200	5.70	0.400	7.00
Turkey							
1965	u	5.100	591.000	14421.000	0.90	0.030	4.10
1966	u	6.700	662.000	16775.000	1.00	0.040	3.90
1967	u	7.600	772.000	18813.000	1.00	0.040	4.10
1968	alloc.	22.100	1013.000	21612.000	2.20	0.100	4.70
1969	alloc.	25.600	1087.000	25697.000	2.40	0.100	4.20
1970	alloc.	16.700	1096.000	26860.000	1.50	0.060	4.10
1971	alloc.	19.500	1937.000	36951.000	1.00	0.050	5.20
1972	alloc.	24.500	2354.000	50310.000	1.00	0.050	4.70
1973	alloc.	24.700	2518.000	61023.000	1.00	0.040	4.10
1974	alloc.	32.900	3406.000	82411.000	1.00	0.040	4.10
1983	alloc.	u	75226.785	2558902.500	u	u	2.90
1984	alloc.	u	100106.514	3211982.000	u	u	3.10
1985	alloc.	3848.936	137462.000	5412082.049	2.80	0.070	2.50
1986	alloc.	6595.692	178261.960	7101500.000	3.70	0.060	2.50
1987	alloc.	7914.920	304420.000	10755000.000	2.60	0.070	2.80
ASIA							
Bangladesh[a]							
1972[o]	alloc.	30.000	60.000	u	50.00	u	u

Table 9. Annual Family Planning, Health, and Total Government Budgets *(continued)*

Country and year	Budget status[b]	Budget in local currency (in millions)			Family planning		Health as % of total budget
		Family planning program	Health ministry	Total government budget	As % of health budget	As % of total budget	
Bangladesh[a] *(continued)*							
1973	alloc.	70.000	421.700	4638.000	16.60	1.500	9.10
1974	alloc.	130.600	402.200	5250.000	32.50	2.500	7.70
1975	alloc.	145.700	576.500	9500.000	25.30	1.500	6.10
1976	alloc.	216.400	340.000	10057.000	63.60	2.100	3.40
1977	alloc.	312.800	430.200	12029.000	72.70	2.600	3.60
1978	alloc.	467.400	476.500	16026.000	98.10	2.900	3.00
1979	alloc.	592.700	700.000	23300.000	84.70	2.500	3.00
1980	alloc.	696.400	658.300	23690.000	105.80	2.900	2.80
1981	alloc.	944.000	840.900	30150.000	112.30	3.100	2.80
1986	alloc.	1674.700[t]	u	u	u	u	u
1987	alloc.	2054.100[t]	u	u	u	u	u
China							
1986	u	3720.000	u	u	u	u	u
Hong Kong							
1982	alloc.	3.800	2135.000	27778.200	0.18	0.014	7.68
1983	alloc.	3.900	2391.500	34597.800	0.16	0.011	6.91
1984	alloc.	4.300	2725.300	33393.100	0.15	0.013	8.16
1985	alloc.	4.900	3118.400	36910.700	0.16	0.013	8.45
1986	alloc.	5.500	3766.900	43444.000	0.15	0.013	8.67
India							
1968	alloc.	370.000[a]	144.200[a]	u	256.00[a]	u	u[a]
1969	alloc.	420.000[a]	295.500[a]	12230.000	142.00[a]	3.400	2.40[a]
1970	alloc.	520.000[a]	332.100[a]	14110.000	156.00[a]	3.700	2.40[a]
1971	alloc.	606.050[a]	380.600[a]	14400.000	159.20[a]	4.200	2.60[a]
1972	alloc.	763.070[a]	404.500[a]	16887.000	188.60[a]	4.500	2.40[a]
1973	alloc.	548.500[a]	305.010[a]	u	179.80[a]	u	u[a]
1974	exp.	696.000	6885.000[h]	148118.000	10.10	0.470	4.60
1975	exp.	894.000	7961.000[h]	181297.000	11.20	0.490	4.40
1976	exp.	1728.000	9927.000[h]	204107.000	17.40	0.850	4.90
1977	exp.	970.000	10472.000[h]	224026.000	9.30	0.430	4.70
1978	exp.	1104.000	12158.000[h]	259051.000	9.10	0.430	4.70
1979	exp.	1218.000	14427.000[h]	291657.000	8.40	0.420	5.00
1980	exp.	1464.000	17640.000[h]	353794.000	8.30	0.410	5.00
1981	exp.	1995.000	20872.000[h]	405649.000	9.60	0.490	5.10
1982	exp.	2946.000	25385.000	480149.000	11.60	0.614	5.29
1982/83	alloc.	2696.000	22640.000	443277.000	11.90	0.610	5.10
1983/84	prop.	4388.000	30678.000	565595.000	14.30	0.776	5.42
1984/85	alloc.	5542.000	32878.000	616021.000	16.86	0.900	5.34
Indonesia[a]							
1969	alloc.	967.000[j]	11564.000	327400.000	8.40	0.300	3.50
1970	alloc.	1433.000[j]	12173.000	416300.000[j]	11.80	0.300	2.90
1971	alloc.	1500.000	15005.000	585200.000	10.00	0.300	2.60
1972	alloc.	2350.000	16539.000	751600.000	14.20	0.300	2.20
1973	alloc.	2500.000	19784.000	862400.000	12.60	0.300	2.30
1974	alloc.	3804.000	u	1933700.000	u	0.200	u
1975	alloc.	5576.000	15222.000	2734700.000	36.60	0.200	0.60
1976	alloc.	7177.000	u	3520600.000	u	0.200	u
1977	alloc.	9149.000	26292.000	4200000.000	34.80	0.200	0.60
1978	alloc.	11691.000	47342.000	4826347.000	24.70	0.200	1.00
1979	alloc.	17580.000	89559.000	6933950.000	19.60	0.300	1.30
1980	alloc.	30934.000	102455.000	9055300.000	30.20	0.300	1.10
1983	alloc.	74718.000	270824.000	10755230.000	27.60	0.700	2.50
1984	alloc.	70399.472	u	u	u	u	u
1985	alloc.	81327.865	u	u	u	u	u
1986	alloc.	90174.290	u	u	u	u	u
Korea, Republic of[m]							
1967	exp.	406.000	1763.000[l]	180900.000	23.00	0.220	0.97
1968	exp.	377.000	2387.000[l]	262100.000	16.00	0.140	0.91
1969	exp.	616.000	3152.000	370882.000	19.50	0.170	0.85

Table 9. Annual Family Planning, Health, and Total Government Budgets (continued)

Country and year	Budget status[b]	Budget in local currency (in millions)			Family planning		Health as % of total budget
		Family planning program	Health ministry	Total government budget	As % of health budget	As % of total budget	
Korea, Republic of[m] *(continued)*							
1970	exp.	716.000	4321.000	446273.000	16.60	0.160	0.97
1971	exp.	674.000	6192.000	659344.000	10.90	0.100	0.94
1972	exp.	657.000	5795.000	709336.000	11.30	0.090	0.82
1973	exp.	765.000	6774.000	659375.000	11.30	0.120	1.03
1974	alloc.	806.000	6303.000	847733.000	12.80	0.100	0.74
1975	alloc.	1177.000	9242.000	1291957.000	12.70	0.090	0.72
1976	alloc.	1859.000	41346.000	2253511.000	4.50	0.080	1.80
1977	alloc.	5401.000	55674.000	2869856.000	9.70	0.190	1.90
1978	alloc.	6300.000	66451.000	3517036.000	9.50	0.180	1.90
1979	alloc.	7577.000	94299.000	5213436.000	8.00	0.150	1.80
1980	alloc.	7816.000	166251.000	5804061.000	4.70	0.130	2.90
1981	exp.	8600.000	251700.000	14322000.000	3.42	0.060	1.76
1982	exp.	10400.000	317400.000	16589900.000	3.28	0.063	1.91
1983	exp.	20600.000	383300.000	18246100.000	5.37	0.113	2.10
1984	exp.	22200.000	375600.000	20306700.000	5.91	0.109	1.85
1985	exp.	30200.000	435200.000	21935000.000	1.98	0.138	1.98
Laos							
1969	u	c	499.000	17344.000	u	u	2.90
1970	u	c	558.000	18273.000	u	u	3.00
1971	u	c	587.000	19200.000	u	u	3.00
1972	u	c	644.000	22808.000	u	u	2.80
1973	u	c	639.000	23006.000	u	u	2.80
Malaysia (Peninsular)[a]							
1966	alloc.	0.249	119.100	1644.000	0.20	0.015	7.30
1967	alloc.	0.900	139.900	1829.000	0.64	0.050	7.60
1968	alloc.	1.600	146.300	1932.000	1.09	0.080	7.60
1969	alloc.	2.000	149.600	1925.000	1.34	0.100	7.80
1970	alloc.	2.216	157.000	2282.000	1.41	0.100	6.90
1971	alloc.	2.213	187.800	2463.000	1.18	0.090	7.60
1972	alloc.	2.100	210.700	2735.000	1.00	0.080	7.70
1973	alloc.	2.690	244.400	3155.000	1.10	0.090	7.70
1974	alloc.	2.960	290.500	3530.000	1.00	0.080	8.20
1975	alloc.	3.660	334.000	4595.000	1.10	0.080	7.30
1976	exp.	8.900	461.800	7324.000	1.90	0.120	6.30
1977	exp.	12.790	541.900	10996.000	2.40	0.120	4.90
1978	exp.	14.280	665.300	12701.000	2.10	0.110	5.20
1979	exp.	15.190	774.800	13170.000	2.00	0.120	5.90
1980	exp.	17.620	860.100	20724.000	2.00	0.090	4.20
1983	exp.	13.775	1034.468	28749.017	1.33	0.048	3.60
1984	exp.	24.617	1101.810	27691.803	2.23	0.089	3.98
1985	exp.	23.146	1256.322	29191.096	1.84	0.079	4.30
1986	exp.	20.120	1333.622	30811.911	1.51	0.065	4.33
1987	alloc.	18.410	1174.786	27411.630	1.57	0.067	4.29
Nepal							
1969	alloc.	4.000[j]	39.500	683.800	10.10	0.500	4.70
1970	alloc.	6.900[j]	51.100	769.500	13.50	0.700	5.30
1971	alloc.	7.500[j]	52.200	889.500	14.40	0.700	4.60
1972	alloc.	5.300[j]	57.900	982.800	9.20	0.400	4.60
1973	alloc.	7.950[j]	63.800	1226.300	10.00	0.400	4.10
1974	alloc.	10.900[j]	93.100	1513.800	11.70	0.600	5.30
1975	alloc.	18.500[j]	120.700	1913.400	9.80	0.600	5.60
1976	alloc.	23.930	162.480	2371.600	14.73	1.009	6.85
1977	alloc.	14.120	164.060	3087.400	8.61	0.457	5.31
1978	alloc.	18.880	178.340	2886.300	10.59	0.654	6.18
1979	exp.	17.450	72.200	2308.600	24.17	0.756	3.13
1980	exp.	24.310	97.800	2731.100	24.86	0.890	3.58
1981	exp.	29.650	152.800	3726.900	19.40	0.796	4.10
1982	exp.	36.150	216.300	4982.100	16.71	0.725	4.34
1983	alloc.	41.710	219.900	5059.900	18.97	0.824	4.34
1984	alloc.	54.710	332.800	6729.900	16.44	0.813	4.94

Table 9.   Annual Family Planning, Health, and Total Government Budgets *(continued)*

Country and year	Budget status[b]	Budget in local currency (in millions)			Family planning		Health as % of total budget
		Family planning program	Health ministry	Total government budget	As % of health budget	As % of total budget	
Pakistan[a]							
1976	u	183.100	540.000	16239.000	33.90	1.130	3.30
1977	u	104.600	512.000	17150.000	20.40	0.600	3.00
1978	u	114.300	569.000	20181.000	20.10	0.570	2.80
1979	u	126.600	717.000	21597.000	17.70	0.590	3.30
1983/84	exp.	118.033	u	u	u	u	u
1984/85	exp.	150.151	u	u	u	u	u
1985/86	exp.	176.925	u	u	u	u	u
1986/87	alloc.	156.112	u	u	u	u	u
1987/88	alloc.	173.927	u	u	u	u	u
Philippines[a]							
1967	exp.	0.520	96.810	2074.000	0.50	0.030	4.70
1968	exp.	1.100	101.450	2276.000	1.10	0.050	4.50
1969	exp.	3.550	146.840	2905.000	2.40	0.120	5.10
1970	exp.	5.260	177.220	3197.000	3.00	0.160	5.50
1971	exp.	14.670	223.830	3394.000	6.60	0.430	6.60
1972	alloc.	7.900	252.300	4303.000	3.10	0.200	5.90
1973	alloc.	26.700	315.200	5702.000	8.50	0.500	5.50
1974	alloc.	58.400	524.800	8711.000	11.10	0.700	6.00
1975	alloc.	60.800	636.100	14500.000	9.60	0.400	4.40
1976	alloc.	110.200	925.900	27919.000	11.90	0.390	3.30
1977	alloc.	74.300	892.900	23759.000	8.30	0.310	3.80
1978	alloc.	122.600	1038.900	28682.000	11.80	0.430	3.60
1979	alloc.	180.500	1372.100	32261.000	13.20	0.560	4.30
1980	alloc.	220.100	1430.900	37894.000	15.40	0.580	3.80
1981	alloc.	283.200	1801.900	50320.000	15.70	0.560	3.60
1982	alloc.	119.800	2149.800	57092.000	13.30	0.500	3.80
1983	alloc.	94.200	2661.000	61838.000	10.40	0.450	4.30
1984	alloc.	118.600	u	u	u	u	u
1985	alloc.	111.600	u	u	u	u	u
1986	alloc.	125.000	u	u	u	u	u
Singapore[a]							
1967	alloc.	0.200	77.600	592.100	0.30	0.030	13.00
1968	alloc.	0.200	77.400	702.000	0.30	0.030	11.00
1969	alloc.	0.200	101.400	1101.500	0.20	0.020	9.20
1970	alloc.	0.200	87.700	1001.000	0.20	0.020	8.80
1971	alloc.	1.000	103.400	1306.800	1.00	0.100	7.90
1972	alloc.	1.200	127.100	1449.000	1.00	0.100	8.80
1973	alloc.	1.800	116.800	1854.000	1.50	0.100	6.30
1974	alloc.	2.400	101.200	2299.000	2.30	0.100	4.40
1975	alloc.	2.200	162.600	2646.000	1.40	0.100	6.10
1976	alloc.	2.400	180.200	3104.000	1.30	0.100	5.80
1977	prop.	2.800	185.600	3362.000	1.50	0.000	5.50
1978	alloc.	2.800	177.600	3668.000	1.60	0.080	4.80
1979	alloc.	2.900	187.800	3885.000	1.50	0.070	4.80
1980	alloc.	3.300	217.000	4113.000	1.50	0.080	5.30
1981	alloc.	3.600	272.300	6335.000	1.30	0.060	4.30
1982	alloc.	3.700	318.700	7638.000	1.20	0.050	4.20
1983	alloc.	3.900	363.500	8871.000	1.10	0.040	4.10
Sri Lanka							
1968	exp.	0.087[k]	206.900	3391.000	0.04[k]	0.000[k]	6.10
1969	alloc.	0.242[k]	220.000	3999.000	0.11[k]	0.000[k]	5.50
1972	u	c	317.000	5151.000	u	u	6.20
1985	exp.	15.369	1955.215	64000.000	0.79	0.024	3.06
1986	alloc.	37.760	2163.049	67000.000	1.74	0.056	3.23
1987	alloc.	39.218	2975.000	72000.000	1.32	0.054	4.13
Taiwan[q]							
1965	exp.	0.000	120.600	2653.000	0.00	0.000	4.50
1966	exp.	1.182	111.500	2929.000	1.10	0.040	3.80
1967	exp.	0.881	125.400	3459.000	0.70	0.040	3.60
1968	exp.	3.780	147.400	3784.000	2.60	0.100	3.90

Table 9. Annual Family Planning, Health, and Total Government Budgets *(continued)*

Country and year	Budget status[b]	Budget in local currency (in millions)			Family planning		Health as % of total budget
		Family planning program	Health ministry	Total government budget	As % of health budget	As % of total budget	
Taiwan *(continued)*							
1969	exp.	7.908	155.200	4355.000	5.10	0.180	3.60
1970	exp.	12.000	192.300	5402.000	6.20	0.220	3.60
1971	exp.	31.000	340.000	44817.000	9.10	0.070	0.80
1972	exp.	41.000	988.000	62153.000	4.20	0.070	1.60
1973	exp.	43.600	1086.000	72335.000	4.00	0.060	1.50
1974	exp.	53.900	778.000	76251.000	6.90	0.070	1.00
1975	exp.	51.400	826.000	96459.000	6.20	0.050	0.90
1976	exp.	88.400	1299.000	135626.000	6.80	0.070	1.00
1977	alloc.	105.900	1462.000	162826.000	7.20	0.070	0.90
1978	alloc.	132.000	1804.000	131244.000	7.30	0.100	1.40
1979	alloc.	128.200	4950.000	155056.000	2.60	0.080	3.20
1980	alloc.	150.000	6616.000	194177.000	2.30	0.080	3.40
1981	alloc.	237.160	9534.000	433221.000	2.50	0.050	2.20
1982	alloc.	316.400	12418.000	493741.000	2.50	0.060	2.50
1983	alloc.	346.440	12820.000	498159.000	2.70	0.070	2.50
1984	alloc.	382.080	16076.000	519049.000	2.40	0.070	3.10
1985	alloc.	386.880	19494.400	563729.000	2.00	0.070	3.50
Thailand							
1968	exp.	0.300	587.900	21262.000	0.05	0.000	2.80
1969	exp.	0.900	643.600	23960.000	0.10	0.000	2.70
1970	exp.	1.800	800.400	27300.000	0.20	0.010	2.90
1971	exp.	2.400	975.400	28645.000	0.20	0.010	3.40
1972	exp.	10.000	972.000	29000.000	1.00	0.030	3.30
1973	exp.	11.000	1023.000	31600.000	1.10	0.030	3.20
1974	exp.	12.500	1114.000	36000.000	1.10	0.030	3.10
1975	alloc.	18.700	1547.000	48000.000	1.20	0.040	3.20
1976	alloc.	22.900	2755.000	62650.000	0.80	0.040	4.40
1977	alloc.	47.900	3522.000	68790.000	1.30	0.070	5.10
1978	alloc.	57.500	3417.000	81000.000	1.70	0.070	4.20
1979	u	u	u	u	u	u	u
1980	exp.	52.000	4495.000	109000.000	1.20	0.050	4.10
1981	exp.	55.500	5572.000	140000.000	1.00	0.040	4.00
1982	exp.	196.000	u	u	u	u	u
1983	exp.	198.000	u	u	u	u	u
1984	alloc.	184.000	8618.000	192000.000	2.14	0.096	4.49
1985	alloc.	196.000	9044.000	209000.000	2.17	0.094	4.33
1986	alloc.	210.000	9447.000	218000.000	2.22	0.096	4.33
1987	alloc.	268.000	9544.000	228000.000	2.81	0.118	4.19

a. The family planning budget is not included in the Ministry of Health budget. Hence, for the column family planning as a percentage of health budget, the figure shown is the ratio of the family planning budget to the (separate) health budget.

b. In this column, "alloc." refers to allocated, "exp." refers to expended, "prop." refers to proposed, and "u" means the status is unknown.

c. Family planning is not budgeted independently in the Ministry of Health budget.

d. For unclear reasons, the figures shown here are only about one-fourth the reported expenditures shown in Table 10.

e. Family planning monies from all sources.

f. Includes an estimate for family planning inputs provided under maternal and child health services. For 1977, this was estimated at $700,000.

g. The family planning budget is not included in the Ministry of Health budget.

h. The Ministry of Health became broad-based in 1974; its budget thereafter includes public health programs, sanitation, water supply, and family welfare services.

i. Expended.

j. The family planning budget includes foreign as well as domestic funds.

k. The family planning budget represents only direct monetary input and excludes the contribution to the program of the personnel and facilities of the health network, into which the program is integrated.

l. Represents health budget only; budget for social affairs is excluded from this figure.

m. The family planning program budget excludes local government funds.

Table 9. Annual Family Planning, Health, and Total Government Budgets *(continued)*

n. Data from the authors' 1987 questionnaire do not agree with figures published in the Nortman Fact Books. The domestic data shown here for 1982–86 exclude international funds. The Nortman data for 1983 and earlier are believed to include them. Previously published data are 285.5 million for 1982 and 275.8 million for 1983.

o. Prior to 1971 (before Bangladesh gained independence), Bangladesh data were included under Pakistan.

p. About half of the family planning program budget is for the maternal and child health component of the MCH/FP budget.

q. Prior to FY 1971, the family planning budget was funded by the provincial government. In 1970, however, the National Health Administration was established, and beginning with FY 1971, figures include funds from the national government, the provincial government, and the Taipei city government, which was separated from Taiwan Province in 1970.

r. In 1987, the family planning budget was integrated into the public health budget.

s. National consolidated budget.

t. Includes international as well as domestic funds. The figures for 1981 and earlier years are believed to have included international funds also. The totals shown here break down for 1986 into 250 million Taka domestic and 1424.7 million Taka international, and for 1987 into 300 million Taka domestic and 1754.1 million Taka international.

Table 10. Annual Total and Per Capita Funding for Family Planning Programs, by Major Source

Country and year	Exchange rate (U.S.$)	Budget status[a]	Funding by major source (000s of U.S.$)					Per capita (U.S. cents)	
			Govt.	International agency	Foreign govt.	Private org.	All sources	Govt.	All sources including govt.
SUB-SAHARAN AFRICA									
Botswana									
1970	0.70	exp.	u	23	u	0	23	u	3.50
1971	0.70	exp.	u	50	u	0	50	u	7.40
1972	0.70	exp.	u	58	u	u	u	u	u
1973	0.70	exp.	u	85	u	u	u	u	u
1974	0.70	exp.	u	68	u	u	u	u	u
1975	0.68	exp.	u	34	u	u	u	u	u
1982	1.02	u	u	3	u	2	5	u	0.47
1983	1.10	u	u	9	u	41	50	u	4.82
1984	1.28	u	u	16	u	68	84	u	7.84
1985	1.89	exp.	44	150	u	16	209	3.93	18.86
Burkina Faso									
1987	300.03	alloc.	325	250	415	170	1160	4.43	15.82
Ethiopia									
1982	2.07	u	u	u	u	600	u	u	u
1983	2.07	u	u	u	u	697	u	u	u
1984	2.07	u	u	u	u	828	u	u	u
1985	2.07	u	u	u	u	858	u	u	u
1986	2.07	u	u	u	u	974	u	u	u
Gambia									
1972	1.96	exp.	0	u	u	u	25	0.00	5.00
1973	1.59	exp.	0	u	u	u	27	0.00	5.40
1974	1.72	alloc.	0	u	u	u	45	0.00	8.90
Ghana									
1970	1.02	alloc.	325	130	705	150	1310	4.00	14.00
1971	1.02	alloc.	733	172	84	0	989	8.00	11.00
1972	1.27	alloc.	391	6	u	165	562	4.00	7.00
1973	1.15	alloc.	653	18	u	178	849	7.00	9.00
1974	1.15	alloc.	1036	3	100	u	1139	11.00	12.00
1975	1.15	exp.	1012	u	262	u	1274	11.00	13.00
1976	1.15	alloc.	1782	u	170	u	1952	18.00	21.00
1977	1.15	prop.	1281	u	164	u	1445	13.00	15.00
Kenya									
1969	7.14	alloc.	28	368	447	95	938	0.25	8.50
Mauritius									
1965	5.56	exp.	18	26	b	0	44	2.42	5.90
1966	5.56	exp.	36	35	b	0	71	4.72	9.30
1967	5.56	exp.	90	87	b	0	167	11.57	21.48
1968	5.56	exp.	75	122	b	0	197	9.00	24.00
1969	5.56	exp.	87	97	b	0	184	10.00	21.90
1970	5.56	exp.	85	131	b	0	216	10.00	26.00
1971	5.00	exp.	82	0	0	131	213	10.00	26.00
1972	5.00	exp.	97	162	0	53	312	12.00	37.00
1973	5.00	exp.	211	340	0	84	635	25.00	75.00
1974	5.00	exp.	353	311	15	178	857	41.00	100.00
1975	5.88	exp.	538	580	20	83	1221	62.00	141.00
1976	6.67	exp.	611	251	0	79	941	69.00	107.00
1978	5.88	exp.	750	172	2	100	1024	84.00	114.00
1979	5.88	exp.	754	392	0	138	1284	82.00	139.00
1980	7.69	exp.	814	133	0	217	1164	87.00	124.00
1981	10.31	exp.	666	97	0	150	913	70.00	96.00
1982	11.36	alloc.	639	94	0	148	881	66.00	91.00
Nigeria									
1984	0.76	exp.	u	826	1840	1342	4008	u	4.34
1985	0.89	exp.	u	1042	3140	1040	5222	u	5.49
1986	1.35	alloc.	u	825	3009	1210	5044	u	5.10
1987	4.00	alloc.	u	203	u	u	u	u	u

Table 10. Annual Total and Per Capita Funding for Family Planning Programs, by Major Source (continued)

Country and year	Exchange rate (U.S.$)	Budget status[a]	Funding by major source (000s of U.S.$)					Per capita (U.S. cents)	
			Govt.	International agency	Foreign govt.	Private org.	All sources	Govt.	All sources including govt.
Somalia									
1982	10.75	exp.	u	285[bb]	u	u	285	u	u
1983	15.79	exp.	u	128[bb]	u	u	128	u	u
1984	20.02	exp.	u	32[bb]	u	u	32	u	u
1985	38.00	exp.	u	77[bb]	u	u	77	u	u
1986	83.61	exp.	u	154[bb]	u	u	154	u	u
Tanzania									
1972	8.00	alloc.	9	0	0	180	189	0.06	1.30
1973	8.00	alloc.	10	0	0	218	228	0.07	1.60
1974	8.00	alloc.	10	0	0	298	308	0.07	2.10
1975	8.00	alloc.	24	0	0	359	383	0.16	2.50
1976	8.00	alloc.	22	0	4	443	469	0.12	2.90
Uganda									
1972	7.14	exp.	126[f]	u	u	u	u	1.20	u
1973	7.14	exp.	u	u	u	u	126	u	1.20
1975	8.33	alloc.	u	u	u	u	170	u	1.50
1976	8.33	alloc.	u	u	u	u	226	u	1.80
Zimbabwe									
1970	0.70	exp.	152	69	0	1	223	2.80	4.20
1971	0.69	exp.	159	u	u	271	512	2.80	9.20
1972	0.62	exp.	183	26	0	318	527	3.00	9.00
1973	0.57	exp.	581	0	0	70	651	10.00	11.00
1974	0.61	exp.	643	0	0	63	707	10.00	11.00
1975	0.56	exp.	858	0	0	66	924	13.00	15.00
1976	0.56	exp.	1132	0	0	38	1170	17.00	17.00
1977	0.70	exp.	1342	0	0	0	1342	20.00	20.00
1978	0.70	exp.	1810	0	0	0	1810	25.00	25.00
1980	0.65	u	3773	u	u	208	3980	51.21	54.02
1981	0.69	u	2132	u	u	u	2132	27.87	27.87
1982	0.76	u	3168	u	106	60	3334	39.94	42.03
1983	1.01	u	3366	u	445	232	4043	40.98	49.22
1984	1.25	u	3675	u	960	212	4847	43.26	57.05
1985	1.61	u	3102	u	1357	203	4662	35.35	53.11
LATIN AMERICA/CARIBBEAN									
Bolivia									
1973	20.00	exp.	0	0	16	0	16	0.00	0.30
1974	20.00	exp.	29	79	0	60	168	0.50	3.00
1975	20.00	exp.	29	0	21	90	140	0.50	2.50
1976	20.00	alloc.	6	300	u	183	489	0.10	10.40
1977	20.00	alloc.	9	0	0	118	127	0.20	2.50
1987	2.60	alloc.	u	u	20	1118	1138	u	16.86
Brazil									
1971	5.26	alloc.	165	u	u	1337	u	0.17	u
1972	5.88	alloc.	61	u	u	2252	u	0.06	u
1973	6.25	alloc.	82	u	u	3163	u	0.08	u
1974	6.67	alloc.	131	u	u	3149	u	1.25	u
1975	7.69	alloc.	105	u	u	3761	u	0.97	u
Brazil (BEMFAM)									
1980	65.49	exp.	0	0	0	5666	5666	0.00	4.60
1981	127.88	exp.	0	0	0	5954	5954	0.00	4.80
1982	252.53	exp.	0	0	0	5215	5215	0.00	4.10
1983	980.39	exp.	0	0	0	4487	4487	0.00	3.40
1984	1904.76	prop.	0	0	0	5291	5291	0.00	3.90
1985	4784.69	prop.	0	0	0	7138	7138	0.00	5.20
1986	7.42	prop.	0	0	0	8810	8810	0.00	6.30
Colombia									
1972	23.81	exp.	1258	2846	680	200	4984	5.00	22.00
1973	23.81	exp.	1369	2791	600	595	5355	6.00	23.00
1974	25.64	exp.	1711	2885	470	469	5535	7.00	23.00

Table 10. Annual Total and Per Capita Funding for Family Planning Programs, by Major Source *(continued)*

Country and year	Exchange rate (U.S.$)	Budget status[a]	Funding by major source (000s of U.S.$)					Per capita (U.S. cents)	
			Govt.	International agency	Foreign govt.	Private org.	All sources	Govt.	All sources including govt.
Colombia *(continued)*									
1979	40.00	exp.	2247	729	u	2591	5567	8.80	21.80
1980	43.48	exp.	2758	u	u	2684	5442	10.60	20.90
1981	52.63	exp.	2850	u	u	3769	6619	10.70	24.90
1982	66.67	exp.	3144	u	u	3250	6394	11.60	23.60
1983	71.43	exp.	3731	u	u	3564	7294	13.50	26.40
Costa Rica									
1971	8.33	exp.	40	41	110	110	301	2.00	17.00
1972	8.33	exp.	49	73	90	156	368	3.00	20.00
1973	8.33	exp.	52	90	113	167	422	3.00	22.00
1974	8.33	exp.	326	413	124	308	1171	16.00	60.00
1975	8.33	exp.	643	466	200	386	1695	33.00	86.00
Dominican Republic									
1968	1.00	u	80	u	21	54	155	2.10	4.10
1969	1.00	exp.	80	20	0	55	155	2.10	4.00
1970	1.00	exp.	295	108	0	108	511	7.10	12.20
1971	1.00	exp.	270	116	0	74	460	6.20	10.60
1972	1.00	exp.	179	25	0	74	278	4.00	6.20
1973	1.00	exp.	159	42	0	37	238	3.80	5.10
1974	1.00	exp.	454[d]	304	0	232	990	9.50	20.70
1975	1.00	exp.	823[d]	362	34	739	1958	16.80	39.90
1976	1.00	exp.	1009[d]	514	0	689	2212	20.20	43.60
1977	1.00	exp.	910[d]	598	0	445	1953	17.50	37.50
El Salvador									
1969	2.50	alloc.	109	172	228	28	537	3.00	16.00
1970	2.50	alloc.	146	217	315	33	711	4.00	20.00
1971	2.50	alloc.	272	231	200	41	744	7.00	20.00
1972	2.50	alloc.	379	242	214	44	878	10.00	23.00
1973	2.50	alloc.	484	340	240	37	1101	12.00	28.00
1975	2.50	alloc.	1517	30	134	11	1692	36.00	40.00
1976	2.50	exp.	4100	510	132	0	4742	95.00	110.00
1977	2.50	exp.	2700	748	245	34	3727	63.00	87.00
1978	2.50	exp.	7300	790	450	130	8670	166.00	197.00
1979	2.50	exp.	7000	1000	228	120	8348	150.00	179.00
1980	2.50	alloc.	6000	1000	760	76	7836	125.00	163.00
Guatemala									
1972	1.00	exp.	14	591	0	100	705	0.25	13.00
1973	1.00	alloc.	34	517	0	105	656	0.60	12.00
1974	1.00	alloc.	16	456	0	181	653	0.29	12.00
Honduras									
1984	2.00	alloc.	0	u	2097	700	2797	u	66.03
1985	2.00	alloc.	0	u	2097	700	2494	u	57.05
1986	2.00	alloc.	0	u	2900	600	2797	u	61.89
1987	2.00	alloc.	0	u	3100	700	3800	u	81.45
Jamaica									
1966	0.42	u	9	u	u	39[e]	48	0.60	3.40
1967	0.42	u	168	u	u	37	205	11.00	13.00
1968	0.42	exp.	380	u	u	177	u	20.00	u
1969	0.80	exp.	548	u	116	u	u	28.00	u
1970	0.80	exp.	721	u	166	u	u	36.00	u
1971	0.80	exp.	1090	u	178	u	u	56.00	u
1972	0.91	exp.	1221	u	222	u	u	63.00	u
1973	0.90	alloc.	1490	u	574	u	u	75.00	u
Mexico									
1972	12.50	exp.	4297	u	u	u	u	8.00	u
1973	12.50	exp.	25656	u	u	u	u	46.00	u
1985[dd]	197.75	alloc.	9388	u	u	u	9388	11.88	11.88
1986[dd]	401.93	alloc.	6953	u	u	u	6953	8.58	8.58
1987[dd]	978.47	alloc.	5871	u	u	u	5871	7.07	7.07

Table 10. Annual Total and Per Capita Funding for Family Planning Programs, by Major Source *(continued)*

Country and year	Exchange rate (U.S.$)	Budget status[a]	Funding by major source (000s of U.S.$)					Per capita (U.S. cents)	
			Govt.	International agency	Foreign govt.	Private org.	All sources	Govt.	All sources including govt.
Panama									
1982	0.91	exp.	1390	u	1159	u	2549	67.94	124.58
1983	0.94	exp.	117	u	664	u	781	5.60	37.35
1984	0.98	exp.	200	u	322	u	522	9.36	24.44
Puerto Rico									
1971	1.00	exp.	1139	u	2877	u	4016	41.00	144.00
1972	1.00	exp.	1558	u	2945	u	4503	54.00	156.00
1973	1.00	exp.	1691	u	3247	u	4938	57.00	167.00
1974	1.00	exp.	2557	u	3825	u	6382	85.00	212.00
1975	1.00	exp.	3647	u	2846	u	6493	117.00	209.00
1976	1.00	alloc.	5095	u	5913	u	11008	159.00	344.00
1977	1.00	prop.	5349	u	6208	u	11557	165.00	355.00
Venezuela									
1975	4.35	alloc.	4000	u	u	u	u	34.00	u
MIDDLE EAST/NORTH AFRICA									
Egypt									
1975	0.43	alloc.	197	1449	u	40	1686	0.50	4.50
1981	0.80	exp.	2375	8950	u	u	u	5.20	u
1982	0.80	exp.	2500	8850	u	u	u	5.60	u
1983	0.83	exp.	2750	2200	u	u	u	6.00	u
1984	0.80	alloc.	u	1400	20000	u	u	u	u
1985	0.80	prop.	u	1300	20000	u	u	u	u
Iran									
1968	75.19	u	532[g]	u	u	50[h]	532	2.00	2.10
1969	75.19	exp.	4500	u	u	93	4600	15.00	17.00
1971	76.92	exp.	4186[i]	1990	100	817	7093[i]	14.00[i]	24.00[i]
1972	66.67	exp.	9000	1600	0	96	10696	29.00	35.00
1973	20.00	exp.	13000	0	0	0	13000	41.00	41.00
1974	66.67	exp.	19830	0	0	0	19830	60.00	60.00
1975	71.43	exp.	28000	0	0	0	28000	85.00	85.00
1976	71.43	exp.	29600	0	0	0	29600	88.00	88.00
1977	71.43	alloc.	31400	0	0	0	31400	92.00	92.00
1983	86.43	alloc.	20	u	u	u	u	0.05	u
1984	90.09	alloc.	20	u	u	u	u	0.05	u
1985	91.07	alloc.	20	u	u	u	u	0.04	u
1986	78.76	alloc.	19	u	u	u	u	0.04	u
Iraq									
1986	0.31	u	200	u	u	90	290	1.21	1.76
Jordan									
1982	0.35	exp.	295	180	u	111	586	9.34	18.55
1983	0.36	exp.	340	19	u	197	556	10.37	16.96
1984	0.39	exp.	359	110	u	266	735	10.57	21.64
1985	0.40	exp.	374	128	343	249	1094	10.64	31.12
1986	0.35	exp.	389	165	779	318	1651	10.60	44.98
Morocco									
1968	5.00	alloc.	172	u	u	u	u	1.10	u
1969	5.00	alloc.	269	u	u	u	u	1.70	u
1970	5.00	alloc.	290	u	u	u	u	1.90	u
1971	4.55	alloc.	277	u	u	u	u	1.80	u
1972	4.55	alloc.	347	u	u	u	u	2.20	u
1973	4.55	alloc.	894	u	u	u	u	5.50	u
1988	8.30	prop.	1363	211	3666	u	5241	5.79	22.26
Tunisia									
1968	0.52	exp.	270	u	427	185	882	5.80	18.90
1969	0.52	exp.	280[j]	u	461	42	783	6.00	16.80
1970	0.52	exp.	129[j]	u	567	u	u	2.50	u
1971	0.52	alloc.	129[j]	0	858	u	987	2.50	18.80
1972	0.47	alloc.	143[j]	0	884	u	1029	2.70	19.30

Table 10. Annual Total and Per Capita Funding for Family Planning Programs, by Major Source *(continued)*

Country and year	Exchange rate (U.S.$)	Budget status[a]	Funding by major source (000s of U.S.$)					Per capita (U.S. cents)	
			Govt.	International agency	Foreign govt.	Private org.	All sources	Govt.	All sources including govt.
Tunisia *(continued)*									
1973	0.40	alloc.	295[j]	0	870	u	1165	5.40	21.40
1974	0.43	alloc.	747	1000	562	u	2309	13.20	40.90
1975	0.43	alloc.	834	1000	877	u	2711	14.90	48.40
1976	0.43	alloc.	888	1000	700	u	2588	15.50	45.40
1977	0.41	alloc.	u	344	365	u	u	u	u
1978	0.40	alloc.	575	604	852	54	2084	10.00	35.00
1979	0.40	alloc.	589	544	839	14·	1986	10.00	32.00
1980	0.39	alloc.	654	628	1022	11	2315	10.00	36.00
1981	0.49	alloc.	u	596	1224	u	u	u	u
Turkey									
1965	9.09	u	562	u	u	u	u	1.80	u
1966	9.09	u	738	u	100[k]	264[h]	1102	2.20	3.30
1967	9.09	u	835	u	571	256	1662	2.50	4.90
1968	9.09	u	1925	u	330	135	2390	5.70	7.10
1969	9.09	u	1375	u	100	90	1565	4.00	4.60
1970	14.93	alloc.	1116	u	33	u	1149	3.10	3.20
1971	14.08	alloc.	1383	u	88	u	1471	3.80	4.10
1972	13.89	alloc.	1763	u	54	u	1817	5.00	5.00
1973	13.33	alloc.	1855	u	38	u	1893	5.00	5.00
1974	14.08	alloc.	2339	134	u	u	2473	6.00	6.00
1975	15.15	alloc.	2000	u	u	u	u	5.00	u
1983	250.00	u	2500	u	u	u	2500	5.28	5.28
1984	400.00	alloc.	2500	350	20	10	2880	5.17	5.96
1985	500.00	alloc.	2566	470	15	5	3056	5.21	6.20
1986	700.28	alloc.	3141	420	30	10	3601	6.24	7.15
1987	820.34	alloc.	3175	302	10	15	3502	6.17	6.81
ASIA									
Bangladesh[m]									
1971	7.14	exp.	2211	390	0	0	2601	3.00	3.50
1972	7.14	prop.	2438	u	1312	u	3750	3.00	5.00
1973	7.14	prop.	3188	u	3062	u	6250	4.00	8.00
1974	7.52	prop.	3143	205	6027	u	9375	4.00	12.00
1975	14.93	prop.	4072	6285	2625	80	13062	5.00	16.00
1976	14.93	alloc.	u	3100	4300	u	u	u	u
1977	14.93	alloc.	u	4500	4690	u	u	u	u
1978	14.93	alloc.	u	4500	6630	u	u	u	u
1979	14.29	u	u	10600	12350	u	u	u	u
1986	31.01	alloc.	54023	8500	28000	u	u	51.96	u
Hong Kong[l]									
1968	6.06	exp.	90	77	u	38	205	2.30	5.20
1969	6.06	exp.	133	108	0	26	267	3.30	6.70
1970	5.95	exp.	229	141	0	37	407	3.40	7.90
1971	5.81	exp.	266	6	0	225	497	3.50	9.20
1972	5.56	exp.	401	6	0	200	607	6.00	11.10
1973	5.00	exp.	533	0	0	417	950	7.00	16.90
1974	5.00	exp.	588	0	0	371	959	8.30	17.00
1975	5.00	exp.	498	0	0	283	781	7.80	14.30
1976	5.00	alloc.	503	0	0	284	787	7.00	14.00
1977	4.55	alloc.	611	1	0	287	899	7.00	15.00
1978	4.55	alloc.	841	4	0	326	1171	7.00	17.00
1979	5.00	alloc.	942	0	0	328	1270	10.00	17.00
1980	5.26	alloc.	1230	0	0	280	1510	12.00	18.00
1981	5.56	alloc.	1375	0	0	156	1531	12.00	30.00
1982	16.00	exp.	1422	0	u	268	1690	27.13	32.24
1983	14.00	exp.	1378	0	u	241	1619	25.79	30.30
1984	7.80	exp.	1560	0	53	180	1793	28.65	32.92
1985	7.80	exp.	1731	0	29	156	1917	31.20	34.55
1986	7.80	exp.	1983	0	39	206	2228	35.13	39.47
India									
1956	4.76	exp.	u	u	u	u	183	u	0.05
1957	4.76	exp.	u	u	u	u	547	u	0.13

Table 10. Annual Total and Per Capita Funding for Family Planning Programs, by Major Source (continued)

Country and year	Exchange rate (U.S.$)	Budget status[a]	Funding by major source (000s of U.S.$)					Per capita (U.S. cents)	
			Govt.	International agency	Foreign govt.	Private org.	All sources	Govt.	All sources including govt.
India (continued)									
1958	4.76	exp.	u	u	u	u	663	u	0.16
1959	4.76	exp.	u	u	u	u	1074	u	0.25
1960	4.76	exp.	u	u	u	u	2072	u	0.48
1961	4.76	exp.	u	u	u	u	2933	u	0.66
1962	4.76	exp.	u	u	u	u	5836	u	1.28
1963	4.76	exp.	u	u	u	u	4573	u	0.98
1964	4.76	exp.	u	u	u	u	13733	u	2.87
1965	7.69	exp.	u	u	u	u	25263	u	5.16
1966	7.69	exp.	u	u	u	u	17840	u	3.55
1967	7.69	exp.	u	u	u	u	35364	u	6.90
1968	7.69	exp.	u	u	u	u	40686	u	7.80
1969	7.52	exp.	u	u	u	u	50785	u	9.50
1970	7.52	exp.	u	u	u	u	65043	u	12.00
1971	7.30	exp.	u	u	u	u	84605	u	15.40
1972	7.30	exp.	u	u	u	u	109248	u	19.60
1973	7.30	exp.	u	u	u	u	79249	u	13.90
1974	8.20	exp.	66209	9492	n	u	75701	11.00	13.00
1975	8.77	exp.	78477	13418	n	u	91895	13.00	15.40
1976	9.09	exp.	175521	14584[n]	n	u	190105	28.00	31.00
1977	8.55	exp.	93682	15526[n]	n	u	109208	15.00	17.00
1978	7.94	exp.	101241	30722[n]	n	u	131963	16.00	20.00
1979	7.97	exp.	120737	16884	11122	0	148743	18.00	22.00
1980	7.97	exp.	160675	13520	2632	0	176827	24.00	26.00
1981	9.00	exp.	184176	19648	10621	0	214445	27.00	31.00
1982	9.00	exp.	260289	24557	35477	0	320323	37.00	45.00
1983	10.00	exp.	331716	23360	19825	0	374900	46.00	52.00
Indonesia									
1968	400.00	exp.	90	67	279	286	722	0.08	0.60
1969	400.00	exp.	250	642	1569	686	3237	0.20	2.70
1970	400.00	exp.	1250	1705	1296	625	4966	1.00	4.10
1971	403.23	alloc.	372	————3795————			7520	3.10	6.30
1972	414.94	alloc.	5663	————4900————			10563	5.00	9.00
1973	414.94	alloc.	6024	————8800————			14824	5.00	12.00
1974	414.94	alloc.	9165	————13490————			22355	7.00	17.00
1975	414.94	alloc.	13436	————12208————			25644	10.00	19.00
1976	414.94	alloc.	17294	————17132————			34426	13.00	25.00
1977[o]	414.94	alloc.	22046	23883	u	u	45929	16.00	32.00
1978[o]	414.94	alloc.	28171	13083	u	u	41254	19.00	28.00
1979[o]	628.93	alloc.	27994	15127	u	u	43121	20.00	31.00
1980[o]	628.93	alloc.	49258	21800	u	u	71058	33.00	48.00
1982	654.02	alloc.	90544	9480	21453	659	122136	u	u
1983	1010.10	alloc.	53778	————19647————			73425	34.00	46.00
1984	1055.97	alloc.	66729	6173	7020	474	80396	u	u
1985	1112.35	alloc.	73071	1166	12949	u	87186	u	u
1986	1126.13	alloc.	80084	21033	16328	u	117444	u	u
Kampuchea									
1973	222.22	exp.	0	4	0	1	5	0.00	0.10
Korea, Republic of									
1962	129.87	exp.	328	u	u	u	u	1.30	u
1963	129.87	exp.	593	u	u	u	u	2.20	u
1964	129.87	exp.	1378	u	u	u	u	5.00	u
1965[p]	270.27	exp.	961	u	u	277[h]	1238	3.40	4.40
1966	270.27	exp.	2046	u	u	106[h]	2152	7.00	7.40
1967	270.27	exp.	2146[q]	u	u	253	2399	7.20	8.10
1968	270.27	exp.	2145[q]	335	2700	780	6000	7.00	19.50
1969	285.71	exp.	1950[q]	473	1500	562	4500	6.00	14.50
1970	303.03	exp.	2670[q]	310	1200	660	4800	8.50	15.00
1971	384.62	exp.	2800[q]	400	2100	600	5800	8.00	18.00
1972	400.00	exp.	3470[q]	100	1112	900	5582	10.00	17.00
1973	400.00	exp.	4061[q]	100	690	1050	5901	11.00	17.00
1974	476.19	exp.	4350[q]	1234	840	870	7294	13.00	21.00
1975	476.19	alloc.	4500[q]	1096	626	683	6905	13.00	19.00

Table 10. Annual Total and Per Capita Funding for Family Planning Programs, by Major Source *(continued)*

Country and year	Exchange rate (U.S.$)	Budget status[a]	Funding by major source (000s of U.S.$)					Per capita (U.S. cents)	
			Govt.	International agency	Foreign govt.	Private org.	All sources	Govt.	All sources including govt.
Korea, Republic of *(continued)*									
1976	476.19	alloc.	7012[q]	1412	43	853	9320	20.00	26.00
1977	476.19	alloc.	14753[q]	1079	135	975	16942	40.00	46.00
1978	476.19	alloc.	17594[q]	696	55	1283	19628	47.00	53.00
1979	476.19	alloc.	20994[q]	821	70	1511	23396	56.00	62.00
1980	666.67	alloc.	15959[q]	——————1450——————			17409	42.00	46.00
1981	700.28	exp.	12356	1156	u	3691	17203	u	u
1982	745.16	exp.	13972	1183	u	2334	17489	u	u
1983	796.18	exp.	25854	1118	u	2911	29883	u	u
1984	827.13	exp.	26877	1064	u	3944	31885	u	u
1985	890.47	exp.	33974	915	u	4364	39253	u	u
1986	861.33	exp.	28545	1088	u	5873	35506	u	u
Laos									
1969	238.10	u	u	u	990	13	1003	u	33.00
1970	238.10	u	u	u	1112	13	1125	u	36.00
1971	238.10	u	u	u	925	20	945	u	30.00
1972	588.24	u	u	6	500	28	534	u	17.00
Malaysia (Peninsular)									
1966	3.00	u	83	u	u	189	272	1.00	3.30
1967	3.00	u	306	u	200	293	799	3.50	8.10
1968	3.00	u	533	50	500	124	1207	6.00	12.20
1969	3.00	u	667	u	u	u	791	7.30	8.60
1970	3.00	alloc.	739	3	46	23	810	7.80	8.60
1971	3.00	alloc.	771	u	u	u	u	8.00	u
1972	4.00	alloc.	827	u	u	u	u	8.00	u
1973	4.17	alloc.	1136	u	u	u	u	11.00	u
1974	2.38	alloc.	1234	u	u	u	1525[r]	12.00	15.00
1975	2.22	alloc.	1665	u	u	u	2227[r]	16.00	21.00
1976	2.50	alloc.	3562	u	u	u	3881[r]	33.00	36.00
1977	2.50	alloc.	5116	u	u	u	5432[r]	46.00	49.00
1978	2.22	alloc.	7139	u	u	u	7510[r]	65.00	68.00
1979	2.13	alloc.	7062	330	u	u	7392	63.00	66.00
1980	2.22	alloc.	6712	2027	21	u	8759	60.00	79.00
1983	2.10	exp.	6560	300	u	133	6993	44.20	47.12
1984	2.30	exp.	10703	476	u	134	11314	70.42	74.44
1985	2.50	exp.	9258	318	u	82	9659	59.51	62.09
1986	2.60	exp.	7738	318	u	95	8151	48.65	51.24
1987	2.50	alloc.	7364	148	u	65	7577	45.31	46.62
Nepal									
1968	10.08	u	10	u	39	u	49	0.10	0.50
1969	10.08	u	88	0	312	0	400	0.80	3.70
1970	10.08	alloc.	156	496	0	0	652	1.30	5.60
1971	10.10	alloc.	185	0	557	0	742	1.60	6.30
1972	10.10	alloc.	185	0	343	0	528	2.00	4.00
1973	10.10	alloc.	214	0	399	0	613	2.00	5.00
1974	10.53	alloc.	435	0	600	0	1035	3.00	8.00
1975	10.53	alloc.	1138	0	302	0	1440	9.00	11.00
1982	14.40	exp.	u	421	u	u	u	u	u
1983	18.00	exp.	u	451	2400[z]	u	u	u	u
1984	21.20	exp.	u	511	2300[z]	u	u	u	u
1985	21.20	exp.	u	413	2600[z]	u	u	u	u
1986	21.20	alloc.	u	816	2100[z]	u	u	u	u
Pakistan									
1965	4.76	exp.	u	u	u	571[s]	5860	u	5.00
1966	4.76	exp.	u	u	u	343[s]	10650	u	8.80
1967	4.76	alloc.	u	378[t]	5875[cc]	26[s]	u	u	u
1968	4.76	exp.	u	u	u	u	20300	u	16.00
1969	4.76	exp.	u	u	u	u	22405	u	17.20
1970	4.76	u	u	u	u	u	u	u	u
1971	4.76	alloc.	2792	u	u	u	u	4.50	u
1972	6.67	exp.	u	u	u	u	3750	u	6.00
1973	10.00	exp.	2000	u	u	u	8339[v]	3.00	13.00

Country and year	Exchange rate (U.S.$)	Budget status[a]	Funding by major source (000s of U.S.$)					Per capita (U.S. cents)	
			Govt.	International agency	Foreign govt.	Private org.	All sources	Govt.	All sources including govt.
Pakistan *(continued)*									
1974	10.00	alloc.	4000	3000	7500	0	14500	6.00	22.00
1975	10.00	alloc.	7500	3000	7100	0	17600	10.00	24.00
1976	10.00	alloc.	8485	12432	0	3383	24300	12.00	34.00
1977	10.00	alloc.	6922	1326	0	16052	24300	9.00	32.00
1978	10.00	alloc.	13770	1650	1500	4080	21000	18.00	27.00
1979	10.00	alloc.	9500	5170	0	2230	16900	12.00	22.00
1983	13.34	exp.	8848	2428	3858	7	15155	9.34	16.01
1984	14.50	exp.	10355	4050	7755	u	22161	10.62	22.72
1985	15.75	exp.	11233	2816	10610	1	24681	11.19	24.59
1986	16.90	alloc.	9237	8454	15215	u	32906	8.99	32.03
1987	17.35	alloc.	10025	u	u	u	32911	9.54	31.31
Philippines									
1967	6.25	exp.	0	0	0	134	134	0.00	0.40
1968	6.25	exp.	0	0	222	61	283	0.00	0.80
1969	6.25	exp.	0	0	697	214	911	0.00	2.50
1970	3.91	exp.	0	0	1187	163	1350	0.00	3.70
1971	6.25	alloc.	56	352	4378	303	5089	0.10	13.40
1972	6.25	alloc.	1259	684	6189	283	8415	3.00	22.00
1973	6.67	alloc.	4008	495	5255	1123	10882	10.00	27.00
1974	6.67	alloc.	8711	1808	5146	1277	16942	21.00	41.00
1975	7.14	alloc.	8691	1986	5921	1294	17892	20.00	43.00
1976	7.14	alloc.	16861	2247	5464	1201	25773	37.00	58.00
1977	7.14	alloc.	10609	1174	5746	290	17819	23.00	40.00
1978	7.14	alloc.	17515	402	4868	492	23277	38.00	51.00
1979	7.69	alloc.	17867	2040	4160	0	24067	38.00	51.00
1980	7.69	alloc.	21400	2941	3679	0	28019	45.00	59.00
1981	7.69	alloc.	23887	5214	7446	0	36546	48.00	74.00
1982	8.54	alloc.	14028	3829	8806	23	26686	27.62	52.54
1983	11.11	alloc.	8479	2799	6607	u	17901	16.30	34.41
1984	16.70	alloc.	7102	2066	4305	u	13473	13.33	25.30
1985	18.62	alloc.	5994	3453	3862	u	13309	11.00	24.42
1986	20.50	alloc.	6098	4351	3507	u	13956	10.93	25.01
Singapore									
1969	3.03	alloc.	67	0	0	261	328[x]	3.30	16.00
1970	3.03	alloc.	67	u	u	31	319[x]	3.20	15.00
1971	3.03	alloc.	290	0	0	20	310[x]	14.00	15.00
1972	2.70	exp.	389	0	0	0	389[x]	18.00	18.00
1973	2.50	alloc.	491	50	0	17	558[x]	25.00	26.00
1974	2.33	alloc.	657	39	0	2	698[x]	30.00	31.00
1975	2.50	alloc.	921	25	0	3	950[x]	41.00	42.00
1976	2.44	alloc.	926	5	0	0	931[x]	41.00	41.00
1977	2.33	alloc.	1142	0	0	0	1142	49.00	49.00
1978	2.33	alloc.	1217	0	0	0	1217	52.00	52.00
1979	2.22	alloc.	1290	0	0	0	1290	54.00	54.00
1980	2.13	alloc.	1529	0	0	0	1529	64.00	64.00
1981	2.13	alloc.	1671	9	0	0	1680	68.00	69.00
1982	2.13	alloc.	1752	0	0	0	1752	71.00	71.00
1983	2.13	alloc.	1810	0	0	0	1810	76.00	76.00
1984	2.19	exp.	1775	u	u	u	1775	69.37	70.16
Sri Lanka									
1971	5.88	exp.	u	u	120	u	120	u	0.90
1972	6.67	exp.	u	u	222	u	222	u	1.70
1973	6.67	exp.	u	755	334	u	1089	u	8.20
1985	2.50	exp.	617	541	u	u	1158	3.81	7.15
1986	2.80	alloc.	1351	330	u	u	1717	8.21	10.43
1987	30.00	alloc.	1310	488	u	u	1798	7.84	10.76
Taiwan									
1964	40.00	exp.	u	———120———			120	u	1.00
1965	40.00	exp.	167	———136———			303	1.30	2.40
1966	40.00	exp.	344	———111———			454	2.73	3.50
1967	40.00	exp.	437	0	0	123	560	3.30	4.30

Table 10. Annual Total and Per Capita Funding for Family Planning Programs, by Major Source (continued)

Country and year	Exchange rate (U.S.$)	Budget status[a]	Funding by major source (000s of U.S.$)					Per capita (U.S. cents)	
			Govt.	International agency	Foreign govt.	Private org.	All sources	Govt.	All sources including govt.
Taiwan *(continued)*									
1968	40.00	exp.	497	0	0	151	648	3.70	4.80
1969	40.00	exp.	570	0	0	119	689	4.10	5.00
1970	40.00	exp.	650	0	0	358	1008	4.60	6.80
1971	40.00	exp.	642	0	0	248	890	4.40	6.00
1972	38.46	exp.	800	0	0	222	1022	5.30	6.80
1973	38.46	exp.	1146	0	0	250	1396	7.00	9.00
1974	38.46	exp.	1418	0	0	225	1643	9.00	10.40
1975	38.46	exp.	1352	0	0	375	1727	8.00	11.00
1976	38.46	exp.	2327	0	0	302	2629	14.00	16.00
1977	38.46	alloc.	2785	0	0	0	2785	17.00	17.00
1978	38.46	alloc.	3495	0	0	0	3495	21.00	21.00
1979	40.00	alloc.	3755	0	0	0	3755	21.00	21.00
1980	40.00	alloc.	4354	0	0	0	4354	24.00	24.00
1981	40.00	exp.	5764	0	0	0	5764	32.02	32.02
1982	40.00	exp.	7077	0	0	0	7077	38.67	38.67
1983	40.00	exp.	7552	0	0	0	7552	40.60	40.60
1984	40.00	exp.	8514	0	0	0	8514	45.05	45.05
1985	40.00	exp.	9060	0	0	0	9060	47.43	47.43
Thailand									
1968	20.00	exp.	15[y]	0	647	206	868[y]	0.60	3.10
1969	20.00	exp.	26[y]	17	813	299	1155[y]	1.40	4.60
1970	20.00	exp.	93[y]	24	1191	459	1757[y]	0.30	5.00
1971	20.00	exp.	120[y]	17	1620	550	2307[y]	0.30	6.40
1972	20.00	exp.	604[y]	150	2050	650	3454[y]	1.60	9.30
1973	20.00	exp.	550[y]	1067	1616	255	3488[y]	1.00	9.00
1974	20.00	exp.	625[y]	1945	2260	129	4959[y]	2.00	12.00
1975	20.00	exp.	935[y]	1896	830	25	3686[y]	2.00	9.00
1976	20.00	alloc.	1144[y]	1200	4100	u	6444[y]	2.70	15.00
1977	20.00	exp.	2344[y]	2282	2365	u	6991[y]	5.80	15.90
1978	20.00	alloc.	3398[y]	2026	1714	3	7138[y]	7.50	15.80
1979	22.88	exp.	2372[y]	11707	0	0	14072[y]	5.20	30.60
1980	22.88	exp.	2269[y]	5453	0	0	7722[y]	5.40	16.40
1981	22.88	exp.	2424[y]	4380	0	0	6804[y]	4.90	14.20
1982	22.88	exp.	8602	3314	0	0	11916	17.80	24.60
1983	26.00	u	8434	423	2808	u	11665	17.05	23.59
1984	26.00	u	7077	385	3385	u	10847	14.03	21.51
1985	26.00	u	7538	708	4492	u	12738	14.66	24.78
1986	26.00	u	8077	381	4127	u	12585	15.45	24.08

u = unknown.

a. In this column, "alloc." refers to allocated, "exp." refers to expended, "prop." refers to proposed, and "u" means the status is unknown.

b. Any foreign government or private organization allocation is included with the international agency allocation.

c. Because the program is integrated into the health network, the contribution to the program of the health network's personnel and facilities has been calculated and presented as an indirect government input.

d. Includes an estimate for family planning input provided under maternal and child health services. For 1977, this was estimated to amount to $700,000.

e. Jamaica Family Planning Association.

f. Allocation from the government to the private family planning association, which was currently implementing the program in its own and in government facilities.

g. Excludes funds for services of government corps. These plus contributions from private agencies in Iran would probably add about seven times the government figure shown.

h. Population Council.

i. Includes funds that also support maternal and child health services other than family planning, but excludes funds utilized for family planning that are not clearly earmarked as a line item in the budget for family planning.

j. The family planning budget represents only direct monetary input and excludes contributions to the program of the personnel and facilities of the health network, into which the program is integrated.

k. From the Swedish International Development Agency for 500,000 cycles of oral contraceptives.

l. For all years after 1969, government sources and totals include fees collected from program clientele. Such fees increased gradually from $96,000 in 1970 to $1,268,000 in 1986.

m. Prior to 1971 (before Bangladesh gained independence), Bangladesh data were included under Pakistan.

n. Includes any foreign government expenditure.

o. Any international agency contributions are included with foreign government funds and all sources.

p. A new exchange rate became effective in May 1965. The apparent decline in funds compared with 1964 stems from the currency devaluation. In local currency, government per capita expenditure in 1965 exceeded that of 1964 by 17 percent.

q. Includes local and provincial as well as national funds.

r. In addition, UNFPA provided supplementary funding for Population Project 1, during 1973–78.

s. Ford Foundation support, administered by Population Council.

t. UNICEF.

v. Mostly USAID-funded.

w. Estimated.

x. Includes proceeds from sales of contraceptives and services.

y. The domestic family planning budget represents only direct monetary input and excludes the contributions to the program of the personnel and facilities to the health network, into which the program is integrated.

z. USAID only.

aa. Figure shown includes receipts and fees, which amount to 57 percent, 61 percent, 64 percent, 63 percent, and 64 percent, in the years 1982–86, respectively.

bb. UNFPA-supported MCH/FP project.

cc. This total breaks down as follows: Swedish International Development Agency, $832,000; U.K. technical assistance, $60,000; USAID, $4,983,000 ($4,200,000 in rupees and $783,000 in dollars).

dd. Social Security system (IMSS) only.

Table 11. Percentage Distribution of Family Planning Program Expenditures, by Type of Expenditure

Country and year	Total expenditure (000s of U.S.$)	Salaries and wages — Medical, para-medical	Field-workers	Admin., clerical	Promotion, information, education	Contra-ceptive supplies	Maint., operation[a]	Capital construction, improvement	Other	Total
SUB-SAHARAN AFRICA										
Ghana										
1973	653[b,c]	0	——38——		49	0	11	2	0	100
1974	901	d	——25——		56	e	12	7	0	100
1975	1488[b]	——24——				10	54	4	8	100
1976	1952[b]	——47——				11	24	8	10	100
1977	1445[f]	——32——				13	19	10	26	100
Sudan										
1986	394[j]	——15——		9	34	u	32	10	u	100
Uganda										
1973	126	18	——39——		13	7	18	0	5	100
Zimbabwe										
1972	628	19	——9——		22	12	37	1	0	100
1978	1810	——41——				25	30	4	0	100
LATIN AMERICA/CARIBBEAN										
Bolivia										
1977	127[b]	35	——16——		14	0	26	0	9	100
Brazil (BEMFAM)										
1975	3784[b]	37	——7——		17	26	7	0	6	100
1979	5662	14	19	4	8	31	10	0	14	100
Colombia (PROFAMILIA)										
1980	5768	33	19	——6——		4	——38——			100
1983	7569	34	——3——		9	11	——43——			100
Costa Rica										
1974	1171	27	——18——		14	4	33	1	3	100
1975	1695	32	——19——		9	6	34	0	0	100
Costa Rica (ADC)										
1987	614	u	u	u	22	23	u	u	54	100
Dominican Republic										
1974	990	40	——20——		10	7	11	2	10	100
1975	1958	39	——14——		7	24	9	2	5	100
1976	2212	36	——14——		4	16	18	0	12	100
1977	1953	21	——23——		9	8	19	3	17	100
El Salvador										
1973	1101[b]	38	——13——		13	12	21	0	3	100
1975	1692[b]	——59——				12	——29——		0	100
1979	8348	——32——				46	2	20	0	100
Honduras										
1986	3500	——36——				15	18	8	23	100
Mexico										
1973	26656[c]	34	0	0	10	35	5	0	16	100
Mexico (IMSS)										
1987	5871	20	64	u	<1	4	1	u	11	100
Puerto Rico										
1975	6493	33	——10——		17	10	5	0	25[g]	100
Puerto Rico (APPBF)										
1986	403	5	20	32	18	11	8	5	<1	100

Table 11. Percentage Distribution of Family Planning Program Expenditures, by Type of Expenditure (continued)

Country and year	Total expenditure (000s of U.S.$)	Salaries and wages — Medical, para-medical	Field-workers	Admin., clerical	Promotion, information, education	Contra-ceptive supplies	Maint., operation[a]	Capital construction, improvement	Other	Total
MIDDLE EAST/NORTH AFRICA										
Egypt										
1986	691	u	u	u	69	u	30	<1	u	100
Iran										
1973	13000	17	——21——		11	23	28	0	0	100
1974	19830	17	——21——		11	23	28	0	0	100
1975	28000	10	——23——		12	32	23	0	0	100
1976	29600	12	——20——		16	33	——19——		0	100
1987	18635	——————60——————				u	u	u	u	100
Iraq										
1986	46	——————41——————				u	21	u	38	100
Jordan										
1986	1651	11	35	2	<1[k]	9	26	u	16	100
Turkey										
1974	2339[c]	——————58——————				1	15	14	12	100
1987	377	——————58——————				m	20	17	3	100
ASIA										
Bangladesh										
1974	5788	——————49——————				22	20	0	9	100
1976	14420[f]	0	——10——		32	35	16	7	0	100
Hong Kong										
1973	837	44	——8——		19	10	17	1	1	100
1975	764	47	——8——		20	7	10	0	8	100
1976	787[b]	44	——8——		20	7	13	6	2	100
1978	1080	45	——12——		21	3	15	3	1	100
1980	1385	45	6	8	20	3	17	1	0	100
1983	1605	45	6	9	15	6	14	3	2	100
1986	2257	42	u	15	15	7	19	2	u	100
Indonesia										
1987	117	u	4	21	19	15	4	1	35	100
Korea, Republic of										
1986	35506	——————16——————				79	<1	u	4	100
Malaysia (Peninsular)										
1975	1642[b]	25	——45——		10	1	17	1	1	100
1976	3100[b]	——37——			3	47	12	0	1	100
1977	4508[b,c]	——38——			3	38	20	0	1	100
1978	7139[c]	——————52——————				37	10	0	1	100
1980	6712[c]	——————58——————				23	16	0	3	100
1987	7364	——————78——————				11	5	4	2	100
Pakistan										
1979	13044[b]	——————77——————				14	7	0	3	100
Singapore										
1972	344[h]	46	——21——		7	5	14	7	0	100
1974	785[b]	47	——7——		15	2	10	4	15[i]	100
1975	835[b]	48	——8——		9	2	13	5	15[i]	100
1976	849[b]	51	——9——		14	0	25	1	0	100
1979	1290[b]	——————66——————				13	20	0	1	100
1981	1671[c]	——————75——————				13	12	0	0	100
1983	1810[c]	——————75——————				13	12	0	0	100
1984	1775	——————86——————				u	14	u	u	100
Sri Lanka										
1986	1714	——————60——————				12	4	<1	23	100

Table 11. Percentage Distribution of Family Planning Program Expenditures, by Type of Expenditure *(continued)*

| Country and year | Total expenditure (000s of U.S.$) | Salaries and wages | | | | Contra-ceptive supplies | Maint., operation[a] | Capital construction, improvement | Other | Total |
		Medical, para-medical	Field-workers	Admin., clerical	Promotion, information, education					
Taiwan 1985	9060	15	17	1	40	10	7	1	9	100

u = unknown.

a. Includes rent, telephone, electricity, postage, stationery, office equipment, computers, and other such costs.

b. Allocated, not expended.

c. Government funds only.

d. Health network medical personnel do not receive specific family planning payments.

e. Received as commodities; no monetary estimate was made.

f. Proposed.

g. Includes sterilization and laboratory expenditures.

h. Expenditures covering public and private programs combined.

i. Includes expenditures on publicity, conferences, and surveys.

j. Expenditures for the national MCH/FP program funded by UNFPA and executed by WHO. Bilateral and NGO funds are not channeled through the government and thus are not included.

k. Expenditures on training and research.

m. Contraceptive supplies donated free of charge; no monetary estimate was made.

Table 12. Percentage Distribution of Family Planning Program Expenditures, by Program Function

Country and year	Total expenditure (000s of U.S.$)[d]	Contraceptive services	Information, education	Research, evaluation	Personnel training	Administration	Other	Total
SUB-SAHARAN AFRICA								
Ghana								
1973	653[a]	4.0	46.0	8.0	10.0	31.0	0.0	100
1974	901	5.0	40.0	7.0	9.0	39.0	0.0	100
1975	1488[a]	17.0	35.0	8.0	9.0	18.0	13.0	100
1976	1952[a]	21.0	30.0	10.0	8.0	22.0	9.0	100
1977	1445[b]	18.0	29.0	9.0	7.0	20.0	17.0	100
Mauritius								
1978	750[c]	53.0	6.0	3.0	0.0	20.0	18.0	100
1980	814	62.0	5.0	4.0	0.0	14.0	14.0	100
1982	639	62.0	6.0	5.0	0.0	13.0	14.0	100
Uganda								
1973	126	50.0	3.0	0.0	0.4	33.0	14.0	100
1975	170[a]	35.0	6.0	23.0	4.0	32.0	0.0	100
Zimbabwe								
1972	628	38.0	43.0	1.0	1.0	16.0	1.0	100
1978	1810	74.0	18.0	0.0	2.0	6.0	0.0	100
LATIN AMERICA/CARIBBEAN								
Bolivia								
1977	127[a]	43.0	12.0	0.0	0.0	45.0	0.0	100
Brazil								
1975	3784[a]	66.0	12.0	3.0	5.0	13.0	1.0	100
Colombia (PROFAMILIA)								
1974	5535	35.0	16.0	12.0	13.0	24.0	0.0	100
1980	5768	81.0	3.0	2.0	0.0	13.0	0.0	100
1983	7569	81.0	2.0	2.0	1.0	13.0	1.0	100
Costa Rica								
1973	632	20.0	15.0	7.0	16.0	32.0	10.0	100
1974	1171	37.0	33.0	3.0	15.0	9.0	3.0	100
1975	1695	53.0	23.0	2.0	13.0	9.0	0.0	100
Costa Rica (ADC)								
1987	614	23.2	15.2	9.4	7.2	u	45.0	100
Dominican Republic								
1974	990	48.0	13.0	5.0	4.0	19.0	11.0	100
1975	1958	73.0	7.0	4.0	4.0	11.0	1.0	100
1976	2212	66.0	7.0	7.0	3.0	17.0	0.0	100
1977	1953	33.0	14.0	14.0	5.0	33.0	1.0	100
El Salvador								
1973	1101[a]	62.0	7.0	14.0	3.0	14.0	0.0	100
1979	8348	46.0	0.0	0.0	1.0	53.0	0.0	100
Guatemala								
1974	653[a]	38.0	20.0	11.0	11.0	18.0	2.0	100
Honduras								
1986	3500	25.7	5.7	17.1	5.7	22.9	22.9	100
Puerto Rico								
1975	6493	67.0	20.0	3.0	1.0	7.0	2.0	100
MIDDLE EAST/NORTH AFRICA								
Iran								
1973	13000	25.0	50.0	8.0	11.0	6.0	0.0	100
1974	19830	25.0	50.0	8.0	11.0	6.0	0.0	100
1975	28000	32.0	41.0	9.0	10.0	8.0	0.0	100
1976	29600	33.0	45.0	7.0	8.0	7.0	0.0	100

Table 12. Percentage Distribution of Family Planning Program Expenditures, by Program Function (continued)

Country and year	Total expenditure (000s of U.S.$)[d]	Contraceptive services	Information, education	Research, evaluation	Personnel training	Administration	Other	Total
Jordan								
1986	1651	43.7	0.2	2.8	13.6	39.7	u	100
Tunisia								
1974	5121[a]	18.0	4.0	1.0	3.0	31.0	43.0	100
ASIA								
Bangladesh								
1972	3351	u	u	u	u	40.0	u	100
1974	5788	26.0	9.0	0.0	8.0	51.0	6.0	100
1976	14420[b]	42.0	28.0	1.0	0.0	29.0	0.0	100
Hong Kong								
1973	837	62.0	21.0	4.0	0.0	11.0	2.0	100
1975	764	55.0	21.0	4.0	0.0	12.0	8.0	100
1976	787[a]	51.0	24.0	4.0	0.0	13.0	8.0	100
1978	1080	53.0	26.0	4.0	0.0	15.0	2.0	100
1980	1385	54.0	26.0	4.0	0.0	9.0	6.0	100
1983	1605	61.0	24.0	3.0	0.0	10.0	2.0	100
1986	2257	62.7	15.1	0.3	3.9	18.0	0.0	100
India								
1972	109248	80.0	4.0	1.0	2.0	1.0	12.0[e]	100
1973	79241	78.0	4.0	2.0	3.0	1.0	12.0[e]	100
1974	75699	80.0	4.0	1.0	3.0	1.0	10.0[e]	100
1975	91920	82.0	3.0	1.0	3.0	1.0	10.0[e]	100
1977	109208	78.0	3.0	1.0	4.0	1.0	13.0[e]	100
1979	148141	81.0	4.0	1.0	5.0	1.0	10.0[f]	100
1980	175909	75.1	3.3	1.4	1.3	2.5	16.4[l]	100
1981	214445	77.7	2.9	1.2	0.9	1.7	15.6[l]	100
1982	320323	60.5	2.4	0.8	0.6	0.5	35.2[g]	100
1983	382984	73.3	2.4	0.6	0.5	1.2	22.0[l]	100
1984	343190	71.2	2.3	0.7	0.7	2.4	22.7[l]	100
Indonesia								
1979	49986[a]	12.0	17.0	1.0	10.0	12.0	49.0	100
1987	117444	6.1	2.2	2.2	4.4	48.2	36.9	100
Kampuchea								
1973	5	10.0	44.0	2.0	10.0	33.0	0.0	100
Korea, Republic of								
1973	5901	65.0	12.0	9.0	4.0	10.0	0.0	100
1976	7619[a]	73.0	8.0	4.0	4.0	11.0	0.0	100
1980	17409[a]	44.0	8.0	4.0	3.0	6.0	36.0[k]	100
Malaysia (Peninsular)								
1974	1234[a]	46.0	13.0	7.0	7.0	26.0	1.0	100
1975	1642[a]	45.0	12.0	8.0	7.0	28.0	0.0	100
1976	3100[a]	22.0	7.0	2.0	4.0	65.0	0.0	100
1977	4508[a,h]	22.0	10.0	5.0	5.0	58.0	0.0	100
1978	7139[h]	25.0	9.0	4.0	6.0	56.0	0.0	100
1979	6712[h]	33.0	12.0	4.0	i	49.0	2.0	100
1987	7364	41.1	10.6	7.6	2.3	13.7	24.7	100
Philippines								
1972	1900[a]	44.0	22.0	11.0	8.0	5.0	9.0	100
1974	11000	42.0	8.0	4.0	13.0	29.0	4.0	100
1978	23277[a]	50.0	3.0	6.0	3.0	12.0	26.0	100
1980	29351	42.0	11.0	7.0	9.0	10.0	21.0	100
1983	22444	51.0	8.0	3.0	5.0	9.0	24.0	100
1986	9862	44.7	8.0	4.1	5.3	19.7	18.2	100
Singapore								
1972	344[j]	55.0	11.0	8.0	1.0	25.0	0.0	100
1974	785[a]	54.0	18.0	10.0	7.0	11.0	0.0	100
1975	835[a]	53.0	23.0	6.0	6.0	12.0	0.0	100

Table 12. Percentage Distribution of Family Planning Program Expenditures, by Program Function *(continued)*

Country and year	Total expenditure (000s of U.S.$)[d]	Contraceptive services	Information, education	Research, evaluation	Personnel training	Administration	Other	Total
Singapore *(continued)*								
1976	849[a]	52.0	17.0	7.0	10.0	14.0	0.0	100
1979	1290[a]	61.0	13.0	7.0	9.0	10.0	0.0	100
1981	1671	64.0	13.0	6.0	6.0	11.0	0.0	100
1983	1810	63.0	12.0	7.0	7.0	11.0	0.0	100
Taiwan								
1978	3469[a]	45.0	9.0	2.0	2.0	26.0	16.0	100
1983	6239	42.0	22.0	3.0	2.0	10.0	21.0	100
1985	9060	46.9	29.9	4.8	2.7	4.5	11.2	100

u = unknown.

a. Allocation, not expenditure.

b. Amount proposed.

c. Allocation of government funds only.

d. Because the figures in this table are generally based on actual expenditures, the totals will not always correspond to those in Table 5, which represent funds allocated, proposed, or expended.

e. This expenditure was used mainly for the India Population Project or construction of new buildings.

f. Includes 3 percent for MCH services, 5 percent for buildings, and 2 percent for IPPF.

g. Includes 12.8 percent for MCH services, 21.3 percent for area and village health projects, and 1.1 percent for buildings.

h. Government funds allocated to the National Family Planning Board.

i. Included in contraceptive services.

j. Covers public and private programs combined.

k. Includes family planning workers' salaries and travel expenses.

l. May include MCH worker or village health guide.

Table 13. Import Regulations, Contraceptive Supplies Available, and Price Range in Private Sector

Country and method	Year	License required	Duty as % of import value	Duty as % of CIF[a]	Total	Imports	Domestic manufacture	Minimum	Maximum
		Import regulations			Supplies available by source (000s)[b]			Price in private sector (U.S.$)[b]	
SUB-SAHARAN AFRICA									
Botswana									
IUD	1975	No	25	u	5.00	5.00	0.00	u	u
IUD	1976	No	25	0	5.00	5.00	0.00	7.40	7.40
IUD	1982	u	u	u	2.00	2.00	0.00	u	u
IUD	1983	No	0	0	23.00	23.00	0.00	13.00	17.00
IUD	1984	u	u	u	24.50	24.50	0.00	u	u
IUD	1985	u	u	u	72.60	72.60	0.00	u	u
IUD	1986	u	u	u	0.00	0.00	0.00	u	u
IUD	1987	No	u	u	u	u	u	14.18	17.34
Orals	1975	No	25	u	100.00	100.00	0.00	1.78	1.78
Orals	1976	No	25	0	100.00	100.00	0.00	1.78	1.78
Orals	1982	u	u	u	223.00	223.00	0.00	u	u
Orals	1983	No	0	0	299.00	299.00	0.00	1.95	4.20
Orals	1984	u	u	u	366.00	366.00	0.00	u	u
Orals	1985	u	u	u	774.00	774.00	0.00	u	u
Orals	1986	u	u	u	336.00	336.00	0.00	u	u
Orals	1987	No	u	u	u	u	u	1.58	4.53
Injectables	1982	u	u	u	6.00	6.00	0.00	u	u
Injectables	1983	No	0	0	6.00	6.00	0.00	u	u
Injectables	1984	u	u	u	13.00	13.00	0.00	u	u
Injectables	1985	u	u	u	20.00	20.00	0.00	u	u
Injectables	1986	u	u	u	23.80	23.80	0.00	u	u
Injectables	1987	No	u	u	u	u	u	8.68	8.68
Condoms	1975	No	50	u	u	u	u	2.88	2.88
Condoms	1976	No	50	0	u	u	0.00	2.90	2.90
Condoms	1982	u	u	u	41.66	41.66	0.00	u	u
Condoms	1983	No	0	0	41.66	41.66	0.00	2.25	3.30
Condoms	1984	u	u	u	41.66	41.66	0.00	u	u
Condoms	1985	u	u	u	40.00	40.00	0.00	u	u
Condoms	1986	u	u	u	40.00	40.00	0.00	u	u
Condoms	1987	No	u	u	u	u	u	4.02	5.79
Diaphragm	1975	No	25	u	0.43	0.43	0.00	15.00	15.00
Diaphragm	1976	No	25	0	0.43	0.43	0.00	4.50	7.50
Diaphragm	1982	u	u	u	0.72	0.72	0.00	u	u
Diaphragm	1983	No	0	0	0.34	0.34	0.00	4.00	4.00
Diaphragm	1984	u	u	u	0.97	0.97	0.00	u	u
Diaphragm	1985	u	u	u	2.19	2.19	0.00	u	u
Diaphragm	1986	u	u	u	0.00	0.00	0.00	u	u
Diaphragm	1987	No	u	u	u	u	u	22.11	22.11
Spermicides	1982	u	u	u	16.50	16.50	0.00	u	u
Spermicides	1983	No	0	0	9.00	9.00	0.00	u	u
Spermicides	1984	u	u	u	13.23	13.23	0.00	u	u
Spermicides	1985	u	u	u	6.48	6.48	0.00	u	u
Spermicides	1986	u	u	u	0.00	0.00	0.00	u	u
Spermicides	1987	No	u	u	u	u	u	10.34	11.18
Burkina Faso									
IUD	1985	u	u	u	28.29	28.29	0.00	u	u
IUD	1987	u	u	u	u	u	u	30.00	30.00
Orals	1985	u	u	u	149.98	149.98	0.00	u	u
Orals	1987	u	u	u	u	u	u	1.00	1.00
Injectables	1987	u	u	u	u	u	u	4.00	4.00
Condoms	1985	u	u	u	29.46	29.46	0.00	u	u
Condoms	1986	u	u	u	60.00	60.00	0.00	u	u
Condoms	1987	u	u	u	u	u	u	0.42	0.42
Spermicides	1985	u	u	u	38.75	38.75	0.00	u	u
Spermicides	1987	u	u	u	u	u	u	8.33	8.33
Chad									
IUD	1985	u	u	u	0.12	0.12[q]	0.00	u	u
IUD	1986	u	u	u	0.00	0.00	0.00	u	u
IUD	1987	No	0	0	u	u	u	21.93	21.93
Orals	1985	u	u	u	12.56	12.56[q]	0.00	u	u
Orals	1986	u	u	u	24.10	24.10[q]	0.00	u	u

70

Table 13. Import Regulations, Contraceptive Supplies Available, and Price Range in Private Sector (continued)

Country and method	Year	Import regulations			Supplies available by source (000s)[b]			Price in private sector (U.S.$)[b]	
		License required	Duty as % of import value	Duty as % of CIF[a]	Total	Imports	Domestic manufacture	Minimum	Maximum
Chad *(continued)*									
Orals	1987	No	0	0	u	u	u	1.29	1.29
Injectables	1985	u	u	u	0.18	0.18[q]	0.00	u	u
Injectables	1986	u	u	u	1.70	1.70[q]	0.00	u	u
Injectables	1987	No	0	0	u	u	u	7.42	7.42
Condoms	1987	No	0	0	0.00	0.00	0.00	3.54	3.54
Côte d'Ivoire									
IUD	1987	u	u	u	u	u	u	300.00	300.00
Orals	1987	u	u	u	u	u	u	2.67	2.67
Injectables	1987	u	u	u	u	u	u	1.00	1.00
Condoms	1987	u	u	u	u	u	u	0.67	0.67
Ethiopia									
IUD	1987	u	u	u	u	u	u	14.49	24.15
Orals	1987	u	u	u	u	u	u	2.41	3.38
Condoms	1987	u	u	u	u	u	u	2.43	5.98
Ghana									
IUD	1975	Yes	0	u	u	u	u	u	u
IUD	1976	Yes	0	0	u	u	u	u	u
IUD	1977	Yes	0	0	u	u	u	u	u
IUD	1978	Yes	0	0	u	u	u	u	u
Orals	1975	Yes	0	u	u	u	u	u	u
Orals	1976	Yes	0	0	u	u	u	u	u
Orals	1977	Yes	0	0	u	u	u	2.60	2.60
Orals	1978	Yes	0	0	u	u	u	2.60	2.60
Condoms	1975	Yes	0	u	u	u	u	u	u
Condoms	1976	Yes	0	0	u	u	u	u	u
Condoms	1977	Yes	0	0	u	u	u	1.74	1.74
Condoms	1978	Yes	0	0	u	u	u	1.74	1.74
Diaphragm	1975	Yes	0	u	u	u	u	u	u
Diaphragm	1976	Yes	0	0	u	u	u	u	u
Diaphragm	1977	Yes	0	0	u	u	u	u	u
Diaphragm	1978	Yes	0	0	u	u	u	u	u
Kenya									
IUD	1987	No	0	0	u	u	u	u	u
Orals	1987	No	0	0	u	u	u	u	u
Injectables	1987	No	0	0	u	u	u	u	u
Condoms	1987	No	0	0	u	u	u	u	u
Diaphragm	1987	No	0	0	u	u	u	u	u
Spermicides	1987	No	0	0	u	u	u	u	u
Norplant	1987	No	0	0	u	u	u	u	u
Lesotho									
IUD	1987	No	0	0	u	u	u	14.07	14.07
Orals	1987	No	0	0	u	u	u	2.01	2.01
Injectables	1987	No	0	0	u	u	u	5.02	5.02
Condoms	1987	No	0	0	u	u	u	5.04	5.04
Diaphragm	1987	No	0	0	u	u	u	5.04	5.04
Spermicides	1987	No	0	0	u	u	u	u	u
Liberia									
Orals	1987	u	u	u	u	u	u	4.52	4.52
Condoms	1987	u	u	u	u	u	u	4.08	4.08
Spermicides (12)	1987	u	u	u	u	u	u	2.93	2.93
Female sterilization	1987	na	na	na	na	na	na	35.00	35.00
Male sterilization	1987	na	na	na	na	na	na	50.00	50.00
Mauritius									
IUD	1976	Yes	0	0	0.10	0.10	0.00	20.00	20.00
IUD	1977	Yes	0	0	0.00	0.00	0.00	20.00	20.00
IUD	1979	Yes	0	0	110.00	110.00	0.00	25.50	25.50
IUD	1981	Yes	0	0	65.00	65.00	0.00	6.50	6.50

71

Table 13. Import Regulations, Contraceptive Supplies Available, and Price Range in Private Sector (continued)

Country and method	Year	Import regulations			Supplies available by source (000s)[b]			Price in private sector (U.S.$)[b]	
		License required	Duty as % of import value	Duty as % of CIF[a]	Total	Imports	Domestic manufacture	Minimum	Maximum
Mauritius *(continued)*									
IUD	1984	Yes	0	0	0.00	0.00	0.00	8.47	8.47
IUD	1988	u	u	u	u	u	u	7.87	7.87
Orals	1976	Yes	0	0	29.50	29.50	0.00	2.00	2.00
Orals	1977	Yes	0	0	40.80	40.80	0.00	2.00	2.00
Orals	1979	Yes	0	0	52.70	52.70	0.00	2.04	2.04
Orals	1981	Yes	0	0	55.50	55.50	0.00	2.86	2.86
Orals	1984	Yes	0	0	11.70	11.70	0.00	2.48	2.48
Orals	1988	u	u	u	u	u	u	1.97	1.97
Injectables	1988	u	u	u	u	u	u	4.72	4.72
Condoms	1976	Yes	0	0	u	u	u	1.25	1.25
Condoms	1977	Yes	0	0	3.60	3.60	u	1.25	1.25
Condoms	1979	Yes	0	0	0.00	0.00	0.00	1.36	1.36
Condoms	1981	Yes	0	0	260.00	260.00	0.00	2.08	2.08
Condoms	1984	Yes	0	0	u	u	0.00	1.81	1.81
Condoms	1988	u	u	u	u	u	u	4.72	4.72
Diaphragm	1976	Yes	0	0	0.40	0.40	0.00	10.00	10.00
Diaphragm	1977	Yes	0	0	0.00	0.00	0.00	10.00	10.00
Diaphragm	1979	Yes	0	0	0.00	0.00	0.00	25.50	25.50
Diaphragm	1981	Yes	0	0	0.00	0.00	0.00	6.50	6.50
Diaphragm	1984	Yes	0	0	0.00	0.00	0.00	5.65	5.65
Diaphragm	1988	u	u	u	u	u	u	7.87	7.87
Spermicides	1988	u	u	u	u	u	u	4.72	4.72
Female sterilization	1988	na	na	na	na	na	na	157.48	157.48
Male sterilization	1988	na	na	na	na	na	na	19.68	19.68
Niger									
IUD	1987	u	30	u	u	u	u	15.00	20.00
Orals	1987	u	u	u	u	u	u	2.00	2.00
Injectables	1987	u	u	u	u	u	u	10.00	10.00
Condoms	1987	u	u	u	u	u	u	8.00	8.00
Spermicides (6)	1987	u	u	u	u	u	u	4.00	4.00
Nigeria									
IUD	1984	No	u	u	u	u	u	u	u
IUD	1987	No	15	u	u	u	u	30.25	130.25
Orals	1984	Yes	u	u	u	u	u	u	u
Orals	1987	No	25	u	u	u	u	0.25	2.38
Injectables	1985	u	u	u	40.00	40.00	0.00	u	u
Injectables	1986	u	u	u	235.60	235.60	0.00	u	u
Injectables	1987	No	25	u	u	u	u	1.75	3.75
Condoms	1984	No	u	u	u	u	u	u	u
Condoms	1987	No	15	u	u	u	u	0.75	1.50
Diaphragm	1984	No	u	u	u	u	u	u	u
Diaphragm	1987	No	15	u	u	u	u	18.75	u
Spermicides (4)	1987	No	25	u	u	u	u	0.75	1.25
Norplant	1987	No	25	u	u	u	u	u	u
Sierra Leone									
IUD	1984	No	0	0	u	u	u	10.00	10.00
Orals	1984	No	0	0	u	u	u	1.00	1.00
Condoms	1984	No	0	0	u	u	u	1.50	1.50
Diaphragm	1984	No	0	0	u	u	u	7.00	7.00
Sudan									
IUD	1986	u	u	u	0.35	0.35	0.00	u	u
IUD	1987	Yes	0	0	u	u	u	30.61	40.82
Orals	1987	Yes	0	0	u	u	u	0.41	1.63
Injectables	1986	u	u	u	9.00	u	u	u	u
Condoms	1986	u	u	u	0.60	u	u	u	u
Condoms	1987	Yes	0	0	u	u	u	u	u
Diaphragm	1987	Yes	0	0	u	u	u	u	u
Spermicides	1987	Yes	0	0	u	u	u	u	u
Norplant	1987	Yes	0	0	u	u	u	u	u

Table 13. Import Regulations, Contraceptive Supplies Available, and Price Range in Private Sector *(continued)*

Country and method	Year	Import regulations			Supplies available by source (000s)[b]			Price in private sector (U.S.$)[b]	
		License required	Duty as % of import value	Duty as % of CIF[a]	Total	Imports	Domestic manufacture	Minimum	Maximum
Tanzania									
IUD	1977	No	0	1	6.00	6.00	0.00	u	u
Orals	1977	Yes	0	1	780.80	780.80	0.00	u	u
Condoms	1977	Yes	0	1	2.40	2.40	0.00	u	u
Diaphragm	1977	Yes	0	1	0.40	0.40	0.00	u	u
Togo									
IUD	1987	No	0	0	u	u	u	3.33	3.33
Orals	1987	No	0	0	u	u	u	0.03	0.03
Injectables	1987	No	0	0	u	u	u	3.33	3.33
Condoms	1987	No	0	0	u	u	u	1.67	1.67
Diaphragm	1987	No	0	0	u	u	u	3.33	3.33
Spermicides (tube)	1987	No	0	0	u	u	u	1.67	1.67
Norplant	1987	No	0	0	u	u	u	u	u
Uganda									
IUD	1976	Yes	50	0	11.00	u	u	2.40	2.40
Orals	1976	Yes	50	0	45.40	u	u	0.60	0.60
Injectables	1976	u	u	u	3.00	u	u	1.20	1.20
Condoms	1976	Yes	50	0	u	u	u	0.72	0.72
Diaphragm	1976	Yes	50	0	u	u	u	1.20	1.20
Zimbabwe									
IUD	1975	u	u	u	0.45	0.45	0.00	2.82	2.82
IUD	1976	u	u	u	1.30	1.30[c,d]	0.00	3.53	3.53
IUD	1979	u	u	u	4.70	u	u	18.98	18.98
IUD	1983	Yes	0	4	10.00	10.00	0.00	u	u
IUD	1985	u	u	u	21.00	u	u	u	u
IUD	1986	u	u	u	11.60	u	u	u	u
IUD	1986	u	u	u	21.00	u	u	u	u
IUD	1987	u	u	u	u	u	u	9.38	9.38
Orals	1975	u	u	u	347.60	347.60[d]	0.00	0.19	0.19
Orals	1976	u		uu	464.90	464.90[d,f]	0.00	0.18	0.18
Orals	1979	u	u	u	622.50	u	u	2.19	2.19
Orals	1983	Yes	0	4	2415.00	2415.00	0.00	u	u
Orals	1985	u	u	u	9200.00	u	u	u	u
Orals	1986	u	u	u	5400.00	u	u	u	u
Orals	1987	u	u	u	u	u	u	1.88	1.88
Injectables	1983	Yes	0	4	100.00	100.00	0.00	u	u
Injectables	1985	u	u	u	0.68	u	u	u	u
Injectables	1986	u	u	u	42.00	u	u	u	u
Condoms	1975	u	u	u	u	u	u	4.52	4.52
Condoms	1976	u	u	u	u	u	u	4.24	4.24
Condoms	1979	u	u	u	330.60	u	u	2.19	2.19
Condoms	1983	Yes	0	4	12552.00	12552.00	0.00	u	u
Condoms	1985	u	u	u	6400.00	u	u	u	u
Condoms	1985	u	u	u	10400.00	u	u	u	u
Condoms	1987	u	u	u	u	u	u	9.38	9.38
Diaphragm	1975	u	u	u	0.20	0.20	0.00	1.88	1.88
Diaphragm	1976	u	u	u	0.50	0.50[c,e]	0.00	2.65	2.65
Diaphragm	1979	u	u	u	0.40	u	u	20.44	20.44
Diaphragm	1985	u	u	u	2.20	u	u	u	u
Diaphragm	1987	u	u	u	u	u	u	9.38	9.38
Spermicides	1986	u	u	u	3.60	u	u	u	u
Female sterilization	1987	na	na	na	na	na	na	75.00	75.00
LATIN AMERICA/CARIBBEAN									
Bolivia									
IUD	1975	No	0	u	11.60	u	u	40.00	40.00
IUD	1976	Yes	4	1	11.60	u	u	15.00	15.00
IUD[h]	1977	No	4	1	3.90	3.90[c,d]	u	20.00	20.00
IUD[h]	1978	No	4	1	5.30	4.00[c,d]	0.00	75.00	75.00
IUD	1987	Yes	22	25	u	u	u	12.31	14.78
Orals	1975	Yes	0	u	30.00	u	u	2.00	2.00
Orals	1976	Yes	4	1	30.00	u	u	1.50	1.50

Country and method	Year	Import regulations			Supplies available by source (000s)[b]			Price in private sector (U.S.$)[b]	
		License required	Duty as % of import value	Duty as % of CIF[a]	Total	Imports	Domestic manufacture	Minimum	Maximum
Bolivia *(continued)*									
Orals[h]	1977	Yes	4	1	9.00	9.00[c,d]	u	2.00	2.00
Orals[h]	1978	Yes	4	1	4.00	4.00[c,d]	0.00	2.00	2.00
Orals	1987	Yes	22	25	u	u	u	1.48	1.48
Injectables	1987	Yes	22	25	u	u	u	1.48	1.48
Condoms	1975	No	0	u	u	u	u	2.00	2.00
Condoms	1976	Yes	4	1	u	u	u	2.00	2.00
Condoms[h]	1977	No	4	1	0.70	0.70[c,d]	u	3.00	3.00
Condoms[h]	1978	No	4	1	3.80	3.80[c,d]	0.00	2.40	2.40
Condoms	1987	Yes	22	25	u	u	u	4.93	4.93
Diaphragm	1975	No	0	u	0.14	u	u	10.00	10.00
Diaphragm	1976	Yes	4	1	0.14	u	u	7.00	7.00
Diaphragm[h]	1977	No	4	1	u	u	u	20.00	20.00
Diaphragm[h]	1978	No	4	1	u	u	u	1.00	1.00
Diaphragm	1987	Yes	22	25	u	u	u	9.85	12.31
Spermicides	1987	Yes	22	25	0.00	0.00	0.00	u	u
Female sterilization	1987	na	na	na	na	na	na	197.00	295.00
Male sterilization	1987	na	na	na	na	na	na	197.00	295.00
Brazil									
All types	1984	Yes	130	u	u	u	u	u	u
IUD	1980	Yes	u	u	0.40	0.40	0.00	u	u
IUD	1987	Yes	u	u	u	u	u	43.00	85.23
Orals	1976	u	u	u	u	u	4000.00	0.27	0.27
Orals	1980	Yes	u	u	3408.00	0.00	3408.00	0.30	0.30
Orals	1987	u	117	u	u	u	u	0.23	0.43
Injectables	1987	Yes	u	u	u	u	u	0.77	1.30
Condoms	1980	Yes	u	u	432.00	432.00	0.00	0.20	0.20
Condoms	1987	Yes	u	u	u	u	u	1.30	4.69
Diaphragm	1987	Yes	u	u	u	u	u	26.00	42.62
Spermicides	1980	Yes	u	164	u	u	u	u	u
Spermicides (tube)	1987	Yes	u	u	u	u	u	2.00	17.05
Female sterilization	1987	na	na	na	na	na	na	320.00	320.00
Male sterilization	1987	na	na	na	na	na	na	850.00	850.00
Norplant	1987	Yes	u	u	u	u	u	u	u
Chile									
IUD	1975	u	u	u	90.30	u	u	u	u
IUD	1987	Yes	u	u	u	u	u	15.49	15.49
Orals	1975	u	u	u	2039.00	u	u	u	u
Orals	1976	Yes	35	0	u	u	u	u	u
Orals	1977	Yes	15	u	1900.00	u	u	u	u
Orals	1987	Yes	u	u	u	u	u	3.31	3.31
Injectables	1987	Yes	u	u	u	u	u	14.30	14.30
Condoms	1976	Yes	u	u	u	u	u	u	u
Condoms	1977	Yes	27	u	16.80	u	u	u	u
Condoms	1987	Yes	u	u	u	u	u	2.38	2.38
Diaphragm	1976	Yes	u	u	u	u	u	u	u
Diaphragm	1977	Yes	27	u	u	u	u	u	u
Diaphragm	1987	Yes	u	u	u	u	u	17.60	17.60
Spermicides	1987	Yes	u	u	u	u	u	2.60	2.60
Colombia									
IUD	1975	Yes	u	6	u	u	u	10.00	10.00
IUD	1976	Yes	0	13	u	u	u	10.00	10.00
IUD	1977	Yes	0	13	u	u	u	10.00	10.00
IUD	1978	Yes	20	12	u	u	u	0.81	0.81
IUD	1981	Yes	26	6	40.00	40.00	0.00	12.25	61.25
IUD	1982	u	u	u	120.00	120.00	0.00	u	u
IUD	1983	u	u	u	120.00	120.00	0.00	u	u
IUD	1984	Yes	u	u	70.00	70.00	0.00	2.07	3.32
IUD	1985	u	u	u	80.00	80.00	0.00	u	u
IUD	1986	u	u	u	70.00	70.00	0.00	u	u
Orals	1975	Yes	u	0	u	u	u	0.75	0.75
Orals	1976	Yes	0	6	u	u	u	0.60	0.60

Table 13. Import Regulations, Contraceptive Supplies Available, and Price Range in Private Sector *(continued)*

Country and method	Year	Import regulations			Supplies available by source (000s)[b]			Price in private sector (U.S.$)[b]	
		License required	Duty as % of import value	Duty as % of CIF[a]	Total	Imports	Domestic manufacture	Minimum	Maximum
Colombia *(continued)*									
Orals	1977	Yes	0	6	u	u	u	0.60	0.60
Orals	1978	Yes	25	6	u	u	u	0.27	0.27
Orals	1981	Yes	25	0	5000.00	0.00	5000.00	0.66	1.23
Orals	1982	u	u	u	2000.00	0.00	2000.00	u	u
Orals	1983	u	u	u	2000.00	0.00	2000.00	u	u
Orals	1984	Yes	u	u	757.00	757.00	0.00	0.29	0.41
Orals	1985	u	u	u	1000.00	400.00	600.00	u	u
Orals	1986	u	u	u	1950.00	750.00	1200.00	u	u
Injectables	1984	Yes	u	u	u	u	u	u	u
Condoms	1975	Yes	u	15	u	u	u	1.20	1.20
Condoms	1976	Yes	0	22	u	u	u	1.20	1.20
Condoms	1977	Yes	0	22	u	u	u	1.20	1.20
Condoms	1978	Yes	55	21	u	u	u	0.97	0.97
Condoms	1981	Yes	36	15	450.00	450.00	0.00	0.98	2.21
Condoms	1984	Yes	u	u	473.00	473.00	0.00	1.82	5.31
Condoms	1985	u	u	u	75.00	75.00	0.00	u	u
Condoms	1986	u	u	u	150.00	150.00	0.00	u	u
Diaphragm	1975	Yes	u	15	u	u	u	17.00	17.00
Diaphragm	1976	Yes	0	13	u	u	u	17.00	17.00
Diaphragm	1977	Yes	0	13	u	u	u	17.00	17.00
Diaphragm	1978	Yes	20	12	u	u	u	2.16	2.16
Diaphragm	1981	Yes	45	22	u	u	u	u	u
Spermicides	1984	Yes	u	u	641.00	191.00	450.00	u	u
Spermicides	1985	u	u	u	40.00	40.00	0.00	u	u
Colombia (PROFAMILIA)									
IUD	1987	Yes	57	u	u	u	u	2.89	2.89
Orals	1987	Yes	57	u	u	u	u	0.21	0.40
Injectables	1987	Yes	57	u	0.00	0.00	0.00	u	u
Condoms	1987	Yes	57	u	u	u	u	0.76	0.76
Diaphragm	1987	Yes	57	u	u	u	u	u	u
Spermicides (tablet)	1987	Yes	57	u	u	u	u	0.10	0.10
Female sterilization	1987	na	na	na	na	na	na	2.07	33.06
Male sterilization	1987	na	na	na	na	na	na	2.07	8.26
Norplant	1987	Yes	57	u	u	u	u	u	u
Costa Rica									
IUD	1982	u	u	u	24.00	24.00	0.00	u	u
IUD	1983	Yes	0	1	15.00	15.00	0.00	17.00	17.00
IUD	1984	u	u	u	12.88	12.88	0.00	u	u
IUD	1985	u	u	u	5.05	5.05	0.00	u	u
IUD	1986	u	u	u	0.81	0.81	0.00	u	u
IUD	1987	Yes	na	u	u	u	u	22.40	29.86
Orals	1982	u	u	u	549.80	549.80	0.00	u	u
Orals	1983	Yes	0	0	349.00	349.00	0.00	3.25	3.25
Orals	1984	u	u	u	1943.13	1943.13	0.00	u	u
Orals	1985	u	u	u	1562.65	1562.65	0.00	u	u
Orals	1986	u	u	u	304.25	304.25	0.00	u	u
Orals	1987	Yes	na	u	u	u	u	2.99	5.97
Injectables	1983	Yes	0	0	23.00	23.00	0.00	u	u
Injectables	1984	u	u	u	0.50	0.50	0.00	u	u
Injectables	1985	u	u	u	3.00	3.00	0.00	u	u
Injectables	1986	u	u	u	2.00	2.00	0.00	u	u
Injectables	1987	Yes	na	u	u	u	u	1.79	3.73
Condoms	1982	u	u	u	242.98	242.98	0.00	u	u
Condoms	1983	Yes	0	11	456.00	456.00	0.00	2.30	2.30
Condoms	1985	u	u	u	139.53	139.53	0.00	u	u
Condoms	1986	u	u	u	411.46	411.46	0.00	u	u
Condoms	1987	Yes	na	22	u	u	u	0.90	2.99
Diaphragm	1986	u	u	u	1.21	1.21	0.00	u	u
Diaphragm	1987	u	u	u	u	u	u	5.23	5.23
Spermicides	1982	u	u	u	149.76	149.76	0.00	u	u
Spermicides	1983	Yes	0	u	99.84	99.84	0.00	u	u
Spermicides	1984	u	u	u	204.41	204.41	0.00	u	u

Table 13. Import Regulations, Contraceptive Supplies Available, and Price Range in Private Sector *(continued)*

Country and method	Year	License required	Duty as % of import value	Duty as % of CIF[a]	Total	Imports	Domestic manufacture	Minimum	Maximum
		Import regulations			Supplies available by source (000s)[b]			Price in private sector (U.S.$)[b]	
Costa Rica *(continued)*									
Spermicides	1985	u	u	u	161.08	161.08	0.00	u	u
Spermicides	1986	u	u	u	76.12	76.12	0.00	u	u
Spermicides	1987	Yes	na	u	u	u	u	2.99	5.97
Female sterilization	1987	na	na	na	na	na	na	149.32	746.61
Male sterilization	1987	na	na	na	na	na	na	44.80	149.32
Cuba									
IUD	1977	u	u	u	96.00	96.00	0.00	1.50	1.50
Orals	1977	u	u	u	204.00	10.00	194.00	u	u
Condoms	1977	u	u	u	819.00	819.00	0.00	0.80	0.80
Diaphragm	1977	u	u	u	9.00	9.00	0.00	u	u
Dominican Republic									
IUD	1975	No	0	u	1.20	1.20	0.00	10.00	25.00
IUD	1976	No	0	0	1.20	1.20	0.00	20.00	30.00
IUD	1977	No	0	0	u	u	0.00	25.00	50.00
IUD	1978	No	10	0	u	u	0.00	40.00	40.00
Orals	1975	No	0	u	0.55	0.55	0.00	2.00	2.00
Orals	1976	No	0	0	0.55	0.55	0.00	1.50	2.00
Orals	1977	No	0	0	u	u	0.00	3.00	3.00
Orals	1978	No	10	0	u	u	0.00	3.00	3.00
Condoms	1975	No	0	u	u	u	u	1.60	1.85
Condoms	1976	No	0	0	u	u	u	3.00	4.00
Condoms	1977	No	0	0	u	u	0.00	3.00	4.00
Condoms	1978	No	10	0	u	u	0.00	2.50	3.00
Diaphragm	1975	No	0	u	u	u	u	13.50	18.50
Diaphragm	1976	No	0	0	u	u	u	10.00	20.00
El Salvador									
IUD	1976	Yes	25	20	u	u	u	20.00	20.00
IUD	1977	Yes	25	20	u	u	u	20.00	20.00
IUD	1984	No	0	0	u	u	u	40.00	40.00
Orals	1976	Yes	50	10	u	u	u	0.80	3.20
Orals	1977	Yes	50	10	u	u	u	0.80	3.20
Orals	1984	No	0	0	u	u	u	4.00	4.00
Condoms	1976	Yes	25	20	u	u	u	0.80	4.00
Condoms	1977	Yes	25	20	u	u	u	0.80	4.00
Condoms	1984	No	0	0	u	u	u	u	u
Diaphragm	1976	Yes	25	20	u	u	u	u	u
Diaphragm	1977	Yes	25	20	u	u	u	u	u
Diaphragm	1984	No	0	0	u	u	u	na	na
Guatemala									
IUD	1981	Yes	u	u	u	u	u	15.00	15.00
Orals	1981	Yes	u	u	u	u	u	2.50	2.50
Condoms	1981	No	u	u	u	u	u	5.00	5.00
Diaphragm	1981	Yes	u	u	u	u	u	6.00	6.00
Haiti									
IUD	1984	u	u	u	4.00	u	u	u	u
IUD	1986	u	u	u	2.10	u	u	u	u
IUD	1987	Yes	0	0	u	u	u	3.00	3.00
Orals	1983	u	u	u	584.40	584.40	0.00	u	u
Orals	1984	u	u	u	967.20	967.20	0.00	u	u
Orals	1985	u	u	u	974.40	974.40	0.00	u	u
Orals	1986	u	u	u	1099.20	1099.20	0.00	u	u
Orals	1987	Yes	0	0	u	u	u	1.80	2.00
Injectables	1987	Yes	0	0	u	u	u	0.80	0.80
Condoms	1982	u	u	u	916.70	916.70	0.00	u	u
Condoms	1983	u	u	u	1052.00	1052.00	0.00	u	u
Condoms	1984	u	u	u	867.50	867.50	0.00	u	u
Condoms	1985	u	u	u	1448.50	1448.50	0.00	u	u
Condoms	1986	u	u	u	1050.50	1050.50	0.00	u	u
Condoms	1987	Yes	0	0	u	u	u	0.60	0.60

Table 13. Import Regulations, Contraceptive Supplies Available, and Price Range in Private Sector *(continued)*

Country and method	Year	Import regulations			Supplies available by source (000s)[b]			Price in private sector (U.S.$)[b]	
		License required	Duty as % of import value	Duty as % of CIF[a]	Total	Imports	Domestic manufacture	Minimum	Maximum
Haiti *(continued)*									
Spermicides	1982	u	u	u	304.80	304.80	0.00	u	u
Spermicides	1983	u	u	u	304.80	304.80	0.00	u	u
Spermicides	1984	u	u	u	912.00	912.00	0.00	u	u
Spermicides	1987	Yes	0	0	u	u	u	1.00	1.00
Female sterilization	1987	na	na	na	na	na	na	350.00	350.00
Male sterilization	1987	na	na	na	na	na	na	250.00	250.00
Honduras									
IUD	1985	u	u	u	8.00	8.00	0.00	u	u
IUD	1986	u	u	u	2.34	2.34	0.00	u	u
Orals	1985	u	u	u	54.00	54.00	0.00	u	u
Orals	1986	u	u	u	216.00	216.00	0.00	u	u
Condoms	1984	u	u	u	198.00	198.00	0.00	u	u
Condoms	1985	u	u	u	12.00	12.00	0.00	u	u
Condoms	1986	u	u	u	198.00	198.00	0.00	u	u
Spermicides	1984	u	u	u	81.60	81.60	0.00	u	u
Spermicides	1986	u	u	u	4.00	4.00	0.00	u	u
Jamaica									
IUD	1975	Yes	0	0	u	u[c]	0.00	u	u
IUD	1982	u	u	u	4.00	u	u	u	u
IUD	1983	u	u	u	22.20	u	u	u	u
IUD	1984	u	u	u	1.00	u	u	u	u
IUD	1985	u	u	u	3.00	u	u	u	u
IUD	1986	u	u	u	3.00	u	u	u	u
IUD	1987	No	15	25	u	u	u	u	u
Orals	1975	Yes	0	0	u	u[c]	0.00	u	u
Orals	1987	Yes	15	60	u	u	u	u	u
Injectables	1982	u	u	u	1462.00	u	u	u	u
Injectables	1983	u	u	u	150.00	u	u	u	u
Injectables	1984	u	u	u	211.77	u	u	u	u
Injectables	1985	u	u	u	75.00	u	u	u	u
Injectables	1986	u	u	u	292.00	u	u	u	u
Injectables	1987	Yes	15	25	u	u	u	u	u
Condoms	1975	Yes	0	0	u	u[c]	0.00	u	u
Condoms	1982	u	u	u	406.50	u	u	u	u
Condoms	1983	u	u	u	285.50	u	u	u	u
Condoms	1984	u	u	u	473.00	u	u	u	u
Condoms	1985	u	u	u	377.50	u	u	u	u
Condoms	1986	u	u	u	87.00	u	u	u	u
Condoms	1987	No	15	60	u	u	u	u	u
Diaphragm	1975	Yes	0	0	u	u[c]	0.00	u	u
Diaphragm	1982	u	u	u	0.12	u	u	u	u
Diaphragm	1984	u	u	u	2.28	u	u	u	u
Diaphragm	1985	u	u	u	0.30	u	u	u	u
Diaphragm	1986	u	u	u	0.50	u	u	u	u
Diaphragm	1987	No	15	25	u	u	u	u	u
Spermicides	1982	u	u	u	0.39	u	u	u	u
Spermicides	1983	u	u	u	28.00	u	u	u	u
Spermicides	1984	u	u	u	18.00	u	u	u	u
Spermicides	1985	u	u	u	12.00	u	u	u	u
Spermicides	1986	u	u	u	18.00	u	u	u	u
Spermicides	1987	No	15	60	u	u	u	u	u
Norplant	1987	Yes	15	25	u	u	u	u	u
Mexico									
IUD	1980	u	u	u	u	u	249.00	u	u
IUD	1982	u	u	u	800.00	u	u	u	u
IUD	1987	Yes	u	u	u	u	u	21.19	21.19
Orals	1980	u	u	u	u	u	14257.00	u	u
Orals	1982	u	u	u	19500.00	u	u	u	u
Orals	1987	Yes	u	u	u	u	u	1.11	1.11
Injectables	1980	u	u	u	u	u	5054.00	u	u
Injectables	1982	u	u	u	6400.00	u	u	u	u

Table 13. Import Regulations, Contraceptive Supplies Available, and Price Range in Private Sector *(continued)*

Country and method	Year	Import regulations			Supplies available by source (000s)[b]			Price in private sector (U.S.$)[b]	
		License required	Duty as % of import value	Duty as % of CIF[a]	Total	Imports	Domestic manufacture	Minimum	Maximum
Mexico *(continued)*									
Injectables	1987	Yes	u	u	u	u	u	2.53	2.53
Condoms	1980	u	u	u	u	u	528.00	u	u
Condoms	1982	u	u	u	12720.00	u	u	u	u
Condoms	1987	Yes	u	u	u	u	u	4.26	4.26
Diaphragm	1982	u	u	u	1500.00	u	u	u	u
Diaphragm	1987	No	u	u	u	u	u	10.59	10.59
Spermicides	1982	u	u	u	12600.00	u	u	u	u
Spermicides	1987	Yes	u	u	0.00	0.00	0.00	u	u
Female sterilization	1987	na	na	na	na	na	na	49.44	141.25
Male sterilization	1987	na	na	na	na	na	na	17.66	70.63
Norplant	1987	Yes	u	u	u	u	u	u	u
Panama									
IUD	1987	u	u	u	u	u	u	35.00	75.00
Orals	1987	u	u	u	u	u	u	1.40	7.96
Injectables	1987	u	u	u	u	u	u	15.00	30.00
Condoms	1987	u	u	u	u	u	u	3.00	6.00
Diaphragm	1987	u	u	u	u	u	u	15.00	20.00
Spermicides (tube)	1987	u	u	u	u	u	u	5.00	5.00
Female sterilization	1987	na	na	na	na	na	na	200.00	500.00
Male sterilization	1987	na	na	na	na	na	na	200.00	300.00
Paraguay									
IUD	1987	u	u	u	u	u	u	3.64	21.82
Orals	1987	u	u	u	u	u	u	0.55	2.73
Injectables	1987	u	u	u	u	u	u	3.64	6.23
Condoms	1987	u	u	u	u	u	u	1.64	4.00
Diaphragm	1987	u	u	u	u	u	u	2.18	2.18
Spermicides (10)	1987	u	u	u	u	u	u	3.55	3.55
Peru									
IUD	1979–80	Yes	0	0	28.90	u	u	u	u
IUD	1986	u	u	u	85.68	85.68	0.00	u	u
IUD	1987	No	0[v]	0[v]	u	u	u	50.18	57.35
Orals	1979–80	Yes	0	0	52.50	u	u	u	u
Orals	1986	u	u	u	1075.70	1075.70	0.00	u	u
Orals	1987	No	0[v]	0[v]	u	u	u	0.80	0.80
Injectables	1987	No	0[v]	0[v]	u	u	u	u	u
Condoms	1979–80	No	0	0	45.80	u	u	u	u
Condoms	1986	u	u	u	1806.79	1806.79	0.00	u	u
Condoms	1987	No	0[v]	0[v]	u	u	u	5.40	5.40
Diaphragm	1979–80	Yes	0	0	u	u	u	u	u
Diaphragm	1987	No	0[v]	0[v]	u	u	u	u	u
Spermicides	1986	u	u	u	17.46	17.46	0.00	u	u
Spermicides	1987	No	0[v]	0[v]	u	u	u	u	u
Female sterilization	1987	na	na	na	na	na	na	645.16	645.16
Male sterilization	1987	na	na	na	na	na	na	430.11	430.11
Norplant	1987	No	u	u	u	u	u	u	u
Puerto Rico									
IUD	1976	Yes	0	0	u	u	u	20.00	20.00
IUD	1987	u	u	u	u	u	u	150.00	150.00
Orals	1976	Yes	0	0	u	u	u	2.50	2.50
Orals	1987	u	u	u	u	u	u	18.00	18.00
Condoms	1976	No	0	0	u	u	u	2.00	2.00
Condoms	1987	u	u	u	u	u	u	3.50	3.50
Diaphragm	1976	Yes	0	0	u	u	u	20.00	20.00
Diaphragm	1987	u	u	u	u	u	u	15.00	15.00
Spermicides (12)	1987	u	u	u	u	u	u	8.50	8.50
Female sterilization	1987	na	na	na	na	na	na	300.00[s]	800.00[s]
Male sterilization	1987	na	na	na	na	na	na	300.00	300.00
Venezuela									
IUD	1975	Yes	150	0	u	u[c,d]	0.00	69.00	69.00

Table 13. Import Regulations, Contraceptive Supplies Available, and Price Range in Private Sector *(continued)*

Country and method	Year	Import regulations			Supplies available by source (000s)[b]			Price in private sector (U.S.$)[b]	
		License required	Duty as % of import value	Duty as % of CIF[a]	Total	Imports	Domestic manufacture	Minimum	Maximum
Venezuela *(continued)*									
Orals	1975	Yes	50	0	u	u[c,d]	0.00	2.53	2.53
Condoms	1975	Yes	20	0	u	u[c,d]	0.00	1.84	11.00
Diaphragm	1975	Yes	20–150	0	u	u[c,d]	0.00	46.00	46.00
MIDDLE EAST/NORTH AFRICA									
Egypt									
IUD	1975	Yes	0	0	80.00	i	i	2.30	2.30
IUD	1977	Yes	0	0	90.00	i	i	2.30	2.30
IUD	1979	Yes	0	0	57.70	57.70	0.00	2.30	2.30
IUD	1981	Yes	0	0	77.70	77.70	0.00	1.45	1.45
IUD	1982	u	u	u	270.00	270.00	0.00	u	u
IUD	1983	u	u	u	325.00	325.00	0.00	u	u
IUD	1984	Yes	0	0	360.00	360.00	0.00	1.20	1.20
IUD	1985	u	u	u	420.00	420.00	0.00	u	u
IUD	1986	u	u	u	600.00	600.00	0.00	u	u
IUD	1987	u	0	0	u	u	u	8.92	8.92
Orals	1975	Yes	0	0	6600.00	i	i	0.30	0.41
Orals	1977	Yes	0	0	6000.00	i	i	0.46	0.46
Orals	1979	Yes	0	0	4629.50	4629.50	0.00	0.46	0.46
Orals	1981	Yes	0	0	3386.40	0.00	3386.40	0.07	0.07
Orals	1982	u	u	u	11100.00	0.00	11100.00	u	u
Orals	1983	u	u	u	10600.00	0.00	10600.00	u	u
Orals	1984	Yes	0	0	12000.00	1300.00	10700.00	0.06	0.06
Orals	1985	u	u	u	11400.00	1400.00	10000.00	u	u
Orals	1986	u	u	u	10900.00	1400.00	9500.00	u	u
Orals	1987	u	0	0	u	u	u	0.07	0.24
Injectables	1984	u	u	u	60.00	60.00	0.00	u	u
Injectables	1985	u	u	u	290.00	290.00	0.00	u	u
Injectables	1986	u	u	u	10.00	10.00	0.00	u	u
Injectables	1987	u	0	0	u	u	u	2.45	2.45
Condoms	1975	Yes	0	0	u	u	u	0.14	0.14
Condoms	1977	Yes	0	0	500.00	i	i	0.14	0.14
Condoms	1979	Yes	0	0	1111.40	1111.40	0.00	0.14	0.14
Condoms	1981	Yes	0	0	8662.10	8662.10	0.00	0.09	0.09
Condoms	1982	u	u	u	13000.00	13000.00	0.00	u	u
Condoms	1983	u	u	u	19000.00	19000.00	0.00	u	u
Condoms	1984	Yes	0	0	22000.00	22000.00	0.00	0.24	0.24
Condoms	1985	u	u	u	26000.00	26000.00	0.00	u	u
Condoms	1986	u	u	u	29000.00	29000.00	0.00	u	u
Condoms	1987	u	0	0	u	u	u	0.28	0.28
Diaphragm	1975	Yes	u	u	3.00	3.00	0.00	2.30	2.30
Diaphragm	1977	Yes	0	0	4.00	i	i	2.30	2.30
Diaphragm	1979	Yes	0	0	6.70	i	i	2.30	2.30
Diaphragm	1981	Yes	0	0	9.30	9.30	0.00	1.45	1.45
Diaphragm	1984	Yes	0	0	0.00	0.00	0.00	0.30	0.30
Diaphragm	1987	u	0	0	u	u	u	0.35	0.35
Spermicides	1982	u	u	u	5000.00	5000.00	0.00	u	u
Spermicides	1983	u	u	u	13000.00	13000.00	0.00	u	u
Spermicides	1984	u	u	u	9000.00	9000.00	0.00	u	u
Spermicides	1985	u	u	u	4500.00	4500.00	0.00	u	u
Spermicides	1986	u	u	u	2000.00	2000.00	0.00	u	u
Spermicides (8)	1987	u	0	0	u	u	u	0.35	0.35
Iran									
IUD	1975	Yes	u	u	u	u	0.00	15.00	15.00
IUD	1976	Yes	u	u	100.00	100.00[c]	0.00	10.00	10.00
IUD	1978	Yes	u	u	100.00	100.00[c]	0.00	10.00	10.00
IUD	1982	u	u	u	u	739.90	u	u	u
IUD	1983	u	u	u	u	799.90	u	u	u
IUD	1984	u	u	u	u	265.00	u	u	u
IUD	1985	u	u	u	u	400.60	u	u	u
IUD	1987	Yes	u	u	u	u	u	135.00	270.00
Orals	1975	Yes	u	u	u	u	u	1.05	1.05
Orals	1976	Yes	u	u	15000.00	10000.00[d,g]	5000.00	1.00	1.00

Table 13. Import Regulations, Contraceptive Supplies Available, and Price Range in Private Sector *(continued)*

Country and method	Year	Import regulations			Supplies available by source (000s)[b]			Price in private sector (U.S.$)[b]	
		License required	Duty as % of import value	Duty as % of CIF[a]	Total	Imports	Domestic manufacture	Minimum	Maximum
Iran *(continued)*									
Orals	1978	Yes	u	u	19327.00	17632.00[d,g]	1695.00	1.00	1.00
Orals	1987	Yes	u	u	u	u	u	1.15	1.15
Condoms	1975	Yes	u	u	u	u	u	0.60	0.60
Condoms	1976	Yes	u	u	u	u	u	0.50	0.50
Condoms	1978	Yes	u	u	1200.00	1200.00	0.00	0.50	0.50
Condoms	1984	u	u	u	33111.00	33111.00	u	u	u
Condoms	1985	u	u	u	10158.90	10158.90	u	u	u
Condoms	1986	u	u	u	9336.10	9336.10	u	u	u
Condoms	1987	Yes	u	u	u	u	u	2.70	2.70
Diaphragm	1975	Yes	u	u	u	u	u	u	u
Diaphragm	1976	Yes	u	u	u	u	u	u	u
Iraq									
IUD	1987	u	u	u	u	u	u	8.53	8.53
Orals	1987	u	u	u	u	u	u	0.97	0.97
Injectables	1987	u	u	u	u	u	u	2.42	2.42
Condoms	1987	u	u	u	u	u	u	3.22	3.22
Spermicides (bottle)	1987	u	u	u	u	u	u	1.93	1.93
Spermicides (20)	1987	u	u	u	u	u	u	2.42	2.42
Jordan									
IUD	1986	u	u	u	12.00	12.00	0.00	u	u
IUD	1987	Yes	u	7[w]	u	u	u	71.00	99.40
Orals	1986	u	u	u	240.00	240.00	0.00	u	u
Orals	1987	Yes	u	7[w]	u	u	u	0.85	0.85
Injectables	1987	No	u	u	u	u	u	u	u
Condoms	1986	u	u	u	6.00	6.00	0.00	u	u
Condoms	1987	Yes	u	32[w]	u	u	u	5.68	5.68
Diaphragm	1987	No	u	u	u	u	u	u	u
Spermicides (20)	1987	Yes	u	7[w]	u	u	u	1.70	1.70
Female sterilization	1987	na	na	na	na	na	na	397.60	397.60
Norplant	1987	No	u	u	u	u	u	u	u
Morocco									
IUD	1974	u	u	u	u	u	u	40.00	65.00
Orals	1974	u	u	u	u	u	u	0.70	1.00
Orals	1987	u	u	u	u	u	u	0.96	2.05
Tunisia									
IUD	1975	No	0	u	u	u	0.00	u	u
IUD	1977	Yes	0	0	u	u	u	20.00	30.00
IUD	1981	Yes	0	0	u	65.60	u	u	u
IUD	1982	u	u	u	137.00	137.00	0.00	u	u
IUD	1983	u	u	u	10.00	10.00	0.00	u	u
IUD	1984	u	u	u	19.40	19.40	0.00	u	u
IUD	1985	u	u	u	136.20	136.20	0.00	u	u
IUD	1986	u	u	u	5.00	5.00	0.00	u	u
IUD	1987	Yes	u	u	u	u	u	u	u
Orals	1975	No	0	u	u	u	0.00	1.27	1.27
Orals	1977	Yes	0	0	u	u	u	6.00	10.00
Orals	1981	Yes	0	0	u	562.70	u	0.13	0.13
Orals	1982	u	u	u	578.68	578.68	0.00	u	u
Orals	1983	u	u	u	1173.20	1173.20	0.00	u	u
Orals	1984	u	u	u	1458.29	1458.29	0.00	u	u
Orals	1985	u	u	u	1335.40	1335.40	0.00	u	u
Orals	1986	u	u	u	500.00	500.00	0.00	u	u
Orals	1987	Yes	u	u	u	u	u	0.06	0.06
Condoms	1975	No	0	u	u	u	0.00	1.48	1.48
Condoms	1977	Yes	0	0	u	u	u	u	u
Condoms	1981	Yes	0	0	u	u	u	0.31	0.31
Condoms	1982	u	u	u	0.42	0.42	0.00	u	u
Condoms	1984	u	u	u	47.28	47.28	0.00	u	u
Condoms	1985	u	u	u	267.00	267.00	0.00	u	u
Condoms	1987	Yes	u	u	u	u	u	0.15	0.15

Table 13. Import Regulations, Contraceptive Supplies Available, and Price Range in Private Sector (continued)

Country and method	Year	Import regulations			Supplies available by source (000s)[b]			Price in private sector (U.S.$)[b]	
		License required	Duty as % of import value	Duty as % of CIF[a]	Total	Imports	Domestic manufacture	Minimum	Maximum
Tunisia (continued)									
Diaphragm	1975	No	0	u	u	u	0.00	u	u
Spermicides	1982	u	u	u	54.22	54.22	0.00	u	u
Spermicides	1983	u	u	u	5.00	5.00	0.00	u	u
Spermicides	1984	u	u	u	57.02	57.02	0.00	u	u
Spermicides	1985	u	u	u	5.04	5.04	0.00	u	u
Spermicides	1986	u	u	u	139.20	139.20	0.00	u	u
Spermicides	1987	Yes	u	u	u	u	u	u	u
Norplant	1987	Yes	u	u	u	u	u	u	u
Turkey									
IUD	1975	Yes[j]	40–50	0	u	u	u	u	u
IUD	1986	u	u	u	703.65	703.65	0.00	u	u
IUD	1987	Yes	u	u	u	u	u	15.00	15.00
Orals	1975	Yes[j]	40–50	0	u	u	u	0.67	0.67
Orals	1986	u	u	u	32.41	32.41	0.00	u	u
Orals	1987	Yes	u	u	u	u	u	1.00	1.00
Injectables	1987	No	u	u	u	u	u	u	u
Condoms	1975	Yes	0	0	u	u	u	0.43	0.85
Condoms	1986	u	u	u	1022.50	1022.50	0.00	u	u
Condoms	1987	Yes	u	u	u	u	u	2.00	2.00
Diaphragm	1975	Yes	0	0	u	u	u	u	u
Diaphragm	1987	No	u	u	u	u	u	u	u
Spermicides	1986	u	u	u	210.00	0.00	210.00	u	u
Spermicides (10)	1987	Yes	u	u	u	u	u	2.00	2.00
Female sterilization	1987	na	na	na	na	na	na	1.50	1.50
Male sterilization	1987	na	na	na	na	na	na	1.50	1.50
Norplant	1987	No	u	u	u	u	u	u	u
ASIA									
Bangladesh									
IUD	1976	Yes	0	0	u	u	u	u	u
IUD	1977	Yes	0	0	0.00	0.00	0.00	u	u
IUD	1981	Yes	0	0	48.00	u	u	u	u
IUD	1984	u	u	u	250.00	250.00	0.00	u	u
IUD	1985	u	u	u	600.00	600.00	0.00	u	u
IUD	1986	u	u	u	786.40	786.40	0.00	u	u
Orals	1976	Yes	0	0	u	u	281.30	0.64	0.64
Orals	1977	Yes	0	0	u	u	350.00	0.64[k]	0.64[k]
Orals	1981	Yes	0	0	4695.00	u	u	0.71	0.71
Orals	1982	u	u	u	2376.00	2376.00	0.00	u	u
Orals	1983	u	u	u	3254.04	3254.04	0.00	u	u
Orals	1984	u	u	u	8259.84	8259.84	0.00	u	u
Orals	1985	u	u	u	3852.36	3852.36	0.00	u	u
Orals	1986	u	u	u	14546.52	14546.52	0.00	u	u
Orals	1987	u	u	u	u	u	u	0.05	0.13
Injectables	1982	u	u	u	299.58	299.58	0.00	u	u
Injectables	1983	u	u	u	593.20	593.20	0.00	u	u
Injectables	1984	u	u	u	0.00	0.00	0.00	u	u
Injectables	1985	u	u	u	325.00	325.00	0.00	u	u
Injectables	1986	u	u	u	262.50	262.50	0.00	u	u
Injectables	1987	u	u	u	250.00	250.00	0.00	u	u
Condoms	1976	Yes	0	0	u	u	u	0.27	0.80
Condoms	1977	Yes	0	0	u	u	u	0.27[k]	0.80[k]
Condoms	1981	Yes	0	0	5468.00	u	u	0.23	0.23
Condoms	1982	u	u	u	3571.00	3571.00	0.00	u	u
Condoms	1983	u	u	u	1895.00	1895.00	0.00	u	u
Condoms	1984	u	u	u	1871.50	1871.50	0.00	u	u
Condoms	1985	u	u	u	5617.50	5617.50	0.00	u	u
Condoms	1986	u	u	u	7307.00	7307.00	0.00	u	u
Condoms	1987	u	u	u	u	u	u	0.14	0.14
Diaphragm	1976	Yes	0	0	0.00	0.00	0.00	u	u
Diaphragm	1977	Yes	0	0	0.00	0.00	0.00	u	u
Diaphragm	1981	Yes	0	0	0.00	0.00	0.00	u	u
Spermicides	1985	u	u	u	50.00	50.00	0.00	u	u

Table 13. Import Regulations, Contraceptive Supplies Available, and Price Range in Private Sector *(continued)*

Country and method	Year	Import regulations			Supplies available by source (000s)[b]			Price in private sector (U.S.$)[b]	
		License required	Duty as % of import value	Duty as % of CIF[a]	Total	Imports	Domestic manufacture	Minimum	Maximum
Bangladesh *(continued)*									
Spermicides (10)	1987	u	u	u	u	u	u	0.08	0.08
China									
IUD	1986	na[t]	u	u	50000.00	u	50000.00	u	u
Orals	1986	na[t]	u	u	3500000.00	u	3500000.00	u	u
Injectables	1986	na[t]	u	u	35000.00	u	35000.00	u	u
Condoms	1986	na[t]	u	u	900000.00	u	900000.00	u	u
Spermicides	1986	na[t]	u	u	1000.00	u	1000.00	u	u
Hong Kong									
IUD	1976	No	u	u	14.60	14.60[e]	0.00	u	11.00
IUD	1981	No	u	u	u	u	u	47.50	47.50
IUD	1984	No	0	0	u	u	u	u	u
IUD	1987	No	u	u	u	u	u	64.10	64.10
Orals	1976	No	u	u	846.00	846.00[l]	u	u	5.50
Orals	1981	No	u	u	u	u	u	0.86	1.14
Orals	1984	No	0	0	u	u	u	0.68	0.68
Orals	1987	Yes	u	u	u	u	u	1.15	1.15
Injectables	1987	Yes	u	u	u	u	u	6.41	6.41
Condoms	1976	No	u	u	u	u	u	u	2.64
Condoms	1981	No	u	u	u	u	u	1.05	1.14
Condoms	1984	No	0	0	u	u	u	1.64	1.64
Condoms	1987	No	u	u	u	u	u	2.56	2.56
Diaphragm	1976	No	u	u	1.40	1.40[c]	0.00	u	2.20
Diaphragm	1981	No	u	u	u	u	u	29.45	29.45
Diaphragm	1984	No	0	0	u	u	u	u	u
Diaphragm	1987	No	u	u	u	u	u	44.87	44.87
Spermicides (12)	1987	No	u	u	u	u	u	2.18	2.18
Female sterilization	1987	na	na	na	na	na	na	320.51	320.51
Male sterilization	1987	na	na	na	na	na	na	128.20	128.20
Norplant	1987	No	u	u	u	u	u	u	u
India									
IUD	1976	Yes	0	0	u	100.00	u	u	u
IUD	1977	Yes	0	0	u	497.00[m]	u	u	u
IUD	1979	Yes	0	0	u	339.00[m]	u	u	u
IUD	1981	Yes	0	0	350.00	350.00	0.00	u	u
IUD	1983	Yes	0	0	3300.00	3300.00	0.00	1.00	1.00
Orals	1976	u	u	u	u	800.00	u	u	u
Orals	1977	Yes	0	0	1800.00	800.00[n]	1000.00	u	u
Orals	1979	Yes	0	0	1600.00	n	n	u	u
Orals	1981	Yes	0	0	1666.00	p	p	u	u
Orals	1983	Yes	0	0	11500.00	11500.00	0.00	0.15	0.15
Condoms	1977	o	u	u	22500.00	0.00	22500.00	0.19	0.19
Condoms	1979	u	0	0	u	u	33333.00	0.12	0.12
Condoms	1981	u	0	0	24167.00	0.00	24167.00	0.13	0.13
Condoms	1983	Yes	0	0	572000.00	100000.00	472000.00	0.37	0.37
Indonesia									
IUD	1975	Yes	0	u	400.00	0.00	400.00	4.80	7.20
IUD	1976	Yes	0	0	300.00	0.00	300.00	4.82	7.23
IUD	1979	Yes	0	0	220.00	220.00	0.00	u	u
IUD	1981	Yes	0	0	581.00	581.00	0.00	u	u
IUD	1982	u	u	u	2452.60	452.60	2000.00	u	u
IUD	1983	Yes	0	0	1552.00	1552.00	0.00	4.95	4.95
IUD	1984	u	u	u	2474.00	200.00	2274.00	u	u
IUD	1985	u	u	u	1522.00	0.00	1522.00	u	u
IUD	1986	u	u	u	337766.00	2555.55	822.10	u	u
IUD	1987	u	0	0	u	u	u	0.17	0.17
Orals	1975	Yes	0	u	1400–2000	0.00	1400–2000	0.84	2.20
Orals	1976	Yes	0	0	u	1400–2000	0.00	0.84	2.17
Orals	1979	Yes	0	0	29055.00	28802.00	253.00	u	u
Orals	1981	Yes	0	0	67483.00	56322.00	11161.00	u	u
Orals	1982	u	u	u	97564.20	70703.40	26860.80	u	u

82

Table 13. Import Regulations, Contraceptive Supplies Available, and Price Range in Private Sector *(continued)*

Country and method	Year	Import regulations			Supplies available by source (000s)[b]			Price in private sector (U.S.$)[b]	
		License required	Duty as % of import value	Duty as % of CIF[a]	Total	Imports	Domestic manufacture	Minimum	Maximum
Indonesia *(continued)*									
Orals	1983	Yes	0	0	103396.33	63880.80	39515.50	1.48	1.48
Orals	1984	u	u	u	124033.78	76250.00	47783.80	u	u
Orals	1985	u	u	u	58245.90	14845.90	43400.00	u	u
Orals	1986	u	u	u	36228.80	14948.12	21280.70	u	u
Orals	1987	u	0	0	u	u	u	0.19	0.19
Injectables	1981	u	u	u	300.00	300.00	0.00	u	u
Injectables	1982	u	u	u	3250.00	0.00	3250.00	u	u
Injectables	1983	Yes	0	0	4647.79	4647.79	0.00	na	na
Injectables	1984	u	u	u	8500.00	0.00	8500.00	u	u
Injectables	1985	u	u	u	7830.00	0.00	7830.00	u	u
Injectables	1986	u	u	u	10945.37	0.00	10945.40	u	u
Injectables	1987	u	0	0	u	u	u	0.79	0.79
Condoms	1975	Yes	0	u	14400.00	u	14400.00	0.48	0.72
Condoms	1976	Yes	0	0	2160.00	2160.00	0.00	0.48	0.72
Condoms	1979	Yes	0	0	3600.00	3600.00	0.00	u	u
Condoms	1981	Yes	0	0	8270.00	8270.00	0.00	u	u
Condoms	1982	u	u	u	215.83	215.83	0.00	u	u
Condoms	1983	Yes	0	0	100.00	100.00	0.00	0.74	0.74
Condoms	1984	u	u	u	150.00	150.00	0.00	u	u
Condoms	1985	u	u	u	60.00	60.00	0.00	u	u
Condoms	1986	u	u	u	110.00	110.00	0.00	u	u
Condoms	1987	u	0	0	u	u	u	0.46	0.46
Diaphragm	1975	Yes	0	u	0.00	0.00	0.00	u	u
Norplant	1987	u	0	0	u	u	u	u	u
Korea, Republic of									
IUD	1975	Yes	u	u	350.00	0.00	350.00	na	na
IUD	1976	Yes	u	u	350.00	0.00	350.00	2.48	2.48
IUD	1977	Yes	u	u	u	u	u	u	u
IUD	1981	Yes	u	u	u	u	u	30.00	30.00
IUD	1982	u	u	u	220.00	0.00	220.00	u	u
IUD	1983	u	u	u	250.00	0.00	250.00	u	u
IUD	1984	u	u	u	210.00	0.00	210.00	u	u
IUD	1985	u	u	u	200.00	50.00	150.00	u	u
IUD	1986	u	u	u	350.00	100.00	250.00	u	u
IUD	1987	Yes	0	0	u	u	u	11.61	17.42
Orals	1975	Yes	u	u	u	u	u	0.52	0.52
Orals	1976	Yes	u	u	1950.00	u	1950.00	0.56	0.56
Orals	1977	Yes	u	u	1932.00	0.00	1932.00	0.52	0.52
Orals	1981	Yes	u	u	2713.00	0.00	2713.00	0.90	1.20
Orals	1982	u	u	u	1500.00	0.00	1500.00	u	u
Orals	1983	u	u	u	1100.00	0.00	1100.00	u	u
Orals	1984	u	u	u	800.00	0.00	800.00	u	u
Orals	1985	u	u	u	600.00	0.00	600.00	u	u
Orals	1986	u	u	u	600.00	0.00	600.00	u	u
Orals	1987	Yes	15	u	u	u	u	1.04	1.28
Injectables	1987	Yes	15	u	u	u	u	na	na
Condoms	1975	Yes	u	u	u	u	u	0.52	0.52
Condoms	1976	Yes	u	u	u	u	u	0.59	0.59
Condoms	1977	Yes	u	u	u	u	u	0.63	0.63
Condoms	1981	Yes	u	u	21899.00	0.00	21899.00	0.75	1.20
Condoms	1982	u	u	u	700.00	0.00	700.00	u	u
Condoms	1983	u	u	u	800.00	0.00	800.00	u	u
Condoms	1984	u	u	u	800.00	0.00	800.00	u	u
Condoms	1985	u	u	u	800.00	0.00	800.00	u	u
Condoms	1986	u	u	u	1500.00	0.00	1500.00	u	u
Condoms	1987	Yes	25	u	u	u	u	1.16	1.74
Diaphragm	1975	Yes	u	u	u	u	u	u	u
Diaphragm	1976	Yes	u	u	0.00	0.00	0.00	u	u
Diaphragm	1977	Yes	u	u	0.00	0.00	0.00	u	u
Diaphragm	1987	Yes	15	u	u	u	u	u	u
Spermicides (12)	1987	Yes	0	0	u	u	u	2.32	2.32
Female sterilization	1987	na	na	na	na	na	na	49.94	81.30
Male sterilization	1987	na	na	na	na	na	na	44.13	69.69

Table 13. Import Regulations, Contraceptive Supplies Available, and Price Range in Private Sector (continued)

Country and method	Year	Import regulations			Supplies available by source (000s)[b]			Price in private sector (U.S.$)[b]	
		License required	Duty as % of import value	Duty as % of CIF[a]	Total	Imports	Domestic manufacture	Minimum	Maximum
Korea, Republic of (continued)									
Norplant	1987	Yes	15.00	na	u	u	u	u	u
Malaysia (Peninsular)									
IUD	1987	Yes	u	u	u	u	u	16.00	32.00
Orals	1987	Yes	u	u	u	u	u	0.80	1.40
Injectables	1987	Yes	u	u	u	u	u	4.00	6.00
Condoms	1987	Yes	u	u	u	u	u	1.28	1.28
Diaphragms	1987	Yes	u	u	u	u	u	8.00	16.00
Spermicides (tube)	1987	Yes	u	u	u	u	u	1.60	2.00
Female sterilization	1987	na	na	na	na	na	na	80.00	160.00
Male sterilization	1987	na	na	na	na	na	na	80.00	160.00
Norplant	1987	Yes	u	u	u	u	u	u	u
Nepal									
IUD	1987	No	0	0	u	u	u	u	u
Orals	1987	No	0	0	u	u	u	0.09	0.14
Injectables	1987	No	0	0	u	u	u	u	u
Condoms	1987	No	0	0	u	u	u	0.28	0.28
Diaphragm	1987	No	0	0	u	u	u	u	u
Spermicides (9)	1987	No	0	0	u	u	u	0.14	0.14
Norplant	1987	No	0	0	u	u	u	u	u
Pakistan									
IUD	1982	u	u	u	120.00	60.00	60.00	u	u
IUD	1983	u	u	u	140.90	0.00	140.90	u	u
IUD	1984	u	u	u	338.18	21.40	316.70	u	u
IUD	1985	u	u	u	45.00	0.00	45.00	u	u
IUD	1987	No	0	0	u	u	u	u	u
Orals	1982	u	u	u	1994.97	1994.97	0.00	u	u
Orals	1984	u	u	u	1110.67	1110.67	0.00	u	u
Orals	1986	u	u	u	1499.40	1499.40	0.00	u	u
Orals	1987	No	0	0	u	u	u	0.30	0.30
Injectables	1984	u	u	u	262.53	262.53	0.00	u	u
Injectables	1985	u	u	u	249.64	249.64	0.00	u	u
Injectables	1986	u	u	u	399.40	399.40	0.00	u	u
Injectables	1987	No	0	0	u	u	u	1.18	1.77
Condoms	1983	u	u	u	1485.70	1485.70	0.00	u	u
Condoms	1984	u	u	u	9336.56	9336.56	0.00	u	u
Condoms	1985	u	u	u	19804.36	19804.36	0.00	u	u
Condoms	1986	u	u	u	8279.87	8279.87	0.00	u	u
Condoms	1987	No	0	0	u	u	u	0.24	0.59
Diaphragms	1987	No	0	0	u	u	u	u	u
Spermicides	1983	u	u	u	59.96	59.96	0.00	u	u
Spermicides	1984	u	u	u	59.76	59.76	0.00	u	u
Spermicides	1986	u	u	u	185.36	185.36	0.00	u	u
Spermicides (bottle)	1987	No	0	0	u	u	u	0.30	0.59
Norplant	1987	No	0	0	0.00	0.00	0.00	u	u
Philippines									
IUD	1977	Yes	0	0	u	u	u	u	u
IUD	1978	Yes	20	0	u	u	0.00	u	u
IUD	1981	Yes	15	0	u	u	u	u	u
IUD	1983	u	u	u	120.00	120.00	0.00	u	u
IUD	1984	u	u	u	u	157.00	u	u	u
IUD	1987	u	u	u	u	u	u	2.44	24.39
Orals	1977	Yes	0	0	u	u	u	0.40	0.40
Orals	1978	Yes	0	0	u	u	0.00	0.42	0.70
Orals	1981	Yes	0	0	u	668.80	u	0.76	0.76
Orals	1982	u	u	u	8871.60	8871.60	0.00	u	u
Orals	1983	u	u	u	2817.60	2817.60	0.00	u	u
Orals	1984	Yes	5	0	11539.20	11539.20	0.00	0.63	0.79
Orals	1986	u	u	u	7369.20	7369.20	0.00	u	u
Injectables	1981	u	u	u	u	36.40	u	u	u
Injectables	1985	u	u	u	u	220.00	u	u	u

84

Table 13. Import Regulations, Contraceptive Supplies Available, and Price Range in Private Sector *(continued)*

Country and method	Year	Import regulations			Supplies available by source (000s)[b]			Price in private sector (U.S.$)[b]	
		License required	Duty as % of import value	Duty as % of CIF[a]	Total	Imports	Domestic manufacture	Minimum	Maximum
Philippines *(continued)*									
Condoms	1977	Yes	0	0	u	u	u	0.64	0.64
Condoms	1978	Yes	7	0	u	u	u	0.56	0.56
Condoms	1981	Yes	0	0	u	23.90	u	3.74	3.74
Condoms	1982	u	u	u	u	2583.50	u	u	u
Condoms	1984	Yes	5	0	31002.00	31002.00	u	2.03	2.03
Condoms	1985	u	u	u	u	1765.50	u	u	u
Diaphragm	1977	Yes	0	0	u	u	u	u	u
Diaphragm	1978	Yes	0	0	u	u	u	u	u
Diaphragm	1981	Yes	0	0	u	u	u	u	u
Singapore									
IUD	1987	u	u	u	u	u	u	71.16	71.16
Orals	1987	u	u	u	u	u	u	2.37	2.37
Injectables	1987	u	u	u	u	u	u	7.12	7.12
Condoms	1987	u	u	u	u	u	u	2.37	2.37
Female sterilization	1987	na	na	na	na	na	na	284.63	284.63
Male sterilization	1987	na	na	na	na	na	na	189.75	189.75
Sri Lanka									
IUD	1983	u	u	u	12.00	12.00	0.00	u	u
IUD	1984	u	u	u	10.00	10.00	0.00	u	u
IUD	1985	u	u	u	50.00	50.00	0.00	u	u
IUD	1986	u	u	u	20.00	20.00	0.00	u	u
Orals	1983	u	u	u	700.00	700.00	0.00	u	u
Orals	1984	u	u	u	1000.00	1000.00	0.00	u	u
Orals	1985	u	u	u	1000.00	1000.00	0.00	u	u
Orals	1986	u	u	u	400.00	400.00	0.00	u	u
Orals	1987	Yes	u	u	u	u	u	0.12	0.12
Injectables	1983	u	u	u	140.00	140.00	0.00	u	u
Injectables	1984	u	u	u	140.00	140.00	0.00	u	u
Injectables	1986	u	u	u	200.00	200.00	0.00	u	u
Injectables	1987	Yes	u	u	u	u	u	2.50	2.50
Condoms	1983	u	u	u	120.00	120.00	0.00	u	u
Condoms	1984	u	u	u	120.00	120.00	0.00	u	u
Condoms	1985	u	u	u	360.00	360.00	0.00	u	u
Condoms	1986	u	u	u	120.00	120.00	0.00	u	u
Condoms	1987	u	u	u	u	u	u	0.13	0.13
Taiwan									
IUD	1975	Yes	u	10	u	u	220.00	5.50	5.50
IUD	1976	No	u	u	u	u	u	5.50	5.50
IUD	1977	No	u	u	u	u	u	5.50	5.50
IUD	1979	No	u	u	u	u	u	5.60	5.60
IUD	1981	Yes	u	u	u	u	u	1.40	1.40
IUD	1982	u	u	u	62.00	62.00	0.00	u	u
IUD	1983	u	u	u	100.00	100.00	0.00	u	u
IUD	1984	Yes	10	0	100.00	100.00	0.00	2.50	25.00
IUD	1987	Yes	10	5	u	u	u	20.00	37.50
Orals	1975	Yes	20	4	u	u	500.00	1.65	1.65
Orals	1976	Yes	20	0	u	u	u	1.65	1.65
Orals	1977	Yes	20	0	u	u	u	1.65	1.65
Orals	1979	Yes	10	u	u	u	u	1.68	1.68
Orals	1981	Yes	5	u	u	u	u	0.28	0.28
Orals	1982	u	u	u	1460.00	0.00	1460.00	u	u
Orals	1983	u	u	u	870.00	0.00	870.00	u	u
Orals	1984	Yes	10	0	1310.00	0.00	1310.00	1.50	2.50
Orals	1985	u	u	u	1310.00	0.00	1310.00	u	u
Orals	1986	u	u	u	1035.00	0.00	1035.00	u	u
Orals	1987	Yes	10	5	u	u	u	1.25	2.00
Injectables	1984	Yes	10	0	u	u	u	u	u
Condoms	1975	No	0	u	u	u	u	1.38	1.38
Condoms	1976	No	u	u	u	u	u	1.38	1.38
Condoms	1977	No	u	u	u	u	u	1.38	1.38
Condoms	1979	No	u	u	u	u	u	1.68	1.68

Table 13. Import Regulations, Contraceptive Supplies Available, and Price Range in Private Sector *(continued)*

Country and method	Year	Import regulations			Supplies available by source (000s)[b]			Price in private sector (U.S.$)[b]	
		License required	Duty as % of import value	Duty as % of CIF[a]	Total	Imports	Domestic manufacture	Minimum	Maximum
Taiwan *(continued)*									
Condoms	1981	Yes	10	u	u	u	u	0.14	0.14
Condoms	1982	u	u	u	1500.00	0.00	1500.00	u	u
Condoms	1983	u	u	u	1170.00	0.00	1170.00	u	u
Condoms	1984	Yes	10	0	2374.00	0.00	2374.00	1.50	1.50
Condoms	1985	u	u	u	2085.00	0.00	2085.00	u	u
Condoms	1986	u	u	u	1800.00	0.00	1800.00	u	u
Condoms	1987	Yes	10	5	u	u	u	1.25	5.00
Diaphragm	1975	No	0	u	u	u	u	u	u
Diaphragm	1981	Yes	u	u	u	u	u	u	u
Diaphragm	1987	Yes	10	5	u	u	u	u	u
Spermicides	1987	Yes	10	5	u	u	u	1.25	11.50
Female sterilization	1987	na	na	na	na	na	na	100.00	100.00
Male sterilization	1987	na	na	na	na	na	na	42.50	42.50
Thailand									
IUD	1975	Yes	10	10[f]	u	u	u	10.00	10.00
IUD	1977	Yes	10	10[f]	u	u	u	5.00	5.00
IUD	1981	Yes	10	0	u	u	u	u	u
IUD	1984	Yes	u	0	u	u	u	10.93	10.93
IUD	1987	u	15	u	u	u	u	0.84	7.94
Orals	1975	Yes	10	10[f]	u	u	u	0.75	0.75
Orals	1977	Yes	10	10[f]	u	u	u	0.75	0.75
Orals	1981	Yes	10	0	7658.00	5493.00	2165.00	1.00	1.00
Orals	1984	Yes	u	0	u	u	u	1.09	1.09
Orals	1987	u	15	u	u	u	u	0.18	0.81
Injectables	1981	u	u	u	1180.00	600.00	580.00	u	u
Injectables	1984	Yes	u	0	u	u	u	u	u
Injectables	1987	u	15	u	u	u	u	0.57	2.40
Condoms	1975	Yes	10	60[f]	u	u	0.00	1.00	1.00
Condoms	1977	Yes	10	60[f]	u	u	0.00	1.20	1.20
Condoms	1981	Yes	10	0	1120.00	1120.00	0.00	1.00	1.25
Condoms	1984	No	u	0	u	u	u	1.57	1.57
Condoms	1987	u	15	u	u	u	u	0.29	0.82
Diaphragm	1975	Yes	u	u	u	u	0.00	5.00	10.00
Diaphragm	1977	Yes	u	u	u	u	0.00	5.00	5.00
Diaphragm	1981	Yes	10	0	u	u	u	u	u
Diaphragm	1987	u	15	u	u	u	u	u	u
Spermicides	1987	u	15	u	u	u	u	u	u
Female sterilization	1987	na	na	na	na	na	na	4.88	35.42
Male sterilization	1987	na	na	na	na	na	na	10.01	14.27

u = unknown.

na = not applicable.

a. Cost insurance freight price.

b. Supplies are given as follows: IUD, units; orals, cycles; injectables, doses; condoms, dozens; diaphragms, units; spermicides, variable, usually unspecified by respondent. Prices of condoms are per dozen, unless otherwise marked. Prices of orals are per cycle.

c. Imports are from the United States.

d. Imports are from West Germany.

e. Imports are from England.

f. Imports are from South Africa.

g. Imports are from the Netherlands.

h. Supply data from PROFAM only, a private agency.

i. Raw, auxiliary, and packaging materials are imported; the product is manufactured and distributed by national companies.

j. The raw materials for local manufacture are imported from the United States.

k. Fee is charged by private physician, but the government subsidizes the commerical sale price at a rate of U.S. $0.05 for a cycle of orals and U.S. $0.11 for a dozen condoms.

l. Approximately 793,000 oral cycles were imported from Germany.

m. The Copper T is imported; contributed by the UNFPA.

n. The raw materials from which the product is manufactured are imported, contributed by the UNFPA.

o. Importation of condoms is banned.

p. The product is manufactured from imported raw materials.

q. Imports are from France.

r. Applies only to supplies entering the country through commercial channels, not to supplies contributed to the national family planning program by donor agencies.

s. U.S. $300 is charged at outpatient clinics. U.S. $800 is charged at private hospitals; this fee includes the cost of hospitalization.

t. All contraceptives are produced domestically.

v. Imported as "donations."

w. Clearance charges of 5 percent are required for all contraceptives.

Table 14. Charges and Payments to Acceptors of Family Planning Services and Supplies

Country and supply or service	Year	Exchange rate (U.S.$)	Fee charged		Payment given	
			Local currency	U.S.$	Local currency	U.S.$
SUB-SAHARAN AFRICA						
Botswana						
IUD insertion	1972	0.70	0.40[a]	0.57[a]	0.00	0.00
IUD insertion	1974	0.70	0.40[a]	0.57[a]	0.00	0.00
IUD insertion	1975	0.68	0.40	0.59	0.00	0.00
IUD insertion	1978	0.83	0.40	0.48	0.00	0.00
Orals	1972	0.70	0.10	0.14	0.00	0.00
Orals	1974	0.70	0.10	0.14	0.00	0.00
Orals	1975	0.68	0.10	0.15	0.00	0.00
Orals	1978	0.83	0.40	0.48	0.00	0.00
Injectables (3-month)	1974	0.70	0.30	0.43	0.00	0.00
Injectables (3-month)	1975	0.68	0.30	0.44	0.00	0.00
Injectables (3-month)	1978	0.83	0.40	0.48	0.00	0.00
Condoms (12)	1972	0.70	0.10	0.14	0.00	0.00
Condoms (12)	1974	0.70	0.05	0.07	0.00	0.00
Condoms (12)	1975	0.68	0.05	0.07	0.00	0.00
Condoms (12)	1978	0.83	0.05	0.06	0.00	0.00
Condoms (12)	1987	1.59	0.05	0.03	0.00	0.00
Sterilization	1972	0.70	0.40	0.57	0.00	0.00
Sterilization	1974	0.70	0.40	0.57	0.00	0.00
Spermicide (tablets)	1974	0.70	0.05	0.07	0.00	0.00
All types	1984	0.65	0.40[b]	0.62[b]	0.00	0.00
All types (except condom)	1987	1.59	0.40	0.25	0.00	0.00
Burkina Faso						
IUD insertion	1987	300.00	800.00	2.67	0.00	0.00
Orals (cycle)	1987	300.00	100.00	0.33	0.00	0.00
Condoms	1987	300.00	25.00	0.08	0.00	0.00
Female sterilization	1987	300.00	0.00	0.00	0.00	0.00
Male sterilization	1987	300.00	0.00	0.00	0.00	0.00
Spermicides	1987	300.00	150.00	0.50	0.00	0.00
Burundi						
All types	1987	116.31	0.00	0.00	0.00	0.00
Ethiopia						
IUD insertion: Loop	1987	2.07	2.00	0.97	0.00	0.00
IUD insertion: CuT	1987	2.07	5.00	2.41	0.00	0.00
Orals	1987	2.07	1.00–1.50	0.48–0.72	0.00	0.00
Condoms (12)	1987	2.07	1.00	0.48	0.00	0.00
Spermicides (tube)	1987	2.07	2.00	0.97	0.00	0.00
Ghana						
IUD insertion	1970	1.02	1.00	0.98	0.00	0.00
IUD insertion	1973	1.26	1.00	0.79	0.00	0.00
IUD insertion	1974	1.15	1.00	0.87	0.00	0.00
IUD insertion	1975	1.15	1.00	0.87	0.00	0.00
IUD insertion	1976	1.15	1.00	0.87	0.00	0.00
IUD insertion	1977	1.15	1.00	0.87	0.00	0.00
IUD insertion	1978	2.78	1.00	0.36	0.00	0.00
IUD insertion	1987	174.00	100.00	0.57	0.00	0.00
Orals	1970	1.02	0.20	0.20	0.00	0.00
Orals	1973	1.26	0.20	0.16	0.00	0.00
Orals	1974	1.15	0.20	0.17	0.00	0.00
Orals	1975	1.15	0.20	0.17	0.00	0.00
Orals	1978	2.78	0.20	0.07	0.00	0.00
Orals	1987	174.00	15.00	0.09	0.00	0.00
Injectables	1987	174.00	40.00	0.23	0.00	0.00
Condoms (3)	1970	1.02	0.10	0.10	0.00	0.00
Condoms (3)	1973	1.26	0.10	0.08	0.00	0.00
Condoms (3)	1974	1.15	0.10	0.09	0.00	0.00
Condoms (3)	1975	1.15	0.10	0.09	0.00	0.00
Condoms (3)	1976	1.15	0.10	0.09	0.00	0.00
Condoms (3)	1977	1.15	0.10	0.09	0.00	0.00
Condoms (3)	1978	2.78	0.10	0.04	0.00	0.00
Condoms (4)	1987	174.00	10.00	0.06	0.00	0.00
Aerosol foam	1970	1.02	0.50	0.49	0.00	0.00

Table 14. Charges and Payments to Acceptors of Family Planning Services and Supplies *(continued)*

Country and supply or service	Year	Exchange rate (U.S.$)	Fee charged		Payment given	
			Local currency	U.S.$	Local currency	U.S.$
Ghana *(continued)*						
Aerosol foam	1973	1.26	0.50	0.40	0.00	0.00
Aerosol foam	1974	1.15	0.50	0.44	0.00	0.00
Aerosol foam	1975	1.15	0.50	0.44	0.00	0.00
Aerosol foam	1976	1.15	0.50	0.44	0.00	0.00
Aerosol foam	1977	1.15	0.50	0.44	0.00	0.00
Aerosol foam	1978	2.78	0.50	0.18	0.00	0.00
Spermicides	1987	174.00	v	v	0.00	0.00
Kenya						
All types	1979	7.41	0.00	0.00	0.00	0.00
All types	1981	6.90	0.00	0.00	0.00	0.00
All types	1987	15.60	0.00	0.00	0.00	0.00
Lesotho						
IUD insertion	1987	2.07	0.60	0.29	0.00	0.00
Orals	1987	2.07	0.60	0.29	0.00	0.00
Injectables	1987	2.07	0.60	0.29	0.00	0.00
Female sterilization	1987	2.07	0.00	0.00	0.00	0.00
Male sterilization	1987	2.07	0.00	0.00	0.00	0.00
Diaphragm	1987	2.07	0.00	0.00	0.00	0.00
Spermicides	1987	2.07	0.00	0.00	0.00	0.00
Other	1987	2.07	0.60	0.29	0.00	0.00
Mauritius						
IUD insertion	1970	5.56	0.50	0.09	0.00	0.00
IUD insertion	1971	5.00	0.50	0.09	0.00	0.00
IUD insertion	1972	5.00	0.00	0.00	0.00	0.00
IUD insertion	1988	12.70	0.00	0.00	0.00	0.00
Orals	1970	5.56	0.50–2.35	0.09–0.42	0.00	0.00
Orals	1971	5.00	0.50–2.35	0.10–0.47	0.00	0.00
Orals	1972	5.00	0.00	0.00	0.00	0.00
Orals	1988	12.70	0.00	0.00	0.00	0.00
Condoms	1970	5.56	0.08–0.25	0.02–0.05	0.00	0.00
Condoms	1972	5.00	0.00	0.00	0.00	0.00
Condoms	1988	12.70	0.00	0.00	0.00	0.00
Injectables	1988	12.70	0.00	0.00	0.00	0.00
Female sterilization	1988	12.70	0.00	0.00	0.00	0.00
Male sterilization	1988	12.70	0.00	0.00	0.00	0.00
Diaphragm	1988	12.70	0.00	0.00	0.00	0.00
Spermicides	1988	12.70	0.00	0.00	0.00	0.00
Rhythm	1970	5.56	2.50	0.45	0.00	0.00
All types	1975	5.00	0.00	0.00	0.00	0.00
All types	1976	5.88	0.00	0.00	0.00	0.00
All types	1977	6.67	0.00	0.00	0.00	0.00
All types	1979	5.88	0.00	0.00	0.00	0.00
All types	1981	7.69	0.00	0.00	0.00	0.00
All types	1984	11.36	0.00	0.00	0.00	0.00
Niger						
All types	1987	300.00	0.00	0.00	0.00	0.00
Nigeria						
All types	1987	4.00	0.00	0.00	0.00	0.00
Sudan						
All types	1987	2.50	0.00	0.00	0.00	0.00
Togo						
All types	1987	300.00	0.00	0.00	0.00	0.00
Uganda						
IUD insertion	1971	7.14	5.00	0.70	0.00	0.00
IUD insertion	1972	7.14	5.00	0.70	0.00	0.00
IUD insertion	1973	7.14	5.00	0.70	0.00	0.00
Orals	1974	7.14	2.00	0.28	0.00	0.00
Injectables (1-month)	1971	7.14	2.00	0.28	0.00	0.00

Table 14. Charges and Payments to Acceptors of Family Planning Services and Supplies *(continued)*

Country and supply or service	Year	Exchange rate (U.S.$)	Fee charged		Payment given	
			Local currency	U.S.$	Local currency	U.S.$
Uganda *(continued)*						
Injectables (1-month)	1972	7.14	2.00	0.28	0.00	0.00
Injectables (3-month)	1971	7.14	5.00	0.70	0.00	0.00
Injectables (3-month)	1972	7.14	5.00	0.70	0.00	0.00
Injectables (3-month)	1974	7.14	5.00	0.70	0.00	0.00
Condoms (1)	1971	7.14	1.00	0.14	0.00	0.00
Condoms (1)	1972	7.14	1.00	0.14	0.00	0.00
Condoms (3)	1974	7.14	1.00	0.14	0.00	0.00
Diaphragm	1971	7.14	10.00	1.40	0.00	0.00
Diaphragm	1972	7.14	10.00	1.40	0.00	0.00
Diaphragm	1974	7.14	10.00	1.40	0.00	0.00
Zimbabwe						
IUD insertion	1973	0.58	0.25	0.43	0.00	0.00
IUD insertion	1974	0.61	0.20	0.33	0.00	0.00
IUD insertion	1975	0.53	0.20	0.38	0.00	0.00
IUD insertion	1976	0.56	2.00	3.54	0.00	0.00
IUD insertion	1979	0.68	22.00	2.92	0.00	0.00
Orals	1973	0.58	0.10	0.17	0.00	0.00
Orals	1974	0.61	0.10	0.16	0.00	0.00
Orals	1975	0.53	0.10	0.19	0.00	0.00
Orals	1976	0.56	0.10	0.18	0.00	0.00
Orals	1979	0.68	0.10	0.15	0.00	0.00
Injectables (3-month)	1974	0.61	0.25	0.41	0.00	0.00
Injectables (3-month)	1975	0.53	0.25	0.47	0.00	0.00
Injectables (3-month)	1977	0.56	0.25	0.44	0.00	0.00
Condoms	1973	0.58	0.03	0.05	0.00	0.00
Condoms (3)	1974	0.61	0.05	0.08	0.00	0.00
Condoms (6)	1975	0.53	0.05	0.09	0.00	0.00
Condoms	1976	0.56	0.00	0.00	0.00	0.00
Condoms	1979	0.68	0.00	0.00	0.00	0.00
Diaphragm	1974	0.61	1.00	1.64	0.00	0.00
Diaphragm	1975	0.53	1.00	1.88	0.00	0.00
Diaphragm	1976	0.56	1.50	2.66	0.00	0.00
Diaphragm	1979	0.68	1.50	2.19	0.00	0.00
All types	1987	0.59	0.00	0.00	0.00	0.00
LATIN AMERICA/CARIBBEAN						
Chile						
All types	1976	10.00	0.00	0.00	0.00	0.00
Colombia						
IUD insertion	1980	40.82	0.00	0.00	0.00	0.00
Orals	1980	40.82	0.00	0.00	0.00	0.00
Condoms (packet)	1980	40.82	0.00	0.00	0.00	0.00
Sterilization (all)	1980	40.82	200.00–400.00	4.90–9.80	0.00	0.00
All types	1974	2.32	0.00	0.00	0.00	0.00
All types	1976	29.85	0.00	0.00	0.00	0.00
All types	1977	37.04	0.00	0.00	0.00	0.00
All types	1987	252.00	0.00	0.00	0.00	0.00
Colombia (PROFAMILIA)						
IUD insertion	1980	40.82	150.00	3.68	0.00	0.00
Orals	1980	40.82	25.00	0.61	0.00	0.00
Condoms (1)	1980	40.82	5.00	0.12	0.00	0.00
Sterilization (all)	1980	40.82	800.00	19.60	0.00	0.00
Costa Rica						
Orals	1984	46.51	0.00–10.00[c]	0.00–0.21[c]	0.00	0.00
All types (except orals)	1984	46.51	0.00	0.00	0.00	0.00
All types	1975	8.33	0.00	0.00	0.00	0.00
All types	1976	8.33	0.00	0.00	0.00	0.00
All types	1987	66.97	0.00	0.00	0.00	0.00
Dominican Republic						
All types	1974	1.00	0.00	0.00	0.00	0.00
All types	1976	1.00	0.00	0.00	0.00	0.00

Table 14. Charges and Payments to Acceptors of Family Planning Services and Supplies *(continued)*

Country and supply or service	Year	Exchange rate (U.S.$)	Fee charged		Payment given	
			Local currency	U.S.$	Local currency	U.S.$
Dominican Republic *(continued)*						
All types	1977	1.00	0.00	0.00	0.00	0.00
All types	1978	1.00	0.00	0.00	0.00	0.00
El Salvador						
All types	1976	2.50	0.00	0.00	0.00	0.00
All types	1980	2.50	0.00	0.00	0.00	0.00
All types	1984	2.50	0.00	0.00	0.00	0.00
Guatemala[d]						
IUD insertion	1971	1.00	0.25	0.25	0.00	0.00
IUD insertion	1972	1.00	0.25	0.25	0.00	0.00
IUD insertion	1974	1.00	0.25	0.25	0.00	0.00
Orals	1971	1.00	0.15	0.15	0.00	0.00
Orals	1972	1.00	0.15	0.15	0.00	0.00
Orals	1974	1.00	0.15	0.15	0.00	0.00
Injectables	1971	1.00	0.50	0.50	0.00	0.00
Injectables	1972	1.00	0.50	0.50	0.00	0.00
Injectables	1974	1.00	0.50	0.50	0.00	0.00
Haiti						
All types	1987	5.00	0.00	0.00	0.00	0.00
Honduras						
IUD insertion	1987	2.00	0.00	0.00	0.00	0.00
Orals	1987	2.00	0.00	0.00	0.00	0.00
Injectables	1987	2.00	0.00	0.00	0.00	0.00
Condoms	1987	2.00	0.00	0.00	0.00	0.00
Female sterilization	1987	2.00	30.00	15.00	0.00	0.00
Male sterilization	1987	2.00	30.00	15.00	0.00	0.00
Spermicides	1987	2.00	0.00	0.00	0.00	0.00
All types	1971	2.00	0.00	0.00	0.00	0.00
Jamaica						
IUD insertion	1970	0.83	0.00	0.00	0.00	0.00
IUD insertion	1971	0.78	0.00	0.00	0.00	0.00
IUD insertion	1972	0.91	0.00	0.00	0.00	0.00
Orals	1970	0.83	0.10	0.12	0.00	0.00
Orals	1971	0.78	0.10	0.13	0.00	0.00
Orals	1972	0.91	0.10	0.11	0.00	0.00
Orals	1975	0.90	0.10[e]	0.11[e]	0.00	0.00
Orals	1976	0.90	0.10[e]	0.11[e]	0.00	0.00
Condoms	1970	0.83	0.00	0.00	0.00	0.00
Condoms	1971	0.78	0.00	0.00	0.00	0.00
Condoms	1972	0.91	0.00	0.00	0.00	0.00
Diaphragm	1970	0.83	0.10	0.12	0.00	0.00
Diaphragm	1971	0.78	0.10	0.13	0.00	0.00
Diaphragm	1972	0.91	0.00	0.00	0.00	0.00
Spermicide (tablets)	1970	0.83	0.10	0.12	0.00	0.00
Spermicide (tablets)	1971	0.78	0.10	0.13	0.00	0.00
Spermicide (tablets)	1972	0.91	0.00	0.00	0.00	0.00
All types	1974	0.90	0.00	0.00	0.00	0.00
Paraguay						
All types	1987	550.00	0.00	0.00	0.00	0.00
Peru						
All types	1987	15.89	3.00	0.19	0.00	0.00
Puerto Rico						
All types	1976	1.00	0.00	0.00	0.00	0.00
All types	1987	1.00	u	u	0.00	0.00
Trinidad and Tobago						
All types	1984	23.81	0.00	0.00	0.00	0.00

Table 14. Charges and Payments to Acceptors of Family Planning Services and Supplies *(continued)*

Country and supply or service	Year	Exchange rate (U.S.$)	Fee charged Local currency	Fee charged U.S.$	Payment given Local currency	Payment given U.S.$
Venezuela						
All types	1972	4.35	0.00	0.00	0.00	0.00
All types	1975	4.35	0.00	0.00	0.00	0.00
MIDDLE EAST/NORTH AFRICA						
Egypt						
IUD insertion	1968	0.43	0.30[f]	0.70[f]	0.00	0.00
IUD insertion	1969	0.43	0.30[f]	0.70[f]	0.00	0.00
IUD insertion	1970	0.43	0.00	0.00	0.00	0.00
IUD insertion	1971	0.43	0.00	0.00	0.00	0.00
IUD insertion	1972	0.43	0.00	0.00	0.00	0.00
IUD insertion	1974	0.43	0.00	0.00	0.00	0.00
IUD insertion	1975	0.43	0.00	0.00	0.00	0.00
IUD insertion	1977	0.43	0.00	0.00	0.00	0.00
IUD insertion	1979	0.70	0.00	0.00	0.00	0.00
IUD insertion	1981	0.69	0.00	0.00	0.00	0.00
IUD insertion	1984	0.83	1.00	1.20	0.00	0.00
Orals	1968	0.43	0.10	0.23	0.00	0.00
Orals	1969	0.43	0.10	0.23	0.00	0.00
Orals	1970	0.43	0.05	0.12	0.00	0.00
Orals	1971	0.43	0.05	0.12	0.00	0.00
Orals	1972	0.43	0.05	0.12	0.00	0.00
Orals	1974	0.43	0.05	0.12	0.00	0.00
Orals	1975	0.43	0.05	0.12	0.00	0.00
Orals	1977	0.43	0.05	0.12	0.00	0.00
Orals	1979	0.70	0.05	0.07	0.00	0.00
Orals	1981	0.69	0.05	0.07	0.00	0.00
Orals	1984	0.83	0.05	0.06	0.00	0.00
Condoms (10)	1974	0.43	0.05	0.12	0.00	0.00
Condoms (10)	1975	0.43	0.05	0.12	0.00	0.00
Condoms (10)	1977	0.43	0.05	0.12	0.00	0.00
Condoms (10)	1979	0.70	0.05	0.07	0.00	0.00
Condoms (10)	1981	0.69	0.05	0.07	0.00	0.00
Condoms (10)	1984	0.83	0.20	0.24	0.00	0.00
Female sterilization	1968	0.43	0.00	0.00	0.00	0.00
Female sterilization	1969	0.43	0.00	0.00	0.00	0.00
Female sterilization	1970	0.43	0.00	0.00	0.00	0.00
Female sterilization	1971	0.43	0.00	0.00	0.00	0.00
Male sterilization	1968	0.43	0.00	0.00	0.00	0.00
Male sterilization	1969	0.43	0.00	0.00	0.00	0.00
Male sterilization	1970	0.43	0.00	0.00	0.00	0.00
Diaphragm	1974	0.43	0.00	0.00	0.00	0.00
Diaphragm	1975	0.43	0.00	0.00	0.00	0.00
Diaphragm	1977	0.43	0.00	0.00	0.00	0.00
Diaphragm	1979	0.70	0.00	0.00	0.00	0.00
Diaphragm	1981	0.69	0.00	0.00	0.00	0.00
Diaphragm	1984	0.83	0.25	0.30	0.00	0.00
All types	1987	1.43	0.00	0.00	0.00	0.00
Iran						
IUD insertion	1968	75.19	0.00	0.00	0.00	0.00
IUD insertion	1969	75.19	0.00	0.00	0.00	0.00
IUD insertion	1970	75.19	0.00	0.00	0.00	0.00
IUD insertion	1987	74.00	0.00	0.00	0.00	0.00
Orals	1968	75.19	10.00	0.13	0.00	0.00
Orals	1969	75.19	10.00	0.13	0.00	0.00
Orals	1970	75.19	10.00	0.13	0.00	0.00
Orals	1987	74.00	0.00	0.00	0.00	0.00
Condoms	1987	74.00	0.00	0.00	0.00	0.00
Female sterilization	1968	75.19	0.00	0.00	0.00	0.00
Female sterilization	1969	75.19	0.00	0.00	0.00	0.00
Female sterilization	1970	75.19	0.00	0.00	0.00	0.00
Male sterilization	1968	75.19	0.00	0.00	0.00	0.00
Male sterilization	1969	75.19	0.00	0.00	0.00	0.00
Male sterilization	1970	75.19	0.00	0.00	0.00	0.00
All types	1971	75.19	0.00–18.00[c]	0.00–0.25[c]	0.00	0.00
All types	1972	68.49	0.00	0.00	0.00	0.00

Table 14. Charges and Payments to Acceptors of Family Planning Services and Supplies *(continued)*

Country and supply or service	Year	Exchange rate (U.S.$)	Fee charged Local currency	Fee charged U.S.$	Payment given Local currency	Payment given U.S.$
Iran *(continued)*						
All types	1974	67.57	0.00	0.00	0.00	0.00
All types	1975	66.67	0.00	0.00	0.00	0.00
All types	1976	71.43	0.00	0.00	0.00	0.00
All types	1977	71.43	0.00	0.00	0.00	0.00
Jordan						
IUD insertion	1987	0.21	2.00	9.68	0.00	0.00
Orals	1987	0.21	0.00	0.00	0.00	0.00
Morocco						
All types	1972	4.55	0.00	0.00	0.00	0.00
All types	1974	4.55	0.00	0.00	0.00	0.00
All types	1975	3.85	0.00	0.00	0.00	0.00
All types	1987	8.70	0.00	0.00	0.00	0.00
Tunisia						
Female sterilization	1975	0.40	0.00	0.00	5.00	12.50
Female sterilization	1976	0.38	0.00	0.00	5.00	13.00
Female sterilization	1977	0.41	0.00	0.00	5.00	11.65
All types	1974	0.40	0.00	0.00	0.00	0.00
All types (including abortion)	1975	0.40	0.00	0.00	0.00	0.00
All types (including abortion)	1976	0.38	0.00	0.00	0.00	0.00
All types (including abortion)	1977	0.41	0.00	0.00	0.00	0.00
Turkey						
IUD insertion	1973	9.09	0.00	0.00	0.00	0.00
IUD insertion	1975	14.71	0.00	0.00	0.00	0.00
IUD insertion	1987	820.00	0.00	0.00	0.00	0.00
Orals	1973	9.09	0.00	0.00	0.00	0.00
Orals	1975	14.71	0.00	0.00	0.00	0.00
Orals	1987	820.00	0.00	0.00	0.00	0.00
Condoms	1987	820.00	0.00	0.00	0.00	0.00
Sterilization (all)	1987	820.00	1640.00	2.00	0.00	0.00
Diaphragm	1987	820.00	0.00	0.00	0.00	0.00
All types	1987	0.80	0.00	0.00	0.00	0.00
ASIA						
Bangladesh						
IUD insertion	1972	7.14	0.00	0.00	0.00	0.00
IUD insertion	1974	7.52	0.00	0.00	0.00	0.00
IUD insertion	1987	31.00	0.00	0.00	15.00	0.48
Orals	1972	7.14	0.25	0.04	0.00	0.00
Orals	1987	31.00	0.00	0.00	0.00	0.00
Condoms	1987	31.00	0.00	0.00	0.00	0.00
Injectables	1987	31.00	0.00	0.00	0.00	0.00
Condoms (12)	1972	7.14	0.30	0.04	0.00	0.00
Sterilization	1987	31.00	0.00	0.00	175.00	5.64
Female sterilization	1981	14.08	0.00	0.00	83.00	5.89
Male sterilization	1972	7.14	0.00	0.00	0.00	0.00
Male sterilization	1976	14.93	0.00	0.00	15.00[g]	1.00[g]
Male sterilization	1977	14.93	0.00	0.00	15.00[g]	1.00[g]
Male sterilization	1981	14.08	0.00	0.00	96.00	6.82
Diaphragm	1987	31.00	0.00	0.00	0.00	0.00
Foam (vial)	1972	7.14	1.00	0.14	0.00	0.00
Spermicides	1987	31.00	0.00	0.00	0.00	0.00
All types	1976	14.93	0.00	0.00	0.00	0.00
All types	1977	14.93	0.00	0.00	0.00	0.00
China						
All types	1987	3.73	0.00	0.00	0.00	0.00
Hong Kong						
IUD insertion	1971	5.56	0.00	0.00	0.00	0.00
IUD insertion	1972	5.68	0.00	0.00	0.00	0.00
IUD insertion	1974	5.00	0.00	0.00	0.00	0.00
IUD insertion	1975	5.00	10.00[c]	2.00[c]	0.00	0.00

Table 14. Charges and Payments to Acceptors of Family Planning Services and Supplies *(continued)*

Country and supply or service	Year	Exchange rate (U.S.$)	Fee charged		Payment given	
			Local currency	U.S.$	Local currency	U.S.$
Hong Kong *(continued)*						
IUD insertion	1977	4.55	5.00[c]	1.10[c]	0.00	0.00
IUD insertion	1979	4.55	25.00[c]	5.50[c]	0.00	0.00
IUD insertion	1981	5.26	25.00[c]	4.75[c]	0.00	0.00
IUD insertion	1984	7.14	0.00–50.00	0.00–6.85	0.00	0.00
IUD insertion	1987	7.80	50.00	6.41	0.00	0.00
Orals	1971	5.56	1.00	0.18	0.00	0.00
Orals	1972	5.68	1.00[c]	0.18[c]	0.00	0.00
Orals	1974	5.00	1.50–2.00[c]	0.30–0.40[c]	0.00	0.00
Orals	1975	5.00	2.00[c]	0.40[c]	0.00	0.00
Orals	1977	4.55	2.00[c]	0.44[c]	0.00	0.00
Orals	1979	4.55	3.00[c]	0.66[c]	0.00	0.00
Orals	1981	5.26	3.00[c]	0.57[c]	0.00	0.00
Orals	1984	7.14	0.00–4.00	0.00–0.55	0.00	0.00
Orals	1987	7.80	4.0–5.000	0.51–0.64	0.00	0.00
Injectables (12-week)	1971	5.56	5.00	0.90	0.00	0.00
Injectables (12-week)	1972	5.68	5.00[c]	0.88[c]	0.00	0.00
Injectables (12-week)	1974	5.00	3.00–5.00[c]	0.60–1.40[c]	0.00	0.00
Injectables (12-week)	1975	5.00	7.00[c]	1.40[c]	0.00	0.00
Injectables (12-week)	1977	4.55	5.00[c]	1.10[c]	0.00	0.00
Injectables (12-week)	1979	4.55	7.00[c]	1.54[c]	0.00	0.00
Injectables (12-week)	1981	5.26	7.00[c]	1.33[c]	0.00	0.00
Injectables	1984	7.14	0.00–10.00	0.00–1.37	0.00	0.00
Injectables	1987	7.80	10.00	1.28	0.00	0.00
Condoms (9)	1971	5.56	1.00	0.18	0.00	0.00
Condoms (9)	1972	5.68	1.00[c]	0.18[c]	0.00	0.00
Condoms (9)	1974	5.00	1.00–1.50[c]	0.20–0.30[c]	0.00	0.00
Condoms (9)	1975	5.00	2.00[c]	0.40[c]	0.00	0.00
Condoms (9)	1977	4.55	2.00[c]	0.44[c]	0.00	0.00
Condoms (9)	1979	4.55	1.50–3.00[c]	0.33–0.66[c]	0.00	0.00
Condoms (9)	1981	5.26	3.00[c]	0.57[c]	0.00	0.00
Condoms (12)	1984	7.14	0.00–10.00	0.00–1.37	0.00	0.00
Condoms (12)	1987	7.80	6.00–10.00	0.76–1.28	0.00	0.00
Female sterilization	1977	4.55	100.00[c]	22.00[c]	0.00	0.00
Female sterilization	1979	4.55	500.00[c]	110.00[c]	0.00	0.00
Female sterilization	1981	5.26	250.00[c]	47.50[c]	0.00	0.00
Female sterilization	1984	7.14	0.00–250.00	0.00–34.25	0.00	0.00
Female sterilization	1987	7.80	250.00	32.05	0.00	0.00
Male sterilization	1974	5.00	25.00–50.00[c]	5.00–10.00[c]	0.00	0.00
Male sterilization	1975	5.00	100.00[c]	20.00[c]	0.00	0.00
Male sterilization	1977	4.55	100.00[c]	22.00[c]	0.00	0.00
Male sterilization	1979	4.55	200.00[c]	44.00[c]	0.00	0.00
Male sterilization	1981	5.26	200.00[c]	38.00[c]	0.00	0.00
Male sterilization	1984	7.14	0.00–200.00	0.00–27.40	0.00	0.00
Male sterilization	1987	7.80	200.00	25.64	0.00	0.00
Diaphragm	1971	5.56	4.00	0.72	0.00	0.00
Diaphragm	1972	5.68	4.00[c]	0.70[c]	0.00	0.00
Diaphragm	1974	5.00	5.00[c]	1.00[c]	0.00	0.00
Diaphragm	1975	5.00	5.00[c]	1.00[c]	0.00	0.00
Diaphragm	1977	4.55	5.00[c]	1.10[c]	0.00	0.00
Diaphragm	1979	4.55	5.00–8.00[c]	1.10–1.76[c]	0.00	0.00
Diaphragm	1981	5.26	8.00[c]	1.52[c]	0.00	0.00
Diaphragm	1984	7.14	0.00–50.00	0.00–6.85	0.00	0.00
Diaphragm	1987	7.80	50.00	6.41	0.00	0.00
Aerosol foam	1979	4.55	3.00[c]	0.66[c]	0.00	0.00
Aerosol foam	1981	5.26	3.00[c]	0.57[c]	0.00	0.00
Aerosol foam	1984	7.14	0.00–5.00	0.00–0.68	0.00	0.00
Spermicides	1987	7.80	8.00	1.06	0.00	0.00
India						
IUD insertion	1968	7.69	0.00	0.00	5.00[h]	0.67[h]
IUD insertion	1969	7.69	0.00	0.00	5.00[h]	0.67[h]
IUD insertion	1970	7.52	0.00	0.00	5.00[h]	0.67[h]
IUD insertion	1972	7.30	0.00	0.00	5.00[h]	0.69[h]
IUD insertion	1974	7.30	0.00	0.00	5.00	0.69
IUD insertion	1975	8.20	0.00	0.00	6.00	0.73
IUD insertion	1976	8.77	0.00	0.00	0.00	0.00

Table 14. Charges and Payments to Acceptors of Family Planning Services and Supplies *(continued)*

Country and supply or service	Year	Exchange rate (U.S.$)	Fee charged Local currency	Fee charged U.S.$	Payment given Local currency	Payment given U.S.$
India *(continued)*						
IUD insertion	1977	9.09	0.00	0.00	6.00	0.66
IUD insertion	1978	7.94	0.00	0.00	6.00	0.76
IUD insertion	1980	7.75	0.00	0.00	6.00	0.77
IUD insertion	1982	10.00	0.00	0.00	9.00	0.90
IUD insertion	1987	13.12	0.00	0.00	9.00	0.68
Orals	1968	7.69	0.00	0.00	0.00	0.00
Orals	1969	7.69	0.00	0.00	0.00	0.00
Orals	1970	7.52	0.00	0.00	0.00	0.00
Condoms	1968	7.69	0.00[i]	0.00[i]	0.00	0.00
Condoms	1969	7.69	0.00[i]	0.00[i]	0.00	0.00
Condoms	1970	7.69	0.00[i]	0.00[i]	0.00	0.00
Female sterilization	1968	7.69	0.00	0.00	40.00[h]	5.33[h]
Female sterilization	1969	7.69	0.00	0.00	40.00[h]	5.33[h]
Female sterilization	1970	7.52	0.00	0.00	15.00[h]	2.00[h]
Female sterilization	1972	7.30	0.00	0.00	15.00[h]	2.06[h]
Female sterilization	1974	7.30	0.00	0.00	15.00	2.06
Female sterilization	1975	8.20	0.00	0.00	25.00	3.05
Female sterilization	1976	8.77	0.00	0.00	150.00	17.10
Female sterilization	1977	9.09	0.00	0.00	70.00	7.70
Female sterilization	1978	7.94	0.00	0.00	70.00	8.82
Female sterilization	1980	7.75	0.00	0.00	70.00	9.03
Female sterilization	1982	10.00	0.00	0.00	100.00	10.00
Female sterilization	1987	13.12	0.00	0.00	100.00	7.62
Male sterilization	1968	7.69	0.00	0.00	10.00[h]	1.33[h]
Male sterilization	1969	7.69	0.00	0.00	10.00[h]	1.33[h]
Male sterilization	1970	7.52	0.00	0.00	10.00[h]	1.33[h]
Male sterilization	1972	7.30	0.00	0.00	35.00[h]	4.80[h]
Male sterilization	1974	7.30	0.00	0.00	10.00	1.33
Male sterilization	1975	8.20	0.00	0.00	20.00	2.44
Male sterilization	1976	8.77	0.00	0.00	150.00	17.10
Male sterilization	1977	9.09	0.00	0.00	70.00	7.70
Male sterilization	1978	7.94	0.00	0.00	70.00	8.82
Male sterilization	1980	7.75	0.00	0.00	70.00	9.03
Male sterilization	1982	10.00	0.00	0.00	100.00	10.00
Male sterilization	1987	13.12	0.00	0.00	100.00	7.62
Indonesia						
IUD insertion	1969	400.00	75.00–150.00	0.19–0.38	0.00	0.00
IUD insertion	1970	400.00	75.00–150.00	0.19–0.38	0.00	0.00
IUD insertion	1971	408.16	0.00	0.00	0.00	0.00
IUD insertion	1972	408.16	0.00	0.00	0.00	0.00
Orals	1969	400.00	16.70	0.04	0.00	0.00
Orals	1970	400.00	100.00	0.26	0.00	0.00
Orals	1971	408.16	0.00	0.00	0.00	0.00
Orals	1972	408.16	0.00	0.00	0.00	0.00
All types	1974	413.22	0.00	0.00	0.00	0.00
All types	1975	414.94	0.00	0.00	0.00	0.00
All types	1976	414.94	0.00	0.00	0.00	0.00
All types	1977	414.94	0.00	0.00	0.00	0.00
All types	1979	621.12	0.00	0.00	0.00	0.00
All types	1981	628.93	0.00	0.00	0.00	0.00
All types	1983	1010.10	0.00	0.00	0.00	0.00
Kampuchea						
IUD insertion	1974	370.37	110.00	0.30	0.00	0.00
Orals	1974	370.37	37.00	0.10	0.00	0.00
Injectables (3-month)	1974	370.37	110.00	0.30	0.00	0.00
Condoms	1974	370.37	0.00	0.00	0.00	0.00
Korea, Republic of						
IUD insertion	1968	270.27	0.00	0.00	0.00	0.00
IUD insertion	1969	270.27	0.00	0.00	0.00	0.00
IUD insertion	1970	270.27	0.00	0.00	0.00	0.00
IUD insertion	1971	384.62	0.00	0.00	0.00	0.00
IUD insertion	1973	400.00	0.00	0.00	0.00	0.00
IUD insertion	1974	400.00	0.00	0.00	0.00	0.00

Table 14. Charges and Payments to Acceptors of Family Planning Services and Supplies *(continued)*

Country and supply or service	Year	Exchange rate (U.S.$)	Fee charged		Payment given	
			Local currency	U.S.$	Local currency	U.S.$
Korea, Republic of *(continued)*						
IUD insertion	1975	476.19	0.00	0.00	0.00	0.00
IUD insertion	1976	476.19	0.00	0.00	0.00	0.00
IUD insertion	1977	476.19	0.00	0.00	0.00	0.00
IUD insertion	1981	666.67	600.00	0.90	0.00	0.00
IUD insertion	1987	861.00	2500.00	2.90	0.00	0.00
Orals	1968	270.27	30.00[j]	0.11[j]	0.00	0.00
Orals	1969	270.27	30.00[j]	0.11[j]	0.00	0.00
Orals	1970	270.27	30.00[j]	0.11[j]	0.00	0.00
Orals	1971	384.62	30.00[j]	0.08[j]	0.00	0.00
Orals	1973	400.00	30.00	0.08	0.00	0.00
Orals	1974	400.00	30.00	0.08	0.00	0.00
Orals	1975	476.19	30.00	0.06	0.00	0.00
Orals	1976	476.19	50.00	0.10	0.00	0.00
Orals	1977	476.19	50.00	0.10	0.00	0.00
Orals	1981	666.67	100.00	0.15	0.00	0.00
Orals	1987	861.00	200.00	0.23	0.00	0.00
Condoms	1973	400.00	0.00	0.00	0.00	0.00
Condoms	1974	400.00	0.00	0.00	0.00	0.00
Condoms	1975	476.19	0.00	0.00	0.00	0.00
Condoms	1976	476.19	0.00	0.00	0.00	0.00
Condoms (6)	1977	476.19	30.00	0.06	0.00	0.00
Condoms (6)	1981	666.67	100.00	0.15	0.00	0.00
Condoms (6)	1987	861.00	200.00	0.23	0.00	0.00
Sterilization	1974	400.00	0.00	0.00	0.00	0.00
Sterilization	1975	476.19	0.00	0.00	0.00	0.00
Sterilization	1977	476.19	0.00	0.00	0.00	0.00
Sterilization	1981	666.67	0.00	0.00	4100.00	6.15
Sterilization	1987	861.00	0.00	0.00	w	w
Female sterilization	1968	270.27	0.00	0.00	800.00	3.00
Female sterilization	1969	270.27	0.00	0.00	800.00	3.00
Female sterilization	1970	270.27	0.00	0.00	800.00	3.00
Female sterilization	1971	384.62	0.00	0.00	0.00	0.00
Female sterilization	1973	400.00	k	k	0.00	0.00
Female sterilization	1976	476.19	10000.00[l]	21.00[l]	5000.00	10.50
Male sterilization	1968	270.27	0.00	0.00	800.00	3.00
Male sterilization	1969	270.27	0.00	0.00	800.00	3.00
Male sterilization	1970	270.27	0.00	0.00	800.00	3.00
Male sterilization	1971	384.62	0.00	0.00	0.00	0.00
Male sterilization	1973	400.00	0.00	0.00	0.00	0.00
Male sterilization	1976	476.19	0.00	0.00	0.00	0.00
Menstrual regulation	1976	476.19	0.00	0.00	0.00	0.00
Other	1968	270.27	0.00	0.00	0.00	0.00
Other	1969	270.27	0.00	0.00	0.00	0.00
Other	1970	270.27	0.00	0.00	0.00	0.00
Other	1971	384.62	0.00	0.00	0.00	0.00
Laos						
IUD insertion	1972	588.24	500.00[e]	0.85[e]	0.00	0.00
Orals	1972	588.24	200.00[e]	0.34[e]	0.00	0.00
Condoms	1972	588.24	0.00	0.00	0.00	0.00
Malaysia (Peninsular)[o]						
IUD insertion	1968	3.00	0.00	0.00	0.00	0.00
IUD insertion	1969	3.00	0.00	0.00	0.00	0.00
IUD insertion	1970	3.00	0.00	0.00	0.00	0.00
IUD insertion	1971	3.00	0.00	0.00	0.00	0.00
IUD insertion	1972	3.94	0.00	0.00	0.00	0.00
IUD insertion	1973	4.17	0.00	0.00	0.00	0.00
IUD insertion	1977	4.00	0.00	0.00	0.00	0.00
IUD insertion	1979	2.17	3.00[e]	1.38[e]	0.00	0.00
IUD insertion	1981	2.22	0.00–3.00	0.00–1.35	0.00	0.00
IUD insertion	1987	2.50	5.00	2.00	0.00	0.00
Orals	1968	3.00	0.00–10.00	0.00–3.33	0.00	0.00
Orals	1969	3.00	0.00–10.00	0.00–3.33	0.00	0.00
Orals	1970	3.00	1.00	0.33	0.00	0.00
Orals	1971	3.00	1.00[e]	0.33[e]	0.00	0.00

Table 14. Charges and Payments to Acceptors of Family Planning Services and Supplies (continued)

Country and supply or service	Year	Exchange rate (U.S.$)	Fee charged		Payment given	
			Local currency	U.S.$	Local currency	U.S.$
Malaysia (Peninsular,[o] continued)						
Orals	1972	3.94	1.00[e]	0.25[e]	0.00	0.00
Orals	1973	4.17	1.00[e]	0.24[e]	0.00	0.00
Orals	1977	4.00	1.00[e]	0.25[e]	0.00	0.00
Orals	1979	2.17	1.00	0.46	0.00	0.00
Orals	1981	2.22	1.00	0.45	0.00	0.00
Orals	1987	2.50	1.60	0.64	0.00	0.00
Injectables	1987	2.50	4.00	1.60	0.00	0.00
Injectables	1979	2.17	1.00	0.46	0.00	0.00
Injectables	1981	2.22	1.00	0.45	0.00	0.00
Condoms	1970	3.00	0.10	0.03	0.00	0.00
Condoms	1971	3.00	0.10[e]	0.03[e]	0.00	0.00
Condoms	1972	3.94	0.10[e]	0.03[e]	0.00	0.00
Condoms	1973	4.17	0.10[e]	0.02[e]	0.00	0.00
Condoms (10)	1979	2.17	1.00	0.46	0.00	0.00
Condoms (10)	1981	2.22	1.00	0.45	0.00	0.00
Condoms (1)	1987	2.50	0.25	0.10	0.00	0.00
Female sterilization	1968	3.00	0.00	0.00	0.00	0.00
Female sterilization	1969	3.00	0.00	0.00	0.00	0.00
Female sterilization	1970	3.00	0.00	0.00	0.00	0.00
Female sterilization	1971	3.00	0.00	0.00	0.00	0.00
Female sterilization	1972	3.94	0.00	0.00	0.00	0.00
Female sterilization	1973	4.17	0.00	0.00	0.00	0.00
Female sterilization	1977	4.00	0.00	0.00	0.00	0.00
Female sterilization	1979	2.17	0.00[n]	0.00[n]	0.00	0.00
Female sterilization	1981	2.22	0.00	0.00	0.00	0.00
Female sterilization	1987	2.50	20.00–30.00[x]	8.00–12.00[x]	0.00	0.00
Male sterilization	1968	3.00	0.00	0.00	0.00	0.00
Male sterilization	1969	3.00	0.00	0.00	0.00	0.00
Male sterilization	1970	3.00	0.00	0.00	0.00	0.00
Male sterilization	1971	3.00	0.00	0.00	0.00	0.00
Male sterilization	1972	3.94	0.00	0.00	0.00	0.00
Male sterilization	1973	4.17	0.00	0.00	0.00	0.00
Male sterilization	1977	4.00	0.00	0.00	0.00	0.00
Male sterilization	1979	2.17	0.00[n]	0.00[n]	0.00	0.00
Male sterilization	1981	2.22	0.00	0.00	0.00	0.00
Male sterilization	1987	2.50	50.00[y]	20.00[y]	0.00	0.00
Diaphragm	1987	2.50	0.00	0.00	0.00	0.00
Spermicides	1987	2.50	0.00	0.00	0.00	0.00
Other	1968	3.00	0.00	0.00	0.00	0.00
Other	1969	3.00	0.00	0.00	0.00	0.00
All types	1975	4.48	0.00	0.00	0.00	0.00
All types	1976	4.00	0.00	0.00	0.00	0.00
Mongolia						
All types	1987	3.36	0.00	0.00	0.00	0.00
Nepal						
Orals	1974	10.00	0.50	0.05	0.00	0.00
Condoms (12)	1974	10.00	0.50	0.05	0.00	0.00
Sterilization	1987	21.50	0.00	0.00	100.00	4.65
All types	1976	10.53	0.00	0.00	0.00	0.00
All types	1977	12.50	0.00	0.00	0.00	0.00
All types (except sterilization)	1987	21.50	0.00	0.00	0.00	0.00
Pakistan						
IUD insertion	1968	4.76	0.00	0.00	2.00	0.42
IUD insertion	1969	4.76	0.00	0.00	0.00	0.00
IUD insertion	1970	4.76	0.00	0.00	0.00	0.00
IUD insertion	1972	10.00	0.50	0.05	0.00	0.00
IUD insertion	1974	10.00	0.50	0.05	0.00	0.00
IUD insertion	1980	9.71	0.00	0.00	0.00	0.00
Orals	1968	4.76	m	m	0.00	0.00
Orals	1969	4.76	m	m	0.00	0.00
Orals	1970	4.76	m	m	0.00	0.00
Orals	1980	9.71	1.00	0.10	0.00	0.00
Orals	1987	17.35	1.00	0.06	0.00	0.00

Table 14. Charges and Payments to Acceptors of Family Planning Services and Supplies *(continued)*

Country and supply or service	Year	Exchange rate (U.S.$)	Fee charged Local currency	Fee charged U.S.$	Payment given Local currency	Payment given U.S.$
Pakistan *(continued)*						
Condoms (12)	1968	4.76	0.25	0.05	0.00	0.00
Condoms (12)	1969	4.76	0.25	0.05	0.00	0.00
Condoms (12)	1970	4.76	0.25	0.05	0.00	0.00
Condoms (12)	1980	9.71	4.00	0.41	0.00	0.00
Condoms	1987	17.35	1.00	0.06	0.00	0.00
Sterilization	1987	17.35	0.00	0.00	50.00	2.88
Female sterilization	1968	4.76	0.00	0.00	25.00	5.25
Female sterilization	1969	4.76	0.00	0.00	25.00	5.25
Female sterilization	1970	4.76	0.00	0.00	25.00	5.25
Female sterilization	1972	10.00	0.00	0.00	20.00	2.00
Female sterilization	1974	10.00	0.00	0.00	20.00	2.00
Female sterilization	1980	9.71	0.00	0.00	0.00	0.00
Male sterilization	1968	4.76	0.00	0.00	20.00	4.20
Male sterilization	1969	4.76	0.00	0.00	20.00	4.20
Male sterilization	1970	4.76	0.00	0.00	20.00	4.20
Male sterilization	1972	10.00	0.00	0.00	15.00	1.50
Male sterilization	1974	10.00	0.00	0.00	15.00	1.50
Male sterilization	1980	9.71	0.00	0.00	0.00	0.00
Spermicide (tablets)	1968	4.76	0.25	0.05	0.00	0.00
Spermicide (tablets)	1969	4.76	0.25	0.05	0.00	0.00
Spermicide (tablets)	1970	4.76	0.25	0.05	0.00	0.00
Spermicide (bottle)	1987	17.35	5.00	0.29	0.00	0.00
Philippines						
All types[p]	1971	6.25	0.00	0.00	0.00	0.00
All types[p]	1972	6.25	0.00	0.00	0.00	0.00
All types[p]	1974	6.67	0.00	0.00	0.00	0.00
All types[p]	1976	7.14	0.00	0.00	0.00	0.00
All types[p]	1977	7.14	0.00	0.00	0.00	0.00
All types[p]	1978	7.14	0.00	0.00	0.00	0.00
All types	1980	7.69	0.00	0.00	0.00	0.00
All types	1983	12.50	0.00	0.00	0.00	0.00
All types	1987	20.50	0.00	0.00	0.00	0.00
Singapore						
IUD insertion[a,f]	1968	3.60	5.00	1.39	0.00	0.00
IUD insertion[a,f]	1969	3.60	5.00	1.39	0.00	0.00
IUD insertion[a,f]	1970	2.97	5.00	1.68	0.00	0.00
IUD insertion[a,f]	1971	3.03	5.00	1.65	0.00	0.00
IUD insertion	1972	2.70	5.00	1.85	0.00	0.00
IUD insertion	1974	2.50	5.00	2.00	0.00	0.00
IUD insertion	1975	2.33	5.00	2.15	0.00	0.00
IUD insertion	1976	2.50	5.00	2.00	0.00	0.00
IUD insertion	1977	2.44	5.00	2.05	0.00	0.00
IUD insertion	1979	2.22	5.00	2.25	0.00	0.00
IUD insertion	1981	2.13	5.00	2.35	0.00	0.00
IUD insertion: Loop	1984	2.13	5.00	2.35	0.00	0.00
IUD insertion: CuT	1984	2.13	30.00	14.08	0.00	0.00
Orals	1968	3.60	1.50	0.42	0.00	0.00
Orals	1969	3.60	1.50	0.42	0.00	0.00
Orals	1970	2.97	1.00	0.34	0.00	0.00
Orals	1971	3.03	1.00	0.33	0.00	0.00
Orals	1972	2.70	1.00	0.37	0.00	0.00
Orals	1974	2.50	1.00	0.40	0.00	0.00
Orals	1975	2.33	1.00	0.43	0.00	0.00
Orals	1976	2.50	1.00	0.40	0.00	0.00
Orals	1977	2.44	1.00	0.41	0.00	0.00
Orals	1979	2.22	1.00	0.45	0.00	0.00
Orals	1981	2.13	1.00	0.47	0.00	0.00
Orals	1984	2.13	1.00	0.47	0.00	0.00
Injectables	1984	2.13	5.00	2.35	0.00	0.00
Injectables	1975	2.33	2.50	1.08	0.00	0.00
Injectables	1976	2.50	2.50	1.00	0.00	0.00
Injectables	1977	2.44	2.50	1.02	0.00	0.00
Injectables	1979	2.22	2.50	1.12	0.00	0.00
Injectables	1981	2.13	2.50	1.18	0.00	0.00

Table 14. Charges and Payments to Acceptors of Family Planning Services and Supplies *(continued)*

Country and supply or service	Year	Exchange rate (U.S.$)	Fee charged Local currency	Fee charged U.S.$	Payment given Local currency	Payment given U.S.$
Singapore *(continued)*						
Condoms	1968	3.60	0.50	0.14	0.00	0.00
Condoms	1969	3.60	1.50	0.14	0.00	0.00
Condoms	1970	2.97	0.50	0.17	0.00	0.00
Condoms (12)	1971	3.03	1.00	0.33	0.00	0.00
Condoms (12)	1972	2.70	1.00	0.37	0.00	0.00
Condoms (12)	1974	2.50	1.00	0.40	0.00	0.00
Condoms (12)	1975	2.33	1.00	0.43	0.00	0.00
Condoms (12)	1976	2.50	1.00	0.40	0.00	0.00
Condoms (12)	1977	2.44	1.00	0.41	0.00	0.00
Condoms (12)	1979	2.22	1.00	0.45	0.00	0.00
Condoms (12)	1981	2.13	1.00	0.47	0.00	0.00
Condoms (10)	1984	2.13	1.00	0.47	0.00	0.00
Sterilization	1974	2.50	5.00	2.00	0.00	0.00
Sterilization	1975	2.33	5.00	2.15	0.00	0.00
Sterilization	1976	2.50	5.00	2.00	0.00	0.00
Sterilization	1977	2.44	5.00	2.05	0.00	0.00
Sterilization	1979	2.22	5.00	2.25	0.00	0.00
Sterilization	1981	2.13	5.00	2.35	0.00	0.00
Sterilization	1984	2.13	5.00	2.35	0.00	0.00
Female sterilization	1968	3.60	0.00	0.00	0.00	0.00
Female sterilization	1969	3.60	0.00	0.00	0.00	0.00
Female sterilization	1970	2.97	5.00	1.68	0.00	0.00
Female sterilization	1971	3.03	5.00	1.65	0.00	0.00
Female sterilization	1972	2.70	5.00	1.85	0.00	0.00
Male sterilization	1968	3.60	0.00	0.00	0.00	0.00
Male sterilization	1969	3.60	0.00	0.00	0.00	0.00
Male sterilization	1970	2.97	5.00	1.68	0.00	0.00
Male sterilization	1971	3.03	5.00	1.65	0.00	0.00
Male sterilization	1972	2.70	5.00	1.85	0.00	0.00
Diaphragm	1972	2.70	2.00	0.74	0.00	0.00
Diaphragm	1974	2.50	2.00	0.80	0.00	0.00
Diaphragm	1975	2.33	2.00	0.86	0.00	0.00
Diaphragm	1976	2.50	2.00	0.80	0.00	0.00
Diaphragm	1977	2.44	2.00	0.82	0.00	0.00
Diaphragm	1979	2.22	2.00	0.90	0.00	0.00
Diaphragm	1981	2.13	2.00	0.94	0.00	0.00
Diaphragm	1984	2.13	13.00	6.10	0.00	0.00
Spermicide (tube)	1984	2.13	3.00	1.41	0.00	0.00
Spermicide (tablets)	1974	2.50	1.00	0.40	0.00	0.00
Sri Lanka						
IUD insertion	1968	5.92	0.00	0.00	0.00	0.00
IUD insertion	1969	5.92	0.00	0.00	0.00	0.00
IUD insertion	1970	5.92	0.00	0.00	0.00	0.00
IUD insertion	1971	5.95	0.00	0.00	0.00	0.00
IUD insertion	1972	6.25	0.00	0.00	0.00	0.00
IUD insertion	1974	6.25	0.00	0.00	0.00	0.00
IUD insertion	1975	6.67	0.00	0.00	0.00	0.00
IUD insertion	1976	7.14	0.00	0.00	0.00	0.00
IUD insertion	1987	30.30	0.00	0.00	0.00	0.00
Orals	1968	5.92	0.75	0.13	0.00	0.00
Orals	1969	5.92	0.75	0.13	0.00	0.00
Orals	1970	5.92	0.75	0.13	0.00	0.00
Orals	1971	5.95	0.75	0.13	0.00	0.00
Orals	1972	6.25	0.75	0.12	0.00	0.00
Orals	1974	6.25	0.75	0.12	0.00	0.00
Orals	1975	6.67	0.75	0.11	0.00	0.00
Orals	1976	7.14	0.75	0.10	0.00	0.00
Orals	1987	30.30	0.50	0.02	0.00	0.00
Injectables	1987	30.30	0.00	0.00	0.00	0.00
Condoms	1968	5.92	0.05	0.01	0.00	0.00
Condoms	1969	5.92	0.05	0.01	0.00	0.00
Condoms	1970	5.92	0.05	0.01	0.00	0.00
Condoms	1971	5.95	0.05	0.01	0.00	0.00
Condoms	1972	6.25	0.05	0.01	0.00	0.00
Condoms	1974	6.25	0.05	0.01	0.00	0.00

Table 14. Charges and Payments to Acceptors of Family Planning Services and Supplies *(continued)*

Country and supply or service	Year	Exchange rate (U.S.$)	Fee charged Local currency	Fee charged U.S.$	Payment given Local currency	Payment given U.S.$
Sri Lanka *(continued)*						
Condoms	1975	6.67	0.05	0.01	0.00	0.00
Condoms	1976	7.14	0.05	0.01	0.00	0.00
Condoms (12)	1987	30.30	0.60	0.02	0.00	0.00
Sterilization	1972	6.25	0.00	0.00	0.00	0.00
Sterilization	1974	6.25	0.00	0.00	0.00	0.00
Sterilization	1975	6.67	0.00	0.00	0.00	0.00
Sterilization	1976	7.14	0.00	0.00	0.00	0.00
Sterilization	1983	25.00	0.00	0.00	0.00	0.00
Female sterilization	1968	5.92	0.00	0.00	0.00	0.00
Female sterilization	1969	5.92	0.00	0.00	0.00	0.00
Female sterilization	1970	5.92	0.00	0.00	0.00	0.00
Female sterilization	1971	5.95	0.00	0.00	0.00	0.00
Female sterilization	1987	30.30	0.00	0.00	500.00	16.50
Male sterilization	1968	5.92	0.00	0.00	0.00	0.00
Male sterilization	1969	5.92	0.00	0.00	0.00	0.00
Male sterilization	1970	5.92	0.00	0.00	0.00	0.00
Male sterilization	1971	5.95	0.00	0.00	0.00	0.00
Male sterilization	1987	30.30	0.00	0.00	500.00	16.50
Diaphragm	1975	6.67	1.50	0.22	0.00	0.00
Diaphragm	1976	7.14	1.50	0.21	0.00	0.00
Spermicide (tablets)	1968	5.92	0.05	0.01	0.00	0.00
Spermicide (tablets)	1969	5.92	0.05	0.01	0.00	0.00
Spermicide (tablets)	1970	5.92	0.05	0.01	0.00	0.00
Spermicide (tablets)	1971	5.95	0.05	0.01	0.00	0.00
Spermicide (tablets)	1972	6.25	0.05	0.01	0.00	0.00
Spermicide (tablets)	1974	6.25	0.05	0.01	0.00	0.00
Spermicide (tablets)	1975	6.67	0.05	0.01	0.00	0.00
Spermicide (tablets)	1976	7.14	0.05	0.01	0.00	0.00
Other	1983	25.00	0.00	0.00	0.00	0.00
Taiwan						
IUD insertion	1968	40.00	0.00–30.00q	0.00–0.75q	0.00	0.00
IUD insertion	1969	40.00	0.00–30.00q	0.00–0.75q	0.00	0.00
IUD insertion	1970	40.00	0.00–30.00q	0.00–0.75q	0.00	0.00
IUD insertion	1971	40.00	0.00–30.00q	0.00–0.75q	0.00	0.00
IUD insertion	1972	38.46	0.00–30.00q	0.00–0.78q	0.00	0.00
IUD insertion	1974	38.46	0.00–30.00q	0.00–0.78q	0.00	0.00
IUD insertion	1975	38.46	0.00–30.00q	0.00–0.78q	0.00	0.00
IUD insertion: Loop	1976	38.46	0.00–30.00	0.00–0.78	0.00	0.00
IUD insertion: Ota Ring	1976	38.46	50.00–80.00	1.30–2.08	0.00	0.00
IUD insertion: Loop	1977	38.46	0.00–30.00	0.00–0.78	0.00	0.00
IUD insertion: Ota Ring	1977	38.46	50.00–80.00	1.30–2.08	0.00	0.00
IUD insertion: Loop	1979	35.71	0.00–30.00	0.00–0.84	0.00	0.00
IUD insertion: Ota Ring	1979	35.71	50.00–80.00	1.40–2.24	0.00	0.00
IUD insertion: Loop	1981	35.71	0.00–30.00	0.00–0.84	0.00	0.00
IUD insertion: Ota Ring	1981	35.71	50.00–80.00	1.40–2.24	0.00	0.00
IUD insertion: Loop	1984	40.00	0.00–30.00	0.00–0.75	0.00	0.00
IUD insertion: CuT	1984	40.00	100.00	2.50	0.00	0.00
IUD insertion: Ota Ring	1984	40.00	50.00–80.00	1.25–2.00	0.00	0.00
IUD insertion: Loop	1987	40.00	0.00	0.00	0.00	0.00
IUD insertion: CuT	1987	40.00	100.00	2.50	0.00	0.00
IUD insertion: Ota Ring	1987	40.00	50.00	1.25	0.00	0.00
Orals	1968	40.00	10.00r	0.25r	0.00	0.00
Orals	1969	40.00	10.00r	0.25r	0.00	0.00
Orals	1970	40.00	1.50	0.04	0.00	0.00
Orals	1971	40.00	1.50	0.04	0.00	0.00
Orals	1972	38.46	5.00	0.13	0.00	0.00
Orals	1974	38.46	5.00	0.13	0.00	0.00
Orals	1975	38.46	10.00	0.26	0.00	0.00
Orals	1976	38.46	10.00	0.26	0.00	0.00
Orals	1977	38.46	10.00	0.26	0.00	0.00
Orals	1979	35.71	10.00	0.28	0.00	0.00
Orals	1981	35.71	10.00	0.28	0.00	0.00
Orals	1984	40.00	20.00	0.50	0.00	0.00
Orals	1987	40.00	20.00	0.50	0.00	0.00
Condoms (12)	1970	40.00	1.00	0.03	0.00	0.00

Table 14. Charges and Payments to Acceptors of Family Planning Services and Supplies (continued)

Country and supply or service	Year	Exchange rate (U.S.$)	Fee charged Local currency	Fee charged U.S.$	Payment given Local currency	Payment given U.S.$
Taiwan (continued)						
Condoms (12)	1971	40.00	1.00	0.03	0.00	0.00
Condoms (12)	1972	38.46	1.00	0.03	0.00	0.00
Condoms (12)	1974	38.46	2.50	0.06	0.00	0.00
Condoms (12)	1975	38.46	5.00	0.13	0.00	0.00
Condoms (12)	1976	38.46	5.00	0.13	0.00	0.00
Condoms (12)	1977	38.46	5.00	0.13	0.00	0.00
Condoms (12)	1979	35.71	5.00	0.14	0.00	0.00
Condoms (12)	1981	35.71	5.00	0.14	0.00	0.00
Condoms (12)	1984	40.00	10.00	0.25	0.00	0.00
Condoms (12)	1987	40.00	10.00	0.25	0.00	0.00
Female sterilization	1968	40.00	q	q	0.00	0.00
Female sterilization	1969	40.00	q	q	0.00	0.00
Female sterilization	1974	38.46	1200.00	31.20	0.00	0.00
Female sterilization	1975	38.46	1200.00	31.20	0.00	0.00
Female sterilization	1976	38.46	aa	15.60–26.00	0.00	0.00
Female sterilization	1977	38.46	aa	26.00–65.52	0.00	0.00
Female sterilization	1979	35.71	aa	14.00–42.00	0.00	0.00
Female sterilization	1981	35.71	1600.00[e]	44.80[e]	0.00	0.00
Female sterilization	1984	40.00	0.00–3000.00	0.00–75.00	0.00	0.00
Female sterilization	1987	40.00	0.00	0.00	0.00	0.00
Male sterilization	1968	40.00	q	q	0.00	0.00
Male sterilization	1969	40.00	q	q	0.00	0.00
Male sterilization	1974	38.46	600.00	15.60	0.00	0.00
Male sterilization	1975	38.46	600.00	15.60	0.00	0.00
Male sterilization	1976	38.46	aa	15.60–26.00	0.00	0.00
Male sterilization	1977	38.46	aa	13.00–31.72	0.00	0.00
Male sterilization	1979	35.71	800.00[e]	22.40[e]	0.00	0.00
Male sterilization	1981	35.71	700.00[e]	19.60[e]	0.00	0.00
Male sterilization	1984	40.00	0.00–2000.00	0.00–50.00	0.00	0.00
Male sterilization	1987	40.00	0.00	0.00	0.00	0.00
Thailand						
IUD insertion	1968	20.00	0.00[s]	0.00[s]	0.00	0.00
IUD insertion	1969	20.00	0.00[s]	0.00[s]	0.00	0.00
IUD insertion	1970	20.00	0.00[s]	0.00[s]	0.00	0.00
IUD insertion	1971	20.00	0.00–20.00	0.00–1.00	0.00	0.00
IUD insertion	1972	20.00	20.00[e]	1.00[e]	0.00	0.00
IUD insertion	1974	20.00	20.00[e]	1.00[e]	0.00	0.00
IUD insertion	1975	20.00	20.00[e]	1.00[e]	0.00	0.00
IUD insertion	1976	20.00	20.00[e]	1.00[e]	0.00	0.00
IUD insertion	1977	20.00	0.00	0.00	0.00	0.00
IUD insertion	1979	20.00	20.00[t]	1.00[t]	0.00	0.00
IUD insertion	1981	20.00	20.00[t]	1.00[t]	0.00	0.00
IUD insertion	1984	23.64	21.80–47.70[z]	0.92–2.02[z]	0.00	0.00
Orals	1968	20.00	0.00[s]	0.00[s]	0.00	0.00
Orals	1969	20.00	0.00[s]	0.00[s]	0.00	0.00
Orals	1970	20.00	0.00[s]	0.00[s]	0.00	0.00
Orals	1971	20.00	0.00–5.00	0.00–0.25	0.00	0.00
Orals	1972	20.00	5.00[e]	0.25[e]	0.00	0.00
Orals	1974	20.00	5.00[e]	0.25[e]	0.00	0.00
Orals	1975	20.00	5.00[e]	0.25[e]	0.00	0.00
Orals	1976	20.00	5.00[e]	0.25[e]	0.00	0.00
Orals	1977	20.00	0.00	0.00	0.00	0.00
Orals	1979	20.00	5.00[t]	0.25[t]	0.00	0.00
Orals	1981	20.00	0.00	0.00	0.00	0.00
Orals	1984	23.64	5.50–8.00[z]	0.23–0.34[z]	0.00	0.00
Injectables	1976	17.24	15.00[e]	0.75[e]	0.00	0.00
Injectables (3-month)	1977	20.00	15.00	0.75	0.00	0.00
Injectables	1981	20.00	15.00[t]	0.75[t]	0.00	0.00
Injectables	1984	23.64	14.80–48.90[z]	0.63–2.07[z]	0.00	0.00
Condoms (12)	1975	20.00	5.00[e]	0.25[e]	0.00	0.00
Condoms (12)	1976	20.00	5.00[e]	0.25[e]	0.00	0.00
Condoms (12)	1977	20.00	0.00	0.00	0.00	0.00
Condoms	1981	20.00	0.00	0.00	0.00	0.00
Condoms	1984	23.64	7.60[z]	0.32[z]	0.00	0.00
Female sterilization	1968	20.00	0.00	0.00	0.00	0.00

Country and supply or service	Year	Exchange rate (U.S.$)	Fee charged		Payment given	
			Local currency	U.S.$	Local currency	U.S.$
Thailand *(continued)*						
Female sterilization	1969	20.00	0.00	0.00	0.00	0.00
Female sterilization	1970	20.00	100.00–600.00	5.00–30.00	0.00	0.00
Female sterilization	1971	20.00	0.00–150.00	0.00–7.50	0.00	0.00
Female sterilization	1972	20.00	150.00[e]	7.50[e]	0.00	0.00
Female sterilization	1974	20.00	150.00[e]	7.50[e]	0.00	0.00
Female sterilization	1975	20.00	150.00[e]	7.50[e]	0.00	0.00
Female sterilization	1976	20.00	150.00[e]	7.50[e]	0.00	0.00
Female sterilization	1977	20.00	t	t	0.00	0.00
Female sterilization	1979	20.00	300.00[t]	15.00[t]	0.00	0.00
Female sterilization	1981	20.00	0.00	0.00	0.00	0.00
Female sterilization	1984	23.64	127.00–371.30[z]	5.37–15.71[z]	0.00	0.00
Male sterilization	1968	20.00	0.00	0.00	0.00	0.00
Male sterilization	1969	20.00	0.00	0.00	0.00	0.00
Male sterilization	1970	20.00	50.00–300.00	2.50–15.00	0.00	0.00
Male sterilization	1971	20.00	0.00–50.00	0.00–2.50	0.00	0.00
Male sterilization	1972	20.00	50.00[e]	2.50[e]	0.00	0.00
Male sterilization	1974	20.00	50.00[e]	2.50[e]	0.00	0.00
Male sterilization	1975	20.00	50.00[e]	2.50[e]	0.00	0.00
Male sterilization	1976	20.00	50.00[e]	2.50[e]	0.00	0.00
Male sterilization	1977	20.00	t	t	0.00	0.00
Male sterilization	1979	20.00	200.00[t]	10.00[t]	0.00	0.00
Male sterilization	1981	20.00	0.00	0.00	0.00	0.00
Male sterilization	1984	23.64	371.00[z]	15.69[z]	0.00	0.00
Vietnam						
All types	1987	80.00	0.00	0.00	0.00	0.00

u = unknown.

a. Includes complete follow-up service.

b. Annual subscription fee for any contraceptive supply during the year.

c. Free to acceptors in the social security system, who account for 53 percent of oral acceptors.

d. IUDs, orals, and injectables are offered free to those unable to pay. Approximately 80 percent of acceptors can afford to pay partial or total fees.

e. Offered free to those unable to pay.

f. In most cases, indigents are not charged.

g. Paid to acceptors to cover transportation costs.

h. In some states, acceptors may have to meet income requirements to receive payment.

i. Free at health centers and sold through commerical channels at subsidized prices.

j. Indigents pay 0–6 won (0–2.2 cents) for each oral cycle.

k. Cost of tubal ligation varies by hospital, but it is not free for most acceptors.

l. The government provides an additional 5000 won (U.S.$10.50) subsidy.

m. Sold commercially at low and variable prices.

n. Free to clients referred by the program to government hospitals.

o. Peninsular Malaysia excludes Sabah and Sarawak.

p. Although the service is free, clinics may request a "voluntary" contribution. On the other hand, in implementing Presidential Decree No. 148, the Department of Labor has issued rules and regulations to the effect that firms are expected to provide bonuses for contraceptive acceptance or continuation, based on the savings in finances and time resulting from employee participation in family planning activities.

q. Offered free to indigents and recent postpartum acceptors at all times, and to others during limited periods of the year.

r. This figure represents a service fee. Orals are given free to indigent IUD dropouts.

s. Donations of 10–20 baht (U.S.$0.50–$1.00) and 2–5 baht (U.S.$0.10–$0.25) are requested for IUDs and orals, respectively.

t. Free in rural outlets.

v. Three types of spermicides are available: Neo Sampoon (tube), for 20 cedis, or U.S.$0.06; Conceptrol (12 tablets), for 25 cedis, or U.S.$0.14; Delfen foam (box), for 60 cedis, or U.S.$0.34.

w. For low-income acceptors, payments are as follows: U.S.$330 if acceptor has one child, U.S.$110 if two, and U.S.$45 if three or more.

Table 14. Charges and Payments to Acceptors of Family Planning Services and Supplies *(continued)*

x. Postpartum program acceptors are charged $20.00 (U.S.$8.00); other acceptors are charged $30.00 (U.S.$12.00).

y. Procedures performed in government hospitals.

z. Free by regulation, but in many localities charges are common. Figures shown are from a 1984 national survey. See J. Knodel et al., *Thailand's Reproductive Revolution*, University of Wisconsin Press, Madison, 1987.

aa. Local currency equivalents to the U.S. dollar amounts shown are as follows: for female sterilization, $NT 600–1000 for 1976, $NT 1000–2520 for 1977, and $NT 500–1500 for 1979; for male sterilization, $NT 600–1000 for 1976, $NT 500–1220 for 1977.

Table 15. Payments to Personnel for Specified Family Planning Services, by Type of Service and Category of Worker

Country and type of service	Year	Exchange rate (U.S.$)	Cash payment in local currency			Cash equivalent in U.S.$		
			Physician	Nurse or midwife	Other[a]	Physician	Nurse or midwife	Other[a]
SUB-SAHARAN AFRICA								
Botswana								
Govt. program: all types	1987	1.59	0.00	0.00	0.00	0.00	0.00	0.00
Burkina Faso								
Govt. program: all types	1987	300.00	0.00	0.00	na	0.00	0.00	na
Burundi								
Govt. program: all types	1987	116.31	0.00	0.00	0.00	0.00	0.00	0.00
Côte d'Ivoire								
Govt. program: all types	1987	300.00	0.00	u	u	0.00	u	u
Ethiopia								
Govt. program: all types	1987	2.07	0.00	0.00	0.00	0.00	0.00	0.00
Ghana								
Govt. program: all types	1987	173.91	0.00	0.00	0.00	0.00	0.00	0.00
Clinic session	1972	1.26	10.00	0.00	0.00	7.94	0.00	0.00
Clinic session	1974	1.15	10.00	0.00	0.00	8.70	0.00	0.00
Clinic session	1975	1.15	10.00	0.00	0.00	8.70	0.00	0.00
Clinic session	1976	1.15	10.00	0.00	0.00	8.70	0.00	0.00
Clinic session	1977	1.15	10.00	0.00	0.00	8.70	0.00	0.00
Clinic session	1978	2.78	10.00	0.00	0.00	3.60	0.00	0.00
Salary (per month)	1972	1.26	0.00	113.00	50.00	0.00	89.72	39.70
Salary (per month)	1974	1.15	0.00	113.00	50.00	0.00	98.00	44.00
Salary (per month)	1975	1.15	0.00	113.00	50.00	0.00	98.00	44.00
Salary (per month)	1976	1.15	0.00	113.00	50.00	0.00	98.31	43.50
Salary (per month)	1977	1.15	0.00	113.00	50.00	0.00	98.31	43.50
Salary (per month)	1978	2.78	0.00	297.00	134.00	0.00	106.92	48.24
Kenya								
Govt. program: all types	1987	15.60	0.00	0.00	0.00	0.00	0.00	0.00
Lesotho								
Govt. program: all types	1987	0.50	0.00	0.00	u	0.00	0.00	u
Mauritius								
IUD insertion	1970	5.56	0.00	0.00	6.00	0.00	0.00	1.08
Orals	1970	5.56	0.00	0.00	6.00	0.00	0.00	1.08
All types (per month)	1975	5.00	2600.00	u	480.00	520.00	u	96.00
All types (per month)	1976	5.88	2500.00	u	400.00	425.00	u	68.00
All types (per month)	1977	6.67	2500.00	u	400.00	375.00	u	60.00
All types (per month)	1979	5.88	3000.00	u	400.00	510.00	u	68.00
All types (per month)	1981	7.69	4600.00	2000.00	1400.00	598.00	260.00	182.00
All types (per month)	1984	11.36	4600.00	2000.00	650–2000[b]	405.00	176.00	57–176[b]
All types	1988	12.70	0.00	0.00	0.00	0.00	0.00	0.00
Case recruitment	1975	5.00	u	u	20.00	u	u	4.00
Case recruitment	1976	5.88	u	u	20.00	u	u	3.40
Case recruitment	1977	6.67	u	u	20.00	u	u	3.00
Case recruitment	1979	5.88	u	u	20.00	u	u	3.40
Case recruitment: IUD, orals	1971	5.00	0.00	0.00	6.00	0.00	0.00	1.20
Case recruitment: IUD, orals	1973	5.00	u	u	6.00[c]	u	u	1.20[c]
Niger								
Govt. program: all types	1987	300.00	0.00	0.00	0.00	0.00	0.00	0.00
Nigeria								
Govt. program: all types	1987	4.00	0.00	0.00	0.00	0.00	0.00	0.00
Togo								
Govt. program: all types	1987	300.00	0.00	0.00	0.00	0.00	0.00	0.00
Uganda								
All types (per hour)	1974	7.14	40.00	20.00	0.00	5.60	2.80	0.00
Clinic session	1971	7.14	40.00	20.00	0.00	5.60	2.80	0.00

Table 15. Payments to Personnel for Specified Family Planning Services, by Type of Service and Category of Worker *(continued)*

Country and type of service	Year	Exchange rate (U.S.$)	Cash payment in local currency			Cash equivalent in U.S.$		
			Physician	Nurse or midwife	Other[a]	Physician	Nurse or midwife	Other[a]
Uganda *(continued)*								
Clinic session	1972	7.14	40.00	20.00	0.00	5.60	2.80	0.00
Salary (per month)	1974	7.14	0.00	0.00	300–650	0.00	0.00	42–91
Zimbabwe								
All types (per month)	1974	0.61	720–800	200.00	65.00	1181–1312	328.00	107.00
All types (per month)	1975	0.53	720–800	200.00	65.00	1346–1496	374.00	122.00
All types (per month)	1976	0.56	600–700	250.00	72.00	1062–1239	442.50	127.44
All types (per month)	1979	0.68	1200.00	310.00	136.00	1752.00	453.00	199.00
Govt. program: all types	1987	0.60	0.00	0.00	0.00	0.00	0.00	0.00
LATIN AMERICA/CARIBBEAN								
Bolivia								
All types (per month)	1976	20.00	5267.00	4242.00	0.00	263.35	212.10	0.00
All types (per month)	1977	20.00	4500.00[d]	4000.00	2500.00	225.00[d]	200.00	125.00
All types (per month)	1978	20.00	4500.00[d]	4000.00	2500.00	225.00[d]	200.00	125.00
Colombia								
Govt. program: all types	1987	242.00	0.00	0.00	0.00	0.00	0.00	0.00
Colombia (PROFAMILIA)								
IUD insertion	1987	242.00	0.00	0.00	0.00	0.00	0.00	0.00
Orals	1987	242.00	0.00	0.00	0.00	0.00	0.00	0.00
Male sterilization	1987	242.00	0.00	0.00	0.00	0.00	0.00	0.00
Female sterilization	1987	242.00	0.00	0.00	0.00	0.00	0.00	0.00
Condoms	1987	242.00	0.00	0.00	0.00	0.00	0.00	0.00
Spermicides	1987	242.00	0.00	0.00	0.00	0.00	0.00	0.00
Costa Rica								
Govt. program: all types	1987	66.97	0.00	0.00	0.00	0.00	0.00	0.00
Dominican Republic								
All types (per month)	1974	1.00	350.00	200.00	90.00	350.00	200.00	90.00
All types (per month)	1975	1.00	350.00[d]	200.00	110.00	350.00[d]	200.00	110.00
All types (per month)	1976	1.00	350.00[d]	350.00	110.00	350.00[d]	350.00	110.00
All types (per month)	1977	1.00	350.00[d]	275.00	110.00	350.00[d]	275.00	110.00
All types (per month)	1978	1.00	350.00[d]	200.00	110.00	350.00[d]	200.00	110.00
Guatemala								
All types	1971	1.00	3.75	100.00	165–250	3.75	100.00	165–250
APROFAM clinics (per hour)	1972	1.00	3.90	0.00	0.00	3.90	0.00	0.00
APROFAM clinics (per hour)	1974	1.00	3.90	0.00	0.00	3.90	0.00	0.00
MOH medical supervisor (per month)	1972	1.00	450.00	100.00	165–200	450.00	100.00	165–200
MOH medical supervisor (per month)	1974	1.00	450.00	100.00	165–200	450.00	100.00	165–200
Haiti								
Govt. program: all types	1987	5.00	0.00	0.00	0.00	0.00	0.00	0.00
Honduras								
IUD insertion	1987	2.00	0.00	0.00	na	0.00	0.00	na
Orals	1987	2.00	0.00	0.00	na	0.00	0.00	na
Male sterilization	1987	2.00	0.00	na	na	0.00	na	na
Female sterilization[r]	1987	2.00	0.00	na	na	0.00	na	na
Condoms	1987	2.00	0.00	0.00	na	0.00	0.00	na
Clinic session (per month)	1971	2.00	800.00	0.00	1200.00	400.00	0.00	600.00
Spermicides	1987	2.00	0.00	0.00	na	0.00	0.00	na
Jamaica								
Clinic session[e]	1969	8.33[f]	90.00	30.00	25.00	10.80	3.60	3.00
Clinic session[e]	1970	8.33	90.00	30.00	25.00	10.80	3.60	3.00
Clinic session[e]	1971	0.78	9.00	3.00	2.50	11.52	3.84	3.20
Clinic session	1974	0.90	12.93	3.00	2.50	14.00	3.33	2.78
Clinic session	1975	0.90	12.93	3.00	2.50	14.00	3.33	2.78
Clinic session: government	1972	0.91	9.00	3.00	2.50	9.90	3.30	2.75

Table 15. Payments to Personnel for Specified Family Planning Services, by Type of Service and Category of Worker *(continued)*

Country and type of service	Year	Exchange rate (U.S.$)	Cash payment in local currency			Cash equivalent in U.S.$		
			Physician	Nurse or midwife	Other[a]	Physician	Nurse or midwife	Other[a]
Jamaica *(continued)*								
Clinic session: private	1972	0.91	11.25	0.00	0.00	12.38	0.00	0.00
Mexico								
Govt. program: all types	1974	12.50	6240.00	0.00	1368.00	499.00	0.00	109.00
Govt. program: all types	1987	1416.43	0.00	0.00	0.00	0.00	0.00	0.00
Clinic session: private (per month)	1972	12.50	4500–6500	1600.00	0.00	360–520	128.00	0.00
Clinic session: private (per month)	1974	12.50	5000.00	2100.00	2300.00	400.00	168.00	184.00
Nicaragua								
All types (per month)	1972	6.99	1000–1400	500–700	300–500	143–200	72–100	43–72
All types (per month)	1974	6.99	1000–1400	500–700	300–500	143–200	72–100	43–72
Paraguay (CEPEP)								
IUD insertion	1987	549.45	0.00	0.00	500.00	0.00	0.00	0.91
Orals	1987	549.45	0.00	0.00	150.00	0.00	0.00	0.27
Male sterilization	1987	549.45	0.00	0.00	0.00	0.00	0.00	0.00
Female sterilization	1987	549.45	0.00	0.00	0.00	0.00	0.00	0.00
Condoms	1987	549.45	0.00	0.00	40.00	0.00	0.00	0.07
Injectables	1987	549.45	0.00	0.00	0.00	0.00	0.00	0.00
Spermicides	1987	549.45	0.00	0.00	0.00	0.00	0.00	0.00
Diaphragm	1987	549.45	0.00	0.00	0.00	0.00	0.00	0.00
Peru								
Govt. program: all types	1987	1.59	u	u	0.00	u	u	0.00
Peru (IPPF)								
IUD insertion	1987	1.59	u	u	2–8	u	u	0.11–0.44
Orals	1987	1.59	u	u	0.10–1.80	u	u	0.01–0.10
Condoms	1987	1.59	u	u	0.03–0.55	u	u	0.00–0.03
Spermicides	1987	1.59	u	u	1–4	u	u	0.06–0.22
Puerto Rico								
Sterilization: all	1976	1.00	50.00	0.00	0.00	50.00	0.00	0.00
Salary (per month)	1976	1.00	1405.00	555.00	0.00	1405.00	555.00	0.00
Venezuela								
Clinic session (per hour)	1972	4.35	25.00	15.00	0.00	5.75	3.45	0.00
Clinic session (per hour)	1975	4.35	25.00	15.00	0.00	5.75	3.45	0.00
Salary (per week)	1972	4.35	0.00	0.00	700.00	0.00	0.00	161.00
Salary (per week)	1975	4.35	0.00	0.00	700.00	0.00	0.00	161.00
MIDDLE EAST/NORTH AFRICA								
Egypt								
IUD insertion[g]	1968	0.43	1.00	0.00	0.30[i]	2.33	0.00	0.70[i]
IUD insertion[g]	1969	0.43	1.00	0.00	0.30[i]	2.33	0.00	0.70[i]
IUD insertion[g]	1970	0.43	0.50	0.25	0.25	1.15	0.58	0.58
IUD insertion	1971	0.43	0.50	0.25	0.25	1.15	0.58	0.58
IUD insertion	1972	0.43	0.50	0.25	0.25	1.15	0.58	0.58
IUD insertion	1974	0.43	0.50	0.25	0.25	1.15	0.58	0.58
IUD insertion	1975	0.43	0.50	0.25	0.25	1.15	0.58	0.58
IUD insertion	1977	0.43	0.50	0.25	0.25	1.15	0.58	0.58
IUD insertion	1978	0.43	0.50	0.25	0.25	1.15	0.58	0.58
IUD insertion	1984	0.83	0.50	0.25	0.25	0.60	0.30	0.30
Orals: rural areas[g]	1968	0.43	0.06	0.00	0.04	0.14	0.00	0.09
Orals: rural areas[g]	1969	0.43	0.06	0.00	0.04	0.14	0.00	0.09
Orals: rural areas[g]	1970	0.43	0.06	0.02	0.02	0.14	0.05	0.05
Orals: rural areas	1971	0.43	0.03	0.02	0.01	0.06	0.05	0.01
Orals: rural areas	1972	0.43	0.03	0.02	0.01	0.06	0.05	0.01
Orals: rural areas	1974	0.43	0.03	0.02	0.01	0.06	0.05	0.01
Orals: rural areas	1975	0.43	0.03	0.02	0.01	0.06	0.05	0.01
Orals: rural areas	1977	0.43	0.03	0.02	0.01	0.06	0.05	0.01
Orals: rural areas	1978	0.43	0.03	0.02	0.01	0.06	0.05	0.01
Orals: urban areas[g]	1968	0.43	0.05	0.00	0.05	0.12	0.00	0.12

Table 15. Payments to Personnel for Specified Family Planning Services, by Type of Service and Category of Worker (continued)

Country and type of service	Year	Exchange rate (U.S.$)	Cash payment in local currency			Cash equivalent in U.S.$		
			Physician	Nurse or midwife	Other[a]	Physician	Nurse or midwife	Other[a]
Egypt (continued)								
Orals: urban areas[g]	1969	0.43	0.05	0.00	0.05	0.12	0.00	0.12
Orals: urban areas[g]	1970	0.43	0.05	0.03	0.03	0.12	0.06	0.06
Orals: urban areas	1971	0.43	0.02	0.02	0.01	0.05	0.05	0.02
Orals: urban areas	1972	0.43	0.02	0.02	0.01	0.05	0.05	0.02
Orals: urban areas	1974	0.43	0.02	0.02	0.01	0.05	0.05	0.02
Orals: urban areas	1975	0.43	0.02	0.02	0.01	0.05	0.05	0.02
Orals: urban areas	1977	0.43	0.02	0.02	0.01	0.05	0.05	0.02
Orals: urban areas	1978	0.43	0.02	0.02	0.01	0.05	0.05	0.02
Orals (per cycle)	1984	0.83	0.02	0.02	0.01	0.02	0.02	0.01
Govt. program: all types	1987	14.29	w	w	w	w	w	w
Case recruitment[g,h]	1968	0.43	0.00	0.00	0.50	0.00	0.00	1.15
Case recruitment[g,h]	1969	0.43	0.00	0.00	0.50	0.00	0.00	0.12
Case recruitment[g]	1970	0.43	0.00	0.00	0.50	0.00	0.00	1.15
Case recruitment	1971	0.43	0.00	0.00	0.50	0.00	0.00	1.15
Case recruitment (at follow-up)[g,h]	1968	0.43	0.00	0.00	0.30	0.00	0.00	0.70
Case recruitment (at follow-up)[g,h]	1969	0.43	0.00	0.00	0.30	0.00	0.00	0.70
Case recruitment (at follow-up)[g,h]	1970	0.43	0.25	0.25	0.25	0.58	0.58	0.58
Case recruitment (at follow-up)	1971	0.43	0.25	0.25	0.25	0.58	0.58	0.58
Iran								
IUD insertion	1972	68.49	250.00	250.00	0.00	3.65	3.65	0.00
IUD insertion[k]	1975	66.67	250.00	250.00	0.00	3.75	3.75	0.00
IUD insertion	1987	74.00	0.00	0.00	0.00	0.00	0.00	0.00
Orals	1972	68.49	100.00	100.00	0.00	1.46	1.46	0.00
Orals	1987	74.00	0.00	0.00	0.00	0.00	0.00	0.00
Oral prescription[k]	1975	66.67	100.00	100.00	0.00	1.50	1.50	0.00
Male sterilization[k]	1975	66.67	1000.00	0.00	0.00	15.00	0.00	0.00
Female sterilization[k]	1975	66.67	2500.00	0.00	0.00	37.50	0.00	0.00
Condoms	1987	74.00	0.00	0.00	0.00	0.00	0.00	0.00
All types (per month)[j]	1971	75.19	y	y	y	379–757	192–384	53–192
Case recruitment: IUD[k]	1972	68.49	0.00	0.00	75.00	0.00	0.00	1.09
Case recruitment: IUD	1975	66.67	0.00	0.00	75.00	0.00	0.00	1.12
Case recruitment: orals[k]	1972	68.49	0.00	0.00	10.00	0.00	0.00	0.15
Case recruitment: orals[k]	1975	66.67	0.00	0.00	10.00	0.00	0.00	0.15
Case recruitment: sterilization	1975	66.67	0.00	0.00	150.00	0.00	0.00	2.25
Fieldwork (per month)[j]	1968	75.19	0.00	0.00	2520–4000	0.00	0.00	33–53
Fieldwork (per month)[j]	1969	75.19	0.00	0.00	2520–4000	0.00	0.00	33–53
Fieldwork (per month)[j]	1970	75.19	0.00	0.00	2520–4000	0.00	0.00	33–53
Salary (per month)	1976	71.43	50000.00	30000.00	10000.00	700.00	420.00	140.00
Salary supplement (per month)	1977	71.43	77000.00	45500.00	21000.00	1078.00	637.00	294.00
Iraq								
Salary (per month)	1987	0.31	50.00	20.00	15.00	161.00	64.40	48.30
Tunisia								
IUD insertion	1975	0.43	0.80	0.20	0.00	1.88	0.47	0.00
IUD insertion	1977	0.43	1.00	1.00	0.00	2.33	2.33	0.00
Male sterilization	1975	0.43	2.30	0.00	0.60	5.40	0.00	1.41
Male sterilization	1977	0.43	2.10	0.00	0.50	4.89	0.00	1.16
Female sterilization	1975	0.43	1.30	0.00	0.60	3.06	0.00	1.41
Female sterilization	1977	0.43	1.10	0.00	0.50	2.56	0.00	1.16
Abortion	1975	0.43	1.20	0.00	0.20	2.82	0.00	0.47
Abortion	1977	0.43	1.00	0.00	0.20	2.33	0.00	0.47
Govt. program: all types	1987	0.80	0.00	0.00	0.00	0.00	0.00	0.00
Turkey								
IUD insertion	1968	9.09	0.00	0.00	10.00	0.00	0.00	1.10
IUD insertion	1969	9.09	0.00	0.00	10.00	0.00	0.00	1.10
IUD insertion	1970	9.09	0.00	0.00	10.00	0.00	0.00	1.10
Govt. program: all types	1987	820.00	0.00	0.00	0.00	0.00	0.00	0.00
Case recruitment[h]	1968	9.09	0.00	0.00	5.00	0.00	0.00	0.55
Case recruitment[h]	1969	9.09	0.00	0.00	5.00	0.00	0.00	0.55
Case recruitment[h]	1970	9.09	0.00	0.00	5.00	0.00	0.00	0.55
Fieldwork	1968	9.09	0.00	0.00	5.00	0.00	0.00	0.55
Fieldwork	1969	9.09	0.00	0.00	5.00	0.00	0.00	0.55

Table 15. Payments to Personnel for Specified Family Planning Services, by Type of Service and Category of Worker *(continued)*

Country and type of service	Year	Exchange rate (U.S.$)	Cash payment in local currency			Cash equivalent in U.S.$		
			Physician	Nurse or midwife	Other[a]	Physician	Nurse or midwife	Other[a]
Turkey *(continued)*								
Fieldwork	1970	9.09	0.00	0.00	5.00	0.00	0.00	0.55
ASIA								
Bangladesh								
IUD insertion	1974	7.52	6.00	0.00	3.00	0.80	0.00	0.40
IUD insertion	1976	14.93	0.00	0.00	3.00	0.00	0.00	0.20
IUD insertion	1977	14.93	0.00	0.00	3.00	0.00	0.00	0.20
IUD insertion	1987	31.00	5.00	5.00	30.00	0.16	0.16	0.97
Orals	1987	31.00	0.00	0.00	0.00	0.00	0.00	0.00
Male sterilization	1981	14.08	16.00	10.00	na	1.14	0.71	na
Male sterilization	1987	31.00	20.00	20.00	45.00[v]	0.64	0.64	1.45
Female sterilization	1981	14.08	14.00	8.00	na	0.99	0.57	na
Female sterilization	1987	31.00	20.00	15.00	45.00[v]	0.64	0.48	1.45
Condoms	1987	31.00	0.00	0.00	0.00	0.00	0.00	0.00
Home visit for FP services	1972	7.14	0.00	0.00	110.00	0.00	0.00	15.40
Case recruitment: vasectomy	1972	7.14	0.00	0.00	15.00	0.00	0.00	2.10
FP supervisor (per month)	1972	7.14	0.00	0.00	400.00	0.00	0.00	56.00
Injectables	1987	31.00	0.00	0.00	0.00	0.00	0.00	0.00
Spermicide	1987	31.00	0.00	0.00	0.00	0.00	0.00	0.00
Diaphragm	1987	31.00	0.00	0.00	0.00	0.00	0.00	0.00
China								
IUD insertion	1987	3.73	0.00	0.00	0.00	0.00	0.00	0.00
Male sterilization	1987	3.73	0.00	0.00	0.00	0.00	0.00	0.00
Female sterilization	1987	3.73	0.00	0.00	0.00	0.00	0.00	0.00
Hong Kong								
Sterilization or subfertility	1984	7.30	250.00[l]	na	na	34.00[l]	na	na
Vasectomy clinic (per 3-hour session)	1974	5.00	200.00	0.00	0.00	40.00	0.00	0.00
Vasectomy clinic (per 3-hour session)	1975	5.00	200.00	0.00	557–1343	40.00	0.00	111–269
Vasectomy clinic (per month)	1974	5.00	0.00	0.00	457–927	0.00	0.00	91–185
Birth control services (per month)	1984	7.30	4870–18170	3160–7540	4870–21610	667–2489	433–1033	667–2961
All types (per month)	1974	5.00	1135–5395	659–1524	0.00	227–1079	132–305	0.00
All types (per month)	1975	5.00	1590–6910	942–2077	557–1098	318–1382	188–415	111–220
All types (per month)	1977	4.55	2000–7795	1210–2720	0.00	440–1715	266–598	0.00
All types (per month)	1979	4.55	2426–3816	1481–3155	0.00	534–839	326–694	0.00
All types (per month)	1981	5.26	3255–12830	2205–4645	0.00	618–2438	419–883	0.00
Govt. program: all types	1987	7.80	0.00	0.00	0.00	0.00	0.00	0.00
Clinics (per 3-hour session)	1977	4.55	60–200	0.00	0.00	13–44	0.00	0.00
Clinics (per 3-hour session)	1979	4.55	120–200	0.00	0.00	26–44	0.00	0.00
Clinics (per 3-hour session)	1981	5.26	250.00	0.00	0.00	48.00	0.00	0.00
Youth advisory/rape victim (per month)	1984	7.30	5120–12060	na	1780–6220	701–1652	na	244–852
Recruitment and motivation (per month)	1974	5.00	0.00	0.00	457–827	0.00	0.00	91–165
India								
IUD insertion	1968	7.52	2.00[m]	0.00	0.00	0.27[m]	0.00	0.00
IUD insertion	1969	7.52	2.00[m]	0.00	0.00	0.27[m]	0.00	0.00
IUD insertion	1970	7.52	2.00[m]	0.00	0.00	0.27[m]	0.00	0.00
IUD insertion	1972	7.30	2.00[m]	0.00	1.00	0.27[m]	0.00	0.14
IUD insertion	1974	7.30	2.00	0.00	1.00	0.27	0.00	0.14
Male sterilization	1972	7.30	10.00	0.00	3.00	1.37	0.00	0.41
Male sterilization	1974	7.30	10.00	0.00	3.00	1.37	0.00	0.41
Male sterilization	1987	13.12	u	u	15.00	u	u	1.14
Male sterilization in camp	1968	7.52	5.00[m]	0.00	0.00	0.63[m]	0.00	0.00
Male sterilization in camp	1969	7.52	5.00[m]	0.00	0.00	0.63[m]	0.00	0.00
Male sterilization in camp	1970	7.52	5.00[m]	0.00	0.00	0.63[m]	0.00	0.00
Male sterilization out of camp	1968	7.52	10.00[m]	0.00	0.00	1.33[m]	0.00	0.00
Male sterilization out of camp	1969	7.52	10.00[m]	0.00	0.00	1.33[m]	0.00	0.00
Male sterilization out of camp	1970	7.52	10.00[m]	0.00	3.00	1.33[m]	0.00	0.40
Female sterilization	1968	7.52	10.00[m]	0.00	0.00	1.33[m]	0.00	0.00
Female sterilization	1969	7.52	10.00[m]	0.00	0.00	1.33[m]	0.00	0.00

Table 15. Payments to Personnel for Specified Family Planning Services, by Type of Service and Category of Worker (continued)

Country and type of service	Year	Exchange rate (U.S.$)	Cash payment in local currency			Cash equivalent in U.S.$		
			Physician	Nurse or midwife	Other[a]	Physician	Nurse or midwife	Other[a]
India (continued)								
Female sterilization	1970	7.52	10.00[m]	0.00	5.00	1.33[m]	0.00	0.63
Female sterilization	1972	7.30	10.00	0.00	5.00	1.37	0.00	0.69
Female sterilization	1974	7.30	10.00	0.00	5.00	1.37	0.00	0.69
Female sterilization	1987	13.12	u	u	30.00	u	u	2.28
Case recruitment[h]	1968	7.52	0.00	0.00	2.00[n]	0.00	0.00	0.27[n]
Case recruitment[h]	1969	7.52	0.00	0.00	2.00[n]	0.00	0.00	0.27[n]
Case recruitment[h]	1970	7.52	0.00	0.00	2.00[n]	0.00	0.00	0.27[n]
Indonesia								
Case recruitment	1971	408.16	200.00	200.00	200.00	0.43	0.43	0.43
Case recruitment	1972	408.16	200.00	200.00	200.00	0.49	0.49	0.49
Case recruitment: IUD	1974	413.22	0.00	0.00	200.00	0.00	0.00	0.48
Case recruitment: orals	1974	413.22	0.00	0.00	100.00	0.00	0.00	0.24
Salary (per month)	1974	413.22	0.00	0.00	5000.00	0.00	0.00	12.00
Salary (per month)	1975	414.94	0.00	0.00	7500.00	0.00	0.00	18.08
Salary supplement (per month)	1976	414.94	5000.00	3750.00	0.00	12.05	9.04	0.00
Salary supplement (per month)	1977	414.94	5000.00	3750.00	2750.00	12.05	9.04	6.63
Salary supplement (per month)	1979	621.12	5000.00	3750.00	2750.00	8.05	6.04	4.43
Salary supplement (per month)	1981	628.93	5000.00	3750.00	2750.00	7.95	5.96	4.37
Kampuchea								
All types (per month)	1974	370.37	37500.00	25000.00	0.00	101.00	68.00	0.00
Korea, Republic of								
IUD insertion	1968	270.27	0.00	0.00	350.00	0.00	0.00	1.25
IUD insertion	1969	270.27	0.00	0.00	350.00	0.00	0.00	1.25
IUD insertion	1970	270.27	u	u	350.00	u	u	1.25
IUD insertion	1971	384.62	500.00	100.00	100.00	1.32	0.26	0.26
IUD insertion	1973	384.62	500.00	100.00	100.00	1.25	0.25	0.25
IUD insertion	1974	400.00	500.00	100.00	100.00	1.25	0.25	0.25
IUD insertion	1975	476.19	500.00	200.00	200.00	1.05	0.42	0.42
IUD insertion	1976	476.19	470.00	200.00	200.00	0.99	0.42	0.42
IUD insertion	1977	476.19	500.00	200.00	200.00	1.05	0.42	0.42
IUD insertion	1981	666.67	1800.00	na	na	2.70	na	na
IUD insertion	1987	861.00	5000.00	0.00	0.00	5.81	0.00	0.00
IUD follow-up	1968	270.27	0.00	0.00	95.00	0.00	0.00	0.35
IUD follow-up	1969	270.27	0.00	0.00	95.00	0.00	0.00	0.35
IUD follow-up	1970	270.27	u	u	95.00	u	u	0.35
Orals	1971	384.62	300.00	u	u	0.79	u	u
Orals	1987	0.00	0.00	0.00	0.00	0.00	0.00	0.00
Medical screening for orals	1968	270.27	0.00	0.00	50.00	0.00	0.00	0.18
Medical screening for orals	1969	270.27	0.00	0.00	50.00	0.00	0.00	0.18
Medical screening for orals	1970	270.27	u	u	50.00	u	u	0.18
Sterilization: all	1973	400.00	3000.00	u	300.00	7.50	u	0.75
Sterilization: all	1974	400.00	3000.00	300.00	300.00	7.50	0.75	0.75
Sterilization: all	1975	476.19	3500.00	300.00	300.00	7.35	0.63	0.63
Male sterilization	1968	270.27	0.00	0.00	900.00	0.00	0.00	3.21
Male sterilization	1969	270.27	0.00	0.00	900.00	0.00	0.00	3.21
Male sterilization	1970	270.27	u	u	900.00	u	u	3.21
Male sterilization	1971	384.62	3000.00	u	300.00	7.89	u	0.79
Male sterilization	1976	476.19	3600.00	350.00	350.00	7.56	0.74	0.74
Male sterilization	1977	476.19	5000.00	350.00	350.00	10.50	0.74	0.74
Male sterilization	1978	476.19	6000.00	0.00	400.00	12.60	0.00	0.84
Male sterilization	1981	666.67	14000.00	na	na	21.00	na	na
Male sterilization	1987	861.00	38000.00	0.00	0.00	44.13	0.00	0.00
Female sterilization	1976	476.19	5000.00	0.00	0.00	10.50	0.00	0.00
Female sterilization	1977	476.19	15000.00	350.00	350.00	31.50	0.74	0.74
Female sterilization	1978	476.19	15000.00	0.00	400.00	31.50	0.00	0.84
Female sterilization	1981	666.67	17000.00	na	na	25.50	na	na
Female sterilization	1987	861.00	43000.00	0.00	0.00	49.94	0.00	0.00
Condoms	1987	0.00	0.00	0.00	0.00	0.00	0.00	0.00
Menstrual regulation	1976	476.19	5900.00	0.00	0.00	12.39	0.00	0.00
Menstrual regulation	1977	476.19	700.00	0.00	0.00	14.70	0.00	0.00
Menstrual regulation	1981	666.67	8800.00	na	na	13.20	na	na
Fieldwork for IUD	1968	270.27	0.00	0.00	50.00	0.00	0.00	0.18

Table 15. Payments to Personnel for Specified Family Planning Services, by Type of Service and Category of Worker *(continued)*

Country and type of service	Year	Exchange rate (U.S.$)	Cash payment in local currency			Cash equivalent in U.S.$		
			Physician	Nurse or midwife	Other[a]	Physician	Nurse or midwife	Other[a]
Korea, Republic of *(continued)*								
Fieldwork for IUD	1969	270.27	0.00	0.00	50.00	0.00	0.00	0.18
Fieldwork for IUD	1970	270.27	u	u	50.00	u	u	0.18
Fieldwork for male sterilization	1968	270.27	0.00	0.00	100.00	0.00	0.00	0.37
Fieldwork for male sterilization	1969	270.27	0.00	0.00	100.00	0.00	0.00	0.37
Fieldwork for male sterilization	1970	270.27	u	u	100.00	u	u	0.37
Laos								
All types (per 3-hour clinic session)	1972	588.24	3000.00	1500.00	0.00	5.10	2.55	0.00
Malaysia (Peninsular)								
All types (per month)	1977	4.00	1930.00	419.00	0.00	482.50	104.75	0.00
All types (per month)	1979	2.17	1900–2125	350–810	180–360	778–874	161–373	83–166
All types (per month)	1981	2.22	1360–2770	540–1120	300–510	612–1247	243–504	135–230
Govt. program: all types	1987	2.50	0.00	0.00	0.00	0.00	0.00	0.00
Nepal								
IUD insertion	1975	10.53	20.00	0.00	0.00	1.90	0.00	0.00
IUD insertion	1976	10.53	5.00	0.00	0.00	0.47	0.00	0.00
IUD insertion	1977	12.50	5.00	3.00	0.00	0.40	0.24	0.00
IUD insertion	1987	21.50	5.00	5.00	u	0.23	0.23	u
Sterilization	1975	10.53	5.00	0.00	0.00	0.47	0.00	0.00
Sterilization	1976	10.53	20.00	0.00	0.00	1.90	0.00	0.00
Male sterilization[j]	1968	10.08	0.00	0.00	20.00	0.00	0.00	1.98
Male sterilization[j]	1969	10.08	0.00	0.00	20.00	0.00	0.00	1.98
Male sterilization	1970	10.08	0.00	0.00	20.00	0.00	0.00	1.98
Male sterilization	1977	12.50	20.00	10.00	0.00	1.60	0.80	0.00
Male sterilization	1987	21.50	100.00[x]	u	u	4.65[x]	u	u
Female sterilization	1987	21.50	100.00[x]	u	u	4.65[x]	u	u
Female sterilization: laparoscopy	1977	12.50	20.00	20.00	0.00	1.60	1.60	0.00
Pakistan								
IUD insertion	1968	4.76	6.00	0.00	3.00	1.26	0.00	0.63
IUD insertion	1969	4.76	6.00	0.00	3.00	1.26	0.00	0.63
IUD insertion	1970	4.76	0.00	0.00	0.00	0.00	0.00	0.00
IUD insertion	1972	10.00	6.00	0.00	0.00	0.60	0.00	0.00
IUD insertion	1974	10.00	6.00	3.00	0.00	0.60	0.30	0.00
IUD insertion	1980	9.71	u	6.00	na	u	0.62	na
IUD insertion	1987	17.35	0.00	0.00	0.00	0.00	0.00	0.00
Orals	1987	17.35	0.00	0.00	0.00	0.00	0.00	0.00
Sterilization: all	1980	9.71	20.00	na	10.00	2.06	na	1.03
Male sterilization	1968	4.76	15.00	0.00	0.00	3.15	0.00	0.00
Male sterilization	1969	4.76	10.00	0.00	0.00	3.15	0.00	0.00
Male sterilization	1970	4.76	10.00	0.00	0.00	2.10	0.00	0.00
Male sterilization	1972	10.00	15.00	0.00	0.00	1.50	0.00	0.00
Male sterilization	1974	10.00	15.00	0.00	0.00	1.50	0.00	0.00
Male sterilization	1987	17.35	z	z	z	z	z	z
Female sterilization	1968	4.76	25.00	0.00	0.00	5.25	0.00	0.00
Female sterilization	1969	4.76	25.00	0.00	0.00	5.25	0.00	0.00
Female sterilization	1970	4.76	25.00	0.00	0.00	5.25	0.00	0.00
Female sterilization	1974	10.00	20.00	0.00	0.00	2.00	0.00	0.00
Female sterilization	1987	17.35	z	z	z	z	z	z
Condoms	1987	17.35	0.00	0.00	0.00	0.00	0.00	0.00
Case recruitment: male sterilization[h]	1968	4.76	0.00	0.00	5.00	0.00	0.00	1.06
Case recruitment: male sterilization[h]	1969	4.76	0.00	0.00	5.00	0.00	0.00	1.06
Case recruitment: male sterilization[h]	1970	4.76	0.00	0.00	5.00	0.00	0.00	1.06
Case recruitment: sterilization	1972	10.00	0.00	0.00	5.00	0.00	0.00	0.50
Case recruitment: sterilization	1974	10.00	0.00	0.00	5.00	0.00	0.00	0.50
Case recruitment: IUD[h]	1968	4.76	0.00	2.50[o]	2.00	0.00	0.53[o]	0.42
Case recruitment: IUD[h]	1969	4.76	0.00	2.50[o]	2.00	0.00	0.53[o]	0.42
Case recruitment: IUD[h]	1970	4.76	0.00	2.50[o]	2.00	0.00	0.53[o]	0.42

Country and type of service	Year	Exchange rate (U.S.$)	Cash payment in local currency			Cash equivalent in U.S.$		
			Physician	Nurse or midwife	Other[a]	Physician	Nurse or midwife	Other[a]
Pakistan *(continued)*								
Case recruitment: IUD	1972	10.00	0.00	0.00	2.00–2.50	0.00	0.00	0.20–0.25
Case recruitment: IUD	1974	10.00	0.00	0.00	2.50	0.00	0.00	0.25
Program supervision (per month)	1968	4.76	0.00	0.00	350.00	0.00	0.00	73.50
Program supervision (per month)	1969	4.76	0.00	0.00	350.00	0.00	0.00	73.50
Program supervision (per month)	1970	4.76	0.00	0.00	350.00	0.00	0.00	73.50
Injectables	1987	17.35	0.00	0.00	0.00	0.00	0.00	0.00
Spermicide	1987	17.35	0.00	0.00	0.00	0.00	0.00	0.00
Diaphragm	1987	17.35	0.00	0.00	0.00	0.00	0.00	0.00
Philippines								
IUD insertion	1987	20.50	———142.25———			———6.94———		
Orals	1987	20.50	———117.65———			———5.74———		
Male sterilization	1984	12.50	120.00	na	na	10.00	na	na
Male sterilization	1987	20.50	———120.00———			———5.85———		
Female sterilization	1984	12.50	200.00	na	na	16.00	na	na
Female sterilization	1987	20.50	———120.00———			———5.85———		
All types (per month)	1971	6.25	400–800	250–450	240–300	64–128	40–72	38–48
All types (per month)	1972	6.25	350–800	300–350	130.00	56–128	48–56	20.80
All types (per month)	1974	6.67	700.00	300–332	130.00	105.00	45–50	20.00
All types (per month)	1975	6.67	700.00	300–350	150.00	105.00	45–53	23.00
All types (per month)	1976	7.14	770.00	330–385	150.00	107.80	46–54	21.00
All types (per month)	1977	7.14	813.00	349–405	390.00	113.82	49–57	54.60
All types (per month)	1979	7.14	970.00	631.00	424.00	135.80	88.34	59.36
All types (per month)	1981	7.69	1200.00	556.00	520.00	156.00	72.26	67.60
All types: itinerant teams (per month)	1984	12.50	2500.00	1255.00	u	200.00	100.00	u
All types: family planning (per month)	1984	12.50	u	735.00	u	u	59.00	u
All types: integrated clinic (per month)	1984	12.50	u	725.00	u	u	58.00	u
Injectables	1987	20.50	———123.00———			———6.00———		
Singapore								
All types (per month)	1971	3.03	1100.00	240.00	0.00	3.67	0.80	0.00
All types (per month)	1972	2.70	1138.00	473.00	385.50	421.06	175.01	142.64
All types (per month)	1974	2.50	1406.00	468.00	540.00	562.00	187.00	216.00
All types (per month)	1975	2.33	1731.00	1288.00	100–705	744.00	554.00	43–303
All types (per month)	1976	2.50	1790.00	617–1240	533–778	716.00	247–496	213–311
All types (per month)	1977	2.44	1914.00	648–1292	552–805	785.00	266–530	226–330
All types (per month)	1979	2.22	2219.00	837–1208	691.00	999.00	377–544	311.00
All types (per month)	1981	2.13	2994.00	2102.00	924.00	1407.00	988.00	434.00
All types (per month)	1984	2.13	3800.00	1440–2035	455–1005[p]	1787.00	678–956	214–603[p]
Sri Lanka								
IUD insertion	1968	5.92	2.50	1.50	0.00	0.42	0.25	0.00
IUD insertion	1969	5.92	2.50	1.50	0.00	0.42	0.25	0.00
IUD insertion	1970	5.92	2.50	1.50	0.00	0.42	0.25	0.00
IUD insertion	1987	30.00	0.00	0.00	0.00	0.00	0.00	0.00
Orals	1968	5.92	0.00	0.00	0.00	0.00	0.00	0.00
Orals	1969	5.92	0.00	0.00	0.00	0.00	0.00	0.00
Orals	1970	5.92	0.00	0.00	0.00	0.00	0.00	0.00
Orals (per cycle)	1975	6.67	0.00	0.15	0.00	0.00	0.02	0.00
Orals (per cycle)	1976	7.14	0.00	0.15	0.00	0.00	0.02	0.00
Orals (per cycle)	1987	30.00	0.00	0.15	na	0.00	0.01	na
Male sterilization	1968	5.92	0.00	0.00	5.00	0.00	0.00	0.85
Male sterilization	1969	5.92	0.00	0.00	5.00	0.00	0.00	0.85
Male sterilization	1970	5.92	0.00	0.00	5.00	0.00	0.00	0.85
Male sterilization	1987	30.00	25.00	7.50	3.00	0.83	0.25	0.10
Female sterilization	1968	5.92	0.00	0.00	5.00	0.00	0.00	0.85
Female sterilization	1969	5.92	0.00	0.00	5.00	0.00	0.00	0.85
Female sterilization	1970	5.92	0.00	0.00	5.00	0.00	0.00	0.85
Female sterilization	1987	30.00	40.00	7.50	10.00	1.33	0.25	0.33
Condoms (per dozen)	1987	30.00	0.00	0.20	na	0.00	0.01	na
Injectables	1987	30.00	0.00	0.00	na	0.00	0.00	na

Table 15. Payments to Personnel for Specified Family Planning Services, by Type of Service and Category of Worker (continued)

Country and type of service	Year	Exchange rate (U.S.$)	Cash payment in local currency			Cash equivalent in U.S.$		
			Physician	Nurse or midwife	Other[a]	Physician	Nurse or midwife	Other[a]
Taiwan								
IUD insertion	1968	40.00	60.00	0.00	0.00	1.50	0.00	0.00
IUD insertion	1969	40.00	60.00	0.00	0.00	1.50	0.00	0.00
IUD insertion	1970	40.00	60.00	0.00	0.00	1.50	0.00	0.00
IUD insertion	1971	40.00	60.00	0.00	0.00	1.50	0.00	0.00
IUD insertion	1972	38.46	60.00	u	u	1.56	u	u
IUD insertion	1974	38.46	60.00	0.00	0.00	1.56	0.00	0.00
IUD insertion	1975	38.46	60.00	0.00	0.00	1.56	0.00	0.00
IUD insertion	1984	40.00	65.00	u	na	1.63	u	na
IUD insertion	1987	40.00	s	s	30–80[aa]	s	s	0.75–2.00[aa]
IUD insertion: Loop	1976	38.46	80.00	0.00	0.00	2.08	0.00	0.00
IUD insertion: Loop	1977	38.46	80.00	0.00	0.00	2.08	0.00	0.00
IUD insertion: Loop	1979	35.71	80.00	0.00	0.00	2.24	0.00	0.00
IUD insertion: Loop	1981	35.71	80.00	0.00	0.00	2.24	0.00	0.00
IUD insertion: Ota Ring	1976	38.46	130.00	0.00	0.00	3.38	0.00	0.00
IUD insertion: Ota Ring	1977	38.46	130.00	0.00	0.00	3.38	0.00	0.00
IUD insertion: Ota Ring	1979	35.71	130.00	0.00	0.00	3.64	0.00	0.00
IUD insertion: Ota Ring	1981	35.71	130.00	0.00	0.00	3.64	0.00	0.00
Orals	1969	40.00	0.00	0.00	1.50	0.00	0.00	0.03
Orals (per cycle)	1970	40.00	0.00	0.00	0.50	0.00	0.00	0.01
Orals (per cycle)	1971	40.00	0.00	0.00	0.50	0.00	0.00	0.01
Orals (per cycle)	1972	38.46	u	u	1.00	u	u	0.03
Orals (per cycle)	1974	38.46	0.00	0.00	0.75	0.00	0.00	0.02
Orals (per cycle)	1975	38.46	0.00	0.00	0.75	0.00	0.00	0.02
Orals (per cycle)	1984	40.00	0.50	1.00	na	0.10	0.03	na
Male sterilization	1968	40.00	200.00	0.00	0.00	5.00	0.00	0.00
Male sterilization	1969	40.00	200.00	0.00	0.00	5.00	0.00	0.00
Male sterilization	1976	38.46	500.00	0.00	0.00	13.00	0.00	0.00
Male sterilization	1977	38.46	500.00	0.00	0.00	13.00	0.00	0.00
Male sterilization	1979	35.71	900.00	0.00	0.00	25.20	0.00	0.00
Male sterilization	1981	35.71	850.00	0.00	0.00	23.80	0.00	0.00
Male sterilization	1984	40.00	650.00	na	na	16.25	na	na
Female sterilization	1968	40.00	300.00	0.00	0.00	7.50	0.00	0.00
Female sterilization	1969	40.00	300.00	0.00	0.00	7.50	0.00	0.00
Female sterilization	1976	38.46	1150.00	0.00	0.00	29.90	0.00	0.00
Female sterilization	1977	38.46	1500.00	0.00	0.00	39.00	0.00	0.00
Female sterilization	1979	35.71	2500.00	0.00	0.00	70.00	0.00	0.00
Female sterilization	1981	35.71	1900.00	0.00	0.00	53.20	0.00	0.00
Female sterilization	1984	40.00	1150.00	na	na	28.75	na	na
Female sterilization	1987	40.00	t	t	100–200[aa]	t	t	2.50–5.00[aa]
Condoms (per dozen)	1970	40.00	0.00	0.00	0.50	0.00	0.00	0.01
Condoms (per dozen)	1971	40.00	0.00	0.00	0.50	0.00	0.00	0.01
Condoms (per dozen)	1972	38.46	u	u	1.00	u	u	0.03
Condoms (per dozen)	1974	38.46	0.00	0.00	0.75	0.00	0.00	0.02
Condoms (per dozen)	1975	38.46	0.00	0.00	0.75	0.00	0.00	0.02
Condoms	1987	40.00	0.00	1.00	1.50	0.00	0.03	0.04
Case recruitment[h]	1968	40.00	0.00	10.00	1200.00	0.00	0.25	30.00
Case recruitment[h]	1969	40.00	0.00	10.00	1200.00	0.00	0.25	30.00
Case recruitment[h]	1970	40.00	0.00	20.00	20.00	0.00	0.50	0.50
Case recruitment[h]	1971	40.00	0.00	20.00	20.00	0.00	0.50	0.50
Case recruitment	1972	38.46	u	20.00	20.00	u	0.52	0.52
Case recruitment	1974	38.46	0.00	20.00	0.00	0.00	0.52	0.00
Case recruitment	1975	38.46	0.00	20.00	0.00	0.00	0.52	0.00
Case recruitment: Loop	1976	38.46	0.00	20.00	0.00	0.00	0.52	0.00
Case recruitment: Loop	1977	38.46	0.00	20.00	0.00	0.00	0.52	0.00
Case recruitment: Loop	1979	35.71	0.00	20.00	0.00	0.00	0.56	0.00
Case recruitment: Loop	1981	35.71	0.00	20.00	0.00	0.00	0.56	0.00
Case recruitment: orals	1976	38.46	0.00	0.00	1.00	0.00	0.00	0.03
Case recruitment: orals	1977	38.46	0.00	0.00	1.00	0.00	0.00	0.03
Case recruitment: orals	1979	35.71	0.00	0.00	1.00	0.00	0.00	0.03
Case recruitment: orals	1981	35.71	0.00	1.50	0.00	0.00	0.04	0.00
Case recruitment: sterilization	1976	38.46	0.00	150.00	0.00	0.00	3.90	0.00
Case recruitment: sterilization	1977	38.46	0.00	150.00	0.00	0.00	3.90	0.00
Case recruitment: condoms	1976	38.46	0.00	0.00	1.00	0.00	0.00	0.03
Case recruitment: condoms	1977	38.46	0.00	0.00	1.00	0.00	0.00	0.03
Case recruitment: condoms	1979	35.71	0.00	0.00	1.00	0.00	0.00	0.03

Table 15. Payments to Personnel for Specified Family Planning Services, by Type of Service and Category of Worker (continued)

Country and type of service	Year	Exchange rate (U.S.$)	Cash payment in local currency			Cash equivalent in U.S.$		
			Physician	Nurse or midwife	Other[a]	Physician	Nurse or midwife	Other[a]
Taiwan (continued)								
Case recruitment: condoms	1981	35.71	0.00	1.00	0.00	0.00	0.03	0.00
Fieldwork (per month)	1969	40.00	0.00	3140.00	0.00	0.00	78.50	0.00
Fieldwork (per month)	1970	40.00	0.00	0.00	3200.00	0.00	0.00	80.00
Fieldwork (per month)	1971	40.00	0.00	0.00	1255.00	0.00	0.00	31.38
Fieldwork (per month)	1972	38.46	u	u	1250.00[q]	u	u	32.50[q]
Fieldwork (per month)	1974	38.46	0.00	0.00	1520.00[q]	0.00	0.00	40.00[q]
Fieldwork (per month)	1975	38.46	0.00	0.00	2100.00[q]	0.00	0.00	55.00[q]
Fieldwork (per month)	1968	40.00	0.00	3140.00	0.00	0.00	78.50	0.00
Village health ed. nurse (per month)	1971	40.00	0.00	0.00	2400.00	0.00	0.00	60.00
Village health ed. nurse (per month)	1972	38.46	u	u	2400.00	u	u	62.40
Village health ed. nurse (per month)	1974	38.46	0.00	0.00	2600.00	0.00	0.00	68.00
Village health ed. nurse (per month)	1975	38.46	0.00	0.00	2600.00	0.00	0.00	68.00
Thailand								
Govt. program: all types	1987	26.00	0.00	0.00	0.00	0.00	0.00	0.00

u = unknown.   na = not applicable.

a. Examples include, but are not limited to, the following occupations: field-worker, motivator, medical assistant, auxiliary worker, practical nurse, social worker, and clerk.

b. Monthly payments were 2,000 rupees (U.S. $176) for supervisors, 1,400 rupees (U.S. $123) for clinical assistants, and 650 rupees (U.S. $57) for motivators.

c. Payment is rationed over a six-month period, contingent upon use by acceptor over that interval.

d. Twenty hours per week.

e. In addition to figures specified, the National Family Planning Board paid annual incentives of U.S. $600 to parish medical officers and U.S. $144 to public health nurses.

f. On September 8, 1969, the Jamaican dollar, equal to one-half the Jamaican pound, was introduced.

g. Top administrative family planning personnel receive 30 percent above the regular health service salary for program supervision.

h. Finder's fees are paid to persons within or outside the program who bring cases into the program.

i. Paid to the rest of the doctor's staff at follow-up. The staff also receives a total of 1 pound per IUD that remains in place all of the first month.

j. Other payments are not specifically given here because the personnel involved are part of the health program.

k. Special project in Najafabad and Shahreza districts.

l. Honorarium

m. Figure represents central government recommendations to the states. The central government contributed to the states 11 rupees per IUD, 30 rupees per vasectomy, and 70 rupees per salpingectomy. These contributions include payments to the clients and other personnel, as well as payments to physicians.

n. Fees vary by state; figure shown here is the normal payment.

o. Payment to dai (village midwife). In addition, each dai receives 15 rupees a month as a retainer fee.

p. Monthly payments were U.S. $473 for family assistants, $307–$406 for office workers, $214–$267 for junior assistants, and $603 for laboratory technicians.

q. In addition, field-workers earned on the average $NT1,800 (U.S. $46.80) in bonuses for performance in 1974 and 1975, and $NT 1,650 (U.S. $42.90) in 1972.

r. Some clinics are reimbursed at U.S. $55 per female sterilization. Public-sector cases are covered on a salary basis.

s. In private contracted hospitals or clinics, the subsidy for IUD insertions goes to medical doctors. For the mobile team program, the subsidy goes to county health bureaus as part of program funds.

t. The subsidy for sterilization operations goes to medical doctors. However, in the public sector, it goes to hospitals and clinics.

v. Field-workers are entitled to this payment only if they themselves refer the case.

w. Proceeds from the sale of contraceptives by each family planning unit are distributed an an incentive among concerned personnel.

x. In addition, physicians receive a hardship allowance of 25–100 percent for operations in remote areas.

y. Payments are 28,400–56,800 rials for physicians, 14,400–28,800 rials for nurses, and 4,000–14,400 rials for other personnel.

z. Institutional reimbursements are made: 135 rupees (U.S. $7.99) to type A centers, 235 rupees (U.S. $13.90) to type B centers, and 200 rupees (U.S. $11.83) to type C centers. These reimbursements are intended to be allocated to the institution itself, medical staff, motivators, and clients (for transportation and nutritional allowance). Nonprogram doctors are paid a fee.

aa. Upper limit applied only in remote areas.

Table 16. Personnel Specifically Allocated for Family Planning Services[a]

Country and year	Total	Physicians[b]	Paramedics[c]	Field-workers[d]	Administrators, managers[e]	Others	MWRA[hh] per family planning staff member
SUB-SAHARAN AFRICA							
Ghana							
1970	110	f	60	50	u	u	11257
1971	159	f	95	64	u	u	8010
1972	158	f	94	64	u	u	8300
1973	353	f	149	204	u	u	3824
1974	439	f	145	294	u	u	3140
1975	500	f	156	344	u	u	2798
1976	503	f	180	323	u	u	2828
1977	503	f	180	323	u	u	2876
Kenya							
1970	90[g]	60	30	u	u	u	16044
1973	10	u	10	u	u	u	u
1978	603	u	u	603[h]	u	u	3466
1980	817	u	u	817[h]	u	u	2765
Liberia (FPAL)							
1986	72[gg]	u	39	26	7	u	4748
Mauritius							
1971	435	8	14	394	19	u	214
1972	471	20	16	394[i]	41	u	205
1974	199	22	19	118	40	u	521
1975	338	18	28	249	43	u	317
1976	329	19	28	260	48	u	336
1978	357	20	27	243	67	u	329
1980	456	18	29	341	68	u	272
1984	580	49[j]	27	429	75	u	242
Niger							
1986	70	15	55	u	u	u	u
Sudan							
1984–85	27388[h]	u	24239	3149	u	u	118
Togo							
1986	56	28	28	u	u	u	7771
Zimbabwe							
1974	138	9	81	u	u	48	u
1975	101	8	93	u	u	u	u
1978	106	4	102	u	u	u	u
1986	920	u	120	800	u	u	1329
Zimbabwe (FPA)							
1972	30	2	28	u	u	u	u
1973	214	7	70	103	u	34	u
LATIN AMERICA/CARIBBEAN							
Bolivia							
1975	36	19	11	6	u	u	17056
1977	28	8	10	u	10	u	23090
Bolivia (PROFAM)							
1976	20	9	11	u	u	u	31516
Brazil (ABEPF)							
1986	2000	u	u	u	u	u	9464
Colombia							
1968	2044	1243	301	500	u	u	1081
1969	1310	507	303	500	u	u	1736
1970	2053	1250	303	500	u	u	1139
1971	3827	677	1150	2000	u	u	628
1972	4150	700	1150	2300	u	u	594
1973	3499	808	505	2186	u	u	723

Table 16. Personnel Specifically Allocated for Family Planning Services[a] (continued)

Country and year	Total	Physicians[b]	Paramedics[c]	Field-workers[d]	Administrators, managers[e]	Others	MWRA[hh] per family planning staff member
Colombia (continued)							
1974	5537	1040	1587	2910	u	u	472
1986	11667[l]	1336	5240	5017	74	u	341
Colombia (PROFAMILIA)							
1980	645	——362——		235	48	u	4931
1987	3765	95	175	3495[z]	u	u	1093
Costa Rica							
1970	1071	152	385	410	u	124	174
1972	391	75	316	u	u	u	525
1974	325	70	255	u	u	u	690
1975	505	92	345	u	u	68	464
Dominican Republic							
1969	69[h]	4	u	7	10	48	7101
1970	286[h]	38	u	9	30	209	1784
1973	142[h]	65	67	u	10	u	4028
1974	211[h]	87	107	u	17	u	2818
1975	400[h]	150	225	u	25	u	1547
1976	370[h]	100	270	u	u	u	1742
1977	444[h]	130	314	u	u	u	1514
Guatemala							
1971	220[k]	89	64	37	30	u	3082
1973	452[k]	89	264	69	30	u	1562
1974	452[k]	89	264	69	30	u	1595
Guatemala (APROFAM)							
1976	61	18	17	7	——19——		12311
1977	66	18	22	7	——19——		11606
Honduras							
1986	6	1	1	1	3	u	406758
Peru (Social Security)							
1986	642	——642——		u	u	u	3904
Puerto Rico (FPA)							
1986	27	12	6	5	4	u	u
MIDDLE EAST/NORTH AFRICA							
Egypt							
1971	11400	3800	5800	1800	u	u	u
1972	11650	3850	6000	1800	u	u	u
1973	12820	3920	6150	1800	950	u	u
1974	13422	4019	6638	1800	965	u	368
1976	14094	4663	6772	1771	888	u	370
1979	15340	5120	7370	1900	950	u	368
Iran							
1968	11780[l]	748	222	10460	350	u	u
1970	11276[l]	252	223	10451	350	u	u
1971	2425[l]	1111	1314	u	u	u	u
1972	4171[l]	1111	1314	1746	u	u	u
1973	5500[l]	1252	1448	2800	u	u	u
1974	4796[l]	1390	2520	886	u	u	989
1975	5610[l]	1450	3210	950	u	u	874
1977	2790[l]	3740	968	u	u	u	1877
1986	5710[l]	u	2875	2835	u	u	1312
Jordan							
1986	485[l]	50	150	u	275	10	691
Tunisia							
1970	218[l]	35	100	20	63	u	2945
1971	218[l]	35	100	20	35	28	2963

Table 16. Personnel Specifically Allocated for Family Planning Services[a] *(continued)*

Country and year	Total	Physicians[b]	Paramedics[c]	Field-workers[d]	Administrators, managers[e]	Others	MWRA[hh] per family planning staff member
Tunisia *(continued)*							
1972	318[l]	38	71	54	25	130	2047
1973	200[l]	30	110	30	u	u	3280
1974	446[l]	89	357	u	u	u	1482
1975	676[l]	40	612	24	u	u	985
Turkey							
1986	21900[l]	5900	16000	u	u	u	366
ASIA							
Bangladesh							
1972	21823	"1000	u	11065	1758	8000[m]	522
1973	14128	1033	501	12000	594	u	836
1974	22009	509	500	20000[n]	1000	u	555
1976	32038	48	u	31990	u	u	408
1980	40388	241	115	19200	457	20375[o]	371
1986	35246	u	7697	25585	1964	u	515
China							
1986	148000	u	u	u	u	ff	1131
Hong Kong							
1971	201	5	64	49	83	u	2189
1972	222	6	73	52	91	u	2020
1973	194	15	65	47	67	u	2356
1974	160	7	57	36	60	u	2910
1976	141	8	41	37	55	u	3422
1978	116	5	37	33	41	u	4547
1980	138	9	42	36	51	u	4148
1984	143	14	45	61	23	u	5004
1986	182	33	44	38	60	7	4374
India							
1972	51445	5107	34988	7319	4031	u	1831
1973	54549	5336	23471	20936	4806	u	1772
1974	52978	5664	23916	19348	4050	u	1872
1975	57038	5056	27299	20379	4304	u	1785
1976	56857	5862	26921	19786	4288	u	1839
1978	48510	6074	———28875———		13561	u	2276
1979	58572	6200	28900	19972	3500	u	1937
1983	113779	6868	80536	20375	6000	u	1116
Indonesia							
1969	620	171	293	u	u	156	30024
1970	4895	1040	1930	u	u	1925	3815
1971	5105	1176	1929	2000	u	u	3670
1972	7228	813	2641	3774	u	u	2601
1973	9629	997	3473	5159	u	u	1959
1974	15714	2223	6630	6861	u	u	1205
1975	14434	2029	5643	6641	u	u	1316
1976	16159	2203	7411	6545	u	u	1180
1978	21717	2872	8248	7010	u	u	996
1980	27751	3807	10228	6838	u	u	873
1983	33000	4500	12000	12000	u	u	794
1986–87	55294	7166	9439	19245[aa]	19444	u	514
Korea, Republic of							
1968	4091	1691[p]	2400[q]	1473	u	u	u
1973	6432	2039[p]	2920	1473	230	u	668
1974	6675	1925[p]	2900	1550	300	u	661
1975	5403	2130[p]	1018	1692	563	u	839
1976	5741	2130[p]	1012	2599	u	u	811
1980	6178	2052[p]	361	2799	966	u	832
1986	6846	2430[p]	———4170[bb]———		246	u	899
Malaysia (Peninsular)							
1967	230[r]	7	92	66	u	65	4813

Table 16. Personnel Specifically Allocated for Family Planning Services[a] (continued)

Country and year	Total	Physicians[b]	Paramedics[c]	Field-workers[d]	Administrators, managers[e]	Others	MWRA[hh] per family planning staff member
Malaysia (Peninsular, continued)							
1968	158[r]	3	———————140———————			u	7437
1969	238[r]	5	203	17	13	u	5227
1971	238[r]	6	120	u	12	100	5798
1973	254[r]	6	235	u	13	u	5972
1974	438[r]	4	419	u	15	u	3621
1975	538[r]	10	505	u	23	u	3074
1976	577[r]	10	540	u	27	u	2984
1978[ii]	3672[s]	208	3458	u	u	6	506
1980[ii]	5831[s]	80	4672	u	88	991	342
1986[jj]	528[r]	12[cc]	510	u	u	6	4623
Nepal							
1970	223	1	37	u	26	159	9722
1971	451	11	256	u	25	159	4892
1972	431	13	388	2	28	u	5207
1974	763	18	710	3	32	u	3047
1975	903	12	850	5	36	u	2622
1976	1002	17	930	5	50	u	2406
1986	4344[h]	46	1096	2500	702	u	680
Pakistan							
1969[t]	95756	2300	u	51330	5126	37000[m]	u
1970[t]	76178	2400	u	41300	2478	30000[m]	u
1972	25911	1363	u	23572	976	u	349
1973	30393	1405	u	24255	1005	3285[m]	311
1974	39736	587	u	35207	1105	2837[m]	249
1979	10246	2508	u	6037[kk]	1047	654[m]	1169
1986	35206	——————6713——————		25000[dd]	3493	u	424
Philippines							
1970	16139[gg]	7132	8945	62	u	u	271
1971	5361	1336	2447	1291	u	287	865
1972	8772	1933	4076	u	u	2763	559
1973	9461	2283	4878	2300	u	u	546
1974	10442	2856	5139	2447	u	u	520
1975	10270	2465	5612	2059	u	144	555
1976	10605	2065	5666	2729	u	142	556
1978	92370	2538	7383	81472[v]	977	u	68
1980	13085	2554	9569	u	962	u	513
1982	71994	2859	17135	52000[w]	u	u	99
Singapore							
1969	96	5	51	u	u	40	2437
1970	116	7	45	u	u	64	2074
1971	106	9	63	u	u	34	2349
1972	117	8	50	2	24	33	2197
1973	98	12	50	2	u	34	2694
1974	149[x]	10	49	14	76	u	1826
1975	168[x]	12	70	12	74	u	1667
1976	164[x]	10	69	12	73	u	1756
1978	182[x]	16	76	13	77	u	1665
1980	172[x]	16	65	18	73	u	1852
1982	162[x]	16	62	18	66	u	2114
1984	155	13	72	u	48	22	2362
Sri Lanka							
1968	3234	663[gg]	1950[gg]	621	u	u	u
1970	2774	112	727	1935	u	u	549
1973	11426[h]	2045	6095	3286	u	u	144
1974	13205[h]	2300	6494	4411	u	u	128
1975	12873[h]	2045	6456	4372	u	u	135
Taiwan							
1968	1669	745[p]	80	814	30	u	1059
1969	1963	706[p]	844	413	u	u	929
1970	2147	934[p]	782	431	u	u	876

Table 16. Personnel Specifically Allocated for Family Planning Services[a] *(continued)*

Country and year	Total	Physicians[b]	Paramedics[c]	Field-workers[d]	Administrators, managers[e]	Others	MWRA[hh] per family planning staff member
Taiwan *(continued)*							
1971	2053	837[p]	782	434	u	u	944
1972	2083	837[p]	782	434	30	u	958
1973	2245	990[p]	776	471	8	u	914
1974	2255	990[p]	782	471	12	u	935
1975	2543	1041[p]	1022	476	4	u	851
1976	2514	1015[p]	1013	476	10	u	884
1978	2497	1023[p]	1013	454	7	u	935
1980	2656	1803[p]	1346	491	16	u	922
1984[ee]	2200	1625[p]	u	559	16	u	1282
1985[ee]	1059	———530———		332	169	28	2753
Thailand							
1968	1311	103	1208	y	u	u	3396
1969	5688	229	3662	1797	u	u	807
1970	5477	311	3780	1386	u	u	864
1971	7213	411[l]	4778[l]	2024	u	u	676
1972	7812	599[l]	5138[l]	2075	u	u	644
1973	27952	6408[l]	21544[l]	u	u	u	185
1975	23566	7181[l]	16375[l]	u	u	u	234
1976	23556	7181[l]	16375[l]	u	u	u	242
1980	29201	6550[l]	22651[l]	u	u	u	223
Vietnam							
1982	153582	15093	134617	u	u	3872	u
1983	157288	16145	137232	u	u	3911	u
1984	162262	17435	141047	u	u	3780	u
1985	170049	19171	147041	u	u	3837	u

u = unknown.

a. Numbers in each personnel category were obtained from the Nortman Fact Books and the 1987 questionnaire.

b. Includes physicians, medical officers, private practitioners, and others.

c. Includes nurses, clinical assistants, midwives, health aides, clinic workers, female inspecting assistants, family planning assistants, laboratory workers, health station personnel, auxiliary midwives, paramedicals, pharmacists, and others.

d. Includes field-workers, motivators, health educators, lady welfare visitors, lady health visitors, contraceptive distributors, outreach workers, supply point officers, social workers, information and education staff, field midwives, public health inspectors, family planning educators, health promoters, community leaders, extension educators, welfare workers, family welfare assistants, and others.

e. Includes administrators, supervisors, family planning officers, administrative assistants, executives, officers, population planning officers, trainers, researchers, evaluators, statistical staff, social scientists, support staff, and others.

f. Many government and private doctors participate on a part-time basis.

g. Personnel trained in family planning by 1970.

h. These personnel provide maternal and child health care and family planning services.

i. Of these, at least 126 are full-time.

j. Of these, only 15 are full-time.

k. APROFAM (private family welfare association) and Ministry of Health personnel.

l. All personnel provide other health services in addition to family planning.

m. Part-time dais (untrained indigenous midwives).

n. Of these, 12,000 provide health as well as family planning services.

o. Dais and traditional birth attendants.

p. The majority of the doctors are in private practice and are paid on a per case basis.

q. Authorized nurses, midwives, and field-workers.

r. National Family Planning Board personnel.

s. National Family Planning Board, Family Planning Association, and Ministry of Health personnel.

t. Prior to the independence of Bangladesh.

v. Includes 30,670 barrio supply-point officers.

Table 16. Number of Personnel Specifically Allocated for Family Planning Services *(continued)*

w. Includes 52,000 village volunteers.

x. Employees of the Singapore Family Planning and Population Board; excludes staff of maternal and child health services who provide family planning services.

y. Numbers of part-time field-workers unavailable.

z. Includes 3,400 community-based distribution workers.

aa. Includes 72,082 community-based distribution workers.

bb. During the period 1974–1986, 1,214 paramedical personnel were trained and authorized to insert IUDs.

cc. Fifty part-time doctors also provide services. Part-time ranges from once a week to once a month.

dd. Community-based distribution workers.

ee. For 1984, numbers are full-time equivalents only for field-workers, administrators, and managers. For 1985, numbers are full-time equivalents for all categories; thus, the number of physicians appears less than it was in 1984.

ff. There are approximately 5 million volunteer workers.

gg. Personnel trained in family planning.

hh. Women aged 15–44 includes those in consensual unions.

ii. Ministry of Health personnel included, as well as personnel from the National Population and Family Development Board and the Family Planning Association, who are included in other years.

jj. National Population and Family Development Board only.

kk. Excludes contraceptive distributors.

Table 17. Facilities Specifically Allocated for Family Planning Services

Country and year	Total facilities[a]	Hospitals[b]	Clinics[c]	Health centers[d]	Community posts[e]	Mobile teams	Research/ training[f]	Other	MWRA per service point
SUB-SAHARAN AFRICA									
Botswana									
1984	776[g]	15	128	7	251	375[h]	u	u	110
Burkina Faso									
1986	53	u	u	u	u	u	u	u	26763
Chad									
1986	7	1	1	5	u	u	u	u	122920
Ghana									
1969	30	i	30	u	u	u	u	u	40067
1971	131	i	131	u	u	u	u	u	9722
1972	140	i	140	u	u	u	u	u	9368
1973	160	u	160	u	u	u	u	u	8438
1974	187	u	187	u	u	u	u	u	7373
1975	189	u	189	u	u	u	u	u	7401
1977	156	u	156	u	u	u	u	u	9274
Kenya									
1968	174[j]	u	u	u	u	8	u	u	7368
1970	262	u	250	u	u	12	u	u	5511
1973	305	u	298	u	u	7	u	u	5531
1978	495	u	166	u	329	u	u	u	4222
1980	631	u	234	u	397	u	u	u	3579
Liberia (FPAL)									
1986	18	u	18	u	u	u	u	u	18992
Mauritius									
1970	99	u	u	u	u	5	u	u	909
1971	94	u	62	32	u	u	u	u	989
1972	109[k]	u	71	12	26	u	u	u	886
1974	160[k]	u	76	54	30	u	u	u	648
1975	185[k]	u	83	56	44	1	u	u	579
1976	185[k]	u	86	56	42	1	u	u	598
1978	299[k]	u	88	168	42	1	u	u	393
1980	118[l]	u	89	u	28	1	u	u	1051
1984	122[m]	u	88	u	33	1	u	u	1153
Nigeria									
1986	728	u	728[n]	u	u	u	u	u	25979
Senegal									
1986	22[o]	u	22	u	u	u	u	u	48792
Sudan									
1984	5281[g]	u	u	1265	4016	u	u	u	613
Togo									
1986	28	17	u	11	u	u	u	u	15542
Zimbabwe (FPA)									
1972	12	u	5	u	u	7	u	u	u
1973	23	u	12	u	u	11	u	u	u
1974	69	u	57	u	u	12	u	u	u
1975	42	u	15	13	u	14	u	u	u
1978	44	u	35	u	u	9	u	u	u
1986	1060	u	36	1000[g]	u	24	u	u	1153
LATIN AMERICA/CARIBBEAN									
Bolivia									
1975	12	1	11	u	u	u	u	u	51167
1976	8	1	7	u	u	u	u	u	78791
Brazil (ABEPF)									
1986	150	u	u	u	u	u	u	u	126188

Table 17. Facilities Specifically Allocated for Family Planning Services (continued)

Country and year	Total facilities[a]	Hospitals[b]	Clinics[c]	Health centers[d]	Community posts[e]	Mobile teams	Research/ training[f]	Other	MWRA per service point
Chile									
1986	901	u	226	u	675	u	u	u	1806
Colombia									
1969	363[l]	u	u	u	u	3	u	u	6264
1970	403[l]	u	u	u	u	3	u	u	5801
1971	563	u	u	u	u	u	u	u	4266
1972	573	u	u	u	u	u	u	u	4302
1973	900	u	u	u	u	u	u	u	2809
1974	978	u	u	u	u	u	u	u	2671
1980	9615[g,l]	583	28	u	9001	3	u	u	331
1986	3648[g]	636	u	722	2290	u	u	u	1090
Costa Rica									
1970	91	u	91	u	u	u	u	u	2044
1972	163	——23——		140	u	u	u	u	1258
1974	131	——16——		101	6	8	u	u	1712
1975	159	11	14	76	51	7	u	u	1473
1987	177	6	30	85	56	u	u	u	2169
Dominican Republic									
1967	13	u	13	u	u	u	u	u	35077
1968	78	u	78	u	u	u	u	u	6051
1969	81	u	78	u	u	3	u	u	6049
1970	82	u	79	u	u	3	u	u	6222
1973	60	42	u	18	u	u	u	u	9534
1974	97	26	23	48	u	u	u	u	6130
1975	319	35	92	67	125[p]	u	u	u	1940
1976	241	35	119	87	u	u	u	u	2675
1977	262	33	134	95	u	u	u	u	2565
Guatemala									
1971	80	u	u	u	u	1	u	u	8475
1972	80	u	u	u	u	1	u	u	8650
1973	80	u	u	u	u	1	u	u	8828
1974	439	24	70	325	u	1	u	19	609
Haiti									
1986	219	213[q]	u	q	u	6	u	u	u
Peru									
1986	3762[r]	146	21	630	2965	u	u	u	666
MIDDLE EAST/NORTH AFRICA									
Egypt									
1971	3113[g]	u	u	u	u	u	u	u	u
1972	3187[g]	u	u	u	u	u	u	u	u
1973	3211[g]	u	u	u	u	u	u	u	u
1974	3319[g]	u	u	u	u	u	u	u	1489
1976	3478[g]	u	u	u	u	u	u	u	1500
1979	4500[g]	u	u	u	u	u	u	u	1254
Iran									
1968	862	u	u	u	u	350[g]	u	u	u
1969	1250	u	u	u	u	738[g]	u	u	u
1971	1393[g]	73	u	915	u	405	u	u	u
1972	1393[g]	73	u	915	u	405	u	u	u
1973	2540[g]	u	2153	u	u	387	u	u	u
1974	2877[g]	u	2480	u	u	397	u	u	1649
1975	2900[g]	u	2550	u	u	350	u	u	1691
1977	3258[g]	u	2848	u	u	410	u	u	1607
Iraq									
1986	129	u	9	120[g]	u	u	u	u	16395
Jordan									
1986	120	u	u	120[g]	u	u	u	u	2793

121

Table 17. Facilities Specifically Allocated for Family Planning Services *(continued)*

Country and year	Total facilities[a]	Hospitals[b]	Clinics[c]	Health centers[d]	Community posts[e]	Mobile teams	Research/ training[f]	Other	MWRA per service point
Tunisia									
1968	221	63	u	89	56	13	u	u	2860
1969	311	63	u	89	56	1	u	102	2048
1971	324	63	u	89	56	14	u	102	1994
1972	387	44	u	82	246	15	u	u	1682
1973	344	45	u	71	208	15	u	5	1907
1974	411	44	u	88	260	19	u	u	1608
1975	434	44	u	88	260	42	u	u	1534
Turkey									
1986	11616[g]	430	u	3186	8000	u	u	u	690
ASIA									
Bangladesh									
1972	454	u	u	u	u	u	u	u	25112
1973	562	u	558	u	u	u	4	u	21020
1974	757	84	449	224	u	u	u	u	16150
1976	931	u	681	250	u	u	u	u	14037
1980	1290	u	7	1227	u	u	56	u	11610
1986	2082	56	u	2026	u	u	u	u	8717
Hong Kong									
1970	44	u	u	u	u	2	u	u	9818
1971	51	u	51	u	u	u	u	u	8628
1972	57	u	57	u	u	u	u	u	7860
1973	65	u	65	u	u	u	u	u	7031
1974	33	u	33	u	u	u	u	u	14121
1976	35	u	35	u	u	u	u	u	13788
1978	32	u	32	u	u	u	u	u	16469
1980	26	u	26	u	u	u	u	u	22038
1984	62	u	25	u	u	u	u	37[s]	11548
1986	61	u	26	u	u	u	u	35[s]	13050
India									
1970	31710	u	u	u	u	256	u	u	2791
1972	40271	u	u	7194	32217	855	5	u	2339
1973	40780	u	u	7162	33048	505	5	60	2370
1974	40905	u	u	7107	33370	363	5	60	2425
1975	42793	u	u	7155	35274	313	7	44	2380
1976	44955[t]	u	u	6988	37690	226	7	44	2326
1978	50660	u	u	7732	42875	u	53	u	2179
1979	58518	u	u	8002	50462	u	54	u	1939
1983	73632	u	u	7938	65643	u	51	u	1724
1984	82392	u	u	8109	74236	u	47	u	1585
Indonesia									
1969	510	u	510	u	u	u	u	u	36500
1970	1300	u	1300	u	u	u	u	u	14364
1971	1805[g]	u	1805	u	u	u	u	u	10378
1972	2067[g]	u	2067	u	u	u	u	u	9094
1973	4430[g]	u	4430	u	u	u	u	u	4258
1974	5832[g]	u	5832	u	u	u	u	u	3246
1975	3000	u	2620[g]	u	u	380	u	u	6331
1976	32905	u	3603[g]	u	27179[p]	2123	u	u	579
1978	36200	u	4116[g]	u	32084[p]	u	u	u	598
1980	55814	u	5609[g]	u	50205[p]	u	u	u	434
1983	60796	u	7064[g]	u	53732[p]	u	u	u	431
Korea, Republic of									
1968	1794[x]	u	u	u	u	38	u	u	u
1970	1794[x]	u	u	u	u	38	u	u	u
1973	1900[x]	60	1628	193	u	19	u	u	2261
1974	302	80	12	193	u	17	u	u	14606
1975	313	75	28	198	u	11	1	u	14476
1976	323	77	36	198	u	11	1	u	14412
1980	2266	——2041——		214	u	11	u	u	2269
1986	6036[x]	u	2455	1569	2000	12	u	u	1019

122

Table 17. Facilities Specifically Allocated for Family Planning Services (continued)

Country and year	Total facilities[a]	Hospitals[b]	Clinics[c]	Health centers[d]	Community posts[e]	Mobile teams	Research/ training[f]	Other	MWRA per service point
Malaysia (Peninsular)									
1967	521	u	u	u	u	u	u	u	2125
1968	576	u	u	u	u	38	u	u	2040
1969	443	u	69	u	u	38	u	u	2808
1970	746	u	492	216	u	38	u	u	1759
1971	472	u	472	u	u	u	u	u	2924
1973	736	u	524	u	u	212	u	u	2061
1974	1551	u	1551	u	u	u	u	u	1023
1975	701	u	688	13	u	u	u	u	2359
1976	581	u	569	12	u	u	u	u	2964
1978	1975	u	1975	u	u	u	u	u	941
1980	2304	u	2304	u	u	u	u	u	866
1986	2495	2	350	122	1462	559[h]	u	u	978
Nepal									
1970	40	u	40	u	u	u	u	u	54200
1971	88	u	86	u	u	2	u	u	25070
1972	88	u	u	u	u	88	u	u	25504
1975	265	u	u	265	u	u	u	u	8934
1986	2708	u	258	u	2450	u	u	u	1090
Pakistan									
1972	963	u	u	u	u	u	u	u	9391
1973	985	u	u	u	u	u	u	u	9606
1979	1055	u	1003	52	u	u	u	u	11349
Philippines									
1970	800	u	800	u	u	u	u	u	5462
1971	1291	u	1291	u	u	u	u	u	3591
1972	1503	u	1274	221	u	8	u	u	3261
1973	2184	u	2175	u	u	9	u	u	2366
1974	2287	u	2274	u	u	13	u	u	2376
1975	2509	u	2493	u	u	16	u	u	2272
1976	2794	u	2774	u	u	20	u	u	2109
1978	3334	u	——3334——		u	u	u	u	1888
1980	3385	——1821——		1549	u	15	u	u	1984
1982	13383	——1763——		1595	10000	25	u	u	534
Singapore									
1968	38	1	37	u	u	u	u	u	6000
1969	38	1	37	u	u	u	u	u	6158
1970	49	1	48	u	u	u	u	u	4911
1971	42	1	40	u	u	1	u	u	5929
1972	53	u	53	u	u	u	u	u	4849
1973	53	u	53	u	u	u	u	u	4981
1974	51	u	51	u	u	u	u	u	5333
1975	42	u	42	u	u	u	u	u	6667
1976	40	u	40	u	u	u	u	u	7200
1978	38	u	38	u	u	u	u	u	7974
1980	38	u	38	u	u	u	u	u	8385
1982	38	u	36	u	u	u	2	u	9011
Sri Lanka									
1970	438	u	u	u	u	1	u	u	3477
1971	415	——414——			u	1	u	u	3772
1972	491	u	490	u	u	1	u	u	3271
1973	521	24	496	u	u	1	u	u	3163
1974	1478	24	506	u	940[p]	8	u	u	1143
1975	2010	30	598	u	1374[p]	8	u	u	862
1986	4758	u	118	740	3900[p]	u	u	u	473
Taiwan									
1968	979	16	u	263	u	u	u	700[v]	1805
1969	1129	16	u	263	u	u	u	850[w]	1616
1971	1137	16	u	346	u	u	u	775[w]	1704
1972	1072	16	u	346	u	10	u	700[v]	1861
1973	1252	16	u	362	u	14	u	860[v]	1638

Table 17. Facilities Specifically Allocated for Family Planning Services (continued)

Country and year	Total facilities[a]	Hospitals[b]	Clinics[c]	Health centers[d]	Community posts[e]	Mobile teams	Research/ training[f]	Other	MWRA per service point
Taiwan (continued)									
1974	1256	16	u	362	u	14	u	864[v]	1678
1975	1073	38	u	362	u	14	u	659[v]	2018
1976	1070	45	u	362	u	10	u	653[v]	2077
1978	1061	45	u	362	u	9	u	645[v]	2201
1980	1328	45	u	363	u	u	u	920[v]	1844
1984	1779	84	u	392	u	12	u	1291[v]	1585
Thailand									
1968	73[g]	u	u	u	u	1	u	u	60986
1969	275[g]	u	u	u	u	1	u	u	16698
1970	275[g]	u	u	u	u	1	u	u	17217
1971	98[g]	94	u	u	u	4	u	u	49775
1972	4781[g]	97	u	4680	u	4	u	u	1052
1973	2512[g]	97	u	2411	u	4	u	u	2064
1975	5231[g]	121	u	5200	u	u	u	u	1055
1976	5231[g]	121	u	5200	u	u	u	u	1090
1980	7007[g]	401	u	6466	u	140	u	u	928
Vietnam									
1981	12576[g]	1150	11227	191	u	u	8	u	u
1982	12992[g]	1186	11595	203	u	u	8	u	u
1983	13048[g]	1191	11662	186	u	u	9	u	u
1984	13155[g]	1222	11728	196	u	u	9	u	u
1985	13096[g]	1211	11666	210	u	u	9	u	u

u = unknown.

a. Numbers in each category were obtained from Nortman Fact Books and the authors' 1987 questionnaire.

b. Hospitals, district hospitals, regional hospitals, university hospitals, and others.

c. Clinics, family planning clinics, family planning centers, and other facilities specifically for family planning.

d. Health centers, health and family welfare centers, MCH/FP centers, health complexes, MCH centers, counseling centers, medical centers, health subcenters, dispensaries, and other facilities.

e. Community posts, rural posts, health posts, dressing stations, PHC units, and other facilities.

f. Research and training facilities.

g. These facilities provide health and family planning services.

h. Number of "mobile stops."

i. Family planning services are available at mission hospitals, which are not included here.

j. Government and private facilities.

k. Government, Action Familiale (Catholic church–approved), and FPA facilities.

l. Government and FPA facilities.

m. Government facilities only.

n. State family planning clinics vary in size, and health centers are often listed as clinics.

o. Senegal Family Health and Population Project facilities only.

p. Community-based distribution centers.

q. Hospitals and health centers are combined in the "Hospitals" column.

r. Ministry of Health and Social Security facilities.

s. Counseling services.

t. Figures include only those facilities run by the state governments.

v. Private doctors' offices.

w. Private doctors' offices and other facilities.

x. Includes private clinics.

Table 18. Family Planning Program Effort Scores, by Effort Level and Program Component, 1982; and Contraceptive Prevalence, Selected Years

Program effort level and country	Total	Program component				Contraceptive prevalence	
		Policy and stage setting	Service and service-related	Record keeping and evaluation	Availability and accessibility	Percentage using a method	Year
Maximum possible score	120.0	32.0	52.0	12.0	24.0		
Strong							
China	101.1	31.0	40.3	6.8	23.0	69.0	1982
Korea, Republic of	94.8	23.5	37.2	10.5	23.6	58.0	1982
Taiwan	94.3	20.1	38.7	11.5	24.0	70.0	1981
Singapore	93.4	21.3	38.6	10.0	23.5	71.0	1977
Indonesia	89.9	24.5	40.6	11.2	13.6	48.0	1982
Colombia	85.3	19.5	34.0	11.0	20.8	51.0	1980
Hong Kong	82.8	17.7	30.2	11.4	23.5	80.0	1981
Mauritius	82.0	25.5	35.3	8.8	12.4	50.6	1981
Sri Lanka	80.4	21.3	35.1	7.1	16.9	57.0	1982
Mexico	79.9	22.7	31.8	7.8	17.6	40.0	1979
Moderate							
India	75.6	23.0	31.5	7.2	13.9	32.4	1982
El Salvador	75.5	17.9	32.6	7.0	18.0	34.4	1978
Thailand	72.9	16.7	27.5	8.6	20.1	59.0	1981
Tunisia	70.2	19.8	25.4	7.5	17.5	31.0	1982
Bangladesh	68.5	18.6	28.5	5.1	16.3	18.6	1981
Dominican Republic	66.3	17.2	27.9	5.7	15.5	43.0	1980
Jamaica	66.0	21.0	21.4	6.2	17.4	55.0	1979
Philippines	65.2	18.2	26.0	5.6	15.4	45.0	1982
Vietnam	64.0	16.8	27.3	5.9	14.0	21.0	1982
Malaysia	61.1	18.9	18.4	8.7	15.1	42.0	1981
Panama	60.8	13.8	16.6	8.3	22.1	63.4	1979
Fiji	59.8	16.9	25.0	4.2	13.7	38.0	1978
Korea, Dem. People's Rep.	59.8	18.3	24.0	2.5	15.0	u	u
Cuba	59.2	8.6	28.8	5.4	16.4	79.0	1980
Trinidad and Tobago	55.9	16.9	19.2	6.0	13.8	54.0	1977
Weak							
Chile	52.3	14.2	19.0	8.2	10.9	43.0	1978
Brazil	51.1	11.6	18.7	8.0	12.8	50.0	1982
Pakistan	48.5	18.8	14.5	6.3	8.9	6.0	1980
Egypt	47.6	16.1	19.8	3.0	8.7	24.0	1980
Nepal	44.7	17.7	15.6	5.0	6.4	7.0	1981
Morocco	43.3	12.6	17.5	4.9	8.3	19.0	1980
Haiti	42.9	14.3	15.3	5.1	8.2	19.0	1977
Ecuador	42.2	11.7	14.8	3.7	12.0	40.0	1979
Costa Rica	40.0	10.3	12.0	4.4	13.3	66.0	1981
Lebanon	39.8	6.0	18.0	5.2	10.6	u	u
Venezuela	37.5	12.7	14.6	2.8	7.4	49.0	1977
Turkey	35.0	19.3	8.2	3.5	4.0	40.0	1978
Guatemala	34.0	5.6	11.5	5.5	11.4	18.2	1978
West Samoa	33.8	13.3	12.0	3.6	4.9	u	u
Kenya	33.7	13.7	12.7	3.8	3.5	7.0	1977
Zimbabwe	32.7	11.0	14.8	1.7	5.2	14.0	1979
Botswana	31.8	12.0	11.5	1.5	6.8	u	u
Guyana	31.7	6.4	14.9	0.9	9.5	u	u
Gambia	31.2	16.6	8.7	1.9	4.0	1.0	1977
Cyprus	30.4	6.0	13.3	3.4	7.7	u	u
Honduras	30.3	7.7	10.2	1.8	10.6	27.0	1981
Algeria	30.0	13.5	10.1	5.2	1.2	7.0	1977
Papua New Guinea	29.7	12.8	8.3	3.1	5.5	5.0	1982
Rwanda	27.6	16.7	8.3	2.0	0.6	u	u
Senegal	27.2	10.3	10.4	3.0	3.5	4.0	1978
Tanzania	26.8	11.1	11.7	2.1	1.9	1.0	1977

Table 18. Family Planning Program Effort Scores, by Effort Level and Program Component, 1982; and Contraceptive Prevalence, Selected Years (continued)

Program effort level and country	Total	Policy and stage setting	Service and service-related	Record keeping and evaluation	Availability and accessibility	Percentage using a method	Year
		Program component				Contraceptive prevalence	
Weak *(continued)*							
Peru	26.3	9.7	7.6	2.5	6.5	43.0	1981
Liberia	25.9	14.1	6.8	2.3	2.7	1.0	1977
Very weak or none							
Nicaragua	23.8	4.7	9.3	2.7	7.1	9.0	1977
Ghana	21.3	10.1	7.6	2.1	1.5	10.0	1977
Uganda	20.5	12.2	5.4	2.0	0.9	1.0	1982
Yemen, South	20.3	7.5	9.2	1.5	2.1	u	u
Mozambique	19.7	9.8	4.7	1.9	3.3	u	u
Sierra Leone	19.3	8.0	6.3	1.3	3.7	4.0	1982
Jordan	19.0	5.2	3.0	1.4	9.4	u	u
Zambia	18.7	9.1	5.5	1.4	2.7	1.0	1977
Congo	18.4	10.1	5.3	1.4	1.6	u	u
Lesotho	16.7	8.6	6.3	0.9	0.9	6.0	1977
Togo	16.7	6.1	7.5	2.3	0.8	u	u
Guinea-Bissau	16.3	6.0	7.8	0.8	1.7	1.0	1977
Zaire	15.5	4.9	5.4	2.5	2.7	3.0	1982
Nigeria	15.4	5.9	5.8	1.3	2.4	6.0	1981
Benin	13.7	3.9	5.0	2.9	1.9	18.0	1982
Mali	13.6	4.5	5.1	2.1	1.9	1.0	1977
Afghanistan	13.5	4.7	6.5	0.5	1.8	u	u
Iran	13.3	4.1	4.8	2.0	2.4	23.0	1978
Syria	12.9	5.4	3.9	1.6	2.0	20.0	1978
Burundi	12.6	9.5	1.7	0.4	1.0	1.0	1977
Central African Republic	12.4	6.9	3.6	1.0	0.9	u	u
Somalia	11.5	6.0	3.6	1.1	0.8	2.0	1982
Madagascar	10.3	2.8	3.3	1.2	3.0	u	u
Cameroon	10.1	3.4	4.3	0.4	2.0	2.0	1978
Paraguay	9.4	2.7	2.0	0.2	4.5	36.0	1979
Yemen, North	9.2	5.6	1.5	0.2	1.9	1.0	1979
Sudan	9.0	5.7	2.8	0.2	0.3	5.0	1978
Bolivia	9.0	2.5	5.0	0.9	0.6	23.6	1983
Chad	8.3	5.0	2.9	0.0	0.4	1.0	1977
Ethiopia	7.4	2.5	3.1	1.0	0.8	2.0	1982
Malawi	6.9	4.0	1.4	0.3	1.2	1.0	1977
Côte d'Ivoire	6.6	3.8	0.6	0.4	1.8	u	u
Kuwait	6.1	3.1	1.0	0.0	2.0	u	u
Niger	5.5	3.0	1.1	0.2	1.2	1.0	1977
Guinea	5.4	2.3	2.1	0.2	0.8	1.0	1977
Burkina Faso	5.2	3.8	0.9	0.2	0.3	1.0	1977
Burma	5.1	1.0	0.0	0.0	4.1	5.0	1980
Mauritania	4.2	1.3	1.4	0.0	1.5	1.0	1977
Iraq	3.7	2.0	0.8	0.0	0.9	u	u
Oman	1.7	0.8	0.0	0.4	0.5	u	u
United Arab Emirates	1.5	0.8	0.0	0.2	0.5	u	u
Saudi Arabia	1.4	0.0	0.8	0.4	0.2	u	u
Equatorial Guinea	0.5	0.0	0.5	0.0	0.0	u	u
Libya	0.0	0.0	0.0	0.0	0.0	u	u
Kampuchea	0.0	0.0	0.0	0.0	0.0	u	1982
Laos	0.0	0.0	0.0	0.0	0.0	u	u
Mongolia	0.0	0.0	0.0	0.0	0.0	u	u
Mean for all countries[a]	**69.5**	**21.0**	**27.8**	**6.1**	**14.6**	**43.0**	

u = unknown.   a. Means weighted by 1982 population size. Countries under 1 million population are retained in this table from the original.

Table 19. Family Planning Activities Performed by Paramedics, 1987

Country	Initial OC screening[d]	Using OC checklist[e]	IUD insertion	Country	Initial OC screening[d]	Using OC checklist[e]	IUD insertion
SUB-SAHARAN AFRICA				**LATIN AMERICA/CARIBBEAN** *(continued)*			
Botswana	Yes	Yes	No	Peru	Yes	No	No
Burkina Faso	u	u	Yes	Puerto Rico	Yes	Yes	No
Cameroon	Yes	Yes	Yes	Trinidad and Tobago	No	na	No
Ethiopia	Yes	Yes	No				
Ghana	Yes	No	Yes	**MIDDLE EAST/NORTH AFRICA**			
Liberia	Yes	Yes	No	Egypt	Yes	Yes	No
Lesotho	No	na	No	Iran	No	na	No
Niger	Yes	Yes	Yes	Iraq	No	na	No
Nigeria	Yes	Yes	Yes	Jordan	No	na	No
Sudan	u	u	Yes[c]	Morocco	Yes[b]	Yes[b]	Yes[b]
Togo	No	na	No	Turkey	Yes	Yes	Yes
Zimbabwe	Yes	Yes	Yes				
				ASIA			
LATIN AMERICA/CARIBBEAN				Bangladesh	Yes	Yes	Yes
Bolivia	No	na	No	Burma	No	na	No
Brazil (BEMFAM)	No	na	No	Hong Kong	No	na	No
Brazil (ABEPF)	Yes	Yes	Yes	India	Yes	No	No
Chile	Yes	Yes	Yes	Korea	Yes	No	Yes
Colombia	Yes	Yes	Yes	Malaysia	Yes	Yes	No
Haiti	Yes[a]	Yes[a]	No	Pakistan	Yes	Yes	Yes
Honduras	u	u	No	Philippines	No	na	No
Jamaica	Yes	Yes	No	Singapore	No	na	No
Mexico (MEXFAM)	Yes	Yes	No	Sri Lanka	Yes	Yes	Yes
Mexico (IMSS)	u	u	No	Taiwan	No	na	No
Panama	No	na	No	Thailand	Yes	Yes	Yes
Paraguay	Yes	Yes	No				

u = unknown.

na = not applicable.

a. In operations research projects only.

b. Visite à Domicile pour Motivation Systematique Project only.

c. In Khartoum area only.

d. Paramedics are permitted to screen clients for the initial supply of oral contraceptives.

e. Paramedics who are permitted to screen use a checklist for medical contraindications.

Table 20. Percentage of Population with Access to Family Planning and Health Services, 1987

Country	IUD insertion	Pill	Injectable	Female sterilization	Male sterilization	Condom	Abortion	Menstrual regulation
SUB-SAHARAN AFRICA								
Burkina Faso	5	7	na	2	na	7	na	na
Urban	57	93	na	20	na	93	na	na
Rural	0	0	na	0	na	0	na	na
Gabon	0	u	0	0	0	u	0	u
Urban	0	u	0	0	0	u	0	u
Rural	0	0	0	0	0	u	0	u
Ghana	15	15	15	15	3	48	15	0
Urban	50	50	50	50	10	100	50	0
Rural	0	0	0	0	0	25	0	0
Liberia	u	u	u	0	u	u	u	u
Urban	u	u	u	1	u	u	u	u
Rural	u	u	u	0	u	u	u	u
Niger	0	20	20	0	1	u	0	0
Togo	22	22	22	u	u	33	u	22
Urban	80	80	80	u	u	80	u	80
Rural	5	5	5	u	u	20	u	5
Zimbabwe	42	58	28	35	35	42	u	u
Urban	80	80	50	80	80	80	u	u
Rural	30	50	20	20	20	30	u	u
LATIN AMERICA/CARIBBEAN								
Bolivia	12	12	3	0	u	25	u	u
Urban	20	20	5	1	u	30	u	u
Rural	5	5	2	0	u	20	u	u
Colombia	97	100	100	95	40	100	7	7
Urban	100	100	100	100	50	100	10	10
Rural	90	100	100	80	10	100	0	0
Honduras	70	70	u	u	u	58	u	u
Urban	100	100	u	100	100	100	u	100
Rural	50	50	u	u	u	30	u	u
Jamaica	64	100	100	64	32	100	32	u
Urban	75	100	100	75	50	100	50	75
Rural	50	100	100	50	10	100	10	na
Paraguay	28	46	19	1	u	49	u	u
Urban	50	75	30	2	u	60	u	u
Rural	10	20	10	1	u	40	u	u
Peru	24	35	24	10	u	49	u	u
Urban	35	50	35	15	u	70	u	u
Rural	3	5	3	1	u	7	u	u
Puerto Rico	90	90	u	90	u	90	u	u
Urban	90	90	u	90	u	90	u	u
Rural	90	90	u	90	u	90	u	u
Trinidad and Tobago	93	100	100	100	100	100	u	93
Urban	100	100	100	100	100	100	u	100
Rural	80	100	100	100	100	100	u	80
MIDDLE EAST/NORTH AFRICA								
Egypt	97	100	32	u	u	100	u	u
Urban	100	100	70	u	u	100	u	u
Rural	95	100	na	u	u	100	u	u
Iran	15	74	u	u	u	12	u	u

Table 20.

ORS[a]	Prenatal care	Postnatal care	Delivery by trained midwife	Delivery at institution	Paramedic care for infants	Infant immuni-zations	Tetanus immunization for women	Country
								SUB-SAHARAN AFRICA
u	u	u	u	29	u	u	u	**Burkina Faso**
u	u	u	u	70	u	u	u	Urban
u	u	u	u	25	u	u	u	Rural
u	88	88	100	u	u	94	94	**Gabon**
u	100	100	100	90	u	100	100	Urban
u	80	80	100	u	u	90	90	Rural
42	80	80	48	48	u	65	65	**Ghana**
80	100	100	100	100	u	100	100	Urban
25	70	70	25	25	u	50	50	Rural
u	44	44	u	u	u	34	u	**Liberia**
u	50	50	u	u	u	40	u	Urban
u	40	40	u	u	u	30	u	Rural
u	u	u	u	u	u	u	u	**Niger**
39	28	33	24	21	24	39	24	**Togo**
70	90	80	90	60	90	70	90	Urban
30	10	20	5	10	5	30	5	Rural
u	60	60	60	60	28	60	60	**Zimbabwe**
u	90	90	90	90	50	90	90	Urban
u	50	50	50	50	20	50	50	Rural
								LATIN AMERICA/CARIBBEAN
25	30	30	40	20	u	70	u	**Bolivia**
20	40	40	50	30	u	80	u	Urban
30	20	20	30	10	u	60	u	Rural
100	97	97	84	70	95	100	100	**Colombia**
100	100	100	100	90	100	100	100	Urban
100	90	90	50	50	80	100	100	Rural
79	79	79	59	52	79	79	79	**Honduras**
100	100	100	50	100	100	100	100	Urban
65	65	65	65	20	65	65	65	Rural
91	100	100	100	100	u	100	100	**Jamaica**
100	100	100	100	100	u	100	100	Urban
80	100	100	100	100	u	100	100	Rural
34	39	39	61	39	u	40	39	**Paraguay**
40	50	50	50	50	u	40	50	Urban
30	30	30	70	30	u	40	30	Rural
54	64	64	58	57	58	68	21	**Peru**
75	80	80	80	80	80	92	30	Urban
10	30	30	15	10	15	20	3	Rural
u	u	u	u	u	u	u	u	**Puerto Rico**
u	u	u	u	u	u	u	u	Urban
u	u	u	u	u	u	u	u	Rural
u	100	100	100	93	u	100	100	**Trinidad and Tobago**
u	100	100	100	100	u	100	100	Urban
u	100	100	100	80	u	100	100	Rural
								MIDDLE EAST/NORTH AFRICA
100	97	97	97	48	97	97	100	**Egypt**
100	100	100	100	80	100	100	100	Urban
100	95	95	95	20	95	95	100	Rural
u	u	u	u	u	u	u	u	**Iran**

Table 20. Percentage of Population with Access to Family Planning and Health Services, 1987 *(continued)*

Country	IUD insertion	Pill	Injectable	Female sterilization	Male sterilization	Condom	Abortion	Menstrual regulation
Jordan	**90**	**95**	**na**	**50**	**na**	**100**	**na**	**55**
Urban	100	100	na	50	na	100	na	60
Rural	60	80	na	50	na	100	na	40
Morocco	**74**	**74**	**na**	**74**	**na**	**74**	**na**	**na**
Turkey	**14**	**24**	**na**	**5**	**u**	**24**	**5**	**5**
Urban	25	40	na	8	u	40	10	10
Rural	5	10	na	2	u	10	na	na
ASIA								
Bangladesh	**65**	**74**	**12**	**38**	**56**	**100**	**6**	**11**
Urban	100	100	30	100	100	100	10	20
Rural	60	70	10	30	50	100	5	10
Hong Kong	**100**	**100**	**100**	**100**	**100**	**100**	**100**	**100**
Urban	100	100	100	100	100	100	100	100
Rural	100	100	100	100	100	100	100	100
Korea, Republic of	**100**	**97**	**na**	**93**	**94**	**100**	**97**	**97**
Urban	100	100	na	100	100	100	100	100
Rural	100	90	na	80	90	100	90	90
Malaysia (Peninsular)	**45**	**87**	**45**	**70**	**30**	**65**	**u**	**u**
Urban	50	90	50	75	35	70	u	u
Rural	40	85	40	65	25	60	u	u
Pakistan	**14**	**39**	**19**	**16**	**15**	**52**	**u**	**u**
Urban	33	80	50	50	50	80	u	u
Rural	6	21	6	2	na	40	u	u
Philippines	**72**	**88**	**19**	**62**	**62**	**94**	**u**	**u**
Urban	90	100	40	80	80	100	u	u
Rural	60	80	5	50	50	90	u	u
Sri Lanka	**u**	**u**	**u**	**75**	**70**	**95**	**u**	**u**
Urban	u	u	u	85	80	100	u	u
Rural	u	u	u	70	60	90	u	u
Taiwan	**99**	**99**	**na**	**99**	**99**	**99**	**99**	**99**
Urban	100	100	na	100	100	100	100	100
Rural	96	98	na	96	96	98	96	96
Vietnam	**100**	**20**	**u**	**100**	**u**	**50**	**80**	**80**

u = unknown.

na = not applicable.

a. Oral rehydration supplies.

Table 20. *(continued)*

ORS[a]	Prenatal care	Postnatal care	Delivery by trained midwife	Delivery at institution	Paramedic care for infants	Infant immuni- zations	Tetanus immunization for women	Country
95	75	35	15	50	90	100	100	**Jordan**
100	80	40	20	65	100	100	100	Urban
80	60	20	10	25	70	100	100	Rural
40	2	u	na	15	na	u	na	**Morocco**
25	24	24	10	9	14	25	10	**Turkey**
30	35	35	15	13	25	30	15	Urban
20	15	15	5	5	5	20	5	Rural
								ASIA
80	12	7	18	14	15	18	14	**Bangladesh**
80	30	20	80	80	50	80	80	Urban
80	10	5	10	5	10	10	5	Rural
100	100	100	100	100	na	100	100	**Hong Kong**
100	100	100	100	100	na	100	100	Urban
100	100	100	100	100	na	100	100	Rural
100	97	97	64	97	100	100	100	**Korea, Republic of**
100	100	100	60	100	100	100	100	Urban
100	90	90	70	90	100	100	100	Rural
u	u	u	u	u	u	u	u	**Malaysia (Peninsular)**
u	u	u	u	u	u	u	u	Urban
u	u	u	u	u	u	u	u	Rural
u	14	14	u	u	u	u	u	**Pakistan**
u	33	33	u	u	u	u	u	Urban
u	6	6	u	u	u	u	u	Rural
u	u	u	u	u	u	u	u	**Philippines**
u	u	u	u	u	u	u	u	Urban
u	u	u	u	u	u	u	u	Rural
u	90	90	92	92	92	95	95	**Sri Lanka**
u	95	95	100	100	100	100	100	Urban
u	85	85	90	90	90	95	95	Rural
u	u	u	u	u	u	u	u	**Taiwan**
u	u	u	u	u	u	u	u	Urban
u	u	u	u	u	u	u	u	Rural
u	u	u	u	u	u	u	u	**Vietnam**

Table 21. Community-Based Distribution Programs, 1987

Country	Number of providers	Number of villages covered	Population covered (000s)	Services provided[e]	Charges for supplies or services
SUB-SAHARAN AFRICA					
Botswana	u	u	u	FP, MCH, Immun	Yes
Burkina Faso	7800	7800	6914	MCH, Immun	u
Gabon	47	50	u	MCH, Immun	u
Kenya	u	u	u	FP, MCH, Immun	u
Liberia	59	5	44	FP	u
Lesotho	u	u	u	FP	Yes
Nigeria (Oyo State)	484	600	225	FP, MCH, Immun	Yes
Sudan	u	150	150	FP, MCH, Immun	u
Zimbabwe	800	u	u	FP, Immun	Yes
LATIN AMERICA/CARIBBEAN					
Brazil (BEMFAM)	2382	946	u	FP, MCH, Immun	u
Colombia	5017	b	u	FP, MCH, Immun	u
Costa Rica	826	u	u	FP, MCH, Immun	No
Haiti	u	u	u	FP, Immun	u
Honduras	1204	1200	u	FP	u
Jamaica	u	u	u	FP	No
Mexico (IMSS)	u	u	u	FP, MCH, Immun	No
Mexico (MEXFAM)	u	u	u	FP, MCH, Immun	u
Paraguay	98	21	563	FP, MCH, Immun	Yes
Peru	300	40	u	FP	Yes
Puerto Rico	10	u	u	FP, MCH, Immun	u
MIDDLE EAST/NORTH AFRICA					
Iraq	u	u	u	Immun	u
Morocco	4000	u	a	FP, MCH, Immun	u
Turkey	11000	20000	u	FP, MCH, Immun	No
ASIA					
Bangladesh	34000	68000	105000	FP, MCH, Immun	No
China	u	u	u	FP, MCH, Immun	u
Hong Kong	6	6	8	FP	Yes
Malaysia (Peninsular)	30	19	21	FP, MCH, Immun	No
Pakistan	23073	15000	25000	FP, Immun	Yes
Philippines	53458	c	u	FP	u
Sri Lanka	3300	12500	14000	FP	u
Thailand	10000	10000	d	FP	Yes

u = unknown.

a. Seventy-four percent of the total population is covered.

b. Approximately 1,000 counties are covered.

c. Approximately 1,800 municipalities are covered.

d. Approximately 20 percent of the total population is covered.

e. FP = family planning, MCH = maternal and child health, Immun = immunizations.

Table 22. Social Marketing Programs

Country and year	Percentage of urban population covered	Percentage of rural population covered	Number of pill cycles sold (000s)	Cost per pill cycle (U.S.$)	Number of condoms sold[c] (000s)	Cost per condom[c] (U.S.$)	Number of spermicides sold (000s)	Cost per spermicide application (U.S.$)
SUB-SAHARAN AFRICA								
Ghana								
1987	u	u	u	0.11	u	0.02	u	0.01
Nigeria								
1986	u	u	728	0.25	93600	0.05	754	0.04
LATIN AMERICA/CARIBBEAN								
Bolivia								
1986	5	2	13	0.25	468	0.02	u	u
Colombia (PROFAMILIA)								
1976	u	u	780	u	2283	u	639	u
1977	u	u	1140	u	4328	u	1608	u
1978	u	u	1548	u	4188	u	2493	u
1979	u	u	3848	u	6382	u	3944	u
1980	u	u	4712	u	6174	u	4525	u
1981	u	u	4844	u	6133	u	3810	u
1982	u	u	5225	u	6272	u	7422	u
1983	u	u	5312	u	5476	u	6528	u
1984	u	u	5795	u	5875	u	6105	u
El Salvador								
1978	u	u	4	u	620	u	0	u
1979	u	u	14	u	816	u	0	u
1980	u	u	70	u	635	u	0	u
1981	u	u	126	u	920	u	43	u
1982	u	u	153	u	1018	u	24	u
1983	u	u	129	u	556	u	44	u
1984	u	u	115	u	606	u	79	u
1985	u	u	u	0.40	u	0.11	u	0.05
Guatemala								
1985	u	u	u	0.61	u	0.17	u	0.09
Honduras								
1986	u	90	194	0.75	336	0.21	u	u
Jamaica								
1975	u	u	54	u	506	u	u	u
1976	u	u	113	u	549	u	u	u
1977	u	u	164	u	746	u	u	u
1978	u	u	175	u	801	u	u	u
1979	u	u	211	u	886	u	u	u
1980	u	u	259	u	948	u	u	u
1981	u	u	305	u	1045	u	u	u
1982	u	u	296	u	1119	u	u	u
1983	u	u	378	u	989	u	u	u
1984	u	u	401	u	1340	u	u	u
1987	u	u	u	0.18	u	0.04	u	u
Mexico								
1979	u	u	372	u	1708	u	3942	u
1980	u	u	778	u	4027	u	3837	u
1981	u	u	281	u	6327	u	2127	u
1982	u	u	142	u	6403	u	142	u
1983	u	u	16	u	6200	u	0	u
1984	u	u	10	u	4658	u	u	u
1985	u	u	u	u	4209	0.22–0.43	u	u
MIDDLE EAST/NORTH AFRICA								
Egypt								
1979	u	u	0	u	753	u	427	u
1980	u	u	0	u	1200	u	549	u
1981	u	u	0	u	1885	u	2033	u
1982	u	u	0	u	3694	u	1994	u

Table 22. Social Marketing Programs *(continued)*

Country and year	Percentage of urban population covered	Percentage of rural population covered	Number of pill cycles sold (000s)	Cost per pill cycle (U.S.$)	Number of condoms sold[c] (000s)	Cost per condom[c] (U.S.$)	Number of spermicides sold (000s)	Cost per spermicide application (U.S.$)
Egypt *(continued)*								
1983	u	u	0	u	6016	u	4835	u
1984	u	u	1289	u	8253	u	2254	u
1986	16	2	99	0.24	1002	0.02	25	0.35
ASIA								
Bangladesh								
1975	u	u	111	u	636	u	0	u
1976	u	u	469	u	9727	u	0	u
1977	u	u	1021	u	17341	u	0	u
1978	u	u	1097	u	22707	u	0	u
1979	u	u	702	u	31564	u	1743	u
1980	u	u	669	u	35750	u	4536	u
1981	u	u	841	u	50377	u	4757	u
1982	u	u	1138	u	66638	u	3297	u
1983	u	u	1638	u	85363	u	4910	u
1984	u	u	2216	u	115023	u	2202	u
1986[a]	60	40	2425	0.09	96240	0.01	34884	0.01
Hong Kong								
1986	u	u	4	0.32	9	0.09	0.01	1.03–1.28
India (Nirodh)								
1969	u	u	na	na	15740	u	na	na
1970	u	u	na	na	29590	u	na	na
1971	u	u	na	na	52710	u	na	na
1972	u	u	na	na	66550	u	na	na
1973	u	u	na	na	78680	u	na	na
1974	u	u	na	na	116230	u	na	na
1975	u	u	na	na	63940	u	na	na
1976	u	u	na	na	79290	u	na	na
1977	u	u	na	na	97940	u	na	na
1978	u	u	na	na	109670	u	na	na
1979	u	u	na	na	107480	u	na	na
1980	u	u	na	na	77780	u	na	na
1981	u	u	na	na	129500	u	na	na
1982	u	u	na	na	166200	u	na	na
1983	u	u	na	na	162700	u	na	na
1984	u	u	na	na	198500	u	na	na
1985	u	u	na	na	u	0.01	na	na
1986	u	u	na	na	228000	u	na	na
Indonesia								
1987	u	u	u	u	u	0.04	u	u
Malaysia (Peninsular)								
1986[b]	u	u	1579	0.32	4320	0.03	u	u
Nepal								
1979	u	u	20	u	953	u	0	u
1980	u	u	27	u	1036	u	0	u
1981	u	u	75	u	1115	u	0	u
1982	u	u	78	u	2110	u	u	u
1983	u	u	105	u	2621	u	161	u
1984	u	u	111	u	3327	u	165	u
1986	100	u	147	0.12	3387	0.02	199	0.02
Pakistan								
1986	97	64	u	u	18096	0.01	u	u
Sri Lanka								
1973	u	u	0	u	1071	u	0	u
1974	u	u	6	u	3956	u	0	u
1975	u	u	6	u	4118	u	0	u
1976	u	u	73	u	5191	u	0	u

Table 22. Social Marketing Programs (continued)

Country and year	Percentage of urban population covered	Percentage of rural population covered	Number of pill cycles sold (000s)	Cost per pill cycle (U.S.$)	Number of condoms sold[c] (000s)	Cost per condom[c] (U.S.$)	Number of spermicides sold (000s)	Cost per spermicide application (U.S.$)
Sri Lanka (continued)								
1977	u	u	160	u	6199	u	0	u
1978	u	u	281	u	6856	u	0	u
1979	u	u	266	u	7426	u	92	u
1980	u	u	321	u	7539	u	93	u
1981	u	u	435	u	6939	u	73	u
1982	u	u	339	u	6863	u	79	u
1983	u	u	338	u	6332	u	100	u
1984	u	u	362	u	4813	u	88	u
1985	u	u	u	0.09–0.13	u	0.01–0.04	u	0.32
1987	u	u	526	u	5031	u	98	u
Taiwan								
1986	98	94	88	0.50	2111	0.03	u	u
Thailand								
1974	u	u	212	u	775	u	u	u
1975	u	u	276	u	817	u	u	u
1976	u	u	831	u	4655	u	u	u
1977	u	u	849	u	3416	u	u	u
1978	u	u	1382	u	3260	u	u	u
1979	u	u	1386	u	3679	u	u	u
1980	u	u	1270	u	4333	u	u	u
1981	u	u	1574	u	6038	u	u	u
1982	u	u	1723	u	4826	u	u	u
1983	u	u	1630	u	4392	u	u	u
1984	u	u	1500	u	4321	u	u	u
1985	u	u	u	0.19–0.33	u	0.03–0.07	u	u

u = unknown.

na = not applicable.

a. Approximately 8,000 doses of injectables at U.S.$0.32 each were distributed through the social marketing program.

b. Approximately 10,000 doses of injectables at U.S.$5 each were distributed through the social marketing program.

c. Individual prices, not per dozen.

Table 23. Number of Acceptors of Family Planning Services (000s), by Method and Year

Country and year	Total[a]	IUD[c]	Orals	Inject.	Sterilization Male	Sterilization Female	Sterilization Total	Other program methods	Abortion[a]
SUB-SAHARAN AFRICA									
Botswana									
1973	3.7	0.1	3.4	u	0.0	0.0	0.0	0.2[d]	0.0
1974	4.7	0.4	4.0	u	u	u	0.1	0.2[d]	0.0
1975	6.2	1.1	4.9	u	u	u	0.1	0.1[d]	0.0
1976	11.5	1.1	5.2	u	u	u	0.2	5.0	0.0
1977	11.3	1.1	5.6	u	u	u	u	4.6	0.0
1978	0.0	u	u	u	u	u	u	u	u
1979	13.2	1.8	6.9	0.9	u	u	u	3.6	0.0
1980	14.4	2.2	7.8	0.9	0.0	0.2	0.2	3.3	0.0
1981	17.5	2.6	8.9	1.2	u	u	u	4.8	0.0
1982	16.9	3.8	8.9	0.3	u	u	u	3.9	u
1983[gg]	22.9	4.2	10.9	1.2	u	u	u	6.6	u
1984	26.0	5.2	13.4	2.1	u	u	u	5.3	u
1985	32.1	5.4	16.4	3.4	u	u	u	6.9	u
Burkina Faso									
1986	13.9	1.1	7.2	0.0	0.0	0.1	0.1	5.4	u
Burundi									
1986	12.8	0.8	4.2	6.7	u	u	u	1.1	u
Ethiopia (FGAE)									
1982	75.3	6.5	63.7	u	u	u	u	5.1	u
1983	104.1	7.4	89.7	u	u	u	u	7.0	u
1984	114.7	8.3	98.4	u	u	u	u	8.0	u
1985	120.9	7.9	104.3	u	u	u	u	8.7	u
1986	171.7	8.1	148.4	u	u	u	u	15.2	u
Ghana									
1969[g]	2.6	2.0	0.3	u	0.0	0.0	0.0	0.3	u
1970[g]	8.3	2.8	2.7	u	0.0	0.0	0.0	2.8	u
1971[g]	22.6	4.6	8.6	u	0.0	0.0	0.0	9.4	0.0
1972[g]	30.5	3.2	16.1	u	0.0	0.0	0.0	11.2	0.0
1973[g]	29.8	2.6	17.6	u	0.0	0.0	0.0	9.6	0.0
1974	34.2	2.8	19.2	u	0.0	0.0	0.0	12.2	0.0
1975	31.2	2.5	17.8	u	0.0	0.0	0.0	10.9	0.0
1976	31.9	2.8	18.3	u	0.0	0.0	0.0	10.8	0.0
1977	33.5	2.7	17.7	u	0.0	0.0	0.0	13.1	0.0
Kenya									
1967	11.0	11.0	0.0	u	0.0	0.0	0.0	u	u
1968	8.8	3.7	4.9	u	0.0	0.0	0.0	0.2	u
1969	26.4	15.5	8.8	u	0.0	0.0	0.0	2.1	u
1970	30.9	18.1	10.3	u	0.0	0.0	0.0	2.5	u
1971	41.0	10.0	27.0	u	0.0	0.0	0.0	4.0	0.0
1972	43.0	4.7	34.0	u	0.0	0.0	0.0	4.3	0.0
1973	47.4	4.7	37.2	u	0.0	0.0	0.0	5.5	0.0
1974	41.0	4.0	32.6	2.4	0.0	0.0	0.0	2.0	0.0
1975	39.0	4.0	30.7	2.3	0.0	0.0	0.0	2.0	0.0
1976	59.0	7.0	45.1	2.9	0.0	0.0	0.0	4.0	0.0
1977	71.0	10.0	52.0	5.0	0.0	0.0	0.0	4.0	0.0
1978	75.0	12.0	53.5	4.5	0.0	0.0	0.0	5.0	0.0
Lesotho									
1983	4.5	1.5	2.5	1.0	u	u	u	0.5	u
1985	9.3	2.6	3.4	1.6	u	u	u	2.4	u
1986	10.8	2.2	4.0	2.6	u	u	u	2.6	u
Liberia									
1983	4.3	u	u	u	u	4.3	4.3	u	u
1984	5.4	u	u	u	u	5.4	5.4	u	u
Mauritius									
1964	0.9	0.0	0.0	u	0.0	0.0	0.0	0.9	u
1965	3.0	0.0	1.1	u	0.0	0.0	0.0	1.9	u
1966	6.8	0.1	3.6	u	0.0	0.0	0.0	3.1	u
1967	13.0	0.9	6.1	u	0.0	0.0	0.0	6.0	u

Table 23. Number of Acceptors of Family Planning Services (000s), by Method and Year *(continued)*

Country and year	Total[a]	IUD[e]	Orals	Inject.	Sterilization Male	Sterilization Female	Sterilization Total	Other program methods	Abortion[a]
Mauritius *(continued)*									
1968	12.6	1.5	4.8	u	0.0	0.0	0.0	6.3	u
1969	8.6	0.3	5.0	u	0.0	0.0	0.0	3.3	u
1970	9.8	0.1	7.0	u	0.0	0.0	0.0	2.7	u
1971	10.0	0.1	7.2	u	0.0	0.0	0.0	2.7	0.0
1972	7.9	0.0	5.4[s]	s	0.0	0.0	0.0	2.5	0.0
1973	15.3	0.1	10.5[s]	s	0.0	0.0	0.0	4.7	0.0
1974	13.6	0.1	9.6[s]	s	0.0	0.0	0.0	3.9	0.0
1975	13.5	0.1	9.6[s]	s	0.0	0.0	0.0	3.8	0.0
1976	12.1	0.1	7.7	0.7	u	u	u	3.6	0.0
1977	11.0	0.0	7.1	0.6	u	u	u	3.3	0.0
1978	10.9	0.1	7.1	0.8	0.0	u	u	2.9	0.0
1979	11.7	0.1	7.2	0.8	0.0	0.6	0.6	3.0	0.0
1980	12.8	0.1	7.8	0.8	0.0	0.6	0.6	3.5	0.0
1981	13.9	0.2	7.8	0.9	0.0	0.6	0.6	4.4	0.0
1982	13.3	0.2	7.0	0.7	0.0	0.8	0.8	4.6	0.0
1983	13.5	0.2	7.3	0.7	0.0	0.7	0.7	4.6	0.0
1984	16.2	0.1	7.5	6.8	u	u	u	1.8	u
1985	12.7	0.1	6.7	0.7	u	u	u	5.2	u
1986	12.8	0.1	6.9	0.8	u	u	u	5.0	u
Mozambique									
1981	13.6	2.3	5.8	0.0	0.0	0.5	0.5	5.0	u
1982	15.1	3.3	9.8	0.1	0.0	0.4	0.4	1.5	u
1983	16.4	3.5	9.6	0.2	0.0	0.4	0.4	2.7	u
Nigeria									
1969[n]	5.3	3.6	1.4	u	0.0	0.0	0.0	0.3	u
1970[n]	7.6	4.6	2.7	u	0.0	0.0	0.0	0.3	u
1971[n]	12.9	5.5	5.9	u	0.0	0.0	0.0	1.5	0.0
1972[n]	17.6	6.6	10.2	u	0.0	0.0	0.0	0.8	0.0
1973[n]	24.5	6.9	13.0	u	0.0	0.0	0.0	4.6	0.0
1974[n]	33.2	8.3	20.9	u	0.0	0.0	0.0	4.0	0.0
1986	209.0	39.5	70.0	22.6	u	1.7	1.7	75.2	u
Sierra Leone									
1979	6.1	1.0	3.1	0.3	0.0	0.0	0.0	1.7	0.0
1980	8.8	0.8	3.7	0.6	0.0	0.0	0.0	3.7	0.0
1981	7.0	0.9	3.5	0.5	0.0	0.1	0.1	2.0	0.0
1982	8.0	1.2	4.2	0.6	0.0	0.1	0.1	1.9	0.0
1983	10.2	1.3	4.7	0.9	0.0	0.1	0.1	3.2	0.0
Tanzania									
1974	33.6	3.4	25.4[s]	s	0.0	0.0	0.0	4.8	0.0
1975	93.6	4.2	82.6[s]	s	0.0	0.0	0.0	6.8	0.0
Togo									
1985	25.7	3.9	1.0	0.3	u	u	u	20.5	u
1986	33.2	5.4	1.7	0.5	u	u	u	25.6	u
Uganda									
1970	3.8	0.9	1.6	0.7	0.0	0.0	0.0	0.6	u
1971	10.9	1.2	4.0	1.5	0.0	0.0	0.0	4.2	0.0
1972	13.8	0.9	6.9	1.5	0.0	0.0	0.0	4.5	0.0
1973	9.2	0.6	5.2	2.2	0.0	0.0	0.0	1.2	u
1974[y]	81.8	1.5	10.5	67.7	u	u	0.1	2.0	0.0
1975	16.1	2.3	13.3	u	0.0	0.0	0.0	0.5	0.0
Zimbabwe									
1971	14.1	0.4	9.8	3.9	u	u	u	u	0.0
1972	18.7	0.3	10.4	8.0	0.0	0.0	0.0	u	0.0
1973	37.6	0.3	16.0	21.3	0.0	0.0	0.0	0.0	0.0
1974	56.8	0.4	18.8	37.5	u	u	0.1	0.0	0.0
1975	322.4	1.4	146.7	170.7	u	u	0.1	3.5	0.0
1976	14.0	0.0	u	u	0.0	0.0	0.0	14.0	0.0
1977	8.6	0.0	u	u	0.0	0.0	0.0	8.6	0.0
1978	27.5	0.0	u	u	0.0	0.0	0.0	27.5	0.0
1984	171.0	u	157.0	5.0	u	u	u	9.0	u

Table 23. Number of Acceptors of Family Planning Services (000s), by Method and Year *(continued)*

Country and year	Total[a]	IUD[e]	Orals	Inject.	Sterilization			Other program methods	Abortion[a]
					Male	Female	Total		
Zimbabwe *(continued)*									
1985	178.7	4.2	160.0	5.0	u	u	u	9.5	u
1986	225.6	10.0	198.0	6.6	u	u	u	11.0	u
LATIN AMERICA/CARIBBEAN									
Bolivia									
1975	7.6	5.6	1.2	u	0.0	0.0	0.0	0.8	u
Brazil (BEMFAM)									
1971	111.0	18.7	90.1	u	0.0	0.0	0.0	2.2	0.0
1972	129.6	28.0	100.2	u	0.0	0.0	0.0	1.4	0.0
1973	147.9	34.6	110.4	u	0.0	0.0	0.0	2.9	0.0
1974	174.8	11.5	160.0	u	0.0	0.0	0.0	3.3	0.0
1975	203.6	3.6	196.4	u	0.0	0.0	0.0	3.6	0.0
1979	214.3	1.0	211.9	0.0	0.0	0.0	0.0	1.4	0.0
1980	203.1	1.3	190.1	0.0	0.0	0.0	0.0	11.7	0.0
1981	261.3	2.3	193.7	0.0	0.0	0.0	0.0	65.3	0.0
1982	363.2	2.2	260.7	0.0	0.0	0.3	0.3	100.0	0.0
1983	332.3	6.6	251.0	0.0	0.0	1.2	1.2	73.5	0.0
Chile									
1964	11.0	11.0	0.0	u	0.0	0.0	0.0	0.0	u
1965	31.9	20.0	9.4	u	0.0	0.0	0.0	2.5	u
1966	55.9	30.0	23.0	u	0.0	0.0	0.0	2.9	u
1967	129.5	81.0	47.0	u	0.0	0.0	0.0	1.5	u
1968	98.9	59.6	29.7	u	u	u	9.6	u	u
1969	88.8	45.8	27.7	u	u	u	15.3	u	u
1970	216.7	167.8	48.9	u	u	u	u	u	u
1971	168.5	129.8	38.7	u	u	u	u	u	0.0
1972[r]	62.6	39.4	22.1	u	0.0	0.0	0.0	1.1	0.0
1973[r]	88.0	54.7	31.4	u	0.0	0.0	0.0	1.9	0.0
1974[r]	164.5	110.1	51.7	u	0.0	0.0	0.0	2.7	0.0
1975[r]	191.4	124.9	62.3	u	0.0	0.0	0.0	4.2	0.0
1976[r]	227.7	153.6	69.3	u	0.0	0.0	0.0	4.8	0.0
1977[r]	265.9	186.4	69.9	u	0.0	0.0	0.0	9.6	0.0
Colombia (MOH)									
1965	4.7	0.4	2.6	u	0.0	0.0	0.0	1.7	u
1967	8.5	5.7	2.5	u	0.0	0.0	0.0	0.3	u
1968	29.3	14.3	13.1	u	u	u	0.2	1.7	u
1969	33.2	13.0	18.7	u	u	u	0.2	1.3	u
1970	47.4	18.5	26.5	u	u	u	0.5	1.9	u
1971	63.1	23.1	36.9	u	u	u	0.6	2.5	u
1972	62.7	22.6	37.6	u	u	u	0.6	1.9	u
1973	76.9	25.6	48.2	u	u	u	0.8	2.3	u
1974	103.5	29.0	69.3	u	u	u	2.1	3.1	u
1975	119.8	33.5	80.3	u	u	u	2.4	3.6	u
1976	78.8	25.6	51.0	u	u	u	u	2.2	u
1977	62.5	21.8	38.7	u	u	u	u	2.0	u
1978	60.6	22.3	29.3	u	0.0	5.0	5.0	4.0	u
1979	63.9	25.4	28.0	u	0.0	6.3	6.3	4.2	u
1980	103.4	66.8	25.9	u	0.0	5.7	5.7	5.0	u
1982	81.8	37.1	28.4	u	u	12.3	12.3	4.0	u
1983	109.8	50.5	36.2	u	u	14.5	14.5	8.6	u
Colombia (PROFAMILIA)[mm]									
1965	0.1	0.1	0.0	0.0	0.0	0.0	0.0	0.0	0.0
1966	6.6	6.5	0.1	0.0	0.0	0.0	0.0	0.0	0.0
1967	22.4	21.8	0.5	0.0	0.0	0.0	0.0	0.1	0.0
1968	18.9	17.0	1.7	0.0	0.0	0.0	0.0	0.2	0.0
1969	41.6	36.0	4.9	0.0	0.0	0.0	0.0	0.7	0.0
1970	51.6	42.4	8.1	0.0	0.1	0.0	0.1	1.0	0.0
1971	60.7	42.1	17.6	0.0	0.6	0.0	0.6	0.4	0.0
1972	73.7	45.7	26.4	0.0	0.9	0.0	0.9	0.7	0.0
1973	86.4	42.1	38.2	0.0	1.0	0.5	1.5	4.6	0.0
1974	97.7	38.5	49.4	0.0	1.1	2.6	3.7	6.1	0.0
1975	212.1	33.0	132.6	0.0	0.9	8.4	9.3	37.2	0.0
1976	284.9	30.3	201.1	0.0	0.8	18.0	18.8	34.7	0.0

Table 23. Number of Acceptors of Family Planning Services (000s), by Method and Year *(continued)*

Country and year	Total[a]	IUD[c]	Orals	Inject.	Sterilization Male	Female	Total	Other program methods	Abortion[a]
Colombia (PROFAMILIA, *continued* **)**									
1977	377.2	30.9	235.4	0.0	0.7	37.1	37.8	73.1	0.0
1978	424.7	32.2	270.0	0.0	0.7	40.4	41.0	81.5	0.0
1979	473.5	35.4	290.1	0.0	0.6	47.6	48.2	99.8	0.0
1980	539.5	37.8	360.2	0.0	0.6	35.1	35.6	105.9	0.0
1981	551.0	40.2	371.9	0.0	0.5	37.6	38.1	100.8	0.0
1982	638.9	49.1	405.0	0.0	0.5	49.2	49.8	135.0	0.0
1983	637.1	49.9	414.3	0.0	0.7	50.6	51.3	121.6	0.0
1984	670.0	48.1	453.1	0.0	0.8	45.1	45.9	122.9	0.0
1985	536.2	46.5	374.4	0.0	1.2	45.7	46.9	68.4	0.0
1986	480.6	45.9	306.2	0.0	2.2	59.7	61.9	66.6	0.0
1987	591.4	50.7	394.6	0.0	2.3	56.8	59.2	86.9	0.0
Colombia (ASCOFAME)									
1968	1.8	1.2	0.4	u	u	u	0.1	0.1	u
1969	23.5	12.8	9.3	u	u	u	0.5	0.9	u
1970	27.1	12.9	12.3	u	u	u	0.5	1.4	u
1971	34.4	15.1	17.2	u	u	u	0.7	1.4	u
1972	31.1	15.3	14.0	u	u	u	0.9	0.9	u
1973	16.5	9.8	5.6	u	u	u	0.8	0.3	u
1974	20.1	12.9	5.0	u	u	u	1.2	1.0	u
1975	7.9	3.4	2.8	u	u	u	1.0	0.7	u
Costa Rica									
1959	0.6	u	u	u	u	u	0.6	u	u
1960	0.5	u	u	u	u	u	0.5	u	u
1961	0.7	u	u	u	u	u	0.7	u	u
1962	0.9	u	u	u	u	u	0.9	u	u
1963	1.0	u	u	u	u	u	1.0	u	u
1964	1.0	u	u	u	u	u	1.0	u	u
1965	1.2	u	u	u	u	u	1.2	u	u
1966	1.3	u	u	u	u	u	1.3	u	u
1967	1.9	u	u	u	u	u	1.9	u	u
1968	12.0	2.8	7.0	u	u	u	2.1	0.1	u
1969	14.8	2.4	9.8	u	u	u	2.1	0.5	u
1970	18.9	2.4	14.7	u	0.0	0.0	0.0	1.8	u
1971	25.4	3.1	18.4	u	0.0	0.0	0.0	3.9	0.0
1972	26.7	2.4	19.7	u	0.0	0.0	0.0	4.6	0.0
1973	34.5	2.2	25.0	u	0.0	0.0	0.0	7.3	0.0
1974	25.7	1.9	18.7[s]	s	0.0	0.0	0.0	5.1	0.0
1975	30.9	2.1	21.6[s]	s	0.0	0.0	0.0	7.2	0.0
1976	28.8	1.6	19.1[s]	s	0.0	0.0	0.0	8.1	0.0
1977	22.6	0.4	15.3[s]	s	0.0	0.0	0.0	6.9	0.0
1978	22.4	0.9	14.6	u	0.0	0.0	0.0	6.9	0.0
1979	20.9	1.1	12.3	0.7	0.0	0.0	0.0	6.8	0.0
1980	20.3	1.0	11.3	0.7	0.0	0.0	0.0	7.3	u
1981	23.3	1.3	13.1	0.8	0.0	0.0	0.0	8.1	u
1982	22.3	0.9	13.1	0.6	0.0	0.0	0.0	7.7	u
Cuba									
1968	u	u	u	u	u	u	u	u	28.5
1969	u	u	u	u	u	u	u	u	46.1
1970	u	u	u	u	u	u	u	u	70.5
1971	u	u	u	u	u	u	u	u	84.8
1972	u	u	u	u	u	u	u	u	100.0
1973	u	u	u	u	u	u	u	u	112.1
1974	u	u	u	u	u	u	u	u	131.4
1975	u	u	u	u	u	u	u	u	126.1
1976	u	u	u	u	u	u	u	u	121.4
1977	u	u	u	u	u	u	u	u	114.8
1978	u	u	u	u	u	u	u	u	110.4
1979	u	u	u	u	u	u	u	u	106.5
1980	u	u	u	u	u	u	u	u	104.0
1981	u	u	u	u	u	u	u	u	108.6
1982	u	u	u	u	u	u	u	u	126.8
1983	u	u	u	u	u	u	u	u	124.8
1984	u	u	u	u	u	u	u	u	139.6

Table 23. Number of Acceptors of Family Planning Services (000s), by Method and Year *(continued)*

Country and year	Total[a]	IUD[e]	Orals	Inject.	Sterilization Male	Sterilization Female	Sterilization Total	Other program methods	Abortion[a]
Dominican Republic									
1968	3.5	1.4	1.3	u	0.0	0.0	0.0	0.8	u
1969	15.5	5.5	6.5	u	0.0	0.0	0.0	3.5	u
1970	17.2	7.0	6.0	u	0.0	0.0	0.0	4.2	u
1971	19.8	6.8	8.1	u	0.0	0.0	0.0	4.9	0.0
1972	18.7	5.7	8.7	u	0.0	0.0	0.0	4.3	0.0
1973	24.4	5.9	12.5	u	0.0	0.0	0.0	6.0	0.0
1974	38.2	6.4	23.7	u	0.0	0.0	0.0	8.1	0.0
1975	58.2	7.4	39.1	u	0.0	0.0	0.0	11.7	0.0
1976	61.5	6.0	41.7	u	0.0	0.0	0.0	13.8	0.0
1977	89.0	5.9	59.5	u	0.0	4.4	4.4	19.2	0.0
1978	14.3	u	u	u	0.0	14.3	14.3	u	u
1979	18.4	u	u	u	0.0	18.4	18.4	u	u
1980	16.1	u	u	u	0.0	16.1	16.1	u	u
1981	9.8	u	u	u	0.0	9.8	9.8	u	u
1982	14.3	u	u	u	0.0	14.3	14.3	u	u
1983	12.9	u	u	u	0.0	12.9	12.9	u	u
Ecuador									
1967	3.3	1.6	1.7	u	0.0	0.0	0.0	0.0	u
1968	3.2	1.5	1.4	u	0.0	0.0	0.0	0.3	u
1969	5.2	3.0	1.8	u	0.0	0.0	0.0	0.4	u
1970	9.1	4.8	3.3	u	0.0	0.0	0.0	1.0	u
1971	14.8	6.5	6.6	u	0.0	0.0	0.0	1.7	0.0
1972	17.4	8.3	7.2	u	0.0	0.0	0.0	1.9	0.0
1973	26.9	13.5	10.9	u	0.0	0.0	0.0	2.5	0.0
1974	35.2	14.4	16.2	u	0.0	0.0	0.0	4.6	0.0
1975	34.4	11.9	17.2	u	0.0	0.0	0.0	5.3	0.0
1976	32.3	11.3	17.1	u	0.0	0.0	0.0	3.9	0.0
1978	0.7	u	u	u	u	0.7	0.7	u	u
1979	2.4	u	u	u	u	2.4	2.4	u	u
1980	3.6	u	u	u	u	3.6	3.6	u	u
1981	4.5	u	u	u	u	4.5	4.5	u	u
1982	4.4	u	u	u	u	4.4	4.4	u	u
El Salvador									
1969	3.9	0.4	3.3	u	0.0	0.0	0.0	0.2	u
1970	6.5	0.5	5.6	u	0.0	0.0	0.0	0.4	u
1971	7.1	0.4	6.1	u	0.0	0.0	0.0	0.6	0.0
1972	7.0	0.4	5.3	u	0.0	0.7	0.7	0.6	0.0
1973	30.7	4.9	20.6	u	0.0	4.6	4.6	0.6	0.0
1974	41.3	7.6	24.3	u	0.0	5.7	5.7	3.7	0.0
1975	43.9	6.7	23.8	u	0.4	10.4	10.8	2.6	0.0
1976	41.9	6.5	19.9	u	0.3	12.0	12.3	3.2	0.0
1977	48.1	7.1	21.1	u	0.3	15.8	16.1	3.8	0.0
1978	46.8	6.0	19.2	u	0.3	18.6	18.9	2.7	0.0
1979	61.7	6.6	37.2	u	0.2	17.3	17.5	0.4	0.0
1980	56.4	6.1	34.0	u	0.1	15.9	16.0	0.3	0.0
1981	50.1	4.7	31.4	u	0.1	13.8	13.9	0.1	0.0
1982	52.1	7.2	30.3	u	0.1	14.4	14.4	0.2	0.0
1983	53.9	8.6	30.3	u	0.1	14.6	14.6[aa]	0.4	0.0
1984	38.8	7.4	17.4	u	u	u	14.0	u	u
Guatemala									
1968[h]	7.6	3.8	3.7	u	0.0	0.0	0.0	0.1	u
1969[h]	12.4	2.9	8.8	u	0.0	0.0	0.0	0.7	u
1970[h]	21.3	3.9	15.2	u	0.0	0.0	0.0	2.2	u
1971[h]	18.1	2.5	14.1	u	0.0	0.0	0.0	1.5	u
1972[h]	18.0	2.8	14.1	u	0.0	0.0	0.0	1.1	u
1973[h]	18.6	3.6	13.4	u	u	u	0.2	1.4	u
1977	3.6	u	u	u	0.6	3.0	3.6	u	u
1978	5.7	u	u	u	0.7	5.0	5.7	u	u
1979	18.0	2.9	5.1	u	0.8	6.9	7.7	2.3	0.0
1980	19.9	2.9	4.1	u	1.0	7.7	8.8	4.1	0.0
1981	8.6	u	u	u	1.5	7.1	8.6	u	u
1982	9.8	u	u	u	1.3	8.5	9.8	u	u

Table 23. Number of Acceptors of Family Planning Services (000s), by Method and Year *(continued)*

Country and year	Total[a]	IUD[e]	Orals	Inject.	Sterilization			Other program methods	Abortion[a]
					Male	Female	Total		
Haiti									
1974	4.6	0.6	1.8	u	0.0	0.0	0.0	2.2	0.0
1975	15.5	1.4	6.4	u	0.0	0.0	0.0	7.7	0.0
1976	16.0	1.5	8.4	u	0.0	0.0	0.0	6.1	0.0
1982	49.3	0.4	32.2	0.1	0.0	1.7	1.7	14.9	u
1983	43.6	0.5	31.5	0.2	0.3	2.2	2.5	8.9	u
1984	55.3	0.2	37.9	0.9	0.4	3.0	3.4	12.9	u
1985	70.6	0.6	52.2	3.2	0.9	3.9	4.8	9.8	u
1986	16.4	0.0	11.8	0.6	0.0	1.2	1.2	2.8	u
Honduras									
1968	3.3	1.9	1.4	u	0.0	0.0	0.0	0.0	u
1969	4.7	1.3	3.4	u	0.0	0.0	0.0	0.0	u
1970	12.7	2.7	10.0	u	0.0	0.0	0.0	0.0	u
1971	14.6	4.6	10.0	u	0.0	0.0	0.0	0.0	u
1972	25.2	6.7	18.1	u	0.0	0.0	0.0	0.4	u
1973	23.1	6.4	16.2	u	0.0	0.0	0.0	0.5	u
1978	1.2	u	u	u	0.0	1.2	1.2[bb]	u	u
1979	3.8	u	u	u	0.0	3.8	3.8[bb]	u	u
1980	3.7	u	u	u	0.0	3.7	3.7[bb]	u	u
1981	3.9	u	u	u	0.0	3.8	3.9[bb]	u	u
1982	5.0	u	u	u	0.0	4.9	5.0[bb]	u	u
Jamaica									
1968	2.1	0.3	1.6	u	u	u	u	0.2	u
1969	28.4	3.9	18.1	u	u	u	u	6.4	u
1970	19.3	2.2	10.2	u	u	u	u	6.9	u
1971	22.2	2.5	12.9	u	u	u	u	6.8	0.0
1972	23.1	1.9	10.3	u	0.0	1.1	1.1	9.8	0.0
1973	28.0	1.8	11.1	u	0.0	2.4	2.4	12.7	0.0
1974	24.7	0.9	10.7	5.7	0.0	2.7	2.7	4.7	0.0
1975	27.0	1.0	11.4	6.2	0.0	3.2	3.2	5.2	0.0
1982	36.5	0.7	15.6	7.8	u	u	3.9	8.5	u
1983	47.1	0.8	20.1	11.0	u	u	5.9	9.3	u
1984	62.9	1.2	29.4	11.2	u	u	6.6	14.5	u
1985	62.2	1.0	31.2	12.0	u	u	5.4	12.6	u
1986	64.6	0.6	29.1	11.3	u	u	5.0	18.6	u
Mexico[p]									
1973	192.2	103.3	79.9	9.0	0.0	0.0	0.0	u	0.0
1974	585.0	285.0	213.0	7.0	u	u	13.0	67.0	0.0
1975	564.0	297.0	169.6	6.4	u	u	15.0	76.0	0.0
1977	911.0	206.0	444.0	u	u	u	147.0	114.0	0.0
1978	1085.0	233.0	604.0[s]	s	u	u	147.0	101.0	0.0
1979	1144.0	225.0	640.0[s]	s	u	u	136.0	143.0	0.0
1980	1314.0	298.0	693.0[s]	s	u	u	134.0	189.0	0.0
1981	1582.0	u	u	u	u	u	u	1582.0[c]	0.0
1982	1600.0	u	u	u	u	u	u	1600.0[c]	0.0
1983	1609.0	425.0	920.0[s]	s	u	u	177.0	87.0	0.0
Mexico (FEPAC)									
1968	10.7	4.2	6.5	u	0.0	0.0	0.0	u	u
1969	19.6	5.6	6.8	7.2	0.0	0.0	0.0	u	u
1970	25.0	8.5	8.7	7.8	0.0	0.0	0.0	u	u
1971	28.9	9.4	13.1	6.4	0.0	0.0	0.0	u	0.0
1972	44.5	13.8	23.1	7.6	0.0	0.0	0.0	u	0.0
Mexico (IMSS)									
1982	898.5	246.2	536.4[s]	s	4.0	111.9	115.9	u	u
1983	992.1	301.2	554.5[s]	s	4.9	131.5	136.4	u	u
1984	1038.4	377.7	495.1[s]	s	5.4	160.2	165.6	u	u
1985	1098.9	437.2	495.9[s]	s	4.8	161.0	165.8	u	u
1986	1099.0	478.4	440.0	9.6	5.0	166.0	171.0	u	u
Mexico (MEXFAM)									
1982	25.3	6.4	14.6	1.5	0.0	0.2	0.2	2.6	u
1983	27.1	6.5	16.1	1.4	0.0	0.2	0.2	2.9	u
1984	34.9	9.7	18.6	1.7	0.0	0.6	0.6	4.3	u

141

Table 23. Number of Acceptors of Family Planning Services (000s), by Method and Year *(continued)*

Country and year	Total[a]	IUD[e]	Orals	Inject.	Sterilization Male	Sterilization Female	Sterilization Total	Other program methods	Abortion[a]
Mexico (MEXFAM, *continued*)									
1985	58.6	7.3	34.0	2.2	0.0	3.5	3.5	11.6	u
1986	174.6	26.8	75.2	7.0	0.3	12.4	12.7	52.9	u
Mexico (MOH)									
1978	425.1	92.8	254.5	16.0	u	u	12.2	49.6	u
1979	476.5	88.6	287.5	24.7	u	u	17.0	58.7	u
1980	524.8	96.5	285.5	51.8	u	u	21.5	69.5	u
1981	485.7	84.6	251.7	61.7	u	u	23.3	64.4	u
1982	569.0	103.0	293.4	68.3	u	u	21.1	83.2	u
1983	529.6	98.4	281.5	56.1	u	u	18.1	75.5	u
1984	548.6	105.1	296.7	43.1	u	u	23.3	80.4	u
1985	523.9	110.6	270.6	37.6	u	u	25.0	80.1	u
Nicaragua									
1968	1.6	0.8	0.7	u	0.0	0.0	0.0	0.1	u
1969	7.3	4.6	2.6	u	0.0	0.0	0.0	0.1	u
1970	10.1	5.3	4.7	u	0.0	0.0	0.0	0.1	u
1971	13.8	5.3	8.2	u	u	u	u	0.3	u
1972	13.6	4.0	9.2	u	u	u	u	0.4	u
1973	15.5	4.7	9.6	u	u	u	u	1.2	u
Panama									
1972	15.4	2.3	8.6	u	u	u	3.7	0.8	0.0
1973	13.7	2.4	7.1	u	u	u	3.4	0.8	0.0
1974	24.1	5.6	13.4	u	u	u	4.5	0.6	0.0
1975	15.1	2.4	7.6	u	u	u	0.8	4.3	0.0
Paraguay									
1974	15.9	3.5	10.3	u	0.0	0.0	0.0	2.1	0.0
1975	20.3	3.8	13.2	u	0.0	0.0	0.0	3.3	0.0
1976	26.0	4.0	17.0	u	0.0	0.0	0.0	5.0	0.0
Paraguay (CEPEP)									
1982	5.3	3.2	1.5	k	u	0.0	0.0	0.6	u
1983	6.4	2.9	2.8	k	u	0.0	0.0	0.7	u
1984	8.8	3.9	3.6	k	u	0.2	0.2	1.1	u
1985	10.6	4.3	5.1	k	u	0.3	0.3	0.9	u
1986	11.0	3.7	5.6	0.1	u	0.5	0.5	1.1	u
Peru (MOH)									
1986	76.8	22.2	26.5	u	u	u	u	28.1	u
Peru (INPPARES)									
1986	86.7	28.5	29.7	u	u	0.1	0.1	28.4	u
Puerto Rico									
1971	28.2	2.0	13.2	u	u	u	3.0	10.0	0.0
1972	43.5	4.6	20.6	u	u	u	1.0	17.3	0.0
1973	28.7	2.3	14.2	u	u	u	1.0	11.2	0.0
1974	47.0	2.9	22.4	u	u	u	5.9	15.8	0.0
1975	53.4	2.7	23.0	u	u	u	9.0	18.7	0.0
1985	10.6	0.4	5.9	u	u	u	0.0	4.3	u
Puerto Rico (APPBF)									
1986	0.3	0.0	u	u	0.0	0.2	0.3	0.0	u
Trinidad and Tobago									
1969	15.4	0.6	11.4	u	0.0	0.0	0.0	3.4	u
1970	10.3	0.5	5.7	u	u	u	0.3	3.8	u
1971	9.0	0.4	4.4	u	u	u	0.3	3.9	u
1972	0.0	u	u	u	u	u	u	u	u
1973	6.2	0.2	2.4	u	0.0	0.0	0.0	3.6	u
1978	0.4	u	u	u	0.0	0.4	0.4[bb]	u	u
1979	0.3	u	u	u	0.0	0.3	0.3[bb]	u	u
1980	0.4	u	u	u	0.0	0.4	0.4[bb]	u	u
1981	10.0	0.3	2.7	0.0	0.0	0.4	0.4[bb]	6.6	0.0
1982	10.9	0.4	2.5	0.0	0.0	0.4	0.4[bb]	7.6	0.0

Table 23. Number of Acceptors of Family Planning Services (000s), by Method and Year *(continued)*

Country and year	Total[a]	IUD[c]	Orals	Inject.	Sterilization Male	Female	Total	Other program methods	Abortion[a]
Trinidad and Tobago *(continued)*									
1983	10.9	0.3	2.2	0.0	0.0	0.0	0.0	8.4	0.0
Venezuela									
1968	9.3	6.3	2.7	u	0.0	0.0	0.0	0.3	u
1969[g]	24.9	15.7	8.5	u	0.0	0.0	0.0	0.7	u
1970[g]	32.7	18.2	12.8	u	0.0	0.0	0.0	1.7	u
1971[g]	44.2	23.1	19.0	u	u	u	0.1	2.0	0.0
1972[g]	82.2	42.7	35.9	u	u	u	0.1	3.5	0.0
1973[g]	88.1	42.4	42.9	u	u	u	0.1	2.7	0.0
1974	86.0	30.0[z]	53.0[z]	u	u	u	u	3.0[z]	0.0
1975	0.0	u	u	u	u	u	u	u	0.0
MIDDLE EAST/NORTH AFRICA									
Egypt									
1967	141.0	51.0	90.0	u	0.0	0.0	0.0	0.0	u
1968	134.0	47.0	87.0	u	0.0	0.0	0.0	0.0	u
1969	148.0	55.0	93.0	u	0.0	0.0	0.0	0.0	u
1970	206.0	57.0	115.0	u	0.0	0.0	0.0	34.0	u
1971	221.0	69.0	87.0	u	0.0	0.0	0.0	65.0	0.0
1972	237.0	85.0	77.0	u	0.0	0.0	0.0	75.0	0.0
1973	150.0	75.0	55.0	u	0.0	0.0	0.0	20.0	0.0
1974	143.0	66.0	48.0	u	0.0	0.0	0.0	29.0	0.0
1975	184.0	76.0	108.0	u	0.0	0.0	0.0	u	0.0
1976	441.6	83.6	347.3	u	0.0	0.0	0.0	10.7	0.0
1977	460.4	94.5	346.6	u	0.0	0.0	0.0	19.3	0.0
1978	346.1	57.7	275.3	0.0	0.0	0.0	0.0	13.1	0.0
1979	327.7	63.7	248.3	0.0	0.0	0.0	0.0	15.7	0.0
1980	1102.7	181.3	699.4	0.0	0.0	0.0	0.0	222.0	0.0
1981	1148.5	205.6	738.9	0.0	0.0	0.0	0.0	204.0	0.0
1982	1315.5	280.4	856.4	0.0	0.0	0.0	0.0	178.7	0.0
1983	1459.0	326.0	814.4	0.0	0.0	0.0	0.0	318.6	0.0
1984	1236.0	u	908.0	16.0	u	u	u	312.0	u
1985	1396.0	146.0	865.0	73.0	u	u	u	312.0	u
1986	1357.0	154.0	875.0	2.0	u	u	u	326.0	u
Iran									
1967	10.3	0.9	9.4	u	0.0	0.0	0.0	u	u
1968	122.4	8.6	113.8	u	0.0	0.0	0.0	u	u
1969	230.5	12.1	218.4	u	0.0	0.0	0.0	u	u
1970	304.1	12.7	291.4	u	0.0	0.0	0.0	u	u
1971	385.0	14.4	370.6	u	0.0	0.0	0.0	u	0.0
1972	445.0	19.0	426.0	u	0.0	0.0	0.0	u	0.0
1973	470.0	19.6	450.4	u	0.0	0.0	0.0	u	0.0
1974	481.0	19.4	461.6	u	0.0	0.0	0.0	u	0.0
1975	506.0	18.0	488.0	u	0.0	0.0	0.0	u	0.0
1976	571.7	25.4	546.0	u	0.1	0.2	0.3	u	0.0
1977	621.3	16.7	603.0	u	0.4	1.2	1.6	u	0.0
1982	1005.8	25.4	431.4[j]	u	u	u	u	549.0[v]	u
1983	990.7	26.9	411.8[j]	u	u	u	u	552.0[v]	u
1984	1131.0	28.8	393.2[j]	u	u	u	u	709.0[v]	u
1985	1131.5	32.4	391.1[j]	u	u	u	u	708.0[v]	u
1986	1284.2	33.3	406.9[j]	u	u	u	u	844.0[v]	u
Iraq									
1986	40.0	7.0	25.0	2.5	u	u	u	5.5	u
Morocco									
1966	6.4	6.4	0.0	u	0.0	0.0	0.0	0.0	u
1967	5.5	5.1	0.0	u	0.0	0.0	0.0	0.4	u
1968	10.3	8.5	0.0	u	0.0	0.0	0.0	1.8	u
1969	21.3	I1.0	9.2	u	0.0	0.0	0.0	1.1	u
1970	25.1	9.8	14.3	u	0.0	0.0	0.0	1.0	u
1971	28.9	7.7	17.9	u	0.0	0.0	0.0	3.3	0.0
1972	28.5	6.3	19.3	u	0.0	0.0	0.0	2.9	0.0
1973	37.0	5.2	27.3	u	0.0	0.0	0.0	4.5	0.0
1974	55.4	6.3	46.2	u	0.0	0.0	0.0	2.9	0.0
1975	72.3	7.5	59.8	u	0.0	0.0	0.0	5.0	0.0

Table 23. Number of Acceptors of Family Planning Services (000s), by Method and Year *(continued)*

Country and year	Total[a]	IUD[e]	Orals	Inject.	Sterilization Male	Sterilization Female	Sterilization Total	Other program methods	Abortion[a]
Morocco *(continued)*									
1976	77.9	6.2	63.7	u	0.0	0.0	0.0	8.0	0.0
1982	180.9	u	180.9	na	na	u	u	u	na
1983	197.2	13.4	182.5	na	na	1.3	1.3	u	na
1984	225.8	25.8	196.9	na	na	3.1	3.1	u	na
1985	242.3	20.3	215.8	na	na	6.2	6.2	u	na
1986	233.2	16.7	210.8	na	na	5.7	5.7	u	na
Tunisia									
1964	1.4	1.1	0.0[f]	u	u	u	0.3	0.0[f]	u
1965	15.0	13.3	0.2[f]	u	0.0	0.4	0.4	1.1[f]	u
1966	17.3	14.1	0.5[f]	u	0.0	0.8	0.8	1.9[f]	1.4
1967	11.4	9.7	0.6[f]	u	0.0	0.7	0.7	0.4	1.2
1968	16.7	9.3	4.8	u	0.0	1.6	1.6	1.0	2.2
1969	20.6	8.7	7.9	u	0.0	2.5	2.5	1.5	2.9
1970	31.6	9.6	10.0	u	0.0	2.5	2.5	9.5	2.7
1971	26.5	12.4	11.8	u	0.0	2.3	2.3	u	3.2
1972	40.0	13.2	12.0	u	0.0	2.5	2.5	12.3	4.6
1973	45.6	16.8	11.2	u	0.0	5.0	5.0	12.6	6.5
1974	51.8	19.1	10.8	u	0.0	10.8	10.8	11.1	12.4
1975	56.6	17.3	16.3	u	0.0	9.9	9.9	13.1	16.0
1976	60.9	17.3	21.6	u	0.0	8.3	8.3	13.7	20.3
1977	64.8	19.1	22.6	u	0.0	8.0	8.0	15.1	21.2
1978	65.0	21.0	21.6	u	0.0	8.8	8.8	13.6	21.0
1979	59.7	20.6	18.9	u	0.0	8.1	8.1	12.1	19.2
1980	64.3	25.4	17.4	u	0.0	8.5	8.5	13.0	20.5
1981	69.8	32.5	16.1	u	0.0	8.7	8.7	12.5	20.7
1982	9.6	u	u	u	0.0	9.6	9.6	u	21.0
1983	0.0	u	u	u	u	u	u	u	20.3
1984	0.0	u	u	u	u	u	u	u	20.9
1985	0.0	u	u	u	u	u	u	u	21.3
1986	0.0	u	u	u	u	u	u	u	20.0
Turkey									
1965	5.0	5.0	0.0	u	0.0	0.0	0.0	0.0	u
1966	33.0	33.0	0.0	u	0.0	0.0	0.0	0.0	u
1967	47.0	47.0	0.0	u	0.0	0.0	0.0	0.0	u
1968	67.8	58.6	9.2	u	0.0	0.0	0.0	0.0	u
1969	77.0	60.3	16.7	u	0.0	0.0	0.0	0.0	u
1970	65.6	57.2	8.4	u	0.0	0.0	0.0	0.0	u
1971	53.6	49.6	4.0	u	0.0	0.0	0.0	0.0	0.0
1972	51.7	46.6	5.1	u	0.0	0.0	0.0	0.0	0.0
1973	58.7	43.7	12.2	u	0.0	0.0	0.0	2.8	0.0
1974	66.7	43.8	13.2	u	0.0	0.0	0.0	9.7	0.0
1981	0.0	u	u	u	u	u	u	u	320.0[m]
ASIA									
Afghanistan									
1974	10.9	1.1	6.4	u	0.0	0.0	0.0	3.4	0.0
1975	12.7	1.2	7.3	u	0.0	0.0	0.0	4.2	0.0
1976	16.6	1.2	9.7	u	0.0	0.0	0.0	5.7	0.0
Bangladesh									
1966	3.9	u	u	u	3.9	u	u	u	u
1967	690.3	299.0	u	u	46.0	u	u	391.3	u
1968	1008.8	397.2	u	u	252.8	u	u	611.6	u
1969[g]	933.0	366.3	u	u	389.5	u	u	566.7	u
1970[g]	159.6	159.6	u	u	314.2	u	u	u	0.0
1971[g]	170.8	27.4	0.6	u	16.6	u	u	142.8	0.0
1972[g]	142.5	8.5	4.4	u	0.3	0.2	0.5	129.1	0.0
1973[g]	205.1	18.6	16.5	u	0.2	0.1	0.4	169.6	0.0
1974	182.6	31.9	54.9	u	0.4	1.0	1.5	94.3	0.0
1975	637.3	67.6	225.0	u	14.5	4.7	19.2	325.5	4.4
1976	946.2	77.8	458.0	0.5	37.8	11.1	48.9	361.0	6.7
1977	764.3	59.4	357.0	0.6	75.1	41.2	116.3	231.0	6.1
1978	1118.0	40.6	577.0	1.1	32.6	44.7	77.3	422.0	4.4
1979	1084.8	22.6	550.0	2.8	24.7	81.7	106.4	403.0	10.5
1980	1092.1	21.8	486.0	6.5	27.5	171.2	198.8	379.0	28.0

144

Table 23. Number of Acceptors of Family Planning Services (000s), by Method and Year *(continued)*

Country and year	Total[a]	IUD[e]	Orals	Inject.	Sterilization Male	Sterilization Female	Sterilization Total	Other program methods	Abortion[a]
Bangladesh *(continued)*									
1981	258.5	u	u	u	26.0	232.5	258.5	u	42.4
1982	2236.9	117.8	630.8	18.2	69.3	232.8	302.1	1168.0	58.6
1983	2754.1	303.3	746.1	30.6	88.5	274.6	363.1	1311.0	56.7
1984	3496.2	432.5	884.6	41.5	281.8	336.8	618.6	1519.0	68.6
1985	1955.8	300.1	930.8	54.1	168.6	143.3	311.8	359.0	u
1986	2867.8	389.2	853.8	49.7	203.3	127.9	331.1	1244.0	u
China									
1971	9141.0	6172.9	u	u	1223.5	1744.6	2968.1	u	3910.0
1972	13023.0	9220.3	u	u	1715.8	2087.2	3803.0	u	u
1973	18838.0	13950.0	u	u	1933.2	2955.6	4888.8	u	u
1974	16301.0	12580.0	u	u	1445.3	2275.7	3721.0	u	u
1975	22676.0	16744.0	u	u	2652.7	3280.0	5932.7	u	u
1976	15830.0	11626.0	u	u	1495.5	2707.8	4203.3	u	u
1977	18368.0	12974.0	u	u	2616.9	2776.4	5393.3	u	u
1978	14241.0	10962.0	u	u	767.5	2511.4	3278.9	u	u
1979	20436.0	13472.0	u	u	1673.9	5289.5	6963.4	u	u
1980	16697.0	11492.0	u	u	1363.5	3842.0	5205.5	u	u
1981	12550.0	10344.0	u	u	649.5	1556.0	2205.5	u	u
1982	19226.0	14069.0	u	u	1230.9	3925.9	5156.8	u	u
1983	38513.0	17756.0	u	u	4359.3	16398.0	20758.0	u	u
1984	18462.0	11751.0	u	u	1293.3	5417.2	6710.5	u	u
Anhui	1008.8	311.1	u	u	235.5	462.2	697.7	u	u
Beijing	99.7	78.7	u	u	0.9	20.1	21.0	u	u
Fujian	607.6	274.6	u	u	52.1	280.9	333.0	u	u
Gansu	280.3	122.3	u	u	0.8	157.2	158.0	u	u
Guangdong	1413.9	633.3	u	u	164.8	615.8	780.6	u	u
Guangxi Zhuang Zizhiqu	447.3	409.8	u	u	14.9	22.6	37.5	u	u
Guizhou	474.6	156.8	u	u	142.4	175.4	317.8	u	u
Hebei	1127.5	755.9	u	u	46.8	324.8	371.6	u	u
Heilongjiang	532.9	285.5	u	u	0.8	246.6	247.4	u	u
Henan	1634.3	1141.8	u	u	106.8	385.7	492.5	u	u
Hubei	923.5	491.9	u	u	51.1	380.5	431.6	u	u
Hunan	1078.7	642.4	u	u	136.3	300.0	436.3	u	u
Jiangsu	1214.3	903.6	u	u	50.1	260.6	310.7	u	u
Jiangxi	744.0	183.0	u	u	7.3	553.7	561.0	u	u
Jilin	320.6	231.5	u	u	0.2	88.9	89.1	u	u
Liaoning	474.6	419.4	u	u	0.5	54.7	55.2	u	u
Nei Menggu Zizhiqu	306.7	153.2	u	u	0.8	152.7	153.5	u	u
Ningxia Hui Zizhiqu	44.3	21.7	u	u	0.0	22.6	22.6	u	u
Qinghai	31.7	14.2	u	u	0.2	17.3	17.5	u	u
Shaanxi	590.5	325.9	u	u	28.3	236.3	264.6	u	u
Shandong	1558.8	1241.8	u	u	160.2	156.8	317.0	u	u
Shanghai	196.3	191.8	u	u	0.5	4.1	4.5	u	u
Shanxi	562.6	334.1	u	u	4.2	224.3	228.5	u	u
Sichuan	1405.3	1091.5	u	u	223.8	90.0	313.8	u	u
Tianjin	95.6	89.5	u	u	0.6	5.5	6.1	u	u
Xinjiang Uighur Zizhiqu	79.4	22.9	u	u	0.8	55.7	56.5	u	u
Xizang Zizhiqu	0.0	0.0	u	u	0.0	0.0	0.0	u	u
Yunnan	440.9	261.2	u	u	56.7	123.0	179.7	u	u
Zhejiang	756.9	516.8	u	u	7.4	232.7	240.1	u	
Hong Kong (Government)[l]									
1973	0.0	0.0	0.0	0.0	0.0	0.0	0.0	0.0	0.2
1974	u	u	u	u	u	u	u	u	0.6
1975	u	u	u	u	u	u	u	u	1.0
1976	34.8	0.8	17.7[s]	s	0.1	0.3	0.4	15.9	2.2
1977	39.6	0.4	23.1[s]	s	u	u	u	16.1	3.8
1978	40.0	0.5	22.6[s]	s	u	u	u	16.9	5.5
1979	40.9	0.5	21.9[s]	s	u	u	u	18.5	7.0
1980	41.5	0.3	21.6[s]	s	u	u	u	19.6	9.4
1981	0.0	u	u	u	u	u	u	u	10.6[dd]
1982	48.9	4.1	25.0	2.1	u	u	u	17.7	12.2[dd]
1983	49.0	4.1	25.3	2.3	u	u	u	17.3	13.4[dd]
1984	0.0	u	u	u	u	u	u	u	14.5[dd]
1985	0.0	u	u	u	u	u	u	u	15.4[dd]

Table 23. Number of Acceptors of Family Planning Services (000s), by Method and Year (continued)

Country and year	Total[a]	IUD[c]	Orals	Inject.	Sterilization Male	Sterilization Female	Sterilization Total	Other program methods	Abortion[a]
Hong Kong (FPA)									
1964	10.0	10.0	0.0	0.0	0.0	0.0	0.0	u	u
1965	36.5	30.0	0.5	0.0	0.0	0.0	0.0	6.0	u
1966	23.1	14.0	0.7	0.0	0.1	0.3	0.4	8.0	u
1967	18.7	6.2	2.5	0.0	0.1	0.7	0.8	9.2	u
1968	26.2	5.5	11.8	0.0	u	u	1.0	7.9	u
1969	30.0	3.8	18.0	0.0	u	u	1.0	7.2	u
1970	29.7	2.8	20.2	0.0	u	u	0.9	5.8	u
1971	30.4	1.8	21.5	0.0	u	u	0.5	6.6	u
1972	31.9	0.6	23.2	u	0.3	0.1	0.4	7.7	u
1973	33.2	0.5	24.3	u	0.3	0.1	0.4	8.0	u
1974	29.8	0.3	20.6	u	0.6	0.1	0.7	8.2	u
1975	23.6	0.2	15.9	u	0.7	0.1	0.8	6.7	u
1976	27.1	0.3	17.1[s]	s	0.7	0.1	0.8	8.9	u
1977	25.8	0.3	14.7[s]	s	0.7	0.3	1.0	9.8	u
1978	25.4	0.3	14.0[s]	s	0.6	0.3	0.9	10.2	u
1979	27.8	0.5	14.7	0.2	0.8	0.5	1.3	11.1	u
1980	31.7	0.8	15.0	0.6	0.6	0.6	1.2	14.1	u
1981	29.6	0.7	13.9	0.3	0.3	0.6	0.9	13.8	u
1982	31.0	0.6	14.6	0.2	0.4	0.6	1.0	14.6	u
1983	31.4	0.8	14.0	0.5	0.5	0.5	1.0	15.1	u
1984[cc]	88.8[cc]	5.2	44.1	3.7	0.6	0.4	1.1	34.7	u
1985[cc]	64.4[cc]	4.3	29.3	3.4	0.5	0.5	1.0	26.4	u
1986[cc]	87.2[cc]	5.9	48.9	3.9	0.5	0.5	1.0	27.5	u
India[i]									
1956	7.0	u	u	u	2.3	4.7	7.0	u	u
1957	13.7	u	u	u	4.1	9.6	13.7	u	u
1958	25.1	u	u	u	9.2	15.9	25.1	u	u
1959	42.3	u	u	u	17.6	24.7	42.3	u	u
1960	64.3	u	u	u	37.6	26.7	64.3	u	u
1961	104.6	u	u	u	63.9	40.7	104.6	u	u
1962	157.9	u	u	u	112.3	45.6	157.9	u	u
1963	170.2	u	u	u	114.6	55.6	170.2	u	u
1964	269.6	0.0	0.0	u	201.2	68.4	269.6	u	u
1965	989.0	318.0	0.0	u	577.0	94.0	671.0	u	u
1966	1858.0	971.0	0.0	u	785.0	102.0	887.0	u	u
1967	2985.0	669.0	1.0	u	1648.0	192.0	1840.0	475.0	u
1968	3115.0	479.0	10.0	u	1383.0	282.0	1665.0	961.0	u
1969[g]	3411.0	459.0	15.0	u	1056.0	366.0	1422.0	1515.0	u
1970[g]	3782.0	476.0	13.0	u	879.0	451.0	1330.0	1963.0	u
1971[g]	5049.0	488.0	20.0	u	1620.0	567.0	2187.0	2354.0	u
1972[g]	5875.0	355.0	u	u	2613.0	509.0	3122.0	2398.0	24.3[t]
1973[g]	4324.0	372.0	u	u	403.0	539.0	942.0	3010.0	44.9[t]
1974[g]	4308.0	433.0	u	u	612.0	742.0	1354.0	2521.0	97.7[t]
1975	6802.0	607.0	32.0	u	1438.0	1230.0	2668.0	3495.0	214.2[t]
1976	12534.0	581.0	58.0	u	6199.0	2062.0	8261.0	3634.0	278.9[t]
1977	4528.0	326.0	78.0	u	188.0	761.0	949.0	3175.0	247.0[t]
1978	5639.0	552.0	82.0	u	391.0	1093.0	1484.0	3521.0	317.7[t]
1979	5470.0	635.0	82.0	0.0	473.0	1305.0	1778.0	2975.0	360.8[t]
1980	6456.0	628.0	91.0	0.0	435.0	1594.0	2029.0	3708.0	388.4[t]
1981	8083.0	751.0	120.0	0.0	570.0	2214.0	2784.0	4428.0	434.0[t]
1982	10997.2	1074.0	179.0	0.0	585.5	3397.7	3983.2	5761.0	506.0[t]
1983	14504.3	2134.1	525.0	0.0	661.0	3871.2	4532.2	7313.0	547.3[t]
1984	6644.2	2561.9	u	u	548.9	3533.4	4082.3	u	573.1[t]
1985	8050.0	3220.0	u	u	u	u	4830.0	u	u
Andhra Pradesh									
1967	224.0	54.0	u	u	u	u	170.0	u	u
1968	222.0	17.0	u	u	u	u	205.0	u	u
1969	218.0	9.0	u	u	u	u	209.0	u	u
1970	235.0	10.0	u	u	u	u	225.0	u	u
1971	2524.4	13.4	u	u	u	u	2511.0	u	u
1972	404.6	14.7	u	u	u	u	339.7	50.2	u
1973	146.5	26.5	u	u	u	u	120.0	u	u
1976	811.2	13.7	1.4	u	u	u	755.6	40.5	u
1977	184.2	10.9	1.8	u	27.1	112.1	139.2	32.3	11.5[t]
1978	245.1	17.6	2.1	u	46.7	145.5	192.2	33.2	13.2[t]

Table 23. Number of Acceptors of Family Planning Services (000s), by Method and Year *(continued)*

Country and year	Total[a]	IUD[e]	Orals	Inject.	Sterilization Male	Sterilization Female	Sterilization Total	Other program methods	Abortion[a]
Andhra Pradesh (continued)									
1979	231.8	12.8	2.4	u	35.0	146.1	181.1	35.5	10.0[t]
1981	308.5	18.1	u	u	u	u	290.4	u	15.1[t]
1982	381.8	24.8	u	u	33.2	324.0	357.0	u	u
1983	421.9	64.1	u	u	32.9	325.9	357.8	u	13.5[t]
1984	451.7	78.1	u	u	29.9	343.7	373.6	u	13.0[t]
Assam									
1967	24.0	21.0	u	u	u	u	3.0	u	u
1968	37.0	22.0	u	u	u	u	15.0	u	u
1969	28.0	10.0	u	u	u	u	18.0	u	u
1970	23.0	6.0	u	u	u	u	17.0	u	u
1971	49.2	7.9	u	u	u	u	41.3	u	u
1972	70.1	4.2	u	u	u	u	60.9	5.0	u
1973	23.3	2.8	u	u	u	u	20.5	u	u
1976	259.2	12.3	0.6	u	u	u	230.4	15.9	u
1977	33.7	3.1	0.4	u	7.9	5.8	13.7	16.5	8.4[t]
1978	55.3	6.6	0.9	u	18.1	7.2	25.3	22.5	9.5[t]
1979	45.7	7.0	0.6	u	14.4	7.9	22.3	15.8	9.9[t]
1981	49.9	15.8	u	u	u	u	34.1	u	9.4[t]
1982	71.3	15.6	u	u	41.8	13.9	55.7	u	u
1983	142.9	16.6	u	u	83.5	42.8	126.3	u	12.3[t]
1984	142.6	17.1	u	u	54.8	70.7	125.5	u	11.9[t]
Bihar									
1967	176.0	32.0	u	u	u	u	144.0	u	u
1968	118.0	25.0	u	u	u	u	93.0	u	u
1969	145.0	48.0	u	u	u	u	97.0	u	u
1970	113.0	40.0	u	u	u	u	73.0	u	u
1971	187.8	49.4	u	u	u	u	138.4	u	u
1972	308.4	24.5	u	u	u	u	267.4	16.5	u
1973	35.6	13.4	u	u	u	u	22.2	u	u
1976	630.5	18.0	0.3	u	u	u	583.3	28.9	u
1977	68.5	7.6	0.8	u	10.0	25.0	35.0	25.1	2.9[t]
1978	156.8	19.1	1.7	u	31.0	57.9	88.9	47.1	6.7[t]
1979	170.8	21.2	2.1	u	25.6	60.0	85.6	61.9	7.4[t]
1981	28.0	28.0	u	u	u	u	u	u	u
1982	396.9	44.8	u	u	35.2	316.9	352.1	u	u
1983	483.0	87.1	u	u	35.2	360.7	395.9	u	13.4[t]
1984	367.8	76.5	u	u	30.1	261.2	291.3	u	13.1[t]
Central Government Institute									
1967	52.0	14.0	u	u	u	u	38.0	u	u
1968	40.0	9.0	u	u	u	u	31.0	u	u
1969	34.0	8.0	u	u	u	u	26.0	u	u
1970	38.0	6.0	u	u	u	u	32.0	u	u
1971	29.9	6.9	u	u	u	u	23.0	u	u
1972	32.0	6.8	u	u	u	u	25.2	u	u
1973	27.0	6.6	u	u	u	u	20.4	u	u
Community Distribution									
1976	1459.3	u	u	u	u	u	u	1459.3	u
1977	1553.1	u	u	u	u	u	u	1553.1	u
1978	1492.8	u	u	u	u	u	u	1492.8	u
1979	1081.5	u	u	u	u	u	u	1081.5	u
Delhi									
1976	314.2	11.7	0.9	u	u	u	141.1	160.5	u
1977	135.0	13.9	0.7	u	0.7	5.0	5.7	114.7	11.8[t]
1978	181.2	24.2	0.7	u	1.3	6.6	7.9	148.4	14.0[t]
1979	187.2	28.1	0.7	u	1.8	10.2	12.0	146.4	15.0[t]
1981	60.4	36.4	u	u	u	u	24.0	u	9.9[t]
1982	82.9	51.7	u	u	6.1	25.1	31.2	u	u
1983	73.1	45.9	u	u	3.9	23.3	27.2	u	28.0[t]
1984	78.0	50.3	u	u	3.7	24.0	27.7	u	13.1[t]
FPA									
1976	2.4	u	2.4	u	u	u	u	u	u

Table 23. Number of Acceptors of Family Planning Services (000s), by Method and Year *(continued)*

Country and year	Total[a]	IUD[e]	Orals	Inject.	Sterilization Male	Sterilization Female	Sterilization Total	Other program methods	Abortion[a]
FPA *(continued)*									
1977	4.5	u	4.5	u	u	u	u	u	u
1978	6.5	u	6.5	u	u	u	u	u	u
1979	6.4	u	6.4	u	u	u	u	u	u
Gujarat									
1967	115.0	30.0	u	u	u	u	85.0	u	u
1968	112.0	12.0	u	u	u	u	100.0	u	u
1969	105.0	11.0	u	u	u	u	94.0	u	u
1970	104.0	9.0	u	u	u	u	95.0	u	u
1971	297.0	8.7	u	u	u	u	288.3	u	u
1972	178.8	9.2	u	u	u	u	96.8	72.8	u
1973	77.1	17.4	u	u	u	u	59.7	u	u
1976	570.1	29.2	10.3	u	u	u	323.0	207.6	u
1977	313.7	30.3	16.6	u	25.5	86.3	111.8	155.0	16.8[t]
1978	438.1	35.3	20.4	u	54.2	143.2	197.4	185.0	23.0[t]
1979	444.5	37.8	17.0	u	53.2	167.0	220.2	169.5	21.3[t]
1981	283.0	45.6	u	u	u	u	237.4	u	22.0[t]
1982	304.6	63.1	u	u	43.0	198.5	241.5	u	u
1983	347.4	111.6	u	u	36.9	198.9	235.8	u	21.0[t]
1984	470.7	214.2	u	u	44.9	211.6	256.5	u	20.0[t]
Haryana									
1967	75.0	58.0	u	u	u	u	17.0	u	u
1968	48.0	29.0	u	u	u	u	19.0	u	u
1969	46.0	27.0	u	u	u	u	19.0	u	u
1970	45.0	23.0	u	u	u	u	22.0	u	u
1971	76.5	30.2	u	u	u	u	46.3	u	u
1972	151.3	16.5	u	u	u	u	55.7	79.1	u
1973	38.5	21.5	u	u	u	u	17.0	u	u
1976	574.0	82.3	0.4	u	u	u	225.2	266.1	u
1977	191.0	24.1	0.2	u	1.0	4.9	5.9	160.8	3.8[t]
1978	167.0	27.9	0.4	u	2.4	11.5	13.9	124.8	3.8[t]
1979	167.7	26.5	1.1	u	4.4	22.6	27.0	113.1	4.6[t]
1981	76.0	31.6	u	u	u	u	44.4	u	6.6[t]
1982	124.3	37.8	u	u	4.9	81.6	86.5	u	u
1983	205.0	102.9	u	u	6.8	95.3	102.1	u	11.5[t]
1984	248.7	159.1	u	u	6.4	83.2	89.6	u	12.4[t]
Himachal Pradesh									
1971	8.9	3.4	u	u	u	u	5.5	u	u
1972	8.6	2.6	u	u	u	u	6.0	u	u
1973	7.7	1.8	u	u	u	u	5.9	u	u
1976	140.3	8.3	u	u	u	u	102.9	29.1	u
1977	17.0	3.4	0.0	u	0.3	1.5	1.8	11.8	1.3[t]
1978	23.4	5.1	0.1	u	2.6	4.4	7.0	11.2	1.9[t]
1979	25.4	6.2	0.2	u	3.8	6.7	10.5	8.5	2.5[t]
1981	30.2	7.6	u	u	u	u	22.6	u	4.3[t]
1982	43.1	9.7	u	u	7.1	26.3	33.4	u	u
1983	46.2	12.2	u	u	7.5	26.5	34.0	u	5.5[t]
1984	47.7	19.8	u	u	5.4	22.5	27.9	u	u
Jammu and Kashmir									
1967	19.0	10.0	0.0	0.0	0.0	0.0	9.0	0.0	0.0
1968	20.0	8.0	0.0	0.0	0.0	0.0	12.0	0.0	0.0
1969	12.0	4.0	0.0	0.0	0.0	0.0	8.0	0.0	0.0
1970	19.0	8.0	0.0	0.0	0.0	0.0	11.0	0.0	0.0
1971	11.4	5.4	0.0	0.0	0.0	0.0	6.0	0.0	0.0
1972	16.9	4.1	0.0	0.0	0.0	0.0	10.3	2.5	0.0
1973	4.0	1.7	u	u	u	u	2.3	u	u
1976	26.5	6.0	0.2	u	u	u	16.1	4.2	u
1977	13.5	2.3	0.1	u	2.7	3.8	6.5	4.6	0.0[t]
1978	19.4	3.9	0.4	u	4.7	4.6	9.3	5.8	1.6[t]
1979	21.7	4.3	1.0	u	3.8	4.6	8.4	8.0	0.1[t]
1981	16.3	5.1	u	u	u	u	11.2	u	u
1982	28.1	8.8	u	u	3.9	15.4	19.3	u	u
1983	33.1	8.3	u	u	3.2	21.6	24.8	u	u
1984	31.0	8.1	u	u	2.8	20.1	22.9	u	u

Table 23. Number of Acceptors of Family Planning Services (000s), by Method and Year *(continued)*

Country and year	Total[a]	IUD[c]	Orals	Inject.	Sterilization Male	Sterilization Female	Sterilization Total	Other program methods	Abortion[a]
Karnataka									
1971	68.3	11.7	u	u	u	u	56.6	u	u
1972	195.1	13.3	u	u	u	u	141.3	40.5	u
1973	75.4	10.5	u	u	u	u	64.9	u	u
1976	531.3	32.4	4.2	u	u	u	439.5	55.2	u
1977	199.0	23.4	3.6	u	8.4	85.7	94.1	77.9	12.1[t]
1978	204.7	33.9	5.8	u	4.9	91.1	96.0	69.0	12.7[t]
1979	255.8	50.8	5.4	u	5.6	111.6	117.2	82.4	14.7[t]
1981	244.2	55.4	u	u	u	u	188.8	u	16.7[t]
1982	301.9	68.9	u	u	2.3	230.7	233.0	u	u
1983	337.0	97.1	u	u	5.1	234.8	239.9	u	16.8[t]
1984	387.4	120.6	u	u	6.9	259.9	266.8	u	18.3[t]
Kerala									
1967	103.0	38.0	u	u	u	u	65.0	u	u
1968	110.0	36.0	u	u	u	u	74.0	u	u
1969	99.0	38.0	u	u	u	u	61.0	u	u
1970	99.0	31.0	u	u	u	u	68.0	u	u
1971	170.1	18.3	u	u	u	u	151.8	u	u
1972	113.4	19.0	u	u	u	u	86.6	7.8	u
1973	64.9	20.6	u	u	u	u	44.3	u	u
1976	255.1	18.9	0.3	u	u	u	210.5	25.4	u
1977	116.9	10.6	0.2	u	15.3	67.5	82.8	23.3	28.8[t]
1978	125.2	12.1	0.2	u	15.1	75.0	90.1	22.8	27.8[t]
1979	134.5	17.0	0.3	u	14.3	84.7	99.0	18.2	32.6[t]
1981	144.4	20.5	u	u	u	u	123.9	u	35.0[t]
1982	172.1	28.1	u	u	17.2	126.8	144.0	u	u
1983	217.2	37.4	u	u	19.7	160.1	179.8	u	40.0[t]
1984	253.2	44.1	u	u	12.1	197.0	209.1	u	44.0[t]
Madhya Pradesh									
1967	208.0	32.0	u	u	u	u	176.0	u	u
1968	171.0	36.0	u	u	u	u	135.0	u	u
1969	169.0	43.0	u	u	u	u	126.0	u	u
1970	110.0	41.0	u	u	u	u	69.0	u	u
1971	132.3	47.2	u	u	u	u	85.1	u	u
1972	438.6	36.7	u	u	u	u	317.6	84.3	u
1973	78.1	35.1	u	u	u	u	43.0	u	u
1976	1108.3	22.4	0.8	u	u	u	1020.1	65.0	u
1977	103.4	13.7	0.9	u	6.5	30.7	37.2	51.6	11.8[t]
1978	164.3	20.1	1.2	u	25.6	54.7	80.3	62.7	13.9[t]
1979	223.3	19.3	1.3	u	48.1	77.7	125.8	76.9	15.4[t]
1981	236.7	23.3	u	u	u	u	213.4	u	19.6[t]
1982	376.9	51.2	u	u	23.3	302.4	325.7	u	u
1983	446.6	114.4	u	u	38.7	293.5	332.2	u	23.0[t]
1984	408.1	154.7	u	u	36.9	216.5	253.4	u	24.8[t]
Maharashtra									
1967	361.0	29.0	u	u	u	u	332.0	u	u
1968	284.0	11.0	u	u	u	u	273.0	u	u
1969	241.0	10.0	u	u	u	u	231.0	u	u
1970	254.0	6.0	u	u	u	u	248.0	u	u
1971	401.7	9.8	u	u	u	u	391.9	u	u
1972	719.5	9.4	u	u	u	u	609.3	100.8	u
1973	209.3	17.3	u	u	u	u	192.0	u	u
1976	1056.9	15.7	6.5	u	u	u	878.7	156.0	u
1977	250.3	15.9	21.3	u	17.3	100.8	118.1	95.0	22.1[t]
1978	338.1	20.7	6.3	u	29.6	148.3	177.9	133.2	30.6[t]
1979	463.6	29.9	6.7	u	108.6	180.6	289.2	137.8	37.8[t]
1981	336.2	40.7	u	u	u	u	295.5	u	36.5[t]
1982	716.6	94.1	u	u	210.8	411.7	622.5	u	u
1983	1378.4	726.0	u	u	215.4	437.0	652.4	u	u
1984	1153.9	601.7	u	u	163.0	389.2	552.2	u	95.8[t]
Manipur									
1972	2.6	1.7	u	u	u	u	0.6	0.3	u
1976	9.3	1.1	0.0	u	u	u	6.4	1.8	u
1977	2.9	0.7	0.1	u	0.6	0.1	0.7	1.4	0.2[t]

149

Table 23. Number of Acceptors of Family Planning Services (000s), by Method and Year *(continued)*

Country and year	Total[a]	IUD[e]	Orals	Inject.	Sterilization Male	Female	Total	Other program methods	Abortion[a]
Manipur (continued)									
1978	4.8	1.2	0.1	u	1.6	0.5	2.1	1.4	0.2[t]
1979	6.6	2.1	0.3	u	1.9	0.6	2.5	1.7	0.9[t]
1981	4.6	2.4	u	u	u	u	2.2	u	1.4[t]
1982	6.4	3.9	u	u	2.0	0.5	2.5	u	u
1983	9.1	3.4	u	u	2.3	3.4	5.7	u	1.9[t]
1984	9.3	3.5	u	u	1.1	4.7	5.8	u	2.5[t]
Meghalaya									
1976	11.5	1.1	0.2	u	u	u	7.7	2.5	u
1977	1.5	0.2	0.1	u	u	u	0.2	1.0	0.8[t]
1978	1.3	0.4	0.1	u	u	u	0.2	0.6	0.7[t]
1979	0.9	0.2	0.1	u	u	u	0.2	0.4	0.3[t]
1981	0.7	0.4	u	u	u	u	0.3	u	0.0[t]
1982	0.6	0.3	u	u	u	0.3	0.3	u	u
1983	0.9	0.5	u	u	0.0	0.4	0.4	u	0.0[t]
1984	0.9	0.5	u	u	u	0.4	0.4	u	0.0[t]
Ministry of Defense									
1976	91.2	3.7	0.6	u	u	u	27.0	59.9	u
1977	81.8	3.7	2.6	u	7.2	7.4	14.6	60.9	1.4[t]
1978	86.1	5.5	0.5	u	8.9	8.8	17.7	62.4	1.6[t]
1979	85.7	5.6	0.8	u	9.1	9.4	18.5	60.8	2.9[t]
1981	31.2	8.2	u	u	u	u	23.0	u	3.4[t]
1982	30.0	8.4	u	u	10.2	11.4	21.6	u	u
1983	30.5	9.5	u	u	8.3	12.7	21.0	u	3.3[t]
1984	23.3	10.4	u	u	6.7	12.9	u	u	3.2[t]
Ministry of Railways									
1976	328.9	5.0	2.3	u	u	u	88.4	233.2	u
1977	168.6	1.1	1.4	u	1.2	4.6	5.8	160.3	2.2[t]
1978	190.0	2.3	1.3	u	2.2	5.4	7.6	178.8	2.4[t]
1979	191.8	2.7	1.3	u	2.1	6.7	8.8	179.0	2.3[t]
1981	21.9	4.4	u	u	u	u	17.5	u	2.8[t]
1982	28.2	4.9	u	u	3.6	19.7	23.3	u	u
1983	27.8	5.5	u	u	2.9	19.4	22.3	u	3.7[t]
1984	25.2	6.1	u	u	2.2	16.9	19.1	u	3.3[t]
Mysore									
1967	151.0	41.0	u	u	u	u	110.0	u	u
1968	112.0	20.0	u	u	u	u	92.0	u	u
1969	62.0	13.0	u	u	u	u	49.0	u	u
1970	57.0	10.0	u	u	u	u	47.0	u	u
1971	66.5	11.7	u	u	u	u	54.8	u	u
1972	197.9	13.3	u	u	u	u	144.1	40.5	u
Nagaland									
1976	0.0	u	u	u	u	u	u	u	u
1977	0.4	u	u	u	u	u	0.1	0.3	0.5[t]
1978	0.3	0.1	0.1	u	u	u	0.1	u	0.6[t]
1979	0.1	u	u	u	u	u	0.1	u	0.6[t]
1981	0.2	0.0	u	u	u	u	0.2	u	u
1982	0.4	0.1	u	u	0.0	0.3	0.3	u	u
1983	0.5	0.3	u	u	0.0	0.2	0.2	u	0.5[t]
1984	0.6	0.4	u	u	0.0	0.2	0.2	u	0.5[t]
Orissa									
1967	127.0	39.0	u	u	u	u	88.0	u	u
1968	97.0	26.0	u	u	u	u	71.0	u	u
1969	139.0	37.0	u	u	u	u	102.0	u	u
1970	156.0	59.0	u	u	u	u	97.0	u	u
1971	140.5	54.4	u	u	u	u	86.1	u	u
1972	183.8	39.9	u	u	u	u	90.6	53.3	u
1973	80.5	27.8	u	u	u	u	52.7	u	u
1976	358.9	18.8	0.4	u	u	u	326.3	13.4	u
1977	130.0	10.4	0.8	u	25.6	56.3	81.9	36.9	8.6[t]
1978	169.5	13.9	1.3	u	26.2	78.9	105.1	49.2	11.0[t]
1979	150.5	17.2	1.1	u	16.2	72.9	89.1	43.1	11.0[t]

Table 23. Number of Acceptors of Family Planning Services (000s), by Method and Year *(continued)*

Country and year	Total[a]	IUD[c]	Orals	Inject.	Sterilization Male	Sterilization Female	Sterilization Total	Other program methods	Abortion[a]
Orissa *(continued)*									
1981	139.2	29.1	u	u	u	u	110.1	u	19.6[t]
1982	177.3	30.6	u	u	21.4	125.3	146.7	u	u
1983	222.2	43.9	u	u	17.0	161.3	178.3	u	23.0[t]
1984	206.1	69.7	u	u	11.1	125.3	136.4	u	22.1[t]
Punjab									
1967	132.0	103.0	u	u	u	u	29.0	u	u
1968	75.0	36.0	u	u	u	u	39.0	u	u
1969	71.0	30.0	u	u	u	u	41.0	u	u
1970	57.0	26.0	u	u	u	u	31.0	u	u
1971	85.8	45.8	u	u	u	u	40.0	u	u
1972	233.3	31.0	u	u	u	u	58.2	144.1	u
1973	43.1	21.8	u	u	u	u	21.3	u	u
1976	330.7	38.9	0.3	u	u	u	142.0	149.5	u
1977	179.0	28.2	0.4	u	1.9	11.1	13.0	137.4	7.4[t]
1978	185.6	34.3	0.4	u	3.1	17.4	20.5	130.4	9.0[t]
1979	176.9	37.8	0.5	u	4.3	23.7	28.0	110.6	9.6[t]
1981	142.5	67.2	u	u	u	u	75.3	u	22.8[t]
1982	296.4	161.3	u	u	9.3	125.8	135.1	u	u
1983	335.3	195.1	u	u	12.4	127.8	140.2	u	25.5[t]
1984	361.0	240.0	u	u	14.8	106.2	121.0	u	24.9[t]
Rajasthan									
1967	60.0	24.0	u	u	u	u	36.0	u	u
1968	59.0	21.0	u	u	u	u	38.0	u	u
1969	65.0	22.0	u	u	u	u	43.0	u	u
1970	48.0	18.0	u	u	u	u	30.0	u	u
1971	50.0	16.4	u	u	u	u	33.6	u	u
1972	119.7	15.7	u	u	u	u	73.4	30.6	u
1973	40.5	15.4	u	u	u	u	25.1	u	u
1976	464.7	11.8	1.0	u	u	u	371.3	80.6	u
1977	92.0	9.0	1.1	u	1.9	10.7	12.6	69.3	6.7[t]
1978	133.2	18.2	2.7	u	4.4	16.5	20.9	91.4	8.3[t]
1979	192.5	24.0	2.7	u	11.0	36.3	47.3	118.5	10.3[t]
1981	160.6	18.5	u	u	u	u	142.1	u	11.7[t]
1982	188.2	21.1	u	u	6.5	160.6	167.1	u	u
1983	220.3	35.9	u	u	8.2	176.2	184.4	u	14.5[t]
1984	200.3	61.8	u	u	5.1	133.4	138.5	u	14.7[t]
Sikkim									
1976	0.0	u	u	u	u	u	u	u	u
1977	1.0	0.4	0.4	u	u	u	0.2	u	u
1978	1.9	0.7	0.9	u	0.2	0.1	0.3	u	u
1979	2.2	0.7	1.1	u	0.2	0.2	0.4	u	u
1981	1.0	0.6	u	u	u	u	0.4	u	u
1982	1.2	0.7	u	u	0.2	0.3	0.5	u	u
1983	1.3	0.8	u	u	0.2	0.3	0.5	u	0.0[t]
1984	1.4	0.8	u	u	0.1	0.5	0.6	u	0.0[t]
Tamil Nadu									
1967	133.0	10.0	u	u	u	u	123.0	u	u
1968	139.0	25.0	u	u	u	u	114.0	u	u
1969	154.0	42.0	u	u	u	u	112.0	u	u
1970	126.0	54.0	u	u	u	u	72.0	u	u
1971	286.9	38.4	u	u	u	u	248.5	u	u
1972	358.0	21.0	u	u	u	u	275.2	61.8	u
1973	122.3	22.1	u	u	u	u	100.2	u	u
1976	788.6	33.7	1.9	u	u	u	580.5	172.5	u
1977	235.4	23.0	2.0	u	20.7	90.9	111.6	98.8	26.1[t]
1978	336.0	36.6	2.5	u	91.3	125.1	216.4	80.5	34.4[t]
1979	262.8	31.2	3.5	u	35.4	122.2	157.6	70.5	32.7[t]
1981	167.0	33.0	u	u	u	u	134.0	u	42.4[t]
1982	303.6	37.3	u	u	15.7	250.6	266.3	u	u
1983	552.6	55.9	u	u	23.6	473.1	496.7	u	68.8[t]
1984	611.3	86.0	u	u	57.3	468.0	525.3	u	65.8[t]

Table 23. Number of Acceptors of Family Planning Services (000s), by Method and Year (continued)

Country and year	Total[a]	IUD[e]	Orals	Inject.	Sterilization Male	Female	Total	Other program methods	Abortion[a]
Tripura									
1972	4.2	0.2	u	u	u	u	2.1	1.9	u
1976	17.3	0.3	0.2	u	u	u	12.9	3.9	u
1977	5.6	0.1	0.1	u	0.3	0.2	0.5	4.9	0.4[t]
1978	4.7	0.2	0.4	u	0.5	0.2	0.7	3.4	0.6[t]
1979	3.9	0.5	0.5	u	0.6	0.3	0.9	2.0	0.9[t]
1981	1.6	0.3	u	u	u	u	1.3	u	u
1982	2.8	0.7	u	u	1.4	0.7	2.1	u	u
1983	6.3	1.2	u	u	3.9	1.2	5.1	u	1.0[t]
1984	7.6	0.9	u	u	1.2	5.5	6.7	u	1.0[t]
Uttar Pradesh									
1967	262.0	103.0	u	u	u	u	159.0	u	u
1968	246.0	91.0	u	u	u u	u	155.0	u	u
1969	159.0	81.0	u	u	u	u	78.0	u	u
1970	175.0	97.0	u	u	u	u	78.0	u	u
1971	238.9	93.3	u	u	u	u	145.6	u	u
1972	480.1	57.1	u	u	u	u	333.3	89.7	u
1973	104.6	77.7	u	u	u	u	26.9	u	u
1976	1164.6	159.0	2.5	u	u	u	853.3	149.8	u
1977	318.0	78.4	4.7	u	1.3	12.2	13.5	221.4	44.0[t]
1978	574.2	195.2	11.2	u	4.6	24.7	29.3	338.5	66.5[t]
1979	591.7	222.4	11.3	u	9.3	47.0	56.3	301.7	84.4[t]
1981	383.5	224.9	u	u	u	u	158.6	u	92.6[t]
1982	709.7	278.9	u	u	9.6	421.2	430.8	u	u
1983	607.3	229.0	u	u	9.3	369.0	378.3	u	97.1[t]
1984	798.4	477.7	u	u	10.6	310.1	320.7	u	103.3[t]
West Bengal									
1967	249.0	22.0	u	u	u	u	227.0	u	u
1968	194.0	22.0	u	u	u	u	172.0	u	u
1969	95.0	10.0	u	u	u	u	85.0	u	u
1970	83.0	9.0	u	u	u	u	74.0	u	u
1971	80.3	8.8	u	u	u	u	71.5	u	u
1972	280.5	9.5	u	u	u	u	226.4	44.6	u
1973	28.9	6.8	u	u	u	u	22.1	u	u
1976	1164.3	28.3	4.9	u	u	u	896.7	234.4	u
1977	123.7	7.1	6.2	u	3.6	32.2	35.8	74.6	13.8[t]
1978	166.1	10.7	5.7	u	10.6	56.9	67.7	82.0	19.2[t]
1979	284.2	21.4	6.4	u	61.7	94.1	155.8	100.6	25.5[t]
1981	249.2	31.9	u	u	u	u	217.3	u	31.2[t]
1982	308.7	39.1	u	u	75.2	194.4	269.6	u	u
1983	416.0	45.0	u	u	82.3	288.7	371.0	u	39.8[t]
1984	317.7	46.1	u	u	40.4	231.2	271.6	u	34.5[t]
Other territories									
1967	42.0	20.0	u	u	u	u	22.0	u	u
1968	48.0	22.0	u	u	u	u	26.0	u	u
1969	39.0	16.0	u	u	u	u	23.0	u	u
1970	36.0	15.0	u	u	u	u	21.0	u	u
1971	29.0	11.0	u	u	u	u	18.0	u	u
1972	35.4	12.0	u	u	u	u	23.4	u	u
1973	29.1	11.6	u	u	u	u	17.5	u	u
1976	51.4	7.3	5.8	u	u	u	19.8	18.5	u
1977	33.2	4.3	6.7	u	0.4	6.0	6.4	15.8	3.8[t]
1978	34.3	5.8	8.5	u	1.0	8.3	9.3	10.7	4.6[t]
1979	33.8	6.8	7.0	u	0.9	8.5	9.4	10.6	5.2[t]
1981	20.0	9.1	u	u	u	u	10.9	u	6.0[t]
1982	25.5	10.8	u	u	1.5	13.2	14.7	u	u
1983	33.2	14.4	u	u	1.8	17.0	18.8	u	7.4[t]
1984	33.2	13.5	u	u	1.5	18.2	19.7	u	6.7[t]
Indonesia[i]									
1967	6.5	6.0	0.3	0.0	0.0	0.0	0.0	0.2	0.0
1968	25.1	13.8	7.6	0.0	0.0	0.0	0.0	3.7	0.0
1969	53.1	29.0	14.6	0.0	0.0	0.0	0.0	9.5	0.0
1970	181.3	76.4	79.8	0.0	u	u	0.2	24.9	0.0
1971	520.8	212.7	281.8	0.0	u	u	1.4	24.9	0.0

Table 23. Number of Acceptors of Family Planning Services (000s), by Method and Year *(continued)*

Country and year	Total[a]	IUD[c]	Orals	Inject.	Sterilization Male	Female	Total	Other program methods	Abortion[a]
Indonesia *(continued)*									
1972	1078.9	380.3	607.0	0.0	u	u	u	91.6	0.0
1973	1369.1	293.2	857.7	0.0	u	u	u	218.2	0.0
1974	1593.0	187.2	1087.8	4.3	2.0	7.7	9.7	304.0	0.0
1975	1966.7	252.0	1330.3	11.5	2.1	12.6	14.7	358.2	0.0
1976	2212.7	400.2	1481.7	27.5	3.5	19.0	22.5	280.8	0.0
1977	2248.4	366.6	1595.5	48.5	9.6	26.1	35.6	202.2	0.0
1978	2216.0	405.7	1524.5	67.6	7.4	32.4	39.9	178.3	0.0
1979	2229.7	398.2	1550.9	64.5	6.0	39.6	45.7	170.4	0.0
1980	3051.2	496.8	2120.9	112.0	5.0	47.3	52.3	269.2	0.0
1981	2967.0	596.8	1908.6	227.7	6.4	57.0	63.5	170.4	0.0
1982	3885.6	892.5	2055.3	660.1	18.9	70.6	89.5	188.2	0.0
1983	5247.2	1425.5	2316.2	1226.0	16.6	93.4	110.0	169.5	0.0
1984	3970.5	979.9	1708.0	1055.0	7.1	83.9	91.0	136.6	0.0
1985	5076.9	1131.4	2054.5	1609.5	12.0	93.3	105.3	176.2	0.0
1986	4930.5	905.5	1887.8	1809.6	7.7[b]	85.5[b]	93.2[b]	234.4	0.0
Java-Bali									
1969	53.1	29.0	14.6	0.0	0.0	0.0	0.0	9.5	0.0
1970	181.3	76.4	79.8	0.0	u	u	0.2	24.9	0.0
1971	520.8	212.7	281.8	0.0	u	u	1.4	24.9	0.0
1972	1078.9	380.3	607.0	0.0	u	u	u	91.6	0.0
1973	1369.1	293.2	857.7	0.0	u	u	u	218.2	0.0
1974	1475.1	162.3	1017.8	14.7[ii]	u	u	ii	280.3	0.0
1975	1786.0	232.2	1214.4	17.9[ii]	u	u	ii	321.5	0.0
1976	1979.4	356.3	1326.2	39.6[ii]	u	u	ii	257.3	0.0
1977	1934.7	328.9	1373.7	58.0[ii]	u	u	ii	174.1	0.0
1978	1797.5	359.5	1222.3	71.9[ii]	u	u	ii	143.8	0.0
1979	1772.1	349.5	1211.2	44.0	u	u	33.0	134.4	0.0
1980	2145.4	407.3	1463.1	62.8	u	u	36.2	176.0	0.0
1981	2075.1	470.0	1284.7	154.6	u	u	47.2	118.6	0.0
1982	2825.9	718.3	1390.9	527.1	u	u	68.5	121.1	0.0
1983	3894.0	1129.7	1625.9	948.4	u	u	88.1	101.9	0.0
Outer islands I									
1974	117.8	20.0	77.8	3.5[ii]	u	u	ii	16.5	0.0
1975	180.7	28.9	124.7	7.2[ii]	u	u	ii	19.9	0.0
1976	233.3	37.3	161.0	9.3[ii]	u	u	ii	25.7	0.0
1977	313.6	43.9	229.0	18.8[ii]	u	u	ii	21.9	0.0
1978	418.2	46.0	313.7	25.1[ii]	u	u	ii	33.4	0.0
1979	400.9	42.2	297.7	17.0	u	u	9.0	35.0	0.0
1980	769.0	67.2	561.6	40.8	u	u	10.9	88.5	0.0
1981	717.1	91.5	515.1	59.4	u	u	13.8	37.3	0.0
1982	851.6	126.2	545.2	100.5	u	u	16.0	63.7	0.0
1983	1009.9	230.3	531.5	178.4	u	u	16.6	53.1	0.0
Outer islands II									
1979	56.8	8.8	38.3	4.0	u	u	1.5	4.2	0.0
1980	137.0	28.8	86.2	9.5	u	u	3.1	9.4	0.0
1981	174.8	37.5	102.8	18.6	u	u	3.6	12.3	0.0
1982	207.9	48.9	107.3	37.8	u	u	4.2	9.7	0.0
1983	341.1	68.5	157.3	96.5	u	u	5.1	13.7	0.0
Kampuchea									
1973	2.8	0.4	2.2	u	u	u	0.1	0.1	u
Korea, Republic of									
1962	3.4	u	u	u	3.4	0.0	3.4	u	u
1963	19.9	u	u	u	19.9	0.0	19.9	u	u
1964	292.3	111.0	0.0	u	26.3	0.0	26.3	155.0	u
1965	429.9	226.0	0.0	u	12.9	0.0	12.9	191.0	u
1966	568.9	380.0	0.0	u	19.9	0.0	19.9	169.0	u
1967	494.7	323.0	0.0	u	19.7	0.0	19.7	152.0	u
1968	488.0	263.0	76.0	u	16.0	0.0	16.0	133.0	u
1969	645.5	229.0	253.0	u	15.5	0.0	15.5	148.0	u
1970	672.3	224.0	268.0	u	17.3	0.0	17.3	163.0	u
1971	669.6	295.0	195.0	u	18.6	0.0	18.6	161.0	0.0
1972	610.7	308.0	126.0	u	16.4	3.3	19.7	157.0	0.0

Table 23. Number of Acceptors of Family Planning Services (000s), by Method and Year (continued)

Country and year	Total[a]	IUD[c]	Orals	Inject.	Sterilization Male	Sterilization Female	Sterilization Total	Other program methods	Abortion[a]
Korea, Republic of *(continued)*									
1973	672.5	337.0	135.0	u	19.7	4.8	24.5	176.0	0.0
1974	676.4	354.0	111.0	u	32.0	5.4	37.4	174.0	0.0
1975	685.6	334.0	97.0	u	43.1	14.5	57.6	197.0	0.0
1976	739.4	298.0	203.0	u	44.9	35.5	80.4	158.0	8.5
1977	799.2	282.0	179.0	u	53.7	181.4	235.2	103.0	22.0
1978	712.3	241.0	130.0	u	36.9	193.4	230.3	111.0	60.8
1979	600.1	189.0	109.0	u	25.9	195.3	221.1	81.0	79.3
1980	571.1	188.0	103.0	u	28.0	179.1	207.1	73.0	70.2
1981	196.1	u	u	u	31.3	164.8	196.1	u	80.5
1982	700.3	199.1	113.0	u	53.1	233.5	286.6	101.6	141.3
1983	849.9	213.1	82.4	u	97.2	329.9	427.1	127.3	244.7
1984	758.6	195.4	54.7	u	123.2	255.6	378.8	129.7	209.7
1985	673.5	176.9	44.0	u	110.1	217.6	327.7	124.9	184.0
1986	700.0	233.4	45.8	u	92.2	220.3	312.5	108.3	196.5
Laos									
1969	0.3	0.3	0.0	u	u	u	u	0.0	u
1970	0.7	0.4	0.2	u	u	u	u	0.1	u
1971	1.5	0.6	0.8	u	u	u	u	0.1	u
1972	3.2	0.5	2.5	u	u	u	u	0.2	u
1973	6.7	0.6	5.4	u	u	u	u	0.7	u
Malaysia (Peninsular)									
1967	20.6	0.7	18.5	u	u	u	0.6	0.8	u
1968	74.9	1.2	69.3	u	u	u	2.6	1.8	u
1969	70.6	1.1	65.6	u	u	u	2.7	1.2	u
1970	56.0	0.8	49.6	u	u	u	3.5	2.1	u
1971	54.8	0.9	47.8	u	u	u	4.0	2.1	0.0
1972	56.4	1.1	48.9	u	0.4	3.5	3.9	2.5	0.0
1973	57.4	0.9	49.9	u	0.4	3.8	4.2	2.4	0.0
1974	61.7	0.8	54.0	u	0.3	3.9	4.2	2.7	0.0
1975	69.4	0.9	61.3	u	0.2	3.7	3.9	3.3	0.0
1976	75.2	1.1	65.7	u	0.2	3.7	3.9	4.5	0.0
1977	80.4	1.1	70.2	u	0.2	3.5	3.7	5.4	0.0
1978	80.2	1.6	66.5	u	0.2	4.6	4.8	7.3	0.0
1979	87.3	2.3	70.2	u	0.2	4.5	4.7	10.1	0.0
1980	81.1	2.6	62.6	u	0.2	4.9	5.1	10.8	0.0
1982	72.4	3.1	52.6	0.6	0.2	5.1	5.3	10.8	u
1983	64.5	3.0	47.1	0.5	0.1	5.0	5.0	8.9	u
1984	55.9	2.9	40.3	0.8	0.0	4.1	4.1	7.8	u
1985	51.3	2.8	37.8	0.8	0.0	3.5	3.5	6.4	u
1986	57.8	2.9	42.2	0.9	0.1	4.0	4.1	7.7	u
Nepal[i]									
1966	0.6	0.6	u	u	u	u	u	u	u
1967	6.4	3.0	0.6	u	1.1	u	1.1	1.7	u
1968	7.8	1.2	1.4	u	3.3	u	3.3	1.9	u
1969	29.8	1.1	10.3	u	3.9	u	3.9	14.5	u
1970	34.4	0.7	10.5	u	4.4	u	4.4	18.8	u
1971	43.9	1.2	15.9	u	3.9	u	3.9	22.9	u
1972	65.1	0.6	24.0	u	4.2	0.6	4.8	35.7	u
1973	86.1	0.3	27.0	0.0	6.1	0.8	6.9	51.9	u
1974	98.3	1.1	26.9	0.1	3.7	0.7	4.4	65.8	u
1975	138.7	1.7	37.6	0.1	9.2	2.2	11.4	87.9	u
1976	126.6	1.1	33.3	1.0	11.0	5.4	16.4	74.8	u
1977	174.2	0.9	44.4	1.7	12.2	7.9	20.1	107.1	u
1978	165.8	1.2	38.0	1.5	7.0	11.2	18.2	106.9	u
1979	196.4	1.0	44.2	1.8	4.3	11.1	15.4	134.0	u
1980	215.9	1.3	49.0	2.2	4.8	18.0	22.8	140.6	u
1981	223.2	1.1	48.9	3.1	10.4	20.2	30.6	139.5	u
1982	284.6	1.7	66.9	4.8	16.5	28.5	45.0	166.2	u
Pakistan[i]									
1965	147.5	38.0	0.0	u	u	u	0.5	109.0	u
1966	1023.2	483.0	1.3	u	u	u	1.9	537.0	u
1967	1005.1	375.8	u	u	u	u	1.7	627.6	u
1968	1324.4	467.6	u	u	u	u	50.2	806.6	u

Table 23. Number of Acceptors of Family Planning Services (000s), by Method and Year *(continued)*

Country and year	Total[a]	IUD[c]	Orals	Inject.	Sterilization Male	Sterilization Female	Sterilization Total	Other program methods	Abortion[a]
Pakistan *(continued)*									
1969	1166.8	371.0	u	u	u	u	28.0	767.8	u
1970	317.5	309.5	u	u	u	u	8.0	u	u
1971	4.0	u	u	u	u	u	4.0	u	u
1972	136.1	136.1	u	u	u	u	u	u	0.0
1973	112.4	109.1	u	u	u	u	3.3	u	0.0
1974	250.1	112.5	132.2	u	u	u	5.4	u	0.0
1975	2085.4	189.0	340.0	u	2.9	8.5	11.4	1545.0	0.0
1976	1443.6	169.0	315.0	u	1.7	12.9	14.6	945.0	0.0
1977	682.2	71.0	109.0	u	0.6	6.6	7.2	495.0	0.0
1978	906.2	78.0	145.0	u	0.7	12.5	13.2	670.0	0.0
1979	1244.9	100.0	268.0	u	0.7	24.2	24.9	852.0	0.0
1982	627.8	95.9	43.9	12.2	u	u	43.7	432.1	u
1983	864.8	152.3	57.0	19.2	u	u	41.1	595.2	u
1984	1175.8	196.6	71.3	22.1	u	u	58.9	826.9	u
1985	1317.9	241.9	98.0	45.0	u	u	70.0	863.0	u
1986	1617.0	312.0	111.5	76.6	u	u	72.0	1044.9	u
Philippines									
1966	8.4	1.8	3.0	u	0.0	0.0	0.0	3.6	u
1967	23.4	8.7	9.3	u	0.0	0.0	0.0	5.4	u
1968	42.8	12.3	22.6	u	0.0	0.0	0.0	7.9	u
1969	85.2	15.1	43.3	u	0.0	0.0	0.0	26.8	u
1970	191.6	41.4	102.0	u	0.0	0.0	0.0	48.2	u
1971	408.8	76.8	230.5	u	0.0	0.0	0.0	101.5	0.0
1972	621.9	83.0	338.2	u	0.0	0.0	0.0	200.7	0.0
1973	737.9	80.2	344.1	u	0.0	0.0	0.0	313.6	0.0
1974	715.0	77.6	381.0	u	0.4	1.0	1.4	255.0	0.0
1975	749.4	51.2	364.6	u	9.2	23.3	32.5	301.1	0.0
1976	643.0	43.1	282.0	u	10.3	37.6	47.9	270.0	0.0
1977	551.5	44.9	229.0	u	8.0	60.6	68.6	209.0	0.0
1978	496.7	35.6	199.0	u	4.3	48.8	53.1	209.0	0.0
1979	488.8	42.6	211.0	4.8	2.0	45.4	47.4	183.0	0.0
1980	433.8	46.6	195.0	4.6	1.9	50.7	52.6	135.0	0.0
1981	448.4	51.5	204.0	6.4	1.8	61.7	63.5	123.0	0.0
1982	432.6	52.3	200.0	0.0	2.4	61.9	64.3	116.0	0.0
1983	229.2	35.1	109.4	u	u	u	30.7	54.0	u
1984	628.2	69.4	134.5	u	u	u	111.3	313.0	u
1985	359.7	u	u	u	u	u	88.5	271.2	u
1986	504.9	47.6	257.6	u	u	u	80.0	119.7	u
Singapore									
1965	10.3	1.0	3.3	u	0.0	0.5	0.5	5.5	u
1966	30.9	2.8	14.0	u	0.0	0.5	0.5	13.6	u
1967	31.7	0.3	18.9	u	0.0	0.7	0.7	11.8	u
1968	36.4	3.7	19.4	u	0.0	1.1	1.1	12.2	u
1969	37.1	1.3	18.3	u	0.0	1.4	1.4	16.1	u
1970	28.6	0.7	12.4	u	0.1	2.3	2.4	13.1	1.9
1971	21.8	0.4	10.0	u	0.1	3.9	4.0	7.4	3.4
1972	23.8	0.2	10.2	u	0.3	5.8	6.1	7.3	3.7
1973	28.3	0.1	11.0	u	0.4	8.9	9.3	7.9	3.0
1974	27.8	0.1	10.7	u	0.3	9.2	9.5	7.5	6.7
1975	26.4	0.1	9.5	u	0.4	9.2	9.6	7.2	10.7
1976	27.6	0.1	9.0	u	0.4	9.5	9.9	8.6	11.7
1977	23.9	0.1	7.6	u	0.3	7.4	7.7	8.5	12.7
1978	22.1	0.1	6.3	0.0	0.3	6.6	6.9	8.8	13.1
1979	21.6	0.1	5.8	0.1	0.5	5.8	6.3	9.3	17.0
1980	20.8	0.2	5.6	0.0	0.4	5.3	5.7	9.3	18.2
1981	21.4	0.1	5.1	0.1	0.5	6.3	6.8	9.3	18.9
1982	21.2	0.1	4.9	0.1	0.5	6.0	6.5	9.6	19.1
1983	19.8	0.2	4.5	0.0	0.5	5.6	6.1	9.0	19.1
1984	12.5	0.4	4.1	u	u	u	u	8.0	22.2
1985	0.0	u	u	u	u	u	u	u	23.5
Sri Lanka									
1966	15.0	9.0	2.0	u	u	u	3.0	1.0	u
1967	36.7	18.5	8.9	u	u	u	3.6	5.7	u
1968	44.5	20.6	16.0	u	u	u	5.2	2.7	u

Table 23. Number of Acceptors of Family Planning Services (000s), by Method and Year *(continued)*

Country and year	Total[a]	IUD[c]	Orals	Inject.	Sterilization Male	Sterilization Female	Sterilization Total	Other program methods	Abortion[a]
Sri Lanka *(continued)*									
1969	54.5	19.5	25.3	u	u	u	2.9	6.8	u
1970	55.3	15.8	26.9	u	u	u	5.0	7.6	u
1971	48.8	11.4	25.8	u	0.2	4.1	4.3	7.3	0.0
1972	70.1	18.6	32.3	u	0.5	9.1	9.6	9.6	0.0
1973	95.2	27.5	34.2	u	1.9	18.4	20.2	13.3	0.0
1974	71.9	29.7	u	u	7.3	34.9	42.2	u	0.0
1975	71.6	32.2	u	u	6.0	33.1	39.4	u	0.0
1976	88.2	27.0	25.6	u	2.9	32.7	35.6	u	u
1977	67.9	21.3	27.5	u	1.3	17.8	19.1	u	u
1978	79.2	23.1	34.2	u	2.3	19.6	21.9	u	u
1979	92.1	20.2	30.4	5.9	5.6	30.0	35.6	u	u
1980	165.3	17.1	35.3	u	51.3	61.6	112.9	u	u
1981	121.7	14.8	22.2	8.1	30.3	46.3	76.6	u	u
1982	112.7	16.1	26.2	10.2	13.1	48.9	60.2	u	u
1983	162.0	15.0	32.2	11.0	44.8	59.0	103.8	u	u
1984	160.0	16.1	32.9	9.7	37.5	63.8	101.3	u	u
1985	138.9	13.9	34.2	19.1	17.4	54.3	71.7	u	u
1986	143.6	12.8	39.9	37.8	12.5	40.6	53.1	u	u
Taiwan									
1964	47.0	47.0	0.0	u	0.0	0.0	0.0	u	u
1965	99.0	99.0	0.0	u	0.0	0.0	0.0	u	u
1966	111.6	111.0	0.0	u	u	u	0.6	u	u
1967	138.6	110.0	28.0	u	u	u	0.6	0.0	u
1968	137.0	101.4	35.6	u	0.0	0.0	0.0	0.0	u
1969	127.4	95.2	32.2	u	0.0	0.0	0.0	0.0	u
1970	247.4	143.3	55.0	u	0.0	0.0	0.0	49.1	u
1971	296.1	155.6	79.2	u	0.0	0.0	0.0	61.3	0.0
1972	272.6	152.2	66.6	u	0.0	0.3	0.3	53.5	0.0
1973	261.1	148.5	58.4	u	0.4	2.0	2.1	52.1	0.0
1974	283.7	156.7	63.9	u	1.0	11.7	12.7	50.4	0.0
1975	291.2	173.4	54.6	u	1.3	15.4	16.7	46.5	0.0
1976	317.7	181.0	45.7	u	2.5	31.0	33.5	57.5	0.0
1977	335.8	177.0	52.4	u	3.7	35.0	38.7	67.7	0.0
1978	348.0	169.0	56.2	0.0	3.6	44.9	48.5	74.3	0.0
1979	359.7	158.6	63.7	0.0	3.9	47.9	51.8	85.6	0.0
1980	370.5	158.8	65.6	0.0	2.9	51.0	53.9	92.2	0.0
1981	392.3	161.6	69.9	0.0	2.9	51.5	54.4	106.4	0.0
1982	393.3	168.5	67.8	0.0	3.0	47.2	50.2	106.8	0.0
1983	399.8	184.9	64.4	0.0	3.0	50.1	53.1	97.4	89.0
1984	403.0	188.0	67.0	u	3.0	50.0	53.0	95.0	108.5
1985	381.0	188.0	59.0	u	3.0	45.0	48.0	86.0	u
1986	343.0	167.0	51.0	u	3.0	44.0	47.0	78.0	u
Thailand									
1964	0.6	0.6	0.0	u	0.0	0.0	0.0	0.0	u
1965	22.4	22.4	0.0	u	0.0	0.0	0.0	0.0	u
1966	28.5	28.5	0.0	u	0.0	0.0	0.0	0.0	u
1967	48.7	32.7	4.0	u	u	u	12.0	0.0	u
1968	57.3	35.2	10.0	u	u	u	12.1	0.0	u
1969	130.3	54.5	60.5	u	u	u	15.3	0.0	u
1970	225.4	74.4	132.4	u	u	u	18.6	0.0	u
1971	404.1	86.0	294.6	u	u	u	23.5	u	0.0
1972	456.8	90.1	327.7	6.3	1.3	31.4	32.7	u	0.0
1973	422.0	93.4	268.6	10.4	2.8	46.8	49.6	u	0.0
1974	494.4	89.7	305.2	19.0	6.8	73.7	80.5	u	0.0
1975	561.8	75.2	345.1	24.6	7.5	82.7	90.2	26.7	0.0
1976	665.0	71.9	376.7	73.4	10.2	95.1	105.3	37.7	0.0
1977	829.0	74.8	488.4	68.7	19.1	106.8	125.9	71.2	0.0
1978	940.8	77.8	557.9	86.6	44.3	124.2	168.5	50.0	0.0
1979	1012.8	78.1	614.5	118.0	35.3	138.7	147.0	55.2	0.0
1980	1121.0	79.4	653.6	149.7	31.1	151.7	182.8	55.5	0.0
1981	1125.7	80.1	634.9	170.5	28.4	149.3	177.7	62.5	0.0
1982	1116.5	83.9	622.3	177.9	23.4	143.6	167.0	65.4	0.0
1983	1183.2	126.9	597.8	206.2	27.1	146.4	173.5	78.8	0.0
1984	1316.4	190.3	581.9	249.6	45.2	164.5	209.7	84.9	u
1985	1419.3	184.6	587.2	373.0	37.4	160.3	197.7	76.8	u

Table 23. Number of Acceptors of Family Planning Services (000s), by Method and Year *(continued)*

Country and year	Total[a]	IUD[e]	Orals	Inject.	Sterilization Male	Sterilization Female	Sterilization Total	Other program methods	Abortion[a]
Thailand *(continued)*									
1986	1547.0	199.9	613.1	450.8	35.8	162.3	198.1	85.1	u
Vietnam									
1975	148.1	145.8	1.0	u	u	u	0.3	1.0	52.1
1976	374.6	361.9	7.1	u	u	u	3.2	2.4	51.0
1977	605.8	364.1	36.3	u	u	u	7.6	197.8	85.0
1978	835.8	348.9	113.9	u	4.2	9.7	12.9	360.1	126.6
1979	865.6	270.8	112.4	u	1.8	13.0	14.8	467.6	161.8
1980	828.9	298.4	121.3	u	1.1	13.2	14.3	394.9	170.6
1982	1165.0	421.0	164.0	u	u	u	16.0	564.0	u
1983	1229.0	534.0	105.0	u	u	u	20.0	570.0	u
1984	1396.0	722.0	41.0	u	u	u	29.0	604.0	u
1985	1662.0	935.0	81.0	u	u	u	31.0	615.0	u
Vietnam (Hanoi Province)									
1981	74.9	25.1	2.0	u	0.0	0.2	0.2	47.6	21.2
1982	109.7	32.5	1.7	u	0.0	0.5	0.5	75.0	23.5
1983	133.0	41.5	1.0	u	0.0	0.6	0.6	89.9	28.3
1984	115.3	57.5	0.6	u	0.1	1.5	1.6	55.6	34.1
1985	145.5	64.3	0.5	u	0.0	0.6	0.6	80.1	40.1
Vietnam, South									
1969	2.5	2.0	0.5	u	0.0	0.0	0.0	u	u
1970	2.4	1.5	0.9	u	0.0	0.0	0.0	u	u
1971	4.5	2.3	2.2	u	0.0	0.0	0.0	u	u
1972	14.7	5.0	7.4	u	0.0	0.0	0.0	2.3	u
1973	23.2	6.8	14.8	u	u	u	0.1	1.5	u

u = unknown.

na = not applicable.

a.   The total excludes abortion acceptors. It is the sum of acceptors of all contraceptive methods, including those in the "other" category. The data for other program methods are often estimates of CYP generated from the quantities of resupply methods not otherwise listed. Cells with a "u" entry are ignored in the total, since in many cases a "u" occurs only for a method not offered by the program in that year—for example, injectables in the early years.

b.   Extrapolation based upon data for the first nine months of the year.

c.   Breakdown by method not available.

d.   Excludes condom acceptors.

e.   Includes reinsertions and first insertions; most countries do not keep separate records. Examples of recent data on reinsertions as a proportion of all insertions are as follows: Paraguay, 6 percent; Korea, 15 percent; Peru, 28 percent; Togo, 30 percent; Lesotho, 36 percent; Taiwan, 39 percent; and Iran, 46 percent.

f.   The annual number of oral acceptors is taken to approximate CYP. CYP, in turn, roughly equals the total of all monthly acceptors times three (three cycles given to each acceptor), divided by 12.

g.   Includes acceptors in the International Postpartum Family Planning Program.

h.   Includes acceptors in the private family planning association.

i.   Data are for fiscal year. In India and Indonesia, the fiscal year begins April 1 of indicated year and ends March 31 of the following year; in Nepal, it begins July 15 of indicated year and ends July 14 of the following year; in Pakistan, it begins July 1 and ends June 30.

j.   Cycles distributed through the program are divided by 13 to estimate CYP.

k.   Fewer than 0.05.

l.   The Family Planning Association of Hong Kong carried out large-scale family planning activities for many years with financial assistance from the government. The government became involved directly in service delivery in 1974; government statistics became available in 1976. FPA activities have continued. Some past data from the Nortman Fact Books have pertained only to the FPA. Other data have been national totals including both government and FPA sectors. In attempting to clarify the historical series, we have assumed that the data for the years 1982–86 constitute national totals. From 1977 on, all sterilization figures have been listed under the FPA; the government also performs sterilizations, but it has been estimated that almost 90 percent of sterilizations are handled by the FPA.

m.   Of these, 290,000 abortions were performed in the private sector and 30,000 in the public sector.

n.   Services thus far have been available only in private clinics cooperating with the national program.

o.   Figure includes 1,886 legal abortions under the 1969 act.

p.   In Mexico, the private association FEPAC carried out family planning activities before the various government agencies began to become active in service delivery in 1973 and 1974. Services developed rapidly thereafter. Data shown here are intended to be national data, covering FEPAC and the major government provider agencies, including IMSS, MOH, and ISSSTE.

Table 23. Number of Acceptors of Family Planning Services (000s), by Method and Year *(continued)*

q. The increase in 1974 over 1973 acceptors results largely from the inclusion of acceptors in selected private-sector service centers that joined the government's reporting system.

r. Data for acceptors in the National Health Service program only.

s. Data for orals include acceptors of injectables.

t. Medical termination of pregnancy is offered in government family hospitals and approved institutions as a health care measure for reducing maternal mortality and morbidity from illegal abortions, not for demographic reasons.

v. Condoms distributed through the program are divided by 149.8 to estimate CYP.

w. Recognized as menstrual regulation rather than abortion.

x. Data only from Family Planning and Population Board clinics.

y. Data for 1974 are not comparable with those of other years. The latter relate only to the private family planning association, an IPPF affiliate.

z. Prorated on the basis of a distribution of 68,000 acceptors by method.

aa. Estimate based on statistical data for January–June 1983.

bb. Estimates are for IPPF affiliate only. They do not reflect total number of sterilization acceptors in the country.

cc. Data for 1984–86 are for government and FPA activities combined.

dd. Includes abortions performed in the public and private sectors. Recent data indicate that 91 percent of abortions are performed in the private sector.

ee. In addition to these numbers, 516,000 and 318,000 abortions were performed in the private sector in 1981 and 1984 respectively, as estimated by the National Fertility and Family Planning Surveys.

ff. Annual number of acceptors is an estimate based on units of contraceptives supplied, assuming that one acceptor accounts for 130 units per year.

gg. Data for July–December 1983, doubled.

hh. Women represent 99.9 percent of all sterilization acceptors.

ii. Sterilization included with injectables.

jj. Includes condoms, rhythm, and diaphragm.

kk. Includes IUD, orals, and injectables.

ll. Postpartum hospitals.

mm. "Other program methods" are condoms and spermicides; this column and that pertaining to orals include both clinical and nonclinical acceptors. Profamilia had only a clinical program from 1967 through 1970. In 1971 it initiated a CBD program, and in 1975 a CSM program. Clinical figures are for new acceptors, and the clinical component is included in all years; however, it is a very small proportion of the total shown from about 1975 on. The CBD and CSM programs maintain data not on new acceptors, but rather on quantitites distributed; these are converted to CYP and presented here. One CYP may represent several persons, each obtaining supplies for less than a year, or one person throughout the year. For this table, one CYP represents one new acceptor if, on average, each new acceptor continues use for a year.

Table 24. Acceptors Distributed by Method and Age of Wife, and Median Age of Wife

Country and method	Year	Number (000s)	<20	20–24	25–29	30–34	35–39	40+	Unknown	Total	Wife's median age[b]
SUB-SAHARAN AFRICA											
Ghana											
IUD and orals	3/1971–11/1972	29.2	3.7	20.9	26.6	24.0	15.7	9.2	0.0	100	29.8
IUD	1973	2.6	2.9	16.3	27.1	25.6	18.3	9.8	0.0	100	30.7
IUD	1974	2.8	2.0	18.0	26.0	24.0	17.0	13.0	0.0	100	30.8
IUD	1976	1.3	2.7	18.6	28.4	24.8	16.3	9.2	0.0	100	30.1
IUD	1–6/1977	1.1	2.8	19.0	27.0	28.2	14.7	8.3	0.0	100	30.2
Orals	1973	17.6	4.9	24.2	27.2	22.1	13.2	8.4	0.0	100	28.8
Orals	1974	19.2	5.0	25.0	27.0	21.0	14.0	8.0	0.0	100	28.7
Orals	1976	9.3	6.0	31.6	28.0	18.4	11.2	4.8	0.0	100	27.2
Orals	1–6/1977	8.1	6.6	30.9	28.2	18.6	10.9	4.8	0.0	100	27.2
All methods	1976	11.1	5.4	29.2	27.8	19.3	12.4	5.9	0.0	100	27.8
All methods	1–6/1977	9.4	6.2	29.3	25.2	20.7	12.4	6.2	0.0	100	27.9
Kenya											
IUD	1970	4.8	—25.0—		29.0	21.0	14.0	11.0	0.0	100	29.3
Orals	1970	8.5	—33.0—		28.0	17.0	12.0	9.0	0.0	100	27.9
Orals	4–6/1971	1.1	10.1	35.0	24.8	14.2	9.6	3.3	3.0	100	25.7
All methods	1974	40.6	10.0	34.0	25.0	15.0	8.0	3.0	5.0	100	25.7
All methods	10–12/1976	10.8	12.0	36.0	26.0	14.0	8.0	4.0	0.0	100	25.4
All methods	1978	61.1	13.0	29.0	25.0	15.0	10.0	8.0	0.0	100	26.6
Mauritius											
Orals	1974	2.0	13.7	37.4	23.7	14.6	7.4	3.2	0.0	100	24.9
Orals	1976	2.0	18.8	38.9	24.1	10.2	5.7	1.8	0.5	100	24.0
Orals	1980	1.6	25.0	42.3	21.9	6.7	2.8	1.3	0.0	100	23.0
Orals	5/1983	0.6	20.4	43.2	20.7	10.9	3.6	1.2	0.0	100	23.4
Injectables	1976	0.2	3.0	13.6	25.1	25.1	15.6	17.1	0.5	100	31.6
Injectables	1980	0.2	12.2	26.4	28.9	18.8	10.1	3.6	0.0	100	27.0
Other	1983	0.3	11.8	39.8	24.9	18.2	4.0	1.3	0.0	100	24.8
All methods	1969	10.5	10.4	30.8	25.0	18.0	11.4	4.3	0.0	100	26.8
Mozambique											
IUD and orals	1981	0.3	4.7	41.1	30.1	13.5	5.3	4.4	0.9	100	25.6
Nigeria											
All methods	1972	14.3	2.9	19.0	27.0	24.7	16.3	9.2	0.8	100	30.1
All methods	1973	23.1	2.6	12.2	24.9	28.2	19.4	12.6	0.1	100	31.8
Sierra Leone											
IUD	1981	0.9	5.7	20.4	22.7	34.1	11.4	5.7	0.0	100	30.2
Orals	1981	3.5	14.4	57.1	28.5	0.0	0.0	0.0	0.0	100	23.1
Other	1982–83	3.3	0.0	33.0	30.0	11.0	10.2	15.8	0.0	100	27.8
LATIN AMERICA/CARIBBEAN											
Bolivia											
IUD	1976	1.1	7.5	28.6	31.3	18.8	11.1	2.7	0.0	100	27.2
Orals	1976	0.8	8.1	24.4	31.1	18.0	13.9	4.4	0.0	100	27.8
All methods	1976	2.5	10.7	17.6	28.7	14.9	23.3	4.8	0.0	100	28.8
Brazil											
IUD	1974	1.0	3.6	22.5	31.5	22.5	12.6	6.8	0.5	100	28.8
Orals	1974	13.6	14.0	32.8	25.3	15.0	8.8	3.7	0.4	100	25.6
All methods	1974	15.4	13.1	32.0	25.6	15.6	9.1	4.1	0.5	100	25.9
Brazil (BEMFAM)											
All methods	1979	168.0	16.3	31.1	23.6	13.7	9.5	4.3	1.4	100	25.4
All methods	1980	166.0	16.4	31.2	22.6	14.4	9.2	5.0	1.3	100	25.4
All methods	1981	230.0	20.6	29.2	21.9	13.3	7.5	5.6	1.9	100	24.9
Brazil (Rio de Janeiro)											
Female sterilization	1983	2.0	0.0	0.2	12.6	41.1	31.6	14.4	0.0	100	34.5
Colombia											
IUD	1–6/1972	6.7	11.3	31.7	25.4	16.7	10.0	4.6	0.3	100	26.3
IUD	1973	69.0	10.5	30.9	26.1	17.2	10.3	3.8	1.2	100	26.5
IUD	1974	73.4	11.4	32.2	25.6	16.3	9.5	3.8	1.2	100	26.1

Table 24. Acceptors Distributed by Method and Age of Wife, and Median Age of Wife *(continued)*

Country and method	Year	Number (000s)	<20	20–24	25–29	30–34	35–39	40+	Unknown	Total	Wife's median age[b]
Colombia *(continued)*											
IUD	1975	59.8	11.0	32.0	26.7	15.2	9.5	4.0	1.6	100	26.2
Orals	1–6/1972	8.1	17.2	35.8	23.5	13.3	7.1	3.1	0.2	100	24.6
Orals	1973	75.0	13.5	33.9	24.1	14.5	9.0	3.6	1.4	100	25.4
Orals	1974	98.7	14.6	34.4	23.8	13.8	8.2	3.3	1.9	100	25.0
Orals	1975	90.0	15.8	35.1	24.1	12.3	7.7	3.0	2.0	100	24.7
All methods	1–6/1972	15.8	13.9	32.8	24.3	15.4	9.1	4.2	0.2	100	25.6
All methods	1973	159.0	11.7	31.8	25.0	16.0	10.1	4.1	1.3	100	26.2
All methods	1974	189.6	12.5	31.8	24.2	15.8	9.8	4.3	1.6	100	26.0
All methods	1975	165.3	12.6	31.4	24.8	15.0	10.1	4.3	1.8	100	26.0
All methods	1979	64.0	14.8	33.2	24.8	14.7	8.7	3.7	0.2	100	25.4
Colombia (PROFAMILIA)											
All methods exc. sterilization	1981	u	11.4	39.1	28.1	13.4	5.5	2.4	0.1	100	24.9
All methods exc. sterilization	1982	u	11.8	38.1	29.2	13.3	5.1	2.5	0.0	100	25.0
All methods exc. sterilization	1983	u	10.7	36.3	29.9	14.2	5.8	3.1	0.0	100	25.5
Female sterilization	1974	6.6	0.3	4.7	19.3	32.5	27.5	14.3	1.4	100	33.8
Female sterilization	1975	11.4	0.7	4.5	21.1	32.5	28.9	11.4	0.9	100	33.6
Female sterilization	1976	u	u	4.8	25.8	31.6	27.9	9.8	0.0	100	33.1
Female sterilization	1977	u	u	5.6	30.5	30.8	23.9	9.2	0.0	100	32.3
Female sterilization	1978	u	u	6.9	32.6	29.9	22.3	8.3	0.0	100	31.8
Female sterilization	1979	u	u	9.5	33.7	29.1	20.6	7.1	0.0	100	31.2
Female sterilization	1980	u	u	6.1	32.1	32.2	21.9	7.7	0.0	100	31.8
Female sterilization	1981	u	0.0	7.6	32.9	31.2	20.6	7.7	0.0	100	31.5
Female sterilization	1982	u	0.0	9.0	35.2	30.3	18.9	6.5	0.1	100	30.9
Female sterilization	1983	u	0.0	10.6	34.1	29.5	19.3	6.5	0.0	100	30.9
Costa Rica											
IUD	1974	1.0	12.5	28.3	24.1	17.1	8.6	6.7	2.7	100	26.6
IUD	1975	2.1	11.0	28.5	24.7	17.9	9.8	6.8	1.3	100	27.0
IUD	1980	1.0	17.7	39.3	24.2	10.8	4.6	2.2	1.2	100	24.0
Orals	1974	8.3	21.6	35.8	21.2	10.9	5.0	2.6	2.9	100	23.8
Orals	1975	20.5	23.5	37.1	20.9	9.9	4.7	2.4	1.5	100	23.5
Orals	1977	14.6	26.9	36.9	19.9	9.2	4.2	1.9	1.0	100	23.1
Orals	1980	11.3	31.6	39.1	17.4	7.0	2.7	1.1	1.1	100	22.3
Injectables	1979	0.7	9.4	13.8	13.2	16.0	21.3	23.5	2.8	100	33.8
Injectables	1980	0.7	11.0	20.4	15.2	15.9	14.7	19.8	3.0	100	30.6
All methods	1974	12.6	18.3	32.2	21.5	13.2	7.3	4.7	2.7	100	24.7
All methods	1975	31.0	20.0	33.2	21.5	12.2	7.1	4.6	1.4	100	24.4
All methods	1978	22.4	23.3	37.0	20.3	9.9	5.0	3.5	1.0	100	23.5
All methods	1980	20.4	28.5	37.4	18.6	8.2	3.9	2.3	1.1	100	22.8
Dominican Republic											
IUD	1972	7.3	11.0	34.2	26.7	16.3	8.7	2.8	0.2	100	25.9
IUD	6–12/1973	2.8	10.0	35.2	26.9	14.8	9.4	3.1	0.6	100	25.8
IUD	1975	7.2	10.5	32.2	26.3	15.8	10.3	4.0	0.9	100	26.3
IUD	1976	6.0	10.1	30.9	27.3	16.5	10.4	4.8	0.0	100	26.6
IUD	1977	5.9	12.0	32.8	27.2	14.8	8.8	4.4	0.0	100	26.0
Orals	1972	8.6	17.6	39.2	23.4	11.9	5.9	2.0	0.0	100	24.1
Orals	6–12/1973	6.2	18.5	41.4	22.7	10.4	5.2	1.4	0.3	100	23.8
Orals	1975	39.9	17.6	38.4	23.9	11.3	6.2	2.0	0.6	100	24.2
Orals	1976	41.7	20.4	39.4	23.4	10.0	5.1	1.7	0.0	100	23.8
Orals	1977	39.6	22.3	41.2	22.4	9.0	3.9	1.2	0.0	100	23.4
All methods	1976	58.2	18.3	33.2	25.7	12.8	7.2	2.8	0.0	100	24.8
All methods	1977	57.1	19.0	37.0	24.0	12.0	—8.0—		0.0	100	24.2
Ecuador											
IUD	1973	5.1	8.8	33.0	29.0	17.5	8.5	2.8	0.4	100	26.4
IUD	1974	14.4	8.0	30.0	30.0	17.0	10.0	4.0	1.0	100	26.9
Orals	1–8/1971	0.9	5.3	24.6	30.3	23.8	10.9	3.9	1.2	100	28.2
Orals	1973	1.2	12.6	35.9	28.0	13.3	6.6	2.9	0.7	100	25.2
Orals	1974	16.2	9.3	32.6	25.6	18.3	9.3	4.4	0.5	100	26.5
El Salvador											
IUD	1984	7.4	29.7	41.6	17.6	6.5	3.1	1.5	0.0	100	22.4
Orals	1984	17.4	31.3	41.8	18.2	6.9	1.4	0.3	0.0	100	22.2
Female sterilization	1–6/1976	5.5	1.1	20.3	36.5	23.7	15.7	2.7	0.0	100	28.9

160

Table 24. Acceptors Distributed by Method and Age of Wife, and Median Age of Wife *(continued)*

Country and method	Year	Number (000s)	<20	20–24	25–29	30–34	35–39	40+	Unknown	Total	Wife's median age[b]
El Salvador *(continued)*											
Female sterilization	1–6/1983	14.6	5.0	30.8	29.8	19.2	10.9	4.3	0.0	100	27.4
Female sterilization	1984	13.9	4.1	31.4	30.0	18.6	11.0	4.9	0.0	100	27.4
Male sterilization	1984	0.1	0.0	8.4	14.1	23.9	28.2	25.4	0.0	100	35.6
All methods	3/1971–8/1972	4.0	9.2	31.6	27.8	16.9	9.2	3.9	1.4	100	26.5
Guatemala											
IUD	2–12/1976	1.3	0.1	44.5	35.2	12.6	5.4	2.2	0.0	100	25.8
Orals	2–12/1976	6.4	0.0	64.5	21.8	8.9	3.5	1.3	0.0	100	23.9
Injectables	2–12/1976	0.5	0.1	23.3	30.7	26.7	13.4	5.8	0.0	100	29.3
All methods	2–12/1976	9.6	0.1	56.8	25.3	11.1	4.7	2.0	0.0	100	24.4
Haiti											
Female sterilization	10/1985–9/1986	3822.0	0.1	3.6	24.2	29.0	27.5	6.9	8.8	100	33.1
Jamaica											
All methods	1969	28.0	11.0	29.0	26.0	16.0	10.0	8.0	0.0	100	26.9
All methods	1970	19.0	14.0	31.0	24.0	15.0	8.0	8.0	0.0	100	26.0
All methods	1971	22.0	16.0	32.0	23.0	13.0	7.0	9.0	0.0	100	25.4
All methods	1972	22.0	20.0	33.0	22.0	12.0	6.0	7.0	0.0	100	24.5
All methods	1973	25.0	23.0	33.0	20.0	11.0	6.0	7.0	0.0	100	24.1
All methods	1974	22.0	23.0	35.0	18.0	11.0	6.0	7.0	0.0	100	23.9
All methods	1975	24.0	26.0	36.0	17.0	10.0	6.0	5.0	0.0	100	23.3
Mexico											
IUD	1972	12.1	4.0	25.0	30.0	23.0	15.0	3.0	0.0	100	28.5
IUD	1973	18.8	7.9	26.9	27.0	20.4	12.9	4.9	0.0	100	27.8
IUD	1977	8.3	9.0	27.0	23.0	14.0	——12.0——		15.0	100	u
Orals	1972	17.7	8.0	31.0	27.0	19.0	12.0	3.0	0.0	100	27.0
Orals	1973	23.1	8.0	27.0	26.9	19.9	13.2	5.0	0.0	100	27.8
Orals	1977	20.1	14.0	29.0	19.0	11.0	——12.0——		15.0	100	u
All methods	1977	42.0	11.0	26.0	20.0	13.0	——14.0——		16.0	100	u
Panama											
IUD	1984	18.5	8.1	38.9	27.0	13.0	7.0	5.9	0.0	100	25.5
Orals	1984	36.4	8.2	32.4	35.7	14.8	5.8	3.0	0.0	100	26.3
Injectable	1984	2.5	4.0	32.0	28.0	20.0	4.0	12.0	0.0	100	27.5
Female sterilization	1984	100.0	0.0	2.9	14.9	26.4	31.3	24.5	0.0	100	35.9
Male sterilization	1984	1.2	0.0	8.3	16.7	33.3	16.7	25.0	0.0	100	33.8
Others	1984	21.1	5.2	22.3	28.4	19.9	10.9	13.3	0.0	100	29.0
Paraguay											
IUD	1986	3.6	10.5	27.0	24.0	18.0	14.7	5.8	0.0	100	27.6
Orals	1986	5.6	10.1	38.1	30.0	12.8	8.0	1.0	0.0	100	25.3
Condom	1986	0.7	13.2	16.2	17.4	17.9	19.0	16.3	0.0	100	30.9
Other	1986	0.5	16.9	17.3	20.6	18.2	16.2	10.8	0.0	100	28.8
Puerto Rico											
IUD	1974–75	2.4	5.8	21.8	29.1	21.9	12.6	8.8	0.0	100	28.8
Orals	1974–75	20.2	23.9	35.5	22.5	10.7	4.9	2.5	0.0	100	23.7
All methods	1974–75	38.8	21.5	31.9	22.4	13.2	6.9	4.1	0.0	100	24.5
MIDDLE EAST/NORTH AFRICA											
Iran											
IUD	9–10/1972	0.4	6.6	21.4	22.9	22.9	20.0	6.3	0.0	100	29.8
IUD	1973	0.3	15.0	33.0	20.0	18.0	10.0	4.0	0.0	100	25.5
IUD	5/1975	1.0	10.7	32.9	22.3	18.5	11.6	4.0	0.0	100	26.4
Orals	9–10/1972	0.6	7.0	21.5	18.0	23.6	19.4	10.5	0.0	100	30.7
Orals	1973	3.9	15.3	21.8	20.4	21.5	14.8	6.2	0.0	100	28.2
Orals	1974	2.3	12.1	30.2	22.8	17.1	11.9	5.8	0.0	100	26.7
Morocco											
IUD	1969	7.7	2.8	13.6	23.6	27.7	22.8	8.6	0.9	100	31.7
Orals	1969	4.8	3.7	16.5	26.2	27.0	19.1	6.5	1.0	100	30.6
All methods	1966–1967	8.3	2.4	14.9	28.9	28.3	18.9	6.6	0.0	100	30.7
All methods	1969	14.3	3.1	14.8	24.7	27.0	21.5	7.7	1.2	100	31.3
All methods	1971	18.6	3.7	14.8	23.1	28.5	22.3	7.6	0.0	100	31.5

Table 24. Acceptors Distributed by Method and Age of Wife, and Median Age of Wife *(continued)*

Country and method	Year	Number (000s)	<20	20–24	25–29	30–34	35–39	40+	Unknown	Total	Wife's median age[b]
Tunisia											
IUD	1966	7.0	0.7	8.9	20.4	29.7	29.1	11.2	0.0	100	33.4
IUD	1969	8.6	1.3	15.0	26.0	27.0	24.2	6.5	0.0	100	31.4
IUD	1970	9.5	1.4	16.2	23.9	27.5	23.3	7.3	0.4	100	31.5
IUD	1972	9.7	1.1	18.7	25.1	24.6	20.6	8.6	1.4	100	30.9
IUD	1974	15.9	1.9	22.7	27.8	22.5	16.8	7.0	1.3	100	29.5
IUD	1975	13.5	2.2	23.1	29.4	21.5	16.8	6.5	0.5	100	29.2
IUD	1986	54.9	u	u	u	u	u	u	u	100	27.7[a]
Orals	1/1969–8/1972	0.9	2.7	19.3	24.0	25.6	17.5	7.9	3.0	100	30.5
Orals	1975	11.6	2.6	24.7	29.6	20.2	15.5	7.0	0.4	100	28.8
Orals	1986	22.4	u	u	u	u	u	u	u	100	28.5[a]
Female sterilization	1969	1.9	0.0	2.3	15.3	28.0	33.8	19.6	1.0	100	35.6
Female sterilization	1974	u	u	u	u	u	u	u	u	u	35.1
Female sterilization	1975	8.0	0.0	0.9	9.7	26.8	43.6	19.0	0.0	100	36.4
Female sterilization	1977	6.6	0.1	1.9	9.0	24.5	42.2	19.1	3.2	100	36.5
Female sterilization	1986	10.4	u	u	u	u	u	u	u	100	35.0[a]
Abortion	1975	10.2	1.6	14.9	24.5	24.2	23.0	10.8	1.0	100	31.8
All methods	1986	u	u	u	u	u	u	u	u	100	29.9[a]
Turkey											
IUD	7–12/1968	26.4	3.3	19.5	24.8	25.2	19.9	6.3	1.0	100	30.4
IUD	1969	52.8	4.0	21.9	25.4	25.1	18.2	5.4	0.0	100	29.7
IUD	1970	53.1	4.1	22.9	25.3	24.6	17.8	5.3	0.0	100	29.5
IUD	1971	45.7	4.4	24.4	25.0	23.4	17.3	5.5	0.0	100	29.2
IUD	1973	28.3	5.1	27.0	26.8	20.3	15.5	5.3	0.0	100	28.3
ASIA											
Bangladesh											
IUD	7/1965–12/1966	1.2	2.6	16.6	28.4	30.1	15.7	6.6	0.0	100	30.4
IUD	10–12/1985	0.1	6.2	20.8	32.3	15.4	13.8	11.5	0.0	100	28.6
Orals	10–12/1985	0.7	2.2	15.7	24.2	24.7	17.6	15.6	0.0	100	31.6
Sterilization	1967–1968	9.4	——5.1——		32.5	39.7	19.0	3.7	0.0	100	31.6
Sterilization	1983	u	0.8	15.8	40.4	30.5	10.2	2.4	0.0	100	29.1
Sterilization	10–12/1985	1.0	1.1	5.9	18.1	30.5	26.8	17.6	0.0	100	34.1
Female sterilization	1–4/1977	25.8	0.0	0.0	37.9	32.6	20.6	8.9	0.0	100	31.9
Female sterilization	1978–1979	0.4	u	u	37.9	32.6	20.6	7.4	1.4	100	31.7
Female sterilization	1978	0.5	u	21.9	43.7	22.1	11.7	0.4	0.0	100	28.2
Spermicides	10–12/1985	0.2	1.3	2.0	6.6	10.5	23.0	56.6	0.0	100	40.6
Male sterilization	1–4/1977	50.1	1.0	7.0	27.6	26.9	26.6	10.9	0.0	100	32.7
Male sterilization	1978–1979	0.3	u	4.1	38.3	45.5	11.7	0.3	0.0	100	30.8
Hong Kong											
IUD	1968	3.0	——15.0——		22.0	27.0	23.0	14.0	0.0	100	32.5
IUD	1972	0.1	2.2	19.4	31.6	18.7	18.0	10.1	0.0	100	29.5
IUD	1974	0.3	1.0	16.0	28.0	24.0	24.0	7.0	0.0	100	31.0
IUD	1975	0.3	1.5	14.0	28.7	21.1	19.2	15.1	0.4	100	31.3
IUD	1976	0.3	0.0	9.4	29.2	22.5	22.2	16.8	0.0	100	32.5
IUD	1978	0.3	0.6	8.5	27.4	24.3	20.1	19.1	0.0	100	32.8
IUD	1979	0.4	0.7	8.2	25.6	30.5	18.6	16.4	0.0	100	32.5
Orals	7/1966–6/1968	1.5	——27.9——		28.2	22.9	16.1	4.9	0.0	100	28.9
Orals	1972	4.3	5.7	40.8	32.0	10.4	7.4	3.7	0.0	100	25.5
Orals	1–3/1973	6.5	12.0	48.0	25.0	8.0	4.0	3.0	0.0	100	24.0
Orals	1974	20.6	8.0	46.0	33.0	7.0	5.0	1.0	0.0	100	24.6
Orals	1975	15.2	8.2	45.7	33.6	6.4	3.8	2.0	0.2	100	24.6
Orals	1976	16.8	8.1	45.6	35.0	6.8	2.9	1.3	0.2	100	24.6
Orals	1978	13.9	8.0	46.9	33.8	8.1	2.4	0.6	0.2	100	24.5
Orals	1980	14.5	5.9	45.8	35.6	8.6	2.2	0.3	1.6	100	24.7
Injectables	1975	0.2	0.0	4.7	14.5	20.6	26.6	33.2	0.4	100	36.9
Injectables	1976	0.2	0.0	4.6	11.3	18.5	22.0	43.6	0.0	100	38.5
Injectables	1977	0.2	0.6	1.2	14.5	24.7	22.3	36.7	0.0	100	37.0
Injectables	1979	0.1	0.0	10.6	12.1	21.2	15.2	39.4	1.5	100	36.8
Female sterilization	1977	0.2	0.0	1.3	25.0	30.2	25.0	17.7	0.8	100	33.9
Female sterilization	1978	0.3	0.7	1.3	22.5	41.6	23.8	9.8	0.3	100	33.0
Female sterilization	1980	0.6	0.0	1.8	20.1	43.8	19.3	15.0	0.0	100	33.2
All methods	1970	30.5	3.4	31.4	26.4	17.2	14.4	7.2	0.0	100	27.9
All methods	1972	5.7	5.1	35.7	30.9	11.9	9.4	6.9	0.0	100	26.5
All methods	1975	21.4	7.2	39.8	33.4	8.7	5.8	4.1	1.0	100	25.4

Table 24. Acceptors Distributed by Method and Age of Wife, and Median Age of Wife *(continued)*

Country and method	Year	Number (000s)	Percentage in wife's age-group								Wife's median age[b]
			<20	20–24	25–29	30–34	35–39	40+	Unknown	Total	
Hong Kong *(continued)*											
All methods	1976	25.5	7.0	41.1	34.4	8.5	4.6	4.2	0.2	100	25.3
All methods	1978	24.2	6.7	40.4	33.5	10.6	4.4	4.2	0.2	100	25.4
All methods	1980	27.5	4.6	36.8	34.0	13.4	4.6	4.4	2.2	100	26.1
India											
IUD	7/1970–1/1971	0.5	——16.7——		17.3	28.5	26.5	11.0	0.0	100	32.8
IUD	1973–1974	249.1	2.8	18.0	30.8	29.7	14.5	4.2	0.0	100	29.7
IUD	1974	363.5	2.5	18.4	31.9	28.4	14.9	4.0	0.0	100	29.6
IUD	4/1975–3/1976	521.2	3.8	20.2	31.3	26.3	14.0	4.4	0.0	100	29.2
IUD	1976	525.1	5.2	24.2	30.8	23.3	12.8	3.7	0.0	100	28.3
IUD	4/1977–3/1978	238.6	4.3	27.5	33.8	22.1	10.1	2.5	0.0	100	27.7
IUD	1978	474.6	4.5	26.1	33.5	22.7	10.6	2.5	0.0	100	27.9
IUD	4/1979–3/1980	529.6	4.8	26.9	33.5	22.1	10.1	2.6	0.0	100	27.7
IUD	1980	563.1	4.4	28.3	34.0	21.8	9.3	2.2	0.0	100	27.5
IUD	1981	750.0	3.8	23.9	29.1	17.4	7.8	1.7	16.3	100	u
IUD	1982	1092.0	3.9	25.0	28.6	17.2	7.1	2.0	16.2	100	u
IUD	1983	1999.8	6.2	33.5	32.9	18.9	7.3	1.2	0.0	100	26.6
Female sterilization	7/1970–1/1971	2.1	——3.0——		21.7	31.3	24.8	19.2	0.0	100	34.0
Female sterilization	1973–1974	335.8	0.1	7.0	30.5	36.3	20.7	5.4	0.0	100	31.7
Female sterilization	1974	461.6	0.2	8.1	29.1	35.5	21.4	5.7	0.0	100	31.8
Female sterilization	4/1975–3/1976	765.5	0.4	7.9	29.6	34.7	22.0	5.4	0.0	100	31.7
Female sterilization	1976	1778.2	0.6	11.0	31.8	32.5	18.8	5.7	0.0	100	31.0
Female sterilization	4/1977–3/1978	541.5	1.0	13.2	36.7	31.7	14.3	3.1	0.0	100	29.9
Female sterilization	1978	999.3	0.6	12.8	36.0	31.9	15.6	3.1	0.0	100	30.1
Female sterilization	4/1979–3/1980	1211.1	0.5	13.1	36.5	31.3	14.9	3.7	0.0	100	30.0
Female sterilization	1980	1524.3	0.5	12.7	36.1	32.0	15.4	3.3	0.0	100	30.1
Female sterilization	1981	2219.0	0.5	11.2	30.6	27.0	13.9	2.9	13.9	100	30.1[b]
Female sterilization	1982	3396.0	0.4	9.2	26.7	25.5	13.3	2.9	22.0	100	u
Female sterilization	1983	3551.6	0.6	13.0	33.9	31.6	17.0	3.9	0.0	100	30.4
Male sterilization	7/1970–1/1971	2.8	——6.0——		15.5	28.2	30.2	20.1	0.0	100	35.0
Male sterilization	1973	230.3	1.6	10.6	21.2	30.9	22.6	13.1	0.0	100	32.7
Male sterilization	1974	458.6	0.8	9.6	22.6	30.3	23.6	13.1	0.0	100	32.8
Male sterilization	4/1975–3/1976	1002.4	1.3	9.4	22.1	29.5	25.9	11.8	0.0	100	32.9
Male sterilization	1976	5388.0	0.8	8.4	21.5	30.4	24.9	14.0	0.0	100	33.2
Male sterilization	4/1977–3/1978	140.4	1.1	12.2	28.5	30.5	19.5	8.2	0.0	100	31.3
Male sterilization	1978	361.2	0.5	9.1	27.1	30.2	22.9	10.2	0.0	100	32.2
Male sterilization	4/1979–3/1980	439.5	0.3	10.2	27.8	32.6	22.2	6.9	0.0	100	31.8
Male sterilization	1980	408.8	0.3	10.4	29.3	33.1	20.1	6.8	0.0	100	31.5
Male sterilization	1981	573.0	0.4	8.6	24.5	29.2	20.4	6.9	10.0	100	32.0[b]
Male sterilization	1982	584.0	0.3	8.3	23.1	29.8	20.3	6.6	11.6	100	32.1[b]
Male sterilization	1983	629.3	1.1	11.6	26.9	28.8	24.2	6.8	0.0	100	31.8
Andhra Pradesh											
IUD	1977	9.0	13.1	33.2	30.4	16.1	6.1	1.1	0.0	100	25.6
IUD	4/1978–3/1979	15.5	8.4	27.9	31.5	21.3	9.1	1.8	0.0	100	27.2
IUD	1979	13.2	13.3	29.5	28.1	16.1	7.7	5.3	0.0	100	26.3
IUD	1982	24.4	13.5	31.1	27.5	15.9	8.4	3.5	0.0	100	26.0
IUD	1983	62.7	11.2	32.0	31.6	17.0	6.8	1.4	0.0	100	26.1
Female sterilization	1977	88.1	2.9	21.8	38.0	25.2	9.3	2.8	0.0	100	28.3
Female sterilization	4/1978–3/1979	124.2	2.2	22.8	36.1	26.3	10.1	2.5	0.0	100	28.5
Female sterilization	1979	146.8	1.8	21.6	34.9	24.9	9.6	7.2	0.0	100	28.8
Female sterilization	1982	318.7	1.1	20.3	36.7	25.7	13.7	3.1	0.0	100	28.9
Female sterilization	1983	317.9	1.8	23.7	38.1	22.9	11.0	2.5	0.0	100	28.2
Male sterilization	1977	23.8	2.9	20.6	30.1	25.9	14.7	5.8	0.0	100	29.4
Male sterilization	4/1978–3/1979	39.1	1.6	16.5	29.7	28.4	16.7	7.1	0.0	100	30.4
Male sterilization	1979	35.6	1.0	18.4	31.3	25.7	15.2	8.4	0.0	100	29.9
Male sterilization	1982	32.7	1.0	19.5	33.3	29.3	13.7	3.2	0.0	100	29.4
Male sterilization	1983	31.9	4.4	18.3	36.2	26.3	12.1	2.7	0.0	100	28.8
Assam											
IUD	1977	3.1	1.0	13.2	32.2	28.0	18.5	6.6	0.0	100	29.0
IUD	4/1978–3/1979	6.6	1.8	13.3	42.4	28.2	13.7	0.6	0.0	100	29.1
IUD	1979	7.0	4.0	6.0	52.1	36.1	1.8	0.0	0.0	100	28.8
IUD	1982	15.6	0.1	24.2	48.4	23.9	3.3	0.1	0.0	100	27.7
IUD	1983	16.6	11.0	21.4	33.4	21.2	12.1	1.1	0.0	100	27.6
Female sterilization	1977	5.8	0.2	4.8	30.0	35.8	19.9	10.2	0.0	100	32.2

Table 24. Acceptors Distributed by Method and Age of Wife, and Median Age of Wife (continued)

Country and method	Year	Number (000s)	<20	20–24	25–29	30–34	35–39	40+	Unknown	Total	Wife's median age[b]
Assam (continued)											
Female sterilization	4/1978–3/1979	7.2	0.9	8.6	18.9	41.9	25.1	4.6	0.0	100	32.6
Female sterilization	1979	7.9	0.0	0.9	53.3	30.0	10.0	5.8	0.0	100	29.6
Female sterilization	1982	14.0	0.0	5.0	33.4	42.3	18.9	0.4	0.0	100	31.4
Female sterilization	1983	42.8	1.5	5.5	15.2	31.7	28.3	17.8	0.0	100	34.4
Male sterilization	1977	7.9	0.0	1.7	6.9	16.6	30.4	44.4	0.0	100	39.1
Male sterilization	4/1978–3/1979	18.1	0.0	0.2	2.6	10.2	43.0	44.0	0.0	100	39.3
Male sterilization	1979	14.4	0.0	0.4	10.0	63.4	25.3	0.9	0.0	100	33.1
Male sterilization	1982	41.8	0.0	0.9	12.7	46.2	34.2	6.0	0.0	100	33.9
Male sterilization	1983	83.5	0.3	2.8	11.1	13.8	58.8	13.2	0.0	100	36.9
Bihar											
IUD	1977	4.2	5.4	26.3	34.6	25.4	7.1	1.2	0.0	100	27.6
IUD	4/1978–3/1979	15.8	6.2	26.8	28.3	25.0	11.5	2.2	0.0	100	28.0
IUD	1979	13.4	6.8	24.8	35.1	23.3	8.3	1.7	0.0	100	27.6
IUD	1983	39.7	9.0	28.0	33.8	19.6	8.7	0.9	0.0	100	26.9
Female sterilization	1977	18.9	1.0	8.5	30.9	37.1	20.3	2.2	0.0	100	31.3
Female sterilization	4/1978–3/1979	45.6	2.1	10.7	24.3	34.8	23.0	5.1	0.0	100	31.9
Female sterilization	1979	39.6	1.6	12.3	30.7	36.0	16.5	2.9	0.0	100	30.8
Female sterilization	1983	167.6	0.8	5.5	26.9	36.7	21.7	8.4	0.0	100	32.3
Male sterilization	1977	8.1	0.0	5.0	21.5	36.4	27.8	9.3	0.0	100	33.2
Male sterilization	4/1978–3/1979	26.2	1.6	8.0	18.6	28.8	27.0	16.0	0.0	100	33.8
Male sterilization	1979	18.3	0.1	6.7	24.3	35.0	25.9	8.0	0.0	100	32.7
Male sterilization	1983	18.6	0.2	5.5	24.5	33.8	24.6	11.4	0.0	100	32.9
Delhi											
IUD	1977	9.0	2.0	27.9	38.9	20.3	8.0	2.9	0.0	100	27.6
IUD	4/1978–3/1979	14.3	3.5	27.0	33.0	23.2	10.1	3.2	0.0	100	28.0
IUD	1979	18.3	3.3	29.9	37.7	19.2	7.7	2.2	0.0	100	27.2
IUD	1982	40.4	2.7	25.2	34.0	27.9	7.7	2.5	0.0	100	28.2
IUD	1983	31.4	3.0	30.9	37.2	19.5	7.4	2.0	0.0	100	27.2
Female sterilization	1977	3.7	0.0	9.9	34.4	33.7	16.1	5.9	0.0	100	30.8
Female sterilization	4/1978–3/1979	4.4	0.1	11.3	36.5	32.2	15.0	4.9	0.0	100	30.3
Female sterilization	1979	6.3	0.2	10.7	39.8	31.4	13.9	4.0	0.0	100	29.9
Female sterilization	1982	19.1	0.1	14.4	32.4	31.5	17.1	4.5	0.0	100	30.5
Female sterilization	1983	22.7	0.1	8.8	36.1	32.3	17.9	4.8	0.0	100	30.8
Male sterilization	1977	0.7	0.0	0.7	18.4	36.0	25.9	19.0	0.0	100	34.3
Male sterilization	4/1978–3/1979	0.8	0.1	4.8	24.8	32.9	23.6	13.8	0.0	100	33.1
Male sterilization	1979	1.3	0.2	4.2	30.5	32.2	21.1	11.8	0.0	100	32.3
Male sterilization	1982	4.6	0.0	10.5	33.0	22.4	20.1	14.0	0.0	100	31.5
Male sterilization	1983	3.1	0.0	3.5	28.1	33.8	22.2	12.4	0.0	100	32.7
Gujarat											
IUD	1977	30.2	2.5	35.4	38.3	17.8	5.1	0.9	0.0	100	26.6
IUD	4/1978–3/1979	35.2	2.7	35.5	37.8	17.5	5.4	1.1	0.0	100	26.6
IUD	1979	37.7	2.5	37.9	33.4	15.9	4.7	0.6	0.0	100	26.1
IUD	1982	62.8	1.7	36.4	40.0	16.4	4.6	0.9	0.0	100	26.5
IUD	1983	110.9	2.8	39.9	37.6	15.0	4.0	0.7	0.0	100	26.0
Female sterilization	1977	86.1	0.4	10.3	37.4	34.8	14.4	2.7	0.0	100	30.3
Female sterilization	4/1978–3/1979	142.8	0.3	8.4	35.0	35.7	17.3	3.3	0.0	100	30.9
Female sterilization	1979	166.9	0.3	8.3	34.6	36.3	17.5	3.0	0.0	100	30.9
Female sterilization	1982	197.5	0.0	9.1	37.6	36.1	14.7	2.5	0.0	100	30.5
Female sterilization	1983	198.0	0.3	11.2	39.7	33.4	12.8	2.6	0.0	100	29.8
Male sterilization	1977	25.4	0.8	11.7	31.7	31.6	18.4	5.8	0.0	100	30.9
Male sterilization	4/1978–3/1979	54.0	0.2	9.8	29.6	31.6	20.7	8.1	0.0	100	31.6
Male sterilization	1979	53.1	0.4	11.2	30.1	30.0	20.8	7.5	0.0	100	31.4
Male sterilization	1982	42.8	0.0	9.0	29.1	31.1	21.8	9.0	0.0	100	31.9
Male sterilization	1983	36.9	0.2	12.6	32.4	30.2	17.4	7.2	0.0	100	30.8
Haryana											
IUD	1977	24.1	1.9	18.9	27.0	27.7	18.8	5.7	0.0	100	30.4
IUD	4/1978–3/1979	27.9	6.5	23.1	29.4	23.2	12.3	5.5	0.0	100	28.5
IUD	1979	26.5	3.5	19.8	31.4	26.2	14.1	5.0	0.0	100	29.3
IUD	1982	37.6	1.6	20.1	30.0	25.7	16.4	5.4	0.0	100	29.6
IUD	1983	102.8	2.8	24.4	30.1	24.0	16.1	2.6	0.0	100	28.8
Female sterilization	1977	5.0	0.2	7.2	29.3	33.7	22.2	7.4	0.0	100	32.0
Female sterilization	4/1978–3/1979	11.5	0.1	7.4	28.8	34.7	21.1	7.9	0.0	100	32.0

Table 24. Acceptors Distributed by Method and Age of Wife, and Median Age of Wife *(continued)*

Country and method	Year	Number (000s)	Percentage in wife's age-group <20	20–24	25–29	30–34	35–39	40+	Unknown	Total	Wife's median age[b]
Haryana *(continued)*											
Female sterilization	1979	22.6	0.0	5.2	28.4	34.9	23.5	8.0	0.0	100	32.3
Female sterilization	1982	81.6	0.0	6.5	29.7	37.0	21.1	5.7	0.0	100	31.9
Female sterilization	1983	95.3	0.0	4.8	30.2	28.4	29.9	6.7	0.0	100	32.6
Male sterilization	1977	1.0	0.2	7.3	26.1	35.3	21.9	9.2	0.0	100	32.3
Male sterilization	4/1978–3/1979	2.4	0.1	7.0	26.9	34.8	20.7	10.5	0.0	100	32.3
Male sterilization	1979	4.4	0.0	4.7	27.2	37.0	22.6	8.5	0.0	100	32.4
Male sterilization	1982	4.9	0.0	4.2	27.7	34.2	24.7	9.1	0.0	100	32.6
Male sterilization	1983	6.8	0.2	5.8	25.7	33.0	26.7	8.6	0.0	100	32.8
Himachal Pradesh											
IUD	1977	3.4	7.6	41.7	27.1	17.7	4.6	1.3	0.0	100	25.1
IUD	4/1978–3/1979	5.2	2.8	36.3	38.7	14.9	6.1	1.2	0.0	100	26.4
IUD	1979	5.7	5.2	34.3	35.4	14.9	7.0	3.2	0.0	100	26.5
IUD	1982	97.0	5.7	34.6	32.5	18.4	7.8	1.0	0.0	100	26.5
IUD	1983	12.2	4.3	37.1	34.3	15.9	6.7	1.7	0.0	100	26.3
Female sterilization	1977	1.5	0.4	21.2	39.2	25.2	11.4	2.6	0.0	100	28.6
Female sterilization	4/1978–3/1979	4.4	0.3	24.7	34.2	26.9	11.2	2.7	0.0	100	28.7
Female sterilization	1979	6.1	0.6	23.1	32.9	20.2	18.2	5.0	0.0	100	29.0
Female sterilization	1982	26.3	0.6	12.8	37.1	29.9	16.1	3.5	0.0	100	29.9
Female sterilization	1983	26.5	0.9	17.2	36.0	27.5	13.7	4.7	0.0	100	29.4
Male sterilization	1977	0.3	0.0	7.7	34.4	38.8	19.1	10.0	0.0	100	31.7
Male sterilization	4/1978–3/1979	2.6	0.4	7.1	23.1	32.0	27.9	9.5	0.0	100	33.0
Male sterilization	1979	3.3	0.7	8.0	24.5	30.7	23.7	12.4	0.0	100	32.7
Male sterilization	1982	7.1	0.4	15.7	32.2	29.9	16.9	4.9	0.0	100	30.3
Male sterilization	1983	7.5	0.3	14.4	34.9	29.6	13.9	6.9	0.0	100	30.1
Jammu and Kashmir											
IUD	1977	2.0	0.7	14.2	39.1	28.2	14.2	3.6	0.0	100	29.5
IUD	4/1978–3/1979	1.6	1.8	18.2	30.9	31.6	14.9	2.6	0.0	100	29.9
IUD	1982	8.7	2.3	17.8	43.3	25.1	9.0	2.5	0.0	100	28.5
IUD	1983	4.0	5.2	22.0	31.9	26.3	11.6	3.0	0.0	100	28.6
Female sterilization	1977	3.5	0.0	7.3	34.0	33.1	21.2	4.4	0.0	100	31.3
Female sterilization	4/1978–3/1979	2.1	0.1	12.8	27.3	30.2	25.5	4.1	0.0	100	31.6
Female sterilization	1982	15.4	0.0	3.7	28.3	34.7	21.5	11.8	0.0	100	32.6
Female sterilization	1983	11.5	0.1	8.5	29.7	40.4	18.0	3.3	0.0	100	31.4
Male sterilization	1977	2.5	0.0	6.1	24.0	36.7	23.6	9.6	0.0	100	32.7
Male sterilization	4/1978–3/1979	2.1	0.0	9.8	23.0	29.9	28.6	8.7	0.0	100	32.9
Male sterilization	1982	3.9	0.1	4.6	27.5	33.9	23.5	10.4	0.0	100	32.6
Male sterilization	1983	1.3	0.0	11.9	25.0	34.3	22.8	6.0	0.0	100	31.9
Karnataka											
IUD	1977	17.4	5.7	26.2	33.0	20.4	10.5	4.2	0.0	100	27.7
IUD	4/1978–3/1979	31.7	6.0	34.5	38.1	15.8	4.8	0.8	0.0	100	26.2
IUD	1979	50.2	5.7	32.4	36.7	17.1	5.4	2.7	0.0	100	26.6
IUD	1982	65.2	8.1	37.5	33.1	15.0	5.5	0.8	0.0	100	25.7
IUD	1983	94.9	7.9	33.1	33.6	17.2	7.2	1.0	0.0	100	26.3
Female sterilization	1977	73.0	0.6	15.5	44.0	27.4	10.3	2.2	0.0	100	28.9
Female sterilization	4/1978–3/1979	78.0	0.4	15.0	45.2	27.5	10.5	1.4	0.0	100	28.8
Female sterilization	1979	106.8	0.5	15.7	44.4	27.1	10.7	1.6	0.0	100	28.8
Female sterilization	1982	229.4	0.9	17.4	40.9	28.1	10.8	1.9	0.0	100	28.9
Female sterilization	1983	233.5	2.4	18.0	42.6	25.8	9.3	1.9	0.0	100	28.5
Male sterilization	1977	7.0	0.2	5.9	21.0	30.3	28.1	14.5	0.0	100	33.8
Male sterilization	4/1978–3/1979	4.4	0.3	4.0	17.1	29.8	29.8	19.1	0.0	100	34.8
Male sterilization	1979	5.3	0.1	5.7	21.5	31.8	26.3	14.6	0.0	100	33.6
Male sterilization	1982	2.3	0.2	8.2	27.0	31.2	24.0	9.4	0.0	100	32.3
Male sterilization	1983	5.0	0.5	5.2	21.9	32.1	28.8	11.5	0.0	100	33.5
Kerala											
IUD	4/1978–3/1979	9.3	6.1	32.0	35.5	17.3	7.0	2.1	0.0	100	26.7
IUD	1979	16.2	4.8	33.6	33.8	18.1	7.2	2.5	0.0	100	26.7
IUD	1982	28.0	15.1	35.8	29.4	12.7	4.8	2.2	0.0	100	24.9
IUD	1983	37.1	10.1	40.9	28.9	12.8	5.2	2.1	0.0	100	24.9
Sterilization	1970	u	u	u	u	u	u	u	u	u	38.9
Sterilization	1971	u	u	u	u	u	u	u	u	u	37.4
Sterilization	1972	u	u	u	u	u	u	u	u	u	35.1
Female sterilization	4/1978–3/1979	56.9	0.7	13.4	36.8	32.4	13.4	3.3	0.0	100	29.9

Table 24. Acceptors Distributed by Method and Age of Wife, and Median Age of Wife *(continued)*

Country and method	Year	Number (000s)	<20	20–24	25–29	30–34	35–39	40+	Unknown	Total	Wife's median age[b]
Kerala (continued)											
Female sterilization	1979	80.5	0.3	19.6	38.8	27.5	11.0	2.8	0.0	100	28.9
Female sterilization	1982	126.7	0.6	28.8	39.8	20.4	8.6	1.8	0.0	100	27.6
Female sterilization	1983	159.0	0.4	28.0	40.2	20.6	8.6	2.2	0.0	100	27.7
Male sterilization	4/1978–3/1979	10.1	1.0	16.2	31.6	32.1	13.2	4.9	0.0	100	30.1
Male sterilization	1979	13.9	0.6	21.5	36.3	24.0	13.3	4.3	0.0	100	28.8
Male sterilization	1982	17.2	1.3	24.7	34.3	21.7	14.7	3.3	0.0	100	28.5
Male sterilization	1983	19.7	0.5	25.1	35.0	23.9	12.7	2.8	0.0	100	28.5
Madhya Pradesh											
IUD	1977	12.5	3.6	30.7	34.4	21.9	8.2	1.2	0.0	100	27.3
IUD	4/1978–3/1979	17.4	3.3	29.5	37.2	20.9	7.9	1.2	0.0	100	27.3
IUD	1979	14.6	3.8	32.0	36.5	20.1	6.1	1.5	0.0	100	26.9
IUD	1982	31.4	4.3	30.6	34.6	21.0	7.7	1.8	0.0	100	27.2
IUD	1983	92.7	6.6	35.1	32.5	18.2	6.6	1.0	0.0	100	26.3
Female sterilization	1977	27.5	0.1	9.7	35.5	37.0	15.7	2.0	0.0	100	30.6
Female sterilization	4/1978–3/1979	48.7	0.1	9.6	34.9	34.7	18.2	2.5	0.0	100	30.8
Female sterilization	1979	61.5	0.3	9.7	35.4	36.2	15.6	2.8	0.0	100	30.6
Female sterilization	1982	176.8	0.2	8.2	32.4	35.4	19.7	4.1	0.0	100	31.3
Female sterilization	1983	225.1	0.7	10.7	31.9	33.2	18.6	4.9	0.0	100	31.0
Male sterilization	1977	5.9	0.4	9.6	29.4	32.3	20.9	7.4	0.0	100	31.6
Male sterilization	4/1978–3/1979	20.1	0.2	7.5	29.0	33.0	24.3	6.0	0.0	100	32.0
Male sterilization	1979	38.4	0.5	9.1	29.7	34.8	19.8	6.1	0.0	100	31.5
Male sterilization	1982	16.6	0.3	8.9	28.5	31.6	22.4	8.3	0.0	100	31.9
Male sterilization	1983	30.3	0.9	10.6	28.7	30.5	22.5	6.8	0.0	100	31.6
Maharashtra											
IUD	1977	15.5	6.0	38.8	38.9	12.1	3.6	0.6	0.0	100	25.7
IUD	4/1978–3/1979	136.1	0.2	9.0	36.9	35.4	15.8	2.7	0.0	100	30.6
IUD	1979	25.2	2.1	26.6	37.2	23.2	8.7	2.2	0.0	100	27.9
IUD	1982	72.1	5.7	39.5	37.4	13.8	3.1	0.5	0.0	100	25.6
IUD	1983	706.2	8.1	39.0	32.7	15.4	4.4	0.4	0.0	100	25.4
Female sterilization	1977	98.8	0.1	8.6	35.5	35.2	16.6	4.4	0.0	100	30.9
Female sterilization	4/1978–3/1979	16.7	2.3	25.1	43.6	21.1	6.7	1.2	0.0	100	27.6
Female sterilization	1979	169.2	0.0	9.3	37.8	35.9	14.7	2.3	0.0	100	30.4
Female sterilization	1982	373.7	0.1	8.7	33.7	37.6	16.6	3.3	0.0	100	31.0
Female sterilization	1983	423.9	0.2	12.4	33.9	31.5	17.6	4.4	0.0	100	30.6
Male sterilization	1977	15.9	0.4	9.6	30.4	35.6	19.6	4.4	0.0	100	31.3
Male sterilization	4/1978–3/1979	28.0	0.5	9.4	30.3	32.1	20.4	7.3	0.0	100	31.5
Male sterilization	1979	104.8	0.1	6.9	26.1	33.3	27.8	5.8	0.0	100	32.5
Male sterilization	1982	196.6	0.4	9.4	27.0	35.2	21.7	6.3	0.0	100	31.9
Male sterilization	1983	214.2	0.7	13.6	29.5	31.9	19.1	5.2	0.0	100	31.0
Manipur											
IUD	4/1978–3/1979	1.2	2.6	14.1	25.6	28.2	21.2	8.3	0.0	100	31.4
IUD	1982	3.9	0.0	24.3	19.6	22.3	23.1	10.7	0.0	100	31.4
IUD	1983	3.4	0.8	15.0	34.1	27.5	16.6	6.0	0.0	100	30.0
Female sterilization	4/1978–3/1979	0.5	0.0	4.1	20.0	39.3	27.8	8.8	0.0	100	33.3
Female sterilization	1982	0.5	0.0	5.2	6.7	62.7	15.4	10.0	0.0	100	33.0
Female sterilization	1983	3.2	0.0	1.9	21.5	39.1	35.7	1.8	0.0	100	33.4
Male sterilization	4/1978–3/1979	1.6	0.1	6.9	21.6	35.3	30.0	6.1	0.0	100	33.0
Male sterilization	1982	2.0	0.0	6.3	11.3	15.8	19.4	47.2	0.0	100	39.3
Male sterilization	1983	2.3	0.0	0.0	12.5	42.5	42.2	2.8	0.0	100	34.4
Meghalaya											
IUD	1979	0.2	11.3	34.8	33.9	10.0	9.2	0.8	0.0	100	25.6
IUD	1982	0.3	5.7	33.1	20.9	24.3	16.0	0.0	0.0	100	27.7
IUD	1983	0.5	0.0	23.4	25.0	29.1	22.5	0.0	0.0	100	30.3
Female sterilization	1979	0.2	0.0	11.8	23.0	21.9	20.9	22.4	0.0	100	33.5
Female sterilization	1982	0.3	0.0	29.3	51.4	10.7	8.6	0.0	0.0	100	27.0
Female sterilization	1983	0.4	0.0	27.1	20.1	25.0	27.8	0.0	0.0	100	30.6
Male sterilization	1979	g	0.0	0.0	50.0	30.0	20.0	0.0	0.0	100	30.0
Male sterilization	1982	g	0.0	26.7	13.3	40.0	20.0	0.0	0.0	100	31.2
Male sterilization	1983	g	0.0	23.1	53.8	15.4	7.7	0.0	0.0	100	27.5
Ministry of Defense											
IUD	1977	3.7	2.6	34.2	43.4	14.2	4.4	1.2	0.0	100	26.5

166

Table 24. Acceptors Distributed by Method and Age of Wife, and Median Age of Wife *(continued)*

Country and method	Year	Number (000s)	<20	20–24	25–29	30–34	35–39	40+	Unknown	Total	Wife's median age[b]
Ministry of Defense (continued)											
IUD	4/1978–3/1979	5.5	2.8	30.2	38.6	20.6	6.1	1.7	0.0	100	27.2
IUD	1979	5.6	2.8	35.9	40.0	16.9	3.6	0.8	0.0	100	26.4
IUD	1982	8.4	9.0	34.5	29.2	20.4	6.1	0.8	0.0	100	26.1
IUD	1983	9.5	3.4	34.4	39.6	16.4	5.3	0.9	0.0	100	26.5
Female sterilization	1977	7.4	0.5	15.6	46.9	26.3	9.3	1.4	0.0	100	28.6
Female sterilization	4/1978–3/1979	8.8	0.1	11.7	48.3	25.2	11.6	3.1	0.0	100	29.0
Female sterilization	1979	9.4	0.1	16.7	45.7	27.5	9.1	0.9	0.0	100	28.6
Female sterilization	1982	11.4	0.0	5.0	17.2	20.3	28.1	29.4	0.0	100	36.3
Female sterilization	1983	12.7	0.4	16.2	44.4	28.3	9.4	1.3	0.0	100	28.8
Male sterilization	1977	7.2	6.3	27.9	38.0	22.4	4.4	1.0	0.0	100	27.1
Male sterilization	4/1978–3/1979	8.9	0.2	6.9	32.2	33.7	22.2	4.8	0.0	100	31.6
Male sterilization	1979	9.1	0.0	7.7	35.6	35.0	17.6	4.1	0.0	100	31.0
Male sterilization	1982	10.2	0.0	2.9	8.1	20.4	33.6	35.0	0.0	100	37.8
Male sterilization	1983	8.3	0.2	10.3	40.1	31.5	14.8	3.1	0.0	100	29.9
Ministry of Railways											
IUD	1977	1.1	2.6	27.5	33.4	23.4	10.6	2.5	0.0	100	28.0
IUD	4/1978–3/1979	2.3	3.2	27.3	36.2	19.8	9.5	2.0	0.0	100	27.6
IUD	1979	2.7	3.0	28.4	34.4	19.5	10.8	3.9	0.0	100	27.7
IUD	1982	4.9	2.4	32.3	34.3	16.8	9.3	4.9	0.0	100	27.2
IUD	1983	5.5	3.7	38.0	33.6	15.2	7.0	2.5	0.0	100	26.2
Female sterilization	1977	4.6	0.3	12.9	37.6	29.0	16.8	3.4	0.0	100	29.9
Female sterilization	4/1978–3/1979	5.4	0.2	16.4	36.7	28.1	15.5	3.1	0.0	100	29.6
Female sterilization	1979	6.7	0.1	15.6	39.6	27.7	14.2	2.8	0.0	100	29.3
Female sterilization	1982	19.7	0.0	15.8	38.4	27.0	14.6	4.2	0.0	100	29.5
Female sterilization	1983	19.4	0.1	16.9	37.6	26.8	14.4	4.2	0.0	100	29.4
Male sterilization	1977	1.2	0.2	8.7	40.4	29.9	16.4	4.4	0.0	100	30.1
Male sterilization	4/1978–3/1979	2.2	0.1	12.4	39.1	25.7	17.9	4.8	0.0	100	29.8
Male sterilization	1979	2.1	0.2	13.6	35.5	26.8	18.4	5.5	0.0	100	30.1
Male sterilization	1982	3.6	0.0	12.6	29.4	26.8	21.5	9.7	0.0	100	31.5
Male sterilization	1983	2.9	0.1	15.4	32.0	28.9	16.0	7.6	0.0	100	30.4
Nagaland											
IUD	1979	g	0.0	0.0	21.6	32.5	27.0	18.9	0.0	100	34.4
IUD	1982	0.1	0.0	26.7	15.1	28.8	21.9	7.5	0.0	100	31.4
IUD	1983	0.3	0.0	12.4	24.7	26.1	21.1	15.7	0.0	100	32.5
Female sterilization	1979	0.1	0.0	13.0	37.0	38.0	12.0	0.0	0.0	100	30.0
Female sterilization	1982	0.3	0.0	0.0	24.2	26.4	36.3	18.1	0.0	100	35.3
Female sterilization	1983	0.2	0.0	0.0	17.3	25.0	41.0	16.7	0.0	100	35.9
Male sterilization	1979	g	0.0	0.0	25.0	33.3	25.0	16.7	0.0	100	33.8
Male sterilization	1982	g	0.0	0.0	0.0	15.4	46.1	38.5	0.0	100	38.8
Male sterilization	1983	g	0.0	0.0	18.8	43.7	25.0	12.5	0.0	100	33.6
Orissa											
IUD	1977	8.9	8.3	32.0	32.4	19.3	7.3	0.7	0.0	100	26.5
IUD	4/1978–3/1979	13.9	8.2	33.0	32.1	17.6	7.4	1.7	0.0	100	26.4
IUD	1979	17.5	8.3	30.3	34.2	20.7	5.7	0.8	0.0	100	26.7
IUD	1982	30.6	7.0	35.9	32.1	17.6	6.6	0.8	0.0	100	26.1
IUD	1983	43.9	6.2	29.0	28.6	25.4	10.0	0.8	0.0	100	27.6
Female sterilization	1977	56.3	0.9	8.8	30.0	35.8	21.2	3.3	0.0	100	31.4
Female sterilization	4/1978–3/1979	78.9	0.2	10.1	28.2	35.7	22.1	3.7	0.0	100	31.6
Female sterilization	1979	73.9	0.2	6.8	28.5	36.1	23.1	5.3	0.0	100	32.0
Female sterilization	1982	125.3	0.3	9.0	36.1	32.3	19.7	2.6	0.0	100	30.7
Female sterilization	1983	161.3	0.3	7.0	27.4	41.8	21.6	1.9	0.0	100	31.8
Male sterilization	1977	25.6	10.4	12.2	21.4	32.9	18.9	4.2	0.0	100	30.9
Male sterilization	4/1978–3/1979	26.2	0.1	9.1	29.9	32.5	21.1	7.3	0.0	100	31.7
Male sterilization	1979	16.8	0.1	9.6	32.3	34.3	19.2	4.5	0.0	100	31.2
Male sterilization	1982	21.4	0.2	7.8	30.0	36.7	21.4	3.9	0.0	100	31.6
Male sterilization	1983	17.0	0.2	8.5	28.5	39.1	20.5	3.2	0.0	100	31.6
Punjab											
IUD	1977	27.6	2.5	21.6	33.4	26.2	14.0	2.3	0.0	100	28.9
IUD	4/1978–3/1979	34.2	2.2	20.7	33.7	27.2	14.0	2.2	0.0	100	29.0
IUD	1979	31.4	1.6	21.7	35.5	27.1	12.8	1.3	0.0	100	28.8
IUD	1982	161.2	2.7	25.8	36.5	22.5	10.3	2.2	0.0	100	27.9
IUD	1983	195.1	1.9	27.7	35.2	23.7	9.9	1.6	0.0	100	27.9

Table 24. Acceptors Distributed by Method and Age of Wife, and Median Age of Wife *(continued)*

Country and method	Year	Number (000s)	<20	20–24	25–29	30–34	35–39	40+	Unknown	Total	Wife's median age[b]
Punjab *(continued)*											
Female sterilization	1977	11.0	6.8	22.5	38.0	27.7	5.0	0.0	0.0	100	27.7
Female sterilization	4/1978–3/1979	17.4	0.0	6.8	23.9	38.8	25.6	4.9	0.0	100	32.5
Female sterilization	1979	20.5	0.0	5.7	25.0	42.2	23.3	3.8	0.0	100	32.3
Female sterilization	1982	125.8	0.0	6.3	29.0	37.8	22.5	4.4	0.0	100	31.9
Female sterilization	1983	127.8	0.0	4.0	25.5	41.5	24.5	4.5	0.0	100	32.5
Male sterilization	1977	1.9	0.0	4.7	17.9	40.5	27.9	9.0	0.0	100	33.4
Male sterilization	4/1978–3/1979	3.1	0.0	5.4	21.3	36.9	28.3	8.1	0.0	100	33.2
Male sterilization	1979	3.8	0.0	4.5	20.6	39.1	29.7	6.1	0.0	100	33.2
Male sterilization	1982	9.3	0.0	8.0	22.9	33.5	25.9	9.7	0.0	100	32.9
Male sterilization	1983	12.4	0.0	2.3	22.3	44.1	25.5	5.8	0.0	100	32.9
Rajasthan											
IUD	1977	8.1	2.2	28.3	32.6	22.8	11.1	3.0	0.0	100	28.0
IUD	4/1978–3/1979	18.2	1.1	26.9	33.3	23.8	12.1	2.8	0.0	100	28.3
IUD	1979	21.0	1.0	22.8	32.6	25.4	13.1	5.1	0.0	100	29.0
IUD	1982	18.9	2.5	31.7	36.4	20.5	7.3	1.6	0.0	100	27.2
IUD	1983	35.5	3.1	26.5	38.4	22.6	7.8	1.6	0.0	100	27.7
Female sterilization	1977	9.2	0.2	13.5	37.5	31.2	13.9	3.7	0.0	100	29.8
Female sterilization	4/1978–3/1979	16.5	0.0	11.1	37.2	32.6	14.7	4.4	0.0	100	30.3
Female sterilization	1979	30.9	0.0	8.0	32.7	34.5	18.2	6.6	0.0	100	31.3
Female sterilization	1982	147.8	0.0	5.3	29.8	38.8	22.2	3.9	0.0	100	31.9
Female sterilization	1983	174.8	0.2	6.4	28.6	39.3	20.8	4.7	0.0	100	31.9
Male sterilization	1977	1.7	0.1	11.3	30.5	32.0	18.7	7.4	0.0	100	31.3
Male sterilization	4/1978–3/1979	4.4	0.1	6.1	31.0	34.1	20.5	8.2	0.0	100	31.9
Male sterilization	1979	9.4	0.1	6.7	27.1	31.9	23.7	10.5	0.0	100	32.5
Male sterilization	1982	5.9	0.0	6.7	30.4	36.0	19.3	7.6	0.0	100	31.8
Male sterilization	1983	8.1	0.2	6.8	25.9	34.4	22.1	10.6	0.0	100	32.5
Sikkim											
IUD	1982	0.7	3.7	30.0	33.6	18.9	9.8	4.0	0.0	100	27.4
IUD	1983	0.8	4.0	30.3	33.2	20.5	8.8	3.2	0.0	100	27.4
Female sterilization	1982	0.3	0.0	15.7	32.1	26.9	18.8	6.5	0.0	100	30.4
Female sterilization	1983	0.3	0.0	16.4	32.2	29.3	16.7	5.4	0.0	100	30.2
Male sterilization	1982	0.2	0.0	6.4	26.8	28.0	24.8	14.0	0.0	100	33.0
Male sterilization	1983	0.2	0.0	6.6	25.3	30.7	20.5	16.9	0.0	100	32.9
Tamil Nadu											
IUD	4/1978–3/1979	36.6	3.4	30.8	35.2	20.1	8.8	1.7	0.0	100	27.2
IUD	1979	31.2	6.8	32.5	33.7	18.6	7.3	1.1	0.0	100	26.6
IUD	1982	36.5	4.6	37.6	32.0	17.4	7.1	1.3	0.0	100	26.2
IUD	1983	51.0	7.4	37.5	31.5	16.0	6.6	1.0	0.0	100	25.8
Female sterilization	4/1978–3/1979	125.1	0.1	13.6	40.9	28.4	14.3	2.7	0.0	100	29.4
Female sterilization	1979	122.2	0.1	16.1	41.3	26.4	13.5	2.6	0.0	100	29.1
Female sterilization	1982	247.3	0.2	12.5	41.8	29.0	14.4	2.1	0.0	100	29.5
Female sterilization	1983	464.4	0.2	15.6	40.9	27.9	13.6	1.8	0.0	100	29.2
Male sterilization	4/1978–3/1979	91.3	0.2	7.8	28.6	31.7	23.3	8.4	0.0	100	32.1
Male sterilization	1979	35.4	0.1	11.6	28.0	28.6	22.6	9.1	0.0	100	31.8
Male sterilization	1982	15.6	0.1	7.2	25.8	30.2	28.6	8.1	0.0	100	32.8
Male sterilization	1983	23.6	0.0	8.4	29.4	31.0	24.7	6.5	0.0	100	32.0
Tripura											
IUD	1977	0.1	4.0	23.0	54.0	9.5	6.8	2.7	0.0	100	27.1
IUD	1979	0.5	5.4	33.8	35.9	24.9	0.0	0.0	0.0	100	26.5
IUD	1982	0.7	0.0	0.0	5.9	41.9	20.1	32.1	0.0	100	35.5
IUD	1983	1.2	8.1	69.1	4.3	0.4	17.5	0.6	0.0	100	23.0
Female sterilization	1979	0.3	1.3	36.1	42.2	9.9	6.4	4.1	0.0	100	26.5
Female sterilization	1982	0.7	0.0	0.0	3.1	43.4	20.9	32.6	0.0	100	35.8
Female sterilization	1983	1.2	0.0	40.9	45.2	2.5	11.4	0.0	0.0	100	26.0
Male sterilization	1979	0.6	5.1	30.9	32.3	17.3	13.3	1.1	0.0	100	27.2
Male sterilization	1982	1.3	0.0	0.2	2.1	43.7	25.8	28.2	0.0	100	35.8
Male sterilization	1983	3.8	0.0	52.0	30.8	5.5	2.1	1.6	0.0	100	24.4
Uttar Pradesh											
IUD	1977	48.9	5.2	23.0	30.9	26.4	11.3	3.2	0.0	100	28.5
IUD	1978	148.6	5.3	20.6	30.4	26.3	13.9	3.5	0.0	100	29.0
IUD	1979	163.6	4.3	20.7	30.6	26.0	14.8	3.6	0.0	100	29.1

Table 24. Acceptors Distributed by Method and Age of Wife, and Median Age of Wife *(continued)*

Country and method	Year	Number (000s)	<20	20–24	25–29	30–34	35–39	40+	Unknown	Total	Wife's median age[b]
Uttar Pradesh (continued)											
IUD	1982	264.9	5.6	25.1	31.4	23.3	11.0	3.9	0.0	100	28.1
IUD	1983	288.3	4.6	26.4	31.3	24.6	10.7	2.4	0.0	100	28.0
Female sterilization	1977	9.1	0.0	7.8	33.9	33.2	20.1	5.0	0.0	100	31.2
Female sterilization	4/1978–3/1979	19.4	0.6	7.8	29.8	37.3	19.6	4.9	0.0	100	31.6
Female sterilization	1979	32.3	0.4	5.9	24.9	35.0	27.5	6.3	0.0	100	32.7
Female sterilization	1982	397.7	0.2	6.3	24.3	36.7	24.6	7.9	0.0	100	32.6
Female sterilization	1983	358.9	0.0	5.3	26.0	38.3	24.7	5.7	0.0	100	32.4
Male sterilization	1977	0.8	0.4	6.7	23.8	35.3	26.4	1.4	0.0	100	32.3
Male sterilization	4/1978–3/1979	3.8	0.0	5.7	23.8	34.7	26.1	9.7	0.0	100	33.0
Male sterilization	1979	6.9	0.2	4.6	23.8	32.7	28.8	9.9	0.0	100	33.3
Male sterilization	1982	8.9	0.0	5.7	27.7	37.6	23.5	5.9	0.0	100	32.2
Male sterilization	1983	9.1	0.0	4.7	21.7	33.5	31.1	9.0	0.0	100	33.5
West Bengal											
IUD	1977	6.3	9.1	37.8	30.7	15.7	5.6	1.1	0.0	100	25.5
IUD	4/1978–3/1979	10.7	11.7	34.1	27.7	15.4	9.3	1.8	0.0	100	25.8
IUD	1979	21.4	15.8	40.4	23.0	14.7	5.4	0.7	0.0	100	24.2
IUD	1982	39.1	10.7	33.1	31.4	16.6	7.1	1.1	0.0	100	26.0
Female sterilization	1977	28.4	0.6	22.4	37.8	25.6	12.1	1.5	0.0	100	28.6
Female sterilization	4/1978–3/1979	56.9	0.6	18.9	41.1	24.8	12.1	2.5	0.0	100	28.7
Female sterilization	1979	94.1	0.6	17.7	39.7	25.4	13.6	3.0	0.0	100	29.0
Female sterilization	1982	193.9	1.3	17.6	35.3	29.5	13.5	2.8	0.0	100	29.4
Female sterilization	1983	288.6	1.0	16.9	33.1	31.6	14.7	2.7	0.0	100	29.8
Male sterilization	1977	2.9	0.8	12.4	23.6	31.0	22.6	9.6	0.0	100	32.1
Male sterilization	4/1978–3/1979	10.6	0.3	11.3	31.5	28.7	20.3	7.9	0.0	100	31.2
Male sterilization	1979	61.7	0.6	13.4	27.7	31.8	19.0	7.5	0.0	100	31.3
Male sterilization	1982	74.8	0.7	10.4	22.2	31.0	24.2	7.6	0.0	100	32.4
Male sterilization	1983	82.3	3.7	14.3	26.2	29.0	20.6	6.2	0.0	100	31.0
Other territories											
IUD	1977	3.5	1.3	27.9	42.0	19.4	7.9	1.4	0.0	100	27.5
IUD	4/1978–3/1979	5.8	2.4	27.5	39.2	21.5	7.7	1.7	0.0	100	27.6
IUD	1979	6.3	3.3	28.3	35.2	19.5	12.3	1.4	0.0	100	27.6
IUD	1982	10.8	5.4	29.8	40.1	18.4	5.3	1.0	0.0	100	26.8
IUD	1982	13.1	0.4	14.0	40.6	31.1	12.6	1.2	0.0	100	29.4
IUD	1983	8.4	7.4	37.5	31.1	17.5	5.3	1.1	0.0	100	25.8
Female sterilization	1977	3.6	0.1	7.4	26.8	37.8	20.7	7.0	0.0	100	32.1
Female sterilization	4/1978–3/1979	8.3	0.3	12.7	35.3	31.1	18.2	2.4	0.0	100	30.3
Female sterilization	1979	6.4	0.6	19.5	34.0	26.9	15.0	3.9	0.0	100	29.4
Female sterilization	1983	14.4	0.5	14.1	37.8	31.1	14.8	1.6	0.0	100	29.7
Male sterilization	1977	0.3	0.0	7.9	19.9	30.6	26.0	15.6	0.0	100	33.6
Male sterilization	4/1978–3/1979	1.0	0.2	13.1	35.1	30.7	15.8	3.0	2.1	100	30.1
Male sterilization	1979	0.9	0.0	9.1	29.0	36.7	19.1	6.1	0.0	100	31.6
Male sterilization	1982	1.5	2.8	22.3	33.1	26.8	12.0	3.1	0.0	100	28.8
Male sterilization	1983	1.1	1.3	14.2	34.9	26.8	17.6	5.2	0.0	100	29.9
Indonesia											
IUD	4–9/1972	10.2	3.7	18.5	29.3	27.5	17.1	3.9	0.0	100	29.7
IUD	7–9/1973	6.3	3.9	19.5	29.4	28.1	15.5	2.4	1.2	100	29.4
IUD	9–12/1974	4.4	5.1	25.4	29.9	23.1	13.8	2.6	0.1	100	28.3
IUD	7–9/1975	3.5	5.6	27.9	31.2	20.3	11.8	3.2	0.0	100	27.6
IUD	10–12/1976	8.1	6.6	28.0	30.3	20.0	12.5	2.6	0.0	100	27.5
IUD	7–9/1978	7.0	7.9	33.3	29.1	15.6	10.8	3.3	0.0	100	26.5
IUD	9–12/1980	9.2	8.5	37.2	28.7	14.7	8.4	2.4	0.1	100	25.7
IUD	4–6/1983	16.9	6.6	35.5	29.7	16.4	9.1	2.7	0.0	100	26.3
Orals	4–9/1972	15.8	6.2	22.9	28.2	23.9	15.2	3.6	0.0	100	28.7
Orals	7–9/1973	13.7	7.2	23.3	28.7	22.7	13.9	3.1	1.2	100	28.3
Orals	9–12/1974	26.3	7.9	26.8	29.4	21.4	11.9	2.5	0.1	100	27.6
Orals	7–9/1975	25.3	9.6	28.5	28.0	19.6	11.7	2.5	0.1	100	27.1
Orals	10–12/1976	20.6	10.5	31.0	27.9	17.5	10.7	2.4	0.0	100	26.5
Orals	7–9/1978	22.9	12.3	33.4	27.3	15.4	9.5	2.0	0.1	100	25.8
Orals	9–12/1980	34.0	11.8	35.7	27.5	14.6	8.3	2.0	0.1	100	25.4
Orals	4–6/1983	20.7	10.3	34.5	27.0	18.3	7.4	2.5	0.0	100	26.0
Injectables	10–12/1976	0.2	3.1	29.4	31.4	19.6	12.4	4.1	0.0	100	27.8
Injectables	7–9/1978	0.7	6.5	28.1	29.7	19.0	12.4	4.3	0.0	100	27.6
Injectables	9–12/1980	1.1	7.9	33.9	30.1	15.7	10.2	2.1	0.1	100	26.4

Table 24. Acceptors Distributed by Method and Age of Wife, and Median Age of Wife *(continued)*

Country and method	Year	Number (000s)	<20	20–24	25–29	30–34	35–39	40+	Unknown	Total	Wife's median age[b]
Indonesia *(continued)*											
Injectables	4–6/1983	13.6	7.1	35.4	29.7	17.1	8.3	2.4	0.0	100	26.3
Condoms	4–6/1983	1.7	6.2	34.4	28.8	17.4	8.1	5.1	0.0	100	26.6
Female sterilization	10–12/1977	0.3	0.6	2.5	20.3	36.9	31.7	7.7	0.3	100	33.6
Female sterilization	7–9/1978	0.4	0.5	3.2	20.3	34.8	31.6	9.1	0.5	100	33.7
Female sterilization	9–12/1980	0.7	0.7	3.3	19.2	35.7	31.1	9.7	0.3	100	33.7
Female sterilization	4–6/1983	1.1	0.7	4.7	22.2	38.6	26.0	7.8	0.0	100	32.9
Male sterilization	10–12/1977	0.2	0.6	5.0	5.6	23.3	37.2	26.7	1.6	100	37.0
Male sterilization	7–9/1978	0.1	0.0	4.1	8.1	21.6	33.8	32.4	0.0	100	37.4
Male sterilization	9–12/1980	0.1	0.0	8.3	10.0	25.0	35.0	18.3	3.4	100	35.7
Male sterilization	4–6/1983	0.3	1.3	4.5	11.8	25.9	24.6	31.9	0.0	100	36.3
All methods	4–9/1972	27.8	5.1	21.0	28.6	25.2	16.1	3.9	0.1	100	29.2
All methods	7–9/1973	23.4	5.9	21.9	28.7	24.2	14.8	3.1	1.4	100	28.7
All methods	9–12/1974	36.7	7.1	25.9	29.1	22.2	12.7	3.0	0.1	100	27.9
Kampuchea											
IUD	1973	0.4	3.0	17.0	35.0	27.0	14.0	4.0	0.0	100	29.3
Orals	1973	2.2	1.7	18.0	32.0	27.0	16.0	5.3	0.0	100	29.7
Korea, Republic of											
IUD	1966	218.4	——0.3——		6.5	22.3	28.9	42.0	0.0	100	38.6
IUD	1969	14.1	——5.0——		23.0	34.0	26.0	12.0	0.0	100	33.2
IUD	1972	7.0	——7.0——		25.0	32.0	25.0	11.0	0.0	100	32.8
IUD	1–6/1975	203.3	0.1	6.4	25.6	31.0	25.5	11.4	0.0	100	32.9
IUD	1980	37.2	——13.7——		36.0	24.7	14.8	9.7	1.1	100	30.0
IUD	1986	233.4	0.0	2.6	51.6	17.6	5.5	2.3	0.0	100	28.6
Orals	1969	7.6	——3.5——		19.0	35.0	30.0	13.0	0.0	100	34.0
Orals	1971	5.0	——5.2——		21.0	34.0	27.0	13.0	0.0	100	33.5
Orals	1986	45.8	u	15.5	31.0	28.6	16.2	8.6	0.0	100	30.6
Condom	1986	108.3	u	9.5	40.6	21.3	19.8	8.9	0.0	100	30.0
Sterilization	1–6/1975	1.4	0.1	1.9	22.5	40.4	27.1	8.0	0.0	100	33.2
Female sterilization	1972	3.0	——1.0——		12.0	29.0	34.0	23.0	1.0	100	36.1
Female sterilization	1973	2.4	——1.0——		11.0	31.0	33.0	23.0	1.0	100	36.0
Female sterilization	1974	3.2	——2.1——		14.5	34.8	31.7	16.0	0.8	100	34.7
Female sterilization	1–6/1975	3.2	——1.3——		16.5	37.3	32.2	12.7	0.0	100	34.3
Female sterilization	1976	12.8	——1.3——		16.1	41.0	33.9	7.7	0.0	100	34.0
Female sterilization	1977	177.7	——2.4——		19.6	38.9	32.2	6.5	0.4	100	33.6
Female sterilization	1978	40.5	——2.7——		20.2	37.9	31.9	9.6	0.4	100	33.7
Female sterilization	1979	35.3	——3.2——		21.9	36.9	29.8	7.7	0.5	100	33.3
Female sterilization	1980	35.2	——3.9——		25.4	36.4	25.0	8.6	0.7	100	32.8
Female sterilization	1981	40.2	——5.0——		29.0	36.0	21.1	7.6	1.3	100	32.1
Female sterilization	1986	220.3	u	11.8	48.2	38.6	1.0	0.3	0.0	100	29.0
Male sterilization	1968	5.4	u	1.8	15.9	35.4	35.0	10.5	1.4	100	34.5
Male sterilization	1969	8.0	0.0	0.6	9.3	31.1	38.3	20.5	0.0	100	36.2
Male sterilization	1970	10.6	0.0	1.0	8.0	32.0	40.0	20.0	0.0	100	36.2
Male sterilization	1971	7.9	0.0	1.0	11.0	35.0	37.0	16.0	0.0	100	35.4
Male sterilization	1972	4.3	——2.0——		17.0	37.0	32.0	11.0	1.0	100	34.1
Male sterilization	1973	3.4	——1.0——		15.0	39.0	34.0	10.0	1.0	100	34.3
Male sterilization	1974	21.2	——2.5——		24.3	40.6	25.7	6.1	0.8	100	32.8
Male sterilization	1–6/1975	22.4	——2.3——		24.3	40.1	26.3	7.0	0.0	100	32.9
Male sterilization	1976	16.5	——2.4——		25.2	38.5	23.6	10.3	0.0	100	32.9
Male sterilization	1977	52.5	——3.3——		26.9	38.8	21.9	7.4	1.7	100	32.4
Male sterilization	1978	18.9	——4.2——		30.5	38.9	19.0	6.4	1.0	100	31.9
Male sterilization	1979	12.6	——3.7——		30.2	39.7	18.1	7.0	1.3	100	31.9
Male sterilization	1980	27.0	——4.7——		33.9	37.7	15.8	6.1	1.8	100	31.4
Male sterilization	1981	31.1	——4.7——		34.7	38.5	14.3	5.8	2.0	100	31.2
Male sterilization	1986	92.2	u	11.1	56.7	31.2	0.8	0.2	0.0	100	28.4
Menstrual regulation	1–6/1975	3.0	0.2	4.0	17.7	32.2	30.7	15.2	0.0	100	34.4
Menstrual regulation	1980	34.4	——5.8——		25.3	33.4	23.8	10.8	0.9	100	32.8
Laos											
Orals (urban)	1972	c	2.0	20.0	32.0	23.0	17.0	6.0	0.0	100	29.4
Orals (rural)	1972	c	1.0	18.0	21.0	27.0	24.0	9.0	0.0	100	31.9
Malaysia (Peninsular)											
IUD	1972	1.1	1.6	18.5	29.9	24.5	17.2	8.3	0.0	100	30.0
IUD	1973	0.9	1.9	19.3	33.3	25.3	14.1	6.1	0.0	100	29.3

Table 24. Acceptors Distributed by Method and Age of Wife, and Median Age of Wife *(continued)*

Country and method	Year	Number (000s)	<20	20–24	25–29	30–34	35–39	40+	Unknown	Total	Wife's median age[b]
Malaysia (Peninsular, *continued***)**											
IUD	1974	0.8	1.9	20.2	33.0	23.9	14.5	6.6	0.0	100	29.2
IUD	1976	1.1	1.3	21.2	32.7	22.3	13.4	9.1	0.0	100	29.2
IUD	1978	1.6	1.8	20.0	33.4	24.5	14.3	6.0	0.0	100	29.2
IUD	1980	2.6	2.1	21.7	34.9	24.5	10.3	6.5	0.0	100	28.8
Orals	1972	48.9	7.6	33.2	27.3	18.0	10.0	3.9	0.0	100	26.7
Orals	1973	49.9	8.4	34.7	27.2	16.4	9.5	3.8	0.0	100	26.3
Orals	1974	53.7	8.9	36.5	27.4	15.1	8.7	3.4	0.0	100	25.8
Orals	1976	65.0	10.0	37.2	28.7	13.0	7.9	3.2	0.0	100	25.5
Orals	1978	65.8	10.2	37.3	29.7	13.3	6.4	3.1	0.0	100	25.4
Orals	1980	61.8	11.0	38.9	28.8	13.4	5.4	2.5	0.0	100	25.0
Injectables	1978	0.7	1.4	19.8	30.3	23.8	14.9	9.8	0.0	100	29.8
Injectables	1980	0.8	3.2	18.6	25.4	25.3	15.0	12.5	0.0	100	30.6
Sterilization	1972	3.9	0.1	4.9	18.8	37.8	28.2	10.2	0.0	100	33.5
Sterilization	1973	4.1	0.1	5.0	22.7	36.7	26.8	8.7	0.0	100	33.0
Sterilization	1976	4.0	0.1	5.7	27.8	31.2	24.8	10.4	0.0	100	32.6
Female sterilization	1974	3.4	0.0	8.0	30.4	20.3	30.7	10.6	0.0	100	32.9
Female sterilization	1975	u	u	u	u	u	u	u	u	u	32.7
Female sterilization	1977	3.6	0.1	5.4	26.5	32.6	24.6	10.8	0.0	100	32.8
Female sterilization	1978	4.6	0.2	4.9	26.9	33.6	24.0	10.4	0.0	100	32.7
Female sterilization	1980	4.9	0.1	4.9	24.0	36.3	22.8	11.9	0.0	100	32.9
Male sterilization	1980	0.2	0.0	3.6	21.0	39.0	24.6	11.8	0.0	100	33.3
All methods	1969	70.6	4.8	23.8	27.9	24.2	13.4	5.9	0.0	100	28.8
All methods	1971	54.7	6.5	29.3	25.9	21.3	12.0	5.0	0.0	100	27.7
All methods	1972	56.4	6.7	30.4	27.0	19.7	11.6	4.6	0.0	100	27.4
All methods	1973	57.3	7.5	31.7	27.2	18.3	11.0	4.3	0.0	100	27.0
All methods	1974	61.7	7.9	33.6	27.5	16.9	10.2	3.9	0.0	100	26.5
All methods	1976	75.2	8.9	34.2	29.0	14.5	9.3	4.1	0.0	100	26.2
All methods	1978	80.2	8.8	33.8	30.1	15.4	8.1	3.8	0.0	100	26.2
All methods	1980	81.1	9.0	34.5	29.7	16.0	7.1	3.7	0.0	100	26.1
Nepal											
IUD	7/1972–7/1973	0.2	3.0	17.0	31.0	23.0	17.0	9.0	0.0	100	29.8
IUD	7/1973–7/1974	0.7	2.1	21.3	25.5	28.3	11.6	9.7	1.5	100	30.1
IUD	1975–1976	0.4	4.2	25.6	27.6	25.0	10.8	6.8	0.0	100	28.7
Orals	4–6/1970	1.9	5.3	22.8	26.6	25.5	12.5	6.6	0.6	100	29.1
Orals	7/1973–7/1974	2.0	4.1	21.1	26.5	27.0	12.9	7.9	0.5	100	29.6
Orals	1975–1976	2.7	4.2	20.6	23.6	27.8	16.6	7.2	0.0	100	30.3
Female sterilization	1975–1976	0.6	0.4	5.8	28.7	34.9	20.9	9.3	0.0	100	32.2
Male sterilization	7/1972–7/1973	1.7	0.0	2.0	13.0	25.0	25.0	35.0	0.0	100	37.0
Male sterilization	7/1973–7/1974	1.8	0.4	10.6	29.3	29.3	17.3	10.3	2.8	100	31.4
Male sterilization	1975–1976	1.3	0.7	11.2	28.6	32.4	19.3	7.8	0.0	100	31.5
Pakistan											
IUD	7/1965–12/1966	1.6	0.5	7.5	16.6	27.4	28.5	19.5	0.0	100	34.6
IUD	1976–1977	32.9	0.5	4.8	15.7	26.7	28.3	21.7	2.3	100	35.2
Orals	1976–1977	123.3	0.8	9.0	21.2	29.2	23.2	15.2	1.4	100	33.1
Sterilization	1967–1968	6.8	——6.6——		22.3	28.0	26.0	17.1	0.0	100	33.8
Female sterilization	1976–1977	7.4	0.2	1.6	9.7	23.4	31.2	30.0	3.9	100	37.1
Male sterilization	1976–1977	1.3	0.0	1.8	8.8	24.1	30.5	30.1	4.7	100	37.1
Philippines											
IUD	10–12/1970	1.4	2.8	17.9	26.4	28.1	17.8	6.0	1.0	100	30.4
IUD	4–6/1972	20.6	4.3	22.0	25.5	24.7	15.7	7.4	0.4	100	29.6
IUD	1–3/1973	2.3	3.9	23.3	28.1	22.1	16.7	5.7	0.2	100	29.0
IUD	7–12/1975	21.7	7.4	30.0	27.2	18.0	12.4	5.0	0.0	100	27.3
IUD	1976	43.1	24.7	23.5	17.0	11.9	8.4	5.3	9.3	100	24.4
IUD	1–8/1978	33.2	5.7	30.4	30.6	16.1	11.2	5.9	0.1	100	27.3
IUD	1980	40.6	12.1	27.3	31.4	17.1	8.2	3.9	0.0	100	26.7
IUD	12/1982	1.9	8.1	34.4	32.1	16.3	6.8	2.0	0.3	100	26.1
Orals	10–12/1970	3.3	3.3	19.7	27.4	24.4	17.6	7.2	0.4	100	29.9
Orals	4–6/1972	86.5	4.4	22.9	27.5	23.3	15.4	6.3	0.2	100	29.1
Orals	1–3/1973	8.7	5.0	23.0	27.9	22.7	14.8	6.3	0.2	100	28.9
Orals	7–12/1975	163.5	8.1	30.3	28.2	17.3	11.9	4.0	0.2	100	27.0
Orals	1976	282.4	29.9	22.5	15.3	11.6	8.0	5.1	7.6	100	23.6
Orals	7–12/1978	170.3	7.2	33.0	31.0	16.4	9.3	2.9	0.2	100	26.6
Orals	1980	170.4	10.8	24.5	32.5	20.0	9.7	2.5	0.0	100	27.3

171

Table 24. Acceptors Distributed by Method and Age of Wife, and Median Age of Wife *(continued)*

Country and method	Year	Number (000s)	<20	20–24	25–29	30–34	35–39	40+	Unknown	Total	Wife's median age[b]
Philippines *(continued)*											
Orals	12/1982	7.9	7.7	33.3	32.2	17.4	8.1	1.2	0.1	100	26.4
Sterilization	6–12/1977	28.7	—9.8—		30.0	32.1	22.1	6.0	0.0	100	31.6
Sterilization	1978	52.8	—11.5—		30.4	31.5	20.7	5.9	0.0	100	31.3
Sterilization	1979	45.6	—10.7—		32.7	32.5	19.3	4.8	0.0	100	31.0
Sterilization	1980	56.6	—10.8—		33.6	33.8	17.4	4.4	0.0	100	30.8
Sterilization	1981	64.4	—11.4—		35.9	32.8	16.2	3.7	0.0	100	30.4
Female sterilization	7–12/1975	13.4	0.3	6.8	27.6	32.2	25.4	7.5	0.1	100	32.4
Female sterilization	1976	37.6	0.5	6.6	18.3	23.9	19.4	12.2	19.1	100	u
Female sterilization	1977	4.5	0.5	9.1	29.9	31.7	22.8	6.0	0.0	100	31.7
Female sterilization	1980	41.2	1.0	8.8	31.4	32.2	19.6	7.1	0.0	100	31.4
Female sterilization	12/1982	1.9	0.3	11.2	36.9	33.3	15.7	2.6	0.0	100	30.2
Male sterilization	7–12/1975	4.1	0.4	7.2	22.0	31.5	26.7	12.1	0.2	100	33.2
Male sterilization	1976	10.3	1.9	13.5	20.2	19.2	16.3	12.5	16.3	100	u
Male sterilization	1–8/1978	3.9	1.7	16.8	32.3	25.9	17.0	5.7	0.6	100	29.8
Male sterilization	1980	1.3	0.9	10.2	34.8	34.3	16.4	3.3	0.0	100	30.6
Other	12/1982	4.4	6.2	27.4	30.7	19.5	11.3	4.3	0.6	100	27.6
All methods	4–6/1972	149.2	3.9	21.0	25.6	23.8	17.3	8.2	0.2	100	29.9
All methods	1–3/1973	15.7	4.4	21.7	26.6	22.9	16.4	7.7	0.2	100	29.5
All methods	7–12/1975	347.3	6.4	25.9	27.5	19.0	14.3	6.7	0.2	100	28.2
All methods	1–8/1978	448.9	5.4	28.1	29.7	19.3	2.4	4.9	0.2	100	26.9
Singapore											
IUD	1979	0.1	4.8	28.3	35.2	19.3	4.8	7.6	0.0	100	27.4
IUD	1980	0.2	3.8	19.2	37.2	28.2	4.5	7.1	0.0	100	28.6
IUD	1983	0.2	2.7	26.0	40.3	16.4	8.7	5.9	0.0	100	27.6
Orals	7/1967–3/1968	3.0	2.1	19.8	31.8	25.7	12.0	8.0	0.5	100	29.4
Orals	1972	8.4	11.2	42.5	27.8	10.4	4.5	2.1	1.5	100	24.5
Orals	1973	10.7	11.0	42.9	30.0	9.1	3.5	1.7	1.8	100	24.4
Orals	1974	5.0	12.0	29.3	43.8	8.7	3.1	1.3	1.8	100	25.9
Orals	1975	9.4	8.3	40.6	35.9	8.8	4.2	2.2	0.0	100	25.2
Orals	1976	9.0	9.6	44.9	33.2	8.1	3.1	1.1	0.0	100	24.5
Orals	1978	6.2	8.3	45.1	33.8	9.4	2.1	1.0	0.3	100	24.6
Orals	1980	5.5	9.0	43.8	32.2	11.7	2.5	0.8	0.0	100	24.7
Orals	1983	4.5	8.3	41.2	35.5	11.3	3.0	0.9	0.0	100	25.1
Condoms	1983	8.8	2.7	28.4	45.7	17.7	4.4	1.1	0.0	100	27.1
Female sterilization	1972	5.8	0.0	6.0	24.0	39.0	22.0	8.0	1.0	100	32.5
Female sterilization	1973	8.7	0.0	6.0	27.0	37.0	22.0	8.0	0.0	100	32.3
Female sterilization	1974	9.2	0.0	7.0	29.0	34.0	22.0	8.0	0.0	100	32.1
Female sterilization	1975	9.2	0.2	8.9	31.3	32.9	20.2	6.1	0.4	100	31.4
Female sterilization	1976	9.5	0.5	8.3	32.2	30.1	20.7	5.8	2.4	100	31.3
Female sterilization	1978	5.9	0.2	7.7	33.6	36.1	17.6	4.8	0.0	100	31.2
Female sterilization	1980	5.3	0.2	7.4	33.7	39.4	14.4	4.9	0.0	100	31.1
Male sterilization	1976	0.4	1.6	17.1	29.1	30.9	13.1	7.7	0.5	100	30.3
Male sterilization	1978	0.3	3.8	27.3	30.7	23.1	8.5	6.0	0.6	100	28.0
Male sterilization	1980	0.4	2.8	24.4	40.8	17.2	14.9	0.0	0.0	100	27.8
All methods	1972	17.7	8.6	37.9	29.7	12.5	6.0	3.5	1.8	100	25.4
All methods	1973	19.1	8.4	38.5	32.0	11.5	4.8	2.7	2.1	100	25.3
All methods	1–6/1974	8.6	9.4	30.7	40.3	10.8	4.3	2.4	2.1	100	26.1
All methods	1975	26.3	5.3	28.9	33.7	17.0	9.7	3.6	1.8	100	27.2
All methods	1976	27.5	4.8	28.8	35.5	17.1	9.7	3.3	0.8	100	27.3
All methods	1977	23.9	4.1	29.1	35.8	18.1	8.3	3.0	1.6	100	27.2
All methods	1980	20.7	4.1	29.6	37.9	20.1	5.9	2.4	0.0	100	27.2
All methods	1983	13.7	4.6	32.5	42.0	15.6	4.1	1.2	0.0	100	26.5
Sri Lanka											
IUD	1974	29.7	4.3	33.0	30.6	17.0	9.0	2.5	3.6	100	26.8
IUD	1–9/1975	24.3	5.1	34.7	31.1	16.3	8.8	2.4	1.6	100	26.5
IUD	1982	16.1	6.2	38.1	29.4	16.5	7.0	2.4	0.4	100	25.9
IUD	1985	13.9	6.3	36.6	30.9	16.2	7.2	2.2	0.5	100	26.1
Orals	1982	26.2	5.3	35.3	32.9	18.1	6.3	1.8	0.3	100	26.4
Orals	1982	13.0	0.5	18.3	34.1	24.1	16.0	3.7	3.3	100	29.3
Orals	1985	34.2	6.1	35.1	33.0	17.7	6.4	1.4	0.3	100	26.3
Injectables	1982	10.2	5.8	38.2	32.1	16.8	5.6	1.2	0.3	100	25.9
Injectables	1985	19.1	5.8	36.2	33.6	16.7	5.9	1.4	0.5	100	26.2
Sterilization	1974	42.2	0.0	6.5	24.0	30.9	23.9	12.3	2.4	100	33.0
Sterilization	1975	39.2	0.1	8.9	30.5	31.6	21.3	6.0	1.6	100	31.5

Table 24. Acceptors Distributed by Method and Age of Wife, and Median Age of Wife (continued)

Country and method	Year	Number (000s)	Percentage in wife's age-group								Wife's median age[b]
			<20	20–24	25–29	30–34	35–39	40+	Unknown	Total	
Sri Lanka *(continued)*											
Female sterilization	1973	20.2	0.0	6.3	24.4	32.6	23.6	7.0	6.0	100	32.5
Female sterilization	1974	34.9	0.1	7.6	26.0	31.9	23.0	9.6	1.7	100	32.4
Female sterilization	1–9/1975	24.9	0.2	9.6	31.0	32.5	20.6	4.3	1.8	100	31.3
Female sterilization	1980	61.6	0.1	10.1	36.4	33.6	16.2	3.4	0.2	100	30.5
Female sterilization	1981	46.3	0.1	11.3	36.4	32.7	15.4	3.2	0.9	100	30.3
Female sterilization	1982	48.9	0.1	14.7	36.7	30.7	14.0	2.6	1.2	100	29.7
Female sterilization	1985	54.3	0.2	14.3	39.4	28.1	14.7	2.8	0.4	100	29.5
Male sterilization	1974	7.3	0.0	1.2	14.3	25.9	27.9	25.0	5.7	100	36.0
Male sterilization	1980	51.3	0.5	11.9	28.2	23.2	17.9	5.6	12.7	100	30.7
Male sterilization	1981	30.3	0.5	12.3	28.9	24.1	19.1	5.5	9.6	100	30.7
Male sterilization	1982	0.7	u	u	15.3	31.2	23.1	30.4	0.0	100	35.8
Male sterilization	1985	17.4	0.4	15.3	35.5	24.8	16.5	5.8	1.7	100	29.7
All methods	1970	55.3	2.3	22.0	29.0	21.6	14.0	3.8	7.1	100	28.8
All methods	1972	71.1	2.5	23.4	29.5	21.0	12.7	3.5	7.5	100	28.5
All methods	1973	95.9	2.5	23.0	28.9	21.8	12.6	3.9	7.3	100	28.6
Taiwan											
IUD	1967–1968	123.7	—10.4—		30.1	30.5	18.8	9.3	0.9	100	31.5
IUD	1971	156.0	1.0	16.6	31.6	26.6	15.5	8.6	0.0	100	30.1
IUD	1972	152.3	1.1	18.6	32.6	25.3	14.3	8.1	0.0	100	29.6
IUD	1973	148.5	1.2	19.8	33.8	23.6	13.6	8.0	0.0	100	29.3
IUD	1974	156.7	1.2	19.5	35.9	22.0	13.3	7.7	0.4	100	29.1
IUD	1975	173.4	—20.5—		37.0	21.0	13.3	7.9	0.3	100	29.0
IUD	1977	177.4	—22.1—		39.5	19.6	11.6	7.1	0.1	100	28.5
IUD	1979	158.6	1.4	21.6	39.7	19.7	10.0	7.4	0.2	100	28.4
IUD	1981	161.6	—24.3—		39.4	21.5	8.4	5.2	1.3	100	28.2
IUD	1985	188.0	1.6	22.3	39.4	22.9	9.0	4.8	h	100	28.3
Orals	1967–1968	59.0	1.0	10.6	31.4	30.7	18.5	7.8	0.0	100	31.1
Orals	1971	79.0	3.1	20.4	28.3	24.9	14.8	8.6	0.0	100	29.7
Orals	1972	66.6	3.5	24.9	28.7	22.8	12.7	7.4	0.0	100	28.8
Orals	1973	58.4	4.1	28.6	29.5	20.5	11.1	6.3	0.0	100	27.9
Orals	1974	64.0	4.4	29.7	30.3	18.7	9.7	5.5	1.7	100	27.5
Orals	1975	54.4	5.0	31.4	31.1	16.5	9.2	5.0	1.8	100	27.0
Orals	1977	52.7	5.9	34.5	34.2	12.5	7.4	4.2	1.3	100	26.3
Orals	1979	63.6	6.3	36.7	35.3	11.2	5.8	3.6	1.1	100	25.9
Orals	1981	68.4	7.0	39.0	35.0	11.0	4.0	3.0	1.0	100	25.5
Orals	1985	57.0	5.3	36.8	36.8	12.3	3.5	1.7	1.7	100	25.8
Condoms	1981	106.2	4.0	33.0	41.0	14.0	5.0	3.0	0.0	100	26.6
Sterilization[d]	1981	51.1	0.0	8.0	45.0	34.0	10.0	3.0	0.0	100	29.7
Sterilization	1985	48.0	h	6.2	39.6	39.6	12.5	4.2	h	100	30.7
Female sterilization	1972	u	—6.7—		38.5	39.3	12.0	2.6	0.9	100	30.6
Female sterilization	1978	46.2	0.2	7.3	42.0	32.5	14.2	3.8	0.0	100	30.1
Female sterilization	1979	49.6	0.2	8.0	43.5	32.2	12.5	3.6	0.0	100	29.8
Female sterilization	1985	45.0	h	6.7	40.0	37.8	11.1	2.2	h	100	30.3
Male sterilization	1978	3.9	0.0	7.8	35.9	33.3	17.9	5.1	0.0	100	30.9
Male sterilization	1979	3.2	0.0	9.3	37.5	31.3	15.6	6.3	0.0	100	30.5
Male sterilization	1985	3.0	h	h	h	33.3	33.3	33.3	h	100	37.5
Other	1985	81.0	3.7	34.6	40.7	14.8	3.7	2.5	1.2	100	26.4
Thailand											
IUD[e]	1965	12.3	3.2	23.1	35.8	22.6	9.2	1.8	4.3	100	28.0
IUD[f]	1/1968–6/1969	5.6	2.7	23.3	31.5	25.9	12.8	3.7	0.1	100	28.8
IUD	1971	1.2	2.7	24.1	27.8	23.2	15.8	5.9	0.5	100	29.1
IUD	1974	1.5	4.8	30.0	29.0	16.6	13.4	5.7	0.6	100	27.6
IUD	1976	1.2	6.7	34.3	28.0	17.0	9.4	4.3	0.3	100	26.6
IUD	1978	1.3	5.4	38.2	28.9	14.3	8.0	5.3	0.0	100	26.1
IUD	1983	1.0	9.1	37.2	27.8	12.4	8.7	4.7	0.1	100	25.7
Orals	1971	3.8	3.9	23.8	24.7	22.9	16.2	7.8	0.7	100	29.4
Orals	1974	5.2	7.5	29.9	25.8	17.1	12.8	5.6	1.3	100	27.3
Orals	1976	6.3	9.9	32.5	25.3	14.2	11.1	6.4	0.6	100	26.4
Orals	1978	8.2	8.0	37.2	26.5	13.7	8.8	6.0	0.0	100	25.9
Orals	1983	4.2	13.6	37.8	25.5	11.8	6.2	4.7	0.4	100	24.8
Injectables	1976	1.1	5.8	26.6	28.4	17.4	13.5	7.7	0.6	100	28.0
Injectables	1978	1.2	3.7	31.5	28.3	17.8	11.9	6.8	0.0	100	27.6
Injectables	1983	1.5	7.4	34.1	28.6	16.5	7.8	5.2	0.4	100	26.5
Sterilization	1974	1.1	1.1	14.7	33.4	26.8	18.1	5.6	0.3	100	30.1

Table 24. Acceptors Distributed by Method and Age of Wife, and Median Age of Wife *(continued)*

Country and method	Year	Number (000s)	Percentage in wife's age-group								Wife's median age[b]
			<20	20–24	25–29	30–34	35–39	40+	Unknown	Total	
Thailand *(continued)*											
Female sterilization	1973	u	u	u	u	u	u	u	u	u	30.9
Female sterilization	1975	u	0.1	15.8	37.0	25.3	16.5	5.0	0.3	100	29.6
Female sterilization	1976	1.5	1.4	17.9	33.9	27.9	14.1	4.3	0.5	100	29.5
Female sterilization	1977	1.7	0.9	19.6	32.8	25.7	16.7	4.3	0.0	100	29.5
Female sterilization	1978	1.2	0.7	22.3	31.8	25.6	14.1	5.4	0.0	100	29.2
Female sterilization	1983	1.1	1.2	22.6	37.3	22.6	10.5	5.5	0.3	100	28.5
Female sterilization	1986	162.3	1.5	22.8	36.0	22.6	13.1	4.0	u	100	28.6
Male sterilization	1976	2.1	0.0	3.8	18.2	28.7	28.2	20.1	1.0	100	34.8
Male sterilization	1977	0.3	0.3	5.5	23.2	26.0	25.7	19.3	0.0	100	34.0
Male sterilization	1978	0.5	0.0	4.5	22.2	23.6	27.1	22.6	0.0	100	34.9
Male sterilization	1983	0.1	7.9	14.0	31.6	25.4	15.8	5.3	0.0	100	29.4
Male sterilization	1986	35.8	0.1	5.9	24.1	28.4	20.1	21.4	u	100	33.5

u = unknown.

a. Mean age.

b. Calculated on the assumption that respondents of unknown age have the same distribution as whose age is specified. This assumption is likely to result in an underestimate of the median age; consequently, the median was not calculated when the unknown percentage was 15 or more.

c. The acceptor sample for rural and urban areas combined is 1,300.

d. Mostly female.

e. Age-groups are one year older than the indicated categories.

f. Excludes IUD acceptors who had given birth in the International Postpartum Family Planning Program.

g. Sample size less than 50.

h. Small base precludes estimate.

Table 25. Acceptors Distributed by Method and Number of Living Children, and Median Number of Living Children

Country and method	Year	Acceptor sample Number (000s)	0 or 1	2	3	4	5	6+	Unknown	Total	Median[d] number of living children
SUB-SAHARAN AFRICA											
Ghana											
IUD	1973	2.6	9.4	13.2	14.1	14.4	12.4	36.5	0.0	100	4.4
IUD	1976	1.3	13.8	17.2	17.0	16.8	13.0	22.2	0.0	100	3.6
IUD	1977	1.1	13.5	16.7	19.0	15.6	12.5	20.4	2.3	100	3.5
Orals	1973	17.6	17.7	14.5	13.4	12.4	10.8	31.2	0.0	100	3.9
Orals	1976	9.3	25.6	20.0	15.7	13.6	9.3	15.8	0.0	100	2.8
Orals	1977	8.1	20.8	20.3	15.6	14.0	9.6	15.3	4.4	100	2.9
All methods	1976	11.1	23.5	19.2	15.7	14.0	10.0	17.6	0.0	100	3.0
All methods	1977	9.7	19.3	19.2	15.7	14.1	10.2	17.4	4.1	100	3.1
Kenya											
IUD	1970	4.0	—16.0—		14.0	14.0	16.0	41.0	0.0	100	4.8
Orals	1970	8.5	—26.0—		15.0	14.0	13.0	32.0	0.0	100	4.1
Orals	1971	1.1	17.3	17.6	11.8	12.9	12.2	27.7	0.7	100	3.7
All methods	1974	40.6	22.0	18.0	14.0	12.0	11.0	23.0	0.0	100	3.2
All methods	1976	10.8	22.0	19.0	15.0	12.0	10.0	22.0	0.0	100	3.1
All methods	1978	61.1	24.0	20.0	10.0	11.0	11.0	20.0	4.0	100	2.9
Mauritius											
Orals	1974	20.0	34.5	20.1	15.1	10.5	8.5	11.3	0.0	100	2.3
Orals	1976	2.0	42.1	22.7	14.0	7.9	5.4	7.7	0.2	100	1.8
Orals	1980	1.6	60.4	21.9	9.5	4.8	1.9	1.5	0.0	100	<1.5
Orals	1983	0.6	63.2	23.2	7.4	3.3	1.6	1.3	0.0	100	<1.5
Injectables	1976	0.2	8.5	8.5	15.1	14.6	13.6	39.7	0.0	100	4.7
Injectables	1976	0.2	8.5	8.5	15.1	14.6	13.6	39.7	0.0	100	4.7
Injectables	1980	0.2	25.4	18.8	18.3	16.7	8.6	12.2	0.0	100	2.8
Other	1983	0.3	55.3	21.3	13.2	7.5	2.0	0.7	0.0	100	<1.5
All methods	1969	10.5	21.3	17.3	16.3	13.6	10.8	20.7	0.0	100	3.2
Nigeria											
All methods	1972	14.3	11.7	13.7	16.6	16.4	17.6	23.9	0.0	100	4.0
All methods	1973	23.1	7.6	13.3	16.3	21.5	13.9	27.3	0.0	100	4.1
LATIN AMERICA/CARIBBEAN											
Bolivia											
IUD	1976	1.1	20.1	29.3	24.6	11.5	7.2	7.3	0.0	100	2.5
Orals	1976	0.8	61.6	12.8	10.8	7.0	3.4	4.4	0.0	100	<1.5
All methods	1976	2.5	37.2	22.7	18.9	9.5	5.2	6.5	0.0	100	2.1
Brazil (BEMFAM)											
IUD	1974	1.0	19.7	23.3	17.9	——37.2——			1.9	100	2.8
Orals	1974	13.6	34.4	21.5	13.2	——26.5——			4.4	100	2.1
All methods	1974	15.4	33.5	21.3	13.4	——27.2——			4.6	100	2.2
All methods	1979	168.0	30.5	19.8	13.8	9.8	—22.2—		3.9	100	2.4
All methods	1980	166.0	31.9	22.1	13.7	9.2	—19.8—		3.3	100	2.2
All methods	1981	230.0	38.8	21.6	12.3	7.6	—14.6—		5.1	100	1.9
Brazil (Rio de Janeiro)											
Female sterilization	1983	2.0	2.0	16.7	24.0	21.1	13.2	23.2	0.0	100	3.8
Colombia											
IUD	1972	6.7	17.6	22.2	16.5	12.7	9.0	21.1	0.7	100	3.1
IUD	1973	69.0	18.9	22.4	16.1	12.1	8.9	19.9	1.7	100	2.9
IUD	1974	73.4	22.9	23.8	16.0	11.3	7.7	17.2	1.1	100	2.7
IUD	1975	59.8	25.1	25.0	16.1	10.6	7.2	14.9	1.1	100	2.5
Orals	1972	8.1	31.2	21.8	14.0	10.4	6.9	14.8	0.9	100	2.4
Orals	1973	75.0	24.3	21.0	14.7	10.6	7.6	18.1	3.7	100	2.7
Orals	1974	98.7	28.8	21.8	14.3	10.1	7.1	16.1	1.8	100	2.4
Orals	1975	77.8	32.4	22.3	14.0	9.3	6.6	13.6	1.8	100	2.2
All methods	1972	15.8	24.3	21.4	15.2	11.5	8.0	18.9	0.8	100	2.8
All methods	1973	159.0	21.3	21.4	15.3	11.4	8.3	19.5	2.8	100	2.9
All methods	1974	189.6	25.2	21.7	15.0	11.0	7.7	17.9	1.5	100	2.7
All methods	1975	165.3	27.4	22.0	14.9	10.6	7.5	16.2	1.4	100	2.5

Table 25. Acceptors Distributed by Method and Number of Living Children, and Median Number of Living Children (continued)

Country and method	Year	Acceptor sample Number (000s)	0 or 1	2	3	4	5	6+	Unknown	Total	Median[d] number of living children
Colombia (PROFAMILIA)											
Orals	1981	u	43.3	31.1	14.0	5.6	2.6	3.4	0.0	100	1.7
Orals	1982	u	44.9	31.1	13.9	4.8	2.3	3.0	0.0	100	1.7
Orals	1983	u	46.1	29.3	13.2	5.4	2.6	3.4	0.0	100	1.6
Sterilization	1974	6.6	1.2	4.6	14.8	19.6	15.7	43.0	1.1	100	5.1
Female sterilization	1975	11.4	0.9	4.3	15.7	20.9	17.4	40.0	0.8	100	4.9
Female sterilization	1976	u	1.0	5.0	17.9	19.5	16.7	39.8	0.0	100	4.9
Female sterilization	1977	u	0.6	5.9	18.6	20.6	16.3	37.9	0.0	100	4.8
Female sterilization	1978	u	0.8	7.6	21.5	21.7	16.6	31.5	0.0	100	4.4
Female sterilization	1979	u	0.7	7.2	22.4	23.2	16.3	30.0	0.0	100	4.3
Female sterilization	1980	u	0.8	7.8	23.7	23.6	16.6	27.3	0.0	100	4.3
Female sterilization	1981	u	0.9	8.3	26.7	23.8	15.2	25.1	0.0	100	4.1
Female sterilization	1982	u	0.9	9.4	27.6	24.1	14.6	23.3	0.0	100	4.0
Female sterilization	1983	u	1.3	11.3	29.1	23.3	14.0	21.0	0.0	100	3.9
Costa Rica											
IUD	1974	1.0	27.3	20.6	13.1	9.4	8.9	19.1	1.6	100	2.6
IUD	1975	2.1	27.3	21.5	17.3	9.6	6.3	16.9	1.1	100	2.5
IUD	1980	1.0	44.0	23.2	14.6	8.7	3.7	5.4	0.4	100	1.8
Orals	1974	8.3	44.8	22.3	11.7	6.4	4.4	8.3	2.0	100	1.7
Orals	1977	14.6	45.6	21.2	11.7	7.2	4.4	9.9	0.0	100	1.7
Orals	1980	11.3	57.6	21.2	9.6	5.0	2.7	3.8	0.1	100	<1.5
Injectables	1979	0.7	30.3	12.6	8.4	10.2	8.3	30.2	0.0	100	3.3
Injectables	1980	0.7	22.5	15.0	11.7	9.0	6.5	35.1	0.2	100	3.6
All methods	1974	12.6	39.1	20.7	12.2	7.6	5.4	13.1	1.9	100	2.0
All methods	1975	31.0	41.4	20.6	12.2	7.4	5.3	11.8	1.3	100	1.9
All methods	1978	22.4	49.3	21.4	10.7	5.9	3.7	7.8	1.2	100	1.5
All methods	1980	20.4	54.3	21.5	10.2	5.4	3.0	5.5	0.1	100	<1.5
Dominican Republic											
IUD	1972	7.3	11.5	19.6	18.6	14.2	11.2	24.8	0.2	100	3.5
IUD	1975	7.2	15.4	21.4	16.9	13.0	10.1	23.2	0.0	100	3.3
IUD	1976	6.0	16.8	21.0	18.2	13.7	9.7	20.6	0.0	100	3.2
IUD	1977	5.5	20.7	18.8	19.8	12.4	9.2	19.1	0.0	100	3.0
Orals	1972	8.7	23.8	22.1	17.5	11.6	8.6	16.3	0.1	100	2.7
Orals	1975	39.9	27.9	23.0	15.7	10.8	7.2	15.4	0.0	100	2.5
Orals	1976	41.7	32.0	23.1	15.4	10.0	6.6	12.9	0.0	100	2.3
Orals	1977	39.7	35.4	24.7	15.1	9.2	5.7	9.9	0.0	100	2.1
All methods	1976	61.5	28.0	22.0	15.7	10.8	7.5	16.0	0.0	100	2.5
Ecuador											
IUD	1971	1.0	9.3	17.0	16.1	16.7	13.7	25.4	1.7	100	4.0
IUD	1973	5.9	11.4	18.9	15.9	16.2	11.2	24.3	2.2	100	3.7
Orals	1971	0.9	15.6	18.6	19.4	17.0	9.7	17.9	1.8	100	3.3
Orals	1973	1.2	25.0	24.3	17.6	11.9	7.1	13.5	0.6	100	2.5
All methods	1974	35.1	17.3	20.6	18.3	12.9	11.2	18.4	1.3	100	3.1
El Salvador											
All methods	1971	4.0	23.4	21.0	16.2	11.7	8.7	19.0	0.0	100	2.8
Haiti											
Female sterilization	1986	3.8	0.3	2.7	15.1	20.2	20.1	36.6	5.0	100	5.0
Jamaica											
Sterilization	1986	5.0	2.7	11.8	18.5	20.2	17.3	29.4	0.2	100	4.3
All methods	1969	28.0	12.0	16.0	16.0	15.0	12.0	27.0	2.0	100	3.8
All methods	1970	19.0	18.0	18.0	16.0	13.0	10.0	25.0	0.0	100	3.4
All methods	1971	22.0	20.0	19.0	15.0	12.0	9.0	22.0	3.0	100	3.1
All methods	1972	22.0	21.0	20.0	15.0	11.0	8.0	23.0	2.0	100	3.0
All methods	1973	25.0	22.0	20.0	15.0	10.0	8.0	24.0	1.0	100	3.0
All methods	1974	22.0	37.0	21.0	13.0	9.0	6.0	13.0	1.0	100	2.1
All methods	1975	24.0	42.0	21.0	12.0	9.0	5.0	11.0	0.0	100	1.9
Mexico											
IUD	1972	12.1	—31.0—		—25.0—		9.0	35.0	0.0	100	4.0

Table 25. Acceptors Distributed by Method and Number of Living Children, and Median Number of Living Children (continued)

Country and method	Acceptor sample Year	Number (000s)	Percentage by number of living children 0 or 1	2	3	4	5	6+	Unknown	Total	Median[d] number of living children
Mexico (continued)											
IUD	1973	18.8	12.0	18.0	17.0	13.0	—40.0—		0.0	100	3.7
Orals	1972	17.7	—32.0—		—29.0—		10.0	29.0	0.0	100	3.7
Orals	1973	23.1	13.0	17.0	17.0	13.0	—40.0—		0.0	100	3.7
Injectables	1973	8.9	5.0	10.0	20.0	22.0	—43.0—		0.0	100	4.2
Paraguay											
IUD	1986	3.6	19.7	23.1	18.8	18.7	10.4	9.2	0.0	100	2.9
Orals	1986	5.6	29.4	21.3	16.5	12.9	10.8	9.0	0.0	100	2.5
Condoms	1986	0.7	23.7	26.8	17.0	13.1	13.2	6.2	0.0	100	2.5
Female sterilization	1986	0.5	0.4	5.1	9.1	15.6	20.0	49.8	0.0	100	5.5
Other	1986	0.5	26.0	22.7	23.2	12.1	8.7	7.4	0.0	100	2.5
Puerto Rico											
IUD	1974	2.4	23.5	—45.8—		—15.7—		14.4	0.6	100	2.6
Orals	1974	20.2	54.5	—31.1—		—8.3—		5.6	0.4	100	<1.5
All methods	1974	38.8	50.0	—31.9—		—10.0—		7.6	0.4	100	1.5
MIDDLE EAST/NORTH AFRICA											
Iran											
IUD	1972	0.4	5.5	14.5	15.7	11.4	16.0	36.9	0.0	100	4.7
IUD	1973	0.3	7.0	18.6	19.8	21.5	15.8	17.3	0.0	100	3.7
Orals	1972	0.6	7.2	14.8	15.7	18.7	15.2	28.4	0.0	100	4.2
Orals	1973	3.9	10.8	21.0	20.6	16.8	13.8	17.0	0.0	100	3.4
Orals	1974	2.3	14.0	23.1	18.0	17.1	11.9	15.8	0.1	100	3.2
Morocco											
All methods	1966	8.3	22.6	22.9	21.0	13.9	7.1	12.5	0.0	100	2.7
All methods	1969	14.3	5.5	8.1	10.1	13.5	15.4	46.8	0.5	100	5.3
All methods	1971	18.6	7.3	10.4	11.9	13.9	14.7	40.8	0.0	100	4.9
Tunisia											
IUD	1966	7.0	2.3	7.0	12.0	18.0	18.6	42.2	0.0	100	5.1
IUD	1969	8.6	6.0	10.5	13.8	18.0	17.5	34.2	0.0	100	4.6
IUD	1970	9.5	6.7	11.9	14.3	17.0	17.0	32.5	0.6	100	4.5
IUD	1972	9.7	7.7	13.7	14.6	17.1	16.2	30.0	0.7	100	4.3
IUD	1974	15.9	10.9	17.3	16.3	17.3	14.2	23.1	0.9	100	3.8
IUD	1975	13.3	11.7	18.6	17.2	17.1	13.2	22.1	0.1	100	3.6
Orals	1975	11.6	17.6	19.0	16.4	15.4	11.6	19.2	0.8	100	3.3
Female sterilization	1969	1.9	0.4	2.0	4.1	12.8	21.9	53.0	5.8	100	5.6
Female sterilization	1975	6.3	1.6	2.1	5.2	16.0	24.6	45.1	5.4	100	5.4
Abortion	1975	10.2	12.6	11.4	12.8	15.9	14.0	29.2	4.1	100	4.2
Turkey											
IUD	1968	26.0	6.3	17.2	21.2	20.1	15.6	19.6	0.0	100	3.8
IUD	1969	53.2	7.4	18.6	21.3	19.4	14.5	18.9	0.0	100	3.6
IUD	1970	26.0	8.5	20.4	21.8	18.7	13.6	16.9	0.0	100	3.5
IUD	1971	53.2	9.0	21.4	21.5	18.7	13.1	16.2	0.0	100	3.4
IUD	1973	28.5	10.5	23.8	22.7	17.8	11.9	13.3	0.0	100	3.2
ASIA											
Bangladesh											
IUD	7/65–12/66	1.2	2.6	7.6	13.3	22.8	18.9	34.7	0.0	100	4.7
Orals[a]	4/76	0.7	5.5	5.9	8.5	13.8	13.8	52.5	0.0	100	5.5
Sterilization	1967–68	9.8	0.1	0.1	17.0	25.4	24.0	33.4	0.0	100	4.8
Sterilization[b]	1983	u	2.4	17.4	24.2	21.8	15.6	18.8	0.0	100	3.8
Sterilization	1985	1.0	5.6	14.4	24.6	24.0	14.9	16.5	0.0	100	3.7
Female sterilization[c]	1978	u	—15.4—		—36.6—		32.8	15.3	0.0	100	4.4
Male sterilization	1968–69	u	—7.6—		—50.6—		31.4	8.9	1.5	100	4.1
Male sterilization[c]	1978	u	—15.7—		—36.3—		35.3	12.7	0.0	100	4.4
Hong Kong											
IUD	1968–69	3.0	—29.0—		19.0	19.0	—34.0—		0.0	100	3.6
IUD	1972	0.1	12.2	25.9	28.8	15.8	6.5	10.8	0.0	100	2.9
IUD	1974	0.3	15.0	29.0	21.0	15.0	9.0	11.0	0.0	100	2.8

Table 25. Acceptors Distributed by Method and Number of Living Children, and Median Number of Living Children *(continued)*

Country and method	Year	Acceptor sample Number (000s)	0 or 1	2	3	4	5	6+	Unknown	Total	Median[d] number of living children
Hong Kong *(continued)*											
IUD	1975	0.3	17.0	29.1	20.0	15.5	6.4	11.7	0.3	100	2.7
IUD	1976	0.3	13.7	35.2	25.4	14.1	6.2	5.4	0.0	100	2.5
IUD	1978	0.3	19.8	36.5	24.0	9.7	5.8	4.2	0.0	100	2.3
IUD	1979	0.4	23.1	34.5	25.3	9.4	3.2	4.5	0.0	100	2.3
Orals	1972	4.3	51.5	22.2	11.2	6.6	4.4	4.1	0.0	100	1.5
Orals	1973	6.5	58.0	19.0	11.0	6.0	3.0	3.0	0.0	100	<1.5
Orals	1974	20.6	66.0	18.0	7.0	4.0	2.0	3.0	0.0	100	<1.5
Orals	1975	15.2	72.4	15.4	6.2	2.9	1.6	1.5	0.0	100	<1.5
Orals	1976	16.8	74.5	15.7	5.4	2.3	0.9	1.0	0.1	100	<1.5
Orals	1978	13.9	76.9	15.3	4.8	1.9	0.6	0.4	0.1	100	<1.5
Orals	1980	14.5	77.4	14.8	4.3	1.3	0.4	0.2	1.0	100	<1.5
Injectables	1975	0.2	4.6	15.4	17.8	17.8	14.5	29.9	0.0	100	4.2
Injectables	1976	0.2	4.1	12.3	21.0	19.0	17.9	25.6	0.0	100	4.2
Injectables	1977	0.2	1.8	21.6	16.9	19.3	16.3	24.1	0.0	100	4.0
Injectables	1979	0.1	7.6	19.7	18.2	24.2	9.1	19.7	1.5	100	3.7
Female sterilization	1977	0.2	0.9	21.6	37.0	20.7	7.8	11.1	0.9	100	3.2
Female sterilization	1978	0.3	3.0	29.5	35.2	17.5	7.4	7.1	0.3	100	3.0
Female sterilization	1980	0.6	1.6	34.6	30.9	19.8	7.6	5.5	0.0	100	2.9
All methods	1975	21.4	66.3	16.2	7.6	4.2	2.4	3.2	0.0	100	<1.5
All methods	1976	25.5	68.2	16.5	7.2	3.8	2.0	2.2	0.1	100	<1.5
All methods	1978	24.2	69.3	17.2	6.8	3.4	1.5	1.5	0.2	100	<1.5
All methods	1980	27.5	66.3	18.5	7.4	3.2	1.4	1.0	2.2	100	<1.5
India											
IUD	1970	0.5	10.1	28.0	13.1	8.2	—40.6—		0.0	100	3.4
IUD	1973	5.3	11.2	23.3	23.3	18.9	11.3	11.6	0.4	100	3.2
IUD	1974	6.7	14.5	26.7	23.7	17.0	9.1	8.8	0.2	100	2.9
IUD	1977	251.7	22.3	32.1	22.8	15.3	—7.5—		0.0	100	2.4
IUD	1978	457.5	18.1	29.4	25.3	16.3	—10.9—		0.0	100	2.6
IUD	1979	530.0	20.2	30.7	24.4	14.8	—9.9—		0.0	100	2.5
IUD	1980	556.5	20.3	32.3	24.8	14.6	—8.0—		0.0	100	2.5
IUD	1981	750.0	16.8	27.9	20.1	10.6	—6.0—		18.6	100	u
IUD	1982	1092.0	18.0	29.3	21.2	9.7	—5.4—		16.4	100	u
IUD	1983	1958.2	27.7	35.8	21.9	10.2	—4.4—		0.0	100	2.1
Female sterilization	1970	2.1	1.9	11.0	15.0	23.7	—48.4—		0.0	100	4.4
Female sterilization	1973	4.5	0.7	6.8	23.5	28.5	19.2	20.5	0.8	100	4.2
Female sterilization	1974	4.9	0.3	5.7	23.6	30.5	20.3	19.4	0.2	100	4.2
Female sterilization	1975	7.2	0.4	7.1	25.2	28.7	19.0	19.6	0.0	100	4.1
Female sterilization	1977	599.9	1.5	19.5	34.1	30.8	—14.1—		0.0	100	3.4
Female sterilization	1978	968.5	1.9	17.7	34.0	25.7	—20.7—		0.0	100	3.4
Female sterilization	1979	1209.1	1.2	16.7	34.4	27.5	—20.2—		0.0	100	3.4
Female sterilization	1980	1508.8	0.6	15.8	35.0	28.9	—19.7—		0.0	100	3.5
Female sterilization	1981	2219.0	0.6	13.9	31.0	23.8	—16.8—		13.9	100	3.4
Female sterilization	1982	3396.0	0.4	12.5	28.1	21.3	—15.5—		22.2	100	u
Female sterilization	1983	3369.4	0.6	18.3	37.1	26.6	—17.4—		0.0	100	3.3
Male sterilization	1970	2.8	3.7	11.3	23.7	23.7	—37.6—		0.0	100	4.0
Male sterilization	1973	4.0	0.6	19.8	28.3	21.8	13.7	15.5	0.3	100	3.6
Male sterilization	1974	6.8	0.9	18.1	28.1	24.9	14.3	13.6	0.1	100	3.6
Male sterilization	1975	8.7	0.6	14.8	27.9	25.1	17.0	14.6	0.0	100	3.8
Male sterilization	1977	138.2	3.2	33.6	29.8	23.8	—9.6—		0.0	100	2.9
Male sterilization	1978	339.5	1.7	27.6	31.9	22.0	—16.8—		0.0	100	3.1
Male sterilization	1979	440.6	1.6	25.3	32.6	23.3	—17.2—		0.0	100	3.2
Male sterilization	1980	412.6	1.0	24.4	34.8	23.6	—16.0—		0.0	100	3.2
Male sterilization	1981	573.0	0.7	22.3	33.6	20.4	—13.2—		9.8	100	3.2
Male sterilization	1982	584.0	0.8	21.9	34.7	19.0	—11.9—		11.7	100	3.1
Male sterilization	1983	609.9	0.9	25.1	36.3	25.1	—12.6—		0.0	100	3.2
Andhra Pradesh											
IUD	1977	9.0	38.0	32.3	17.1	6.7	—5.9—		0.0	100	1.9
IUD	1978	15.5	26.0	29.2	21.7	16.2	—6.9—		0.0	100	2.3
IUD	1979	12.7	20.2	32.6	26.0	13.4	—7.8—		0.0	100	2.4
IUD	1982	23.7	30.3	33.9	20.8	9.7	—5.3—		0.0	100	2.1
IUD	1983	62.6	30.3	33.1	20.3	9.7	—6.2—		0.0	100	2.1
Female sterilization	1977	88.1	5.7	24.6	34.5	21.8	—13.4—		0.0	100	3.1

Table 25. Acceptors Distributed by Method and Number of Living Children, and Median Number of Living Children (continued)

Country and method	Year	Acceptor sample Number (000s)	Percentage by number of living children 0 or 1	2	3	4	5	6+	Unknown	Total	Median[d] number of living children
Andhra Pradesh (continued)											
Female sterilization	1978	124.2	3.2	24.6	35.3	23.6	—13.3—		0.0	100	3.1
Female sterilization	1982	295.6	1.4	24.4	43.0	24.2	—7.0—		0.0	100	3.2
Female sterilization	1983	319.2	0.3	27.4	41.5	20.6	—10.2—		0.0	100	3.0
Male sterilization	1977	23.8	8.8	35.4	27.0	16.3	—12.5—		0.0	100	2.7
Male sterilization	1978	39.0	4.1	30.1	29.3	19.1	—17.4—		0.0	100	3.0
Male sterilization	1979	34.4	2.0	29.6	29.3	21.2	—17.9—		0.0	100	3.1
Male sterilization	1982	32.4	1.2	31.3	39.3	16.5	—11.7—		0.0	100	2.9
Male sterilization	1983	31.9	0.8	33.4	38.0	18.8	—9.0—		0.0	100	2.9
Assam											
IUD	1978	6.6	3.4	21.8	56.9	12.4	—5.5—		0.0	100	2.9
IUD	1979	7.0	1.0	3.6	18.2	48.6	—28.1—		0.0	100	4.1
IUD	1982	15.6	3.4	30.7	47.5	17.2	—0.2—		0.0	100	2.8
IUD	1983	16.6	11.5	24.8	37.4	15.8	—10.5—		0.0	100	3.0
Female sterilization	1978	7.2	0.0	2.9	24.9	66.9	—5.3—		0.0	100	3.8
Female sterilization	1982	14.0	0.0	1.5	56.8	34.9	—6.8—		0.0	100	3.5
Female sterilization	1983	42.3	0.1	6.8	28.5	35.2	—29.4—		0.0	100	3.9
Male sterilization	1978	18.1	0.0	8.4	20.0	46.0	—25.6—		0.0	100	4.0
Male sterilization	1979	14.4	0.0	4.8	11.3	34.7	—49.2—		0.0	100	4.5
Male sterilization	1982	41.8	0.0	6.0	69.1	8.2	—16.7—		0.0	100	3.1
Male sterilization	1983	82.8	0.0	9.0	31.6	44.2	—15.2—		0.0	100	3.8
Bihar											
IUD	1977	2.5	19.7	29.3	23.6	17.0	—10.4—		0.0	100	2.5
IUD	1979	13.1	12.7	33.7	32.1	14.0	—7.5—		0.0	100	2.6
Female sterilization	1977	12.0	2.1	22.7	32.2	27.3	—15.7—		0.0	100	3.3
Male sterilization	1977	4.9	2.0	18.9	34.1	31.2	—13.8—		0.0	100	3.5
Male sterilization	1979	18.7	0.3	23.0	34.0	25.9	—16.8—		0.0	100	3.3
Delhi											
IUD	1978	14.6	18.9	32.5	26.7	21.0	—0.9—		0.0	100	2.5
IUD	1979	17.2	20.7	40.5	22.8	15.6	—0.4—		0.0	100	2.3
IUD	1982	39.5	21.2	42.6	25.6	9.6	—1.0—		0.0	100	2.3
IUD	1983	31.4	25.1	39.2	22.8	12.2	—0.7—		0.0	100	2.2
Female sterilization	1978	4.0	0.2	9.1	33.5	45.1	—12.1—		0.0	100	3.7
Female sterilization	1982	22.6	0.1	9.7	36.6	47.8	—5.8—		0.0	100	3.6
Female sterilization	1983	22.7	2.0	17.3	48.2	27.7	—4.8—		0.0	100	3.2
Male sterilization	1978	0.4	0.5	22.8	34.8	39.6	—2.3—		0.0	100	3.3
Male sterilization	1979	1.1	0.3	24.3	36.1	33.5	—5.8—		0.0	100	3.3
Male sterilization	1982	4.2	0.2	29.1	37.5	23.3	—9.9—		0.0	100	3.2
Male sterilization	1983	3.1	10.9	24.6	35.0	21.6	—8.0—		0.0	100	3.0
Gujarat											
IUD	1977	30.2	22.0	35.2	22.5	——20.3——			0.0	100	2.3
IUD	1978	35.2	23.6	35.9	22.0	10.6	—7.9—		0.0	100	2.2
IUD	1979	37.7	25.4	37.0	22.2	9.5	—5.9—		0.0	100	2.2
IUD	1982	62.8	27.7	39.1	20.5	8.3	—4.4—		0.0	100	2.1
IUD	1983	110.0	30.0	36.5	20.9	8.1	—4.5—		0.0	100	2.0
Female sterilization	1977	86.2	0.4	11.2	30.9	——57.5——			0.0	100	4.0
Female sterilization	1978	142.7	0.7	11.6	30.2	26.8	—30.7—		0.0	100	3.8
Female sterilization	1982	197.5	0.6	15.7	33.5	25.7	—24.5—		0.0	100	3.5
Female sterilization	1983	198.8	1.0	17.8	34.1	24.8	—22.4—		0.0	100	3.4
Male sterilization	1977	25.4	1.9	27.2	29.1	——41.8——			0.0	100	3.2
Male sterilization	1978	54.0	2.1	27.6	29.7	20.1	—20.5—		0.0	100	3.2
Male sterilization	1979	53.1	2.4	30.9	30.0	19.3	—17.4—		0.0	100	3.1
Male sterilization	1982	42.8	2.4	30.6	32.6	19.3	—15.1—		0.0	100	3.0
Male sterilization	1983	36.8	2.2	25.4	34.6	18.8	—19.0—		0.0	100	3.1
Haryana											
IUD	1977	24.1	13.6	23.7	24.7	20.4	—17.6—		0.0	100	3.0
IUD	1978	27.9	15.8	23.7	27.5	19.9	—13.1—		0.0	100	2.9
IUD	1979	26.5	14.4	24.1	30.0	19.9	—11.6—		0.0	100	3.0
IUD	1982	37.6	6.9	27.6	33.5	20.4	—11.5—		0.0	100	3.1
IUD	1983	102.9	11.7	34.5	27.9	17.7	—8.2—		0.0	100	2.6

Table 25. Acceptors Distributed by Method and Number of Living Children, and Median Number of Living Children (continued)

Country and method	Year	Acceptor sample Number (000s)	0 or 1	2	3	4	5	6+	Unknown	Total	Median[d] number of living children
Haryana (continued)											
Female sterilization	1977	4.9	0.0	5.7	28.3	34.1	—31.9—		0.0	100	4.0
Female sterilization	1978	11.5	0.1	6.0	31.2	34.7	—28.0—		0.0	100	3.9
Female sterilization	1982	81.6	0.0	5.7	34.0	32.8	—27.5—		0.0	100	3.8
Female sterilization	1983	95.2	1.0	8.8	36.1	35.9	—18.2—		0.0	100	3.6
Male sterilization	1977	1.0	0.1	6.7	26.9	38.8	—27.5—		0.0	100	3.9
Male sterilization	1978	2.4	0.2	8.8	38.0	29.8	—23.2—		0.0	100	3.6
Male sterilization	1979	4.4	0.2	9.5	35.1	33.9	—21.3—		0.0	100	3.7
Male sterilization	1982	4.9	0.0	10.3	38.5	30.6	—20.6—		0.0	100	3.5
Male sterilization	1983	6.8	0.6	11.2	33.4	34.5	—20.3—		0.0	100	3.6
Himachal Pradesh											
IUD	1977	3.4	22.9	38.4	22.3	11.4	—5.0—		0.0	100	2.2
IUD	1978	5.2	22.9	39.3	24.8	7.9	—5.1—		0.0	100	2.2
IUD	1979	6.1	22.0	41.5	23.0	9.6	—3.9—		0.0	100	2.2
IUD	1982	9.7	29.3	38.5	20.2	7.9	—4.1—		0.0	100	2.0
IUD	1983	12.2	29.7	39.0	20.0	8.3	—3.0—		0.0	100	2.0
Female sterilization	1977	1.5	2.1	16.2	40.3	24.6	—16.8—		0.0	100	3.3
Female sterilization	1978	4.4	0.4	21.9	41.4	21.3	—15.0—		0.0	100	3.2
Female sterilization	1982	26.3	0.3	19.0	38.9	25.8	—16.0—		0.0	100	3.3
Female sterilization	1983	26.5	0.3	22.0	35.9	26.7	—15.1—		0.0	100	3.3
Male sterilization	1977	0.3	0.3	28.5	34.1	25.9	—11.2—		0.0	100	3.1
Male sterilization	1978	2.6	0.2	28.0	40.6	18.2	—13.0—		0.0	100	3.0
Male sterilization	1979	3.6	0.3	20.1	40.8	33.2	—5.6—		0.0	100	3.3
Male sterilization	1982	7.1	0.8	24.9	42.7	21.5	—1.1—		0.0	100	3.0
Male sterilization	1983	7.5	1.0	31.2	41.0	16.2	—10.6—		0.0	100	2.9
Jammu and Kashmir											
IUD	1982	8.1	0.0	15.9	42.6	28.7	—12.8—		0.0	100	3.3
IUD	1983	4.0	22.6	29.9	27.3	12.8	—7.4—		0.0	100	2.5
Female sterilization	1982	15.4	0.0	13.7	33.8	27.9	—24.6—		0.0	100	3.6
Female sterilization	1983	11.5	0.0	12.2	32.0	28.1	—27.7—		0.0	100	3.7
Male sterilization	1982	3.9	0.0	23.3	36.6	23.9	—16.2—		0.0	100	3.2
Male sterilization	1983	1.3	0.1	26.8	39.4	22.8	—10.9—		0.0	100	3.1
Karnataka											
IUD	1977	21.9	26.1	34.0	21.3	10.3	—8.3—		0.0	100	2.2
IUD	1978	31.7	20.6	33.2	23.9	12.8	—9.5—		0.0	100	2.4
IUD	1979	49.2	26.8	32.7	22.4	11.0	—7.1—		0.0	100	2.2
IUD	1982	65.0	28.1	34.0	21.6	10.4	—5.8—		0.0	100	2.1
IUD	1983	94.6	29.0	34.6	20.6	10.8	—5.0—		0.0	100	2.1
Female sterilization	1977	73.0	1.4	25.1	34.6	22.3	—16.6—		0.0	100	3.2
Female sterilization	1978	1.0	1.0	16.9	35.9	26.9	—19.3—		0.0	100	3.4
Female sterilization	1982	229.0	1.4	21.1	36.4	24.1	—17.0—		0.0	100	3.3
Female sterilization	1983	233.4	2.1	22.8	36.0	23.3	—15.8—		0.0	100	3.2
Male sterilization	1977	7.0	3.8	45.0	23.5	16.0	—11.7—		0.0	100	2.6
Male sterilization	1978	4.4	2.0	23.9	30.3	23.3	—20.5—		0.0	100	3.3
Male sterilization	1979	5.3	2.8	25.4	33.2	23.3	—15.3—		0.0	100	3.2
Male sterilization	1982	2.3	2.9	28.2	30.2	26.0	—12.7—		0.0	100	3.1
Male sterilization	1983	5.0	2.2	24.0	34.5	25.4	—13.9—		0.0	100	3.2
Kerala											
IUD	1978	12.2	24.6	36.5	20.0	11.9	—7.0—		0.0	100	2.2
IUD	1979	16.2	29.3	36.4	19.0	8.8	—6.5—		0.0	100	2.1
IUD	1982	27.8	34.7	39.4	18.2	5.2	—2.5—		0.0	100	2.0
IUD	1983	37.1	32.5	37.4	20.5	6.1	—3.5—		0.0	100	2.1
Female sterilization	1978	71.8	10.9	31.9	34.0	13.0	—10.2—		0.0	100	2.7
Female sterilization	1982	126.2	0.1	33.6	42.8	16.4	—7.1—		0.0	100	2.9
Female sterilization	1983	158.9	0.3	32.6	42.4	15.4	—9.3—		0.0	100	2.9
Male sterilization	1978	15.1	3.8	42.5	31.8	13.1	—8.8—		0.0	100	2.6
Male sterilization	1979	13.9	16.6	31.0	28.2	15.0	—9.2—		0.0	100	2.6
Male sterilization	1982	17.2	0.9	46.2	33.0	13.2	—6.7—		0.0	100	2.6
Male sterilization	1983	19.5	0.2	49.9	32.2	10.8	—6.9—		0.0	100	2.5

Table 25. Acceptors Distributed by Method and Number of Living Children, and Median Number of Living Children *(continued)*

Country and method	Year	Acceptor sample Number (000s)	0 or 1	2	3	4	5	6+	Unknown	Total	Median[d] number of living children
Madhya Pradesh											
IUD	1977	12.5	17.9	31.7	24.6	15.5	—10.3—		0.0	100	2.5
IUD	1978	17.9	18.7	32.2	25.0	13.8	—10.3—		0.0	100	2.5
IUD	1979	14.9	20.6	33.1	24.5	12.6	—9.2—		0.0	100	2.4
IUD	1982	31.4	21.0	37.2	23.7	11.0	—7.1—		0.0	100	2.3
IUD	1983	92.6	24.3	34.4	23.7	12.0	—5.6—		0.0	100	2.2
Female sterilization	1977	27.5	0.5	9.9	30.7	29.1	—29.8—		0.0	100	3.8
Female sterilization	1978	48.5	0.7	11.3	31.2	29.2	—27.6—		0.0	100	3.7
Female sterilization	1982	176.8	0.4	10.4	32.1	27.3	—29.8—		0.0	100	3.8
Female sterilization	1983	223.6	0.8	12.7	33.4	27.4	—26.0—		0.0	100	3.6
Male sterilization	1977	5.9	1.1	24.1	29.8	24.0	—21.0—		0.0	100	3.3
Male sterilization	1978	22.2	2.1	17.7	30.6	26.8	—22.8—		0.0	100	3.5
Male sterilization	1979	38.7	1.0	22.6	33.8	23.2	—19.4—		0.0	100	3.3
Male sterilization	1982	16.6	0.9	20.6	36.0	24.2	—18.3—		0.0	100	3.3
Male sterilization	1983	30.2	1.1	20.5	33.4	24.9	—20.1—		0.0	100	3.4
Maharashtra											
IUD	1977	15.5	37.5	44.1	12.6	3.9	—1.9—		0.0	100	1.9
IUD	1978	16.7	28.0	33.7	19.8	13.5	—5.0—		0.0	100	2.2
IUD	1979	25.2	29.8	39.9	18.0	7.1	—5.2—		0.0	100	2.0
IUD	1982	79.7	34.9	42.9	16.9	4.3	—1.0—		0.0	100	1.9
IUD	1983	706.2	36.0	38.8	17.2	6.3	—1.7—		0.0	100	2.0
Female sterilization	1977	98.8	0.4	10.7	38.4	31.2	—19.3—		0.0	100	3.5
Female sterilization	1978	136.1	1.6	10.6	36.3	29.8	—21.7—		0.0	100	3.6
Female sterilization	1982	372.7	0.7	14.4	36.6	29.2	—19.1—		0.0	100	3.5
Female sterilization	1983	423.9	0.7	16.6	39.3	27.0	—16.5—		0.0	100	3.3
Male sterilization	1977	15.9	1.0	37.3	32.6	19.8	—9.3—		0.0	100	2.9
Male sterilization	1978	28.0	1.6	18.8	31.9	23.9	—23.8—		0.0	100	3.4
Male sterilization	1979	6.0	0.8	21.1	34.1	24.1	—19.9—		0.0	100	3.3
Male sterilization	1982	196.8	1.2	25.8	36.5	22.6	—13.9—		0.0	100	3.1
Male steriization	1983	21.2	0.9	27.5	37.6	22.0	—12.0—		0.0	100	3.1
Manipur											
IUD	1978	1.2	10.5	17.6	21.3	20.9	—29.7—		0.0	100	3.5
IUD	1982	3.9	16.5	21.2	27.3	15.8	—19.2—		0.0	100	3.1
IUD	1983	3.4	7.5	13.3	33.3	14.2	—31.7—		0.0	100	3.4
Female sterilization	1978	0.5	0.2	2.1	10.8	28.5	—58.4—		0.0	100	5.3
Female sterilization	1982	0.5	3.8	15.8	25.2	21.2	—34.0—		0.0	100	3.7
Female sterilization	1983	3.4	0.0	0.4	1.2	56.8	—41.6—		0.0	100	4.4
Male sterilization	1978	1.6	0.1	10.7	28.7	38.4	—22.1—		0.0	100	3.8
Male sterilization	1982	2.0	1.5	13.7	25.7	23.7	—35.4—		0.0	100	3.9
Male sterilization	1983	2.3	0.0	0.7	2.4	53.0	—43.9—		0.0	100	4.4
Meghalaya											
IUD	1979	0.2	27.6	35.6	11.3	15.5	—10.0—		0.0	100	2.1
IUD	1982	0.3	10.6	21.7	27.4	35.7	—4.6—		0.0	100	3.1
IUD	1983	0.5	27.2	17.0	41.0	12.3	—2.5—		0.0	100	2.5
Female sterilization	1982	0.3	0.0	46.5	2.8	50.1	—0.6—		0.0	100	3.5
Female sterilization	1983	0.4	0.0	20.1	29.5	25.9	—24.5—		0.0	100	3.5
Male sterilization	1979	m	0.0	10.0	60.0	20.0	—10.0—		0.0	100	3.2
Male sterilization	1982	u	0.0	46.7	33.3	13.3	—6.7—		0.0	100	2.6
Male sterilization	1983	m	0.0	30.8	46.1	15.4	—7.7—		0.0	100	2.9
Ministry of Defense											
IUD	1978	5.5	21.1	40.3	24.7	9.5	—4.4—		0.0	100	2.2
IUD	1979	5.6	24.5	43.2	19.7	8.9	—3.7—		0.0	100	2.1
IUD	1982	8.4	22.7	43.1	28.3	4.7	—1.2—		0.0	100	2.2
IUD	1983	9.5	33.6	45.2	15.8	4.3	—1.1—		0.0	100	1.9
Female sterilization	1978	8.8	1.4	17.3	40.8	27.4	—13.1—		0.0	100	3.3
Female sterilization	1982	11.4	0.1	15.5	60.1	19.3	—5.0—		0.0	100	3.2
Female sterilization	1983	12.7	2.4	23.5	44.5	22.0	—7.6—		0.0	100	3.0
Male sterilization	1978	8.9	4.9	29.6	39.0	20.3	—6.2—		0.0	100	2.9
Male sterilization	1979	9.1	0.7	22.9	43.9	24.4	—8.1—		0.0	100	3.2
Male sterilization	1982	10.1	0.2	20.0	61.2	15.6	—3.0—		0.0	100	3.0
Male sterilization	1983	8.3	4.9	35.1	44.0	11.8	—4.2—		0.0	100	2.8

Table 25. Acceptors Distributed by Method and Number of Living Children, and Median Number of Living Children (continued)

Country and method	Year	Acceptor sample Number (000s)	Percentage by number of living children 0 or 1	2	3	4	5	6+	Unknown	Total	Median[d] number of living children
Ministry of Railways											
IUD	1978	2.3	17.6	36.4	24.5	12.5	—9.0—		0.0	100	2.4
IUD	1979	2.7	17.5	34.0	24.2	13.8	—10.5—		0.0	100	2.5
IUD	1982	4.9	21.6	37.3	23.1	8.9	—9.1—		0.0	100	2.3
IUD	1983	5.5	21.6	41.3	21.7	8.4	—7.0—		0.0	100	2.2
Female sterilization	1978	5.4	0.2	8.8	31.7	29.8	—29.5—		0.0	100	3.8
Female sterilization	1982	19.7	0.1	12.0	33.0	27.1	—27.8—		0.0	100	3.7
Female sterilization	1983	19.4	0.1	12.1	36.2	25.6	—26.0—		0.0	100	3.6
Male sterilization	1978	2.2	0.5	19.9	36.9	22.8	—19.9—		0.0	100	3.3
Male sterilization	1979	2.1	0.4	21.0	38.2	21.6	—18.8—		0.0	100	3.2
Male sterilization	1982	3.6	0.2	20.7	37.8	22.2	—19.1—		0.0	100	3.3
Male sterilization	1983	2.9	0.1	22.4	41.0	20.1	—16.5—		0.0	100	3.2
Nagaland											
IUD	1979	m	0.0	16.7	50.0	33.3	—0.0—		0.0	100	3.2
IUD	1982	0.1	19.2	21.2	35.6	13.7	—10.3—		0.0	100	2.8
IUD	1983	0.3	12.8	23.4	28.6	13.1	—22.1—		0.0	100	3.0
Female sterilization	1982	0.3	0.0.	25.4	33.4	38.2	—3.0—		0.0	100	3.2
Female sterilization	1983	0.1	0.0	18.2	22.4	46.1	—13.3—		0.0	100	3.7
Male sterilization	1979	m	0.0	33.3	33.4	33.3	—0.0—		0.0	100	3.0
Male sterilization	1982	u	0.0	30.8	23.1	46.2	—0.0—		0.0	100	3.2
Male sterilization	1983	m	0.0	18.6	12.5	43.9	—25.0—		0.0	100	4.0
Orissa											
IUD	1977	8.9	22.1	30.6	23.7	14.3	—9.3—		0.0	100	2.4
IUD	1978	13.9	20.8	32.2	25.0	15.1	—6.9—		0.0	100	2.4
IUD	1979	17.5	22.0	31.0	25.6	12.8	—8.6—		0.0	100	2.4
IUD	1982	30.6	23.7	31.9	24.0	12.6	—7.8—		0.0	100	2.3
IUD	1983	43.9	17.4	26.9	31.0	19.6	—5.1—		0.0	100	2.7
Female sterilization	1977	56.3	0.9	16.8	30.8	26.9	—24.6—		0.0	100	3.6
Female sterilization	1978	78.9	0.5	15.3	29.9	30.3	—24.0—		0.0	100	3.6
Female sterilization	1982	125.3	0.2	13.4	32.9	31.2	—22.3—		0.0	100	3.6
Female sterilization	1983	161.3	0.4	14.8	36.4	31.4	—17.0—		0.0	100	3.5
Male sterilization	1977	25.6	2.5	29.6	32.1	21.0	—14.8—		0.0	100	3.1
Male sterilization	1978	26.2	0.3	24.9	32.0	25.1	—17.7—		0.0	100	3.3
Male sterilization	1979	16.8	1.2	24.7	33.1	24.5	—16.5—		0.0	100	3.2
Male sterilization	1982	21.4	0.2	25.3	35.8	21.2	—17.5—		0.0	100	3.2
Male sterilization	1983	17.0	0.8	28.1	36.3	23.3	—11.5—		0.0	100	3.1
Punjab											
IUD	1977	25.4	23.6	30.7	24.5	—21.2———			0.0	100	2.4
IUD	1978	31.0	17.9	27.0	26.7	—28.4———			0.0	100	2.7
IUD	1979	34.2	18.1	32.1	27.2	13.5	—9.1—		0.0	100	2.5
IUD	1982	160.6	21.9	35.9	26.2	10.7	—5.3—		0.0	100	2.3
IUD	1983	195.1	26.1	35.2	24.8	11.1	—2.8—		0.0	100	2.3
Female sterilization	1977	10.6	0.1	8.4	32.2	—59.3———			0.0	100	4.1
Female sterilization	1978	16.7	0.1	7.0	32.9	—60.0———			0.0	100	4.0
Female sterilization	1982	125.4	0.1	10.8	45.3	32.3	—11.5—		0.0	100	3.4
Female sterilization	1983	127.8	0.4	16.4	37.3	32.2	—13.7—		0.0	100	3.4
Male sterilization	1977	1.8	0.1	11.0	33.5	—55.4——			0.0	100	3.8
Male sterilization	1978	3.0	0.0	9.0	37.2	—53.8——			0.0	100	3.6
Male sterilization	1979	4.0	0.1	9.1	37.3	31.5	—22.0—		0.0	100	3.6
Male sterilization	1982	9.3	0.4	10.3	43.3	33.6	—12.4—		0.0	100	3.4
Male sterilization	1983	12.4	1.5	14.2	39.9	30.9	—13.5—		0.0	100	3.5
Rajasthan											
IUD	1977	8.1	16.8	32.1	22.4	14.3	—14.4—		0.0	100	2.5
IUD	1978	18.2	13.0	26.1	24.0	16.9	—20.0—		0.0	100	3.0
IUD	1979	21.0	11.8	24.9	24.1	17.4	—21.8—		0.0	100	3.1
IUD	1982	18.9	18.6	34.1	23.3	13.2	—10.8—		0.0	100	2.4
IUD	1983	35.3	17.8	35.9	24.4	13.5	—8.4—		0.0	100	2.4
Female sterilization	1977	9.2	0.4	7.8	32.2	30.2	—29.4—		0.0	100	3.8
Female sterilization	1978	16.5	0.6	7.0	32.2	30.1	—30.1—		0.0	100	3.8
Female sterilization	1982	147.4	0.1	7.9	27.8	30.9	—33.3—		0.0	100	4.0
Female sterilization	1983	160.3	0.3	0.9	29.4	37.6	—31.8—		0.0	100	4.0

182

Table 25. Acceptors Distributed by Method and Number of Living Children, and Median Number of Living Children (continued)

Country and method	Acceptor sample		Percentage by number of living children								Median[d] number of living children
	Year	Number (000s)	0 or 1	2	3	4	5	6+	Unknown	Total	
Rajasthan (continued)											
Male sterilization	1977	1.7	0.9	27.0	32.7	19.3	—20.1—		0.0	100	3.2
Male sterilization	1978	4.4	0.5	16.2	34.1	26.3	—22.9—		0.0	100	3.5
Male sterilization	1979	9.4	0.3	12.3	29.0	29.7	—28.7—		0.0	100	3.8
Male sterilization	1982	5.9	0.2	16.7	34.3	29.8	—19.0—		0.0	100	3.5
Male sterilization	1983	8.1	0.4	11.6	30.9	33.8	—23.5—		0.0	100	3.7
Sikkim											
IUD	1982	0.7	13.7	33.4	27.0	13.8	—12.1—		0.0	100	2.6
IUD	1983	0.8	14.5	35.8	22.4	13.6	—13.7—		0.0	100	2.5
Female sterilization	1982	0.3	0.0	9.2	32.1	27.6	—31.1—		0.0	100	3.8
Female sterilization	1983	0.3	0.6	15.8	36.0	19.3	—28.3—		0.0	100	3.4
Male sterilization	1982	1.6	1.9	16.6	38.9	22.9	—19.7—		0.0	100	3.3
Male sterilization	1983	0.2	1.2	11.5	27.1	25.3	—34.9—		0.0	100	3.9
Tamil Nadu											
IUD	1977	23.0	24.9	36.3	22.7	10.4	—5.7—		0.0	100	2.2
IUD	1978	36.6	21.5	34.6	24.0	13.6	—6.3—		0.0	100	2.3
IUD	1979	31.2	28.5	34.5	22.0	9.8	—5.2—		0.0	100	2.1
IUD	1982	36.5	24.0	38.3	23.4	9.6	—4.7—		0.0	100	2.2
IUD	1983	51.0	27.3	40.2	21.9	7.4	—3.2—		0.0	100	2.2
Female sterilization	1977	90.9	0.9	34.9	35.1	18.5	—10.6—		0.0	100	2.9
Female sterilization	1978	125.1	0.5	27.3	36.5	19.5	—16.2—		0.0	100	3.1
Female sterilization	1982	246.5	0.1	25.1	39.8	22.8	—12.2—		0.0	100	3.1
Female sterilization	1983	464.1	0.0	23.9	41.1	22.3	—12.7—		0.0	100	3.1
Male sterilization	1977	20.7	2.2	50.1	28.7	12.1	—6.9—		0.0	100	2.5
Male sterilization	1978	91.3	0.8	36.6	35.1	17.3	—10.2—		0.0	100	2.9
Male sterilization	1979	35.4	1.4	38.5	34.9	16.5	—8.7—		0.0	100	2.8
Male sterilization	1982	15.6	0.2	31.5	37.1	21.6	—9.6—		0.0	100	3.0
Male sterilization	1983	23.2	0.3	28.4	41.1	19.9	—10.3—		0.0	100	3.0
Tripura											
IUD	1979	0.5	0.0	32.5	32.9	30.1	—4.5—		0.0	100	3.1
IUD	1982	0.6	9.6	46.8	31.2	8.8	—3.6—		0.0	100	2.5
IUD	1983	1.2	17.3	42.2	39.3	0.8	—0.4—		0.0	100	2.2
Female sterilization	1982	0.7	1.5	42.6	32.5	18.0	—5.4—		0.0	100	2.7
Female sterilization	1983	1.2	5.4	43.4	48.0	2.8	—0.4—		0.0	100	2.5
Male sterilization	1979	0.6	0.0	33.9	29.5	19.6	—17.0—		0.0	100	3.0
Male sterilization	1982	1.2	4.5	59.6	20.7	9.9	—5.3—		0.0	100	2.3
Male sterilization	1983	3.8	6.1	50.2	41.0	1.0	—1.6—		0.0	100	2.4
Uttar Pradesh											
IUD	1977	48.9	15.5	26.3	25.9	18.2	—14.1—		0.0	100	2.8
IUD	1978	148.5	12.9	24.5	26.9	20.3	—15.4—		0.0	100	3.0
IUD	1979	163.5	15.6	25.1	26.0	19.4	—13.9—		0.0	100	3.0
IUD	1982	263.3	14.7	29.7	29.0	16.4	—10.2—		0.0	100	2.7
IUD	1983	288.2	16.4	30.6	28.0	15.4	—9.6—		0.0	100	2.6
Female sterilization	1977	9.1	1.0	11.8	31.7	29.1	—26.4—		0.0	100	3.7
Female sterilization	1978	19.4	0.3	13.7	27.9	28.8	—29.3—		0.0	100	3.8
Female sterilization	1982	393.9	0.1	6.6	27.7	33.0	—32.6—		0.0	100	4.0
Female sterilization	1983	359.4	0.0	7.9	31.5	33.2	—27.4—		0.0	100	3.8
Male sterilization	1977	0.8	0.4	12.8	29.5	29.5	—27.8—		0.0	100	3.7
Male sterilization	1978	3.8	0.2	11.1	31.8	31.9	—25.0—		0.0	100	3.7
Male sterilization	1979	7.0	0.2	11.3	28.6	28.8	—31.1—		0.0	100	3.8
Male sterilization	1982	8.8	0.0	10.9	31.4	36.3	—21.4—		0.0	100	3.7
Male sterilization	1983	9.1	0.0	15.2	33.4	30.2	—21.1—		0.0	100	3.5
West Bengal											
IUD	1977	6.3	37.6	32.4	18.5	——11.5——			0.0	100	1.9
IUD	1978	10.7	33.4	34.0	18.0	8.8	—5.8—		0.0	100	2.0
IUD	1979	21.4	27.3	38.1	21.3	9.9	—3.4—		0.0	100	2.1
IUD	1982	39.1	28.1	36.8	22.5	9.3	—3.3—		0.0	100	2.2
IUD	1983	45.0	28.6	39.5	20.4	9.2	—2.3—		0.0	100	2.0
Female sterilization	1977	28.4	0.7	23.2	37.0	——39.1——			0.0	100	3.2
Female sterilization	1978	56.9	1.1	20.2	38.9	23.5	—16.3—		0.0	100	3.2

Table 25. Acceptors Distributed by Method and Number of Living Children, and Median Number of Living Children (continued)

Country and method	Acceptor sample Year	Number (000s)	Percentage by number of living children 0 or 1	2	3	4	5	6+	Unknown	Total	Median[d] number of living children
West Bengal (continued)											
Female sterilization	1982	193.4	0.6	22.6	37.8	28.0	—11.0—		0.0	100	3.2
Female sterilization	1983	288.7	0.9	25.8	38.7	24.6	—10.0—		0.0	100	3.1
Male sterilization	1977	2.9	0.5	24.9	35.6	———39.0———			0.0	100	3.2
Male sterilization	1978	10.6	0.7	27.1	36.7	21.6	—13.9—		0.0	100	3.1
Male sterilization	1979	61.7	0.9	30.1	35.4	25.3	—8.3—		0.0	100	3.0
Male sterilization	1982	74.8	0.5	27.9	35.4	26.6	—9.6—		0.0	100	3.1
Male sterilization	1983	82.3	0.5	29.4	38.6	24.3	—7.3—		0.0	100	3.0
Other territories											
IUD	1978	5.8	20.5	41.6	20.4	11.5	—6.0—		0.0	100	2.2
IUD	1979	6.3	18.7	30.6	30.0	11.1	—9.5—		0.0	100	2.5
IUD	1982	10.8	20.4	48.4	18.1	7.0	—6.0—		0.0	100	2.1
IUD	1983	8.4	24.3	36.3	19.9	10.5	—9.0—		0.0	100	2.2
Female sterilization	1978	8.3	0.8	11.1	29.2	28.6	—30.3—		0.0	100	3.8
Female sterilization	1982	13.1	0.3	10.2	37.2	29.9	—22.4—		0.0	100	3.6
Female sterilization	1983	14.4	0.3	12.1	35.5	29.3	—22.8—		0.0	100	3.6
Male sterilization	1978	1.0	1.0	21.8	32.8	26.7	—17.7—		0.0	100	3.3
Male sterilization	1979	0.8	0.9	32.4	33.1	17.1	—16.4—		0.0	100	3.0
Male sterilization	1982	1.5	0.7	23.1	37.1	22.1	—17.0—		0.0	100	3.2
Male sterilization	1983	1.1	0.6	31.5	38.0	18.2	—11.6—		0.0	100	3.0
Indonesia											
IUD	1973	6.3	11.3	19.6	19.7	17.3	13.5	18.6	0.0	100	3.5
IUD	1974	4.3	16.9	23.6	19.7	13.9	11.5	14.4	0.0	100	3.0
IUD	1975	3.5	17.0	24.3	20.6	14.4	9.5	14.2	0.0	100	2.9
IUD	1976	8.1	21.6	25.6	18.6	13.1	9.4	11.6	0.1	100	2.7
IUD	1978	7.0	23.5	27.1	18.9	11.8	8.2	10.5	0.0	100	2.5
IUD	1980	9.2	27.2	28.3	19.5	11.7	6.3	7.0	0.0	100	2.3
Orals	1973	13.7	20.6	20.1	18.4	15.3	11.2	14.4	0.0	100	3.0
Orals	1974	26.3	26.3	22.1	17.2	13.0	9.8	11.4	0.2	100	2.6
Orals	1975	25.3	27.1	21.1	17.3	12.9	9.2	12.3	0.2	100	2.6
Orals	1976	20.6	29.8	21.8	17.2	12.3	8.6	10.2	0.1	100	2.4
Orals	1978	22.9	30.9	23.1	16.9	11.9	8.3	8.9	0.0	100	2.3
Orals	1980	34.0	32.1	24.1	17.9	11.4	7.0	7.5	0.0	100	2.2
Injectables	1977	0.7	15.1	21.4	21.1	13.4	11.9	17.1	0.0	100	3.1
Injectables	1978	0.7	14.7	21.6	20.9	15.9	8.9	18.0	0.0	100	3.2
Injectables	1980	1.1	19.9	26.1	19.9	15.1	7.6	11.4	0.0	100	2.7
Female sterilization	1977	0.3	1.5	1.8	11.8	20.9	24.3	39.7	0.0	100	5.0
Female sterilization	1978	0.4	3.4	1.2	10.8	24.3	22.1	38.2	0.0	100	5.0
Female sterilization	1980	0.7	2.4	2.2	15.3	24.8	23.8	31.5	0.0	100	4.7
Male sterilization	1977	0.2	2.2	6.1	17.8	18.9	23.3	31.7	0.0	100	4.7
Male sterilization	1978	0.1	0.0	4.1	23.0	29.7	14.8	28.4	0.0	100	4.3
Male sterilization	1980	0.1	8.3	6.7	25.0	26.6	16.7	16.7	0.0	100	3.9
All methods	1971	38.7	10.6	15.6	17.8	17.4	14.2	23.6	0.7	100	3.8
All methods	1973	23.4	17.3	19.5	18.7	15.9	12.2	16.5	0.0	100	3.2
All methods	1974	36.7	23.8	21.8	17.7	13.4	10.5	12.6	0.2	100	2.7
Kampuchea											
IUD	1973	0.4	4.0	11.0	16.0	20.0	17.0	32.0	0.0	100	4.5
Orals	1973	2.2	9.0	16.0	19.0	16.0	14.0	26.0	0.0	100	3.9
Korea, Republic of											
IUD	1966	218.4	1.6	8.2	17.5	24.8	24.9	23.0	0.0	100	4.4
IUD	1969	14.0	—20.0—		23.0	25.0	—33.0—		0.0	100	3.8
IUD	1972	7.0	7.0	17.0	24.0	24.0	17.0	11.0	0.0	100	3.6
IUD	1975	203.3	8.5	21.9	24.9	21.4	14.3	8.9	0.1	100	3.3
IUD	1980	37.2	17.2	34.7	23.7	13.7	6.7	3.8	0.2	100	2.4
IUD	1986	233.4	53.0	37.6	5.3	———4.1———			0.0	100	1.5
Orals	1969	7.5	—17.0—		23.0	27.0	—34.0—		0.0	100	3.9
Orals	1971	5.0	6.0	14.0	25.0	25.0	17.0	14.0	0.0	100	3.7
Orals	1986	45.8	28.6	34.1	23.4	———14.0———			0.0	100	2.1
Condoms	1986	108.3	28.0	47.5	19.4	———5.2———			0.0	100	2.0
Sterilization	1972	4.0	1.0	14.0	30.0	27.0	16.0	11.0	1.0	100	3.7
Sterilization	1975	1.4	2.9	25.9	34.4	20.4	10.6	5.8	0.0	100	3.1

184

Table 25. Acceptors Distributed by Method and Number of Living Children, and Median Number of Living Children (continued)

Country and method	Year	Acceptor sample Number (000s)	Percentage by number of living children 0 or 1	2	3	4	5	6+	Unknown	Total	Median[d] number of living children
Korea, Republic of (continued)											
Sterilization	1986	312.5	15.6	66.3	9.2	——8.8——			0.0	100	2.0
Female sterilization	1972	3.1	6.0	13.0	22.0	26.0	19.0	13.0	1.0	100	3.8
Female sterilization	1973	2.4	4.0	15.0	25.0	27.0	17.0	11.0	1.0	100	3.7
Female sterilization	1974	3.2	5.0	15.2	27.9	26.3	15.0	9.7	0.9	100	3.6
Female sterilization	1975	3.2	3.2	16.0	34.3	27.1	12.3	6.4	0.5	100	3.4
Female sterilization	1976	12.8	1.3	20.9	40.7	23.8	9.1	3.6	0.6	100	3.2
Female sterilization	1977	177.7	0.9	24.0	39.3	23.0	9.1	3.3	0.3	100	3.1
Female sterilization	1978	44.9	1.0	25.9	37.3	22.1	9.5	4.0	0.2	100	3.1
Female sterilization	1979	35.3	1.2	27.9	36.3	20.9	9.4	4.1	0.2	100	3.1
Female sterilization	1980	35.3	1.2	30.2	37.4	19.0	8.1	3.7	0.3	100	3.0
Female sterilization	1981	40.2	1.5	33.9	37.9	16.9	6.7	2.9	0.2	100	2.9
Female sterilization	1986	220.3	11.3	69.6	10.9	——8.2——			0.0	100	2.1
Male sterilization	1968	u	u	u	u	u	u	u	0.0	100	4.4
Male sterilization	1969	9.7	0.5	5.4	20.8	28.0	23.8	21.4	0.0	100	4.3
Male sterilization	1970	u	1.0	5.0	17.0	29.0	—48.0—		0.0	100	4.4
Male sterilization	1971	u	1.0	8.0	25.0	29.0	—36.0—		1.0	100	4.0
Male sterilization	1972	4.3	1.0	14.0	30.0	27.0	16.0	11.0	1.0	100	3.7
Male sterilization	1973	3.4	1.0	16.0	33.0	26.0	15.0	8.0	1.0	100	3.5
Male sterilization	1974	21.2	1.8	23.8	35.6	22.9	10.3	5.1	0.4	100	3.2
Male sterilization	1975	22.4	2.1	30.0	37.5	19.6	7.3	3.2	0.3	100	3.0
Male sterilization	1976	16.5	2.9	36.9	35.7	16.2	5.8	2.3	0.2	100	2.8
Male sterilization	1977	52.5	3.9	40.2	34.3	14.3	4.9	2.0	0.4	100	2.7
Male sterilization	1978	18.7	4.4	44.7	32.4	12.1	4.1	1.7	0.6	100	2.5
Male sterilization	1979	12.6	5.1	48.0	31.4	10.1	4.7	1.3	0.7	100	2.4
Male sterilization	1980	27.0	5.0	48.7	31.0	9.3	2.6	1.0	1.4	100	2.4
Male sterilization	1981	31.1	5.6	52.7	29.9	8.2	2.2	0.8	0.6	100	2.3
Male sterilization	1986	92.2	25.9	58.6	5.2	——10.3——			0.0	100	1.9
Menstrual regulation	1975	3.0	4.6	16.7	26.0	24.9	16.4	10.4	1.0	100	3.6
Menstrual regulation	1980	34.3	5.0	30.6	32.7	18.1	8.7	4.7	0.2	100	2.9
Laos											
Orals (urban)	1972	e	—17.0—		—31.0—		—49.0—		3.0	100	4.5
Orals (rural)	1972	e	—26.0—		—31.0—		—43.0—		0.0	100	4.0
Malaysia (Peninsular)											
IUD	1971	0.9	5.9	12.3	13.3	18.4	14.1	36.0	0.0	100	4.5
IUD	1972	1.1	7.2	13.7	18.0	18.8	13.0	29.3	0.0	100	4.1
IUD	1973	0.9	10.3	21.3	17.8	15.9	11.9	22.8	0.0	100	3.5
IUD	1974	0.8	11.0	20.6	19.7	16.0	10.1	22.6	0.0	100	3.4
IUD	1976	1.1	13.9	25.6	19.2	14.3	9.9	17.0	0.0	100	3.0
IUD	1978	1.6	14.4	27.2	23.1	16.3	8.6	10.4	0.0	100	2.9
IUD	1980	2.6	19.5	28.7	20.6	13.7	7.7	9.8	0.0	100	2.6
Orals	1971	47.8	21.5	19.5	15.3	12.2	9.6	21.9	0.0	100	3.1
Orals	1972	48.9	23.4	20.7	15.1	11.8	9.3	19.7	0.0	100	2.9
Orals	1973	49.9	25.9	21.4	14.6	11.5	8.6	18.0	0.0	100	2.7
Orals	1974	53.7	29.4	22.0	14.7	10.6	7.7	15.6	0.0	100	2.4
Orals	1976	65.0	33.9	23.3	13.8	9.6	6.6	12.8	0.0	100	2.2
Orals	1978	65.8	36.3	24.9	14.1	9.2	5.9	9.6	0.0	100	2.1
Orals	1980	61.8	39.4	25.6	14.0	8.7	5.0	7.3	0.0	100	1.9
Injectables	1978	0.7	3.7	12.6	20.9	21.4	13.4	28.0	0.0	100	4.1
Injectables	1980	0.8	7.4	17.7	18.6	16.2	13.5	26.6	0.0	100	3.9
Sterilization	1971	4.0	0.4	2.6	6.8	11.7	16.3	62.3	0.0	100	5.7
Sterilization	1972	3.9	0.5	3.1	7.2	13.5	17.5	58.2	0.0	100	5.6
Sterilization	1973	4.1	0.6	2.9	9.3	15.5	17.4	54.3	0.0	100	5.6
Sterilization	1974	4.1	0.3	3.0	9.2	17.6	18.7	51.2	0.0	100	5.5
Sterilization	1976	4.0	0.8	5.3	13.4	19.8	19.5	41.2	0.0	100	5.0
Sterilization	1977	3.6	0.7	4.6	14.2	22.0	18.1	40.4	0.0	100	5.0
Female sterilization	1978	4.6	0.7	5.6	16.7	21.8	20.4	34.8	0.0	100	4.8
Female sterilization	1980	4.9	1.1	6.9	17.9	24.3	19.3	30.5	0.0	100	4.5
Male sterilization	1980	0.2	1.0	15.4	25.1	26.7	16.4	15.4	0.0	100	3.8
All methods	1972	56.4	21.5	19.2	14.6	12.1	9.9	22.7	0.0	100	3.1
All methods	1973	57.3	23.9	19.9	14.2	11.8	9.3	20.9	0.0	100	2.9
All methods	1974	61.7	27.1	20.4	14.4	11.2	8.5	18.4	0.0	100	2.7
All methods	1976	75.2	31.4	22.1	13.9	10.3	7.5	14.8	0.0	100	2.3

Table 25. Acceptors Distributed by Method and Number of Living Children, and Median Number of Living Children (continued)

Country and method	Year	Acceptor sample Number (000s)	Percentage by number of living children 0 or 1	2	3	4	5	6+	Unknown	Total	Median[d] number of living children
Malaysia (Peninsular, continued)											
All methods	1978	80.2	33.4	23.6	14.6	10.2	6.8	11.4	0.0	100	2.2
All methods	1980	81.1	36.3	24.2	14.6	9.9	6.1	8.9	0.0	100	2.1
Nepal											
IUD	1973	0.2	5.0	19.0	20.0	23.0	14.0	20.0	0.0	100	3.8
IUD	1974	0.7	9.6	22.7	20.6	17.0	11.1	16.3	2.7	100	3.3
IUD	1975	0.4	8.6	23.2	25.0	16.6	12.1	14.5	0.0	100	3.2
Orals	1970	1.9	15.6	15.8	21.7	17.2	12.8	16.9	0.0	100	3.4
Orals	1974	2.0	13.4	17.2	20.7	18.2	12.9	16.5	1.1	100	3.4
Orals	1975	2.7	12.3	17.5	23.1	17.6	13.5	16.0	0.0	100	3.4
Female sterilization	1975	0.6	0.9	3.4	20.5	25.9	25.2	24.1	0.0	100	4.5
Male sterilization	1973	1.7	0.0	6.0	19.0	22.0	20.0	33.0	0.0	100	4.6
Male sterilization	1974	1.8	0.2	7.5	18.4	23.9	19.7	30.0	0.3	100	4.5
Male sterilization	1975	1.3	0.2	5.3	21.7	24.2	19.8	28.8	0.0	100	4.4
Pakistan											
IUD	1966	1.6	3.1	7.3	12.3	17.4	19.7	40.2	0.0	100	5.0
IUD	1976	32.9	2.1	7.8	12.9	17.4	18.8	40.8	0.2	100	5.0
Orals	1976	123.3	4.8	11.7	16.2	18.3	17.4	31.1	0.5	100	4.4
Sterilization	1967	6.7	0.2	7.3	21.8	22.0	18.0	30.7	0.0	100	4.4
Female sterilization	1976	7.4	1.2	4.8	9.3	15.1	19.9	49.5	0.2	100	5.5
Male sterilization	1976	1.3	2.0	3.8	11.3	16.3	22.3	43.2	1.1	100	5.2
Philippines											
IUD	1970	1.4	7.3	13.2	16.6	16.1	—46.0—		0.7	100	4.3
IUD	1972	20.6	9.3	18.4	16.9	15.1	20.7	19.3	0.3	100	3.9
IUD	1973	2.3	16.9	17.2	16.2	14.8	12.4	22.2	0.4	100	3.5
IUD	1975	21.9	21.0	23.7	16.9	13.7	7.8	16.9	0.0	100	2.8
IUD	1978	33.2	20.8	—44.4—		—20.8—		13.6	0.4	100	2.8
IUD	1980	40.6	21.2	27.8	20.2	12.6	7.5	10.7	0.0	100	2.5
IUD	1982	1.9	—50.2—		—32.6—		—16.6—		0.6	100	2.5
Orals	1970	3.3	9.8	15.8	15.7	15.0	—42.9—		0.8	100	4.1
Orals	1972	86.5	13.7	17.8	16.1	13.9	21.5	16.4	0.6	100	3.7
Orals	1973	8.7	19.7	18.8	15.8	13.8	11.5	19.8	0.6	100	3.2
Orals	1975	163.5	27.3	21.4	15.6	12.2	8.3	15.2	0.0	100	2.6
Orals	1978	170.3	27.2	—42.9—		—18.8—		10.8	0.3	100	2.6
Orals	1980	170.4	23.0	22.5	19.3	14.6	8.7	11.9	0.0	100	2.7
Orals	1982	7.9	—50.0—		—32.0—		—15.0—		3.0	100	2.5
Sterilization	1977	29.1	—8.7—		—44.2—		—47.0—		0.0	100	4.4
Sterilization	1978	53.4	—10.3—		—44.9—		—44.8—		0.0	100	4.3
Sterilization	1979	49.4	—9.2—		—49.0—		—41.8—		0.0	100	4.2
Sterilization	1980	61.5	—9.1—		—51.3—		—39.6—		0.0	100	4.1
Sterilization	1981	65.5	—8.3—		—53.0—		—38.7—		0.0	100	4.1
Female sterilization	1975	13.2	0.8	6.0	16.7	24.2	18.2	34.1	0.0	100	4.6
Female sterilization	1977	4.5	1.7	7.6	21.0	23.0	16.7	30.0	0.0	100	4.4
Female sterilization	1980	41.2	1.7	10.5	26.5	24.0	14.4	22.9	0.0	100	4.0
Female sterilization	1982	2.0	—8.9—		—53.2—		—36.8—		1.1	100	4.0
Male sterilization	1975	4.2	2.4	11.9	19.0	21.4	16.7	28.6	0.0	100	4.3
Male sterilization	1977	0.5	11.5	11.5	20.2	19.7	14.6	22.5	0.0	100	3.8
Male sterilization	1978	3.9	—43.0—		—38.2—		18.6	0.2	0.0	100	2.9
Male sterilization	1980	1.3	0.7	7.2	24.5	27.1	17.3	23.2	0.0	100	4.1
Male sterilization	1982	0.1	—38.1—		—34.1—		—27.8—		0.0	100	3.2
Other	1982	4.4	—45.3—		—30.3—		—22.0—		2.4	100	2.7
All methods	1972	149.2	12.9	17.3	16.2	13.9	21.4	17.7	0.6	100	3.8
All methods	1973	15.7	19.3	18.0	15.4	14.0	11.9	20.7	0.6	100	3.3
All methods	1975	347.3	24.3	20.0	15.6	12.8	9.4	17.9	0.0	100	2.9
All methods	1978	422.8	21.6	—39.5—		—24.0—		14.6	0.3	100	2.9
Singapore											
IUD	1979	0.1	59.3	28.2	5.5	2.8	—2.1—		0.0	100	<1.5
IUD	1980	0.2	50.6	32.7	11.5	1.9	—3.2—		0.0	100	1.5
IUD	1983	0.2	56.2	31.5	9.1	1.8	1.4	0.0	0.0	100	<1.5
Orals	1968	3.0	23.4	18.6	15.4	11.6	10.0	20.7	0.3	100	3.0
Orals	1973	10.7	71.5	15.6	4.9	2.3	1.3	2.2	2.1	100	<1.5

Country and method	Acceptor sample Year	Acceptor sample Number (000s)	Percentage by number of living children 0 or 1	2	3	4	5	6+	Unknown	Total	Median[d] number of living children
Singapore *(continued)*											
Orals	1974	5.0	73.0	14.9	4.4	2.2	1.1	2.2	2.2	100	<1.5
Orals	1975	9.4	76.1	14.7	4.1	1.5	1.0	1.2	1.4	100	<1.5
Orals	1976	9.0	78.5	14.0	3.3	1.4	0.7	1.0	1.1	100	<1.5
Orals	1978	6.2	83.0	12.4	2.5	1.1	0.4	0.3	0.3	100	<1.5
Orals	1980	5.5	81.3	14.4	2.9	1.0	—0.4—		0.0	100	<1.5
Orals	1983	4.4	79.7	15.5	3.3	0.9	0.3	0.3	0.0	100	<1.5
Condoms	1983	8.8	79.7	15.5	3.3	0.9	0.3	0.3	0.0	100	<1.5
Sterilization	1975	9.6	1.5	14.9	34.3	22.9	11.2	14.8	0.4	100	3.5
Female sterilization	1972	5.8	2.0	14.0	24.0	19.0	13.0	27.0	1.0	100	4.0
Female sterilization	1973	8.7	3.0	16.0	28.0	20.0	12.0	21.0	0.0	100	3.6
Female sterilization	1974	9.2	4.0	20.0	28.0	20.0	11.0	17.0	0.0	100	3.4
Female sterilization	1976	9.5	1.7	17.5	39.2	21.4	—19.8—		0.4	100	3.3
Female sterilization	1977	7.4	1.6	19.5	41.2	21.7	15.5	u	0.5	100	3.2
Female sterilization	1978	6.6	2.6	22.5	43.0	19.0	6.2	6.2	0.5	100	3.1
Female sterilization	1980	5.3	3.1	26.4	45.4	17.1	—7.9—		0.0	100	2.9
Male sterilization	1976	0.4	1.3	45.9	27.2	12.3	—12.0—		1.3	100	2.6
Male sterilization	1977	0.3	2.6	65.8	19.3	7.9	4.4	u	0.0	100	2.2
Male sterilization	1978	0.3	4.4	71.2	14.6	5.1	1.6	2.8	0.3	100	2.1
Male sterilization	1980	0.4	11.8	70.8	11.5	4.4	—1.5—		0.0	100	2.0
All methods	1973	19.1	67.6	16.2	5.9	2.9	1.7	3.3	2.5	100	<1.5
All methods	1974	8.6	68.8	15.8	5.6	2.6	1.5	2.7	3.0	100	<1.5
All methods	1975	26.3	48.3	14.9	15.1	9.4	4.8	6.3	1.2	100	1.6
All methods	1976	27.5	49.9	16.1	16.4	8.5	4.0	4.2	0.9	100	1.5
All methods	1977	23.9	53.7	16.8	15.6	7.8	—5.9—		0.2	100	<1.5
All methods	1980	20.7	61.0	17.7	13.8	5.1	—2.5—		0.0	100	<1.5
All methods	1983	13.7	81.1	14.7	2.9	0.8	0.3	0.2	0.0	100	<1.5
Sri Lanka											
IUD	1974	29.7	18.9	25.1	18.3	12.4	8.0	12.5	4.8	100	2.7
IUD	1982	16.1	27.8	36.3	19.3	8.7	3.9	3.2	0.8	100	2.1
IUD	1985	13.9	31.7	37.6	17.8	7.0	2.9	2.1	1.0	100	2.0
Orals	1982	26.2	29.6	33.0	18.3	8.8	4.2	4.2	1.9	100	2.1
Orals	1985	34.2	35.6	33.2	16.7	7.2	3.0	2.9	1.5	100	1.9
Injectables	1982	10.2	24.0	36.8	20.4	8.8	4.4	4.7	0.9	100	2.2
Injectables	1985	19.1	28.7	36.3	19.5	8.1	3.5	2.8	1.0	100	2.1
Sterilization	1974	42.2	0.9	6.9	20.8	22.0	17.6	29.8	2.0	100	4.4
Female sterilization	1973	20.2	0.5	3.7	14.4	19.7	18.8	38.1	4.8	100	5.0
Female sterilization	1975	39.2	0.6	6.2	21.4	22.4	18.2	29.7	1.5	100	4.4
Female sterilization	1975	24.9	0.4	4.2	20.6	22.5	18.9	31.8	1.7	100	4.6
Female sterilization	1980	61.6	0.2	5.4	29.8	29.7	17.5	17.2	0.3	100	4.0
Female sterilization	1981	46.3	0.2	6.2	33.4	28.2	15.7	15.3	1.0	100	3.8
Female sterilization	1982	48.9	0.3	7.3	36.2	26.5	14.7	14.0	1.0	100	3.7
Female sterilization	1985	54.3	0.4	7.4	43.1	27.1	12.4	9.0	0.6	100	3.5
Male sterilization	1975	4.6	1.8	17.9	24.6	19.7	13.2	20.1	2.8	100	3.7
Male sterilization	1980	51.3	0.1	19.3	33.6	20.4	11.5	12.9	2.2	100	3.4
Male sterilization	1981	30.3	0.4	20.1	35.2	19.4	11.3	12.3	1.3	100	3.3
Male sterilization	1982	13.0	0.4	25.3	38.2	18.0	9.2	8.8	0.1	100	3.1
Male sterilization	1985	17.4	0.2	22.6	48.1	18.1	6.6	4.4	0.1	100	3.1
All methods	1970	55.3	—26.2—		—29.5—		—35.7—		8.6	100	3.8
All methods	1972	71.1	—30.6—		—30.4—		18.7	12.5	7.7	100	3.5
All methods	1973	95.9	13.9	18.1	17.1	13.9	10.5	18.7	7.8	100	3.3
Taiwan											
IUD	1967	123.7	3.9	14.9	25.2	24.0	14.9	15.9	1.2	100	3.7
IUD	1971	156.0	6.8	19.5	28.4	22.7	12.2	10.5	0.0	100	3.3
IUD	1972	152.3	8.1	21.5	29.2	21.4	11.0	8.8	0.0	100	3.2
IUD	1973	148.5	9.7	23.2	29.0	20.4	10.0	7.7	0.0	100	3.1
IUD	1974	156.7	10.9	23.7	28.7	19.5	9.3	6.6	1.3	100	3.0
IUD	1975	173.4	11.6	24.3	29.4	18.8	8.6	5.8	1.5	100	3.0
IUD	1977	177.4	15.2	28.0	28.9	16.6	6.9	4.2	0.2	100	2.7
IUD	1979	158.6	17.7	31.5	28.8	13.8	5.2	2.8	0.2	100	2.5
IUD	1981	161.6	20.7	34.2	27.9	11.5	3.7	1.8	0.2	100	2.4
IUD	1985	188.0	26.6	40.4	22.9	6.9	2.1	1.1	g	100	2.1
Orals	1967	59.0	3.8	15.2	27.4	25.2	14.8	13.6	0.0	100	3.6

187

Table 25. Acceptors Distributed by Method and Number of Living Children, and Median Number of Living Children *(continued)*

Country and method	Acceptor sample Year	Acceptor sample Number (000s)	0 or 1	2	3	4	5	6+	Unknown	Total	Median[d] number of living children
Taiwan *(continued)*											
Orals	1971	79.0	11.3	18.9	25.8	21.1	11.7	11.3	0.0	100	3.3
Orals	1972	66.6	13.8	21.9	26.3	18.7	10.3	9.1	0.0	100	3.0
Orals	1973	58.4	18.2	23.6	25.6	17.0	8.5	7.2	0.0	100	2.8
Orals	1974	64.0	21.4	24.5	24.8	15.5	7.3	5.6	0.8	100	2.6
Orals	1975	54.4	23.9	25.1	24.0	14.2	6.6	5.1	1.1	100	2.5
Orals	1977	52.7	29.1	28.1	22.3	11.4	5.1	3.4	0.6	100	2.2
Orals	1979	63.6	32.8	30.1	21.4	9.4	3.6	2.2	0.5	100	2.1
Orals	1981	68.4	38.0	31.0	20.0	8.0	2.0	1.0	0.0	100	1.9
Orals	1985	57.0	43.9	31.6	15.8	3.5	1.8	g	3.5	100	1.6
Condoms	1981	106.2	43.0	30.0	18.0	6.0	2.0	1.0	0.0	100	1.7
Sterilization	1972	0.8	1.9	8.0	23.7	31.6	21.1	12.2	1.4	100	4.0
Sterilization	1976	40.6	0.8	10.8	37.0	31.0	12.9	6.7	0.8	100	3.5
Sterilization	1979	52.8	0.9	13.2	42.7	28.7	9.6	4.5	0.3	100	3.3
Sterilization	1981	51.1	0.9	16.0	44.6	26.6	8.3	3.4	0.2	100	3.2
Sterilization	1985	48.0	2.1	27.1	45.8	18.8	4.2	2.1	g	100	2.9
Female sterilization	1978	46.2	0.9	11.3	40.3	30.5	11.0	5.6	0.4	100	3.4
Female sterilization	1979	49.6	0.8	12.1	42.8	29.5	9.9	4.7	0.2	100	3.4
Female sterilization	1985	45.0	2.2	24.4	46.7	17.8	4.4	2.1	g	100	3.0
Male sterilization	1978	3.9	0.0	28.9	42.1	21.0	5.3	2.6	0.0	100	3.0
Male sterilization	1979	3.2	3.0	30.3	39.4	18.2	6.1	3.0	0.0	100	2.9
Male sterilization	1985	3.0	g	66.7	33.3	g	g	g	g	100	2.3
Other	1985	81.0	53.1	28.4	12.3	2.5	1.2	g	2.5	100	<1.5
Thailand											
IUD	1965	12.3	4.2	17.2	22.3	20.6	14.5	20.4	0.8	100	3.8
IUD[f]	1968	5.6	9.5	21.2	21.3	17.5	12.0	18.1	0.4	100	3.4
IUD	1971	1.2	11.0	19.2	18.8	16.9	12.6	21.4	0.1	100	3.6
IUD	1974	1.5	16.6	25.0	20.2	12.9	11.1	14.2	0.0	100	2.9
IUD	1976	1.2	21.9	29.4	20.2	9.7	8.8	9.7	0.3	100	2.5
IUD	1978	1.3	29.2	30.1	18.0	9.4	5.9	7.3	0.0	100	2.2
IUD	1983	0.1	38.4	32.2	14.4	6.8	4.5	3.4	0.3	100	1.9
Orals	1971	3.8	14.7	19.6	17.6	15.5	11.9	19.9	0.8	100	3.4
Orals	1974	5.0	24.7	23.7	16.5	12.4	8.8	13.8	0.0	100	2.6
Orals	1976	6.3	33.4	22.6	14.6	9.8	7.3	11.1	1.2	100	2.2
Orals	1978	8.1	38.3	25.2	14.4	8.2	5.9	8.0	0.0	100	2.0
Orals	1983	4.2	49.8	25.1	11.3	5.1	3.7	3.8	1.2	100	1.5
Injectables	1976	1.1	25.3	27.3	17.5	10.5	8.8	10.3	0.3	100	2.4
Injectables	1978	1.2	19.0	35.5	18.2	11.4	6.1	9.8	0.0	100	2.4
Injectables	1983	1.5	29.4	39.8	15.2	8.1	3.4	3.7	0.4	100	2.0
Sterilization	1973	u	1.3	8.5	25.9	26.3	17.8	20.2	0.0	100	4.0
Sterilization	1974	1.1	0.9	11.4	31.4	23.8	13.2	19.3	0.0	100	3.8
Sterilization	1975	u	1.1	15.9	27.6	23.2	14.9	16.8	0.4	100	3.7
Female sterilization	1976	1.5	2.2	16.9	31.5	21.6	12.6	14.2	1.0	100	3.5
Female sterilization	1977	1.7	1.2	18.8	30.5	21.8	13.0	14.9	0.0	100	3.5
Female sterilization	1978	1.2	0.6	23.2	32.5	21.1	9.7	12.8	0.0	100	3.3
Female sterilization	1983	1.1	1.9	32.8	36.3	14.6	6.6	6.5	1.3	100	2.9
Male sterilization	1976	2.1	0.9	23.4	23.0	20.6	11.5	17.8	2.8	100	3.6
Male sterilization	1977	0.3	3.3	24.1	26.1	17.6	13.7	15.3	0.0	100	3.4
Male sterilization	1978	0.5	3.9	29.1	17.9	19.1	11.8	18.2	0.0	100	3.4
Male sterilization	1983	0.1	5.3	42.1	21.9	14.9	5.3	9.6	0.9	100	2.6

u = unknown.

a. Contraceptive prevalence in Matlab Thana.

b. Government programs.

c. Dhaka.

d. Calculated on the assumption that respondents with unknown number of living children have the same distribution as those with number specified. This assumption may lead to errors in the mean when the unknown percentage is large; consequently, the median was not calculated when the unknown percentage was 15 or greater.

e. The acceptor sample for rural and urban areas combined is 1300.

f. Excludes direct IUD acceptors in the International Postpartum Family Planning Program.

g. Small base precludes estimate.

Table 26. Contraceptive Prevalence: Percentage of Married Women of Reproductive Age (or Spouses) Currently Using Each Method

Country	Year	All methods	Modern methods[a]	Female sterilization	Male sterilization	Orals	Injectables	IUD
SUB-SAHARAN AFRICA								
Angola	1977	1	u	u	u	u	u	u
Benin	1977	1	u	u	u	u	u	u
Benin	1981[b]	9	0	0	0	0	0	0
Botswana	1976	8	u	u	u	u	u	u
Botswana	1984	29	18	1	0	10	1	5
Burundi	1977	1	u	u	u	u	u	u
Burundi	1987[b]	9	1	0	0	0	1	0
Cameroon	1978	3	u	0	0	0	0	0
Chad	1977	1	u	u	u	u	u	u
Côte d'Ivoire	1981[b]	3	0	0	0	0	0	0
Ethiopia	1981	2	u	u	u	u	u	u
Ghana	1976	2	u	u	u	u	u	u
Ghana	1978	4	u	u	u	u	u	u
Ghana	1980[b]	10	3	0	0	3	0	0
Guinea	1977	1	u	u	u	u	u	u
Kenya	1967	6	u	u	u	u	u	u
Kenya	1978[c]	7	4	1	0	2	1	1
Kenya	1984[b]	17	9	3	0	3	1	3
Lesotho	1977[b]	5	3	1	0	1	0	0
Liberia	1977	1	u	u	u	u	u	u
Liberia	1986[b]	6	5	1	0	3	0	1
Malawi	1977	1	u	u	u	u	u	u
Mali	1977	1	u	u	u	u	u	u
Mauritania	1977	1	u	u	u	u	u	u
Mauritania	1981[b]	1	0	0	0	0	0	0
Mauritius	1971	25	u	u	u	u	u	u
Mauritius	1975[b]	46	24	0	0	21	2	1
Mauritius	1977	48	u	u	u	u	u	u
Mauritius	1981	51	u	u	u	u	u	u
Mauritius	1985[b]	75	34	5	0	21	6	2
Niger	1977	1	u	u	u	u	u	u
Nigeria	1982[b]	5	1	0	0	0	0	0
Nigeria (Ondo State)	1986	6	3	0	0	1	1	1
Rwanda	1983[c]	10	1	0	0	0	0	0
Senegal	1978[b]	4	1	0	0	0	0	0
Senegal	1986[b]	12	3	0	0	1	0	1
Sierra Leone	1982	4	u	u	u	u	u	u
Somalia	1977	1	u	u	u	u	u	u
Somalia	1982	2	u	u	u	u	u	u
Sudan (North)	1979[c]	5	4	0	0	3	0	0
Tanzania	1977	1	u	u	u	u	u	u
Uganda	1982	1	u	u	u	u	u	u
Zaire	1977	1	u	u	u	u	u	u
Zambia	1977	1	u	u	u	u	u	u
Zimbabwe	1976	5	u	u	u	u	u	u
Zimbabwe	1979	14	u	u	u	u	u	u
Zimbabwe	1984	40	27	1	0	24	0	1
LATIN AMERICA/CARIBBEAN								
Bolivia	1983	26	10	3	0	3	1	4
Brazil	1970	32	u	u	u	u	u	u
Brazil	1976	47	u	u	u	u	u	u
Brazil	1980	52	u	u	u	u	u	u
Brazil	1986	65	54	27	1	25	0	1
Chile	1978	43	u	u	u	u	u	u
Colombia	1969	28	10	1	0	6	0	3
Colombia	1974	31	u	u	u	u	u	u

190

Table 26.

Condoms	Vaginal methods	Rhythm	Withdrawal	Abstinence	Other[o]	Year	Country
							SUB-SAHARAN AFRICA
u	u	u	u	u	u	1977	Angola
u	u	u	u	u	u	1977	Benin
0	0	1	2	5	0	1981[b]	Benin
u	u	u	u	u	u	1976	Botswana
1	0	0	0	9	0	1984	Botswana
u	u	u	u	u	u	1977	Burundi
0	0	5	1	2	0	1987[b]	Burundi
0	0	1	0	0	0	1978	Cameroon
u	u	u	u	u	u	1977	Chad
0	0	0	0	2	0	1981[b]	Côte d'Ivoire
u	u	u	u	u	u	1981	Ethiopia
u	u	u	u	u	u	1976	Ghana
u	u	u	u	u	u	1978	Ghana
1	2	1	0	3	0	1980[b]	Ghana
u	u	u	u	u	u	1977	Guinea
u	u	u	u	u	u	1967	Kenya
0	0	1	0	1	0	1978[c]	Kenya
0	0	4	1	3	0	1984[b]	Kenya
0	0	0	3	0	0	1977[b]	Lesotho
u	u	u	u	u	u	1977	Liberia
0	0	0	0	1	0	1986[b]	Liberia
u	u	u	u	u	u	1977	Malawi
u	u	u	u	u	u	1977	Mali
u	u	u	u	u	u	1977	Mauritania
0	0	0	0	0	0	1981[b]	Mauritania
u	u	u	u	u	u	1971	Mauritius
5	0	14	1	0	1	1975[b]	Mauritius
u	u	u	u	u	u	1977	Mauritius
u	u	u	u	u	u	1981	Mauritius
11	1	17	13	0	0	1985	Mauritius
u	u	u	u	u	u	1977	Niger
0	0	0	0	4	0	1982[b]	Nigeria
0	0	0	0	2	0	1986	Nigeria (Ondo State)
0	0	———9———			0	1983[c]	Rwanda
0	0	0	0	3	0	1978[b]	Senegal
0	0	1	0	7	1	1986[b]	Senegal
u	u	u	u	u	u	1982	Sierra Leone
u	u	u	u	u	u	1977	Somalia
u	u	u	u	u	u	1982	Somalia
0	0	1	0	0	0	1979[c]	Sudan (North)
u	u	u	u	u	u	1977	Tanzania
u	u	u	u	u	u	1982	Uganda
u	u	u	u	u	u	1977	Zaire
u	u	u	u	u	u	1977	Zambia
u	u	u	u	u	u	1976	Zimbabwe
u	u	u	u	u	u	1979	Zimbabwe
1	0	1	7	u	5	1984	Zimbabwe
							LATIN AMERICA/CARIBBEAN
0	1	14	1	0	0	1983	Bolivia
u	u	u	u	u	u	1970	Brazil
u	u	u	u	u	u	1976	Brazil
u	u	u	u	u	u	1980	Brazil
2	1	4	5	0	0	1986	Brazil
u	u	u	u	u	u	1978	Chile
2	2	5	8	0	2	1969	Colombia
u	u	u	u	u	u	1974	Colombia

191

Table 26. Contraceptive Prevalence: Percentage of Married Women of Reproductive Age (or Spouses) Currently Using Each Method (continued)

Country	Year	All methods	Modern methods[a]	Female sterilization	Male sterilization	Orals	Injectables	IUD
LATIN AMERICA/CARIBBEAN (continued)								
Colombia	1976	45	27	4	0	14	1	9
Colombia	1978	48	36	7	0	19	1	8
Colombia	1980	51	40	11	0	19	2	8
Colombia	1984	55	u	u	u	u	u	u
Colombia	1986[b]	63	45	17	0	16	2	10
Costa Rica	1976	67	46	12	1	25	2	6
Costa Rica	1978	65	44	——14——		25	u	5
Costa Rica	1981	66	47	16	1	22	2	6
Costa Rica	1986	68	44	16	1	19	2	7
Cuba	1972	53	u	u	u	u	u	u
Cuba	1980	60	u	u	u	u	u	u
Cuba	1982	60	44	0	0	7	0	37
Dominican Republic	1975	33	24	12	0	8	0	3
Dominican Republic	1977	31	23	——12——		8	u	3
Dominican Republic	1980[b]	42	32	21	0	9	0	2
Dominican Republic	1983	47	40	27	0	9	0	4
Dominican Republic	1986[b]	50	45	33	0	9	0	3
Ecuador	1979	35	25	8	0	11	1	5
Ecuador	1982	40	30	12	0	10	1	6
Ecuador	1987[b]	44	34	15	0	8	1	10
El Salvador	1975	22	19	——10——		7	0	2
El Salvador	1978	34	31	18	0	9	0	3
El Salvador	1985[b]	47	43	32	1	7	1	3
Guatemala	1974	4	u	u	u	u	u	u
Guatemala	1978	18	13	6	0	5	1	1
Guatemala	1983	25	19	10	1	5	0	3
Guatemala	1987	23	18	10	1	4	1	2
Guyana	1975	35	27	9	0	10	0	8
Haiti	1977[c]	19	4	0	0	4	0	0
Haiti	1983[b]	7	3	1	0	2	0	0
Honduras	1981[b]	27	23	8	0	12	0	2
Honduras	1984	35	29	12	0	13	0	4
Jamaica	1976	40	29	8	0	13	7	2
Jamaica	1979	55	48	10	0	24	12	2
Jamaica	1983	52	41	11	0	20	8	2
Mexico	1973	13	u	u	u	u	u	u
Mexico	1976[b]	30	21	3	0	11	2	6
Mexico	1977[d]	27	u	3	u	9	u	5
Mexico	1978	41	32	7	0	15	3	7
Mexico	1979	40	30	——9——		13	1	7
Mexico	1982[b]	48	40	13	0	14	5	7
Mexico	1987	53	43	19	1	10	3	10
Nicaragua	1977	9	u	u	u	u	u	u
Nicaragua	1981[b]	27	19	7	0	10	u	2
Panama	1976	56	45	20	1	19	1	4
Panama	1979	62	54	——30——		19	1	4
Panama	1984	61	54	35	1	12	0	6
Paraguay	1977	29	20	——3——		12	1	4
Paraguay	1979	39	22	2	0	13	2	6
Paraguay	1987	45	26	4	0	14	4	5
Peru	1970[b]	26	6	2	0	3	0	1
Peru	1977	33	11	3	0	5	1	2
Peru	1981	43	16	4	0	5	2	4
Peru	1986[b]	46	22	6	0	6	1	7
Puerto Rico	1947	u	u	——7——		u	u	u
Puerto Rico	1953	u	u	——16——		u	u	u

Table 26.
(continued)

Condoms	Vaginal methods	Rhythm	Withdrawal	Abstinence	ᵕOther°	Year	Country
							LATIN AMERICA/CARIBBEAN
2	3	5	5	0	0	1976	Colombia
1	2	4	4	0	0	1978	Colombia
1	2	5	2	0	0	1980	Colombia
u	u	u	u	u	u	1984	Colombia
2	2	u	6	6	1	1986[b]	Colombia
9	2	5	5	0	0	1976	Costa Rica
9	u	u	u	u	12	1978	Costa Rica
9	1	6	3	0	0	1981	Costa Rica
12	1	7	0	0	5	1986	Costa Rica
u	u	u	u	u	u	1972	Cuba
u	u	u	u	u	u	1980	Cuba
7	0	0	0	0	9	1982	Cuba
2	2	1	4	0	1	1975	Dominican Republic
u	u	u	u	u	8	1977	Dominican Republic
2	2	2	3	0	2	1980[b]	Dominican Republic
1	0	1	3	0	0	1983	Dominican Republic
1	0	1	2	0	1	1986[b]	Dominican Republic
1	2	5	2	0	1	1979	Ecuador
1	2	5	2	0	1	1982	Ecuador
1	1	6	2	u	0	1987[b]	Ecuador
1	0	0	0	0	0	1975	El Salvador
2	0	2	0	0	0	1978	El Salvador
1	0	2	1	u	0	1985[b]	El Salvador
u	u	u	u	u	u	1974	Guatemala
1	0	3	0	0	1	1978	Guatemala
1	1	3	0	0	1	1983	Guatemala
1	0	3	1	u	0	1987	Guatemala
3	2	1	1	0	0	1975	Guyana
1	0	4	5	4	0	1977[c]	Haiti
1	0	1	2	0	0	1983[b]	Haiti
0	1	1	2	0	0	1981[b]	Honduras
1	0	3	0	0	2	1984	Honduras
7	2	0	2	0	0	1976	Jamaica
7	1	0	1	0	0	1979	Jamaica
8	1	1	2	0	0	1983	Jamaica
u	u	u	u	u	u	1973	Mexico
1	2	3	4	0	0	1976[b]	Mexico
u	u	3	u	u	7	1977[d]	Mexico
1	u	3	3	u	1	1978	Mexico
u	u	u	u	u	10	1979	Mexico
1	1	4	0	0	2	1982[b]	Mexico
2	u	u	u	u	9	1987	Mexico
u	u	u	u	u	u	1977	Nicaragua
1	u	u	u	u	6	1981[b]	Nicaragua
1	2	3	3	2	1	1976	Panama
1	1	3	1	1	1	1979	Panama
2	2	2	1	0	0	1984	Panama
3	1	2	3	0	0	1977	Paraguay
2	1	4	2	0	7	1979	Paraguay
2	1	6	3	u	7	1987	Paraguay
3	1	7	4	0	5	1970[b]	Peru
1	1	12	4	0	4	1977	Peru
1	1	18	4	0	3	1981	Peru
1	1	18	4	u	2	1986[b]	Peru
u	u	u	u	u	u	1947	Puerto Rico
u	u	u	u	u	u	1953	Puerto Rico

Table 26. Contraceptive Prevalence: Percentage of Married Women of Reproductive Age (or Spouses) Currently Using Each Method (continued)

Country	Year	All methods	Modern methods[a]	Female sterilization	Male sterilization	Orals	Injectables	IUD
LATIN AMERICA/CARIBBEAN (continued)								
Puerto Rico	1965	u	u	——32——		u	u	u
Puerto Rico	1968[b]	60	49	34	1	11	0	2
Puerto Rico	1974[b]	61	52	——28——		20	u	4
Puerto Rico	1976	69	58	39	3	13	0	3
Puerto Rico	1982	70	58	40	4	9	0	4
Trinidad and Tobago	1970	44	22	2	0	17	0	3
Trinidad and Tobago	1977	55	26	4	0	19	1	2
Venezuela	1977	49	32	7	0	15	0	8
MIDDLE EAST/NORTH AFRICA								
Algeria	1977	7	u	u	u	u	u	u
Egypt	1974	26	23	0	0	20	0	3
Egypt	1980	25	22	1	0	17	0	4
Egypt (rural)	1980[b]	17	u	u	u	u	u	u
Egypt	1981	19	16	u	u	11	u	5
Egypt	1982	34	29	1	0	20	0	7
Egypt	1984	30	27	2	0	17	0	8
Iran	1969	3	u	u	u	u	u	u
Iran	1978	23	u	u	u	u	u	u
Iraq	1974	14	10	1	0	8	1	1
Jordan	1972[b]	22	16	——1——		14	0	1
Jordan	1976	26	17	2	0	13	0	2
Jordan	1983[b]	26	20	3	0	8	0	9
Jordan	1985[k]	26	22	5	0	6	0	11
Lebanon	1971	55	17	1	0	14	0	1
Morocco	1974	7	u	u	u	u	u	u
Morocco	1980	20	17	1	2	15	0	0
Morocco	1981	25	u	u	u	u	u	u
Morocco	1983	27	22	2	0	18	0	2
Morocco	1987[b]	36	28	2	0	23	0	3
Syria	1978[b]	20	13	0	0	12	0	1
Tunisia	1971	12	u	u	u	u	u	u
Tunisia	1978[b]	31	23	8	0	7	0	9
Tunisia	1980[b]	27	u	u	u	u	u	u
Tunisia	1983[b]	41	31	13	0	5	0	13
Turkey	1963	22	1	u	u	1	u	u
Turkey	1968	32	2	u	u	2	u	u
Turkey	1973	38	5	u	u	5	u	u
Turkey	1978	40	11	0	0	6	0	3
Turkey	1983	50	16	1	0	7	0	7
Yemen, North	1979[e]	1	1	0	0	1	0	0
ASIA								
Afghanistan	1972	2	1	0	0	1	0	0
Afghanistan	1976	2	u	u	u	u	u	u
Bangladesh	1965	3	u	u	u	u	u	u
Bangladesh	1969[j]	4	u	u	u	u	u	u
Bangladesh	1975	8	4	0	1	3	0	1
Bangladesh	1976[e]	8	4	0	1	3	0	0
Bangladesh	1979	13	7	2	1	4	0	0
Bangladesh	1981	19	9	4	1	4	0	0
Bangladesh	1983[b]	20	13	6	2	3	0	1
Bangladesh	1985[b]	25[bb]	16	8	2	5	1	1
Burma	1980	5	u	u	u	u	u	u
China	1981[m,n,y]	79	75	21	8	6	u	40
China	1982[m,y]	69[l]	65	18	7	6	0	35
China	1985[m,y]	81	77	30	9	5	u	32
Anhui	1981	76	74	18	6	7	u	42

Table 26.
(continued)

Condoms	Vaginal methods	Rhythm	Withdrawal	Abstinence	Other[o]	Year	Country
							LATIN AMERICA/CARIBBEAN
u	u	u	u	u	u	1965	Puerto Rico
2	0	2	4	0	4	1968[b]	Puerto Rico
3	u	u	u	u	6	1974[b]	Puerto Rico
4	0	2	1	0	3	1976	Puerto Rico
5	0	6	0	0	3	1982	Puerto Rico
10	4	2	4	1	1	1970	Trinidad and Tobago
16	5	3	3	1	1	1977	Trinidad and Tobago
5	1	4	5	0	3	1977	Venezuela
							MIDDLE EAST/NORTH AFRICA
u	u	u	u	u	u	1977	Algeria
u	u	u	u	u	4	1974	Egypt
1	0	1	0	0	0	1980	Egypt
u	u	u	u	u	u	1980[b]	Egypt (rural)
u	u	u	u	u	3	1981	Egypt
1	1	1	u	u	2	1982	Egypt
1	1	1	0	0	1	1984	Egypt
u	u	u	u	u	u	1969	Iran
u	u	u	u	u	u	1978	Iran
1	1	1	0	0	0	1974	Iraq
1	0	2	3	1	1	1972[b]	Jordan
1	0	2	3	0	3	1976	Jordan
1	0	3	2	0	0	1983[b]	Jordan
0	0	3	1	u	u	1985[k]	Jordan
7	0	6	25	0	0	1971	Lebanon
u	u	u	u	u	u	1974	Morocco
0	0	1	1	0	1	1980	Morocco
u	u	u	u	u	u	1981	Morocco
u	u	u	u	u	5	1983	Morocco
1	0	2	3	0	1	1987[b]	Morocco
1	1	3	2	0	1	1978[b]	Syria
u	u	u	u	u	u	1971	Tunisia
1	1	4	2	0	1	1978[b]	Tunisia
u	u	u	u	u	u	1980[b]	Tunisia
1	2	4	2	0	1	1983[b]	Tunisia
4	u	u	10	u	7	1963	Turkey
4	u	u	18	u	8	1968	Turkey
5	u	u	24	u	4	1973	Turkey
3	0	1	18	0	7	1978	Turkey
4	2	1	25	0	2	1983	Turkey
0	u	u	u	u	u	1979[e]	Yemen, North
							ASIA
0	u	u	u	u	1	1972	Afghanistan
u	u	u	u	u	u	1976	Afghanistan
u	u	u	u	u	u	1965	Bangladesh
u	u	u	u	u	u	1969[j]	Bangladesh
1	0	1	1	1	0	1975	Bangladesh
1	0	1	1	1	0	1976[e]	Bangladesh
2	0	2	0	1	1	1979	Bangladesh
2	0	4	2	1	1	1981	Bangladesh
3	0	2	1	0	1	1983[b]	Bangladesh
2	0	4	1	1	2	1985[b]	Bangladesh
u	u	u	u	u	u	1980	Burma
2	u	u	u	u	2	1981[m,n,y]	China
1	0	0	0	0	3	1982[m,y]	China
3	u	u	u	u	2	1985[m,y]	China
1	u	u	u	u	1	1981	Anhui

Table 26. Contraceptive Prevalence: Percentage of Married Women of Reproductive Age (or Spouses) Currently Using Each Method *(continued)*

Country	Year	All methods	Modern methods[a]	Female sterilization	Male sterilization	Orals	Injectables	IUD
ASIA *(continued)*								
Anhui	1982	73	71	16	6	12	0	36
Anhui	1985	83	79	30	14	7	u	29
Beijing	1981	78	58	10	1	27	u	19
Beijing	1982	77	57	15	1	26	0	16
Beijing	1985	78	62	11	1	14	u	37
Fujian	1981	78	75	25	10	1	u	40
Fujian	1982	73	69	29	11	2	0	26
Fujian	1985	82	78	39	11	2	u	27
Gansu	1981	78	75	32	1	3	u	39
Gansu	1982	70	70	23	0	4	0	43
Gansu	1985	81	78	48	1	3	u	26
Guangdong	1981	71	67	19	7	3	u	38
Guangdong	1982	57	53	18	4	3	0	28
Guangdong	1985	80	76	39	12	2	u	21
Guangxi Zhuang Zizhiqu	1981	56	51	5	1	8	u	37
Guangxi Zhuang Zizhiqu	1982	54	43	4	1	5	0	32
Guangxi Zhuang Zizhiqu	1985	69	64	6	3	7	u	49
Guizhou	1981	62	60	9	8	2	u	43
Guizhou	1982	58	55	5	6	2	0	42
Guizhou	1985	72	70	23	17	2	u	28
Hebei	1981	75	70	8	2	7	u	53
Hebei	1982	73	67	8	1	10	0	48
Hebei	1985	81	76	34	4	6	u	34
Heilongjiang	1981	82	78	29	1	3	u	45
Heilongjiang	1982	76	71	22	0	3	0	45
Heilongjiang	1985	85	80	40	1	4	u	35
Henan	1981	76	74	26	7	2	u	39
Henan	1982	75	73	25	5	2	0	41
Henan	1985	84	80	40	9	2	u	29
Hubei	1981	76	74	22	5	6	u	42
Hubei	1982	73	68	21	5	7	0	35
Hubei	1985	82	78	35	7	7	u	30
Hunan	1981	74	71	32	9	3	u	26
Hunan	1982	71	68	32	8	2	0	26
Hunan	1985	83	80	42	11	3	u	24
Jiangsu	1981	82	79	25	5	9	u	41
Jiangsu	1982	76	73	22	5	7	0	39
Jiangsu	1985	86	83	28	6	8	u	43
Jiangxi	1981	73	71	28	1	3	u	39
Jiangxi	1982	62	61	24	1	2	0	34
Jiangxi	1985	73	72	51	1	2	u	17
Jilin	1981	81	76	24	0	4	u	48
Jilin	1982	83	78	21	0	3	0	54
Jilin	1985	83	78	31	0	5	u	41
Liaoning	1981	82	75	28	1	6	u	41
Liaoning	1982	78	72	22	1	7	0	41
Liaoning	1985	82	78	29	0	5	u	44
Nei Menggu Zizhiqu	1981	69	64	20	1	16	u	29
Nei Menggu Zizhiqu	1982	67	57	19	0	12	0	26
Nei Menggu Zizhiqu	1985	81	75	39	1	9	u	26
Ningxia Hui Zizhiqu	1981	73	71	32	0	22	u	17
Ningxia Hui Zizhiqu	1982	64	59	22	0	26	1	10
Ningxia Hui Zizhiqu	1985	74	67	29	0	20	u	19
Qinghai	1981	49	45	7	0	18	u	20
Qinghai	1982	37	36	6	0	13	0	17
Qinghai	1985	63	54	16	0	20	u	17

Table 26.
(continued)

Condoms	Vaginal methods	Rhythm	Withdrawal	Abstinence	Other[o]	Year	Country
							ASIA *(continued)*
1	u	u	0	u	2	1982	Anhui
2	u	u	u	u	1	1985	Anhui
13	u	u	u	u	7	1981	Beijing
11	u	u	0	u	8	1982	Beijing
13	u	u	u	u	3	1985	Beijing
2	u	u	u	u	2	1981	Fujian
2	u	u	0	u	2	1982	Fujian
2	u	u	u	u	1	1985	Fujian
2	u	u	u	u	1	1981	Gansu
0	u	u	0	u	1	1982	Gansu
2	u	u	u	u	1	1985	Gansu
2	u	u	u	u	2	1981	Guangdong
1	u	u	0	u	3	1982	Guangdong
2	u	u	u	u	2	1985	Guangdong
1	u	u	u	u	4	1981	Guangxi Zhuang Zizhiqu
1	u	u	0	u	11	1982	Guangxi Zhuang Zizhiqu
2	u	u	u	u	3	1985	Guangxi Zhuang Zizhiqu
1	u	u	u	u	1	1981	Guizhou
0	u	u	0	u	3	1982	Guizhou
1	u	u	u	u	1	1985	Guizhou
4	u	u	u	u	2	1981	Hebei
2	u	u	0	u	4	1982	Hebei
3	u	u	u	u	1	1985	Hebei
3	u	u	u	u	1	1981	Heilongjiang
2	u	u	0	u	3	1982	Heilongjiang
4	u	u	u	u	1	1985	Heilongjiang
2	u	u	u	u	1	1981	Henan
0	u	u	0	u	1	1982	Henan
2	u	u	u	u	4	1985	Henan
1	u	u	u	u	2	1981	Hubei
2	u	u	0	u	3	1982	Hubei
2	u	u	u	u	2	1985	Hubei
2	u	u	u	u	1	1981	Hunan
1	u	u	0	u	2	1982	Hunan
2	u	u	u	u	1	1985	Hunan
1	u	u	u	u	2	1981	Jiangsu
1	u	u	0	u	2	1982	Jiangsu
1	u	u	u	u	1	1985	Jiangsu
1	u	u	u	u	1	1981	Jiangxi
0	u	u	0	u	1	1982	Jiangxi
1	u	u	u	u	1	1985	Jiangxi
3	u	u	u	u	2	1981	Jilin
1	u	u	0	u	3	1982	Jilin
4	u	u	u	u	1	1985	Jilin
6	u	u	u	u	2	1981	Liaoning
3	u	u	0	u	2	1982	Liaoning
3	u	u	u	u	1	1985	Liaoning
3	u	u	u	u	1	1981	Nei Menggu Zizhiqu
5	u	u	0	u	3	1982	Nei Menggu Zizhiqu
3	u	u	u	u	2	1985	Nei Menggu Zizhiqu
2	u	u	u	u	0	1981	Ningxia Hui Zizhiqu
0	u	u	0	u	4	1982	Ningxia Hui Zizhiqu
3	u	u	u	u	5	1985	Ningxia Hui Zizhiqu
2	u	u	u	u	2	1981	Qinghai
1	u	u	0	u	1	1982	Qinghai
5	u	u	u	u	3	1985	Qinghai

Table 26. Contraceptive Prevalence: Percentage of Married Women of Reproductive Age (or Spouses) Currently Using Each Method (continued)

Country	Year	All methods	Modern methods[a]	Female sterilization	Male sterilization	Orals	Injectables	IUD
ASIA (continued)								
Shaanxi	1981	76	72	11	1	5	u	55
Shaanxi	1982	74	70	13	1	5	0	52
Shaanxi	1985	76	74	26	3	4	u	41
Shandong	1981	78	77	22	15	2	u	39
Shandong	1982	77	75	18	18	2	0	37
Shandong	1985	86	81	24	17	4	u	35
Shanghai	1981	77	68	21	4	21	u	22
Shanghai	1982	76	62	13	3	19	1	25
Shanghai	1985	79	68	13	2	13	u	40
Shanxi	1981	76	72	16	0	7	u	49
Shanxi	1982	72	65	14	0	10	0	39
Shanxi	1985	82	78	30	1	7	u	40
Sichuan	1981	78	75	9	30	3	u	33
Sichuan	1982	80	75	9	30	2	0	33
Sichuan	1985	83	79	10	34	3	u	33
Tianjin	1981	76	59	10	2	19	u	27
Tianjin	1982	72	54	9	1	29	0	14
Tianjin	1985	81	64	13	1	9	u	41
Xinjiang Uighur Zizhiqu	1981	65	56	21	1	21	u	14
Xinjiang Uighur Zizhiqu	1982	39	35	14	0	8	0	12
Xinjiang Uighur Zizhiqu	1985	45	38	15	0	13	u	9
Xizang Zizhiqu	1985	u	u	u	u	u	u	u
Yunnan	1981	54	50	8	4	5	u	33
Yunnan	1982	47	46	11	4	8	0	23
Yunnan	1985	64	59	14	7	6	u	33
Zhejiang	1981	73	69	29	3	10	u	26
Zhejiang	1982	70	64	29	2	8	0	25
Zhejiang	1985	85	80	42	3	7	u	28
Hong Kong	1967[f]	42	u	u	u	u	u	u
Hong Kong	1969	42	u	u	u	16	u	u
Hong Kong	1972[b]	50	36	——11——		18	2	5
Hong Kong	1976[b]	72	u	19	u	25	u	3
Hong Kong	1977[b]	72	47	——19——		23	2	3
Hong Kong	1979	75	48	——18——		25	2	3
Hong Kong	1981	80	u	17	2	32	u	2
Hong Kong	1982	77	50	——22——		21	3	4
Hong Kong	1984	73	u	——21——		22	u	4
India	1969	8	u	u	u	u	u	u
India	1970	14[r]	7	3	4	0	0	1
India	1970–71	12	10	——8——		0	0	2
India	1974–75	15	8	3	4	0	u	1
India	1975–76	19	15	——14——		0	0	1
India	1976–77[q]	u	24	——21——		2[s]	u	1
India	1977–78[q]	u	22	——20——		2[s]	u	1
India	1978–79[q]	u	22	——20——		2[s]	u	1
India	1979–80[q]	u	22	——20——		1[s]	u	1
India	1980	34[r]	23	11	11	1	0	0
India	1980–81[q]	u	23	——20——		2[s]	u	1
India	1981–82[q]	u	24	——21——		2[s]	u	1
India	1982–83[q]	u	26	——22——		2[s]	u	1
India	1983–84[q]	u	30	——24——		4[s]	u	2
India	1984–85[q]	u	32	——25——		4[s]	u	3
India	1985–86[q]	u	35	——26——		5[s]	u	4
Andhra Pradesh	1970	14	11	——10——		u	u	1
Andhra Pradesh	1980	34	31	——31——		0	u	0
Andhra Pradesh	1985	u	30	——29——		u	u	1

198

Table 26.
(continued)

Condoms	Vaginal methods	Rhythm	Withdrawal	Abstinence	Other[o]	Year	Country
							ASIA *(continued)*
2	u	u	u	u	2	1981	Shaanxi
1	u	u	0	u	3	1982	Shaanxi
2	u	u	u	u	1	1985	Shaanxi
1	u	u	u	u	0	1981	Shandong
1	u	u	0	u	1	1982	Shandong
4	u	u	u	u	1	1985	Shandong
7	u	u	u	u	3	1981	Shanghai
8	u	u	1	u	5	1982	Shanghai
8	u	u	u	u	3	1985	Shanghai
3	u	u	u	u	1	1981	Shanxi
1	u	u	0	u	6	1982	Shanxi
3	u	u	u	u	2	1985	Shanxi
2	u	u	u	u	1	1981	Sichuan
1	u	u	0	u	3	1982	Sichuan
2	u	u	u	u	2	1985	Sichuan
13	u	u	u	u	5	1981	Tianjin
8	u	u	2	u	7	1982	Tianjin
14	u	u	u	u	3	1985	Tianjin
5	u	u	u	u	4	1981	Xinjiang Uighur Zizhiqu
2	u	u	0	u	2	1982	Xinjiang Uighur Zizhiqu
4	u	u	u	u	4	1985	Xinjiang Uighur Zizhiqu
u	u	u	u	u	u	1985	Xizang Zizhiqu
2	u	u	u	u	2	1981	Yunnan
1	u	u	0	u	1	1982	Yunnan
2	u	u	u	u	2	1985	Yunnan
2	u	u	u	u	3	1981	Zhejiang
2	u	u	0	u	3	1982	Zhejiang
2	u	u	u	u	3	1985	Zhejiang
u	u	u	u	u	u	1967[f]	Hong Kong
u	u	u	u	u	26	1969	Hong Kong
4	4	3	u	u	4	1972[b]	Hong Kong
u	u	u	u	u	25	1976[b]	Hong Kong
13	4	8	u	u	1	1977[b]	Hong Kong
14	5	8	u	u	1	1979	Hong Kong
u	u	u	u	u	27	1981	Hong Kong
16	u	u	u	u	12	1982	Hong Kong
13	4	u	u	u	9	1984	Hong Kong
u	u	u	u	u	u	1969	India
3	u	u	u	u	4	1970	India
u	u	u	u	u	2	1970–71	India
u	u	u	u	u	7	1974–75	India
u	u	u	u	u	3	1975–76	India
u	u	u	u	u	u	1976–77	India
u	u	u	u	u	u	1977–78	India
u	u	u	u	u	u	1978–79	India
u	u	u	u	u	u	1979–80	India
4	u	——————7——————			0	1980	India
u	u	u	u	u	u	1980–81	India
u	u	u	u	u	u	1981–82	India
u	u	u	u	u	u	1982–83	India
u	u	u	u	u	u	1983–84	India
u	u	u	u	u	u	1984–85	India
u	u	u	u	u	u	1985–86	India
0	u	——————2——————			0[v]	1970	Andhra Pradesh
1	u	——————2——————			0[w]	1980	Andhra Pradesh
u	u	u	u	u	2	1985	Andhra Pradesh

199

Table 26. Contraceptive Prevalence: Percentage of Married Women of Reproductive Age (or Spouses) Currently Using Each Method *(continued)*

Country	Year	All methods	Modern methods[a]	Female sterilization	Male sterilization	Orals	Injectables	IUD
ASIA *(continued)*								
Assam	1970	9	4	——2——		u	u	2
Assam	1985	u	21	——20——		u	u	1
Bihar	1970	5	3	——2——		u	u	1
Bihar	1980	20	13	——12——		1	u	0
Bihar	1985	u	17	——15——		u	u	1
Delhi[t]	1970	21	9	——8——		u	u	1
Delhi	1980	64	27	——23——		1	u	3
Delhi	1985	u	28	——21——		u	u	7
Gujarat	1970	22	11	——10——		u	u	1
Gujarat	1980	45	37	——35——		1	u	1
Gujarat	1985	u	37	——33——		u	u	4
Haryana	1985	u	32	——24——		u	u	8
Himachal Pradesh	1980	47	27	——27——		u	u	0
Himachal Pradesh	1985	u	31	——28——		u	u	3
Jammu and Kashmir	1985	u	14	——12——		u	u	1
Karnataka	1970	8	5	——5——		u	u	0
Karnataka	1980	30	24	——23——		0	u	1
Karnataka	1985	u	29	——26——		u	u	3
Kerala	1970	27	18	——16——		u	u	2
Kerala	1980	61	50	——49——		1	u	0
Kerala	1985	u	38	——36——		u	u	2
Madhya Pradesh	1970	7	5	——5——		u	u	0
Madhya Pradesh	1980	28	22	——22——		0	u	0
Madhya Pradesh	1985	u	24	——22——		u	u	2
Maharashtra	1970	23	16	——15——		u	u	1
Maharashtra	1980	43	35	——33——		1	u	1
Maharashtra	1985	u	46	——39——		u	u	7
Orissa	1970	16	7	——7——		u	u	0
Orissa	1980	40	24	——23——		1	u	u
Orissa	1985	u	28	——26——		u	u	2
Punjab and Haryana	1980	49	26	——25——		0	u	1
Punjab	1985	u	39	——26——		u	u	13
Rajasthan	1970	8	4	——4——		u	u	0
Rajasthan	1980	22	17	——17——		0	u	0
Rajasthan	1985	u	17	——16——		u	u	1
Tamil Nadu	1970	18	4	——4——		u	u	0
Tamil Nadu	1980	45	23	——22——		0	u	1
Tamil Nadu	1985	u	36	——34——		u	u	1
Uttar Pradesh	1970	7	3	——2——		u	u	1
Uttar Pradesh	1980	22	11	——9——		1	u	1
Uttar Pradesh	1985	u	13	——10——		u	u	3
West Bengal	1970	21	7	——7——		u	u	1
West Bengal	1980	49	27	——23——		4	u	0
West Bengal	1985	u	29	——27——		u	u	1
Indonesia	1979[b,z]	31	23	0	0	17	u	6
Indonesia	1979[p,z]	26	24	u	u	17	u	7
Indonesia	1980[b,z]	27	21	u	u	14	u	7
Indonesia	1980[p,z]	32	29	u	u	20	u	9
Indonesia	1985	40	38	1	0	16	8	12
Indonesia	1987[b]	48	42	3	0	16	10	13
Java-Bali	1973	10	9	u	u	5	u	4
Java-Bali	1976	28	22	u	u	16	u	6
Java-Bali	1979[b]	36	28	u	u	20	u	8
Java-Bali	1979[p]	37	34	u	u	24	u	10
Java-Bali	1980[b]	31	25	u	u	17	u	8
Java-Bali	1980[p]	43	38	u	u	26	u	12

Table 26.
(continued)

Condoms	Vaginal methods	Rhythm	Withdrawal	Abstinence	Other[o]	Year	Country
							ASIA *(continued)*
2	u		4		0[v]	1970	Assam
u	u	u	u	u	4	1985	Assam
1	u		1		u[v]	1970	Bihar
2	u		5		u[w]	1980	Bihar
u	u	u	u	u	1	1985	Bihar
8	u		5		0[v]	1970	Delhi[t]
24	u		11		2[w]	1980	Delhi
u	u	u	u	u	10	1985	Delhi
3	u		7		1[v]	1970	Gujarat
3	u		5		0[w]	1980	Gujarat
u	u	u	u	u	7	1985	Gujarat
u	u	u	u	u	15	1985	Haryana
6	u		13		u[w]	1980	Himachal Pradesh
u	u	u	u	u	3	1985	Himachal Pradesh
u	u	u	u	u	1	1985	Jammu and Kashmir
2	u		1		0[v]	1970	Karnataka
2	u		4		0[w]	1980	Karnataka
u	u	u	u	u	3	1985	Karnataka
4	u		5		0[v]	1970	Kerala
6	u		4		u[w]	1980	Kerala
u	u	u	u	u	3	1985	Kerala
1	u		0		0[v]	1970	Madhya Pradesh
3	u		2		0[w]	1980	Madhya Pradesh
u	u	u	u	u	5	1985	Madhya Pradesh
4	u		3		1[v]	1970	Maharashtra
4	u		4		0[w]	1980	Maharashtra
u	u	u	u	u	6	1985	Maharashtra
2	u		8		u[v]	1970	Orissa
2	u		14		u[w]	1980	Orissa
u	u	u	u	u	3	1985	Orissa
13	u		12		0[w]	1980	Punjab and Haryana
u	u	u	u	u	12	1985	Punjab
3	u		1		u[v]	1970	Rajasthan
2	u		2		0[w]	1980	Rajasthan
u	u	u	u	u	2	1985	Rajasthan
2	u		12		1[v]	1970	Tamil Nadu
2	u		19		u[w]	1980	Tamil Nadu
u	u	u	u	u	1	1985	Tamil Nadu
2	u		2		0[v]	1970	Uttar Pradesh
6	u		6		0[w]	1980	Uttar Pradesh
u	u	u	u	u	3	1985	Uttar Pradesh
5	u		8		2[v]	1970	West Bengal
6	u		15		0[w]	1980	West Bengal
u	u	u	u	u	1	1985	West Bengal
1	u	1	0	0	6	1979[b,z]	Indonesia
1	u	u	u	u	1	1979[p,z]	Indonesia
1	u	u	u	u	5	1980[b,z]	Indonesia
2	u	u	u	u	1	1980[p,z]	Indonesia
1	0	0	0	0	2	1985	Indonesia
2	u	u	u	u	4	1987[b]	Indonesia
<1	u	u	u	u	1	1973	Java-Bali
2	u	u	u	u	5	1976	Java-Bali
1	u	u	u	u	5	1979[b]	Java-Bali
2	u	u	u	u	1	1979[p]	Java-Bali
1	u	u	u	u	4	1980[b]	Java-Bali
3	u	u	u	u	1	1980[p]	Java-Bali

Table 26. Contraceptive Prevalence: Percentage of Married Women of Reproductive Age (or Spouses) Currently Using Each Method (continued)

Country	Year	All methods	Modern methods[a]	Female sterilization	Male sterilization	Orals	Injectables	IUD
ASIA (continued)								
Java-Bali	1985[c]	43	42	u	u	u	u	u
Java-Bali	1987	51	46	3	<1	16	11	15
West Java	1973	6	5	u	u	4	u	1
West Java	1976	17	14	u	u	13	u	1
West Java	1979[b]	24	20	u	u	18	u	2
West Java	1980[b]	22	17	u	u	14	u	3
West Java	1985[b]	43	u	u	u	u	u	u
West Java	1987[b]	46	43	2	<1	18	13	9
Jakarta	1973	15	u	u	u	u	u	u
Jakarta	1976	29	14	u	u	10	u	4
Jakarta	1979[b]	29	19	u	u	12	u	7
Jakarta	1980[b]	25	17	u	u	10	u	7
Jakarta	1985[b]	44	u	u	u	u	u	u
Jakarta	1987[b]	54	44	6	<1	11	12	15
Central Java	1973	10	8	u	u	4	u	4
Central Java	1976	30	23	u	u	17	u	6
Central Java	1979[b]	35	27	u	u	21	u	7
Central Java	1980[b]	32	26	u	u	18	u	7
Central Java	1985[b]	39	u	u	u	u	u	u
Central Java	1987[b]	54	49	4	1	15	11	19
Yogyakarta	1973	13	10	u	u	3	u	7
Yogyakarta	1976	43	12	u	u	4	u	8
Yogyakarta	1979[b]	39	22	u	u	13	u	9
Yogyakarta	1980[b]	40	25	u	u	14	u	11
Yogyakarta	1985[b]	53	u	u	u	u	u	u
Yogyakarta	1987[b]	68	52	5	1	7	7	32
East Java	1973	15	13	u	u	8	u	5
East Java	1976	34	29	u	u	20	u	9
East Java	1979[b]	47	39	u	u	26	u	14
East Java	1980[b]	38	33	u	u	21	u	12
East Java	1985[b]	40	u	u	u	u	u	u
East Java	1987[b]	50	46	4	0	18	9	15
Bali	1973	23	21	u	u	3	u	18
Bali	1976	39	33	u	u	6	u	27
Bali	1979[b]	46	37	u	u	7	u	30
Bali	1980[b]	47	36	u	u	6	u	30
Bali	1985[b]	60	u	u	u	u	u	u
Bali	1987[b]	69	65	5	<1	5	6	49
Kalimantan	1979[b]	23	11	u	u	10	u	1
Kalimantan	1979[p]	7	7	u	u	6	u	1
Kalimantan	1980[b]	18	12	u	u	11	u	1
Kalimantan	1980[p]	11	10	u	u	9	u	1
Kalimantan	1985[c]	31	u	u	u	u	u	u
Sulawesi	1979[b]	31	15	u	u	11	u	4
Sulawesi	1979[p]	8	7	u	u	6	u	1
Sulawesi	1980[b]	23	15	u	u	12	u	3
Sulawesi	1980[p]	15	14	u	u	11	u	3
Sulawesi	1985[c]	33	u	u	u	u	u	u
Sumatra	1979[b]	20	8	u	u	7	u	1
Sumatra	1979[p]	9	7	u	u	6	u	1
Sumatra	1980[b]	16	11	u	u	9	u	2
Sumatra	1980[p]	13	10	u	u	8	u	2
Sumatra	1985[c]	31	u	u	u	u	u	u
Other islands	1979[b]	13	7	u	u	6	u	1
Other islands	1979[p]	4	3	u	u	2	u	1
Other islands	1980[b]	12	7	u	u	5	u	2

Table 26.
(continued)

Condoms	Vaginal methods	Rhythm	Withdrawal	Abstinence	Other[o]	Year	Country
							ASIA *(continued)*
u	u	u	u	u	u	1985[e]	Java-Bali
2	u	u	u	u	3	1987	Java Bali
0	u	u	u	u	1	1973	*West Java*
1	u	u	u	u	3	1976	*West Java*
<1	u	u	u	u	4	1979[b]	*West Java*
<1	u	u	u	u	4	1980[b]	*West Java*
u	u	u	u	u	u	1985[b]	*West Java*
1	u	u	u	u	3	1987[b]	*West Java*
u	u	u	u	u	u	1973	*Jakarta*
4	u	u	u	u	10	1976	*Jakarta*
2	u	u	u	u	7	1979[b]	*Jakarta*
1	u	u	u	u	7	1980[b]	*Jakarta*
u	u	u	u	u	u	1985[b]	*Jakarta*
5	u	u	u	u	5	1987[b]	*Jakarta*
1	u	u	u	u	1	1973	*Central Java*
3	u	u	u	u	4	1976	*Central Java*
2	u	u	u	u	5	1979[b]	*Central Java*
2	u	u	u	u	4	1980[b]	*Central Java*
u	u	u	u	u	u	1985[b]	*Central Java*
2	u	u	u	u	2	1987[b]	*Central Java*
1	u	u	u	u	2	1973	*Yogyakarta*
7	u	u	u	u	24	1976	*Yogyakarta*
6	u	u	u	u	11	1979[b]	*Yogyakarta*
7	u	u	u	u	8	1980[b]	*Yogyakarta*
u	u	u	u	u	u	1985[b]	*Yogyakarta*
4	u	u	u	u	12	1987[b]	*Yogyakarta*
0	u	u	u	u	1	1973	*East Java*
1	u	u	u	u	4	1976	*East Java*
1	u	u	u	u	6	1979[b]	*East Java*
1	u	u	u	u	4	1980[b]	*East Java*
u	u	u	u	u	u	1985[b]	*East Java*
1	u	u	u	u	2	1987[b]	*East Java*
0	u	u	u	u	2	1973	*Bali*
4	u	u	u	u	2	1976	*Bali*
1	u	u	u	u	7	1979[b]	*Bali*
2	u	u	u	u	9	1980[b]	*Bali*
u	u	u	u	u	u	1985[b]	*Bali*
2	u	u	u	u	2	1987[b]	*Bali*
1	u	u	u	u	11	1979[b]	Kalimantan
0	u	u	u	u	0	1979[p]	Kalimantan
0	u	u	u	u	5	1980[b]	Kalimantan
0	u	u	u	u	0	1980[p]	Kalimantan
u	u	u	u	u	u	1985[e]	Kalimantan
0	u	u	u	u	15	1979[b]	Sulawesi
0	u	u	u	u	1	1979[p]	Sulawesi
0	u	u	u	u	7	1980[b]	Sulawesi
0	u	u	u	u	1	1980[p]	Sulawesi
u	u	u	u	u	u	1985[e]	Sulawesi
1	u	u	u	u	11	1979[b]	Sumatra
1	u	u	u	u	1	1979[p]	Sumatra
1	u	u	u	u	4	1980[b]	Sumatra
2	u	u	u	u	1	1980[p]	Sumatra
u	u	u	u	u	u	1985[e]	Sumatra
0	u	u	u	u	5	1979[b]	Other islands
0	u	u	u	u	0	1979[p]	Other islands
0	u	u	u	u	4	1980[b]	Other islands

Table 26. Contraceptive Prevalence: Percentage of Married Women of Reproductive Age (or Spouses) Currently Using Each Method (continued)

Country	Year	All methods	Modern methods[a]	Female sterilization	Male sterilization	Orals	Injectables	IUD
ASIA (continued)								
Other islands	1980[p]	5	5	u	u	4	u	1
Other islands	1985[e]	24	u	u	u	u	u	u
Korea, Republic of	1964	9	u	u	u	u	u	u
Korea, Republic of	1965	16	u	u	u	u	u	u
Korea, Republic of	1966	20	12	——2——		1	0	9
Korea, Republic of	1967	26	u	u	u	u	u	u
Korea, Republic of	1971	25	18	2	2	7	0	7
Korea, Republic of	1972	30	24	——3——		9	0	12
Korea, Republic of	1973	36	21	——5——		8	u	8
Korea, Republic of	1974[b]	35	24	4	3	9	0	8
Korea, Republic of	1976	44	27	——8——		8	0	11
Korea, Republic of	1978	49	34	11	6	7	u	10
Korea, Republic of	1979	55	38	15	6	7	0	10
Korea, Republic of	1982	58	40	23	5	5	0	7
Korea, Republic of	1984	70	54	34	7	6	0	7
Korea, Republic of	1985	70	52	32	9	4	0	7
Malaysia, Peninsular	1966	9	5	——1——		4	u	0
Malaysia, Peninsular	1974	35	22	3	0	18	0	1
Malaysia, Peninsular	1981	42	u	u	u	u	u	u
Malaysia, Peninsular	1984	51	22	8	0	12	1	2
Nepal	1976[b]	2	u	0	2	0	u	0
Nepal	1981[b]	7	7	2	3	1	0	0
Nepal	1986[b]	15	14	7	6	1	0	0
Pakistan	1968[b]	6	u	u	u	u	u	u
Pakistan	1975[b]	5	2	1	0	1	0	1
Pakistan	1979[b]	3	u	u	u	u	u	u
Pakistan	1985[b]	8	5	2	0	1	1	1
Philippines	1968	16	2	0	0	1	0	0
Philippines	1972	23	u	u	u	u	u	u
Philippines	1973	24	11	——1——		7	0	3
Philippines	1978	37	13	5	1	5	0	2
Philippines	1983	u	17	9	1	5	0	3
Philippines	1986	44	20	10	1	6	0	2
Singapore	1970	45	u	u	u	38	u	u
Singapore	1973	60	35	11	0	22	0	3
Singapore	1977	71	42	21	1	17	u	3
Singapore	1983	74	35	22	1	12	0	0
Sri Lanka	1975[b]	43	18	8	1	2	0	6
Sri Lanka	1975	34	18	10	1	2	0	5
Sri Lanka	1977[z]	41	20	12	2	2	0	4
Sri Lanka	1981[b]	43	28	18	4	2	1	3
Sri Lanka	1982	58	29	——22——		3	1	3
Sri Lanka	1987[b,h]	62	39	25	5	4	3	2
Taiwan	1965[i]	24	u	u	u	u	u	u
Taiwan	1967[i]	34	28	6	0	3	0	19
Taiwan	1970[i]	44	u	u	u	u	u	u
Taiwan	1971[i]	44	28	u	u	8	u	20
Taiwan	1973[i]	57	43	——9——		6	0	28
Taiwan	1976[i]	63	46	——11——		7	0	28
Taiwan	1980[i]	70	46	——18——		6	0	22
Taiwan	1981[i]	70	51	18	2	6	u	25
Taiwan	1984[i]	74	u	u	u	u	u	u
Taiwan	1985[i]	78	50	26	0	5	0	19
Taiwan	1986[i]	75	56	23	2	6	0	24
Thailand	1970	15	14	5	2	4	0	2
Thailand	1972	26	26	6	3	11	1	5

Table 26.
(continued)

Condoms	Vaginal methods	Rhythm	Withdrawal	Abstinence	Other[o]	Year	Country
							ASIA *(continued)*
0	u	u	u	u	0	1980[p]	Other islands
u	u	u	u	u	u	1985[e]	Other islands
u	u	u	u	u	u	1964	Korea, Republic of
u	u	u	u	u	u	1965	Korea, Republic of
6	u	u	u	u	2	1966	Korea, Republic of
u	u	u	u	u	u	1967	Korea, Republic of
3	0	0	0	0	4	1971	Korea, Republic of
u	u	u	u	u	5	1972	Korea, Republic of
7	u	u	u	u	9	1973	Korea, Republic of
u	u	u	u	u	13	1974[b]	Korea, Republic of
6	u	u	u	u	11	1976	Korea, Republic of
6	u	u	u	u	10	1978	Korea, Republic of
5	1	7	4	0	0	1979	Korea, Republic of
7	u	u	u	u	10	1982	Korea, Republic of
6	u	u	u	u	10	1984	Korea, Republic of
8	2	0	0	0	8	1985	Korea, Republic of
1	0	u	u	u	2	1966	Malaysia, Peninsular
3	0	4	2	2	2	1974	Malaysia, Peninsular
u	u	u	u	u	u	1981	Malaysia, Peninsular
6	0	7	4	2	10	1984	Malaysia, Peninsular
0	u	u	u	0	u	1976[b]	Nepal
0	0	0	0	0	0	1981[b]	Nepal
1	0	0	0	0	0	1986[b]	Nepal
u	u	u	u	u	u	1968[b]	Pakistan
1	0	0	0	1	0	1975[b]	Pakistan
u	u	u	u	u	u	1979[b]	Pakistan
2	0	0	1	u	0	1985[b]	Pakistan
0	0	5	7	0	1	1968	Philippines
u	u	u	u	u	u	1972	Philippines
1	0	7	4	2	0	1973	Philippines
4	0	9	10	2	1	1978	Philippines
2	0	8	u	1	u	1983	Philippines
1	0	12	9	2	1	1986	Philippines
u	u	u	u	u	7	1970	Singapore
17	0	0	0	0	7	1973	Singapore
21	u	u	u	u	u	1977	Singapore
24	0	0	0	0	16	1983	Singapore
2	u	12	7	u	5	1975[b]	Sri Lanka
3	3	8	2	0	0	1975	Sri Lanka
3	0	u	u	u	18	1977[b]	Sri Lanka
2	0	9	3	0	0	1981[b]	Sri Lanka
3	u	14	5	u	7	1982	Sri Lanka
2	0	15	3	3	0	1987[b,h]	Sri Lanka
u	u	u	u	u	u	1965[i]	Taiwan
2	0	0	0	0	4	1967[i]	Taiwan
u	u	u	u	u	u	1970[i]	Taiwan
u	u	u	u	u	16	1971[i]	Taiwan
3	u	u	u	u	10	1973[i]	Taiwan
4	u	u	u	u	13	1976[i]	Taiwan
8	u	u	u	u	15	1980[i]	Taiwan
u	u	u	u	u	19	1981[i]	Taiwan
u	u	u	u	u	u	1984[i]	Taiwan
14	0	0	0	0	14	1985[i]	Taiwan
12	0	u	u	u	7	1986[i]	Taiwan
0	0	0	0	0	1	1970	Thailand
0	u	u	u	u	1	1972	Thailand

Table 26. Contraceptive Prevalence: Percentage of Married Women of Reproductive Age (or Spouses) Currently Using Each Method *(continued)*

Country	Year	All methods	Modern methods[a]	Female sterilization	Male sterilization	Orals	Injectables	IUD
ASIA *(continued)*								
Thailand	1975	37	32	8	2	15	2	6
Thailand	1978	53	47	13	3	22	5	4
Thailand	1981	59	54	19	4	20	7	4
Thailand	1984	65	60	24	4	20	8	5
Thailand	1987[b]	68	66	22	6	20	9	7
Vietnam	1982	20	u	u	u	u	u	u
Vietnam	1985	44	35	——1——		1	u	32
Vietnam	1986	58	49	——2——		1	u	46

u = unknown.   Note: Includes cohabiting women.

a. Female sterilization, male sterilization, oral contraceptives, injectables, and IUD.

b. Married women aged 15–49.

c. Married women aged 15–50.

d. Married women aged 20–44.

e. Married women aged <50.

f. Married women aged 15–45.

g. Married women aged 10–49.

h. Two northern zones of the country are omitted because of civil conflicts.

i. Married women aged 22–39.

j. Married women aged <56.

k. Survey of husbands aged 17–51.

l. Seventy-three percent of married women aged 15–44 were using contraceptives in 1982.

m. All national and provincial data are based on married women aged 15–49.

n. Percentage based on the number of married women 15–49 in 1982.

o. May include user coded "u" in preceding columns.

p. From service statistics.

q. The percentage of couples effectively protected by contraception was calculated from service statistics on the annual numbers of acceptors of sterilization, IUD insertions, and distribution of condoms and pills. Attrition rates were applied to sterilization and IUD acceptors that take into account their age distribution, joint survival ratios of husbands and wives in different age-groups, and termination of IUD use. Couples effectively protected were arrived at by multiplying the couples currently

Table 26.
(continued)

Condoms	Vaginal methods	Rhythm	Withdrawal	Abstinence	Other[o]	Year	Country
							ASIA *(continued)*
0	0	1	1	1	0	1975	Thailand
2	u	u	u	u	4	1978	Thailand
2	u	u	u	u	3	1981	Thailand
2	0	0	0	0	3	1984	Thailand
1	0	u	1	1	0	1987	Thailand
u	u	u	u	u	u	1982	Vietnam
9	u	u	u	u	u	1985	Vietnam
9	u	u	u	u	u	1986	Vietnam

q. *(continued)* protected by the level of use-effectiveness for the particular method. The 1976 data shown here are for the 1976–77 Indian year, 1977 data are for Indian year 1977–78, etc.

r. National and state figures for 1970 and 1980 are based upon surveys, which permit estimates for such methods as rhythm, withdrawal, and abstinence. For other years, estimates for these methods are not available from the service statistics. Consequently, the total for all methods cannot be calculated for such years; a total for modern methods is shown, however, since they are largely program-provided.

s. Includes oral contraceptives and condoms.

t. Also includes Haryana, Himachal Pradesh, and Punjab.

v. Includes oral contraceptives, diaphragm, jelly, foam tablets, and other spermicidal methods.

w. Other modern methods.

x. Ages 15–44 unless otherwise noted.

y. The 1981 and 1985 national and provincial data are based upon service statistics, which may be somewhat inflated. The 1982 data are based upon a survey.

z. The 1979 survey (listed first) agreed with the service statistics (listed second) for modern methods, and recorded additional use of traditional methods not offered by the program. The 1980 census (listed first) is thought to have suffered from undercounting of contraceptive users, which more than offset its inclusion of traditional methods not offered by the program.

aa. Total prevalence (all methods) was 49 percent among nonpregnant married women aged 15–49. Note that two surveys, both dated 1975, agreed on the proportion using modern methods but differed on traditional methods. The same pattern occurred in the 1981 and 1982 surveys.

bb. The 1985 Bangladesh survey obtained different estimates of contraceptive prevalence, ranging from 25.3 percent to 34.9 percent. The "eligible women" sample, drawn from 200 districts, gave 25.3 percent (all female respondents). The "couple" sample, drawn from a randomly selected 50 of the 200 districts (with interviews done in households different from those that fell into the "eligible women" sample) gave two estimates: 32.9 percent from the wives and 34.9 percent from the husbands (interviewed separately). Finally, a "working rate" was calculated, at 29.8 percent, assuming that each sex reported its own methods reliably; for modern methods the female estimate came from the large sample of eligible women, and the male estimate from men in the sample of couples. The entire traditional methods estimate came from reports by women in the eligible women sample, since that was the lower, more conservative figure. See Mitra and Associates, *Bangladesh Contraceptive Prevalence Survey—1985,* n.d., pp. 42–43.

Table 27. Contraceptive Prevalence by Sector: Percentage of Married Women of Reproductive Age (or Spouses) Obtaining Contraception[a] through the Public and Private Sectors

Country and method	Year	Public sector	Private sector	Country and method	Year	Public sector	Private sector
SUB-SAHARAN AFRICA				**Mauritius (continued)**			
Burundi				All methods	1981	39.4	11.2
Orals	1987[f]	0.2	<0.1	IUD	1981	1.9	0.5
Injectables	1987[f]	0.5	<0.1	Orals	1981	23.5	1.5
Sterilization	1987[f]	0.3	<0.1	Injectables	1981	5.0	0.1
				Other methods	1981	9.0	1.2
Ghana				Rhythm	1981	0.0	7.9
All methods	1975	1.4	u	All methods	1984	44.3	11.2
IUD	1975	0.2	u				
Orals	1975	1.1	u	**Nigeria (Ondo State)**			
Other methods	1975	0.1	u	Modern methods	1986[x]	3.0	2.7
All methods	1976	2.0	u	Supply methods[y]	1986[x]	2.5	2.7
IUD	1976	0.2	u	Clinic methods[z]	1986[x]	0.6	<0.1
Orals	1976	1.1	u				
Other methods	1976	0.7	u	**Senegal**			
All methods	1977	2.1	u	Modern methods	1986[x]	1.2	1.4
IUD	1977	0.2	u				
Orals	1977	1.2	u	**Zimbabwe**			
Other methods	1977	0.7	u	All methods	1984	23.2	15.2
All methods	1978	4.4	u	Traditional methods	1984	0.0	11.8
IUD	1978	0.4	u				
Orals	1978	2.4	u	**LATIN AMERICA/CARIBBEAN**			
Other methods	1978	1.6	u	**Brazil**			
				Orals	1977	u	11.0
Kenya				All methods	1986	17.5	47.0
All methods	1969	<1.0[b]	<1.0[b]				
All methods	1970	<1.0[b]	<1.0[b]	**Colombia**			
All methods	1971	2.2	u	All methods	1974	14.0	17.0
IUD	1971	1.5	u	All methods	1977[f]	26.1	22.5
Orals	1971	0.7	u	IUD	1977[f]	10.1	0.0
All methods	1979	6.7	u	Orals	1977[f]	12.7	3.5
				Female sterilization	1977[f]	1.4	5.2
Liberia				Male sterilization	1977[f]	0.2	0.0
Modern methods	1986[x]	2.2	4.8	Other methods	1977[f]	1.8	13.8
Supply methods[y]	1986[x]	1.2	4.1	All methods	1984	23.9	31.2
Clinic methods[z]	1986[x]	1.0	0.7				
				Costa Rica			
Mauritius				IUD	1970	1.4	u
All methods	1971	25.0[c]	d	Orals	1970	4.1	u
IUD	1971	2.0[c]	d	All methods	1978[f]	26.0	38.0
Orals	1971	14.0[c]	d	IUD	1978[f]	3.0	2.0
Other methods	1971	9.0[c]	d	Orals	1978[f]	17.0	6.0
All methods	1972	16.8	4.3	Injectables	1978[f]	1.0	1.0
IUD	1972	2.1	0.3	Sterilization	1978[f]	0.0	15.0[g]
Orals	1972	10.9	1.7	Condoms	1978[f]	4.0	5.0
Other methods	1972	4.5	2.4	Other methods	1978[f]	0.3	9.0
All methods	1975	52.2	4.0	All methods	1981	25.0	41.0
IUD	1975	1.9	0.0	IUD	1981	3.0	3.0
Orals	1975	30.1	3.5	Orals	1981	15.0	6.0
Other methods	1975	20.2	0.5	Injectables	1981	1.5	0.7
All methods	1976	33.5[e]	3.4	Female sterilization	1981	0.0	17.0
IUD	1976	0.4[e]	0.0	Male sterilization	1981	0.0	1.0
Orals	1976	21.6[e]	3.0	Condoms	1981	5.0	4.0
Other methods	1976	11.4[e]	0.4	Other methods	1981	1.0	9.0
All methods	1977	44.2	3.5	All methods	1984	26.4	38.5
IUD	1977	1.4	0.0				
Orals	1977	24.8	3.1	**Dominican Republic**			
Injectables	1977	2.9	0.0	All methods	1976	12.8	11.2
Other methods	1977	7.9	0.4	IUD	1976	2.5	0.0
Rhythm	1977	7.2	0.0	Orals	1976	8.0	0.9
All methods	1979	49.7	3.5	Other methods	1976	2.3	10.2
IUD	1979	1.7	0.0	All methods	1977	10.0	21.0
Orals	1979	27.5	3.1	IUD	1977	1.5	1.5
Injectables	1979	3.2	0.0	Orals	1977	6.0	2.0
Other methods	1979	10.2	0.4	Sterilization	1977	0.0	12.0
Rhythm	1979	7.0	0.0	Other methods	1977	2.0	6.0

Table 27. Contraceptive Prevalence by Sector: Percentage of Married Women of Reproductive Age (or Spouses) Obtaining Contraception[a] through the Public and Private Sectors (continued)

Country and method	Year	Public sector	Private sector	Country and method	Year	Public sector	Private sector
Ecuador				**Egypt** (continued)			
All methods	1974	2.0	1.0	All methods	1970	u	4.0
IUD	1974	1.0	1.0	IUD	1970	u	1.0
Orals	1974	1.0	0.2	Orals	1970	>5.0	3.0
Other methods	1974	0.2	0.0	All methods	1971	6.0	4.0
				IUD	1971	3.0	1.0
El Salvador				Orals	1971	3.0	3.0
All methods	1976	7.3	14.5	Other methods	1971	0.4	u
IUD	1976	1.3	0.7	Orals	1972	8.0	3.0
Orals	1976	3.8	3.6	Other methods	1972	1.0	u
Sterilization	1976	2.1	7.7	All methods	1973	15.8	4.9
Other methods	1976	0.1	2.5	IUD	1973	6.2	1.7
				Orals	1973	8.5	2.8
Guatemala				Other methods	1973	1.1	0.4
All methods	1972	2.1[h]	5.0[h]	All methods	1974	16.8	3.7
IUD	1972	0.4[h]	u	All methods	1975	17.3	3.8
Orals	1972	10.0[h]	u	IUD	1975	7.5	1.7
Other methods	1972	0.2[h]	u	Orals	1975	9.2	1.6
All methods	1973	2.7	1.0	Other methods	1975	0.6	0.5
IUD	1973	0.6	u	All methods	1981	10.0	8.5
Orals	1973	1.9	u	IUD	1981	4.2	0.5
Other methods	1973	0.2	u	Orals	1981	5.6	5.4
All methods	1974	3.0	1.4	Other methods	1981	0.2	2.6
IUD	1974	0.7	u	All methods	1984	6.2	15.1
Orals	1974	2.1	u				
Other methods	1974	0.2	u	**Iran**			
All methods	1977	7.0	u	All methods	1969	1.5	>1.2
All methods	1987	8.4	14.3	IUD	1969	0.4	u
IUD	1987	0.2	1.6	Orals	1969	1.0	1.2
Orals	1987	1.8	2.1	Other methods	1969	0.1	u
Injectables	1987	0.1	0.4	All methods	1970	6.0	>1.2
Female sterilization	1987	4.5	5.9	IUD	1970	1.0	u
Male sterilization	1987	0.1	0.8	Orals	1970	5.0	1.2[j]
Condoms	1987	0.2	0.9	Other methods	1970	0.0	u
Other methods	1987[aa]	2.0	1.9	All methods	1971	u	>1.7[j]
				IUD	1971	0.6	u
Mexico				Orals	1971	7.0	1.7
All methods	1973	1.0	12.2	All methods	1974	11.0	3.0
IUD	1973	0.3	0.8	IUD	1974	2.0	u
Orals	1973	0.4	11.1	Orals	1974	9.0	3.0
Other methods	1973	0.2	0.3	Other methods	1974	1.0	u
All methods	1975	9.0	5.0	All methods	1975	12.6	3.9
All methods	1976	12.0	9.0	IUD	1975	1.7	u
IUD	1976	7.0	1.0	Orals	1975	10.0	3.9
Orals	1976	3.0	6.0	Other methods	1975	0.9	u
Injectables	1976	0.1	1.6	All methods	1977	16.0	7.0
All methods	1978[f]	19.0	21.0	IUD	1977	2.0	u
Sterilization	1978[f]	5.0	2.0	Orals	1977	13.0	7.0
All methods	1979	19.5	18.3	Other methods	1977	1.0	u
All methods	1982	20.6	17.4	All methods[k]	1978	15.0	8.0
				IUD	1978	0.8	u
Paraguay				Orals	1978	13.0	8.0
All methods	1975	10.0	u	Sterilization	1978	0.0	u
All methods	1977[i]	7.8	7.7	Other methods	1978	1.0	u
Puerto Rico[f]				**Jordan**			
IUD	1982	1.5	1.8	All methods	1985	8.3	13.9
Orals	1982	3.5	1.9	IUD	1985	3.6	7.2
Female sterilization	1982	16.5	20.8	Orals	1985	0.7	5.3
Male sterilization	1982	1.3	3.1	Injectables	1985	0.0	0.1
Condoms	1982	1.2	1.2	Female sterilization	1985	3.8	1.1
				Condoms	1985	0.2	0.2
MIDDLE EAST/NORTH AFRICA							
Egypt				**Morocco**			
All methods	1969	6.0	4.0	All methods	1969	0.4	0.6
IUD	1969	1.0	1.0	IUD	1969	0.4	0.0
Orals	1969	5.0	3.0	Orals	1969	<0.1	0.6

Table 27. Contraceptive Prevalence by Sector: Percentage of Married Women of Reproductive Age (or Spouses) Obtaining Contraception[a] through the Public and Private Sectors (continued)

Country and method	Year	Public sector	Private sector	Country and method	Year	Public sector	Private sector
Morocco (continued)				**Tunisia** (continued)			
Other methods	1969	0.0	<0.1	IUD	1977	6.2	0.2
All methods	1970	0.4	0.6	Orals	1977	2.2	2.7
IUD	1970	0.4	0.0	Female sterilization	1977	5.5	0.0
Orals	1970	<0.1	0.6	Abortion	1977	2.5	u
Other methods	1970	0.0	0.1	Other methods	1977	0.6	u
All methods	1971	1.2	2.0	All methods	1982	19.6	u
IUD	1971	0.7	0.0	IUD	1982	9.8	u
Orals	1971	0.5	2.0	Orals	1982	3.3	u
Other methods	1971	0.0	0.0	Female sterilization	1982	4.5	u
All methods	1972	1.1	3.1	Other methods	1982	2.1	u
IUD	1972	0.9	0.0	All modern methods	1983	27.1	7.0
Orals	1972	0.2	3.1	IUD	1983	11.7	1.5
Other methods	1972	0.0	0.0	Orals	1983	2.4	2.9
All methods	1973	2.1	3.5	Injectables	1983	0.2	0.2
IUD	1973	1.0	0.0	Female sterilization	1983	12.1	0.4
Orals	1973	1.1	3.5	Condoms	1983	0.6	0.7
Other methods	1973	1.0	0.0	Spermicides	1983	0.2	1.3
All methods	1974	2.6	4.1				
IUD	1974	0.9	0.1	**Turkey**			
Orals	1974	1.3	4.0	All methods	1969	1.7[b]	u
Other methods	1974	0.3	0.1	IUD	1969	1.7	u
				Orals	1969	u	1.5
Tunisia				All methods	1970	2.6	u
All methods	1969	5.4	2.8	IUD	1970	2.3	u
IUD	1969	4.2	u	Orals	1970	0.3	1.5
Orals	1969	0.4	1.2	Other methods	1970	0.0	u
Sterilization	1969	0.5	u	All methods	1971	3.0	u
Other methods	1969	0.2	1.5	IUD	1971	2.7	u
All methods	1970	6.8	2.8	Orals	1971	0.3	u
IUD	1970	4.1	u	Other methods	1971	0.0	u
Orals	1970	1.5	1.2	All methods	1973[m]	2.5	u
Sterilization	1970	0.8	u	IUD	1973[m]	2.4	u
Other methods	1970	0.4	1.5	Orals	1973[m]	0.2	u
All methods	1971	9.0	2.8	Other methods	1973[m]	0.0	u
IUD	1971	5.0	u	All methods	1974[m]	2.5	u
Orals	1971	2.0	1.2	IUD	1974[m]	2.4	u
Sterilization	1971	1.0	u	Orals	1974[m]	0.2	u
Other methods	1971	1.0	1.2	Other methods	1974[m]	0.0	u
All methods	1972	6.0	u				
IUD	1972	3.0	u	**ASIA**			
Orals	1972	1.0	u	**China**			
Sterilization	1972	1.0	u	All methods	1982	69.5	0.0
Other methods	1972	0.4	u				
All methods	1973	6.4	u	**Hong Kong**			
IUD	1973	3.4	u	IUD	1969	4.5	u
Orals	1973	1.3	u	Orals	1969	2.8	12.8
Sterilization	1973	1.3	u	Sterilization	1969	0.4	u
Other methods	1973	0.4	u	All methods	1970	17.0	33.0
All methods	1974	7.8	u	IUD	1970	6.0	u
IUD	1974	4.1	u	Orals	1970	7.0	u
Orals	1974	1.1	1.4	Sterilization	1970	1.0	u
Sterilization	1974	2.2	u	Other methods	1970	3.0	u
Other methods	1974	0.3	u	All methods	1971	18.0	34.0
All methods	1975	12.6	u	IUD	1971	5.0	u
IUD	1975	6.5	u	Orals	1971	8.0	u
Orals	1975	1.1	1.4	Sterilization	1971	1.0	u
Sterilization	1975	2.8	u	All methods	1972	19.0	35.0
Abortion	1975	1.7[l]	u	IUD	1972	4.0	u
Other methods	1975	0.5	u	Orals	1972	10.0	u
All methods	1976	13.7	u	Sterilization	1972	1.0	u
IUD	1976	5.0	u	Other methods	1972	4.0	u
Orals	1976	1.5	1.6	All methods	1973	25.2	27.1
Sterilization	1976	4.6	u	IUD	1973	5.6	0.7
Abortion	1976	2.0	u	Orals	1973	11.8	11.1
Other methods	1976	0.6	0.7	Sterilization	1973	0.0[n]	5.3
All methods	1977	17.0	u	Other methods	1973	7.8	10.0

Table 27. Contraceptive Prevalence by Sector: Percentage of Married Women of Reproductive Age (or Spouses) Obtaining Contraception[a] through the Public and Private Sectors (continued)

Country and method	Year	Public sector	Private sector	Country and method	Year	Public sector	Private sector
Hong Kong (continued)				**India** (continued)			
All methods	1974	27.0	28.0	IUD	1975	1.3	u
All methods	1975	29.0	28.0	Sterilization	1975	12.2	u
IUD	1975	5.0	0.0	Other methods	1975	2.2	u
Orals	1975	13.0	11.0	All methods	1976	16.9	u
Sterilization	1975	7.0	6.0	IUD	1976	1.4	u
Other methods	1975	4.0	11.0	Sterilization	1976	13.0	u
All methods	1976	34.0[e]	27.0	Other methods	1976	2.5	u
IUD	1976	5.0[e]	0.0	All methods	1977	23.9	u
Orals	1976	16.0[e]	10.0	IUD	1977	1.6	u
Sterilization	1976	8.0[e]	6.0	Sterilization	1977	20.6	u
Other methods	1976	5.0[e]	11.0	Other methods	1977	1.7	u
All methods	1977	36.0	28.0	All methods	1979	22.6	u
IUD	1977	3.0	0.0	IUD	1979	0.9	u
Orals	1977	16.0	11.0	Sterilization	1979	20.1	u
Female sterilization	1977	9.0	6.0	Other methods	1979	1.6	u
Male sterilization	1977	2.0	0.0	All methods	1981	22.6	u
Other methods	1977	6.0	10.0	IUD	1981	1.0	u
All methods	1979	46.4	32.6	Sterilization	1981	20.0	u
IUD	1979	1.9	0.6	Other methods	1981	1.6	u
Orals	1979	17.3	11.0	All methods	1984	24.5	1.4
Female sterilization	1979	17.3	0.0				
Male sterilization	1979	1.1	0.0	**Indonesia**			
Other methods	1979	8.8	21.0	All methods	1969	0.1	u
All methods	1981	46.5	33.1	All methods	1970	0.2	u
IUD	1981	1.7	0.5	All methods	1971	0.5	u
Orals	1981	18.5	11.5	IUD	1971	0.3	u
Injectables	1981	1.2	1.0	Orals	1971	0.2	u
Female sterilization	1981	16.5	0.0	Other methods	1971	0.0	u
Male sterilization	1981	1.2	0.0	All methods	1972	3.3[m]	u
Other methods	1981	7.3	20.1	IUD	1972	1.3[m]	u
All methods	1982	40.4	22.8	Orals	1972	1.7[m]	u
IUD	1982	1.7	1.4	Other methods	1972	0.2[m]	u
Orals	1982	10.9	7.4	All methods	1974	7.4	u
Injectables	1982	0.6	2.1	IUD	1974	3.7	u
Female sterilization	1982	15.4	0.0	Orals	1974	3.6	u
Male sterilization	1982	0.9	0.0	Other methods	1974	0.1	u
Diaphragm	1982	0.2	0.2	All methods	1975	10.5	u
Condoms	1982	5.5	7.6	IUD	1975	4.2	u
Other methods	1982	4.9	2.4	Orals	1975	5.9	u
Spermicides	1982	0.4	1.7	Other methods	1975	0.5	u
All methods	1984	41.0	31.4	All methods	1976	14.8	u
				IUD	1976	4.7	u
India				Orals	1976	9.1	u
All methods	1969	7.0	0.3	Sterilization	1976	0.1	u
IUD	1969	1.0	u	Other methods	1976	0.9	u
Orals	1969	0.0	0.1	All methods	1977	18.0	u
Sterilization	1969	5.0	u	IUD	1977	6.2	u
Other methods	1969	<1.0	0.2	Orals	1977	10.7	u
All methods	1970	8.0	3.3	Sterilization	1977	0.2	u
IUD	1970	1.4	u	Other methods	1977	0.9	u
Orals	1970	0.0	0.1	All methods	1979	24.0	u
Sterilization	1970	6.0	3.0	IUD	1979	7.2	u
Other methods	1970	1.0	0.2[o]	Orals	1979	14.8	u
All methods	1972	13.2	u	Injectables	1979	0.3	u
IUD	1972	1.6	u	Sterilization	1979	0.5	u
Sterilization	1972	9.3	u	Other methods	1979	1.2	u
Other methods	1972	2.3	u	All methods	1981	36.2	u
All methods	1973	13.6	u	IUD	1981	10.0	u
IUD	1973	1.4	u	Orals	1981	22.5	u
Sterilization	1973	10.2	u	Injectables	1981	0.6	u
Other methods	1973	2.0	u	Sterilization	1981	1.0	u
All methods	1974	15.1	u	Other methods	1981	2.1	u
IUD	1974	1.3	u	All methods	1984	39.9	u
Sterilization	1974	11.4	u	All methods	1987[f]	37.2	10.7
Other methods	1974	2.4	u	IUD	1987[f]	11.9	1.4
All methods	1975	15.8	u	Orals	1987[f]	14.0	2.2

Table 27. Contraceptive Prevalence by Sector: Percentage of Married Women of Reproductive Age (or Spouses) Obtaining Contraception[a] through the Public and Private Sectors (continued)

Country and method	Year	Public sector	Private sector	Country and method	Year	Public sector	Private sector
Indonesia (continued)				**Malaysia (Peninsular)**			
Injectables	1987[f]	7.2	2.3	All methods	1969	3.4	u
Female sterilization	1987[f]	2.9	0.2	IUD	1969	0.1	u
Male sterilization	1987[f]	0.2	0.0	Orals	1969	3.1	u
Condoms	1987[f]	0.6	1.0	Sterilization	1969	0.2	u
Norplant	1987[f]	0.4	0.0	Other methods	1969	<0.1	u
Traditional methods	1987[f]	0.0	3.6	All methods	1970	5.1	1.2[p]
				IUD	1970	0.1	u
Korea, Republic of				Orals	1970	4.6	1.1[p]
All methods	1969	21.0	4.0	Sterilization	1970	0.3	u
IUD	1969	15.0	u	Other methods	1970	0.1	<0.1[p]
Orals	1969	1.0	2.0	All methods	1971	6.5	1.2[p]
Sterilization	1969	3.0	u	IUD	1971	0.1	u
Other methods	1969	2.0	2.0[o]	Orals	1971	5.9	1.1[p]
All methods	1970	28.0	4.0	Sterilization	1971	0.6	0.0
IUD	1970	19.0	u	Other methods	1971	0.0	<0.1[p]
Orals	1970	3.0	2.0	All methods	1972	8.0[q]	u
Sterilization	1970	3.0	u	All methods	1973	9.3[q]	u
Other methods	1970	3.0	2.0[o]	All methods	1975[r]	10.0	33.0
All methods	1971	36.0	6.0	All methods	1976	24.0	10.0
IUD	1971	20.0	u	Orals	1976	19.0	8.0
Orals	1971	7.0	4.0	Sterilization	1976	2.6	0.4
Sterilization	1971	3.0	u	Other methods	1976	2.7	1.5
Other methods	1971	6.0	2.0[o]	All methods	1979	17.4	18.6
All methods	1972	24.0	6.0	IUD	1979	0.5	0.5
IUD	1972	12.0	0.0	Orals	1979	12.7	12.3
Orals	1972	5.0	4.0	Sterilization	1979	2.7	3.3
Sterilization	1972	3.0	0.0	Other methods	1979	1.5	2.5
Other methods	1972	4.0	2.0	All methods	1981	26.0	16.3
All methods	1974	24.5	6.0	IUD	1981	0.6	0.2
IUD	1974	11.7	0.0	Orals	1981	12.7	4.2
Orals	1974	8.4	3.0	Injectables	1981	0.3	0.1
Sterilization	1974	3.4	0.7	Sterilization	1981	3.8	1.2
Other methods	1974	4.0	2.3	Other methods	1981	8.6	10.6
All methods	1975	27.0	7.0	All methods	1984[f]	16.3	14.6
IUD	1975	12.0	0.0	IUD	1984[f]	1.2	1.0
Orals	1975	6.0	3.0	Orals	1984[f]	7.0	4.6
Sterilization	1975	4.0	1.0	Injectables	1984[f]	0.1	0.4
Other methods	1975	4.0	2.0	Female sterilization	1984[f]	5.5	1.9
All methods	1976	25.5	8.7	Male sterilization	1984[f]	0.2	0.0
IUD	1976	12.6	u	Condoms	1984[f]	2.2	5.4
Orals	1976	5.0	4.7	Other methods	1984[f]	u	1.2
Sterilization	1976	3.9	u	Spermicides	1984[f]	0.1	0.1
Other methods	1976	4.0	4.0				
All methods	1977	22.2	21.7	**Nepal**			
IUD	1977	9.5	1.0	All methods	1969	0.3	u
Orals	1977	4.7	3.0	IUD	1969	0.1	u
Female sterilization	1977	1.1	2.9	Orals	1969	<0.1	u
Male sterilization	1977	3.7	0.5	Sterilization	1969	0.1	u
Other methods	1977	3.2	14.3	Other methods	1969	0.1	u
All methods	1978	24.8	24.3	All methods	1970	0.7	u
Sterilization	1978	12.4	4.2	IUD	1970	0.1	u
All methods	1980	29.5	25.0	Orals	1970	0.1	u
IUD	1980	9.0	0.6	Sterilization	1970	0.2	u
Orals	1980	3.7	3.5	Other methods	1970	0.2	u
Injectables	1980	0.0	0.2	All methods	1971	2.5	u
Female sterilization	1980	9.8	4.7	IUD	1971	0.1	u
Male sterilization	1980	5.4	0.5	Orals	1971	0.6	u
Other methods	1980	1.6	15.5	Sterilization	1971	0.4	u
All methods	1985	39.7	30.7	Other methods	1971	1.3	u
IUD	1985	4.3	3.1				
Orals	1985	0.8	3.5	**Pakistan**			
Female sterilization	1985	26.1	5.5	All methods	1969	17.0	u
Male sterilization	1985	7.4	1.5	IUD	1969	6.0	u
Condoms	1985	1.1	6.1	Orals	1969	0.0	u
Other methods	1985	0.0	11.0	Sterilization	1969	3.0	u

Table 27. Contraceptive Prevalence by Sector: Percentage of Married Women of Reproductive Age (or Spouses) Obtaining Contraception[a] through the Public and Private Sectors (continued)

Country and method	Year	Public sector	Private sector	Country and method	Year	Public sector	Private sector
Pakistan (continued)				**Singapore** (continued)			
Other methods	1969	8.0	u	Sterilization	1972[v]	2.8	u
IUD	1970	7.0	u	Orals	1973[v]	12.3	0.0
Orals	1970	0.0	u	Sterilization	1973[v]	6.0	0.0
Sterilization	1970	4.0	u	IUD	1974[v]	0.0	3.3
IUD	1971	7.0	u	Orals	1974[v]	21.7	0.0
Orals	1971	0.0	u	Sterilization	1974[v]	10.8	0.0
Sterilization	1971	5.0	u	All methods	1976	61.4	15.7
All methods	1980	6.4	u	IUD	1976	2.3	0.5
IUD	1980	1.1	u	Orals	1976	24.2	3.0
Orals	1980	0.6	u	Sterilization	1976	14.2	3.2
Sterilization	1980	0.6	u	Other methods	1976	20.7	9.0
Condoms	1980	4.1	u	All methods	1978	53.0	18.0
				IUD	1978	2.0	1.0
Philippines				Orals	1978	14.0	3.0
All methods	1972	8.1	s	Female sterilization	1978	20.0	1.0
IUD	1972	1.9	s	Male sterilization	1978	1.0	0.0
Orals	1972	4.9	s	Other methods	1978	16.0	13.0
Other methods	1972	1.3	s				
All methods	1973	11.0	s	**Sri Lanka**			
IUD	1973	2.0	s	All methods	1969	4.2	u
Orals	1973	7.0	s	IUD	1969	2.3	u
Other methods	1973	2.0	s	Orals	1969	0.8	1.3
All methods	1974	15.0	s	Sterilization	1969	0.7	u
IUD	1974	4.0	s	Other methods	1969	0.4	u
Orals	1974	9.0	s	All methods	1970	6.9	u
Other methods	1974	3.0	s	IUD	1970	3.4	u
All methods	1976	21.7	s	Orals	1970	2.0	1.3
IUD	1976	3.8	s	Sterilization	1970	1.0	u
Orals	1976	10.9	s	Other methods	1970	0.5	u
Sterilization	1976	0.8	s	All methods	1987[bb]	35.6	4.7
Condoms	1976	2.8	s	IUD	1987[bb]	2.0	0.1
Other methods	1976	0.3	s	Orals	1987[bb]	2.8	1.3
Rhythm	1976	3.1	s	Injectables	1987[bb]	1.8	0.9
All methods	1977	22.0	s	Female sterilization	1987[bb]	24.0	0.7
IUD	1977	3.8	s	Male sterilization	1987[bb]	4.3	0.5
Orals	1977	10.5	s	Modern methods	1987[bb]	34.9	3.5
Sterilization	1977	1.6	s	Condom/diaphragm	1987[bb]	0.7	1.2
Other methods	1977	6.0	s				
All methods	1979	16.4	20.6	**Taiwan**			
IUD	1979	2.5	0.0	All methods	1969	17.0	16.0
Orals	1979	4.1	0.9	IUD	1969	14.0	u
Injectables	1979	0.2	0.3	Orals	1969	2.0[b]	3.0
Female sterilization	1979	3.7	0.0	Sterilization	1969	<0.1	u
Male sterilization	1979	0.5	0.0	Other methods	1969	u	>12.0
Other methods	1979	5.3	19.5	All methods	1970	20.0	16.0
All methods	1981	27.0	21.0	IUD	1970	16.0	u
IUD	1981	1.0	3.0	Orals	1970	3.0	3.0
Orals	1981	6.0	10.0	Sterilization	1970	<0.1	u
Sterilization	1981	3.0	0.0	Other methods	1970	u	>12.0
Other methods	1981[t]	16.0	8.0	All methods	1971	24.0	20.0
All methods	1983	28.6	u	IUD	1971	19.0	u
				Orals	1971	4.0	3.6
Singapore				Sterilization	1971	0.0	u
All methods	1969[v]	9.0[b]	28.0	Other methods	1971	u	16.4
Orals	1969[v]	u	28.0	All methods	1972	25.0	31.0
All methods	1970[v]	27.0	18.0[b]	IUD	1972	20.0	11.0
IUD	1970[v]	2.0	u	Orals	1972	3.0	1.0
Orals	1970[v]	20.0	18.0	Sterilization	1972	0.0	8.0
Sterilization	1970[v]	1.0	u	Other methods	1972	1.0	11.0
Other methods	1970[v]	3.0	u	All methods	1973	27.0	30.0
All methods	1971[v]	25.0	u	IUD	1973	23.0	10.0
IUD	1971[v]	1.9	u	Orals	1973	3.0	1.0
Orals	1971[v]	16.6	u	Sterilization	1973	0.0	9.0
Sterilization	1971[v]	2.2	u	Other methods	1973	1.0	10.0
Other methods	1971[v]	4.3	u	All methods	1974[w]	21.0	34.0
Orals	1972[v]	15.6	u	IUD	1974[w]	15.0	12.0

213

Table 27. Contraceptive Prevalence by Sector: Percentage of Married Women of Reproductive Age (or Spouses) Obtaining Contraception[a] through the Public and Private Sectors (continued)

Country and method	Year	Public sector	Private sector	Country and method	Year	Public sector	Private sector
Taiwan *(continued)*				**Thailand** *(continued)*			
Orals	1974[w]	4.0	2.0	IUD	1971	3.0	u
Sterilization	1974[w]	0.1	9.0	Orals	1971	2.8	3.3[j]
Other methods	1974[w]	2.0	11.0	Sterilization	1971	0.7	u
All methods	1977	27.0	34.0	Other methods	1971	0.0	u
IUD	1977	19.0	9.0	All methods	1972	13.3	5.4
Orals	1977	3.0	3.0	IUD	1972	4.0	u
Female sterilization	1977	3.0	7.0	Orals	1972	7.1	5.4
Male sterilization	1977	0.3	0.7	Sterilization	1972	2.2	u
Condoms	1977	2.0	14.0	All methods	1973	17.7	8.0
All methods	1979	34.6	30.9	IUD	1973	4.8	u
IUD	1979	19.0	8.0	Orals	1973	10.3	4.9
Orals	1979	4.0	3.0	Sterilization	1973	2.6	u
Female sterilization	1979	7.0	7.0	Other methods	1973	u	3.1
Male sterilization	1979	0.6	0.9	All methods	1974	17.7	7.1
Condoms	1979	4.0	12.0	IUD	1974	4.5	u
All methods	1981	47.0	23.0	Orals	1974	9.4	7.1
IUD	1981	22.9	2.5	Sterilization	1974	3.5	u
Orals	1981	3.0	2.9	Other methods	1974	0.3	u
Injectables	1981	0.0	0.1	All methods	1975	19.0	7.6
Female sterilization	1981	11.6	6.5	IUD	1975	5.4	u
Male sterilization	1981	0.8	0.8	Orals	1975	8.8	7.6
Condoms	1981	8.7	3.2	Sterilization	1975	4.3	u
Other methods	1981	0.0	7.0	Other methods	1975	0.5	u
All methods	1984	44.8	29.3	All methods	1976	23.7	8.3
All methods	1986	55.7	19.6	IUD	1976	5.5	u
IUD	1986	21.0	3.4	Orals	1976	12.2	8.3
Orals	1986	5.4	0.7	Injectables	1976	0.7	u
Injectables	1986	0.0	<0.1	Sterilization	1976	5.3	u
Female sterilization	1986	19.7	3.3	IUD	1977	6.9	0.0
Male sterilization	1986	1.4	0.6	Injectables	1977	0.5	0.7
Diaphragm	1986	0.0	<0.1	Female sterilization	1977	9.0	0.0
Condoms	1986	8.2	3.9	Male sterilization	1977	0.7	0.0
Other methods	1986	0.0	7.3	All methods	1979	34.0	5.0
Spermicides	1986	0.0	0.3	All methods	1981	51.6	u
				IUD	1981	5.1	u
Thailand				Orals	1981	26.9	u
All methods	1969	4.1	>3.3	Injectables	1981	4.3	u
IUD	1969	1.8	u	Sterilization	1981	15.3	u
Orals	1969	0.3	3.3	All methods	1984	59.1	u
Sterilization	1969	2.2	u	All methods	1987	54.8	12.6
Other methods	1969	0.0	u	IUD	1987	6.9	0.3
All methods	1970	4.3	>3.3	Orals	1987	14.3	5.7
IUD	1970	2.0	u	Injectables	1987	8.0	1.2
Orals	1970	1.0	3.3	Female sterilization	1987	20.6	1.8
Sterilization	1970	1.3	u	Male sterilization	1987	4.4	1.1
Other methods	1970	0.0	u	Condoms	1987	0.6	0.6
All methods	1971	6.5	>3.3[j]				

u = unknown.

a. Supplies and services, including sterilization.

b. Estimate of uncertain quality.

c. Based on a survey covering current practice, not on method continuation rates.

d. The Mauritius national program operates through two private associations; therefore, the private sector is presumed to be incorporated into the program.

e. Government-supported as well as government-operated facilities.

f. Based on married women aged 15–49.

g. Predominantly female. Although more than four-fifths of these sterilizations were performed in Social Security or Ministry of Health facilities, they are not considered to have been supplied through the public sector because sterilization is not an official program method.

h. Denominator includes women living in consensual unions.

i. Based on all women aged 15–44.

Table 27. Contraceptive Prevalence by Sector: Percentage of Married Women of Reproductive Age (or Spouses) Obtaining Contraception[a] through the Public and Private Sectors *(continued)*

j. Represents estimate as of January.

k. The basis for this estimate is uncertain, but the amount suggests that it reflects distribution of orals without the necessary allowance for discontinuation of use.

l. Abortion is also included in total for all methods.

m. Rough estimate.

n. Sterilization applicants were referred to Hong Kong hospitals for the operation and were not considered program acceptors.

o. Mainly condoms.

p. Includes only users who obtained contraceptive supplies at subsidized prices from the Family Planning Association. An estimated 6 percent of married women aged 15–44 obtained supplies from other private sources.

q. Mainly oral contraceptives.

r. The total number of users is derived from data in the 1974 Second Malaysian Fertility and Family Survey. The private-sector figures are residuals between totals and program estimates. The main method is oral contraception.

s. Most private supplies and services are provided by clinics that receive financial support from the government, and acceptors at these clinics are reported in the program data. Private use through other channels is considered too small to affect the total.

t. Mostly condoms and rhythm in the public sector (in almost equal proportions); mostly condoms in the private sector.

v. The distinction between the government program and other sources is not well defined. Late in 1968 the government took over the operation of the private family planning association, and even during the earlier years the family planning association had extensive use of government funds and facilities.

w. Based on a KAP survey of married women aged 20–39.

x. Based on all women aged 15–49.

y. Orals, injectables, vaginal methods, and condoms.

z. IUD and sterilization.

aa. Rhythm, Billings method, and withdrawal.

bb. The 1987 survey excluded districts in the north and east.

Table 28. Adolescents: Vital Statistics for Women 15–19

Country and year	Number of women 15–19[a] (000s)	Percent currently married[a]	Children ever born (CEB) per woman[p]	Children still living (CSL) per woman[p]	Ratio of CSL to CEB	Age-specific fertility rate[b]	Percent probability of dying (15–19)[c]	Percent using contraception[d]
SUB-SAHARAN AFRICA								
Angola								
1980–85	u	u	u	u	u	203	u	u
Benin								
1979	132.3	u	u	u	u	u	u	u
1981–82	u	u	u	u	u	u	u	12
1980–85	u	u	u	u	u	216	u	u
Botswana								
1981	49.5	7.0	0.253	u	u	u	1.24	u
1984	u	u	u	u	u	u	u	20
1980–85	u	u	u	u	u	204	u	u
Burkina Faso								
1975	262.6[f]	53.4	u	u	u	u	u	u
1980–85	u	u	u	u	u	218	u	u
Burundi								
1979	247.1	18.6	u	u	u	u	u	u
1980–85	u	u	u	u	u	211	u	u
1985	233.6	19.2	u	u	u	u	u	u
Cameroon								
1978	u	u	u	u	u	u	u	2
1980–85	u	u	u	u	u	189	u	u
1986	498.3	44.5[g]	u	u	u	u	u	u
Central African Republic								
1975	92.4	45.5	u	u	u	u	u	u
1980–85	u	u	u	u	u	192	u	u
1985	128.8[e]	u	u	u	u	u	u	u
Chad								
1978	208.9[e]	u	u	u	u	u	u	u
1980–85	u	u	u	u	u	192	u	u
Congo								
1980–85	u	u	u	u	u	196	u	u
1985	111.1[e]	u	u	u	u	u	u	u
Côte d'Ivoire								
1978	373.8	52.5	u	u	u	u	u	u
1980–81	u	u	u	u	u	u	u	2
1980–85	u	u	u	u	u	206	u	u
Ethiopia								
1978	1466.0[e]	56.3	u	u	u	u	u	u
1982	1479.2[e]	53.2	u	u	u	u	u	u
1980–85	u	u	u	u	u	206	u	u
1983	1523.0[e]	53.1	u	u	u	u	u	u
1984	1836.7	53.1	u	u	u	u	u	u
1985	1898.2	41.7	u	u	u	u	u	u
Gabon								
1980–85	u	u	u	u	u	139	u	u
Ghana								
1979–80	u	u	u	u	u	u	u	5
1980–85	u	u	u	u	u	200	u	u
Guinea								
1980–85	u	u	u	u	u	198	u	u
Kenya								
1977–78	u	u	u	u	u	u	u	2

Table 28. Adolescents: Vital Statistics for Women 15–19 *(continued)*

Country and year	Number of women 15–19[a] (000s)	Percent currently married[a]	Children ever born (CEB) per woman[p]	Children still living (CSL) per woman[p]	Ratio of CSL to CEB	Age-specific fertility rate[b]	Percent probability of dying (15–19)[c]	Percent using contraception[d]
Kenya *(continued)*								
1980–85	u	u	u	u	u	244	u	u
Lesotho								
1977	u	u	u	u	u	u	u	2
1980–85	u	u	u	u	u	69	u	u
Liberia								
1971	u	u	u	u	u	u	1.88	u
1974	83.5	40.9	u	u	u	u	u	u
1977	93.5	u	u	u	u	u	u	u
1980–85	u	u	u	u	u	208	u	u
Libya								
1974	80.5[f]	36.7	u	u	u	u	u	u
1980–85	u	u	u	u	u	112	u	u
Madagascar								
1972	u	u	u	u	u	u	1.74	u
1974–75	u	u	u	u	u	u	3.40	u
1975	413.8	32.4	u	u	u	u	u	u
1980–85	u	u	u	u	u	188	u	u
Malawi								
1970–72	u	u	u	u	u	u	7.93	u
1977	280.0	47.3[g]	0.496	0.373	0.753	u	3.00	u
1980–85	u	u	u	u	u	230	u	u
1983	343.6	u	u	u	u	u	u	u
Mali								
1976	u	u	u	u	u	u	2.11	u
1980–85	u	u	u	u	u	205	u	u
1985	409.0[e]	u	u	u	u	u	u	u
Mauritania								
1977	70.8	36.9	u	u	u	u	u	u
1980–85	u	u	u	u	u	232	u	u
Mauritius								
1971–73	u	u	u	u	u	u	0.57	u
1972	50.4	12.5	u	u	u	u	u	u
1982–84	u	u	u	u	u	u	0.45	u
1983	52.2	47.9[g]	u	u	u	u	u	u
1980–85	u	u	u	u	u	79	u	u
Mozambique								
1980	540.6	u	u	u	u	u	u	u
1980–85	u	u	u	u	u	200	u	u
Namibia								
1980–85	u	u	u	u	u	200	u	u
Niger								
1980–85	u	u	u	u	u	239	u	u
Nigeria								
1981–82	u	u	u	u	u	u	u	4
1980–85	u	u	u	u	u	219	u	u
Rwanda								
1978	286.7	14.6	0.092	0.080	0.869	u	2.55	u
1980–85	u	u	u	u	u	219	u	u
Senegal								
1976	87.9[f]	37.3[g,i]	u	u	u	u	u	u
1978	u	u	u	u	u	u	u	5

Table 28. Adolescents: Vital Statistics for Women 15–19 *(continued)*

Country and year	Number of women 15–19[a] (000s)	Percent currently married[a]	Children ever born (CEB) per woman[p]	Children still living (CSL) per woman[p]	Ratio of CSL to CEB	Age-specific fertility rate[b]	Percent probability of dying (15–19)[c]	Percent using contraception[d]
Senegal *(continued)*								
1980–85	u	u	u	u	u	218	u	u
Sierra Leone								
1980–85	u	u	u	u	u	200	u	u
Somalia								
1983	u	u	u	u	u	u	u	u
1983 (Hargeisa, urban)	u	u	u	u	u	u	u	4
1980–85 (Hargeisa, urban)	u	u	u	u	u	200	u	u
South Africa								
1980	1296.5	5.5[g]	u	u	u	u	u	u
1980–85	u	u	u	u	u	163	u	u
Sudan								
1973	505.3[j]	41.0	u	u	u	u	u	u
1978–79	u	u	u	u	u	u	u	4[k]
1980	944.0[e]	u	u	u	u	u	u	u
1980–85	u	u	u	u	u	110	u	u
Tanzania								
1978	853.8	35.0	u	u	u	u	u	u
1980–85	u	u	u	u	u	219	u	u
1985	1179.0[e]	u	u	u	u	u	u	u
Togo								
1980–85	u	u	u	u	u	200	u	u
Uganda								
1980–85	u	u	u	u	u	226	u	u
Zaire								
1980	1383.5[e]	u	u	u	u	u	u	u
1980–85	u	u	u	u	u	200	u	u
1982–84 (Kananga, urban)	u	u	u	u	u	u	u	10
1982–84 (Kinshasa, urban)	u	u	u	u	u	u	u	39
1982–84 (Kisangani, urban)	u	u	u	u	u	u	u	19
1982–84 (Lubumbasi, urban)	u	u	u	u	u	u	u	34
Zambia								
1977	276.0[e]	u	u	u	u	u	u	u
1980–85	u	u	u	u	u	207	u	u
Zimbabwe								
1982	412.6	24.5	u	u	u	u	u	u
1980–85	u	u	u	u	u	202	u	u
1984	u	u	u	u	u	u	u	25
LATIN AMERICA/CARIBBEAN								
Argentina								
1969–71	u	u	u	u	u	u	0.42	u
1975–80	u	u	u	u	u	u	0.39	u
1980	1398.3[n]	10.1[g,n]	0.136[n]	0.128[n]	0.942	u	u	u
1980–85	u	u	u	u	u	80	u	u
1985	1207.3	u	u	u	u	u	u	u
Bolivia								
1976	248.9	15.6	u	u	u	u	u	u
1980–85	u	u	u	u	u	90	u	u
1983	u	u	u	u	u	u	u	13
1985	332.4	u	u	u	u	u	u	u
Brazil								
1960–70	u	u	u	u	u	u	0.95	u
1985	6941.0[e]	u	u	u	u	u	u	u

Table 28. Adolescents: Vital Statistics for Women 15–19 *(continued)*

Country and year	Number of women 15–19[a] (000s)	Percent currently married[a]	Children ever born (CEB) per woman[p]	Children still living (CSL) per woman[p]	Ratio of CSL to CEB	Age-specific fertility rate[b]	Percent probability of dying (15–19)[c]	Percent using contra-ception[d]
Brazil *(continued)*								
1980–85	u	u	u	u	u	57	u	u
1978 (São Paulo)	u	u	u	u	u	u	u	43
1979 (Piauí)	u	u	u	u	u	u	u	16
1980 (Piauí)	6864.1[f,o]	14.2[g]	0.137	0.122	0.889	u	u	u
1982 (Piauí)	u	u	u	u	u	u	u	15
1980 (Northeast region)	u	u	u	u	u	u	u	18
1981 (Southern region)	u	u	u	u	u	u	u	45
1982 (Amazones, urban)	u	u	u	u	u	u	u	21
Chile								
1969–70	u	u	u	u	u	u	0.51	u
1976	566.5	9.7[g]	u	u	u	u	u	u
1977	576.8	9.7[g]	u	u	u	u	u	u
1978	587.0	9.7[g]	u	u	u	u	u	u
1979	599.0	10.3[g]	u	u	u	u	u	u
1980	603.8	10.3[g]	u	u	u	u	u	u
1981	603.9	10.3[g]	u	u	u	u	u	u
1982	u	u	u	u	0.911	u	u	u
1982	652.6	9.0[g]	u	u	u	u	u	u
1980–85	u	u	u	u	u	62	0.34	u
1983	593.3	10.3[g]	u	u	u	u	u	u
1984	586.5	10.3[g]	u	u	u	u	u	u
1985	581.5	10.3[g]	u	u	u	u	u	u
1986	617.3	u	u	u	u	u	u	u
Colombia								
1974	1226.1	12.8	u	u	u	u	u	u
1976	u	u	u	u	u	u	u	27
1978	u	u	u	u	u	u	u	21
1980	u	u	u	u	u	u	u	25
1980–85	u	u	u	u	u	66	u	u
1985	1672.5	u	u	u	u	u	u	u
Costa Rica								
1978	u	u	u	u	u	u	u	48
1981	u	u	u	u	u	u	u	47
1980–85	u	u	u	u	u	100	u	u
1984	139.1[f]	15.1[g]	0.167	0.164	0.980	u	u	u
Cuba								
1981	572.9	24.2[g]	0.174	0.171	0.982	u	u	u
1980–85	u	u	u	u	u	68	u	u
1985	570.3	u	u	u	u	u	u	u
Dominican Republic								
1975	u	u	u	u	u	u	u	13
1980	316.4	u	u	u	u	u	u	u
1980–85	u	u	u	u	u	76	u	u
1983	u	u	u	u	u	u	u	19
Ecuador								
1974–79	u	u	u	u	u	u	1.15	u
1979	u	u	u	u	u	u	u	14
1982	440.3[p]	16.6[i]	u	u	u	u	u	u
1980–85	u	u	u	u	u	74	u	u
1984	498.2	u	u	u	u	u	u	u
El Salvador								
1978	u	u	u	u	u	u	u	8
1980–85	u	u	u	u	u	116	u	u
1985	265.5	u	u	u	u	u	u	u
Guatemala								
1978	u	u	u	u	0.886	u	u	5
1981	335.0[e]	26.4	u	u	u	u	u	u

Table 28. Adolescents: Vital Statistics for Women 15–19 *(continued)*

Country and year	Number of women 15–19[a] (000s)	Percent currently married[a]	Children ever born (CEB) per woman[p]	Children still living (CSL) per woman[p]	Ratio of CSL to CEB	Age-specific fertility rate[b]	Percent probability of dying (15–19)[c]	Percent using contraception[d]
Guatemala *(continued)*								
1980–85	u	u	u	u	u	121	u	u
1983	u	u	u	u	u	u	u	9
1985	414.8[e]	u	u	u	u	u	u	u
Guyana								
1975	u	u	u	u	u	u	u	15
1980	48.9	11.6	0.172	u	u	u	u	u
Haiti								
1977	274.9[e]	5.4[g]	u	u	u	u	u	17
1978	280.7[e]	5.5[g]	u	u	u	u	u	u
1979	285.7[e]	5.5[g]	u	u	u	u	u	u
1980	270.4[e]	5.5[g]	u	u	u	u	u	u
1981	275.6[e]	5.5[g]	u	u	u	u	u	u
1982	259.6[e]	6.5[g]	0.108	u	u	u	u	u
1980–85	u	u	u	u	u	112	u	u
1983	u	u	u	u	u	u	u	4
1984	262.4[e]	6.5[g]	u	u	u	u	u	u
1985	271.0[e]	u	u	u	u	u	u	u
Honduras								
1981	u	u	u	u	u	u	u	8
1980–85	u	u	u	u	u	129	u	u
1985	237.1[e]	u	u	u	u	u	u	u
Jamaica								
1975–76	u	u	u	u	u	u	u	31
1982	138.1	5.4[g,i]	0.207	u	u	u	u	u
1980–85	u	u	u	u	u	107	u	u
1983	u	u	u	u	u	u	u	34
Mexico								
1975	3159.7[e]	20.2[g]	u	u	u	u	u	u
1976	3290.1[e]	20.2[g]	u	u	u	u	u	u
1976–77	u	u	u	u	u	u	u	14
1977	3405.1[e]	20.2[g]	u	u	u	u	u	u
1978	3534.8[e]	20.2[g]	u	u	u	u	u	24
1979	3569.5[e]	20.2[g]	u	u	u	u	u	20
1980	3889.9	19.6	0.179	u	u	u	u	u
1980–85	u	u	u	u	u	76	u	u
1985	4445.8	u	u	u	u	u	u	u
Nicaragua								
1980–85	u	u	u	u	u	141	u	u
Panama								
1979–80	u	u	u	u	u	u	u	29
1980	100.6	18.0[g]	0.205	0.189	0.921	u	u	u
1980–85	u	u	u	u	u	100	u	u
1984	118.6	u	u	u	u	u	u	u
Paraguay								
1977	u	u	u	u	u	u	u	14
1979	u	u	u	u	u	u	u	19
1982	166.9	15.8[g]	0.167	0.148	0.884	u	u	u
1980–85	u	u	u	u	u	72	u	u
Peru								
1977–78	u	u	u	u	u	u	u	17
1980	698.2	16.1[g]	u	u	u	u	u	u
1981	936.7	13.7[g]	0.133	0.122	0.919	u	u	22
1980–85	u	u	u	u	u	85	u	u
1985	1045.8[e]	u	u	u	u	u	u	u

Table 28. Adolescents: Vital Statistics for Women 15–19 *(continued)*

Country and year	Number of women 15–19[a] (000s)	Percent currently married[a]	Children ever born (CEB) per woman[p]	Children still living (CSL) per woman[p]	Ratio of CSL to CEB	Age-specific fertility rate[b]	Percent probability of dying (15–19)[c]	Percent using contraception[d]
Puerto Rico								
1980	168.7	12.4[g]	u	u	u	u	u	u
1980–85	u	u	u	u	u	74	u	u
1985	166.0	u	u	u	u	u	u	u
Trinidad and Tobago								
1977	u	u	u	u	u	u	u	32
1980	39.8	11.3	u	u	u	u	u	u
1982	70.6	u	u	u	u	u	u	u
1980–85	u	u	u	u	u	64	u	u
Uruguay								
1974–76	u	u	u	u	u	u	0.30	u
1975	119.0[e]	12.8	u	u	u	u	u	u
1980	123.5[e]	u	u	u	u	u	u	u
1980–85	u	u	u	u	u	63	u	u
Venezuela								
1975–80	u	u	u	u	u	u	0.40	u
1977	u	u	u	u	u	u	u	29
1981	823.8	16.8[g]	0.219	0.213	0.974	u	u	u
1980–85	u	u	u	u	u	95	u	u
1986	933.6	u	u	u	u	u	u	u
MIDDLE EAST/NORTH AFRICA								
Algeria								
1982	u	u	u	u	u	u	0.89	u
1980–85	u	u	u	u	u	92	u	u
1984	1142.0[e]	u	u	u	u	u	u	u
Egypt								
1978	1420.0[h]	21.1	u	u	u	u	u	u
1980	u	u	u	u	u	u	u	4
1980 (rural)	u	u	u	u	u	u	u	2
1980–85	u	u	u	u	u	97	u	u
1983	2331.0[e]	u	u	u	u	u	u	u
Iran								
1976	1781.7	33.9	u	u	u	u	1.96	u
1980–85	u	u	u	u	u	76	u	u
1984	2120.8[e]	u	u	u	u	u	u	u
Iraq								
1977	522.0	31.5	u	u	u	u	u	u
1980–85	u	u	u	u	u	111	u	u
Jordan								
1976	u	u	u	u	u	u	u	9
1980–85	u	u	u	u	u	115	u	u
1983	u	u	u	u	u	u	u	4
Kuwait								
1975	41.8	28.7	u	u	u	u	u	u
1980	55.5	18.5	0.132	0.128	0.973	u	u	u
1980–85	u	u	u	u	u	108	u	u
1985	73.1	14.3	u	u	u	u	u	u
Lebanon								
1980–85	u	u	u	u	u	55	u	u
Morocco								
1979–80	u	u	u	u	u	u	u	10
1982	1134.2	16.9	u	u	u	u	u	u
1980–85	u	u	u	u	u	110	u	u
1983–84	u	u	u	u	u	u	u	11

Table 28. Adolescents: Vital Statistics for Women 15–19 *(continued)*

Country and year	Number of women 15–19[a] (000s)	Percent currently married[a]	Children ever born (CEB) per woman[p]	Children still living (CSL) per woman[p]	Ratio of CSL to CEB	Age-specific fertility rate[b]	Percent probability of dying (15–19)[c]	Percent using contra- ception[d]
Saudi Arabia								
1980–85	u	u	u	u	u	112	u	u
Syria								
1977	u	u	u	u	u	u	1.31	u
1978	u	u	u	u	u	u	u	9
1980–85	u	u	u	u	u	112	u	u
1986	499.0[e]	u	u	u	u	u	u	u
Tunisia								
1978	u	u	u	u	u	u	u	8
1980–85	u	u	u	u	u	32	u	u
1984	391.9[e]	u	u	u	u	u	u	u
Turkey								
1975	2155.1	21.2	u	u	u	u	u	u
1980	2404.4	20.8	u	u	u	u	u	u
1980–85	u	u	u	u	u	67	u	u
United Arab Emirates								
1975	14.8	55.0	u	u	u	u	u	u
Yemen, North								
1980–85	u	u	u	u	u	111	u	u
Yemen, South								
1980–85	u	u	u	u	u	111	u	u
ASIA								
Afghanistan								
1984	719.9[e]	u	u	u	u	u	u	u
1980–85	u	u	u	u	u	153	u	u
Bangladesh								
1974	u	u	u	u	u	u	2.70	u
1975–76	u	u	u	u	u	u	u	4
1979–80	u	u	u	u	u	u	u	6
1981	4017.4	65.4	u	u	u	u	1.21	u
1980–85	u	u	u	u	u	218	u	u
Bhutan								
1980–85	u	u	u	u	u	75	u	u
Burma								
1978	u	u	u	u	u	u	0.99	u
1980–85	u	u	u	u	u	65	u	u
1983	1891.0	15.9	0.094	0.086	0.916	u	u	u
China								
1982	61462.9	4.3	0.014	0.013	0.919	u	u	u
Hong Kong								
1976	255.6[l]	3.9	u	u	u	u	u	u
1981	271.3	3.4	0.020	u	u	u	u	u
1980–85	u	u	u	u	u	15	u	u
1986	216.4	2.0	u	u	u	u	u	u
India								
1981	30150.0	43.5	0.173	0.153	0.885	u	u	u
1980–85	u	u	u	u	u	56	u	u
1986	39385.0[e]	u	u	u	u	u	u	u
Indonesia								
1976	u	u	u	u	u	u	u	13
1980	7770.7	27.3	0.178	0.155	0.870	u	u	u
1980–85	u	u	u	u	u	87	u	u

222

Table 28. Adolescents: Vital Statistics for Women 15–19 *(continued)*

Country and year	Number of women 15–19[a] (000s)	Percent currently married[a]	Children ever born (CEB) per woman[p]	Children still living (CSL) per woman[p]	Ratio of CSL to CEB	Age-specific fertility rate[b]	Percent probability of dying (15–19)[c]	Percent using contra-ception[d]
Indonesia *(continued)*								
1983 (Jakarta)	u	u	u	u	u	u	u	25
1983 (Medan)	u	u	u	u	u	u	u	11
1983 (Semarang)	u	u	u	u	u	u	u	38
1983 (Surabaya)	u	u	u	u	u	u	u	18
1983 (Ujung Pandang)	u	u	u	u	u	u	u	8
1984	8400.9[e]	u	u	u	u	u	u	u
Kampuchea								
1980–85	u	u	u	u	u	57	u	u
Korea, Dem. People's Rep.								
1980–85	u	u	u	u	u	29	u	u
Korea, Republic of								
1970	u	u	u	u	u	u	0.71	u
1974	u	u	u	u	u	u	u	13
1975	2022.8	2.6	u	u	u	u	u	u
1978–79	u	u	u	u	u	u	0.43	u
1979	u	u	u	u	u	u	u	11
1980	2052.8	1.7	0.008	0.008	0.986	u	u	u
1980–85	u	u	u	u	u	8	u	u
1985	2071.6	0.9	u	u	u	u	u	u
1986	2180.4[e]	u	u	u	u	u	u	u
Laos								
1980–85	u	u	u	u	u	84	u	u
Malaysia								
1974	u	u	u	u	u	u	u	15
1978	u	u	u	u	u	u	0.36[m]	u
1979	u	u	u	u	u	u	0.37[m]	u
1980	631.5	8.2	0.058	u	u	u	u	u
1980–85	u	u	u	u	u	24	u	u
1984	688.5[e]	u	u	u	u	u	u	u
Mongolia								
1980–85	u	u	u	u	u	49	u	u
Nepal								
1976	u	u	u	u	u	u	u	u
1981	632.7	50.1	0.222	0.159	0.714	u	u	u
1980–85	u	u	u	u	u	104	u	u
1986	794.0[e]	u	u	u	u	u	u	u
Pakistan								
1976	2538.7	29.3	u	u	u	u	u	u
1976–78	u	u	u	u	u	u	1.31	u
1978	2509.9	23.6	u	u	u	u	u	u
1979	2518.8	21.6	u	u	u	u	u	u
1981	3619.5	29.1	u	u	u	u	u	u
1980–85	u	u	u	u	u	139	u	u
Papua New Guinea								
1980	135.7	16.7	0.107	0.099	0.933	u	u	u
1980–85	u	u	u	u	u	90	u	u
1985	178.5[e]	u	u	u	u	u	u	u
Philippines								
1975	2496.1[f]	12.1	u	u	u	u	u	u
1978	u	u	u	u	u	u	u	16
1980	2688.8	13.9	0.100	0.096	0.965	u	u	u
1980–85	u	u	u	u	u	33	u	u
1984	2956.7[e]	u	u	u	u	u	u	u

Table 28. Adolescents: Vital Statistics for Women 15–19 *(continued)*

Country and year	Number of women 15–19[a] (000s)	Percent currently married[a]	Children ever born (CEB) per woman[p]	Children still living (CSL) per woman[p]	Ratio of CSL to CEB	Age-specific fertility rate[b]	Percent probability of dying (15–19)[c]	Percent using contra-ception[d]
Singapore								
1970	u	u	u	u	u	u	0.26	u
1980	139.2	2.3	0.012	u	u	u	0.22	u
1980–85	u	u	u	u	u	10	u	u
1986	110.8[e]	u	u	u	u	u	u	u
Sri Lanka								
1975	u	u	u	u	u	u	u	13
1981	790.4	9.7	u	u	u	u	0.71	u
1982	u	u	u	u	u	u	u	28
1980–85	u	u	u	u	u	31	u	u
1986	845.0[e]	u	u	u	u	u	u	u
Thailand								
1975	u	u	u	u	u	u	u	18
1978	u	u	u	u	u	u	u	31
1980	2711.6	15.6	0.094	0.090	0.961	u	u	u
1981	u	u	u	u	u	u	u	29
1980–85	u	u	u	u	u	46	u	u
1985	2998.0[e]	u	u	u	u	u	u	u
Vietnam								
1980–85	u	u	u	u	u	36	u	u

u = unknown.

a. UN Statistical Office, DIESA, *Demographic Yearbook:* 1982 edition, Table 40, and 1987 edition, Table 29 (forthcoming).

b. UN Population Division (unpublished).

c. Life-table probability of death between exact ages 15.0 and 20.0, given in percentage terms. For example, in Botswana 1.24 percent of 15-year-olds die before age 20. Special tabulations from the UN Statistical Office, and *Demographic Yearbook,* 1985 edition, Table 35.

d. K. London, et al., "Fertility and Family Planning Surveys: An Update," *Population Reports,* series M, no. 8, 1985, Table 4. Base is married or cohabiting women.

e. UN Statistical Office: population estimates provided by countries.

f. De jure population.

g. Includes consensually married.

h. Includes 16–19-year-old Egyptian nationals.

i. Women of unknown marital status (5 percent) distributed proportionately across categories of marital status.

j. Includes urban and settled population only.

k. Urban Sudan.

l. Based on sample survey for Hong Kong.

m. Peninsular Malaysia only.

n. Includes 14–19-year-olds.

o. Excludes Indian jungle population.

p. UN Statistical Office, DIESA, *Demographic Yearbook,* 1986 edition, Tables 50 and 51.

Table 29. Health Manpower Coverage

Country	Year	Number of: Hospital beds	Physicians	Nurses	Midwives	Population per: Hospital bed	Physician	Nurse	Midwife
SUB-SAHARAN AFRICA									
Angola	1973	19666	383	3115	284	300	15404	1894	20774
Benin	1980	5064	204	1294	312	705	17500	2759	11442
Botswana	1980	u	111	574	714	u	7378	1427	1147
Burkina Faso	1981	u	127[b]	1927[b]	281[b]	u	55858	3681	25245
Burundi	1974	4489	81	590	89	857	45432	6237	41348
Cameroon	1979	20624	603	4320	2266	400	13681	1910	3641
Central African Republic	1980	3605	99	900	367	616	22434	2468	6052
Chad	1978	3373[a]	90[b]	933[b]	96[b]	1278	47889	4620	44896
Congo	1978	6876	274	1915	413	212	5328	762	3535
Côte d'Ivoire	1975	8346	321	2859	453	586	15234	1710	10795
Ethiopia	1980	11147	428	7547	u	2787	72582	4116	u
Gabon	1977	4046	207	u	u	129	2560	u	u
Gambia	1978	699	49	179	91	815	11632	3184	6263
Ghana	1981	17026	1665	17758	6728	665	7245	679	1793
Guinea	1981	u	100[b]	570[b]	329[b]	u	8100	1421	2462
Kenya	1978	24708	1466[c]	14296[c]	u	601	10136	1039	u
Lesotho	1977	2564	67	u	u	488	18657	u	u
Liberia	1977	u	u	u	u	u	21800	3100	6600
Madagascar	1981	u	901	3779	1423	u	9939	2370	6293
Malawi	1977	u	116	——1437——		u	47638	——3846——	
Mali	1980	u	264[b]	2054[b]	831[b]	u	26447	3399	8402
Mauritania	1977	545[a]	99	438	79	2569	14141	3196	17721
Mauritius	1982	u	u	u	u	300	1500	600	1700
Mozambique	1980	13087	309	2156	457[b]	800	33883	4856	22910
Niger	1978	3165	134	1080	2006	1577	37238	4620	2487
Nigeria	1980	61628	8037	37370	27983	1251	9591	2063	2755
Rwanda	1981	7882	1182	517[b]	616[b]	4210	28071	64178	53864
Senegal	1981	u	449[c]	2360	401	u	12942	2462	14491
Sierra Leone	1980	3930	190	——1758——		884	18284	——1976——	
Somalia	1980	u	299	1834	556	u	12191	1988	6556
Sudan	1981	17328	2169[b]	13693[b]	376[b]	1091	8714	1380	50268
Swaziland	1978	1717	75	131	731	294	7200	4122	739
Tanzania	1977	33714	960	5658	1400	464	16282	2763	11165
Togo	1980	3346	139	1575	559	739	19417	1714	4828
Uganda	1981	19782	611	——6778——		688	22291	——2009——	
Zaire	1979	79244	1900	14661	3043	323	13452	1743	8399
Zambia	1981	20638	821	3550	1620	289	7261	1679	3680
Zimbabwe	1980	21418	1148	5258	2351	344	6411	1400	3131
LATIN AMERICA/CARIBBEAN									
Argentina	1980	150010	u	u	u	188	u	u	u
Bolivia	1976	u	u	u	u	400	1800	2300	u
Brazil	1974	341322	62743	42985	u	300	1632	2382	u
Chile	1979	27306	5671[b]	24066[b]	1962[b]	400	1926	454	5567
Colombia	1977	41743	12720	19971	u	600	1969	1254	u
Costa Rica	1983	u	u	u	u	300	1100	300	u
Cuba	1979	39809[a]	13531	26457	u	245	722	369	u
Dominican Republic	1976	6914	1203	2254	u	700	4023	2147	u
Ecuador	1977	15117	4660	1225	u	500	1622	6170	u
El Salvador	1981	7375[a]	1793	1734[e]	u	661	2718	2810	u
Guatemala	1979	11750	819[b]	4345	u	600	8608	1623	u
Guyana	1979	4002	85[b]	881[b]	546[b]	205	9647	931	1502
Haiti	1979	3785	600[b]	1486[b]	2425[b]	1300	8200	3311	2029
Honduras	1979	5086	1141	5126	3791	700	3120	694	939
Jamaica	1979	7648[a]	759	3430[b]	485	282	2845	630	4452
Mexico	1976	u	u	u	u	900	1000	1000	u
Nicaragua	1980	5459	1212[b]	4687	u	500	2252	582	u

225

Table 29. Health Manpower Coverage *(continued)*

Country	Year	Number of:				Population per:			
		Hospital beds	Physicians	Nurses	Midwives	Hospital bed	Physician	Nurse	Midwife
LATIN AMERICA/CARIBBEAN *(continued)*									
Panama	1981	u	1913	1630	u	u	1045	1226	u
Paraguay	1979	4243	1700	2636	783	700	1747	1127	3793
Peru	1979	34579	11682	16696	2147	500	1480	1036	8053
Puerto Rico	1980	13958	4057	14392	199	264	907	256	18491
Trinidad and Tobago	1980	5848	786	2837	u	200	1488	412	u
Uruguay	1979	11559	5400	15200	1206	249	533	189	2387
Venezuela	1978	41386	14771	38061	u	317	888	345	u
MIDDLE EAST/NORTH AFRICA									
Egypt	1982	87685	58761	28113	9004[b]	509	760	1589	4960
Iran	1983	67734	15945	29486	2202	601	2551	1379	18472
Iraq	1981	u	7634	6082	2267	u	1772	2224	5967
Jordan	1982	4364	2662	2739	272	717	1175	1142	11499
Kuwait	1982	5754	2470	8579[b]	u	273	635	183	u
Lebanon	1979	u	5030	3681	614	u	260	355	2130
Libya	1982	16061[a]	5210[b]	9495[b]	1218[b]	201	619	340	2648
Morocco	1982	24913[a]	1308	22147	56	859	16355	966	382006
Saudi Arabia	1981	14451[a]	3576[b]	——6706[b]——		645	2606	——1390——	
Syria	1981	10308	4165	6557	1776	903	2236	1420	5244
Tunisia	1981	u	1800	6866	784	u	1800	472	4133
Turkey	1982	98382	30320	26784	13575	471	1527	1729	3411
Yemen, North	1981	u	896[b]	1665[b]	87[b]	u	6629	3567	68271
Yemen, South	1980	2770[a]	258	2250	329	713	7654	878	6002
ASIA									
Afghanistan	1982	4837	1160[b]	1054[b]	529[b]	3470	14471	15926	31732
Bangladesh	1981	19727	10065	3769	2239	4545	8908	23789	40044
Burma	1981	31510	7321	6978[b]	15543	1140	4940	5183	2327
China	1983	2109571	587564[d]	849652	75792	493	1769	1223	13714
Hong Kong	1982	22110	3626[c]	——17401[c]——		237	1443	——301——	
India	1981	1066164[a]	268712[c]	150339[c]	217981[c]	641	2545	4549	3137
Indonesia	1982	u	u	u	u	1500	10000	——4000——	
Kampuchea	1973	u	u	u	u	1000	15300	2000	5000
Korea, Dem. People's Rep.	1979	210000	40750[d]	u	u	83	429	u	u
Korea, Republic of	1982	63804	28365	16651[e]	5403	607	1366	2327	7171
Laos	1976	3232	156	1028	352	401	21667	3288	9602
Malaysia (Peninsular)	1982	32135	4234	27518	12412	370	u	u	u
Mongolia	1982	18901	4405[b]	7595[b]	963[b]	90	3984	2311	18224
Nepal	1980	2556	486	438[b]	1443[b]	5470	28767	31920	9689
Pakistan	1982	50335	29931[c]	10554[c]	9947[c]	1731	2911	8256	8759
Papua New Guinea	1980	12697	192	——3228——		243	16052	——955——	
Philippines	1981	93374	7373[b]	9644[b]	9470[b]	518	6713	5132	5226
Singapore	1981	9899	2219	7240	766	247	1101	337	3189
Sri Lanka	1982	43389[a]	2035[b]	7173[b]	3808[b]	350	7464	2118	3989
Thailand	1981	u	u	u	u	700	7100	2500	2700
Vietnam	1981	202259[a]	13517	44080	13752	272	4067	1247	3998

u = unknown.

a. Government establishments only.

b. Government employees only.

c. Number registered; not all are resident and working in the country.

d. Including dentists.

e. Incomplete data.

Table 30. Numbers of Infant and Child Deaths, 1987

Country	Ages 0–1	Ages 1–5	Ages 0–5	Country	Ages 0–1	Ages 1–5	Ages 0–5
SUB-SAHARAN AFRICA				**LATIN AMERICA/CARIBBEAN** *(continued)*			
Angola	59580	47840	107420	Haiti	28480	14850	43330
Benin	23400	17440	40840	Honduras	13520	7840	21360
Botswana	3670	1480	5150	Jamaica	1080	300	1380
Burkina Faso	49550	39570	89120	Mexico	128350	60080	188430
Burundi	26790	20440	47230	Nicaragua	9250	5070	14320
Cameroon	46540	32180	78720	Panama	1380	600	1980
Central African Republic	15050	11970	27020	Paraguay	5730	2730	8460
Chad	30310	24110	54420	Peru	60260	25340	85600
Congo	6080	3750	983	Puerto Rico	1120	150	1270
Côte d'Ivoire	46940	24880	71820	Trinidad and Tobago	610	90	700
Ethiopia	314380	255300	569680	Uruguay	1530	170	1700
Gabon	4740	3410	8150	Venezuela	20470	4550	25020
Ghana	60630	41090	101720				
Guinea	46910	37980	84890	**MIDDLE EAST/NORTH AFRICA**			
Kenya	86930	53120	140050	Algeria	70480	31430	101910
Lesotho	6580	2570	9150	Egypt	148760	73500	222260
Liberia	13930	10850	24780	Iran	205910	103920	309830
Madagascar	29370	16430	45800	Iraq	52210	20430	72640
Malawi	59860	52680	112540	Jordan	6560	1940	8500
Mali	69430	60390	129820	Kuwait	1460	220	1680
Mauritania	11560	9100	20660	Lebanon	3050	780	3830
Mauritius	500	130	630	Libya	14370	6840	21210
Mozambique	94100	76750	170850	Morocco	67360	32040	99400
Namibia	7890	5810	13700	Saudi Arabia	36450	14890	51340
Niger	45190	35820	81010	Syria	23040	7510	30550
Nigeria	533590	386220	919810	Tunisia	16770	6850	23620
Rwanda	41320	32180	73500	Turkey	117660	26320	143980
Senegal	41260	32750	74010	Yemen, North	42190	9140	51330
Sierra Leone	30660	26670	57330	Yemen, South	12510	8960	21470
Somalia	35700	28990	64690				
South Africa	91430	31750	123180	**ASIA**			
Sudan	109660	79660	189320	Afghanistan	160960	146010	306970
Tanzania	129040	93740	222780	Bangladesh	512110	335670	847780
Togo	14410	9920	24330	Bhutan	8080	4920	13000
Uganda	86470	62120	148590	Burma	72770	27720	100490
Zaire	141010	99280	240290	China	659830	247430	907260
Zambia	27910	17790	45700	Hong Kong	0720	160	880
Zimbabwe	31850	19460	51310	India	2537440	1409690	3947130
				Indonesia	412260	256270	668530
LATIN AMERICA/CARIBBEAN				Kampuchea	44270	24520	68790
Argentina	23580	4420	28000	Korea, Dem. People's Rep.	15410	4500	19910
Bolivia	31250	19600	50850	Korea, Republic of	21510	6270	27780
Brazil	261170	99490	360660	Laos	19810	10090	29900
Chile	5360	1070	6430	Malaysia	12590	4360	16950
Colombia	37760	18880	56640	Nepal	95320	58080	153400
Costa Rica	1400	310	1710	Pakistan	504150	291390	795540
Cuba	2760	550	3310	Papua New Guinea	8510	3160	11670
Dominican Republic	13760	4020	17780	Philippines	84000	54140	138140
Ecuador	21980	9070	31050	Singapore	400	90	490
El Salvador	13350	5880	19230	Sri Lanka	13780	4180	17960
Guatemala	20160	14690	34850	Thailand	53460	13710	67170

Table 31. Infant Mortality: Proportion[a] of Infants Dying Before Age One

Country	1955–1960	1960–1965	1965–1970	1970–1975	1975–1980	1980–1985	1985–1990	1990–1995	1995–2000
SUB-SAHARAN AFRICA									
Angola	215[b]	200	186	173	160	149	137	127	117
Benin	193	176	160	151	130	120	110	101	93
Botswana	122	115	110	95	82	76	67	58	50
Burkina Faso	232	207	183	162	157	150	139	128	116
Burundi	160	145	140	135	130	124	114	105	96
Cameroon	172	154	136	119	111	103	94	86	77
Central African Republic	188	178	160	148	145	142	132	122	112
Chad	200	189	179	166	154	143	132	122	112
Congo	154	131	110	90	85	81	73	65	57
Côte d'Ivoire	212	188	164	153	121	110	100	91	82
Ethiopia	180	170	162	155	155	155	149	138	127
Gabon	179	163	147	132	122	112	103	94	85
Ghana	137	127	118	110	103	98	90	81	73
Guinea	213	202	192	181	171	159	147	136	126
Kenya	130	118	108	98	88	80	72	64	57
Lesotho	152	145	140	130	123	111	100	89	79
Liberia	185	176	167	155	143	132	122	112	103
Madagascar	114	104	94	84	75	67	59	52	45
Malawi	209	204	197	191	177	163	150	136	127
Mali	211	208	206	203	191	180	169	160	149
Mauritania	193	176	166	157	149	137	127	117	107
Mauritius	79	61	67	55	38	28	23	20	17
Mozambique	175	173	170	168	165	153	141	'30	120
Namibia	159	150	142	134	126	116	106	97	89
Niger	196	186	176	166	157	146	135	124	114
Nigeria	194	185	172	148	124	114	105	96	87
Rwanda	150	142	140	140	140	132	122	112	103
Senegal	184	176	168	162	154	142	131	121	111
Sierra Leone	225	224	218	203	191	180	169	160	149
Somalia	180	170	162	155	155	155	149	138	127
South Africa	140	130	120	110	95	83	72	62	52
Sudan	175	165	156	145	131	118	106	94	83
Tanzania	150	143	135	130	125	115	106	97	88
Togo	193	170	141	121	111	102	93	85	77
Uganda	140	125	118	116	114	112	103	94	85
Zaire	151	146	137	127	117	107	98	90	81
Zambia	140	130	115	100	94	88	80	72	64
Zimbabwe	113	106	101	93	86	80	72	64	57
LATIN AMERICA/CARIBBEAN									
Argentina	62	60	56	49	41	36	32	29	26
Bolivia	170	164	157	151	138	124	110	93	74
Brazil	122	109	100	91	79	71	63	57	51
Chile	117	111	95	70	46	23	20	19	18
Colombia	102	84	74	65	55	50	46	42	39
Costa Rica	87	81	66	51	30	20	18	17	16
Cuba	68	56	49	36	23	17	15	13	11
Dominican Republic	132	117	105	94	84	75	65	57	49
Ecuador	129	119	107	95	82	70	63	57	52
El Salvador	154	131	112	97	82	70	59	48	40
Guatemala	131	119	108	95	82	70	59	48	40
Haiti	205	188	172	155	139	128	117	106	95
Honduras	152	136	123	110	95	82	69	57	46
Jamaica	71	54	45	36	25	21	18	16	14
Mexico	98	86	79	69	60	53	47	41	37
Nicaragua	148	131	115	100	93	76	62	50	41
Panama	75	63	52	43	32	26	23	21	19

Table 31. Infant Mortality: Proportion[a] of Infants Dying Before Age One (continued)

Country	1955–1960	1960–1965	1965–1970	1970–1975	1975–1980	1980–1985	1985–1990	1990–1995	1995–2000
LATIN AMERICA/CARIBBEAN (continued)									
Paraguay	91	81	67	53	49	45	42	39	36
Peru	148	136	126	110	105	99	88	76	66
Puerto Rico	51	45	33	25	20	17	15	13	11
Trinidad and Tobago	64	44	41	30	26	24	20	16	15
Uruguay	53	48	48	47	44	30	27	25	23
Venzuela	89	73	60	49	43	39	36	33	31
MIDDLE EAST/NORTH AFRICA									
Algeria	175	160	150	132	112	88	74	61	50
Egypt	183	175	170	150	120	100	85	71	56
Iran	175	163	150	129	120	115	107	96	84
Iraq	148	130	111	96	83	77	69	56	46
Jordan	145	125	102	82	65	54	44	36	30
Kuwait	101	77	55	43	34	23	20	17	15
Lebanon	73	62	52	48	48	48	39	32	26
Morocco	170	155	138	122	110	97	82	66	56
Libya	170	150	130	117	107	97	82	66	56
Oman	220	207	186	160	135	117	100	84	69
Saudi Arabia	180	160	140	120	100	85	71	58	48
Syria	145	125	107	88	70	59	46	39	33
Tunisia	163	155	138	120	102	85	71	59	48
Turkey	203	176	153	138	120	92	76	64	52
United Arab Emirates	160	130	85	57	46	36	32	27	23
Yemen, North	220	207	186	168	150	135	120	106	93
Yemen, South	220	207	186	168	150	135	120	106	93
ASIA									
Afghanistan	219	211	203	194	194	194	183	172	162
Bangladesh	162	150	140	140	137	128	119	108	96
Bhutan	191	182	164	153	147	139	128	118	109
Burma	166	140	110	85	75	70	63	56	49
China	179	121	81	61	41	39	32	27	23
Hong Kong	54	33	23	17	13	10	9	7	7
India	173	157	145	135	126	110	99	88	77
Indonesia	145	133	120	105	95	84	74	64	55
Kampuchea	152	140	130	181	263	160	130	116	102
Korea, Dem. People's Rep.	100	70	58	47	35	30	24	21	17
Korea, Republic of	100	70	58	47	35	30	24	21	17
Laos	160	150	147	145	135	122	110	97	85
Malaysia	82	63	50	42	34	30	26	22	19
Nepal	191	182	164	153	147	139	128	118	109
Pakistan	170	155	145	140	130	120	109	98	88
Papua New Guinea	175	155	130	105	85	74	62	51	42
Philippines	83	76	70	64	54	51	45	40	35
Singapore	41	30	24	19	13	10	9	8	7
Sri Lanka	76	65	61	56	48	39	33	28	24
Thailand	111	95	84	65	56	48	39	32	27
Vietnam	163	148	133	120	90	76	67	58	49

a. Deaths per 1000.

b. Of 1000 births, 215 infants die before age one.

Table 32. Child Mortality Between Ages One and Five: Proportion[a] of One-Year-Olds Dying Before Age Five

Country	1955–1960	1960–1965	1965–1970	1970–1975	1975–1980	1980–1985	1985–1990	1990–1995	1995–2000
SUB-SAHARAN AFRICA									
Angola	182[b]	168	155	143	131	120	110	100	89
Benin	161	146	131	123	103	93	82	73	63
Botswana	65	60	56	46	36	33	27	21	16
Burkina Faso	233	199	168	135	128	122	111	101	91
Burundi	131	118	113	108	102	97	87	76	67
Cameroon	142	125	109	92	83	74	65	57	49
Central African Republic	157	148	131	120	117	114	105	95	84
Chad	168	158	149	137	126	115	105	95	84
Congo	125	104	82	61	56	52	45	38	32
Côte d'Ivoire	162	138	114	103	73	61	53	46	40
Ethiopia	149	140	132	126	126	126	121	110	100
Gabon	148	133	120	105	95	84	74	65	56
Ghana	110	101	90	82	74	69	61	52	45
Guinea	181	170	160	151	142	130	119	109	99
Kenya	103	90	80	70	60	52	44	38	31
Lesotho	73	68	63	57	53	46	39	33	27
Liberia	154	146	138	126	116	105	95	84	74
Madagascar	87	75	65	56	47	40	33	27	21
Malawi	202	195	186	177	162	147	132	117	103
Mali	205	201	198	194	177	162	147	132	120
Mauritania	162	146	137	128	120	110	100	89	79
Mauritius	43	30	27	23	10	8	6	4	3
Mozambique	156	153	149	146	140	128	115	103	90
Namibia	130	122	114	106	99	88	78	68	60
Niger	165	155	146	137	128	118	107	97	87
Nigeria	163	154	142	120	97	87	76	67	59
Rwanda	124	114	113	113	113	105	95	84	74
Senegal	167	157	146	135	125	115	104	94	83
Sierra Leone	223	222	214	194	177	162	147	132	120
Somalia	149	140	132	126	126	126	121	110	100
South Africa	68	62	55	48	38	31	25	19	14
Sudan	155	140	127	117	104	90	77	65	55
Tanzania	122	115	108	103	98	87	77	68	59
Togo	162	140	113	94	83	73	64	56	48
Uganda	113	97	90	88	86	84	74	65	56
Zaire	123	118	110	100	89	79	69	61	52
Zambia	113	103	87	72	65	59	51	44	37
Zimbabwe	85	77	72	64	57	52	44	38	31
LATIN AMERICA/CARIBBEAN									
Argentina	18	14	13	10	7	7	6	5	5
Bolivia	144	133	121	109	96	83	69	54	38
Brazil	54	48	43	38	30	27	24	22	20
Chile	35	28	18	10	6	5	4	4	4
Colombia	64	55	49	40	30	26	23	19	17
Costa Rica	46	34	24	14	6	4	4	4	3
Cuba	31	22	12	9	5	3	3	1	1
Dominican Republic	95	76	59	43	29	21	19	16	14
Ecuador	71	63	54	45	37	28	26	23	21
El Salvador	80	67	33	45	35	30	26	22	19
Guatemala	127	113	96	75	61	51	43	35	29
Haiti	127	115	103	91	79	70	61	53	46
Honduras	112	96	82	69	58	48	40	33	27
Jamaica	30	23	18	12	7	6	5	4	3
Mexico	61	45	38	33	29	25	22	20	17
Nicaragua	87	76	66	56	52	42	34	27	22
Panama	41	37	32	27	16	12	10	10	9

Table 32. Child Mortality Between Ages One and Five: Proportion[a] of One-Year-Olds Dying Before Age Five

Country	1955–1960	1960–1965	1965–1970	1970–1975	1975–1980	1980–1985	1985–1990	1990–1995	1995–2000
LATIN AMERICA/CARIBBEAN *(continued)*									
Paraguay	55	49	41	31	27	23	20	17	15
Peru	115	97	84	63	57	49	37	26	20
Puerto Rico	16	10	6	3	3	2	2	1	1
Trinidad and Tobago	18	10	9	7	6	4	3	3	2
Uruguay	6	6	6	6	5	4	3	3	2
Venezuela	39	33	26	19	13	8	8	7	7
MIDDLE EAST/NORTH AFRICA									
Algeria	133	113	94	78	60	44	33	24	17
Egypt	155	139	133	106	75	54	42	32	22
Iran	106	97	87	69	64	60	54	46	38
Iraq	115	89	64	46	37	33	27	19	13
Jordan	110	82	53	36	25	18	13	9	7
Kuwait	52	33	19	13	8	4	3	3	2
Lebanon	31	23	18	15	15	15	10	7	5
Libya	145	112	86	71	59	50	39	29	21
Morocco	133	112	95	77	62	50	39	29	21
Oman	218	199	171	132	96	78	63	49	36
Saudi Arabia	162	131	103	76	51	38	29	21	14
Syria	110	82	59	40	28	21	15	10	8
Tunisia	122	107	84	68	53	40	29	21	15
Turkey	93	76	63	53	44	25	17	12	8
United Arab Emirates	131	89	38	20	14	10	7	5	4
Yemen, North	218	199	171	147	116	101	86	72	60
Yemen, South	218	199	171	147	116	101	86	72	60
ASIA									
Afghanistan	216	205	194	181	181	181	166	152	137
Bangladesh	134	117	103	103	98	87	78	68	58
Bhutan	140	132	115	103	98	89	78	68	58
Burma	99	80	57	38	32	28	24	19	15
China	77	47	36	23	17	16	12	9	7
Hong Kong	29	15	9	4	3	2	2	1	1
India	152	128	110	96	84	64	55	46	38
Indonesia	117	106	93	76	66	56	46	37	30
Kampuchea	89	80	72	109	168	95	72	60	50
Korea, Dem. People's Rep.	44	32	20	15	13	9	7	5	4
Korea, Republic of	44	32	20	15	13	9	7	5	4
Laos	95	87	86	84	76	66	56	47	38
Malaysia	42	31	24	20	13	11	9	7	5
Nepal	140	132	115	103	98	89	78	68	58
Pakistan	148	124	110	100	80	71	63	54	46
Papua New Guinea	106	91	72	53	39	31	23	17	12
Philippines	65	56	48	40	37	34	29	23	19
Singapore	17	12	8	5	3	3	2	2	1
Sri Lanka	52	38	27	24	19	14	10	8	6
Thailand	57	46	38	28	20	15	10	7	5
Vietnam	97	86	74	63	42	32	26	21	15

a. Deaths per 1000.

b. Of 1000 children at age one, 182 die before age five.

Table 33. Child Mortality through Age Five: Proportion[a] of Infants Dying before Age Five

Country	1955–1960	1960–1965	1965–1970	1970–1975	1975–1980	1980–1985	1985–1990	1990–1995	1995–2000
SUB-SAHARAN AFRICA									
Angola	358[b]	334	312	291	271	251	232	214	195
Benin	323	296	270	255	220	202	184	167	150
Botswana	179	168	160	136	115	106	92	78	65
Burkina Faso	411	365	320	275	265	254	235	217	198
Burundi	270	246	237	228	219	209	191	173	157
Cameroon	290	260	230	200	185	170	153	138	123
Central African Republic	315	300	270	250	245	240	223	205	186
Chad	334	318	302	281	261	241	223	205	186
Congo	260	222	184	145	137	129	115	101	87
Côte d'Ivoire	340	300	260	240	185	165	148	133	118
Ethiopia	302	286	273	262	262	262	252	233	215
Gabon	300	275	250	223	205	186	169	153	137
Ghana	232	215	197	183	169	161	145	129	115
Guinea	355	338	321	305	289	269	249	230	212
Kenya	219	197	179	161	143	128	113	99	86
Lesotho	214	203	194	180	169	152	135	119	104
Liberia	310	296	282	262	242	224	206	187	170
Madagascar	191	171	153	135	119	104	90	77	65
Malawi	368	359	347	334	310	287	263	239	217
Mali	372	367	363	358	335	312	291	271	251
Mauritania	323	296	281	266	251	232	214	195	178
Mauritius	119	89	93	77	48	36	28	24	20
Mozambique	304	300	294	289	282	262	241	219	199
Namibia	269	254	240	226	212	194	176	159	143
Niger	329	312	296	281	266	246	228	209	191
Nigeria	325	310	290	250	209	191	173	157	141
Rwanda	255	240	237	237	237	223	205	186	169
Senegal	320	305	290	275	259	240	222	204	186
Sierra Leone	398	396	385	358	335	312	291	271	251
Somalia	302	286	273	262	262	262	252	233	215
South Africa	199	184	168	153	129	112	96	80	65
Sudan	303	282	263	245	221	198	175	153	133
Tanzania	254	242	228	219	210	192	174	158	142
Togo	323	287	238	204	186	168	152	136	121
Uganda	237	210	197	194	190	186	169	153	137
Zaire	256	246	232	214	195	178	161	145	129
Zambia	237	219	192	164	153	142	127	113	99
Zimbabwe	188	175	165	151	137	128	113	99	86
LATIN AMERICA/CARIBBEAN									
Argentina	78	72	68	58	48	42	38	34	31
Bolivia	289	275	259	244	221	197	171	143	110
Brazil	169	152	139	125	107	96	86	77	69
Chile	148	136	112	79	52	28	24	23	22
Colombia	160	135	119	102	83	75	68	61	55
Costa Rica	130	112	88	64	35	24	22	21	20
Cuba	97	77	61	45	28	20	18	15	12
Dominican Republic	215	184	158	132	111	94	82	72	63
Ecuador	191	175	156	136	116	96	87	79	72
El Salvador	221	190	161	137	114	98	84	69	58
Guatemala	241	218	193	162	139	118	99	82	68
Haiti	306	281	257	232	207	189	170	153	137
Honduras	246	218	195	171	147	126	106	89	72
Jamaica	99	77	62	48	32	27	23	20	17
Mexico	153	127	113	100	87	77	68	60	53
Nicaragua	223	197	173	150	140	115	93	76	63
Panama	113	97	82	68	47	37	33	30	28

Table 33. Child Mortality through Age Five: Proportion[a] of Infants Dying before Age Five (continued)

Country	1955–1960	1960–1965	1965–1970	1970–1975	1975–1980	1980–1985	1985–1990	1990–1995	1995–2000
LATIN AMERICA/CARIBBEAN (continued)									
Paraguay	141	126	105	82	74	67	61	55	50
Peru	246	220	200	167	156	143	122	100	85
Puerto Rico	66	54	39	29	22	19	17	15	12
Trinidad and Tobago	81	53	50	37	32	28	23	20	17
Uruguay	59	53	54	52	49	34	30	27	25
Venezuela	125	103	84	67	56	47	43	40	37
MIDDLE EAST/NORTH AFRICA									
Algeria	285	255	230	200	165	128	105	84	66
Egypt	310	290	280	240	186	148	124	100	80
Iran	263	244	224	190	176	168	155	138	118
Iraq	246	207	168	138	117	107	94	74	59
Jordan	239	197	150	116	88	72	57	45	37
Kuwait	148	107	73	55	42	27	23	19	17
Lebanon	101	84	69	62	62	62	49	39	32
Libya	290	245	205	180	160	142	118	96	76
Morocco	280	250	220	190	165	142	118	96	76
Oman	390	365	325	271	218	186	157	129	103
Saudi Arabia	313	270	228	186	146	120	98	77	61
Syria	239	197	160	125	97	79	63	49	40
Tunisia	265	245	210	180	150	121	99	79	63
Turkey	277	239	206	184	159	115	92	75	60
United Arab Emirates	270	207	120	76	59	47	38	32	27
Yemen, North	390	365	325	290	249	223	196	171	148
Yemen, South	390	365	325	290	249	223	196	171	148
ASIA									
Afghanistan	368	372	357	340	340	340	318	298	277
Bangladesh	274	250	228	228	221	204	188	168	149
Bhutan	304	290	260	240	230	215	196	178	161
Burma	249	209	160	120	105	97	85	74	63
China	242	162	113	83	58	55	44	36	30
Hong Kong	82	47	32	21	16	12	10	9	8
India	299	265	239	218	199	167	148	130	112
Indonesia	245	225	201	173	155	135	117	99	83
Kampuchea	227	208	193	271	367	239	192	169	148
Korea, Dem. People's Rep.	140	99	76	61	48	39	31	26	21
Korea, Republic of	140	99	76	61	48	39	31	26	21
Laos	239	224	221	217	201	180	160	139	120
Malaysia	121	91	72	62	46	41	35	28	24
Nepal	304	290	260	240	230	215	196	178	161
Pakistan	293	260	239	226	200	182	165	147	130
Papua New Guinea	262	232	193	152	121	103	84	67	53
Philippines	142	128	114	101	89	83	72	62	53
Singapore	57	42	31	23	16	12	11	10	8
Sri Lanka	124	101	87	79	66	52	43	36	30
Thailand	162	136	118	91	75	61	49	39	32
Vietnam	244	221	197	175	128	105	91	77	64

a. Deaths per 1000.

b. Of 1000 births, 358 die before age five.

Table 34. Estimates of Maternal Mortality, by Region, ca. 1983

Region[a]	Maternal mortality rate (per 100,000 live births)	Live births (millions)	Maternal deaths (000s)	Lifetime chance of maternal death[b]
WORLD	390	128.3	500	**1 in 58**
DEVELOPED WORLD	30	18.2	5	**1 in 1389**
DEVELOPING WORLD	450	110.1	495	**1 in 44**
AFRICA	640	23.4	150	**1 in 21**
Northern	500	4.8	24	1 in 28
Eastern	660	7.0	46	1 in 19
Middle	690	2.6	18	1 in 20
Western	700	7.6	53	1 in 19
Southern	570	1.4	8	1 in 29
LATIN AMERICA/CARIBBEAN	270	12.6	34	**1 in 72**
Middle	240	3.7	9	1 in 72
Caribbean	220	0.9	2	1 in 140
Tropical South America	310	7.1	22	1 in 66
Temperate South America	110	0.9	1	1 in 244
ASIA	420	73.9	310	**1 in 54**
East	55	21.8	12	1 in 722
Southeastern	420	12.4	52	1 in 44
Southern	650	35.6	231	1 in 26
Western	340	4.1	14	1 in 34

a. Regions as defined in UNDIESA, *Demographic Indicators of Countries: Estimates and Projections as Assessed in 1980,* New York, 1982.

b. The lifetime risk of maternal death, R, may be expressed by the formula $R = 1 - (1-r)^{1.2TFR}$, where r is the maternal mortality rate expressed as a decimal, and the TFR (total fertility rate) is expressed as births per woman. The TFR is multiplied by 1.2 to allow for pregnancies not ending in live births. Thus, for example, the worldwide chance of maternal death is $1 - (1-0.00390)^{1.2(3.7)}$, which equals 0.0172, or 1 in 58, as shown in the first row. In effect, the formula calculates the chance of surviving all pregnancies and then subtracts this value from unity to obtain the chance of dying sometime during the series of pregnancies.

Table 35. Immunization Coverage as of 1984–87

Country	Newborns, 1986 (000s)	Infant mortality rate,[k] 1986	Surviving infants,[a] 1986 (000s)	Percentage immunized[b] BCG	DPT 3	Polio 3	Measles	Tetanus 2
SUB-SAHARAN AFRICA								
Angola[e]	424	137	366	25	6	u	26	9
Benin	205	137	177	27	17	16	23	u
Botswana	56	71	52	67	64	60	62	16
Burkina Faso	326	137	281	17	u	u	38	4
Burundi[f]	229	127	200	80	60	61	57	17
Cameroon	445	107	398	77	50	43	39	8
Central African Republic[f]	119	132	103	53	24	24	30	u
Chad[e]	227	132	197	u	1	u	u	u
Congo[f]	79	114	70	80	59	59	52	u
Côte d'Ivoire	461	112	409	u	u	u	u	u
Ethiopia	2212	132	1920	12	7	6	13	3
Gabon[f]	39	103	35	79	48	48	55	u
Gambia	32	179	26	92	77	55	83	24
Ghana[e]	658	90	599	31	19	17	1	7
Guinea	291	147	248	u	u	u	u	u
Kenya[f]	1166	72	1082	86	75	75	60	u
Lesotho[f]	66	101	59	91	82	80	73	82
Liberia[f]	110	103	99	33	11	12	36	6
Madagascar	461	59	434	10	30	30	10	10
Malawi	387	152	329	79	54	55	42	18
Mali[c]	427	137	369	19	u	u	u	1
Mauritania[f]	97	127	85	91	62	61	69	u
Mauritius	19	25	19	86	84	84	70	55
Mozambique	646	101	580	47	29	25	39	40
Namibia	72	106	64	u	u	u	u	u
Niger[c]	320	129	279	28	6	6	19	3
Nigeria	4958	105	4437	30	14	14	16	11
Rwanda[f]	325	100	293	92	87	86	78	u
Senegal	306	130	267	32	54	54	40	8
Sierra Leone[f]	174	186	141	45	12	9	21	45
Somalia	228	132	198	29	18	18	26	7
South Africa	1285	28	1249	u	u	u	u	u
Sudan	1017	106	909	23	14	14	11	6
Tanzania	1134	90	1032	84	65	65	68	32
Togo	138	103	124	u	u	u	u	u
Uganda	805	85	736	37	14	13	17	u
Zaire	1409	98	1271	57	37	34	40	50
Zambia	331	92	301	71	58	50	49	u
Zimbabwe[f]	408	61	384	87	66	61	53	30
LATIN AMERICA/CARIBBEAN								
Argentina	741	35	715	89	63	69	67[g]	u
Bolivia	291	110	259	24	33	30	21	u
Brazil	2650	61	2489	58	62	86	63	u
Chile	273	20	268	90	89	89	91[g]	u
Colombia	908	49	863	62	61	62	53	u
Costa Rica	87	19	86	85	75	75	81[g]	u
Cuba	184	17	181	98	91	88[h]	85	u
Dominican Republic	212	32	205	51	18	18	24	25
Ecuador	216	54	204	99	41	39	54	11
El Salvador[e]	147	35	142	50	54	54[h]	71	20
Guatemala[d]	314	71	292	30	21	21[h]	23	1
Guyana	23	22	23	98	75	77	40	u
Haiti	224	97	202	57	19	19	21	u
Honduras	175	69	163	65	59	58	53	10
Jamaica	56	24	54	51	60	58	64	u
Mexico	2637	33	2550	16	40	67	64[g]	u
Nicaragua	150	75	138	97	35	70	49	u
Panama	59	20	58	94	73	71	83	u
Paraguay[d]	136	44	130	99	54	97	46	6
Peru[d]	717	91	652	70	48	47	53	4

Table 35. Immunization Coverage as of 1984–87 *(continued)*

Country	Newborns, 1986 (000s)	Infant mortality rate,[k] 1986	Surviving infants,[a] 1986 (000s)	Percentage immunized[b]				
				BCG	DPT 3	Polio 3	Measles	Tetanus 2
LATIN AMERICA/CARIBBEAN *(continued)*								
Puerto Rico	68	16	67	u	u	u	u	u
Trinidad and Tobago	35	16	34	u	75	74	32	u
Uruguay[d]	54	30	52	92	63	58[h]	59[g]	11
Venezuela	558	26	544	92	49	59	56	u
MIDDLE EAST/NORTH AFRICA								
Algeria	898	93	815	89	69	69	67	u
Egypt	1837	70	1708	84	87	86	85	8
Iran	2196	88	2003	75	69	72	73	28
Iraq[f]	462	61	434	78	91	91	75	53
Jordan[f]	163	53	154	u	88	88	64	27
Kuwait[f]	61	18	60	4	90	90	5	2
Lebanon	80	39	77	u	30	30	30	u
Libya	138	46	132	77	62	62	50	12
Morocco	887	84	812	70	53	53	48	u
Oman[f]	60	108	54	95	77	77	78	70
Saudi Arabia[f]	502	86	459	66	75	76	67	u
Syria[f]	466	7	463	82	73	73	70	19
Tunisia	239	39	230	80	70	70	65	11
United Arab Emirates	41	12	40	88	72	72	66	u
Yemen, North	343	138	296	28	16	16	19	3
Yemen, South	111	124	97	12	6	5	6	5
ASIA								
Afghanistan	906	190	734	16	9	9	12	10
Bangladesh	3543	105	3172	5	5	4	3	5
Bhutan	56	132	48	32	16	16	14	4
Burma	1072	47	1021	32	20	4	3	21
China[f]	18740	33	18120	67	74[h]	84	83	u
Hong Kong	79	8	78	99	87	92	u	u
India	25860	106	23120	29	53[i]	45[i]	1	40
Indonesia	5347	76	4941	67	48	46	47	26
Kampuchea	340	130	296	u	u	u	u	u
Korea, Dem. People's Rep.	637	28	619	53	61	62	44	u
Korea, Republic of	964	25	940	47	76	80	88[g]	u
Laos[f]	172	110	153	10	5	5	4	6
Malaysia	492	24	481	100	59	58	20	24
Mongolia	73	43	69	52	81	86	10[j]	u
Nepal	710	132	616	67	38	34	66	13
Pakistan	4250	108	3791	68	55	55	40	28
Papua New Guinea	113	79	104	78	42	37	29	u
Philippines	1619	42	1551	72	55	55	53	49
Singapore	43	9	43	72	78	81	73[g]	u
Sri Lanka	400	30	388	76	77	77	47	44
Thailand	1110	42	1064	83	62	62	39	45
Vietnam	1890	76	1746	57	43	44	37	u

u = unknown.

a. Number of newborns surviving to age one, calculated as the product of the number of newborns and the complement of the infant mortality rate. For example, in Angola, 424 x (1–0.137) = 366; thus, 366,000 infants survive to age one.

b. Denominator for estimating coverage with BCG, DPT 3 (three-shot series), Polio 3 (three-shot series), and measles is the number of surviving infants. Denominator for estimating coverage with Tetanus 2 (two-shot series) is the number of newborns.

c. 1981 data.

d. 1982 data.

e. 1983 data.

f. Survey data.

g. Immunization given at, or later than, 12 months and up to 60 months.

h. Two doses only.

i. Less than 24 months of age

j. Policy is to immunize children 13–24 months of age.

k. Deaths before age one per 1000 births.

Table 36. Availability and Use of Oral Rehydration Solution

Country	Cost per ORS packet (U.S.$)			% of cases treated (1987)	Packets used per 100 episodes (1985)	% of population with access (1987)	Government promotion of home-mix ORS (1985)
	1984	1985	1987				
SUB-SAHARAN AFRICA							
Angola	u	u	u	u	17	u	u
Benin	u	u	u	u	12	u	u
Botswana	u	u	u	u	38	u	u
Burkina Faso	u	u	u	u	8	u	Yes
Burundi	u	u	0.00	u	26	u	u
Cameroon	u	u	u	u	1	u	u
Central African Republic	u	u	u	u	23	u	u
Chad	u	u	u	u	28	u	u
Congo	u	u	u	14	23	u	u
Côte d'Ivoire	u	0.22	0.32	u	17	u	Yes
Ethiopia[h]	u	0.15	0.10	u	38	40[f]	Yes
Gabon	u	u	u	u	27	u	u
Ghana	u	u	u	u	26	42	u
Guinea	u	u	0.17	u	2	u	u
Kenya	u	u	u	u	10	u	u
Lesotho	u	u	0.12	u	41	u	u
Liberia	u	u	0.25–0.50	u	5	u	u
Malawi	u	u	u	u	9	u	u
Mali	u	0.06	0.20–0.40	u	8	u	Yes
Mauritania	u	u	u	u	2	30[g]	No
Mauritius	u	u	0.00	u	12	u	u
Mozambique	u	u	u	u	10	u	u
Niger	u	0.13[d]	u	36	2	u	u
Nigeria	u	u	u	u	2	u	Yes
Rwanda	u	0.02	0.03	38	24	u	No
Senegal	u	u	0.00	u	10	u	u
Sierra Leone	u	u	0.00	10	57	u	u
Somalia	u	0.00	0.00	5[a]	27	u	Yes
Sudan	u	0.00	0.08	25–30	87	u	Yes
Tanzania	u	u	0.08	u	36	u	u
Togo	u	u	0.00	27	21	39	u
Uganda	u	u	u	u	21	u	u
Zaire	u	u	u	u	4	u	u
Zambia	36–50[d]	0.00	u	u	42	u	Yes
Zimbabwe	u	u	u	u	4	u	u
LATIN AMERICA/CARIBBEAN							
Argentina	u	u	u	u	13	u	u
Bolivia	u	u	0.10	u	97	25	u
Brazil	u	0.00	u	5–10	28	u	Yes
Chile	u	u	u	u	3	u	u
Colombia	u	u	0.08	42	53	100	u
Costa Rica	u	u	u	u	67	u	u
Dominican Republic	u	u	u	u	152	u	u
Ecuador	u	u	u	21[c]	34	u	No
El Salvador	u	u	u	30	64	u	u
Guatemala	u	u	0.07	u	11	u	u
Guyana	u	u	0.00	u	14	u	u
Haiti	u	u	0.15	30	7	u	u
Honduras	u	u	u	40[c]	120	79	No
Jamaica	u	u	u	u	u	91	u
Mexico	u	u	u	u	18	u	u
Nicaragua	u	u	0.01	85	92	u	u
Panama	u	u	0.06	u	18	u	u
Paraguay	u	u	u	u	10	34	u
Peru	0.15	0.20	0.12	30	15	54	Yes

237

Table 36. Availability and Use of Oral Rehydration Solution *(continued)*

Country	Cost per ORS packet (U.S.$)			% of cases treated (1987)	Packets used per 100 episodes (1985)	% of population with access (1987)	Government promotion of home-mix ORS (1985)
	1984	1985	1987				
LATIN AMERICA/CARIBBEAN *(continued)*							
Trinidad and Tobago	u	u	u	u	18	u	u
Uruguay	u	u	u	u	21	u	u
Venezuela	u	u	u	u	58	u	u
MIDDLE EAST/NORTH AFRICA							
Algeria	u	u	u	u	22	u	u
Egypt	u	u	u	i	21	100	No
Iran	u	u	u	u	11	u	u
Iraq	u	u	u	u	39	u	No
Jordan	u	u	u	u	61	95	No
Lebanon	u	u	u	u	2	u	u
Morocco	0.14	u	0.22^d	24	18	40	u
Syria	u	0.50^d	0.20	60–70^e	6	u	No
Tunisia	u	u	u	u	106	u	u
Turkey	0.00	u	0.15	u	3	25	u
Yemen, North	0.60	0.00	0.00	u	20	u	No
Yemen, South	u	u	0.00	u	105	u	Yes
Rural	u	u	u	24	u	u	u
Urban	u	u	u	50	u	u	u
ASIA							
Afghanistan	u	0.00	u	b	37	u	Yes
Bangladesh	0.15	0.06	0.13	u	18	80	Yes
Bhutan	u	u	0.00	70	21	u	u
Burma	0.03	0.25^d	0.45^d	u	84	u	Yes
Rangoon	u	u	u	69	u	u	u
Hong Kong	u	u	u	u	u	100	u
India	0.18–0.50	0.20	0.20	u	5	u	Yes
Indonesia	u	0.35–1.80	0.12–0.16	52^c	22	u	Yes
Rural	u	u	u	26	u	u	u
Urban	u	u	u	33	u	u	u
Kampuchea	u	0.05–0.50^d	0.06	u	91	u	No
Phnom Penh	u	u	u	61	u	u	u
Korea, Republic of	u	u	u	u	u	100	u
Laos	u	u	u	u	34	u	u
Malaysia (Peninsular)	u	u	0.60	u	19	u	u
Mongolia	u	u	u	u	20	u	u
Nepal	0.07	0.05	0.05	14	14	u	Yes
Pakistan	u	u	u	u	28	u	u
Philippines	u	u	0.00	16	19	u	u
Singapore	u	u	0.24	10	u	u	u
Sri Lanka	u	u	u	u	59	u	u
Thailand	u	u	u	u	34	u	u
Vietnam	u	u	u	u	10	u	u

u = unknown.

a. Use varies widely by region.

b. In Kabul, approximately 80 percent of all mothers use ORS.

c. Percentage of children, not cases, treated.

d. ORS is also available free of charge through government facilities.

e. In some areas.

f. Percentage of children with access.

g. All who have access to basic health coverage (30 percent of the population) are thought to have access to ORS.

h. Different respondents and sources of information are contradictory.

i. Forty percent of all women know about and use ORS; 25 percent know about it but have not used it.

Table 37. Percentage of Births Attended by Trained Health Personnel, 1984

Country	Percentage	Country	Percentage
SUB-SAHARAN AFRICA		**LATIN AMERICA/CARIBBEAN** (*continued*)	
Angola	15	Peru	44
Benin	34	Trinidad and Tobago	90
Botswana	52[a]	Venezuela	82
Burundi	12		
Ethiopia	58	**MIDDLE EAST/NORTH AFRICA**	
Ghana	73	Egypt	46
Lesotho	28	Iraq	60
Liberia	89	Jordan	75
Madagascar	62	Kuwait	99
Malawi	59	Lebanon	45
Mauritania	23	Libya	76
Mauritius	84	Oman	60
Mozambique	28	Saudi Arabia	78
Niger	47	Syria	37
Sierra Leone	25	Tunisia	60
Somalia	2	Turkey	78[b]
Sudan	20	United Arab Emirates	96
Tanzania	74	Yemen, North	12
Zimbabwe	69	Yemen, South	10
LATIN AMERICA/CARIBBEAN		**ASIA**	
Brazil	73	Bhutan	3
Chile	95	Burma	97
Colombia	51	India	33
Costa Rica	93	Indonesia	43
Dominican Republic	98	Korea, Dem. People's Rep.	99
Ecuador	27	Malaysia (Peninsular)	82
El Salvador	35	Nepal	10
Guyana	93	Pakistan	24
Haiti	20	Papua New Guinea	34
Honduras	50	Singapore	100
Jamaica	89	Sri Lanka	87
Panama	83	Thailand	33
Paraguay	22	Vietnam	99

a. 1986 data.

b. 1983 data.

Table 38. Prevalence and Duration of Breast-Feeding

Country and area[a]	Year	Sample Type	Sample Size[cc]	Ever	At 3 months	At 6 months	At 12 months	Median duration of breast-feeding (in months)
SUB-SAHARAN AFRICA								
Benin								
National sample: WFS	1981–82	u	220	98	90	90	76	18
National sample: WFS	1981–82	Rural	158	97	89	90	75	19
Botswana								
National sample	1984	u	1494	99	96	93	73	19
National sample	1984	Urban	281	99	96	91	69	18
National sample	1984	Rural	1213	99	96	93	74	20
Cameroon								
National sample	1977–78	u	2371	99	99[b]	u	98[c]	u
National sample	1977–78	Rural	1641	99	99[b]	99[d]	99[c]	u
National sample: WFS	1978	u	377	98	92	90	77	17
National sample: WFS	1978	Rural	305	99	91	91	77	18
Côte d'Ivoire								
National sample: WFS	1980–81	u	311	98	87	84	78	18
National sample: WFS	1980–81	Rural	192	98	89	82	82	20
Ethiopia								
Site unspecified	1975–76	Urban[e]	292	91	59	59	35	u
Site unspecified	1975–76	Urban[f]	591	97	87	81	76	u
Site unspecified	1975–76	Rural	594	99	99	99	98	u
Addis Ababa, others	1981	Urban[e]	600	92	u	83	u	u
Addis Ababa, others	1981	Urban[f]	507	96	u	94	u	u
Kembata, others	1981	Rural	1930	99	u	99	u	u
Ghana								
National sample	1962	u	2463	99	99	94	67	16
National sample: WFS	1979–80	u	270	98	91	90	72	17
National sample: WFS	1979–80	Rural	189	98	91	93	76	18
Kenya								
National sample: WFS	1977–78	u	463	98	86	82	67	u
National sample: WFS	1977–78	Rural	413	98	86	84	68	u
Lesotho								
National sample	1976	Urban	222	u	90	87	75	19
National sample	1976	Rural	1007	99	99	98	90	22
National sample: WFS	1977	u	181	96	93	89	76	u
National sample: WFS	1977	Rural	169	97	94	89	77	u
Liberia								
National sample	1976	u	1939	u	u	97	89	u
Mali								
Bamako[g]	1979–80	Urban	3240	98	96[b]	u	82[h]	u
Mauritania								
National sample: WFS	1981	u	202	98	91	86	67	17
National sample: WFS	1981	Rural	118	98	90	86	66	18
Mauritius								
National sample	1983	Urban	710	88[i]	59	34	26	u
National sample	1983	Rural	1582	94[i]	81	65	46	u
National sample	1983	u	2292	92[d]	79[d]	55[d]	40[d]	u
Nigeria								
Ibadan	1975–76	Urban[e]	235	99	96	32	u	6
Ibadan	1975–76	Urban[j]	577	99	99	91	22	11
Ibadan	1975–76	Urban[f]	636	99	99	97	97	u
North Ibadan	1975–76	Rural	668	99	99	99	97	u
Benin City	1980	u	1228	99	u	92	43	u

240

Table 38. Prevalence and Duration of Breast-Feeding (continued)

Country and area[a]	Year	Sample Type	Sample Size[ee]	Ever	At 3 months	At 6 months	At 12 months	Median duration of breast-feeding (in months)
Rwanda								
Site unspecified	1976	u	324	u	94[k]	85[l]	75	21[d]
Senegal								
National sample	1978	u	2392	98	98	97	88	20[m]
National sample: WFS	1978	u	207	98	94	94	82	u
National sample	1978	Rural	140	99	95	95	84	u
South Africa								
Cape Town	1978	u	126	81[i]	40[n]	u	u	u
Port Elizabeth	1978	Urban[p]	1000	30[o]	11	u	u	u
Port Elizabeth	1979	Urban[j]	1000	42[o]	23	12	u	u
Port Elizabeth	1979	q	532	68[o]	39	19	u	u
Pretoria	1980	p	2087	71[r]	21	u	u	u
Sudan								
North Sudan: WFS	1978–79	u	186	u	91	86	72	16
North Sudan: WFS	1978–79	Rural	138	98	93	86	75	17
Tanzania								
Lindi	1977	Rural	419	99[d]	99	99	99	u
Morogoro	1977	Rural	882	99[d]	99	99	97	u
Mwanza	1977	Rural	478	99[d]	u	97	89	u
Ruvuma	1977	Rural	301	99[d]	u	98	96	u
Dar es Salaam[g]	1979	Urban[s]	565	90[d]	58	37	u	u
Kilimanjaro	1979	Rural	150	99[d]	u	99	85	u
Togo								
National sample	1976–77	u	5435	99[d]	u	99[d]	90[d]	23[d]
Zaire								
Kinshasa	1974	Urban	2039	99	98	94	58	13
Kinshasa	1979	f	1149	99	96	u	90	u
Kinshasa	1980	Urban[f]	1989	99[d]	98	98[d]	91[d]	u
Matadi, bas Zaire	1981	Urban	948	99[d]	u	99[t]	95[v]	18
Songololo, bas Zaire	1981	Rural	923	99	u	99[t]	99[v]	21
Zimbabwe								
National sample	1984	u	u	u	98	96	84	19
LATIN AMERICA/CARIBBEAN								
Argentina								
Site unspecified	1981–82	Urban[f]	1027	94	66	36	14	u
Bolivia								
Montero	1977	Rural	887	96	93	91	45	12
Brazil								
Site unspecified	1981–82	Urban[f]	2542	91[i]	56	31	21	u
National sample: DHS	1986	u	1960	u	66[w]	58[x]	34[y]	56
Amazonas	1982	u	1285	u	u	u	u	6
Bahia	1980	u	748	86	u	u	u	8
Bahia	1980	Urban	465	84	u	u	u	7
Bahia (Greater Salvador)	1980	Urban	271	87	u	u	u	6
Greater Recife	1981	u	300	88	31	12	u	2
Northeast states	1980	u	2654	79	u	u	u	7[m]
Northeast states	1980	Urban	1443	77	u	u	u	6[m]
Northeast states	1980	Rural	1211	81	u	u	u	7[m]
Paraíba	1980	u	629	74	u	u	u	5[m]
Paraná	1981	u	967	u	u	u	u	10[m]
Pernambuco	1980	u	614	68	u	u	u	5[m]
Pernambuco	1983	Rural	225	71	45	23	u	u
Piauí	1982	u	1893	u	u	u	u	10[m]
Piauí	1982	Urban	u	u	u	u	u	9[m]
Piauí	1982	Rural	u	u	u	u	u	11[m]
Rio Grande do Sul	1974	Urban[f]	1100	76	u	u	u	u

Table 38. Prevalence and Duration of Breast-Feeding (continued)

Country and area[a]	Year	Sample Type	Sample Size[cc]	Percentage breast-feeding Ever	At 3 months	At 6 months	At 12 months	Median duration of breast-feeding (in months)
Brazil (continued)								
Rio Grande do Sul (Pelotas)	1984	Urban	5163	92	54	30	16	3
Santa Catarina	1981	u	706	u	u	u	u	8[m]
São Paulo	1978	u	1736	u	u	u	u	5[m]
São Paulo	1984–85	u	1003	93	58	33	19	4
Chile								
15 rural communities	1969–70	Rural	1627	86[i]	71	53	u	u
Site unspecified	1981–82	Urban[f]	528	96	81	48	24	u
Arica	1977–79	u	2820	88	u	u	32[h]	u
Santiago Province	1975–76	Urban[e]	295	93	56	28	u	4
Santiago Province	1975–76	Urban[f]	296	92	80	39	20	5
Santiago Province	1975–76	Rural	443	95	76	46	40	6
Valdivia	1977–79	u	1970	89	u	u	22[h]	u
Colombia								
National sample: WFS	1976	u	174	90	70	54	39	7
Site unspecified	1981–82	Urban[f]	504	88	59	42	43	u
Costa Rica								
National sample: WFS	1976	u	129	74	35	36	u	2
National sample: CPS	1981	u	4580	90[i]	61	38	22	7
Dominican Republic								
National sample: WFS	1975	u	125	89	70	56	27	7
Ecuador								
National sample: WFS	1979–80	u	260	93	86	74	48	12
National sample: WFS	1979–80	Rural	156	95	95	84	57	14
Site unspecified	1981–82	Urban[f]	522	97	98	84	68	u
El Salvador								
National sample	1977–79	u	u	88[i]	u	75	53	13[m]
San Salvador	1977–79	Urban	u	67[i]	u	35	11	4[m]
Other urban	1977–79	Urban	u	89[i]	u	74	49	12
Rural	1977–79	Rural	u	90[i]	u	80	61	15
National sample: DHS	1985	u	1845	u	85[z]	77[aa]	55[bb]	15[m]
Guatemala								
National sample	1978	u	2684	90[i]	u	84	74	24
Sample survey: CPS	1983	u	u	u	u	u	u	18
Guyana								
National sample: WFS	1975	u	173	88	62	38	22	5
National sample: WFS	1975	Rural	116	89	65	40	30	5
Haiti								
National sample: WFS	1977	u	114	97	93	85	72	15
National sample: WFS	1977	Rural	85	98	93	92	80	19
Honduras								
National sample: CPS	1983–84	u	1746	u	u	u	u	9
Jamaica								
National sample: WFS	1975–76	u	119	94	74	50	24	6
National sample	1982	Urban[j]	302	67[i]	96	48	25	u
National sample	1982	Urban[f]	292	99[i]	99	92	46	u
National sample	1982	Rural	1414	97[i]	94	86	47	u
National sample	1982	u	u	96[i]	95	82	43	12[m]
Mexico								
National sample: WFS	1976–77	u	393	80	62	52	39	7
National sample: WFS	1976–77	Urban	115	74	50	44	22	3
National sample: WFS	1976–77	Rural	187	87	73	68	56	13
National sample	1979	u	5998	78	62	52	36	u
National sample	1979	Urban	u	72	u	u	u	u

Table 38. Prevalence and Duration of Breast-Feeding *(continued)*

Country and area[a]	Year	Sample Type	Sample Size[cc]	Ever	At 3 months	At 6 months	At 12 months	Median duration of breast-feeding (in months)
Mexico *(continued)*								
National sample	1979	Rural	u	86	u	u	u	u
Site unspecified	1981–82	Urban[f]	859	87	78	53	42	u
Panama								
National sample: WFS	1975–76	u	139	79	52	43	30	4
National sample	1980	u	3332	85	62	53	55	u
National sample	1980	Urban	960	73	36	25	18	u
National sample	1980	Rural	2372	89	73	65	55	u
Paraguay								
National sample: WFS	1979	u	u	92	80	77	49	12
National sample: WFS	1979	Urban	u	94	88	80	42	11
National sample: WFS	1979	Rural	2522	95	84	81	43	u
Peru								
National sample: WFS	1977–78	u	334	93	81	71	54	13
National sample: WFS	1977–78	Urban	134	92	83	68	52	12
National sample: WFS	1977–78	Rural	129	97	92	84	69	18
Trinidad and Tobago								
National sample: WFS	1977	u	116	80	68	53	25	6
Venezuela								
National sample: WFS	1977	u	148	82	50	40	30	3
MIDDLE EAST/NORTH AFRICA								
Algeria								
Algiers	1974–75	Urban	1461	u	73	55	41	11
Wilaya d'Algier	1974–75	Rural	498	u	90	87	80	18
Egypt								
Cairo[g]	1977–78	Urban	2893	89	81	73	42	11
National sample: WFS	1980	u	463	95	89	82	66	17
Cairo: WFS	1980	Urban	93	92	85	74	55	13
National sample: WFS	1980	Rural	285	97	92	87	71	20
National sample: CPS	1984	u	10013	92	90	87	81	17
Iran								
Teheran	1977–78	u	14392	83	67[b]	u	54[h]	u
Jordan								
National sample: WFS	1976	u	276	92	84	64	48	9
National sample: WFS	1976	Urban	97	92	81	62	49	8
National sample: WFS	1976	Rural	96	93	86	74	54	13
National sample	1980	u	3800	93	u	u	u	14
Kuwait								
National sample	1978–79	u	966	75	47	32	12	u
Morocco								
National sample: WFS	1980	u	224	92	83	75	62	16
National sample: WFS	1980	Rural	154	94	87	83	74	17
Saudi Arabia								
Site unspecified	1982	u	u	78	u	u	u	u
Syria								
National sample: WFS	1978	u	333	96	88	72	41	9
National sample: WFS	1978	Urban	108	94	84	70	46	9
National sample: WFS	1978	Rural	186	97	93	72	41	10
Tunisia								
National sample: WFS	1978	u	245	96	83	74	52	14
National sample: WFS	1978	Rural	143	97	90	81	62	18

Table 38. Prevalence and Duration of Breast-Feeding (continued)

Country and area[a]	Year	Sample Type	Sample Size[cc]	Ever	At 3 months	At 6 months	At 12 months	Median duration of breast-feeding (in months)
Turkey								
National sample	1974	u	5370	90	83	53	26	u
National sample: DHS	1983	u	5712	92	u	u	u	14[m]
Yemen, North								
National sample: WFS	1979	u	175	93	73	67	29	8
National sample: WFS	1979	Rural	155	93	74	69	32	9
ASIA								
Afghanistan								
Greater Kabul	1973–74	Urban	8120	u	u	u	u	18[m]
Kabul	1983	u	535	99	u	u	u	u
Bangladesh								
National sample: WFS	1975–76	u	325	98	91	86	82	31
National sample: WFS	1975–76	Rural	298	98	91	86	82	31
Site unspecified	1978	Rural	910	99	99	97	97	27[m]
China								
Site unspecified	1983	Urban	62167	u	43[cc]	34	u	u
Site unspecified	1985	Rural	33411	u	70[cc]	60	u	u
Hong Kong								
Site unspecified	1980	u	877	13	u	u	u	u
India								
Hyderabad	1975–76	Urban[e]	863	96	84	49	33	u
Hyderabad	1975–76	Urban[j]	994	96	78	72	58	15
Hyderabad	1975–76	Urban[f]	980	99	95	88	93	u
Indonesia								
National sample: WFS	1976	u	382	97	90	86	82	22
National sample: WFS	1976	Rural	217	98	91	88	87	24
Jakarta: CPS	1983	u	u	94	89	86	79	20
Medan: CPS	1983	u	u	92	91	87	73	15
Semarang: CPS	1983	u	u	90	91	89	81	25
Surabaya: CPS	1983	u	u	92	86	82	73	18
Ujang Pandang: CPS	1983	u	u	94	93	92	84	23
Korea								
National sample: WFS	1974	u	244	93	86	86	64	17
National sample: WFS	1974	Rural	100	96	87	92	73	19
KIFP survey	1978	u	1040	76	58	40	27	u
Malaysia (Peninsular)								
Site unspecified	1973–74	u	8755	64	u	u	u	u
Site unspecified	1973–74	Urban	3807	47	50	35	u	3[m]
Site unspecified	1973–74	Rural	4948	78	67	52	u	6[m]
National sample: WFS	1974	u	307	73	47	34	19	3
National sample: WFS	1974	Rural	218	79	54	40	22	4
Nepal								
National sample: WFS	1976	u	298	98	92	92	82	24
National sample: WFS	1976	Rural	286	98	92	92	92	24
Pakistan								
National sample: WFS	1975	u	275	95	90	86	78	19
National sample: WFS	1975	Rural	201	96	92	88	83	20
NWFP	1979–80	u	466	94	u	u	u	15[m]
National sample	1979–80	u	4405	94	u	u	u	15[m]
National sample	1979–80	Urban	1196	92	u	u	u	12[m]
National sample	1979–80	Rural	3209	95	u	u	u	16[m]
National sample	1980–81	u	1250	97	u	91	81	u
National sample: IFWP	1981	u	u	99	u	78	u	u
National sample: DDFP	1984	u	u	u	u	92	70	u

244

Table 38. Prevalence and Duration of Breast-Feeding *(continued)*

Country and area[a]	Year	Sample Type	Sample Size[ee]	Percentage breast-feeding Ever	At 3 months	At 6 months	At 12 months	Median duration of breast-feeding (in months)
Philippines								
National sample: WFS	1978	u	545	86	79	70	53	13
National sample: WFS	1978	Urban	95	77	67	54	42	9
National sample: WFS	1978	Rural	395	91	84	80	61	14
Singapore								
Hospital	1985	Urban[e]	202	60[d]	u	u	u	u
Hospital	1983	Urban[f]	310	36[d]	u	u	u	u
Sri Lanka								
National sample: WFS	1975	u	295	95	83	88	73	21
National sample: WFS	1975	Rural	243	95	84	89	75	22
National sample	1982	u	2729	99	95	81	68	u
National sample	1982	Urban[dd]	912	92	95	79	65	u
National sample	1982	Urban	910	98	93	73	59	u
National sample	1982	Rural	907	99	96	89	84	u
CPS survey	1982	u	u	99	u	u	u	23[m]
CPS survey	1982	Urban	u	99	u	u	u	23[m]
CPS survey	1982	Rural	u	99	u	u	u	25[m]
National sample: DHS	1987	u	2360	u	94	92	81	23
Thailand								
National sample: WFS	1975	u	179	92	82	68	67	19
National sample: WFS	1975	Rural	157	94	82	81	74	21
National sample: CPS	1981	u	u	91	82	76	66	17[m]
National sample: CPS	1981	Urban	u	83	57	45	34	5
National sample: CPS	1981	Rural	u	93	88	82	73	19
National sample: CPS	1984	u	u	94	83	79	68	18[m]
National sample: CPS	1984	Urban	u	88	56	46	29	4[m]
National sample: CPS	1984	Rural	u	95	90	86	77	18[m]

u = unknown.

a. World Fertility Surveys, Contraceptive Prevalence Surveys, and Demographic and Health Surveys are designated by WFS, CPS, and DHS, respectively.

b. At 3–5 months.

c. At 6–11 months.

d. Estimate.

e. Upper socioeconomic group.

f. Low socioeconomic group.

g. Clinic, dispensary.

h. At 9–11 months.

i. At 1 month.

j. Middle socioeconomic group.

k. At 0–5 months.

l. At 6–11 months.

m. "Average" duration.

n. At 3 to 4.5 months.

o. At 2 weeks.

p. White population.

q. Black population.

r. At hospital discharge.

s. Indian Ishmaeli.

t. At 6 months or less.

v. At 7–12 months.

w. At 2–3 months.

x. At 4–5 months.

y. At 10–11 months.

z. At 3–4 months.

aa. At 5–6 months.

bb. At 11–12 months.

cc. At 4 months.

dd. Midsize city.

ee. Some sample sizes appear small; this is typically because attention was focused upon a subgroup, such as women whose last birth was within a year of the survey.

Table 39. Percentage of Population with Access to Safe Drinking Water and Sanitation, Early 1980s

Country	Safe drinking water			Sanitation services		
	Total	Urban	Rural	Total	Urban	Rural
SUB-SAHARAN AFRICA						
Angola	31	90	12	18	29	15
Benin	19	26	15	21	48	4
Botswana	57	98	47	36	90	23
Burkina Faso	31	27	31	8	38	5
Burundi	24	90	22	52	50	52
Congo	21	42	7	u	u	u
Ghana	52	72	39	28	47	16
Guinea	17	69	2	13	54	1
Kenya	28	61	21	45	75	39
Lesotho	13	37	11	14	13	14
Liberia	40	71	20	u	24[a]	20
Madagascar	23	73	9	u	3[a]	u
Malawi	51	66	49	u	75	u
Mali	16	46	8	21	91	3
Mauritania	u	80	u	u	4[a]	0
Mauritius	99	100	98	96	100	90
Niger	34	41	33	8	36	3
Nigeria	37	60	30	u	30[b]	u
Rwanda	60	55	60	60	60	60
Senegal	45	69	27	u	87	u
Sierra Leone	22	61	6	22	52	10
Somalia	36	65	21	20	48	5
Sudan	51	100	31	u	73	u
Tanzania	46	88	39	52	83	47
Togo	34	68	26	11	24	8
Uganda	u	45[c]	12	u	34[a]	10
Zaire	22	43	5	u	u	10
Zambia	49	65	33	74	100	48
LATIN AMERICA/CARIBBEAN						
Argentina	64	72	17	84	94	32
Bolivia	41	78	12	23	40	9
Brazil	77	86	53	u	33[a]	u
Chile	86	100	18	84	100	4
Colombia	u	77[c]	u	69	96	13
Costa Rica	90	100	82	93	100	87
Dominican Republic	62	85	32	27	41	9
Ecuador	58	98	21	44	64	26
El Salvador	52	67	40	49	80	26
Guatemala	52	90	26	36	48	28
Guyana	73	100	60	86	100	80
Haiti	34	58	25	20	41	12
Honduras	69	91	55	44	50	40
Mexico	76	91	40	58	78	12
Nicaragua	58	91	10	u	35[a]	u
Panama	63	97	26	u	61	u
Paraguay	25	46	10	87	92	84
Peru	55	73	18	39	57	1
Trinidad and Tobago	97	100	96	97	100	96
Uruguay	81	95	3	u	5[a]	u
Venezuela	u	u	65	u	u	u
MIDDLE EAST/NORTH AFRICA						
Egypt	75	88	64	26	45	10
Iran	68	82	50	72	96	43
Iraq	84	100	46	75	100	15
Jordan	88	100	65	73	94	34
Kuwait	87	86	100	100	100	100

Table 39. Percentage of Population with Access to Safe Drinking Water and Sanitation, Early 1980s *(continued)*

Country	Safe drinking water			Sanitation services		
	Total	Urban	Rural	Total	Urban	Rural
MIDDLE EAST/NORTH AFRICA *(continued)*						
Libya	96	100	90	90	100	72
Morocco	u	100	u	u	u	u
Oman	23	100	16	21	100	13
Saudi Arabia	91	100	68	82	100	33
Syria	80	100	61	u	66[a]	29
Tunisia	u	100	u	u	u	u
Turkey	78	95	62	u	56	u
United Arab Emirates	92	95	81	77	93	22
Yemen, North	37	100	21	u	75	u
Yemen, South	53	73	39	47	69	33
ASIA						
Afghanistan	22	39	18	u	3[b]	u
Bangladesh	41	29	43	4	21	2
Bhutan	u	40[c]	14	u	u	u
Burma	26	36	21	21	34	15
Hong Kong	99	100	93	u	u	u
India	55	80	47	8	30	1
Indonesia	32	40	29	30	31	30
Korea, Republic of	77	86	60	100	100	100
Laos	21	28	20	5	13	4
Malaysia (Peninsular)	79	97	71	72	100	59
Nepal	14	71	11	2	16	1
Pakistan	40	78	24	20	53	6
Papua New Guinea	16	55	10	16	91	3
Philippines	54	53	55	58	75	47
Singapore	u	100	na	u	100	na
Sri Lanka	37	76	26	67	80	63
Thailand	67	50	70	45	50	44
Vietnam	u	u	31	u	u	70

u = unknown.

na = not applicable.

a. Sewerage only.

b. Sanitation by nonsewerage means only.

c. Drinking water by house connection only.